1980

Front pages upside down

# Maps

# Contents

those in "The Rise of Modern Europe" series edited by W. L. Langer (Torchbooks); in the multivolumed *Oxford History of England;* and in R. R. Palmer and J. Colton, *A History of the Modern World* (Knopf, 1970). For historical fiction, one may consult two older specialized guides: E. A. Baker, *A Guide to Historical Fiction* (Macmillan, 1914) and J. Nield, *A Guide to the Best Historical Novels and Tales* (Elkins, Mathews, and Marrot, 1929). The more recent *Fiction Catalogue* (Wilson, 1951), while covering much besides historical fiction, does furnish keys to books that cover particular countries and particular historical eras.

What is much more difficult than assembling titles is securing an evaluation of individual books. For older books the *Guide to Historical Literature,* already mentioned, gives the most useful references to critical reviews of the titles it discusses. *The Book Review Digest* gives capsule reviews and references to longer ones. For current books the weekly book section of *The New York Times* and *The Times Literary Supplement* (published in London) usually provide informative reviews of historical works soon after they are published. Later—sometimes as much as three years later—full scholarly appraisals are published in the *American Historical Review,* its British equivalent, the *English Historical Review,* and in more specialized reviews, such as the *Journal of Modern History, Speculum* (for medieval studies), *The Middle East Journal,* and many others. An American scholarly journal, *History and Theory,* covers a field of great interest to historians today. By reading a few reviews of a book one can usually get a fair indication of its scope and quality. In our reading suggestions we have tried, within a very brief compass, to give comparable indications.

## A Note on the Reading Suggestions

A list of reading suggestions is appended to each chapter of this book. Almost all historical bibliographies nowadays begin with the statement that they are highly selective and do not, of course, aspire to be exhaustive. This apology is hardly necessary, for the fact is that in most fields of history we have outrun the possibility of bringing together in one list all the books and articles in all languages on a given topic. There are for the wide fields of this book, and in English alone, thousands of volumes and hundreds of thousands of articles in periodicals. The brief lists following each chapter are simply suggestions to the reader who wishes to explore a given topic further.

Each list attempts to give important and readable books, with special attention to paperbacks (noted in the list with an asterisk), which are often the editions most available in a college community. A useful guide is *Paperbound Books in Print,* a monthly review of new paperbacks, with encyclopedic cumulative issues published three or four times a year. In addition, good readings in original sources, the contemporary documents and writings of an age, are sometimes listed, though the reader can supplement these listings from the text itself and from the footnotes. In addition, there are many good collections of sources for European history, notably the *Introduction to Contemporary Civilization in the West* (3rd ed., 1960), prepared by faculty members at Columbia University; this begins with the Middle Ages and gives much longer selections from the sources than such compilations usually do. Other good collections are to be found in the Portable Readers (published by Viking). There are also many sourcebooks and pamphlets on central or controversial problems in European history. A good example is K. M. Setton and H. R. Winkler, eds., *Great Problems in European Civilization* (Prentice-Hall, 2nd ed., 1966). Another is the series of pamphlets edited by R. W. Greenlaw under the general title "Problems in European Civilization" (D. C. Heath).

Our lists also include historical novels and, occasionally, dramas. Professional historians are likely to be somewhat severe in their standards for a historical novel. They naturally want its history to be sound, and at bottom they are likely to be somewhat prejudiced against the form. The historical novels listed here are all readable and all reasonably good as history. But note that historical novels, like historical films, though accurate on such material matters as authentic settings and appropriate costumes, often fail to capture the immaterial aspects—the psychology, the spirit—of the age they are written about. Many such novels motivate their characters, especially in love, as if they were modern Europeans and Americans. Exceptions to this rule are noted in the lists.

It is easy to assemble more material on a given topic than is furnished by our reading lists. American libraries, large and small, have catalogs with subject and title listings, as well as a section of reference books with encyclopedias and bibliographies. Many libraries have open shelves where, once a single title is discovered, many others may be found in the immediate area. Perhaps the first printed list of books to be consulted is *A Guide to Historical Literature* (Macmillan, 1931) and its sequel, *The American Historical Association's Guide to Historical Literature* (Macmillan, 1961). For more recent books one can turn, for American history, to the *Harvard Guide to American History* (Belknap, 1954), edited by O. Handlin and others. And for the history of Europe and other areas there are many good bibliographies; see, for example,

# *Preface*

In preparing this fourth edition of *A History of Civilization* we have tried to incorporate the new discoveries that continue to add to our knowledge of the past, especially the remote past. Where new theories or approaches to a major subject have seemed to warrant change, we have made the change. We have recorded and sought to interpret the events of the years since 1967, when the third edition was published. Perhaps naturally, we regard this latest edition as a better book than its predecessors.

In particular, there is now a wholly new chapter on the ancient Near East, and there are wholly rewritten chapters on the Greeks and the Romans. The medieval chapters have also undergone substantial revision, especially in those sections that deal with letters and with art. Throughout the rest of the work, especially of course in Chapters 30 and 31, which deal with the quarter century since the end of World War II, we have recast and reinterpreted our materials. Extensive revisions have brought abreast of recent scholarship the chapters on the Reformation, the seventeenth century, and the economic and intellectual revolutions of the nineteenth century. We think the new illustrations are perhaps more successfully married to the text than ever before, and there are more of them in full color than there have been in earlier editions. Finally, our book is now available in three paperback volumes, with the chronological breaks coming at 1300 and 1815, as well as in two hardbound volumes dividing at 1715; the innovation, we hope, offers more flexibility for courses such as those scheduled on a quarter or trimester basis.

Our senior co-author, Crane Brinton, died on September 7, 1968, and we have had to try to carry on without him. His extraordinary gift for hitting off what he called the style—or essence—of a period, a nation, even a whole civilization, we shall always admire, and we have greatly missed. But the reader of this edition will find, we hope, that much of the substance and all of the spirit of his contributions to the earlier editions have been maintained.

We should like here to thank Elizabeth Genovese for her taste and resourcefulness in obtaining illustrative materials; Mark A. Binn and Helen Maertens of the Project Planning Department at Prentice-Hall, who have applied their skills and energies most generously and effectively; and Cecil Yarbrough, Project Planning editor, whose ingenuity, efficiency, wisdom, and tact have made the preparation of these volumes a pleasure.

**A History of Civilization**

1300 to 1815, Fourth Edition

Brinton, Christopher, and Wolff




*Library of Congress Catalog Card Number 70-140094.*
*Printed in the United States of America;*
*color plates printed in Holland.*
*Cover: Detail of The Harvesters,*
*by Pieter Brueghel the Elder.*
*The Metropolitan Museum of Art, Rogers Fund, 1919.*

*Design by Mark A. Binn*

*Maps by Vincent Kotschar*

PRENTICE-HALL INTERNATIONAL, INC., *London*
PRENTICE-HALL OF AUSTRALIA, PTY. LTD., *Sydney*
PRENTICE-HALL OF CANADA, LTD., *Toronto*
PRENTICE-HALL OF INDIA PRIVATE LTD., *New Delhi*
PRENTICE-HALL OF JAPAN, INC., *Tokyo*

Current printing:
2 3 4 5 6 7 8 9 10

0-13-389510-6

# *Civilization*

## 1300 to 1815

**Fourth Edition**

*Prentice-Hall, Inc., Englewood Cliffs, New Jersey*

# *A History of*

**Crane Brinton**

**John B. Christopher**

*University of Rochester*

**Robert Lee Wolff**

*Archibald Cary Coolidge Professor of History, Harvard University*

# *A History of Civilization*

# 1300 to 1715

# II

# *The Renaissance*

*Above: Brunelleschi's dome for the Cathedral in Florence. Above right: (near) Michelangelo's marble statue of David, 1501–1504; (far) Donatello's bronze David, ca. 1430–1432. Right: Pieter Brueghel the Elder's "The Blind Leading the Blind," 1563.*

## I Introduction

The remarkable outburst of literary, artistic, and intellectual energy that occurred during the centuries of transition from the medieval to the modern world is generally called the Renaissance. It began about 1300 and came to an end during the late 1500's and early 1600's, when Europe had already entered the era of religious and dynastic wars. The first writer to show some of the marks of the Renaissance style, though he belonged primarily to the Middle Ages, was Dante. The last major literary figures of the Renaissance were Shakespeare and Cervantes, who lived three centuries after Dante, and John Milton, who lived still later, in the mid-seventeenth century England of revolution and civil war. All three, incidentally, are discussed in later chapters, since the present chapter is focused on the fourteenth, fifteenth, and sixteenth centuries.

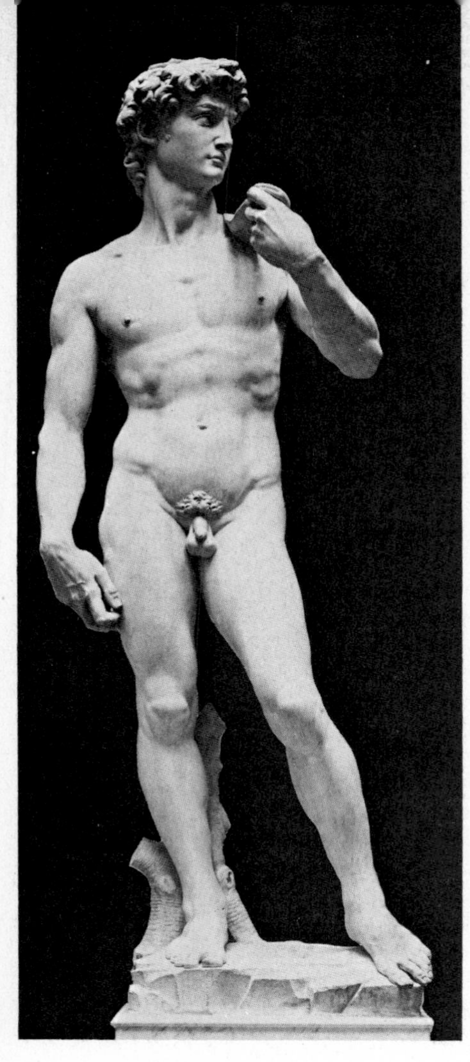

In Italian these centuries are called *trecento, quattrocento,* and *cinquecento* (literally, 300's, 400's, 500's in abbreviated reference to the 1300's, 1400's, 1500's), and the practice is widely followed among historians of the Renaissance, especially of Renaissance art. The convention is appropriate, for Italy was the homeland of the Renaissance, the Italy of aggressive—and cultivated—businessmen and politicians. As time went on the cultural and intellectual currents arising in Italy reached France, Germany, and the Low Countries as well as England. They touched Spain and Portugal more tangentially, and affected the Scandinavian states hardly at all.

The chronological and geographical delimitation of the Renaissance, however, does not hint at the basic historical problems it poses. Like many labels attached to broad historical movements—the Decline and Fall of Rome or the Dark Ages, for instance—the term "Renaissance" has aroused lively controversy among scholars and evoked a bewildering variety of interpretations and reinterpretations. The word itself means simply "rebirth," in this instance the rebirth of the classical values of ancient Greece and Rome. But was Greco-Roman culture actually reborn at the close of the Middle Ages? And, even if it was, could this rebirth alone possibly account for the extraordinarily productive careers of legions of writers, sculptors, painters and all the other luminaries of the era?

Until the middle of the nineteenth century most educated men would have given a simple affirmative response to both questions. The chief reason for the classical revival appeared to be the capture of Constantinople by the Turks in 1453 and the subsequent flight of Greek scholars to Italy and other countries of western Europe, bringing the thousand years of medieval gloom to an end at long last. The eighteenth-century historian Gibbon saluted the event in his characteristically majestic prose:

> Before the revival of classical literature, the barbarians in Europe were immersed in ignorance; and their vulgar tongues were marked with the rudeness and poverty of their manners. The students of the more perfect idioms of Rome and Greece were introduced to a new world of light and science; to the society of the free and polished nations of antiquity; and to a familiar converse with those immortal men who spoke the sublime language of eloquence and reason. . . . As soon as it had been deeply saturated with the celestial dews, the soil was quickened into vegetation and life; the modern idioms were refined; the classics of Athens and Rome inspired a pure taste and a generous emulation; and in Italy, as afterwards in France and England, the pleasing reign of poetry and fiction was succeeded by the light of speculative and experimental philosophy.*

Today, however, these simple answers no longer suffice. We cannot attribute such exaggerated importance to the fall of Byzantium. Well before 1453, knowledge of Greek writings was filtering into the West from Muslim Spain, from Sicily, and from Byzantium itself. Moreover, Greek influence was by no means the only decisive factor in promoting the Renaissance. In an influential study first published in 1860, Professor Jacob Burckhardt of the University of Basel in Switzerland insisted that much of the credit for Renaissance productivity must go also to the genius and individualism of Italians, from despots and condottieri to artists and writers. Burckhardt, however, accepted the traditional contrast between medieval darkness and Renaissance light that had first been drawn by the men of the Renaissance themselves. Today, of course, it is almost universally agreed that a great Christian civilization had in fact come to maturity during the Middle Ages, and that culture, even in the narrow sense of the heritage from classical antiquity, had never actually disappeared from the medieval West. It is both inaccurate and presumptuous to speak of a literal "rebirth" of culture at the close of the Middle Ages. Some historians have contended that the cultural rebirth had occurred much earlier than the trecento, with the "Carolingian Renaissance" for example, or with the "Renaissance of the twelfth century" centered at the court of Eleanor of Aquitaine.

But to find that the germ or the foundation of everything characteristic of the Renaissance had already existed long before 1300—to deny any originality to the Renaissance, as a few historians do—is to push the pendulum of reinterpretation too far. Unquestionably, the men of the Renaissance owed a large debt to the scholarship and art of their medieval predecessors, as we shall see. Unquestionably, the men of the Renaissance were often as religious, as credulous, as caste-

*Edward Gibbon, *The Decline and Fall of the Roman Empire,* Chap. LXVI.

conscious, and as "feudal" as their forbears. But they were also materialistic, skeptical, and individualistic to a degree almost unknown in the Middle Ages. The Renaissance most decidedly had a style of its own, neither fully medieval nor fully modern but rather a transition between the two.

The distinguished Italian historian Federico Chabod has observed that the new secular elements in this style may be summed up as "art for art's sake, politics for politics' sake, science for science's sake."* In other words, men were attempting to do things and study things as ends in themselves rather than as the means to the glorification of God and the salvation of humanity, much as Machiavelli divorced political thought from theology or as Machiavellian rulers cultivated power politics.

We shall now survey these attempts, first in literature and thought, then in art and science. The task is not easy, for we are confronting an age swept by contradictory currents and the new elements will be found intermingled with the old, not neatly isolated or compartmentalized.

## II The Vernaculars and Humanism

### The Rise of the Vernaculars

The vernacular—"native" or "local"—languages of the western European countries developed slowly, arising deep in the Middle Ages as the spoken language of the people, then extending gradually to popular writing and later to formal and official works. Many of the vernaculars—Spanish, Portuguese, Italian, and French—developed from Latin; these were the Romance (Roman) languages. Castilian, the core of modern literary Spanish, attained official status early; the king of Castile ordered that it be used for government records in the thirteenth century. In Italy, the vernacular scarcely existed as a literary language until the eve of the Renaissance when Dante turned to the dialect of his native Tuscany as the medium for the *Divine Comedy,* and it was not until the early sixteenth century that Tuscan Italian won out over the rival dialect of Rome as the standard medium for vernacular expression.

In medieval France, two families of vernaculars appeared. Southern Frenchmen spoke the *langue d'oc,* so called from their use of *oc* (the Latin *hoc*) for "yes"; their northern cousins spoke the *langue d'oïl,* in which "yes" was *oïl,* the ancestor of the modern *oui*. The epic verses of the *Song of Roland,* the rowdy *fabliaux,* and the chronicles of Villehardouin and Joinville were all composed in the *langue d'oïl,* while the troubadours at the court of Eleanor of Aquitaine sang in Provençal, a variety of the *langue d'oc*. By 1400, the *langue d'oïl* of the Paris region was well on its way to replacing Latin as the official language of the whole kingdom. Yet a century later champions of this French tongue were complaining that it was used only for frivolous writings, while Latin still monopolized serious ideas. Provençal eventually died out; however, another offshot of the *langue d'oc* survives in Catalan, used on both the French and Spanish sides of the Pyrenees, and the name Languedoc is still applied to southern France west of the Rhone.

In Germany and in England, the vernaculars were derived ultimately not from Latin but from an ancient Germanic language. The minnesingers of thirteenth century Germany composed their poetry in Middle High German, the predecessor of modern literary German. The Anglo-Saxons of England had spoken a dialect of Low German which incorporated some words of Scandinavian or Celtic origin and later added many borrowings from Norman French and Latin to form the English vernacular. As we have already noted, English achieved official recognition in the fourteenth century; meantime, it was also coming into its own as a literary language with such popular works as *Piers Plowman* and Chaucer's *Canterbury Tales.* Today though Chaucer's language seems stranger and more difficult than Shakespeare's, it is still recognizable as English.

The rise of vernaculars often paralleled and assisted the growth of nationalism. Use of a common language undoubtedly heightened among Englishmen a common sense of national purpose and a common mistrust of foreigners who did not speak the King's English. The ver-

* F. Chabod, *Machiavelli and the Renaissance* (London, 1958), p. 184.

naculars quickened the emergence of distinctive national styles in England, in France, and in Spain. Yet the triumph of particularism in fifteenth-century Germany and Italy demonstrated that the vernaculars could not by themselves create national political units. Nor did the vernaculars divide Western culture into watertight national compartments. Translations kept ideas flowing across national frontiers, and some of the vernaculars themselves became international languages. In the Near East, for instance, the Italian that had been introduced by the Crusaders was the *lingua franca,* the Western tongue most widely understood.

## Humanism

Despite the success of the vernaculars, Latin remained the international language of the Church and of the academic world. Scholars worked diligently to perfect their Latin and, in the later Renaissance, to learn at least the rudiments of Greek and sometimes of Hebrew too. They called themselves humanists, that is, devotees of what Cicero had termed *studia humanitatis,* or humane studies. While these were more restricted than the "humanities" or "liberal arts" of the twentieth century, they usually included rhetoric, grammar, history, poetry, and ethics. Reverence for the classics did not exclude enthusiasm for the vernaculars, which found enthusiastic advocates among the humanists. The reverse was also true, as vernacular writers established a tradition of studying Cicero and other classical masters to improve their own style (the passage from Gibbon quoted earlier in this chapter is a good example of Ciceronian English).

Humanism was far more than a linguistic term, and the humanist was usually much more than a philologist. His studies of the great men and great ideas of the classical past led him to cherish the values of antiquity, pagan though they might be, as much as Christian teachings or even more. Machiavelli, as the preceding chapter noted, found greater virtue in pre-Christian Greece and Rome than he did in the nominally Christian society of his own day. Other humanists, we shall find, sought a kind of highest denominator in the best ancient moral doctrines and in the loftiest Christian aspiration.

Altogether, humanism revolutionized men's attitudes toward the classical heritage. The medieval schoolmen had not disdained this heritage; they admired and copied its forms but transformed or adapted its ideas to fortify their own Christian views. They found in Vergil's *Aeneid,* for instance, not only the splendor of epic poetry but also an allegory of man's sojourn on earth. The humanists of the Renaissance, in turn, transformed their medieval heritage in the more secular spirit of their own age and in the light of their own more extensive knowledge of the classics. They revered both the style and the content of the classics and began to study them for their own sake, not to strengthen or enrich their faith. The two literary trends we have been sketching, the rise of the vernaculars and the evolution of humanism, may now be traced in more detail through the great writers of the Renaissance, beginning with Dante Alighieri (1265–1321).

## Dante

Much of Dante's career, outlook, and writing bore the stamp of the Middle Ages. The grand theme of the *Divine Comedy* was medieval, and the chivalric concept of disembodied love inspired his poems to Beatrice, who was married to another and whom he seldom ever saw. While hostile to the political ambitions of Pope Boniface VIII, Dante was no Machiavellian anticlerical but a good Christian who simply wanted the pope to keep out of politics.

Yet Dante also forshadowed developments that were to characterize the Renaissance. He not only chose the vernacular for the *Divine Comedy* but also wrote in Latin a plea for toleration of the vernacular by pedants who refused to read Italian. He modeled the style of the *Comedy* on the popular poetry of the Provençal troubadours rather than on the epic verse of the ancients. He gave the classics their due by including among the characters of the *Comedy* a host of figures from antiquity, both real and mythological. The Trojan Hector, Homer, Vergil's Aeneas. Vergil himself, Euclid, Plato, Socrates, Caesar, and other virtuous pagans dwell forever in Limbo on the edge of Hell, suffering only the hopelessness of the unbaptized who can never reach God's presence. Dante took from ancient mythology the tormentors of the damned—the Minotaur, the Furies, and Cerberus, the three-headed hound of Hell and the symbol of gluttony.

*Portrait of Dante attributed to the school of Giotto.*

Moreover, the concerns of this world are constantly with Dante in the other world. The lost souls are real people, from Judas through corrupt medieval clerics down to Dante's own fellow Florentines. Finally, Dante was not one of the medieval intellectuals who withdrew from society to the sanctuary of holy orders. Deeply involved in Florentine politics, he became a refugee from Guelf factionalism, and adopted the good Renaissance expedient of obtaining the patronage of a minor despot, the ruler of Verona. As a man of letters, he achieved a remarkable popular success during his own lifetime. Half a century after his death, a group of Florentine citizens honored the memory of their exiled compatriot by founding a public lectureship for a person "well trained in the book of Dante."

## Petrarch

Popular fame and classical enthusiasm positively obsessed the next important Italian literary figure, Francesco Petrarca (1304–1374), better known as Petrarch. His father, like Dante, was a political exile from Florence, and Petrarch himself spent much of his youth at the worldly court of the popes in Avignon. First and last a professional man of letters, Petrarch exhibited a remarkable zeal for collecting and copying the manuscripts of ancient authors. He assembled a splendid private library and found in an Italian cathedral some dusty and forgotten letters by Cicero which threw new light on Cicero's political career. He assembled and edited the first accurate manuscript of the Roman historian Livy. Petrarch so admired the past that he addressed a series of affectionate letters to Cicero and other old masters, and composed a Latin epic in the manner of the *Aeneid* to celebrate Scipio Africanus, the hero of the Second Punic War. Although he never learned to read Greek, he would gaze reverently at his manuscripts of Homer and Plato. On the other hand, he disliked Aristotle, not so much because of what he had written as because of his reputation for preeminence and infallibility in the world of medieval Scholasticism, to which Petrarch had been exposed while attending the law school at the University of Bologna. Petrarch believed that Scholastic Aristotelianism opposed all the values of humanism.

Petrarch's youthful attainments led the Senate of Rome (in his day a kind of municipal council) to revive the Greco-Roman custom of extending official recognition to excellence and crown him with a wreath of laurel in an elaborate ceremony. The new laureate reveled in the honor, for he wanted desperately to be ranked with the ancient Romans to whom he addressed his letters. Ironically, the writings of Petrarch most admired in modern times are not those in his cherished Latin but those he esteemed the least, the vernacular love poems he addressed to his adored Laura, whom he courted in vain until she died during the Black Death. In these lyrics, Petrarch perfected the verse form known as the Italian sonnet, fourteen lines long, divided into one set of eight lines and another of six, each with its own rhyme scheme. The word "sonnet" literally means a little song, and Petrarch developed his from vernacular folk songs. Almost despite himself, therefore, he proved to be one of the founders of modern vernacular literature.

Petrarch exemplified the emerging humanism of the Renaissance through his devotion to the classics and also through his deep feeling for the beauties of this world; he regarded Laura as a real woman, not as a disembodied chivalric heroine. His responses were sometimes complex and unpredictable; witness these excerpts from his famous account of climbing Mont Ventoux, near Avignon:

> At first I stood there almost benumbed, overwhelmed by a gale such as I had never felt before and by the unusually open and wide view. I looked around me: clouds were gathering below my feet, and Athos and Olympus grew less incredible, since I saw on a mountain of lesser fame what I had heard and read about them. From there I turned my eyes in the direction of Italy, for which my mind is so fervently yearning. The Alps were frozen stiff and covered with snow—those mountains through which that ferocious enemy of the Roman name once passed blasting his way through the rocks with vinegar if we may believe tradition.*

Then Petrarch's report takes a medieval turn:

> I admired every detail, now relishing earthly enjoyment, now lifting up my mind to higher spheres after the example of my body, and I thought it fit to look into the volume of Augustine's *Confessions*. . . . I happened to hit upon the tenth book of the work. My brother stood beside me, intently expecting to hear something from Augustine on my mouth. I ask God to be my witness and my brother who was with me: Where I fixed my eyes first it was written: "And men go to admire the high mountains, the vast floods of the sea, the huge streams of the rivers, the circumference of the ocean, and the revolutions of the stars—and desert themselves." I was stunned, I confess. I bade my brother, who wanted to hear more, not to molest me, and closed the book, angry with myself that I still admired earthly things.†

While the story may sound too pat, it is known that Petrarch owned a small manuscript of Augustine which could have fitted handily into a climber's kit.

It is also known that Petrarch admired Augustine almost as much as he admired Cicero. The religious teachings of the one and the Stoic morality of the other could fortify him against the materialism of his own contemporaries. In one of his letters to ancient worthies he wrote to Livy: "I am filled with bitter indignation against the mores of today when men value nothing except gold and silver and desire nothing except sensual pleasures."* We shall encounter other humanists who shared Petrarch's low estimate of existing society and his belief that classical learning and Christian precepts could each contribute to ennoble the human spirit. This was an excellent instance of the intermixture of new and old in the Renaissance. Many humanists also echoed Petrarch's criticism of the medieval Schoolmen for their rationalism, their dependence on Aristotle, and their preoccupation with detail. In their concern with the letter of Christianity, he felt that they missed its spirit—they "desert themselves," as he read in Augustine on Mont Ventoux.

* Quoted in E. Cassirer, P. O. Kristeller, and J. H. Randall, Jr., *The Renaissance Philosophy of Man* (Chicago, 1948), p. 41.

† Ibid., p. 44.

### Boccaccio

Another humanist attitude was demonstrated by another famous Florentine, Petrarch's friend and pupil, Giovanni Boccaccio (1313–1375). This was the light-hearted and matter-of-fact view of human frailty which permeates the *Decameron,* the first major prose work in the Italian vernacular. The *Decameron* recounts the stories told by a company of young Florentines to enliven their exile in a country villa where they have fled to escape the Black Death. Here is the gist of one of the stories:

> You must know, then, that there was once in our city a very rich merchant called Arriguccio Berlinghieri, who . . . took to wife a young gentle woman ill sorting with himself, by name Madam Sismonda, who, for that he, merchant-like, was much abroad and sojourned little with her, fell in love with a young man called Ruberto.†

Arriguccio discovers his wife's infidelity and gives her the beating of her life—or so he thinks. The beating occurs in a darkened room, Sismonda has directed her maid to take her place,

* As translated and quoted by M. P. Gilmore, *Humanists and Jurists* (Cambridge, Mass., 1963), p. 6.

† This and the following quotations are from the eighth story of the seventh day, as translated in the Modern Library edition of the *Decameron.*

and it is actually the maid whom Arriguccio had thrashed. He, ignorant of the deception, plays the wronged husband to the hilt and summons Sismonda's brothers to witness her disgrace. "The brothers,—seeing her seated sewing with no sign of beating on her face, whereas Arriguccio avouched that he had beaten her to a mummy,—began to marvel." Sismonda immediately accuses her hapless husband of "fuddling himself about the taverns, foregathering now with this lewd woman and now with that and keeping me waiting for him . . . half the night." The result: the brothers give Arriguccio a thorough beating. And Boccaccio's moral:

> Thus the lady, by her ready wit, not only escaped the imminent peril but opened herself a way to do her every pleasure in time to come, without evermore having any fear of her husband.

Most of the plots in the *Decameron* were not original with Boccaccio, who borrowed freely from classic and Eastern sources and from the bawdy *fabliaux* of medieval France, particularly those exposing clerical peccadilloes. Where Boccaccio did make an original contribution was in telling these earthy tales in a graceful, entertaining, and dramatic fashion and with a worldly disenchantment based on his own experiences. The son of a Florentine banker, he spent part of his youth at the rather frivolous court of the Angevin kings of Naples. He turned to letters after his apprenticeship in banking left him disillusioned by the gap between the sharp business practices of wealthy Florentines and their professed Christian ideals. His anticlericalism reflected the same kind of disillusion with the corruption of the clergy. Boccaccio himself was no dilettante but a serious humanist who held the Dante memorial lectureship at Florence, succeeded more than Petrarch in learning Greek, and aided his master in tracking down old manuscripts, once finding a copy of Tacitus in the Benedictine abbey on Monte Cassino.

The men of letters who followed Petrarch and Boccaccio may be divided into three groups. First, there were the conservers of classical culture, the bookworms, scholars, cultivated despots and businessmen, all the heirs of Petrarch's great humanistic enthusiasm for classical antiquity. Second were the vernacular writers—many of them not Italians—who took the path marked out by the *Decameron,* from Chaucer at the close of the fourteenth century down to Rabelais and to Cervantes in the sixteenth. And third there were the synthesizers, headed by Pico della Mirandola and Erasmus, who endeavored to fuse Christianity, classicism, and other elements into a universal philosophy of man.

## Classical Scholarship

The devoted antiquarians of the fifteenth century uncovered a really remarkable number of ancient manuscripts. They ransacked monasteries and other likely places, in Italy and Germany, in France and Spain. They pieced together the works of Cicero, Tacitus, Lucretius, and other Latin authors. Collecting Greek manuscripts became a regular business, transacted for Italian scholars and patrons by agents who were active in Constantinople both before and after the city's fall in 1453. They did their work so thoroughly that almost all the Greek classics we now possess reached the West before 1500.

To preserve, catalog, and study these literary treasures, the first modern libraries were created. Cosimo de' Medici supported three separate libraries in and near Florence and employed forty-five copyists. The humanist popes founded the library of the Vatican, today one of the most important collections in the world. Even a minor state, like the Duchy of Urbino in northern Italy, had a major library, assembled by its cultivated duke.

Greek scholars as well as Greek manuscripts made the journey from Byzantium to Italy. One of the earliest of them, Manuel Chrysoloras, came to Italy in the closing years of the fourteenth century seeking help for the Byzantine Empire against the Ottomans, then turned from diplomacy to teach at Florence and Milan. He did the realm of letters a great service by insisting that translations into Latin from the Greek should not be literal, as they had been in the past, but should convey the message and spirit of the original. The revival of Greek studies reached maturity in the 1460's with the emergence of the informal circle of Florentine humanists known as the Platonic Academy. Greek, however, never began to equal Latin in popularity because of the difficulty of the language, which discouraged interest in the Greek drama and led most humanists to study Plato in Latin translation.

The classicists of the fifteenth century made a fetish of pure and polished Latin. The learned composed elaborate letters designed less for private reading than for the instruction of their colleagues. Papal secretaries began to make ecclesiastical correspondence conform to what we should call a manual of correct style. At their worst, these men were pedants, exalting manner over matter, draining vitality from the Latin language; a contemporary complained of the

> chattering flock who, in order to appear highly literate to the crowd, proclaim in the square how many dipthongs the ancients had and why only two are known today. . . . They say poetic stories are fairy tales for women and children and that the sweet recounter of these, Giovanni Boccaccio, did not know grammar. . . . They make fun of the works of the poet laureate Petrarch. . . . And then to show the mob how very well educated they are they say that the most famous and honoured Dante was only a shoemaker's poet.*

At their best, the fifteenth-century classicists were keen and erudite scholars who sifted out the inaccuracies and forgeries in defective manuscripts to establish definitive texts of ancient writings.

Lorenzo Valla (1407–1457) represented classical scholarship at its best. One of the few important figures of the Italian Renaissance not identified with Florence, Valla was reared in Rome and passed much of his adult life there and at Naples. Petty and quarrelsome, fond of exchanging insults with rival humanists, he also commanded both immense learning and the courage to use it against the most sacred targets. He wrote (in Latin, of course) *The Elegances of the Latin Language,* a most popular study (it went through sixty printings within a century) which criticized the supposedly flawless prose of Cicero. He took Thomas Aquinas to task for his failure to know Greek and therefore to possess adequate scholarly equipment. His own expert knowledge of the language led him to point out errors and misinterpretations in the Vulgate, as compared to the Greek New Testament, and thereby to lay the foundation for humanist biblical scholarship.

* Cino Rinuccini, *Invective against Certain Calumniators of Dante, Petrarch, and Boccaccio,* trans. George Holmes in *The Florentine Enlightenment, 1400–1450* (New York, 1969), pp. 1–2.

Valla's fame rests above all on his demonstration that the Donation of Constantine, long a basis for sweeping papal claims to temporal dominion, was actually a forgery. He proved his case by showing that both the Latin in which the Donation was written and the events to which it referred dated from an era several centuries after Constantine, who had been emperor in the early fourth century. For example, the Donation (here called the "privilege") mentioned Constantinople as the seat of a patriarch:

> How in the world . . . could one speak of Constantinople as one of the patriarchal sees, when it was not yet a patriarchate, nor a see, nor a Christian city, nor named Constantinople, nor founded, nor planned! For the "privilege" was granted, so it says, the third year after Constantine became a Christian; when as yet Byzantium, not Constantinople, occupied that site.*

When Valla published this exposure in 1440, he was secretary to Alfonso the Magnanimous, king of Aragon, whose claim to Naples was being challenged by the papacy on the basis of the Donation itself. The pope might well have been expected to condemn Valla as a heretic. Nothing of the kind occurred, and Valla soon accepted a commission to translate Thucydides under papal auspices, with no strings attached. The climate of opinion had indeed changed since the high Middle Ages; it is hard to imagine that Gregory VII or Innocent III would have treated Valla so indulgently.

## Chaucer and Rabelais

The second group of literary men, the vernacular writers, illustrate once again the broad range of the Renaissance. Geoffrey Chaucer (1340–1400), like Dante, belongs both to the Middle Ages and to the Renaissance. His *Canterbury Tales* have a medieval setting; they are told by pilgrims on their way to the shrine of the martyred Becket, not by the secular young people of the *Decameron.* Yet Chaucer's tales are not unlike Boccaccio's; he, too, uses the vernacular, and borrows stories from the *fabliaux.* Although Chaucer apparently had not actually read the

* *The Treatise of Lorenzo Valla on the Donation of Constantine,* ed. C. B. Coleman (New Haven, 1922), p. 95.

*Decameron,* he was familiar enough with other writings of Boccaccio to use the plot of one for his Knight's Tale and of another for *Troilus and Criseyde,* the long narrative poem about two lovers in the Trojan War. The Clerk's Tale, he reveals, "I Lerned at Padowe of a worthy clerk . . ., Fraunceys Petrark, the laureat poete," and the Wife of Bath mentions "the wyse poete of Florence That Highte Dant."

Chaucer came to know Italian literature in the course of several trips to Italy on official business for the English king. He led a busy and prosperous life in the thick of politics, domestic and international. Coming from a family of well-to-do London merchants, he was a justice of the peace in Kent, represented the county in the House of Commons, and filled the important posts of Controller of Customs and Clerk of the King's Works. The writings of Chaucer showed that the English vernacular was coming of age and that in England, as in Italy, the profession of letters was no longer a clerical monopoly.

The medieval values still evident in the writings of Chaucer had largely vanished a century and a half later in the works of the Frenchman François Rabelais (ca. 1494–1553). Rabelais contributed far more to literature than the salacious wit for which he is famous. He studied the classics, particularly Plato and the ancient physicians; practiced and taught medicine; and created two of the great comic figures of letters, Gargantua and his son Pantagruel. The two are giants, and everything they do is of heroic dimensions. The abbey of Theleme, which Gargantua helps to found, permits its residents a wildly unmonastic existence:

> All their life was spent not in lawes, statutes or rules, but according to their own free will and pleasure. They rose out of their beds, when they thought good: they did eat, drink, labour, sleep, when they had a minde to it and were disposed for it. . . . In all their rule, and strictest tie of their order, there was but this one clause to be observed,
>
> DO WHAT THOU WILT.*

While Rabelais accepted the self-indulgence of the age, he also recommended self-improvement, and also on a grand scale. Gargantua exhorts Pantagruel to learn everything: he is to master Arabic in addition to Latin, read the New Testament in Greek and the Old in Hebrew, and study history, geometry, architecture, music, and civil law. He must also know "the fishes, all the fowles of the aire, all the several kinds of shrubs and trees," "all the sorts of herbs and flowers that grow upon the ground: all the various metals that are hid within the bowels of the earth." "In brief," Gargantua concludes, "let me see thee an Abysse, and bottomless pit of knowledge."* Both his insatiable appetite for knowledge and the exuberant yet exhausting fashion in which Rabelais wrote about it represent an important aspect of the Renaissance style.

* Rabelais, *Gargantua and Pantagruel,* Urquhart trans. (New York, 1883), Book I, Chap. 57.

* Ibid., Book I, Chap. 8.

## The Platonic Revival

Another facet of the Renaissance style was highlighted by the third group of writers, the philosophical humanists, who aspired not only to universal knowledge but also to a universal truth and faith. They were centered first at Florence, attracted by the Platonic Academy founded in 1462 by Cosimo de' Medici, two years before his death, when he decided to underwrite the translation of Plato's works into Latin. He entrusted the commission to Marsilio Ficino (1433–1499), a medical student turned classicist, who translated not only the whole body of Plato's writings but some of the Neoplatonists' works as well. These followers of Plato, who flourished in the third century A.D. and later, long after the master, cultivated the search for God through mystical experiences. The opportunity for stressing the compatibility of this strain of Platonism with Christianity exerted a strong attraction on Ficino and his circle.

Ficino, who was also a priest, argued that religious feeling and expression were as natural to man as barking was to dogs or neighing to horses. Man, he wrote, has the unique faculty called intellect which he described as an "eye turned toward the intelligible light" or God. He coined the term "Platonic love" to describe the love that transcends the senses and may also lead man to mystical communion with God. He supported his arguments with appeals to a wide range of authorities—the wise men of the ancient Near

East, the prophets of the Old Testament, the apostles of the New, and the Greek philosophers, including Pythagoras and Aristotle in addition to Plato. Ficino seemed to be attempting a synthesis of all philosophy and religion.

The attempt was pressed further by Ficino's pupil, Pico della Mirandola (1463–1494). Pico crowded much into his thirty-one years and would have delighted Rabelais's Gargantua, for he knew Arabic and Hebrew in addition to Greek and Latin and studied Jewish allegory, Arab philosophy, and medieval Scholasticism, which, almost alone among humanists, he respected. Pico's tolerance was as broad as his learning. In his short *Oration on the Dignity of Man,* he cited approvingly Chaldean and Persian theologians, the priests of Apollo, Socrates, Pythagoras, Cicero, Moses, Paul, Augustine, Mohammed, Francis, Thomas Aquinas, and many others.

In all the varied beliefs of this galaxy, Pico hoped to find the common denominator of a universal faith. This process of syncretism, of borrowing and assimilating from many sources, he was unable to complete, but he, together with Ficino, did help to found the great humane studies of comparative religion and comparative philosophy. And he reaffirmed and strengthened Ficino's idea that man was unique, the link between the mortal physical world and the immortal spiritual one, the hinge of the universe, so to speak. This concept of the uniqueness of man and his central position in the universe lay at the core of the Renaissance style. Yet among the Platonic humanists, the medieval element also remained strong; Pico, in his final years, gave away his worldly possessions and became an ardent supporter of the fanatical preacher Savonarola.

### Erasmus

The man who gave the most mature expression of the humanist impulse to draw on all wisdom was not Italian but Dutch. Erasmus (1466–1536), the "Prince of Humanists," dominated the intellectual life of Europe as few other men have done. He was in fact a cosmopolitan, the foremost citizen of the Republic of Letters. He studied, taught, and lived at Oxford, Cambridge and Paris, and in Italy, and he particularly enjoyed the free atmosphere of semi-independent cities like Louvain in the Low Countries, Basel in Switzerland, and Freiburg in the Rhineland. Building on Valla's scholarship, he published a scholarly edition of the Greek New Testament. He carried on a prodigious correspondence in Latin and compiled a series of *Adages* and *Colloquies* to give students examples of good Latin composition. Because Erasmus never regarded elegance of style as an end in itself, he assailed the "knowledge factories" of the grammarians in the satirical *Praise of Folly:*

> As for those stilted, insipid verses they display on all occasions (and there are those to admire them), obviously the writer believes that the soul of Virgil has transmigrated into his own breast. But the funniest sight of all is to see them admiring and praising each other, trading compliment for compliment, thus mutually scratching each other's itch.*

In exposing human weaknesses, Erasmus played no favorites; he mocked any group or class inflated by a sense of its own importance—merchants, churchmen, scientists, philosophers, courtiers, and kings. He was one of the very first to puncture the pretensions and hypocrisies of nationalism:

> And now I see that it is not only in individual men that nature has implanted self-love. She implants a kind of it as a common possession in the various races, and even cities. By this token the English claim . . . good looks, music, and the best eating as their special properties. The Scots flatter themselves on the score of high birth and royal blood, not to mention their dialectical skill. Frenchmen have taken all politeness for their province. . . . The Italians usurp *belles lettres* and eloquence; and they all flatter themselves upon the fact that they alone, of all mortal men, are not barbarians. . . . The Greeks, as well as being the founders of the learned disciplines, vaunt themselves upon their titles to the famous heroes of old.†

In appraising human nature, however, Erasmus tempered criticism with geniality. In what proportions, asks an ironic passage in *Praise of Folly,* did Jupiter supply men with emotion and reason?

> Well, the proportions run about one pound to half an ounce. Besides, he imprisoned reason in a cramped corner of the head, and turned over all the rest of the body to the emotions. After that

* Erasmus, *Praise of Folly,* trans. H. H. Hudson (Princeton, 1941), pp. 71–72.

† Ibid., p. 61.

*Hans Holbein the Younger's portrait of Erasmus.*

he instated two most violent tyrants, as it were, in opposition to reason: anger, which holds the citadel of the breast, and consequently the very spring of life, the heart; and lust, which rules a broad empire lower down. . . .*

So, Erasmus concludes, we must cherish particularly the few outstanding individuals who have led great and good lives. Christ heads his list of great men; Cicero and Socrates rank very high. Plato's account of the death of Socrates moved Erasmus so deeply that he wanted to cry out, "Pray for us, Saint Socrates."

Erasmus possessed most of the main attributes of Renaissance humanism. He coupled a detached view of human nature with faith in the dignity of man or at least of a few individuals. He joined love of the classics with respect for Christian values. While he was both testy and vain, he had little use for the fine-spun arguments of Scholasticism and was a tireless advocate of what he called his "philosophy of Christ," the application, in the most humane spirit, of the doctrines of charity and love taught by Jesus. Yet, though Erasmus always considered himself a loyal son of the Church, he nevertheless helped to destroy the universality of Catholicism. His edition of the Greek New Testament raised disquieting doubts about the accuracy of the Latin translation in the Vulgate and therefore of Catholic biblical interpretations. His repeated insistence on elevating the spirit of piety above the letter of formal religious acts seemed to diminish the importance of the clergy, and his attacks on clerical laxity implied that the wide gap between the lofty ideals and the corrupt practices of the Church could not long endure. A famous sixteenth-century epigram states: "Where Erasmus merely nodded, Luther rushed in; where Erasmus laid the eggs, Luther hatched the chicks; where Erasmus merely doubted, Luther laid down the law." When Luther did lay down the law in the Protestant revolt, however, the growing dogmatism and belligerence of the rebels soon alienated Erasmus. Both his fidelity to the Christian tradition, as he understood it, and his humanist convictions committed Erasmus to the position that the only weapons worthy of man were reason and discussion.

## III The Arts

### Main Traits

Influenced by the humanists' enthusiasm for classical antiquity, Renaissance artists, too, looked back to Rome for models, and influenced by the secularism and individualism of the age, they experimented with new techniques and new forms. Painting and sculpture were emancipated from their medieval subordination to architecture, now no longer "queen of the arts." Whereas statues, carvings, altarpieces, and stained glass had contributed magnificently to the glory of Romanesque and Gothic churches, they had almost never been entities in themselves but only parts of a larger whole. In the Renaissance the number of "freestanding" pictures and statues—independent aesthetic objects—steadily increased, though many great artists continued to decorate ecclesiastical structures. The artist

* Ibid., p. 23.

himself gained increasing status as a professional man and as a creative personality. The celebrated individualism of the Renaissance was replacing the anonymous or community character of much medieval art.

Reflecting the classical revival, the fashion in building changed from the soaring Gothic to adaptations of the ancient Roman temple, emphasizing symmetry, solidity, and the horizontal line. The contrast may be observed by comparing a Gothic cathedral like Chartres with a Renaissance monument like St. Peter's at Rome. Reflecting the increasing security, wealth, and materialism of the age, palaces and private residences began to rival cathedrals and churches in magnificence. The arts as a whole, like society and culture in general, became less Christian and more secular than they had been in the Middle Ages. For patrons, artists turned increasingly to men of state and business; for subjects they chose their patrons and pagan gods as well as the traditional Virgin, Christ, and saints. Interest in the things of this world, however, did not exclude concern with the next world; the Renaissance was both worldly and otherworldly.

The artists of the Renaissance, even more than its writers and thinkers, displayed an extraordinary range of talents and interests. They produced both secular and sacred works; they imitated classical antiquity and launched bold new experiments in artistic expression; they took pride in their individual achievements, even boasted of them. Some of the very greatest were also the most versatile. Michelangelo executed heroic frescoes and heroic statues, and helped to plan St. Peter's on a truly heroic scale. Giotto designed buildings, painted, wrote verses, and did handsomely in business. Leonardo da Vinci was a jack of all trades and a master of many—painter and sculptor, musician and physicist, anatomist and geologist, inventor and city-planner.

Twentieth-century scholarship has underlined the manysidedness and cosmopolitanism of Renaissance art, and particularly its debt to sources outside Italy and to its medieval forerunners. A Gothic strain persisted throughout the Renaissance, symbolized by the gradual completion of the grandiose "wedding-cake" cathedral in Milan. And the technical inventiveness, the decorative richness, and the almost photographic realism of natural details in late Gothic art made a particular contribution to the Renaissance style. Botanists, for example, can identify dozens of flowers and plants in the Ghent altarpiece of the Van Eyck brothers, a product of the late Gothic in the early fifteenth century, and also in Botticelli's *Primavera* (Spring), a product of the Florentine Renaissance at the end of the same century. Much of this Gothic contribution originated in northern Europe, particularly in Ghent and other cities of the Low Countries during the Burgundian ascendancy. The well-established commercial connections between Flemish and Italian cities promoted cultural intercourse. Wealthy Italians, for instance, were eager to purchase paintings by Flemish masters like the Van Eycks. The music and the fashions of the Burgundian court also had many Italian admirers. In the realm of the artist, as in that of the humanist, there were many major figures outside Italy to belie the implication of monopoly in the old term "Italian Renaissance."

And yet in art many of the greatest names were Italian, and their dazzling achievements could probably be credited more to their own genius than to the guidance of their classical or Gothic mentors. Without them the Renaissance would never had been one of the great ages in the history of art. In sculpture it rivaled the golden centuries of Greece, and in painting it was more than a rebirth: it was the transformation of an old restricted medium of expression into a thrilling new aesthetic instrument. Our survey begins with painting when elements of the Renaissance style first started to emerge in the work of a contemporary of Dante, Giotto.

## Giotto

Before 1300 Italian artists, following the Byzantine tradition, generally produced paintings that were flat and two-dimensional, lacking in depth. Giotto (1276–1337), though not entirely forsaking Byzantine models, experimented to make painting less stiff and austere and more lifelike and emotional. He learned much from the realistic statues of Italian sculptors, who had been influenced by those striking sculptures decorating the portals of Gothic cathedrals in France. The most extensive examples of Giotto's work are the frescoes he executed for the Arena Chapel at Padua, near Venice. In the *Return of Joachim to the Sheepfold,* the sheep are natural and lively, and the dog welcomes his master with right forepaw raised to greet him. In a much more solemn scene, *The Lamentation,* the mood of grief at the burial of Christ is intensified because, above the Virgin and the human mourners, angels are flying, not serenely but beating their wings in anguish. The sense of movement and drama is evident, too, in the frescoes completed by Giotto somewhat later in the Bardi and Peruzzi chapels of the Franciscan church of Santa Croce in Florence. *The Trial by Fire,* for instance, pictures Saint Francis at a critical moment before an imperious Muslim sultan, who appears to dominate the scene from his elevation on a throne but still calls attention to the saint by gesturing in his direction.

By resourceful experimentation Giotto created a three-dimensional quality, an impression of depth, in his paintings. The flatness of medieval painting stemmed from the artists' use of the same tone color throughout a picture; Giotti varied the brightness of his colors and introduced contrasts of light and shade, the technique that goes by the Italian name of *chiaroscuro* (bright-dark). Giotto also paid close attention to perspective and foreshortening, accented the geometrical qualities of the background of the subject, and suggested the living attributes of clothed figures by hinting at the human body beneath the drapery.

*Giotto's "Presentation in the Temple."*

As a person, Giotto anticipated the proud and versatile man of the Renaissance bent on worldly success. He was no anonymous craftsman, dedicated and withdrawn, content to work in obscurity, but a many-sided man, hungry for fame, and famous in his own day for his verses and his witty remarks as well as for his artistic accomplishments. His artistic commissions netted him a sizable fortune, which he augmented through a variety of business enterprises: lending money, running a debt-collection service, and renting looms (at stiff fees) to poor woolen weavers. Giotto had many connections with the great and wealthy; he won the patronage of Roman cardinals, the king of Naples, and the great Florentine banking families of the Bardi and Peruzzi. The richest man in Padua, Enrico Scrovegni, following a custom prevalent in the later Middle Ages, commissioned him to paint the frescoes in the Arena Chapel on behalf of the soul of his father, which Dante had assigned to Hell in the *Divine Comedy* because he was a notorious usurer.

## Patrons, Subjects, and Techniques

Thus, in the time of Giotto, art was beginning to attract the patronage of secular individuals in addition to that of the churchmen who had been its chief sponsors in the Middle Ages. During the next two centuries, more and more despots, kings, and merchant princes joined the ranks of patrons. This is one of the main strands in the history of Renaissance painting. A second strand is the introduction of humanistic and secular themes, and a third is technical: the advances in the use of chiaroscuro, perspective, color, oils, precise anatomical detail—all the techniques that expanded the potentialities of the medium.

By 1500, almost all the Italian states and many states outside Italy had their court painters. In Florence, the government, the guilds, the wealthy magnates, and the churches and monasteries had all been patronizing artists since the time of Giotto, in a sustained campaign for civic beauty. Lorenzo the Magnificent subsidized a great painter like Botticelli as well as the humanists of the Platonic Academy. Il Moro, the Sforza usurper in Milan, made Leonardo da Vinci in effect his Minister of Fine Arts, Director of Public Works, and Master of the Revels. After the collapse of Il Moro's fortunes, Leonardo found new patrons in Cesare Borgia, the pope, and the French kings Louis XII and Francis I, ambitious rulers all. The popes employed Leonardo, Botticelli, Raphael, Michelangelo, and many other leading artists, for they had a keen appreciation of aesthetic values, and favored projects that would add to the luster of their rule. They intended to make St. Peter's the largest and the most resplendent church in Christendom, and, further, to make Rome the artistic capital of the world.

The confusion of secular and religious elements was also evident in the paintings themselves. Sacred subjects predominated, but individual artists interpreted the Madonna, the Nativity, the Crucifixion, and the rest of the great Christian themes in their own particular ways, realistically or piously. And the artists applied equal skill to scenes from classical mythology, portraits of their secular contemporaries, and other matter remote from the Christian tradition. Often the sacred and the secular could be found in the same picture. In the Arena Chapel, in the fresco of the Last Judgment, Giotto portrayed not only the saints but also and on the same scale the donor, Enrico Scrovegni, presenting a model of the chapel to the Virgin. In the Peruzzi Chapel in Florence Giotto framed religious frescoes with a border of medallions depicting members of the Peruzzi family. Giotto's successors maintained the custom, sometimes introducing the whole family of the donor, as in Botticelli's *Adoration of the Magi*, which shows Cosimo and Lorenzo de' Medici as well as the artist himself. While the patron usually assumed a reverent posture, the artist often revealed the acumen and ambition that had won him worldly success and permitted him to afford the luxury of commissioning a work of art. It is hard to tell whom such paintings were intended to honor, God or the donor.

Ambiguities also complicated the treatment of pagan and classical themes in Renaissance painting. At first, artists took figures like Jupiter and Venus out of their Olympian context and made them just another lord and lady of the chivalric class; the sense of historical appropriateness was conspicuously missing. Later painters attempted to depict the gods and goddesses in a proper classical setting, sometimes in a pagan state of undress, but not at all pagan in the sense of glorifying the flesh. For example, when Botticelli (1445–1510), another in the long file of talented Florentines, was commissioned by the Medici to paint the *Birth of Venus,* he made Venus more ethereal than sensual and arranged the figures against a background of water in the fashion traditionally used to depict the baptism of Christ. In his *Primavera,* a pagan allegory of spring, the chief figures—Mercury, the messenger of the gods; the Three Graces; Venus (again, rather ethereal); the goddess Flora, bedecked with blossoms; and Spring herself, blown in by the West Wind—are all youthful and delicate; all have tiny feet and an air of otherworldly serenity, as if this were springtime in some ideal Platonic realm.

Indeed, Botticelli was to painting what the mystics of the Platonic Academy were to humanism. He seems to have moved in the circle of Pico della Mirandola at Florence, and his paintings often suggest an aspiration to some mystic Platonic realm. Yet he also knew the drive of raw religious emotion, and when Savonarola prescribed the burning of all worldly "vanities," so the story has it, Botticelli threw some of his own paintings of nudes onto the flames.

The most significant contributor to the technique of painting after Giotto was Masaccio (1401- ca. 1428), yet another talented Florentine. Masaccio followed the anatomical realism of sculptors and also made bold experiments with chiaroscuro and perspective. In depicting saints, as one critic has observed, he made them as sturdy and down-to-earth as the peasants of Tuscany. In painting the expulsion from the Garden of Eden, he conveyed the shame and the sorrow of Adam and Eve both by their facial expressions and by the forlorn posture of their bodies. And he intensified the sense of tragedy by employing bold contrasts of light and shadow on the bodies. Masaccio had the rare gift of reducing a situation to its essentials.

Where Masaccio relied, as it were, on mass and perspective to achieve his artistic effects, others turned to line and to color. Botticelli was a superb colorist, and such a painstaking draftsman that he seems to have brushed in every single hair on a human head. A great step forward in the use of color came with the introduction of oil paints, developed first in Flanders and brought to Italy in the latter part of the fifteenth century. Until then, painters had generally worked in fresco or tempera or a combination of the two. Fresco, the application of pigments to the wet plaster of a wall, required the artist to work swiftly before the surface dried and set and thus discouraged the showing of details. Tempera (or distemper) painting, in which the pigments were tempered by being mixed with a sizing, often of eggs, enabled the artist to work on a wall after the wet plaster had dried. It permitted him to paint more slowly and in more detail, but had the disadvantage of making the end product rather muddy-looking. Oils overcame the shortcomings of fresco and tempera, by allowing leisurely, delicate work and ensuring clearer and more lasting colors.

*Masaccio's "The Tribute Money," ca. 1425.*

*Self-portrait of Leonardo da Vinci.*

### The High Renaissance in Italy

The major developments we have been following in technical proficiency and secularization of patronage and subject matter reached a climax with the masters of the High Renaissance, the late fifteenth century and the first half or two-thirds of the sixteenth in Italy, in art-historical terms. The quantity of great names is almost overwhelming—Leonardo, Michelangelo, Titian, Botticelli, Raphael, Giorgione, Carpaccio, Tintoretto, Veronese, and still others. Here we shall look at the achievements of the first three of them to suggest the variety and brilliance of the age.

Compared with other great masters Leonardo da Vinci (1452–1519) completed relatively few pictures. His scientific activities and his innumerable services of every kind for his patrons demanded a large part of his time and energies. Some of his paintings deteriorated because of his unsuccessful innovations in mixing paints, and the *Last Supper* began to suffer during Leonardo's own lifetime because of the mold on the damp wall of the Milan monastery where he had painted it. Fortunately, Leonardo's talent and his extraordinary range of interests may be sampled in the voluminous collections of his drawings and notebooks. The drawings include every sort of sketch, from preliminary work for paintings through realistic human embryos and fanciful war machines to mere "doodles." From the notebooks comes this characteristic advice of Leonardo:

> . . . Since, as we know, painting embraces and contains within itself . . . whatever can be comprehended by the eyes, it would seem to me that he is but a poor master who makes only a single figure well.
>
> For do you not see how many and how varied are the actions which are performed by men alone? Do you not see how many different kinds of animals there are, and also of trees and plants and flowers? What variety of hilly and level places, of springs, rivers, cities, public and private buildings; of instruments fitted for man's use; of divers costumes, ornaments and arts?—Things which should be rendered with equal facility and grace by whoever you wish to call a painter.
>
> . . . . . .
>
> The painter will produce pictures of little merit if he takes the works of others as his standard; but if he will apply himself to learn from the objects of nature he will produce good results.*

Leonardo followed his own advice about studying nature afresh. He investigated plants, animals, and fossils. From his intensive study of human anatomy, he drew up rules for indicating the actions of human muscles and for establishing the proportions between the parts of the

**The Notebooks of Leonardo da Vinci,* ed. Edward MacCurdy (New York, n.d.), II, 256, 276.

human body. He made many sketches of the deformed and of people suffering intense strain and anguish, combining a zeal for scientific precision with a taste for the grotesque that recalls the gargoyles of a Gothic cathedral.

Leonardo made the *Last Supper* in part an exercise in artistic geometry, arranging the apostles in four groups of three men each, around the central figure of Christ, and keeping the background deliberately simple to accent the lines of perspective. Yet he did not make the picture superficially realistic; it would have been physically impossible for thirteen men to have eaten together at the relatively small table provided by Leonardo. Older painters had usually shown the group at the solemn yet peaceful moment of the final communion, and had suggested the coming treachery of Judas by placing him in isolation from the others. Not Leonardo. He chose the tense moment when Jesus announced the coming betrayal, and he placed Judas among the apostles, relying on facial and bodily expression to convey the guilt of the one and the consternation of the others. In less ambitious paintings, too, Leonardo showed a concern for both the architecture of the picture and the meticulous execution of detail. In the *Madonna of the Rocks,* the plants and flowers have the accuracy of plates in a textbook. The arrangement of the figures in a pyramid—the Madonna flanked by the young Saint John and by an angel supporting the Christ child—the foreshortening of the arms, and the careful painting of hair and draperies show Leonardo's geometrical sense and expert draftsmanship.

In contrast to Leonardo, who got on quite well with his patrons, his strong-minded contemporary Michelangelo Buonarotti (1475–1564) quarreled repeatedly with the imperious pope Julius II (1503–1513). It was a measure of his extraordinary gifts that, when he quit Rome and fled to Florence, the pope reacted with unaccustomed mildness to woo him back, writing to officials in Florence: "Michelangelo the sculptor, who left us without reason and in mere caprice, is afraid, as we are informed, of returning; though we for our part are not angry with him, knowing the humours of such men of genius."* Michelangelo's Roman commission, and the only painting assignment he deemed challenging enough for a sculptor, was to create frescoes for the ceiling and walls of the Sistine Chapel, added to the Vatican some decades earlier by Julius II's uncle, Pope Sixtus IV. The Sistine ceiling is in every respect a prodigious piece of work, often proclaimed the greatest fresco in the world. The area is approximately 54 by 134 feet, and Michelangelo covered it with 343 separate figures. He executed the whole in the space of four years, working almost single-handed, assisted only by a plasterer and a color mixer, painting uncomfortably on his back atop a scaffolding, sometimes not bothering to descend for his night's rest, and arguing stormily with the impatient pope.

For this massive undertaking, Michelangelo boldly chose not a simple subject but a series of the grandest scenes from Genesis. They are arranged in a sequence that reflects Michelangelo's Neoplatonic convictions of the ascent from the very fleshly to the sublime, beginning over the entrance with the *Drunkenness of Noah* and culminating over the altar with the *Creation.* Throughout, the recurring form is that most appropriate to a master sculptor-painter, the human figure. In this vast gallery of nudes in all types of poses, Michelangelo summed up all that Renaissance art had learned about perspective, anatomy, and motion. The Sistine ceiling also comes close to summarizing man's concepts

*Titian's portrait of Ranuccio Farnese: detail.*

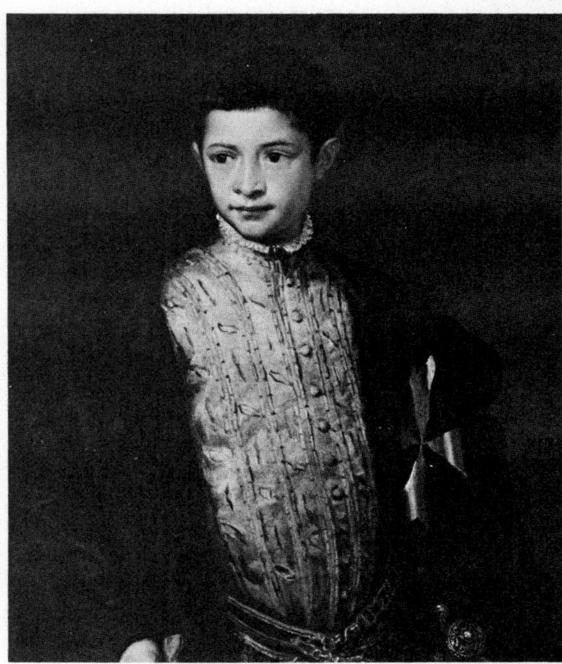

* As quoted in the *New Cambridge Modern History.* Vol. I: *The Renaissance, 1493–1520,* p. 153.

*Dürer's self-portrait of 1500.*

of God; no medieval artist would have dared to represent the deity so directly. God appears repeatedly, draped in a mantle, an ever-changing patriarch. Hovering over the waters, he is benign; giving life to the motionless Adam or directing Eve to arise, he is gently commanding; creating the sun and moon, he is the all-powerful deity, formidable and urgent as a whirlwind.

Both Michelangelo and Leonardo had received their artistic training in Florence; Titian (1477–1576) was identified with Venice. Titian's longevity was staggering: for eighty years he enjoyed almost unbroken professional success and produced an average of one picture a month. Even a partial listing of the commissions that he received underscores again the sweep of Renaissance painting and patronage. At the start of his career in Venice, Titian was hired to do frescoes for the headquarters of the German merchant colony. Then he undertook portraits for rich merchants, altarpieces and madonnas for churches and monasteries, and a great battle scene for the palace of the doge. In the middle decades of the sixteenth century, Titian had become so famous that he received offers from half the despots of Italy and crowned heads of Europe. Pope Paul III, the Hapsburg emperor Charles V, and Charles' son Philip II of Spain, became his patrons.

A gallery of Titian's portraits would make a splendid introduction to the high politics of the sixteenth century. There is Paul III, one of the last of the Renaissance popes, ambitious and authoritative; there is a condottiere at once handsome and worn, cultivated and shrewd, from the successful family of the della Rovere (which had produced Popes Sixtus IV and Julius II). Titian even accomplished the feat of making undistinguished-looking Charles V appear reasonably imperial. Rich, intense colors, especially purples and reds, are Titian's hallmark, and through them he transferred to paint the flamboyance and pageantry identified with Venice.

### The Northern Renaissance

The fame and influence of Titian and many other Italians helped to stimulate the flowering of northern European painting in the sixteenth century. This northern Renaissance also grew out of native traditions of Gothic art passed down from the Middle Ages. It was on the whole more moralistic and less exuberant than the Italian, just as the northern humanism of Erasmus was less flamboyant and more concerned with the search for a reasonable middle way between extremes. In painting the northern Renaissance centered in southern Germany and in the Low Countries: its leaders were Albrecht Dürer (1471–1528) and Hans Holbein (1497?–1543), both from Bavaria, and Pieter Brueghel the Elder (1520?–1569), who was born near Brussels. These northerners, too, had their share of artistic temperament and pride and won the patronage of the mighty. Dürer received commissions from the emperor Maximilian and Brueghel had the support of businessmen in Antwerp and Brussels. Armed with an introduction from Erasmus, Holbein moved to England, where he soon won the custom of humanists, aristocrats, and the court of King Henry VIII. Holbein executed handsome portraits of his benefactors, including the very familiar representation of Henry VIII and a likeness of Erasmus that seems to catch the great humanist's wit and intelligence.

Dürer was in many ways the Leonardo of Germany. His realistic yet compassionate portrait of his aged and homely mother might almost have been taken from da Vinci's sketchbook. He collected monkeys and other tropical specimens, painted the Virgin in the unusual pose of a *Madonna with Many Animals,* and, in the clos-

*Jan van Eyck's "Madonna with the chancellor Rolin," ca. 1434.*

ing years of his career, wrote treatises on perspective and human proportions. By sensitive use of line and shading, Dürer revolutionized the hitherto primitive techniques of copper engraving and woodcuts. These innovations permitted the reproduction of drawings in many copies and enabled artists to illustrate whole editions of volumes prepared by the new process of printing. They brought Dürer closer than any Italian painter to the rapidly expanding public of readers; they made him in effect the first artist in history to become a "bestseller."

Northern painters did not always share Italian tastes in subject matter; often they were more down-to-earth. Brueghel, for example, delighted in scenes of peasant life—weddings, dances, and festivals, executed with Rabelaisian gusto. He also painted a series of lovely landscapes—another form neglected in Italy—showing the cycle of farming activities during the various months of the year. Apparently Brueghel was not striving deliberately to be popular, as Dürer had sought popularity through the mass production of engravings and woodcuts; wealthy individuals commissioned most of Brueghel's plebeian subjects.

Northern art retained the old medieval fascination with the monstrous and the supernatural. Dürer showed this Gothic strain in a series of sixteen woodcuts depicting the Four Horsemen and the other grim marvels of the Apocalypse. In Brueghel, the strain is almost obsessive. His bizarre *Battle of the Angels and the Demons* is full of "things" whose nearest

*Detail of Donatello's statue of Mary Magdalen, ca. 1454–1455.*

relatives populate the science fiction and the surrealist art of the twentieth century—coats-of-arms that actually fight, shellfish that fly, hybrids with insect wings, artichoke bodies, and flower heads. Most of these fantasies were designed to teach a moral lesson; they were sermons in paint or ink, almost as the Gothic cathedrals had been sermons in stone. The painting of northern Europe demonstrates once more the superficiality of the old notion that the men of the Renaissance had cast off all the traditions and values of the Middle Ages.

### Sculpture

In the Renaissance, sculpture and painting maintained a close organic relationship. Italian pictures owed their three-dimensional qualities partly to the painters' study of the sister art; some of the finest painters were also accomplished sculptors—Giotto, Leonardo, Michelangelo. Sculptors, too, turned to classical models and secular themes, studied human anatomy, and experimented with new techniques.

Many of these innovations are evident in Donatello (1386?–1466), a Florentine and the first great name in Renaissance sculpture. Donatello's equestrian statue of the condottiere Gattamelata in Padua is a landmark in artistic history. The subject is secular; the treatment is classical (Gattamelata looks like the commander of a Roman legion); and the material is bronze, not the stone that sculptors had been accustomed to use during the Middle Ages. In freestanding statues of religious figures, Donatello sometimes stressed physical realism and beauty to the exclusion of any spiritual quality. His bronze David, the first statue of a nude male since antiquity, is a handsome youth rather than the divinely inspired slayer of Goliath. In a masterpiece like the statue of Mary Magdalen, however, Donatello transcended literal realism. A critic has called her "an emaciated monster." Emaciated the figure certainly is, all skin and bone, lank hair, and tattered clothing; but everything about her accents the vertical line and contributes to the statue's extraordinary quality. Mary Magdalen is a saint who looks the part.

Verrocchio (1435–1488), yet another gifted Florentine, consciously strove to outdo Donatello and chose similar subjects—the youthful nude (David), the saint (doubting Thomas), and the condottiere. He succeeded best with the last, the Colleoni statue in Venice. Another of the "universal men" of the Renaissance—painter, goldsmith, and student of architecture, geometry, music, and philosophy as well as sculptor—Verrocchio was also celebrated as the teacher of Leonardo, who worked with him for fourteen years. Equaling Verrocchio in versatility was Benvenuto Cellini (1500–1571), goldsmith, engraver, devotee of high living, author of a famous autobiography, who boasted as patrons two popes, King Francis I of France, and the Medici duke of Tuscany. Only in middle age did he turn to sculpture, and confound skeptics by producing an elegant statue of Perseus which still commands a place of honor in a loggia facing a central square in his native Florence.

As sculptors, however, the reputation of Verrocchio and Cellini has been eclipsed by the genius of Michelangelo, who brought the art to the highest summit it had reached since the Age of Pericles, perhaps the highest in its entire history. The man who painted the Sistine ceiling brought the same daring conceptions and concentrated energy to his sculptures. Early in his career, when the government of Florence offered him the exacting task of creating something beautiful from an enormous chunk of marble that another artist had already seemingly spoiled, Michelangelo produced the renowned colossal statue of David, more than sixteen feet tall. His later unfinished figures of Dawn, Day, Dusk, and Night, which adorn the tombs of the Medici in Florence, represent another successful solution of a difficult problem. The figures recline on sloping cornices yet do not look to be about to slide off. Michelangelo gave them repose and yet suggested tremendous latent power, especially in the exuberantly muscled nudes of Day and Dusk. Even more than Donatello, Michelangelo gave his best work a realism surpassing the merely literal. His remarkable statue of Moses, commissioned by Pope Julius II for his tomb, makes a good counterpart to his depictions of God on the Sistine ceiling: one side of the prophet's face shows compassion, the other reveals the stern and wrathful law-giver. In portraying the *Pietà,* the Virgin grieving over the dead Christ, Michelangelo brilliantly solved the difficult technical problem of posing a seated woman with an adult corpse lying across her lap, and he triumphantly called attention to his feat by executing the work in highly polished marble. The face of Mary is sorrowful yet composed, and younger than that of the dead Christ. She is the eternal Virgin, Michelangelo explained, and so is always youthful and does not grieve as an earthly mother would.

### Architecture

In 1546, at the age of seventy, Michelangelo shouldered one more artistic burden: he agreed to be the chief architect of St. Peter's. Though he died long before the great Roman basilica was finally completed in 1626, and his successors altered many of his details, the huge dome, the key feature of the whole structure, followed Michelangelo's basic design. St. Peter's shows most of the characteristics that separate the architectural style of the Renaissance from the Gothic of the High Middle Ages. Gone are the great spires and towers: in their place is Michelangelo's dome, which rises 435 feet above the floor below yet is almost dwarfed in mass by the immense building underneath. While Gothic structures, with their great windows, pointed arches, and high-flung vaults, create an impression of strain and instability, St. Peter's, with its round arches, heavier walls, and stout columns, seems indestructible.

St. Peter's also has the symmetry so admired by Renaissance builders; everything about it fits into a tidy geometrical pattern. Michelangelo cast that pattern in the shape of a Greek cross, which has four arms of equal length, whereas the Gothic cathedral had taken the form of a Latin cross, with the nave in the long arm. Though the Greek-cross design was later modified, St. Peter's still retains many traces of the original plan. The balanced character of the whole edifice is enhanced by the magnificent curving colonnades which were built in the early seventeenth century in the great square outside the basilica and which carry the eye of the approaching visitor straight to the church of the pope.

One great source of the new interest in classical architecture was the study of ruins from Roman antiquity. The pioneering student was Brunelleschi (1377?–1446), whose innovative contributions to building may be compared to those of Giotto and Masaccio in painting and Donatello in sculpture. Brunelleschi surprised and delighted Florence when he designed the Foundlings' Asylum (Ospedale degli Innocenti) with an arcade of graceful Roman arches and other delicate classical details. Brunelleschi's major achievement was the erection of a monumental dome atop the cathedral in Florence, the prototype of that designed for St. Peter's by Michelangelo. Beautifully proportioned, with more accent on the vertical than the domes of classical antiquity, it covered a space 350 feet wide and 300 feet high; its 25,000 tons of stone were hoisted into place without immense scaffolding in a tour de force of engineering.

Another element in Renaissance architecture was the learning of the humanists, particularly Platonic and Pythagorean concepts of perfect ideas and perfect geometric forms. Palladio (1518–1580), the foremost architectural theorist of the age, praised the Greek-cross plan for churches because of its symbolic values. If the apses (at the ends of the four arms) were rounded, and if the spaces between the arms were filled with rounded chapels, then the whole structure became an almost perfect circle. And the circle, according to Palladio, "demonstrates extremely well the unity, the infinite essence, the uniformity, and the justice of God."* Some

* Quoted by Rudolf Wittkower, *The Architectural Principles of the Age of Humanism* (London, 1949), p. 21.

scholars have taken the change in the plan of the church structure from the Latin cross to the circled Greek cross to symbolize a shift in religious emphasis. The Gothic stress on the sacrifice of Christ yields to the Renaissance celebration of the perfection of God.

Palladio himself designed many structures—villas, palaces, a church, a theater—characterized by the grace and elegance that have given the adjective "Palladian" its meaning. The total architectural record of the Renaissance, while including St. Peter's and other churches, is notable for the large number of purely secular buildings. This conspicuous display of worldly wealth was partly an example of the decline of medieval values in the face of mounting materialism, political ambition, and other forms of secular pride. But it was also a simple question of economics and security. The expansion of business gave private individuals the money to finance the construction of lavish residences. The gradual growth of effective government meant that, even in country districts, a man's home could be a showplace and no longer had to be, quite literally, his castle.

Elaborately symmetrical villas now ornamented the countryside; in the cities the characteristic structure was the *palazzo* or palace, usually not a royal or official establishment but an imposing private townhouse combining business offices and residential apartments. Palaces by the dozen went up in Rome and Florence; in Venice they lined the Grand Canal almost solidly from one end to the other. The usual palazzo was three-storied and rectangular, with its windows arranged in symmetrical rows. Architects relieved the effect of monotonous regularity by such decorative devices as pillars, pilasters, and cornices, and by using a different finish of stone for each story, with the roughest at the bottom. The dimensions of the largest palazzi rivaled the monuments of ancient Rome; the Pitti Palace, erected in Florence by a millionaire rival of the Medici, was 475 feet long and 114 feet high.

The fame of Italian builders soon spread throughout Europe, even to distant Moscow, where Italian experts supervised the remodeling of the Kremlin for Ivan III. Most countries did not copy the Italian style straight-out, but grafted

*Palladio's Palazzo Chiericati, Vicenza.*

it onto the older native architecture. The resulting compound occasionally produced some strikingly elegant buildings, particularly the great chateaux constructed in the Loire valley of central France during the sixteenth century. The combination of elements taken from the feudal castle, the Gothic church, and the Italian palace gives these chateaux some of the magic and the unreality of a fairy tale.

### Music

The structure of music is often called architectural. A musical composition, like a building, has its basic skeleton or form, its over-all line, and also its surface decorations and embellishments. The sacred music of the Middle Ages, had achieved very complex and elaborate combinations of form, line, and decoration. Piling voice upon voice in complicated harmony, a technique known as polyphony, fusing a multitude of parts into a single whole, these ecclesiastical compositions have sometimes been compared to Gothic cathedrals. In the late Middle Ages, the center of Gothic music was the Burgundian domain in northern France and the Low Countries. By the fifteenth century French and Flemish musicians were journeying to Italy, where a process of mutual influence developed. The northerners took up the simple tunes of southern folk songs and dances; the Italians, in turn, added a strain of Gothic complexity to the austere plainsong, which had long been the mainstay of their sacred music. The end products of the interaction were the sacred and secular polyphonic compositions of the internationally renowned Flemish composer Josquin des Prez (ca. 1450–1521) and the hundred odd masses of the Italian composer Palestrina (ca. 1526–1594). Much of this music sounds quite otherworldly today, since it lacks the dissonances and the strong rhythms and climaxes to which we are accustomed.

Musicians, too, were affected by the secularism and individualism of the Renaissance and by its taste for experimentation. The Flemings sometimes based even their masses on rowdy popular tunes. Composers and performers began to lose the anonymity associated with the Middle Ages, although the era of prima donnas and other "stars" had not quite arrived. Paid professional singers staffed the famous choirs of Antwerp cathedral and of the Vatican. Josquin des Prez found patrons at the courts of Milan, Rome, and Paris, and both the pope and various cardinals commissioned Palestrina to write masses. Musicians developed or imported a variety of new instruments—the violin, doublebass, and harpsichord; the organ, with its complement of keyboards, pedals, and stops; the kettledrum, which was adopted from the Polish army; and the lute, which had originally been developed in medieval Persia and reached Italy by way of Spain.

A retinue of musicians became a fixture of court life, with the dukes of Burgundy, Philip the Good and Charles the Bold, leading the way. In the third estate German artisans, calling themselves mastersingers, organized choral groups; the most famous of them, Hans Sachs, a cobbler in Nuremberg in the 1500's, was later immortalized in Wagner's opera *Die Meistersinger*.

The mastersingers followed directly in the tradition of the thirteenth-century minnesingers. And princely patronage of music went back at least to the twelfth-century court of Eleanor of Aquitaine and its chivalric troubadours. Musicians as well as poets, the troubadours and minnesingers had sung of the great secular subjects, war and love. Once again, the history of music underlines the important fact that the Renaissance did not represent a sharp break with the past but instead built on the legacy it had received from the Middle Ages.

## IV Science

### An Age of Preparation

In science, particularly, the term "Renaissance" must not be applied in its literal meaning of "rebirth." A scientific revolution did occur in early modern times, but it came in the seventeenth century of Galileo and Newton after the Renaissance had run its course. In the history of science, the fourteenth, fifteenth, and sixteenth centuries were a time of preparation. Men of science absorbed, enlarged, criticized, and modified the body of scientific knowledge handed down to them from the Middle Ages and from antiquity. The followers of the old Scholastic tradition, the new humanists, and artists and craftsmen of every kind, all contributed to this important work of preparation.

Medieval Scholasticism had been by no means antiscientific. The intellectual discipline of the Schoolmen, their habit of systematic work, and their enthusiasm for Aristotle made them, in a sense, precursors of the scientific revolution. These Scholastic traditions remained very much alive after the eclipse of the Schoolmen themselves toward the close of the Middle Ages. Despite the bias of humanism against Aristotle, Aristotelian studies continued to be pursued vigorously at the universities of Paris and of Padua, in northern Italy. Meantime, the humanists steadily increased the amount of ancient scientific writing available to the scholarly world; Galen, Ptolemy, Archimedes, and others were for the first time translated from Greek into the more accessible Latin.

Humanism, however, also thwarted the advance of science; the worship of classical antiquity tended to put old authorities high on a pedestal, beyond the reach of criticism. Few men of the Renaissance believed it possible to improve on the astronomy taught by Ptolemy during the second century A.D., or on the medicine taught by Galen in the same century. Galen, for example, had advanced the erroneous theory that the blood moved from one side of the heart to the other by passing through invisible pores in the thick wall of tissue separating the two sides of the organ. Actually, as Harvey was to discover in the seventeenth century, the blood gets from the one side to the other by circulating through the body and lungs. Galen's theory of invisible pores, however, was enough to keep Leonardo from anticipating Harvey. Leonardo's anatomical studies led him up to the brink of discovery; then he backed away, for he was certain that Galen could not have been wrong.

Leonardo, in fact, illustrates both the shortcomings and the achievements of Renaissance science. On the one hand, he took notes in a hit-or-miss fashion, and in a secretive left-handed writing which must be held up to a mirror to be read. He exerted little direct influence, because he did not have the modern scientist's concern for the systematic cataloging of observations and the frequent publication of findings and speculations. On the other hand, Leonardo showed remarkable inventiveness, drawing plans for lathes, pumps, war machines, flying machines, and many other contraptions, not all of them workable, but all highly imaginative. He had a passionate curiosity for anatomy and proportions, and for almost everything about man and nature. His accurate drawings of human embryos differed radically from the older notion of the fetus as a perfectly formed miniature human being. Moreover, Leonardo did not always bow before established authority, as he did before Galen. His geological studies convinced him that the earth was far older than the men of his time thought it to be. The Po River, he estimated, must have been flowing for about 200,000 years to wash down the sediments forming its alluvial plain in northern Italy.

### Technology and Invention

The best-known invention of the Renaissance—the printed book—furnishes an instructive case history of the way in which many technological advances contributed to the end result. The revolution in book production began when medieval Europeans imported paper, a Chinese invention, and found it to be cheaper than the lambskin or sheepskin previously used by copyists. The next step came when engravers, pioneering in the methods later used by Dürer, made woodcuts or copper plates that could produce many copies of the same drawing. Then sentences were added to the cuts or plates to explain the sketches. Finally, movable type was devised. Each piece of type was simply a minute bit of engraving which could be combined with other pieces to form words, sentences, a whole page, and then salvaged to be used over and over again. This crucial invention occurred during the 1440's, almost certainly in the German Rhineland; Johann Gutenberg, who used to receive the credit for it, has been the focus of a scholarly controversy that has deflated his old heroic reputation.

The new invention gained wide popularity. By 1500, Italy alone had seventy-three presses employing movable type; the most famous was the Aldine Press in Venice, named for its founder, Aldus Manutius (1450–1515). The Aldine Press won its reputation by selling at reasonable prices scholarly editions of the classics printed in a beautiful typeface which, reportedly, was modeled on the handwriting of Petrarch and is the source of modern italics. Everywhere the printing press suddenly made both classical and vernacular literature available to large numbers of people who could never have afforded hand-copied manuscripts. Without the perfection of printing, Erasmus might not have become the acknowledged arbiter of European letters. Without it, Luther could not have secured the rapid distribution of his antipapal tracts, and the Protestant Reformation might not have rent Christian Europe asunder.

Although no other single invention can be compared with printing on the score of quick and decisive effects, many innovations ultimately had comparable influence. Gunpowder, for example, brought from China to medieval Europe, was used in the fighting of the early 1400's, notably the later campaigns of the Hundred Years' War. Improved firearms and artillery were to doom both the feudal knight and the feudal castle, for both were vulnerable to the new weapons. In navigation, as we have seen, the Venetians made galleys swifter, more capacious, and more seaworthy. At the same time, important marine aids came into general use, particularly the magnetic compass and the sailing charts which, at least for the Mediterranean, established a high level of accuracy. By the close of the fifteenth century, Europeans possessed the equipment needed for the oncoming age of world discovery.

On land, the mining industry scored impressive technological advances. The engineers of the late medieval centuries solved some of the problems of extracting and smelting silver, iron, and other ores. Then, in 1556, a German physician and mining expert published a comprehensive treatise on the practices of the industry. Following the custom of the day, he called himself Agricola, a Latinized version of his German name, Bauer which means peasant. His treatise, *De Re Metallica* (*All About Metals*), was translated from Latin into English in 1912 by a famous American mining engineer and his wife, Mr. and Mrs. Herbert Hoover. Agricola's treatise was an early specimen of those handbooks that are indispensable to the engineer. And its detailed observations on soil structures also made it a pioneer study in geology.

### Medicine

Medical knowledge and skills advanced unevenly during the Renaissance. Anatomical studies moved ahead, aided by a partial lifting of the old ban on dissecting human cadavers and by the wide dissemination of printed books with clear and fairly accurate biological illustrations. Pharmacology also progressed, thanks to experiments with the chemistry of drugs made by the eccentric Swiss physician Paracelsus (Theophrastus Bombastus von Hohenheim, 1493–1541). Despite his classical name, Paracelsus delighted in iconoclastic gestures, like insisting on lecturing in German and burning the works of Galen to show his contempt for classical authority. The French surgeon Ambroise Paré (1517–1590), who also had little reverence for antiquity, laid the foundations for modern surgery by developing new techniques, notably that of sewing up blood vessels with stitches rather than cauterizing them with a hot iron. Many so-called physicians, however, were quacks, and many teachers of medicine continued to repeat for their classes the demonstrations that Galen had made more than a thousand years before, without attempting to test the validity of his findings. A striking exception to this rule was furnished by the physicians and scholars of the University of Padua. Protected against possible ecclesiastical censorship by the overlordship of Venice, which controlled the city, they maintained a lively tradition of scientific inquiry that presaged the seventeenth-century triumphs of the experimental method.

In 1537, a young Belgian named Vesalius (1514–1564), trained at Paris, took a teaching post at Padua. Vesalius repeated the dissections of Galen, but always with an open mind, always on the lookout for errors. Thus he rejected Galen's notion of invisible pores in the wall of tissue within the heart, because he could not find such pores. In 1543, Vesalius published *De Humanis Corporis Fabrica* (*Concerning the Structure of the Human Body*). This great anatomical study, while largely confirming the teachings of older authorities, did not hesitate to point out some of their shortcomings. Vesalius prepared the work with admirable concern for accuracy and detail, and provided elaborate woodcuts for illustrations.

### Astronomy

The year 1543 marked not only the appearance of Vesalius' treatise but also the launching of modern astronomical studies with the publication of Copernicus' *De Revolutionibus Orbium Coelestium* (*Concerning the Revolutions of Heavenly Bodies*). Born in Poland, of German extraction, Copernicus (1473–1543) studied law and medicine at Padua and other Italian universities, spent thirty years as canon of a cathedral near Danzig, and made his real career in mathematics and astronomy. His scientific work led him to attack the traditional hypothesis of the geocentric (earth-centered) universe derived from Ptolemy and other astronomers of antiquity. In its place, he advanced the revolutionary new hypothesis of the heliocentric (sun-centered) universe.

The concept of the geocentric universe generally accepted in the sixteenth century included an elaborate system of spheres. Around the stationary earth there revolved some eighty spheres, each, as it were, a separate sky containing some of the heavenly bodies, each moving on an invisible circular path, each transparent so that we mortals could see the spheres beyond it. This imaginative and symmetrical picture of the universe had already come under attack before the time of Copernicus, for observers had had trouble making it agree with the actual behavior of heavenly bodies. Copernicus used both these earlier criticisms and his own computations to arrive at the heliocentric concept. He prefaced this explanation to *De Revolutionibus:*

> . . . What moved me to consider another way of reckoning the motions of the heavenly spheres was nothing else than my realisation that Mathematicians were not agreed about the matter of their research. . . . In setting out the motions of the Sun and Moon and of the five other planets they did not in each case employ the same principles, assumptions and demonstrations of apparent revolutions and motions. For some used concentric circles only, others eccentrics and epicycles, by which, none the less, they were not able to fully arrive at what they sought. . . .
>
> And so after long consideration of the uncertainty of the mathematical traditions about the inferring of the motions of the spheres, it began to vex me that no more certain system of the motions of the machine of the world . . . could be agreed upon by the philosophers. . . .
>
> I . . . began to think about the mobility of the earth. And although it seemed an absurd opinion, . . . I discovered by much and long observation, that if the motions of the rest of the planets are compared with the motion of the earth, . . . not only do their appearances follow therefrom, but the system moreover so connects the orders and sizes both of the planets and of their orbits, and indeed the whole heaven, that in no part of it can anything be moved without bringing to confusion the rest of the parts and the whole universe.*

The Copernican hypothesis of a moving earth had quite radical implications. It destroyed the idea of the earth's uniqueness by suggesting that it acted like other heavenly bodies, and it opened the door to attacks on the uniqueness of the earth's human inhabitants. Nevertheless, once Copernicus had reversed the roles of the sun and the earth, his universe retained many Ptolemaic characteristics. Its heavens were still filled with spheres revolving along their invisible orbits. Only they now moved about a stationary sun, instead of the stationary earth, and Copernican astronomy required only thirty-four of them, not eighty. The revolution in astronomy begun by Copernicus did not reach its culmination for a hundred and fifty years. The circular orbits of Copernicus had to yield to elliptical orbits; the scheme of thirty-four spheres had to be modified; and a theory explaining the forces that kept the universe together had to be put forward. And all these developments had to await the genius of Galileo and Newton, and the observations made possible by the invention of the telescope.

## V Religion

### The Impact of the Renaissance

Although Copernicus dedicated his great book to the pope, Christendom did not welcome a theory that challenged the orthodox belief in an earth-centered and man-centered universe. By the time Copernicus published, however, Western Christendom was split into the warring factions of Catholic and Protestant. To what extent was the Renaissance responsible for the shattering religious crisis of the Reformation? There is no simple answer to this question. The

* Quoted in F. Sherwood Taylor, *A Short History of Science and Scientific Thought* (New York, 1949), pp. 83–84.

next chapter examines in more detail the reasons for the Protestant revolt; here a few conclusions about the relationship between the Renaissance and religion may be suggested.

First, the Renaissance did not make the Reformation inevitable. It is an oversimplification to suppose that the religious individualism of Luther arose directly out of the more general individualism of the Renaissance. Looking back over the checkered culture of the age, one can find many elements—materialism, self-indulgence, power politics—that are hard to reconcile with traditional Christian values. If pushed to extremes, these elements could indeed become anti-Christian—but they were seldom pushed to extremes. Even the most ruthless condottieri of politics and business, men like Cesare Borgia and Jacob Fugger, remained nominal Christians. Also, a pronounced anticlerical like Machiavelli reserved his most stinging criticism for the pope's claim to temporal authority, not his claim to ecclesiastical supremacy. And, in rebuking the pope for political maneuvering, he was following the example of the profoundly Christian Dante.

*Fresco by Melosso da Forli showing Pope Sixtus IV appointing the Vatican librarian, 1475.*

Second, the most characteristic intellectual movement of the Renaissance—humanism—did not propose to replace the traditional Christian values of the Middle Ages with a whole new set of values. On a lower level, much of the fun in the *Decameron* derives from that time-honored object of satire, often lampooned in the Middle Ages, the misbehaving cleric. On a higher level, men like Pico and Erasmus proposed to enrich or purify Christianity; they did not intend to subvert it. As a matter of fact, the Neoplatonic doctrines cherished by Pico and the Platonic Academy had long been identified with the mystical aspects of the Catholic faith. Erasmus, perhaps the most representative thinker of humanism, was too strongly attached to Catholicism and too moderate in temperament to be a revolutionary.

Finally, a religious crisis was indeed gathering during the Renaissance, but it was more internal than external. That is, the Church was only to a limited extent the victim of outside forces operating beyond its control, like the challenge presented to its old international dominion by the new national monarchies. If the Church of the 1400's had been strong and healthy, it might have met such external challenges successfully. Except in Spain, however, the Church was neither strong nor healthy.

## The Condition of the Church

The Renaissance Church as a whole had a low moral tone, although many honorable exceptions to the prevailing laxity and backwardness could be found. Priests were often illiterate, underpaid, and immoral, with little preparation for the effective exercise of their responsibilities. Many bishops—following good medieval precedent, it must be admitted—behaved as politicians, not as churchmen. Perhaps the worst shortcomings existed at the top, in the papacy itself. In the fourteenth and early fifteenth centuries, the papacy experienced a series of crises—the Babylonian Captivity, the Great Schism, and the Conciliar Movement. It emerged from the ordeal with its power reinvigorated, notably by its victory over the reformers who sought to make church councils a check against unlimited papal absolutism. But the triple crisis gravely damaged the spiritual prestige of the office.

*Pope Alexander VI, from a lunette, "The Resurrected Christ," in the Vatican.*

Sixtus IV, Alexander VI, Julius II, and the other popes of the High Renaissance did little to repair the damage. For three quarters of a century after 1450, the see of Peter was occupied by men who scored political and military successes or who were munificent patrons of art and learning. The modern world is indebted to them for the Vatican Library, the beginning of the Basilica of St. Peter, the Sistine Chapel and its frescoes, and a long roster of other works of art. Yet their magnificence cost immense sums of money, increased the burden of ecclesiastical taxation and other fiscal demands, and increased also the resentment that higher levies usually arouse. Their indifference to their spiritual functions enfeebled the Church at a time when it needed firm and dedicated control. The Church was ruled by connoisseurs and condottieri when it needed reformers.

Intellectually, too, the clergy were losing the vitality they had possessed in the age of Abelard and Aquinas. Some of the monks and friars on university faculties hardly qualified as teachers; they blindly defended a decadent Scholasticism against the new humanist studies. These reactionary educators provoked the most blistering satire of the Renaissance, *The Letters of Obscure Men.* It all began when Johann Reuchlin (1455–1522), a German humanist working with Pico at Florence, caught his enthusiasm for comparative religious studies and learned Hebrew in order to read the great books of Judaism. On returning to Germany, Reuchlin aroused the wrath of theological faculties by suggesting that a knowledge of Hebrew and of the sacred Jewish writings might enable a man to be a better-informed Christian. Arraigned in an ecclesiastical court, Reuchlin, who was a layman, assembled in his defense testimonials from leading humanists, *The Letters of Eminent Men.* Then, in 1516 and 1517, a couple of his friends published *The Letters of Obscure Men,* supposedly exchanged between Reuchlin's clerical opponents but actually a hoax designed to laugh the opposition out of court by mocking the futility of theological hair-splitting. One of the "obscure men" related an experience in a Roman tavern:

For you must know that we were lately sitting in an inn, having our supper, and were eating eggs, when on opening one, I saw that there was a young chicken within.

This I showed to a comrade; whereupon quoth he to me, "Eat it up speedily, before the taverner sees it, for if he mark it, you will have to pay for a fowl."

In a trice I gulped down the egg, chicken and all.

And then I remembered that it was Friday!

Whereupon I said to my crony, "You have made me commit a mortal sin, in eating flesh on the sixth day of the week!"

But he averred that it was not a mortal sin—nor even a venial one, seeing that such a chickling is accounted merely as an egg, until it is born.

Then I departed, and thought the matter over.

And by the Lord, I am in a mighty quandary, and know not what to do.

It seemeth to me that these young fowls in eggs are flesh, because their substance is formed and fashioned into the limbs and body of an animal, and possesseth a vital principle.

It is different in the case of grubs in cheese, and such-like, because grubs are accounted fish, as I learnt from a physician who is also skilled in Natural Philosophy.

Most earnestly do I entreat you to resolve the question that I have propounded. For if you hold that the sin is mortal, then, I would fain get shrift here, ere I return to Germany.*

While Reuchlin lost his case, he never paid the costs of the trial, as he was sentenced to do.

## Attempts at Renewal and Reform

Dedicated Christians, both lay and clerical, were aware that the Church needed a thorough cleansing. Fresh attempts within the ecclesiastical hierarchy to increase the powers of representative church councils failed, however, in the face of papal opposition. And the great renovation of the Spanish church fostered by Queen Isabella and Cardinal Jiménez was restricted to Spanish lands.

Meantime, a quiet kind of Catholic renewal had been advanced by the activities of the Brothers and Sisters of the Common Life. Founded in the Low Countries in the 1370's, they consisted of lay people who pooled their resources in communal living and followed the spiritual discipline of a monastic order without, however, taking religious vows. They also emphasized service to one's fellow man as a way of practicing the high ideals of Christianity. Opposed to Scholasticism, the Brethren of the Common Life started schools of their own, which had a high reputation in fifteenth-century Europe. Erasmus, who was educated in one of them, complained that the curriculum was too orthodox and rigid, yet he adopted the goals of the Brethren in his own "philosophy of Christ," with its belief that men should be guided in their daily lives by the example of Jesus. A similar theme, expressed in more mystical terms, ran through the devotional book *Imitation of Christ,* written by Thomas à Kempis, one of the Brethren. While the book soon won enormous popularity, its message, like that of the Brothers of the Common Life, was addressed to the inner spiritual life of the individual rather than to the reform of the Christian community or its institutions.

A more radical and sweeping reform movement was launched by the Dominican friar Savonarola (1452–1498), who won the favor of the Medici through the influence of Pico. His eloquent sermons and reputed gift of predicting the future soon made him the most popular preacher in Florence. Sparing no one in his denunciations of un-Christian conduct he delivered this typical tirade:

> You Christians should always have the Gospel with you, I do not mean the book, but the spirit, for if you do not possess the spirit of grace and yet carry with you the whole book, of what advantage is it to you? And again, all the more foolish are they who carry round their necks Breviaries, notes, tracts and writings, until they look like pedlars going to a fair. Charity does not consist in the writing of papers. The true books of Christ are the Apostles and saints, and true reading consists in imitating their lives. But in these days men are like books made by the Devil. They speak against pride and ambition and yet they are immersed in them up to their eyes. They preach chastity and maintain concubines. They enjoin fasting and partake of splendid feasts. . . . Only look to-day at the prelates. They are tied to earthly vanities. They love them. The cure of souls is no longer their chief concern. . . . In the Primitive Church the chalices were made of wood and the prelates of gold—today—chalices of gold, prelates of wood!*

He particularly abominated Pope Alexander VI, whom he cursed for "a devil" and "a monster" presiding over a "ribald" and "harlot" Church.

In the political confusion following the death of Lorenzo the Magnificent (1492), Savonarola rapidly gained power and prestige in Florence. He attracted many enthusiastic supporters, among them Pico, Botticelli, and Michelangelo. By 1497, he was virtual dictator of the republic and organized troops of boys and girls to tour the city, collect all "vanities," from cosmetics to pagan books and paintings, and burn them on public bonfires. This hysterical pitch of zeal could not be sustained for long, however. Alexander VI placed Florence under an interdict and excommunicated Savonarola, whose popular following began to disperse, especially after he had failed in his promise to bring a miracle to pass. He promised to demonstrate his divine inspiration by going unscathed through the ordeal by fire, but the spectacle was canceled at the last moment. Within a short time, Savonarola was condemned for heresy; on May 23, 1498, he was hanged and his body was burnt.

Savonarola perished not only by the hands of his political and ecclesiastical enemies but also through his own fanaticism. Like most extreme

* Adapted from *Epistolae Obscurorum Virorum,* ed. F. G. Stokes (New Haven, 1925), pp. 445–447.

* Quoted by Piero Misciatelli, *Savonarola* (New York, 1930), pp. 60–61.

puritans, he did not realize that morals could not be transformed overnight; he was in a sense too unworldly to survive. But the Church that he sought to purge was too worldly to survive without undergoing the major crisis of the Reformation.

## VI Conclusion

It is not easy to define an era as complex as the Renaissance. No definition in fact can take in all its currents and cross-currents or encompass such extraordinarily different personalities as Erasmus and Savonarola. No single man of the time, no single masterpiece of art or literature, was fully typical of the Renaissance. And yet there is something about most of its great men and most of its great books, paintings, and sculptures that sets them apart from the great figures and works of other ages. Humanists like Petrarch, Pico, and Erasmus do differ from Thomas Aquinas; Cesare Borgia, Lorenzo the Magnificent, and Louis XI of France have very little in common with Louis IX; the sculpture of Michelangelo does not resemble that of Chartres, nor does a painting by Masaccio much resemble stained glass; St. Peter's belongs to an era unlike that of Mont-Saint-Michel or Notre Dame. The men of the Renaissance lived in a world no longer medieval but not yet fully modern. Their changing values and ideals were presented most sympathetically and disarmingly in a dialogue on manners published in 1528, *The Courtier* by Castiglione.

A book of etiquette may often reveal much about a way of life. Castiglione knew his subject; himself an elegant aristocrat, he had spent years on diplomatic missions and at the highly civilized court of Urbino. He begins his delineation of the ideal courtier with a group of traits differing very little from those commended in the paladins of medieval chivalry:

> I will have this our Courtier to be a gentleman born and of a good house. For it is a great deal less dispraise for him that is not born a gentleman to fail in the acts of virtue than for a gentleman.
>
> I will have him by nature to have not only a wit and a comely shape of person and countenance, but also a certain grace, and, as they say, a hue, that shall make him at the first sight acceptable and loving unto who so beholdeth him.
>
> I judge the principal and true profession of a Courtier ought to be in feats of arms, the which above all I will have him to practise lively.*

The chivalry of Castiglione has all the patronizing attitude of the patrician toward the plebeian, yet it never gets out of hand; it is restrained by the sense of balance and grasp of reality that we have already found in some of the humanists. In love, the perfect gentleman should adore in his lady "no less the beauty of the mind than of the body." In duels and private quarrels, he should be far more moderate than the medieval knight thought to be honorable. He should excel in sport, like the knight of old, should hunt, wrestle, swim, "play at tennis." Again Castiglione sounds the note of balance:

> Therefore will I have our Courtier to descend many times to more easy and pleasant exercises. And to avoid envy and to keep company pleasantly with every man, let him do whatsoever other men do.†

The courtier should also receive a good education

> . . . in those studies which they call Humanity, and . . . have not only the understanding of the Latin tongue, but also of the Greek, because of the many and sundry things that with great excellency are written in it. Let him much exercise himself in poets, and no less in orators and historiographers, and also in writing both rhyme and prose, and especially in this our vulgar tongue.‡

Here in *The Courtier* we encounter once again the celebrated Renaissance concept of the universal man that we have already met in the writings of Pico and Rabelais and witnessed in the

* Adapted from Castiglione, *The Courtier*, trans. T. Hoby, modernized (1907), pp. 21, 23, 26.

† Ibid., p. 35.

‡ Ibid., p. 70.

# *The Renaissance*

Influenced by the humanists' enthusiasm for classical antiquity, Renaissance artists looked back to Rome for models, and influenced by the secularism and individualism of the age, they experimented with new techniques and new forms. Painting and sculpture were emancipated from their medieval subordination to architecture, now no longer "queen of the arts." Whereas statues, carvings, altarpieces, and stained glass had contributed magnificently to the glory of Romanesque and Gothic churches, they had almost never been entities in themselves but only parts of a larger whole. In the Renaissance the number of "freestanding" pictures and statues—independent aesthetic objects — steadily increased, though many great artists continued to decorate ecclesiastical structures. The artist himself gained increasing status as a professional man and as a creative personality. The celebrated individualism of the Renaissance was replacing the anonymous or community character of much medieval art.

*Saint John the Baptist, by Donatello.*

European Art Color, Peter Adelberg, N.Y.C.

*The Lamentation, by Giotto: detail.*
Scrovegni Chapel, Padua. Scala.

*Virgin and Child, by Sandro Botticelli. Poldi Pezzoli, Milan.*

European Art Color, Peter Adelberg, N.Y.C.

The Metropolitan Museum of Art, gift of Henry G. Marquand, 1889.

The Metropolitan Museum of Art, The Jules S. Bache Collection, 1949.

*Francesco Sassetti and His Son Teodoro, by Domenico Ghirlandaio.*

*Opposite: Portrait of a Man and a Woman at a Casement, from the workshop of Fra Filippo Lippi.*

*Detail of Piero della Francesca's fresco cycle, The Legend of the True Cross, in the Church of S. Francesco, Arezzo, 1452–1459.*

European Art Color, Peter Adelberg, N.Y.C.

*Ginevra de' Benci, by Leonardo da Vinci. National Gallery of Art, Washington.*

The Granger Collection

*The Three Graces: detail of a fresco by Raphael. Villa Farnesina, Rome.*

European Art Color, Peter Adelberg, N.Y.C.

*Pendentive, west wall, the Sistine Chapel: David and Goliath, by Michelangelo.*

European Art Color, Peter Adelberg, N.Y.C.

*Venus and the Lute Player, by Titian.*

The Metropolitan Museum of Art, Munsey Fund, 1936.

*Opposite: The Madonna with the Long Neck, by Parmigianino. Uffizi Gallery, Florence.*

European Art Color, Peter Adelberg, N.Y.C.

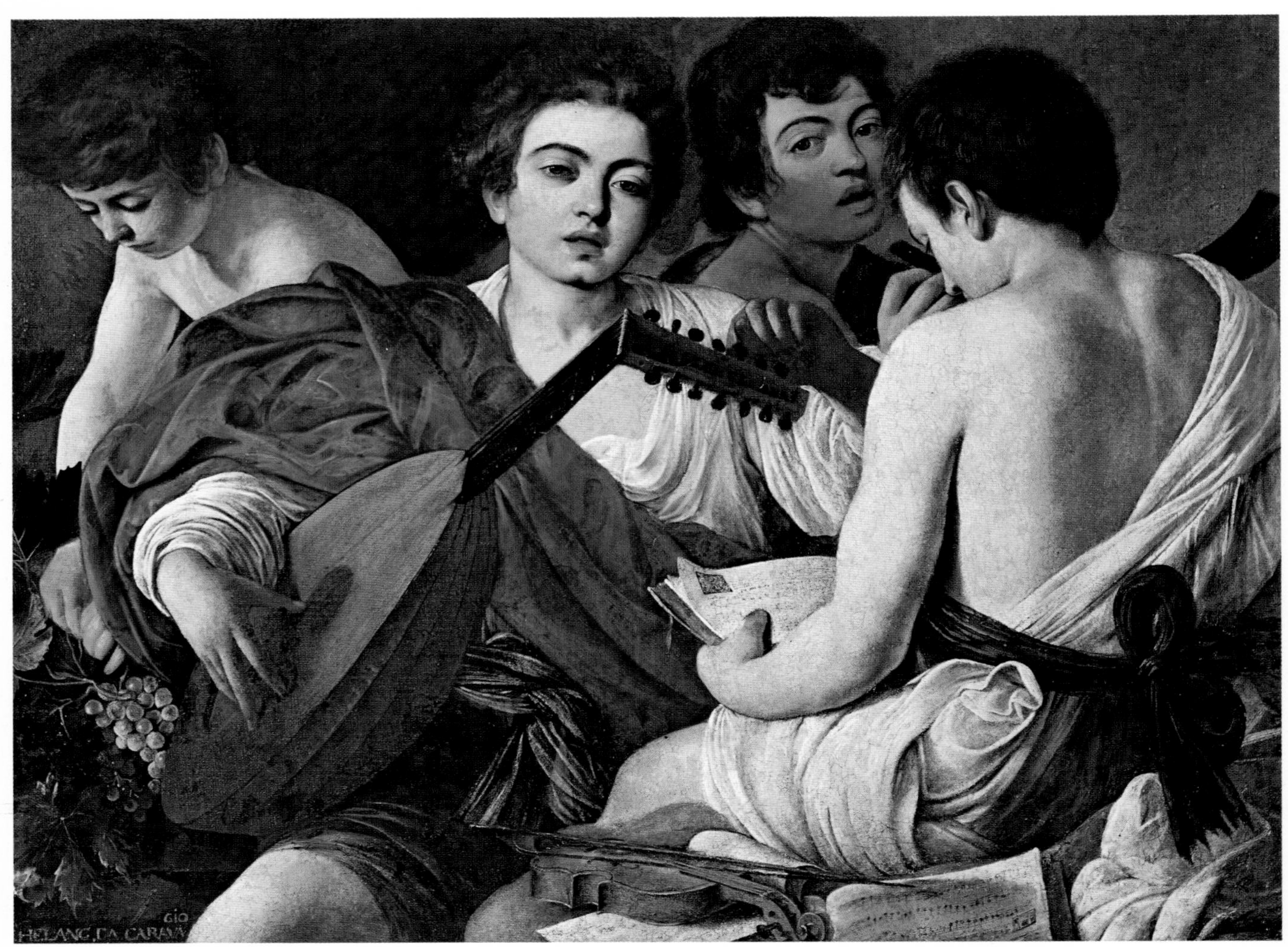

*The Musicians, by Caravaggio.*

The Metropolitan Museum of Art, Rogers Fund, 1952.

*The Harvesters, by Pieter Brueghel the Elder: detail.*

The Metropolitan Museum of Art, Rogers Fund, 1919.

*The Virgin and Child with Saint Anne, by Albrecht Dürer.*
The Metropolitan Museum of Art, bequest of Benjamin Altman, 1913.

*Opposite: The Judgment of Paris, by Lucas Cranach the Elder.*
The Metropolitan Museum of Art, Rogers Fund, 1928.

*Henry VIII, by Hans Holbein the Younger.*

Sammlung Thyssen Bornemisza, Castagnola, Switzerland.

wide-ranging careers of Giotto, Leonardo, Michelangelo, and others.

Finally, when Castiglione praises the beauty of the world (which is, of course, Ptolemaic, not Copernican), he puts into words more eloquently than any of his contemporaries the style of the Renaissance:

> Behold the state of this great engine of the world, which God created for the health and preservation of everything that was made: The heaven round beset with so many heavenly lights; and in the middle the Earth environed with the elements and upheld with the very weight of itself. . . . These things among themselves have such force by the knitting together of an order so necessarily framed that, with altering them any one jot, they should all be loosed and the world would decay. They have also such beauty and comeliness that all the wits men have can not imagine a more beautiful matter.
>
> Think now of the shape of man, which may be called a little world, in whom every parcel of his body is seen to be necessarily framed by art and not by hap, and then the form altogether most beautiful. . . . Leave Nature, and come to art. . . . Pillars and great beams uphold high buildings and palaces, and yet are they no less pleasureful unto the eyes of the beholders than profitable to the buildings. . . . Besides other things, therefore, it giveth a great praise to the world in saying that it is beautiful. It is praised in saying the beautiful heaven, beautiful earth, beautiful sea, beautiful rivers, beautiful woods, trees, gardens, beautiful cities, beautiful churches, houses, armies. In conclusion, this comely and holy beauty is a wondrous setting out of everything. And it may be said that good and beautiful be after a sort one self thing. . . .*

A medieval man might also have coupled the good and the beautiful, but he would have stressed the good, the mysterious ways in which God led man to righteousness. Medieval man had a vision of God's world. The age of Leonardo and of humanism, which Castiglione interpreted so faithfully, had a vision not only of God's world but also of nature's world and man's world.

* Ibid., pp. 348–349.

## Reading Suggestions on the Renaissance

GENERAL ACCOUNTS

E. P. Cheyney, *The Dawn of a New Era, 1250–1453* and M. P. Gilmore, *The World of Humanism, 1453–1517* (*Torchbooks). The first two volumes in the important series "The Rise of Modern Europe" Gilmore's is particularly informative on the topics considered in this chapter.

*The New Cambridge Modern History*. Vol. I: *The Renaissance* (Cambridge Univ. Press, 1957). Chapters by experts in many fields; uneven in quality, but useful for reference.

J. R. Major, *The Age of the Renaissance and Reformation* (*Lippincott), and E. F. Rice, Jr., *The Foundations of Early Modern Europe, 1460–1559* (*Norton). Up-to-date general introductions.

J. H. Plumb, *The Italian Renaissance* (*Torchbooks). Concise historical and cultural survey.

D. Hay, *The Renaissance in its Historical Background* (*Cambridge Univ. Press). Valuable treatment of the topic by a British scholar.

G. Mattingly et al., *Renaissance Profiles* (*Torchbooks). Lively sketches of nine representative Italians, including Petrarch, Machiavelli Leonardo, and Michelangelo.

INTERPRETATIONS

J. Burckhardt, *The Civilization of the Renaissance in Italy,* 2 vols. (*Torchbooks). The classic statement of the view that the Renaissance was unique and revolutionary.

J. A. Symonds, *The Renaissance in Italy,* 5 vols. (*Capricorn). A detailed study a century old, often sharing Burckhardt's views.

D. Hay, ed., *The Renaissance Debate* (*Holt). Excerpts illustrating contrasting points of view.

W. K. Ferguson, *The Renaissance in Historical Thought: Five Centuries of Interpretation* (Houghton, 1948). Valuable and stimulating monograph; may be supplemented by the same scholar's *Renaissance Studies* (Univ. of Western Ontario, 1963).

F. Chabod, *Machiavelli and the Renaissance* (*Torchbooks). The chapter on "The Concept of the Renaissance" is most suggestive.

L. Olschki, *The Genius of Italy* (Cornell Univ. Press, 1954). Scholarly essays on many aspects of the Renaissance.

LITERATURE, THOUGHT AND RELIGION

R. R. Bolgar, *The Classical Heritage and Its Beneficiaries from the Carolingian Age to the End of the Renaissance* (*Torchbooks). The last third of this scholarly study treats the Renaissance.

G. Highet, *The Classical Tradition: Greek and Roman Influences on Western Literature* (*Galaxy). Lively general survey.

R. Weiss, *The Spread of Italian Humanism* (Hutchinson's Univ. Library, 1964). Lucid introduction.

H. O. Taylor, *Thought and Expression in the Sixteenth Century,* 2 vols. (Macmillan, 1920). Standard older study, sections of which have been reprinted in paperback (*Collier) under various titles.

P. O. Kristeller, *Renaissance Thought,* 2 vols. (*Torchbooks). Valuable study, stressing its diversity, by a ranking scholar.

M. P. Gilmore, *Humanists and Jurists* (Belknap-Harvard Univ., 1963). Six essays, especially instructive on Erasmus.

G. Holmes, *The Florentine Enlightenment, 1400–1450* (Pegasus, 1969). Informative monograph on humanists obsessed with classicism.

N. A. Robb, *Neoplatonism of the Italian Renaissance* (Allen & Unwin, 1953). Good solid treatment of an intellectual common denominator of the age.

J. Huizinga, *Erasmus and the Age of the Reformation* (*Torchbooks). Excellent analysis by a distinguished Dutch scholar.

A. Hyma, *The Christian Renaissance* (Shoe String, 1965). Reprint of an older study stressing an aspect of the Renaissance often neglected.

R. Ridolfi, *Savonarola* (Knopf, 1959). Biography of the famous Florentine preacher-dictator.

THE ARTS

H. Wölfflin, *Classic Art: An Introduction to the Italian Renaissance,* 3rd. ed. (*Praeger). Old but still very enlightening.

B. Berenson, *The Italian Painters of the Renaissance* (*Meridian). Opinionated essays by the famous collector and promoter.

J. White, *Art and Architecture in Italy, 1250–1400* (Penguin, 1966). Detailed scholarly volume in the valuable series "The Pelican History of Art."

F. Antal, *Florentine Painting and Its Social Background* (Kegan Paul, 1948). An attempt to relate art to economic and social currents.

E. Panofsky, *Renaissance and Renascences in Western Art* and *Studies in Iconology: Humanistic Themes in the Renaissance* (*Torchbooks). Stimulating studies by a distinguished scholar.

K. M. Clark, *Leonardo da Vinci* (*Penguin). Lively and perceptive study of his art.

E. MacCurdy, *The Mind of Leonardo da Vinci* (Dodd, Mead, 1928). Standard appraisal.

O. Benesch, *The Art of the Renaissance in Northern Europe* (Harvard, 1945). Examines the interrelations of artistic, religious, and intellectual history.

E. Panofsky, *The Life and Art of Albrecht Dürer* (Princeton, 1955). Definitive evaluation of the great German artist.

R. Wittkower, *Architectural Principles in the Age of Humanism,* 3rd ed. (A. Tiranti, 1962). Important assessment of the connections between humanism and architecture.

B. Lowry, *Renaissance Architecture* (Braziller, 1962). Brief introduction.

E. J. Dent, *Music of the Renaissance in Italy* (British Academy, 1935). Meaty lecture by a great authority.

G. Reese, *Music in the Renaissance* (Norton, 1954). Full and detailed.

SCIENCE

M. Boas, *The Scientific Renaissance, 1450–1630* (*Torchbooks). Helpful detailed account.

H. Butterfield, *The Origins of Modern Science, 1300–1800,* rev. ed. (*Free Press). A controversial interpretation, minimizing the scientific contribution of the Renaissance.

A. C. Crombie, *Medieval and Early Modern Science,* 2nd ed. (Harvard Univ. Press, 1963). Volume II of this standard survey treats the Renaissance.

G. Sarton, *Six Wings: Men of Science in the Renaissance* (*Meridian), *The Appreciation of Ancient and Medieval Science during the Renaissance* (*A. S. Barnes), and *The History of Science and the New Humanism* (*Indiana Univ. Press). Clear studies by a pioneering historian of science.

L. Thorndike, *Science and Thought in the Fifteenth Century* (Columbia Univ. Press, 1929). By a specialist on medieval science.

C. Singer et al., *A History of Technology* (Clarendon, 1954–1958). Volumes 2 and 3 of this multivolumed work relate to the Renaissance.

A. Castiglioni, *A History of Medicine,* 2nd ed., rev. (Knopf, 1958). An excellent manual.

SOURCES AND FICTION

J. B. Ross and M. M. McLaughlin, *The Portable Renaissance Reader* (*Viking).

W. L. Gundesheimer, ed., *The Italian Renaissance* (*Prentice-Hall). Selections from eleven representative writers, including Valla, Pico, Leonardo, and Castiglione.

E. Cassirer et al., *The Renaissance Philosophy of Man* (*Phoenix). Excerpts from Petrach, Pico, Valla, and other humanists, with helpful commentary.

Erasmus, *The Praise of Folly* (*Ann Arbor).

S. Putnam, ed., *The Portable Rabelais: Most of Gargantua and Pantagruel* (*Viking).

J. P. Richter, ed., *The Notebooks of Leonardo da Vinci* (*Dover).

A. H. Popham, ed., *The Drawings of Leonardo da Vinci* (*Harvest).

D. Merezhkovsky, *The Romance of Leonardo* (*Signet). The best novel on the Renaissance, romanticized but based on Leonardo's notebooks.

# 12

# *The Protestant Reformation*

An den Christli
chen Adel deüt
scher Nation.
von des Christ
lichen standes
besserung D.
Martinus
Luther
Wittenberg.

*Above: Title page of Luther's "To the Christian Nobility of the German Nation."*
*Right: The emperor Charles V, by Titian.*

## I Luther

On October 31, 1517, the Augustinian monk Martin Luther nailed his Ninety-Five Theses to the door of the court church at Wittenberg in the German electorate of Saxony, and thereby touched off the sequence of events that produced the Protestant Reformation. The term "Protestant" dates from 1529, when a meeting of the Diet of the Holy Roman Empire at Speyer rescinded a grant of toleration to Lutherans it had made three years earlier. A minority of delegates —six Lutheran princes and fourteen Lutheran city delegates—thereupon lodged a formal "protest" with the diet. In Europe the term "Reformed" is often used synonymously with "Protestant," and "Reformation" is the accepted word for the Protestant movement everywhere except in Catholic tradition, which refers to the Protestant "revolt." The difference is significant, because early Protestant leaders like Luther and

MDXLVIII

Calvin did not conceive of themselves as rebels or initiators, as beginning new churches, but as going back to the true old Church.

In fact, however, the Protestant leaders did prove to be revolutionaries in spite of themselves. The Reformation not only created a major schism in the Church but also constituted a major social, economic, and intellectual revolution. In the Middle Ages the Catholic church had faced many reform movements—the Cluniac, the Cistercian, the Franciscan, and, in the century or so before Luther, movements like those of Wycliffe and Hus that anticipated Protestant doctrines and had almost ended by setting up separate or schismatic religious bodies. The Reformation came in a time when the authority of the pope was no longer automatically accepted but had been brought under open discussion by the conciliar movement, though the movement itself had failed to set general church councils above the pope.

More important, the Reformation came in a time when men were still groping to replace the old values and institutions being dissolved by the Renaissance. It came in a time of great religious ferment, of economic change, of violence, uncertainty, even a sense of doom—in short, in times well described by the phrase of the distinguished Dutch historian Huizinga as "the autumn of the Middle Ages." Men everywhere were seeking something, characteristically not usually specific political or economic reforms, but something less readily definable or understandable by most of us today—spiritual salvation, renewal, the better world of Christian promise. Luther, notably, appealed from what he held to be existing evil to a potential—indeed, in men's souls already real—good. Hence the Lutheran appeal from *works,* from the conventions of established things, to *faith,* to something not evident to the outward eye, but there, inside us all, if we could but see it.

Although Luther, when he posted his theses, had no clear intention of setting up a separate religious body, he did live to see a church now called the Lutheran, organized outside the Catholic communion. The Lutheran was but the first of such Protestant churches or "denominations." Within the very generation that had seen the posting of the Ninety-Five Theses, dozens of them were organized—Anglican, Calvinist, Anabaptist, and many more. The medieval unity of Catholic Christendom had given way to the multiplicity of churches we know so well.

## Young Luther

Martin Luther (1483–1546) was a professor of theology at the University of Wittenberg. When he posted his theses in 1517, he had recently experienced a great religious awakening, in effect a conversion, after a long period of spiritual despair. Luther's parents were of peasant stock; his father, authoritarian in discipline as medieval fathers seemed to be, became a miner and in time a prosperous investor in a mining enterprise. Very ambitious for his son, he was able to send him to the University of Erfurt, then the most prestigious in Germany, for the study of law as preparation for a career in a profession. The young man, however, yearned instead to enter the religious life and took the decisive step in 1505 as a result of a traumatic experience. On his way back to Erfurt he was terrified by a severe thunderstorm and prayed to the patron saint of miners—"Help, Saint Anne, I will become a monk!" ("I want to become a monk" is another translation). Against his father's opposition, Luther joined the Augustinian friars (or canons), an elite order both socially and intellectually.

While Luther's lifelong enthusiasm for music found satisfaction in the Augustinian devotion to psalm-singing, he himself underwent a prolonged and intense personal crisis. Luther was convinced that he was lost—literally lost, for as the distinguished psychoanalyst Erik Erikson points out in his *Young Man Luther,* modern depth psychology calls his an "identity crisis." None of Luther's good works, neither the monastic discipline of his order nor his pilgrimage in 1510 to Christian shrines in Rome, could free him of the gnawing feeling that he could not attain God's grace and was destined for the hell of lost souls. Finally, a wise confessor advised the desperate young man to study the Bible and to become a teacher of scripture. Through his reading in the Epistles of Paul and the writings of Augustine, Luther gradually found a positive answer to his anxiety. The answer was that man should have faith in God, faith in the possibility of his own salvation. This answer had indeed long been the answer of the Roman church; what later separated Luther doctrinally from this church was his emphasis on faith alone, to the exclusion of works.

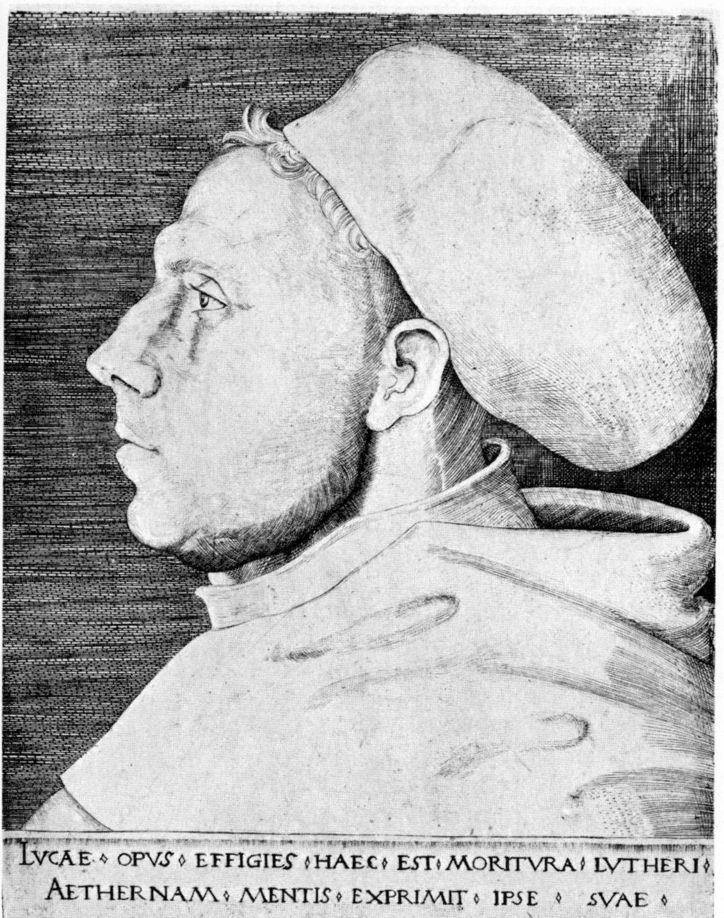


*Martin Luther, by Lucas Cranach the Elder.*

Fortified by his intense personal conviction of the great importance of faith, Luther questioned Catholic practices which in his view were abuses and tended to corrupt or weaken faith. He cast his questions in the form of the Ninety-Five Theses, written in Latin and in the manner of medieval Scholasticism as a challenge to academic debate. A casual observer who saw the manuscript on the door of the Wittenberg church might well have thought that here was another professor "sounding off." Yet this apparently academic exercise in Latin was the trigger-pull for revolution; translated into German, the Theses gained wide circulation and aroused much discussion.

## Indulgences and the Ninety-Five Theses

The specific abuse that Luther sought to prove un-Christian in the Ninety-Five Theses was what he called the "sale" of indulgences, and in particular, the activities of a talented ecclesiastical fundraiser, a Dominican named Tetzel. In today's language, Tetzel was conducting a "campaign" or "drive" for voluntary contributions of money to help fill the treasury of a great institution, an institution which like the state possessed taxing powers, but which like many modern states could not in fact extend those taxing powers to keep up with the rising cost of an era of inflation and luxurious living. Tetzel was raising money to rebuild the great basilica of St. Peter's in Rome, and he had papal authorization for his campaign. One of the great German ecclesiastical princes also had a stake in the indulgences. This was Albert, brother of the elector of Brandenburg, who held two major sees, the archbishopric of Mainz and that of Magdeburg, and had paid a very large sum to the papacy for a dispensation permitting him to do so. To raise the money he had borrowed extensively from the Fuggers, and to repay them he would use his share in the proceeds of the indulgences.

The theory of indulgences concerned the remission of the punishment of sins. Only God can forgive a sin, but the repentant sinner also has to undergo punishment on earth in the form of penance and after death in purgatory, where sinners repentant on earth atone by temporary but painful punishment for their sins and are prepared for heaven. Indulgences could not assure the forgiveness of sins, according to the theory advanced by the medieval Schoolmen, but they could remit penance and part or all of the punishment in purgatory. The Church claimed authority to grant such remission by drawing on the Treasury of Merit, a storehouse of surplus good works accumulated by the holy activities of Christ, the Virgin, and the saints. Only the priest could secure for a layman a draft, as it were, on this heavenly treasury. The use of the word "sale" in connection with indulgences was a form of propaganda useful for the Protestants; the Catholics insist that indulgence was "granted" by the priest, and any monetary contribution thereupon made by the recipient was a freewill offering.

The doctrine of indulgences was thus a complex matter, too complex for the ordinary layman to grasp completely. To the man in the street in sympathy with the reformers, it must have looked as though a sinner could obtain not only remission of punishment but also forgiveness of sin if only he secured enough indulgences. Men like Tetzel, by making extravagant claims for the power of their indulgences, strengthened this popular feeling, summed up in the saying "The moment the money tinkles in the collecting box, a soul flies out of purgatory."* Luther objected not only to Tetzel's perversion of indulgences but also to the whole doctrine behind them. He phrased his objections with great vehemence in the Ninety-Five Theses:

> 23. If any complete remission of penalties can be given to anyone it is sure that it can be given only to the most perfect; that it, to very few.
>
> 24. And therefore it follows that the greater part of the people is deceived by this indiscriminate and liberal promising of freedom from penalty.†

At the highest level of formal theological thought, Luther's quarrel with his ecclesiastical superiors was over one of the oldest and most abiding tensions of Christian thought, the tension between faith and good works. Faith is inward and emotional belief, and good works are the *outward* demonstration of that belief expressed by doing good deeds, by partaking of the sacraments, and by submitting to the discipline of penances. Indulgences, certainly to the ordinary believer, permitted men to secure extra good works by drawing on those stored up in the Treasury of Merit. Now, Christian practice usually insists on the need for *both* faith and good works. But at times of crisis some men pursue one extreme, others the other. In the years of crisis immediately after the posting of the Ninety-Five Theses, the challenged papal party stiffened into a resistance that in turn drove the Lutherans into further resistance. Moreover, Luther's own increasing hostility to things-as-they-were in his Germany drove him to emphasize things-as-they-ought-to-be—that is, drove him to minimize, and at his most excited moments to deny, the uses of the outward, the visible, the here-and-now which is works, and to insist on the inward, the spiritual, the Church invisible which is faith.

*Quoted in O. Chadwick, *The Reformation* (Grand Rapids, Michigan, 1965), p. 42.

†*Documents of the Christian Church,* ed. Henry Bettenson (New York, 1947), p. 265.

In Luther's personal spiritual struggle, faith had helped him immensely, and good works had helped him not at all. In the Ninety-Five Theses, he did not attack all works, but only those he felt to be wrong:

> 43. Christians are to be taught that to give to the poor or to lend to the needy is a better work than the purchase of pardons, i.e., indulgences.
>
> 44. And that because through a work of charity, charity is increased and a man advances in goodness; whereas through pardons there is no advance in goodness but merely an increased freedom from penalty.*

The theses, however, as our earlier quotation from them shows, put great stress on the abuses, and Luther made some very harsh statements about the pope. Soon, under pressure of combat, Luther took a more extreme position on works: Men are saved by *faith alone*. Soon, he was driven to deny that the priest is at all necessary and to affirm the priesthood of all true believers, or, in the American phrase, the doctrine of "every man his own priest."

## The Clash with Authority

The Roman church was quickly alerted to the high importance of the issues that Luther had raised. Tetzel had aroused such indignation that he dared not appear in public, and the archbishop of Mainz complained to the pope of the disastrous financial implications. Pope Leo X (1513–1521), a Medici and the son of Lorenzo the Magnificent but possessing little of the family's intelligence or decisiveness, soon had to give up the pretense that the storm over the Ninety-Five Theses was a tempest in a teapot. Accordingly, in 1518, at Augsburg, Luther was summoned before a papal legate, Cardinal Cajetan, and was directed to recant some of his propositions on indulgences; Luther quietly defied the legate. In 1519, at Leipzig, a learned theologian, John Eck, taxed

*Ibid., p. 267.

Luther in debate with disobeying the authoritative findings of popes and church councils. Luther denied that popes and councils were necessarily authoritative and, carrying his revolt further, explicitly declared adherence to some of Hus's teachings which had been declared heretical by the Council of Constance a century earlier. In 1520, Luther brought his defiance to its highest pitch by publishing a pamphlet, *The Appeal to the Christian Nobility of the German Nation on the Improvement of the Christian Estate,* which stated in part:

> There has been a fiction by which the Pope, bishops, priests, and monks are called the "spiritual estate"; princes, lords, artisans, and peasants are the "temporal estate." This is an artful lie and hypocritical invention, but let no one be made afraid by it, and that for this reason: that all Christians are truly of the spiritual estate, and there is no difference among them, save of office. As St. Paul says (1 Cor. xii), we are all one body, though each member does its own work so as to serve the others. This is because we have one baptism, one Gospel, one faith, and are all Christians alike; for baptism, Gospel, and faith, these alone make spiritual and Christian people.*

Luther's adherence to justification by faith alone had now led him to deny totally the central Catholic doctrine of works, that only the priest had the God-given power to secure for the layman remission of punishment for sin. In *The Appeal to the Christian Nobility* he swept aside the distinction between clergy and laity and declared the priesthood of all believers. The complete break between the rebel and the Church was now at hand. Late in 1520, the pope issued a bull condemning Luther's teachings; Luther burnt the bull. In 1521, Luther was excommunicated and made an outlaw, the political consequence of being excommunicated. The emperor Charles V and the imperial diet passed the sentence of outlawry in a most dramatic session at Worms. Luther was asked, once again, if he would recant. He replied:

> Your Imperial Majesty and Your Lordships demand a simple answer. Here it is, plain and unvarnished. Unless I am convicted of error by the testimony of Scripture or (since I put not trust in the unsupported authority of Pope or of councils, since it is plain that they have often erred and often contradicated themselves) by manifest reasoning I stand convicted by the Scriptures to which I have appealed, and my conscience is taken captive by God's word, I cannot and will not recant anything, for to act against our conscience is neither safe for us, nor open to us.
>
> On this I take my stand. I can do no other. God help me. Amen. [Hier stehe ich. Ich kann nicht anders. Gott helff mir. Amen.]*

*Ibid., p. 274.

These last words are the most famous Luther ever spoke, but it must be recorded as an anticlimax that modern scholarship can find no evidence that he uttered them in exactly this way.

The empire and the papacy took their drastic actions in vain. Luther was already gathering a substantial following and becoming a national hero. He had the protection of the ruler of his own German state, the elector Frederick the Wise of Saxony (1463–1525), and was soon to secure the backing of other princes. Frederick arranged to "kidnap" the outlaw on his way back from Worms, and Luther vanished into seclusion at the castle of the Wartburg, where he began work on his celebrated translation of the Bible into vigorous and effective German. In the next year, Luther returned to Wittenberg; appalled by the vandalism of extremists during his absence, he remodeled the church in Saxony more soberly according to his own views. His revolt was a success.

## Why Luther Succeeded

More than theology was at issue in Luther's revolt and its success. The Church that Luther attacked was, especially in its center at Rome, under the influence of the half-pagan Renaissaince, with its new wealth and new fashion of good living. The papacy, triumphant over the councils, had been drawn into Italian politics. The Rome Luther visited in his younger days, when the warlike Julius II was pope, presented a shocking spectacle of intrigue, display, and corruption. Some part of Luther's success lies in the fact that he was attacking practices revolting to decent men.

* Ibid., p. 285.

*Frederick the Wise: painting from the workshop of Lucas Cranach the Elder.*

There is a second great reason for his success: in the name of good Germans he was attacking the practices of Italians and Italianate Germans. Tetzel was in the eyes of Luther and his followers not only extending an abuse theologically and morally outrageous; the money he was raising was going to enrich Italy, and that was one more step in the exploitation of Germans by Italians.

> For Rome is the greatest thief and robber that has ever appeared on earth, or ever will. . . . Poor Germans that we are—we have been deceived! We were born to be masters, and we have been compelled to bow the head beneath the yoke of our tyrants. . . . It is time the glorious Teutonic people should cease to be the puppet of the Roman pontiff.*

While the nationalistic and economic factors present in the Lutheran movement help explain its success, they do not in and of themselves wholly account for it. As always in human affairs, ideas and ideals worked together with material interests and powerful emotions such as patriotism to move the men of the Reformation.

The princes who supported Luther stood to gain financially, not only by the cessation of the flow of German money to Italy, but by the confiscation of Catholic property, especially monastic property, which was not needed for the new Lutheran cult. Luther gave them a new weapon in the eternal struggle against their feudal overlord, the emperor. The princes were also moved by Luther's German patriotism, and some, like Frederick the Wise of Saxony, sympathized with many of his ideas. Philip of Hesse found Luther obliging enough to condone bigamy, when Philip, who had a sensitive conscience, took a second wife without attempting to divorce the first.

While it is true enough that what Luther started was soon taken out of his hands by princes who joined the reform movement to strengthen their political power and fill their treasuries, Lutheranism without Luther is inconceivable, save perhaps to single-minded devotees of the economic interpretation of history. Luther wrote the pamphlets that did for this revolution what Tom Paine and the Declaration of Independence did for the American Revolution. He put his *Appeal to the Christian Nobility of the German Nation* in the vernacular German, not the academic Latin, so that it became a "best-seller" overnight. Note that printing at this time first made possible wide popular dissemination of ideas. Luther's defiance of the papal legate Cajetan, of the papal champion Eck, and of the Pope himself—indeed all his actions—helped to focus German sentiments on what was, though not of course on our contemporary scale, already a mass movement influenced by mass media. Luther's marriage to a former nun and their rearing of a large family dramatized the break

*Ibid., pp. 278–279.

with Rome. The hymns he composed—*Ein feste Burg* (*A Mighty Fortress*), above all—and his translation of the scriptures became a part of German life and made Luther's language one of the bases of modern literary German. And back of all this—whether or not he actually said *Ich kann nicht anders*—was Luther's passionate conviction that he was doing what he had to do. His power and intensity may still be be sensed over the centuries—Erik Erikson prefaces his *Young Man Luther* with a pertinent reminiscence:

> In my youth, as a wandering artist I stayed one night with a friend in a small village by the Upper Rhine. His father was a Protestant pastor; and in the morning, as the family sat down to breakfast, the old man said the Lord's Prayer in Luther's German. Never having "knowingly" heard it, I had the experience, as seldom before or after, of poetry fusing the esthetic and the moral: those who have once suddenly "heard" the Gettysburg Address will know what I mean.*

Moreover, Luther's doctrine of justification by faith alone has been attractive to many religious dispositions, responding in a more general way to the same sort of needs that the Brethren of the Common Life had tried to meet. Saint Paul at the very beginnings of Christianity set up the contrast between the Spirit—invisible, in a sense private to the believer—and the Letter—only too visible, only too public. Established churches have always tended to balance spirit and letter, invisible and visible, internal and external, faith and works; but to the ardent, crusading Christian even a working successful balance of this sort seems a yielding to a gross materialism. He will have none of this compromise, but will imperiously assert the primacy of the spirit. In Luther's day, the established Roman church had lost its medieval balance; the world was too much with it. The Lutheran felt the new church offered him something he could not get in the old.

## The Opposition to Luther

A final reason for Luther's success—and this may well be true of revolutionary movements generally—lay in the relative weakness of the forces that opposed him. The opposition can be divided into the religious and the political, though the two were really inseparably connected. Religious opposition centered in the top levels of the Catholic bureaucracy; Pope Leo X did not so much head it as prove its willing instrument. Moderate Catholics, anxious to compromise and avert a schism, existed both within the Church and on its margin among the humanist scholars of the Renaissance, notably Erasmus. It is tempting to agree with the great liberal Catholic historian Lord Acton that had there been at the head of the Catholic church a pope willing to reform in order to conserve, willing to make concessions that did not destroy the basic position of the Church as God's chosen instrument on earth, even Luther might have been reconciled. Luther's ablest associate, Melanchthon, was a moderate and a humanist (his great uncle was John Reuchlin, the "hero" of the *Letters of Obscure Men*). Yet the historian can hardly avoid comparing this revolution with other great modern revolutions, the English, the French, the Russian, and noting that in all of them the moderates—gifted, numerous, and active though they were—could not hold up against the extremists. Once Leo X had excommunicated Luther in 1520, the way to compromise was probably blocked, for Luther's associates could have been won away from him only by concessions too great for a Catholic to make.

Politically, the opposition in these critical early years centered in the young emperor Charles V, who came to the imperial throne in 1519. Charles of Hapsburg was the fruit of a series of marriages that gave rise to the famous epigram "Let others wage war; thou, happy Austria, marry." The combined inheritance of his Austrian father and Spanish mother made Charles ruler of the German Empire, the Low Countries, Spain, the Spanish Indies, Hungary, and parts of Italy. This looks on the map like the nearest thing to a real European superstate since Charlemagne, and Charles wanted very much to make it such a state in reality. The activities of Luther's princely German supporters seemed to him a threat to his hold over Germany, and might in themselves have sufficed to turn him against Luther. But Charles, though by no means a mere papal instrument, was by upbringing a good conventional Catholic, in no state of mind to throw his great influence on the side of the

*E. H. Erikson, *Young Man Luther* (London, 1958), p. 10.

moderate group within the Catholic church. He decided to fight—and had to fight the rest of his reign, thus gainsaying the famous epigram about his house.

Charles V entrusted the government of the Germans to his younger brother Ferdinand, who formed alliances with Bavaria and other Catholic German states to oppose the Lutheran states. Thus began a long series of alliances and combinations within the Germanies, the fruits of which were the religious wars of the next few generations, and the division of Germany into, roughly, a Protestant north and east and a Catholic south and west, which has endured to this day. The fact that Charles himself did not directly lead the fight in Germany gives another clue to the success of the Protestant movement in breaking down the unity of Western Christendom. Charles had too many other fights on his hands to concentrate on Germany. Spanish cities rose in revolt early in his reign, the Low Countries were chronically restless, and the Ottoman Turks, who annexed most of Hungary in the 1520's and then besieged Vienna, continued to threaten Charles' frontiers in central Europe and his lines of communication on the Mediterranean. Above all, Charles' huge inheritance encircled the only remaining great power on the Continent, France, which was already engaged with the Hapsburgs in a struggle for control of Italy. The struggle broadened into an intermittent general war between Charles V and the French king, Francis I, which outlasted both monarchs and prevented anything like sustained pressure on the German Protestants by imperial Hapsburg power.

The military arm of the Protestants was the League of Schmalkalden (named for the town where it was founded in 1531), linking cities and princes, with Philip of Hesse in the van. When Charles finally crushed the League with Spanish troops in 1547, his victory was short-lived because it threatened to upset the power balance and therefore alarmed both the papacy and the German princes, Catholic as well as Protestant. In 1555, in the twilight of his reign, Charles felt obliged to allow the German religious settlement negotiated by the Diet and known as the Peace of Augsburg.

The peace formally recognized the Lutherans as established in the German states where they held power at the time. Its guiding principle was expressed in the Latin *cuius regio eius religio* ("he who rules may establish the religion"), which meant in practice that, since the elector of Saxony was Lutheran, all his subjects should be too, whereas, since the ruler of Bavaria was Catholic, all Bavarians should be Catholic. No provision was made for Catholic minorities in Lutheran states, or Lutheran minorities in Catholic. A second respect in which the settlement fell short of full toleration was its failure to recognize any Protestants except Lutherans; the growing numbers of militant Calvinists were bound to press for equal treatment in the future. Finally, more trouble was bound to arise later on from the failure to solve the matter of "ecclesiastical reservation," that is, of what should be done with the property of the Church in a state ruled by a Catholic prelate who had converted to Protestantism. Yet with all these deficiencies the peace of Augsburg was a very important beginning, which made possible the permanent establishment of Protestantism on a peaceful footing in Germany.

## Luther the Conservative

Thus far we have been observing Luther in the role of the great revolutionary and examining some of the revolutionary consequences of his revolt. Now we turn to the issues on which he took a fundamentally conservative stand. Luther did not, for example, push his doctrines of justification by faith and the priesthood of all believers to their logical extreme, which is anarchy. If religion is wholly a matter between each man and his maker, an organized church becomes unnecessary if not impossible, or else there is as many churches as there are individuals. When radical reformers inspired by Luther attempted to apply these anarchical concepts to the churches of Saxony in the early 1520's, the results were immense confusion and popular unrest. Luther, who had no sympathy with such anarchistic experiments, left his sanctuary in the Wartburg, returned to Wittenberg, and drove out the radicals. He and his followers then proceeded to organize a Saxon church that permitted its clergy to marry and magnified the importance of sermons but that also possessed ordained clergymen, ritual, dogmas, even some sacraments—a whole apparatus of good works. Even the Lutheran "faith alone, scripture alone, grace alone" could become a formula and partake of Saint Paul's Letter as well as his Spirit.

The Lutherans did not found their church as an alternative to the Roman Catholic but as the one true church. Where a Lutheran church was founded, a Catholic church ceased to be; the Lutherans commonly just took over the church building. Stimulated by Luther and his clerical and academic disciples, this process at first went on among the people of Germany almost spontaneously, without the intervention of political leaders. But very soon the lay rulers of certain of the half-independent, or rather nine-tenths independent, German states took a hand. In Saxony, Hesse, Brandenburg, Brunswick, and elsewhere in northern Germany, princes and their administrators superintended and hastened the process of converting the willing to Lutheranism and evicting the unwilling. Much excitement was caused in 1525 when the head of the Teutonic Knights, the crusading order controlling Prussia at the eastern corner of the Baltic, turned Lutheran, dissolved the order, and became the first duke of Prussia. Meantime, many of the free cities also opted for Lutheranism, usually not on the initiative of the municipal government but as a result of pressure from the guilds.

Still other social groups took the occasion of the Lutheran revolt to assert themselves. Just beneath the princes, lay and ecclesiastical, in the German social pyramid and like them a legacy of the Middle Ages were the knights, the lesser nobility. Some of them held a castle and a few square miles direct from the emperor, and were in theory as "independent" as an elector of Saxony; others were simply minor feudal lords. Many were younger sons, landless but still gentlemen, who could hardly have a career save that of arms. The class as a whole was losing power to the princes and was also caught in the squeeze of rising prices and the need for maintaining aristocratic standards of living. Luther's challenge to the established order, above all the chance it seemed to give for taking over ecclesiastical holdings, was too good an opportunity for many of these knights to miss. Under the leadership of Ulrich von Hutten and Franz von Sickingen, they rose in 1522 in what is called the Knights' War. They were put down by the bigger lords, but only after a struggle, and their rising added to the confusion of the time.

The really bitter social struggle of the early German Reformation was the Peasants' Rebellion of 1524–1525. In many ways, the German rising resembles the peasant revolts of the fourteenth century in England and France. Like them, it was directed against attempts by money-hungry lords, lay and ecclesiastical, to increase manorial dues; like them, it lacked coordination and effective military organization and was cruelly put down by the possessing classes who did have command over military power. Like them, too, it was a rising, not of peasants who were in the very lowest state of oppression, but of peasants who were beginning to enjoy some degree of prosperity and who wanted more. The German Peasants' Rebellion centered not in those eastern parts of the country where serfdom was most complete, where the status of the peasant was lowest, but in the south and southwestern parts where the peasantry were beginning to emerge as free, landowning farmers.

Yet in one very important respect this sixteenth-century German uprising looks more modern, more democratic, than its medieval counterparts in western Europe. Even more clearly than the English Peasants' Revolt, which had been influenced by Wycliffe and the Lollards, it was led by educated men who were not themselves peasants and who had a program, a set of revolutionary ideas of what the new social structure should be. Their leaders drew up a set of demands known as the Twelve Articles, which were given various regional forms. They were generally moderate enough, and were usually couched in biblical language, which shows clearly their relation to the Reformation. Important articles demanded that each parish have the right to choose its own priest, that the tithes paid to the clergy and the dues paid to the lord be reduced, and that the peasants be allowed to take game and wood from the forests.

Luther's reaction to the Peasants' Rebellion was thoroughly conservative. He was horrified at what the peasants' leaders had found in the Bible he had translated into German so that they might read it. He burst into impassioned abuse that sounds even stronger than his abuse of the Catholics, writing a tract entitled *Against the Murdering Thieving Hordes of Peasants,* for example. From this time on, Luther turned definitely to the princes, and the church he founded became itself an established church, respectful toward civil authority. Luther indeed is quoted in his *Table Talk* as saying: "The princes of the world are gods, the common people are Satan."

*Woodcut from a Lutheran attack against the Peasants' Rebellion, 1525.*

In fairness to Luther, it may be said that his conservatism in social, economic, and political matters is by no means inconsistent with his fundamental spiritual position. For if the visible, external world is really wholly subordinate to the invisible, spiritual world, the most one can hope for in this world of politics is that it be kept in as good orderliness, in as little imperfection as possible, so that the spiritual may thrive. Authority, custom, law, existing institutions combine to provide this orderliness. Kings and princes are better for this wretched world than democratically chosen representatives of the people; obedience is better than discussion.

Luther's conservative views on social and political questions had two important results. First, he won increasing support from kings and princes. By the mid-sixteenth century, Lutheranism had become the state religion in most of the principalities of northern Germany and in the Scandinavian kingdoms, Sweden and Denmark, together with the Danish dependencies of Norway and Iceland, and the Swedish province of Finland. The Scandinavian monarchs, in particular, appear to have been attracted to the Reformation for secular reasons, for the opportunities it presented both to curb unruly bishops and to confiscate monastic wealth. Second, it should hardly be surprising that after the Peasants' Rebellion the initiative in the Protestant movement passed to other hands than those of the Lutherans.

## II Other Protestant Founders

Many of the things that had troubled Luther about the Church had long been troubling his contemporaries. Sensitive men, especially humanists like Erasmus, the Englishmen John Colet and Sir Thomas More, and the Frenchman Lefèvre d'Etaples, condemned the worldliness and corruption of the Church and the oversubtleties of late Scholasticism. They had been seeking in their writing and preaching for a renewal of evangelical Christianity, for a return to what most of them held to be an earlier and better faith that had somehow gone wrong. Many of these reform-minded men wanted the Catholic church to be reformed from within. They were shocked by Luther's intransigent revolt, and sought to tame the movement he had unloosed. Others, however, went on to a break more complete in many ways than Luther's. Of these other main founders of Protestantism the first in time was Zwingli and the first in importance was Calvin.

### Zwingli

Almost contemporaneously with Luther's spectacular revolt, another German, Ulrich Zwingli (1484–1531), began in the Swiss city of Zurich a quieter reform that soon spread to cities elsewhere—Bern and Basel in Switzerland, Augsburg and others in southern Germany. The movement produced no great single organized church, and when it was only a decade old its founder died in battle against the staunchly Catholic forest cantons of Switzerland. Zwingli's reform proved significant because it extended and deepened some of the fundamental theological and moral concepts of Protestantism, and had a wide influence on some of its less conservative and more austere forms. Zwingli was a scholarly humanist trained in the tradition of Erasmus. Like Luther, he sought to combat what seemed to him the perversion of primitive Christianity that made the consecrated priest an agent,

*Ulrich Zwingli: a contemporary painting.*

indeed a sharer, of a miraculous power not possessed by the layman. But, where the doctrine of the priesthood of the true believer drove the emotional Luther to the edge of anarchism, the humanistic Zwingli saw that individuals might achieve a community discipline that would promote righteous living. This discipline would arise from the social conscience of enlightened and emancipated people led by their pastors.

Zwingli believed in a personal God and in the miraculous origin of the Christian religion. Indeed, his God was a highly transcendental one, so powerful, so real, and yet so far above this petty world of sense experience that to Zwingli he was not to be approached by mere sacraments. Hence Zwingli is fundamentally, basically antisacramental in a way Luther was not. Hence Zwingli distrusted what many Protestants feel is the continuous appeal of the Catholics to "superstition," to belief in saints, to the use of images, to incense and candles, and of course to indulgences. In the early 1520's, Zwingli began the process of making the church building an almost undecorated hall, of making the service a sermon and responsive reading, of abolishing the Catholic liturgy, and of replacing the elevated altar with a simple communion table in the midst of the congregation. He thus started on the way toward the puritanical simplicity of the later Calvinists.

A good concrete example of Zwingli's attitude is his doctrine of the Eucharist. The Catholic doctrine of transubstantiation holds that by the miraculous power of the priest the elements in communion, the bread and the wine, become in substance the body and blood of Christ, although their accidents, their make-up as far as chemistry or common sense sees them, remain those of bread and wine. Luther stubbornly refused to eliminate the miraculous completely and, in an acrimonious meeting with Zwingli arranged by Philip of Hesse, insisted that Christ had meant himself to be taken literally when he offered bread to his disciples and said "This is my body." While rejecting transubstantiation, Luther adhered to a difficult and confusing doctrine called consubstantiation to account for the presence of Christ's body in the communion bread. Zwingli, however, went all the way to what is the usual Protestant doctrine that when we partake of the elements in communion we are indeed commemorating Christ's last supper, but only in a symbolic way. We are not, in short, sharing through a sacrament in a miracle; we are simply sharing anew the eternal memory of Christ's stay on earth.

## Calvin

One more Swiss city was ripe for Protestant domination, French-speaking Geneva whose citizens in 1536 won a ten-year struggle with their Catholic bishop, who was also their political lord. A new religious and political regime developed under the leadership of the French-born Jean Cauvin (1509–1564), better known as Calvin, the Latin form of his name. Under Calvin, the Protestant movement was shaped as a faith, a way of life, that gave it a European and not merely a German and Scandinavian basis. Particularly in early Protestant history "Reformed" meant Calvinist, as opposed to Lutheran. Today, the historian finds it useful to take Calvinism as the middle—to borrow a political term, the center—of Protestant beliefs. In Germany and Scandinavia the Lutherans, and in England the Anglican Church remained in doctrine what we may call to the right of Calvinism. In England, the

*John Calvin in 1534.*

Low Countries, and Germany there grew up radical sects like the Anabaptists, who were to the left of Calvinism.

Calvin's career had many parallels with Luther's. Both men had ambitious fathers who had made their way up the economic and social ladder. The senior Calvin had risen from an artisan to the performer of clerical and legal services for the municipal and ecclesiastical authorities in a French town and had eventually gained the considerable distinction of admission to citizenship in the town. Both fathers gave their sons superior education; the young Calvin studied theology and, in deference to his father, law. Both young men experienced spiritual crises, Calvin's resulting in his conversion to Protestantism in his early twenties, though apparently with little of the storm and stress experienced by Luther. Both men took wives (as Zwingli did, too). In temperament, however, the two men differed markedly: in contrast to the emotional, outgoing Luther, Calvin was a very private person, an intellectual, a humanist scholar much interested in Roman Stoic philosophy with its puritanical morality, an austere man, earnest, high-minded, very certain of his convictions and of his vocation in persuading others to accept them.

With the moral and theological ideas of Calvin the next section of this chapter deals in more detail. In 1536 he published his *Institutes of the Christian Religion,* which laid a firm doctrinal foundation for a Protestantism that, like Zwingli's, broke completely with Catholic church organization and Catholic ritual. The very title, *Institutes,* suggested Justinian's code; and Calvin's system, reflecting his legal training, had a logical rigor and completeness that gave it great conviction. In 1536 he also arrived in Geneva, from which he was expelled for three years by the city council (1538–1541), and invited back to rescue the citizens from religious and political confusion. This time he remained until his death, organizing his City of God and making Geneva a Protestant Rome. To Geneva came Protestant refugees from many parts of Europe, there to receive indoctrination in Calvin's faith, and to return, sometimes at the risk of their lives, to spread the word in their own countries. Within a generation or two, Calvinism had spread to Scotland, where it was led by a great preacher and organizer, John Knox; to England, whence it was brought to Plymouth in New England; to parts of the Rhineland; to the Low Countries, where it was to play a major role in the Dutch revolt against Spanish rule; and even to Bohemia, Hungary, and Poland.

In France—where the intellectual classes have long been very serious-minded, contrary to the common concept of all Frenchmen as pleasure-loving and irresponsible—concern over the worldliness of the Catholic church was strong. From Jean Gerson, one of the leaders of the Conciliar Movement, to the humanist Lefèvre d'Etaples, Frenchmen had been seeking ways of reform. Calvin's ideas found ready acceptance among many Frenchmen, and soon there were organized Protestant churches, especially in the southwest, called Huguenot (probably from the German, *Eidgenossen,* "covenanted"). But France was a centralized monarchy. King Francis I (1515–1547) was not eager, as so many of the German princes were, to stir up trouble with Rome. In 1516, he had signed with the pope the Concordat of Bologna, an agreement that increased the royal authority over the Gallican church. In the mid-sixteenth century, only a very few intellectuals could even conceive of the possibility of citizens or subjects of the *same* political unit professing and practicing *different* religious faiths. Protestantism in France had to fight, not for toleration, but to succeed Catholicism as the established religion of Frenchmen. The attempt failed, as the next chapter will show, but only after the long hard struggle of the French wars of religion, only after Protestantism had left its mark on the French conscience.

## Henry VIII

In strict chronology, the first great religious overturn outside the Germanies was in England. The signal for the English Reformation was something very different from the Ninety-Five Theses of Luther: it was the desire of King Henry VIII (1509–1547) to put aside his wife, Catherine of Aragon, who had given him no male heir. The house of Tudor had only recently achieved the crown, and Henry felt very strongly that he must have a male heir. In 1529 he decided to rest his case against Catherine on the fact that she had been married first to his deceased brother Arthur, and that marriage with the widow of a deceased brother was against canon law. Henry's case was hardly strength-

*Catherine of Aragon (left) and Anne Boleyn.*

ened by the circumstance that he had taken nearly twenty years to discover the existence of this impediment. Moreover, Catherine was aunt to the emperor Charles V, whom the pope could scarcely risk offending by granting an annulment, the more so since Charles' troops had staged a terrible sack of Rome in 1527. Nevertheless, Henry tried hard through his minister, Cardinal Wolsey, who was dismissed in disgrace for his failure. Henry then put his case to universities in England and on the Continent, and got a few favorable replies. Finally, in 1533 he married Anne Boleyn, who had become pregnant, and Cranmer, the obliging archbishop of Canterbury whom Henry had recently appointed, pronounced an annulment of the marriage with Catherine. The pope excommunicated Henry and declared the annulment invalid. Henry's answer was the Act of Supremacy in 1534, which set the king up as supreme head of the Church in England.

Much more than the private life of Henry VIII was involved in this English Reformation. Henry could not have secured the Act of Supremacy and other Protestant legislation from Parliament if there had not been a considerable body of English opinion favorable to the breach with Rome, particularly among the sizable and prosperous middle classes. Antipapal sentiment, which was an aspect of English nationalism, had long existed; it had motivated the fourteenth-century statutes of Provisors and Praemunire, which limited the right of the pope to intervene in the affairs of the English church. Anticlericalism went back to the days of Wycliffe; in the days of Henry VIII it was aimed particularly at the monasteries, which were still wealthy landowners but had degenerated since their great medieval days. In the eyes of many Englishmen, the monasteries had outlived their purpose and needed to be reformed or abolished. Moreover, the ideas of Luther and other continental Protestants quickly won a sympathetic hearing in England. Many English scholars were in touch with continental reformers; one of them, Tyndale, studied with Luther and published an English translation of the New Testament in 1526.

Henry VIII sponsored measures in addition to the Act of Supremacy which found favor with Protestant opinion in England. Most important, he closed the monasteries and confiscated their property; the larger establishments were not directly suppressed but persuaded to "dissolve" voluntarily. During the 1540's the Crown sold much of the loot, usually at a price twenty times the yearly income from the parcel. The principal purchasers, aside from short-term speculators, were members of the rising merchant class, of the nobility, and, above all, of the country gentry or "squirearchy." The dissolution of the monasteries, by increasing the wealth of the landed aristocracy, amounted to a social and economic revolution; it contributed to the high rate of economic growth in Tudor England and also to the dislocations accompanying that growth. It is another illustration of how closely the religious and the secular threads were interwoven in the Reformation.

Yet Henry VIII, though he must be numbered among the founders of Protestantism, did not really consider himself a Protestant. The church set up by the Act of Supremacy was in his eyes—and remains today in the eyes of some of its communicants—a Catholic body. Henry hoped to retain Catholic doctrines and ritual, doing no more than abolish monasteries and deny the pope's position as head of the church in England. Inevitably, his policies aroused opposition. Part of that opposition was Roman Catholic, for some Englishmen greatly resented the break with Rome. And part, the more pressing and the larger part, was militantly Protestant. Hardly had Henry given the signal for the break with Rome when groups began even within the new Church of England to introduce such Protestant practices as marriage of the clergy, use of English instead of Latin in the ritual, abolition of auricular confession, abolition of the invocation of saints.

Henry used force against the Catholic opposition, and executed some of its leaders, notably John Fisher, a cardinal and bishop of Rochester who had stoutly defended Catherine of Aragon, and Sir Thomas More, author of *Utopia,* who had succeeded Wolsey as chancellor. Henry tried to stem the Protestant tide by appealing to a willing Parliament, many members of which were enriched by the spoliation of the Catholic church. In 1539, Parliament passed the statute of the Six Articles, reaffirming transubstantiation, celibacy of the priesthood, confession, and other Catholic doctrines and ritual, and making their denial heresy. By this definition, indeed by almost any possible definition, there were far too many heretics to be repressed. The patriotic Englishman was against Rome and all its works. England from now on was to be a great center of religious variation and experimentation, much (though not all) of it peaceful. The Church of England, substantially more Protestant, less like the Roman Catholic, than Henry had intended, became a kind of central national core of precarious orthodoxy.

## The Radicals

One major item is left to consider in this survey of Protestant origins. Socially and intellectually less "respectable" than the soon-established Lutheran and Anglican churches, or the sober Calvinists, was a whole group of radical sects, the left wing of the Protestant revolution. In the sixteenth century, most of them were known loosely as Anabaptists, from the Greek for "baptizing again." Some of Zwingli's followers had come to hold that the Catholic sacrament of baptism of infants had no validity, since the infant could not possibly be said to "believe" or "understand." Here again the relation to Luther's basic doctrine of faith as a direct relation between the believer and God is clear—only for the Anabaptist it is a relation of rational understanding by the believer; here also can be seen one of the clearest elements of much Protestantism, an appeal to individual understanding or conscience. It was not an appeal to understanding in the sense of "scientific" or "commonsense" reason, as it was to be with the eighteenth-century Enlightenment.

The Anabaptists in these early years "baptized again" when the believer could hold that he was voluntarily joining the company of the elect. Later generations were never baptized until they came of age, so the prefix "ana" was dropped, and we have the familiar Baptists of our time. The assumption that the beneficiaries of adult baptism were in effect "saved" could lead to exclusiveness, smugness, and a kind of spiritual snobbery that brought accusations of self-righteousness against radical congregations.

Baptism, indeed, was but one of many questions separating the radicals from other Protestants. A modern scholar defines Anabaptists as those "who gathered and disciplined a 'true church' upon the apostolic pattern as they understood it."* The issue of what the primitive church had been like in the days of the apostles had been joined as early as 1521 when the extremists tried to impose their convictions on the church at Wittenberg during Luther's absence in the Wartburg. Anabaptist preaching of the need to reform both Church and society contributed to the demands put forward by the rebellious German peasants in 1524–1525 and also to the violence sometimes employed by the rebels and always used by those suppressing them.

The Anabaptists split under the pressure of persecution and with the spread of private reading of the Bible. Indeed, for some Catholic observers, the proliferation of Protestant sects seems due inevitably to the Protestant practice of seeking in the Bible for an authority they refused to find in the established dogmas of Catholic authority. The Bible is—from the historian's point of view—a complex record of several thousand years of Jewish history, and it contains an extraordinary variety of religious experience from rigorous ritual to intense emotional commitment and mystical surrender. Especially the apocalyptic books of the Old Testament and the Revelation of Saint John the Divine of the New can be made to yield almost anything a lively imagination wants to find. Many of the leaders of these new sects were uneducated men with a sense of grievance against the established order, seeking to bring heaven to earth, quickly. They were proletarians in not quite the Marxist sense and were in large part landowning farmers, miners, or artisans, all of whom were feeling the pinch of inflation.

Their best-known early manifestation in the Reformation gave the conservatives and moderates as great a shock as had the German Peasants' Rebellion. In the mid-1530's, a group of Anabaptists under the leadership of John of Leiden, a Dutch tailor, got control of the city of Münster in northwest Germany, expelled its prince-bishop, and set up a biblical utopia. We know about them chiefly from their opponents, who certainly exaggerated their doctrines and practices. Still, even if we allow for the distortions of propaganda, it seems clear that the Anabaptists of Münster were behaving in ways that Western traditions do not permit large groups to adopt. For one thing, they preached, and apparently practiced, polygamy; John of Leiden was reported to have taken sixteen wives, one of whom he later decapitated in public when she displeased him. They pushed the Lutheran doctrine of justification by faith to its logical extreme in anarchism, or, in theological language, antinomianism, from the Greek "against law." Each man was to be his own law, or rather, to find God's universal law in his own conscience, not in *written* law and tradition. They did not believe in class distinctions or in the customary forms of private property. They were disturbers of an established order that was strong enough to put them down by force; their leaders were executed and the rank and file either slain or dispersed.

The great majority of Anabaptists were very far from being such wild fanatics as the men of Münster. Many Anabaptist groups sought to bring the Christian life to earth in quieter and more constructive ways. They established communities where they lived as they thought the primitive Christians had lived, in brotherhood, working, sharing, and praying together. These communities bore many resemblances to monasteries, though their members had taken no vows and did not observe celibacy. As we shall see in the next section of this chapter, some of the Anabaptist ideas—quietism, asceticism, the high sense of community—made a lasting contribution to the Protestant tradition. This sober majority of Anabaptists, too, met violent persecution in the sixteenth century but survived thanks to the discipline and to the repeated Christian turning of the other cheek insisted upon by their gifted leader, Menno Simons, a Dutch ex-priest. Something of their spirit lives on today in such diverse groups as the Baptists, the Friends, the Hutterites of Canada, and the Mennonites and Amish among the "Pennsylvania Dutch."

Two other radical strains in Protestantism were the mystical and the Unitarian. The former, often misleadingly referred to as Spiritualist, was exemplified by one of the few aristocratic reformers, Caspar von Schwenkfeld, a former Teutonic Knight and a convert to Lutheranism. More and more he came to feel that the true

* F. H. Littell, *The Anabaptist View of the Church* (Starr King Press, 1958), p. xvii.

church was to be found not in any outward observances but solely in the inner spirit of the individual. His stress on the spiritual and the mystical and his antagonism toward formalistic religion contributed later to the development of German pietism. Some of his eighteenth-century followers settled in eastern Pennsylvania, where there are still Schwenkfelder churches.

Unitarianism is the denial of the Trinity and therefore of the full divinity of Christ. Today it is usually identified with the rejection of the Trinity on the grounds that it is an irrational concept and with the view that Christ was simply a particularly inspired human being. But this version of Unitarianism derives largely from the rationalistic Enlightenment of the eighteenth century. Sixteenth-century Unitarianism was a very different matter and much more mystical in outlook. Its most famous advocate, the Spanish physician Servetus (1511–1553), believed that though Christ was not eternal, he was indeed the Son of God. His concept made Christ, as it were, less removed from man but not less removed from God. Thereby Servetus hoped to make it easier for humanity to acquire a mystic identification with Christ and thus to achieve salvation; he also hoped it would be possible to reconcile the Jewish and Muslim traditions of Spain with the Christian. His teachings greatly alarmed not only Catholics but also many Protestants. Servetus was finally prosecuted for heresy at Geneva by Calvin himself and burnt at the stake in 1553. Other Unitarian victims of persecution were the Socinians of Poland, Hungary, and Transylvania, who were never fully stamped out. They acquired their name and their doctrines from the far-traveling Italian theologian Fausto Sozzini (Socinus in Latin, 1539–1604).

## III Protestant Beliefs and Practices

### Common Denominators

It is very difficult to establish a common denominator for Protestant beliefs. Henry VIII, Luther, Zwingli, Calvin, John of Leiden, and Servetus make a most disparate group. Obviously they all, even the Anglican High Churchmen, repudiated the claim of the Roman Catholic church to be the one true faith. They were all hostile to the Church of Rome.

One other generalization is almost as universally valid, if less obvious in the more ecumenical world today. In the sixteenth century, each Protestant sect was convinced that it was the one true faith, that it and not Rome was the true successor of Christ and his apostles. Even the Antinomians, who believed that each man carried the truth in his own bosom, believed that if all the perversions that custom, education, and bad environment generally had set up as obstacles to the penetration of truth were swept away, each man would find the *same* truth in his bosom. Some early Protestants held that, though their own belief was the sole true belief, its ultimate prevailing on earth must be the slow process of educating men, of convincing them, of converting them. Others, however, could not wait for this slow process. Though they had once been persecuted themselves, they did not hesitate to persecute in their turn when they rose to power. Witness Calvin's condemnation of Servetus.

At this point it must be emphasized that what we nowadays in the United States accept as normal—that is, the peaceful coexistence of many different churches, "freedom of religion," "separation of church and state"—were certainly not normal, widespread concepts in the sixteenth-century, nor even in the seventeenth-century, Western world. Religious toleration itself is a complex matter, based at one extreme on sheer necessity (the impossibility of bringing the sects together) and at the other extreme on a belief that religious divergences are in themselves good, and toleration a positive benefit for all.

Only with the late seventeenth- and early eighteenth-century Enlightenment did the doctrine of religious toleration emerge into full prominence; and in that period many "enlightened" individuals were essentially nonbelievers in Christianity, for whom toleration was a way of letting Christianity wither on the vine. Nevertheless, the era of the Renaissance and Reformation saw the gradual emergence of a characteristic form of positive belief in religious toleration —that is, the belief that although there is indeed a single true religion which men may one day find, each man must find his own way to it freely, unforced by any external pressures. Consequently, there must be no established church, no enforced conformity, no persecution. Many humanists held this view. One of them, Sebastian Castellio, or Châteillon, wrote in 1554 a book in Latin on "whether heretics are to be persecuted," attacking Calvin for the execution of Servetus in 1553. In this book one may discern clearly the positive doctrine of religious toleration: force must never be used to attempt to change a man's ideas about religion. But, as the experience of Roger Williams in seventeenth-century New England was to show, such ideas were only very slowly accepted in the Western world. As a denial of the wisdom and rightness of actual persecution, religious toleration is now firmly established in the West, though there is still debate as to whether religious variation, and religious indifference, are in themselves good.

Even the conservative established churches of the Reformation—the Anglican and the Lutheran—shared with the more radical Protestants certain reductions in organization, ritual, and other external manifestations of belief. All the sects relaxed the requirement of clerical celibacy and either banned or very sharply curtailed monasticism. All reduced somewhat the seven sacraments; a general Protestant minimum was to retain baptism and communion. But the Protestant theological justification of these sacraments could range very widely, from Luther's consubstantiation to the symbolic view of the Eucharist, from an almost Roman acceptance of the miraculous to an almost secularist denial of the miraculous. Veneration of saints, pilgrimages, rosaries, amulets, and such "papist" practices disappeared even among the right-wing Protestants; the left wing also banished musical instruments (if not singing), stained glass and other forms of painting, indeed all the arts except the oratorical.

To these outward signs there corresponds an inner link that ties Protestantism together, loosely indeed, and often uncomfortably. All Protestants were rebels in origin. They had protested almost always in the name of an older, purer, primitive church, almost always maintaining that Rome was the real innovator, the wicked revolutionist. (This attempt of the rebel not to seem to be rebelling, his appeal to the past as legitimatizing his revolt, often recurs in Western history.) The Protestants had appealed from an established order to a "higher law" not concretely established in institutions on this earth. That is to say, all Protestantism has at least a tinge of the Lutheran appeal from works to faith, from the Letter to the Spirit; it has at least a tinge of an appeal to individual judgment. This individualism is an important legacy of early Protestantism to the modern world.

The divergent beliefs of the separate Protestant churches may most conveniently be arranged in order of their theological distance from Roman Catholicism, beginning with those nearest Rome. But it must be noted that the political and social distance is not always the same as the theological.

### Anglicanism

The Church of England contains communicants who think of themselves as Catholics; they represent the High Church point of view. But the Church of England also includes members who take a Low Church view; they are more Protestant in outlook, and some come very close to being Unitarians. The Church of England keeps a modified form of the Catholic hierarchy, with archbishops and bishops, though of course without acknowledging the authority of the pope. Yet it permits its clergy to marry and, although it does nowadays have religious orders, it does not put anything like the Catholic emphasis on the regular clergy. Historically speaking, the Church of England has somehow managed to contain elements from almost the whole range of Protestant belief, though Anglicans have not been very cordial toward the more demonstrative types of Protestantism.

Perhaps the central core of Anglicanism has been a tempered ritualism, a tempered belief in hierarchy, in discipline from above, a tempered acceptance of this imperfect world—a moderate attitude really not very far from the Catholicism of Thomas Aquinas. Indeed, Richard Hooker, who wrote a great defense of the Anglican Church in the 1590's (*The Laws of Ecclesiastical Polity*), relied heavily on Aquinas. It is significant, too, that Hooker is usually called "the judicious Hooker," because of his efforts to reconcile divergent points of view and adjust them to Anglicanism.

On the other hand, there has also always been a strong puritanical or evangelical current in the broad stream of Anglicanism. Some Puritans, for the most part only reluctantly, left the Anglican communion in the late sixteenth and early seventeenth century, and many of them stayed within it. This is not so much what later became the Low Church strain in Anglicanism or, in America, Episcopalianism, as it is a strain of earnest, evangelical piety, social service, plain living and high thinking—in short Puritanism.

The Church of England assumed its definitive form during the reign of Elizabeth I (1558–1603), daughter of Henry VIII and Anne Boleyn. The Thirty-Nine Articles enacted by Parliament in 1563 were a kind of constitution for the church. The Articles rejected the more obvious forms of Romanism—the use of Latin, auricular confession, clerical celibacy, the allegiance to the pope. They also affirmed the Protestant stand on one of the great symbolic issues of the day—whether only the communion bread should be given to the laity (the Catholic tradition) or both the bread and the wine should be offered (long the reformers' demand). The Church of England gave laymen both the bread and the wine. In interpreting the Lord's Supper the Articles sought a compromise somewhere in the uncertain middle ground between Catholic transubstantiation, which the Articles rejected, and Zwinglian symbolism, which they also rejected. Finally, the Thirty-Nine articles sought very emphatically to avoid the anarchistic dangers implicit in the doctrines of justification by faith and the priesthood of the believer.

The Church of England has always seemed to its enemies, and even to some of its friends, a bit too acquiescent in the face of civil authority. In what was once a word of abuse, the Church of England has seemed Erastian, a term named after Erastus, a sixteenth-century Swiss physician and theologian who by no means held the doctrines attributed to him. These doctrines assert that the state is all-powerful against the church, that the clergy are but the moral police force of the state; in short, that the government in power is always right. This extreme statement is indeed a caricature of Anglican practice. But a touch of subservience to political authority, a modified Erastianism, does remain in the Church of England. We shall encounter it in the English civil and religious struggles of the seventeenth century.

### Lutheranism

The first section of this chapter has already presented the main beliefs of the other great conservative Protestant church, the Lutheran. Once it had become established, Lutheranism preserved many practices which seem to outsiders Catholic in origin, but which to Luther represented a return to early Christianity before the corruption by Rome. Lutheranism preserved the Eucharist, now interpreted according to the mysterious doctrine of consubstantiation. It also preserved the notion of hierarchy, bishops, gowns, and something of the plastic arts. The tradition of good music in the church was not only preserved but greatly fortified.

Luther, like so many others upon whom character and fate have thrust rebellion, was at heart a conservative about things of this world, as we have seen. In his own lifetime he really wanted the forms of Lutheran worship to recall the forms he was used to. The Lutheran church, like the Anglican, had its high or conservative party. Yet it also had a strong evangelical party and a tradition of Bible reading. To outsiders, the Lutheran church has seemed even more Erastian than the Anglican. As the state church in much of north Germany and in Scandinavia, it was often a docile instrument of its political masters. And in its close association with the rise of Prussia—though Prussia's Hohenzollern rulers later became Calvinist—it was inevitably brought under the rule of the strongly bureaucratic Prussian state. Yet modern-day Lutherans often stood out more firmly against Hitler than did other Germans.

### Calvinism

The Protestant center is Calvinism, and the main theological problem of Calvinism is not so much Luther's problem of faith against good works as the related problem of predestination against free will. It is a problem that must seem tortured, unreal to many people, but the historian must record the fact that it keeps cropping up in Western history—even in Marxism. The problem is an old one in Christianity, already evident in the fifth-century struggle over the heresy of Pelagius, the problem of the conflict between God's goodness and man's sinfulness. To the logical mind, the problem arises from the Christian concept that God is all-powerful, all-good, all-knowing. If this is so, he must will, must determine, everything that happens. He must will that the sinner shall sin. For if he did not so will, the individual would be doing something God did not want him to do, and God would not be all-powerful. But there is a grave moral difficulty here. If God wills that the sinner sin, the sinner cannot help himself, cannot be "blamed" for his sin. We seem to be at a dead end, where the individual can always say, no matter what he does, that he is doing what God makes him do. We seem, in short, to have cut the ground from individual moral responsibility. And—at least from their enemies' reports—that is just what John of Leiden and his Antinomians did. When they took several wives at once, they argued that God must want them to, since they wanted to.

The dilemma is clear: If the individual can choose for himself between good and evil acts, if in theological terms he has free will to do what God does not want him to do—then it looks as if God were not all-powerful; if he has no such choice, if in theological terms he is subject to predestination—then it looks as if the individual were morally irresponsible. Both these conclusions are repugnant to the general nature of historical Christianity.

To an outsider, it looks as if most Christians most of the time solved the dilemma by embracing both horns at once—by holding that God determines every human act, and yet that human beings may do things God does not want them to do. Theologians do not of course put the matter this way. Most of their basic solutions preserve the moral responsibility of the individual by asserting the profound distance between God and man, a distance that the miracle—the grace— of faith alone can bridge. In terms of everyday life, this means that for the individual to claim that whatever he does is what God wants him to do is to make the incredibly presumptuous claim that he knows God's will, that his petty human understanding is on a par with God's. The individual can never be certain that what he wants to do is what God wants him to do. Therefore he should look about him and see what signs he can, limited though his vision be, of God's intentions. These he will find in Christian tradition and Christian history. To be concrete: If the individual is tempted to commit adultery, he will not follow the Antinomian and say that God wants him to do so; he will follow Christian tradition, and recognize the adulterous desire as an indication that he is being tempted to do wrong, and that if he does it he will not be saved, but damned.

Calvin himself, though he would certainly not have put it this way, would have reached the same conclusion. But he was, as we have noted, a logician. Both his temperament and his environment led him to reject what he believed to be the Catholic emphasis on easy salvation by indulgences and the like. He put his own emphasis on the hard path of true salvation, on the majesty of God and the littleness of man. He evolved therefore a very extreme form of the doctrine of predestination.

In Calvin's system, Adam's original sin was unforgivable. God, however, in his incomprehensible mercy, sent Jesus Christ to this earth and let him die on the cross to make salvation possible for some—but emphatically not all, nor by any means a majority—of Adam's progeny, stained though they were by original sin. Very few—in fact, only the elect—could attain this salvation, and that through no merit of their own, and certainly not on the wholesale scale the Roman Catholic church of the sixteenth century was claiming. The elect were saved only through God's free and infinite grace, by means of which they were given the strength to gain salvation. Grace is not like anything else that touches human life on earth. It is not of a piece with law, morals, philosophy, and other human ways of relating man to his environment—to hold that it is was to Calvin one of the errors of the Catholic. But it is not wholly divorced from these earthly relations—to hold that it is, is the error of the Antinomian. The elect actually tend to behave in a certain way, an identifiable way, a way not wholly misrepresented if it is called puritanical.

Our modern world has certainly exaggerated the gloom of Calvinist puritanism, and the spiritual pride and exclusiveness of its adherents. Yet there is the bite of reality behind Robert Burns' *Holy Willie's Prayer:*

*O Thou that in the heavens does dwell!*
*Wha, as it pleases best Thysel,*
*Sends one to heaven and ten to hell,*
*A' for Thy glory;*
*And no for ony guid or ill*
*They've done before Thee!*

*Yet I am here, a chosen sample,*
*To show Thy grace is great and ample.*
*I'm here, a pillar o' Thy temple.*
*Strong as a rock;*
*A guide, a ruler, and example*
*To a' Thy flock**

* *Poetical Works of Robert Burns,* ed. William Wallace (Chambers, 1958), p. 63.

Where the Calvinists were in complete control of an area (as in sixteenth-century Geneva) or in partial control of larger areas (as in England, Scotland, the Netherlands, or Puritan Massachusetts), they censored, forbade, banished, and punished. Particularly in Geneva, where all trace of the Roman hierarchy had vanished along with the prince-bishop, the Catholic tradition of scrutinizing the morals of the populace continued on an intensive scale. Every week a consistory composed of pastors and of lay elders appointed by the city council met and passed judgment on all accused of improper behavior. Though the consistory sometimes failed to get its decisions enforced, twentieth-century critics condemn its activities as a Protestant inquisition, harsh and inhuman. Yet in their own minds the members of the Geneva consistory and other representatives of puritan spiritual police were God's agents, doing God's work. These firm believers in the inability of human efforts to change anything were among the most ardent of workers toward getting men to change their behavior. To an amazing extent, they succeeded. They helped make the Industrial Revolution and the modern world.

The note of Christianity the Calvinists most clearly emphasized is not so much asceticism or other-worldliness as austerity. The Calvinist did not seek to annihilate the senses but sought rather to select among his worldly desires those that would further his salvation, and to curb or suppress those that would not. The Calvinist thought the world a very serious place indeed, in which laughter was somewhat out of order. This world is for most of us, the Calvinist believed, an antechamber to hell and eternal suffering; if you really feel this, you are not likely to be much amused. The Calvinist thought that many pleasures to which the human race is addicted—music, dancing, gambling, fine clothes, drinking, playgoing, and fortune-telling, among others—were the kind of thing Satan liked. Although the Calvinist did not hold that all sexual intercourse is sinful, he believed firmly that the purpose God had in mind in providing sexual intercourse was the continuation of the race, and not the sensuous pleasures of the participants. Those pleasures are all the more dangerous since they may lead to extramarital indulgence, which is a very great sin.

Calvinism also sounded very loudly the ethical note of Christianity. The Calvinist had a high moral code; he was always trying to live up to his code, and to see that other people did so too. Both inward and outward directions of this effort are important. The Calvinist certainly felt the "civil war in the breast," the struggle between what has become famous as the Puritan conscience and the temptations of this world. This notion of a higher part of human consciousness that can and should censor and suppress the promptings of a lower part has left a firm imprint on the West, an imprint especially strong where Calvinism has set the dominant tone. In its outgoing direction, this Calvinist ethical concern has taken many forms other than that of the outright, police-enforced prohibition. The Calvinist also believed in persuasion; he made the sermon a central part of his worship. He believed in hellfire and in the moral uses of fear of hellfire; he believed in emotional conversion, and was a good missionary, though not at his best among primitive peoples.

Calvinism appears in pure or diluted form in many sects, Presbyterian and Congregational in Britain, Reformed on the Continent. It influenced almost all the other sects, even the Anglican and the Lutheran. Theologically, its main opponent is a system of ideas called Arminianism, from Jacob Arminius, a late sixteenth-century Dutch divine. Arminianism may be classified among the free-will theologies, for Arminius held that election (and of course damnation) were conditional in God's mind—not absolute as Calvin had maintained—and that therefore what a man did on earth could change God's mind about the man's individual fate. Generally, Arminianism was more tolerant of the easy ways of this world than Calvinism, less "puritanical," more Erastian.

Calvinism can hardly be accused of being Erastian. Where it did become the established state church—in Geneva, in the England of the 1650's, in Massachusetts, for instance—the Calvinist church ran or tried to run the state. This is, of course, theocracy, not Erastianism, and even in Calvin's own Geneva it was never fully realized in practice, since the city council refused to surrender all its prerogatives. Where Calvinism had to fight to exist, it preached and practiced an ardent denial of the omnipotence of the state over the individual, made affirmations of popular rights which later generations turned to the uses of their own struggle against kings—and churchmen. In this sense, Calvinism helped create modern democracy. Its basic original concepts are not, however, democratic, if democracy is based as we think it is, on equalitarian principles and on a generally compassionate and hopeful view of human beings, a minimizing of the legacy of original sin.

Finally, we must point out once more that Calvinism is no longer the vigorous, in a sense, fundamentalist, and certainly fighting, creed it was in the sixteenth century. Its churches almost everywhere have gone part way along toward a kindlier view of human nature and human potential, toward optimism, a milder reforming zeal. Arminianism, with help from the eighteenth-century Enlightenment, has triumphed. But would Calvin recognize his twentieth-century children?

## The Left Wing

The sects of the Protestant left wing were usually greatly influenced by Calvinist theology and by Calvinist example. The Anabaptists, too, broke sharply with Catholic forms of worship, in which the congregation, if not quite passive in the presence of age-old rites, was at least quiet and orderly. In the new sects, the congregation sometimes shouted and danced and sang hymns with great fervor. Here again, however, the varieties of practice were almost infinite; some of the Mennonites, for instance, put great stress on silent prayer and meditation. Among the radicals preaching was even more important than in more conservative forms of Protestantism, and more emotionally charged with hopes of heaven and fears of hell. Many of the sects were vigorously chiliastic—that is, they expected an immediate second coming of Christ and the end of this world. Many were in aim, and among themselves in practice, economic equalitarians, communists of a sort. They did not share wealth, however, so much as the poverty that had seemed to Saint Francis, and now seemed to them, an essential part of the Christian way.

Almost all of them had some beliefs, some goals, that alarmed many ordinary, conventional men and women. Many refused to take oaths on grounds of conscience. Most distrusted the state, regarding it as a necessary instrument operated by sinners to punish other sinners, an institution from which true Christians should hold aloof. What is most striking about these sects is the extraordinary range of their ideals and behavior. Some of them really behaved as badly—as insanely—as their conservative enemies have charged. John of Leiden, crowned at Münster as "King David" with two golden, jeweled crowns, one kingly, one imperial, with his "Queen Divara" and a whole harem in attendance, seems a mad parody of the Protestant appeal to the Bible. Yet the Anabaptists already scattered about northwestern Europe at the time were shocked by what went on in Münster; and if one examines their ideas and practices one finds, for the most part, pious and earnest pacifist Christians, living simply and productively as do their modern successors, Mennonites, Baptists, and Quakers.

These left-wing sects often display an illogical and magnificent combination of pacifist principles and ardent combativeness (as long as the weapons are not physical ones, conventional means of inflicting bodily harm). These men are fighting to end fighting. Here is Jacob Hutter, who founded the Hutterite sect of Moravian Anabaptists, addressing the governor-general of Moravia, Ferdinand of Hapsburg, a good Catholic who was ruling the Germanies for his brother Charles V:

> Woe, woe! unto you, O ye Moravian rulers, who have sworn to that cruel tyrant and enemy of God's truth, Ferdinand, to drive away his pious and faithful servants. Woe! we say unto you, who fear that frail and mortal man more than the living, omnipotent, and eternal God, and chase from you, suddenly and inhumanly, the children of God, the afflicted widow, the desolate orphan, and scatter them abroad. . . . God, by the mouth of the prophet, proclaims that He will fearfully and terribly avenge the shedding of innocent blood, and will not pass by such as fear not to pollute and contaminate their hands therewith. Therefore, great slaughter, much misery and anguish, sorrow and adversity, yea, everlasting groaning, pain and torment are daily appointed you.*

Given the pacifist basis of most Anabaptist cults, the violence of this letter is extraordinary, even for the time. Yet these men did know how to die. They, too, were martyrs. And they were persecuted by the more moderate reformers with a violence as firm and principled as that which Protestant tradition attributes to the Catholic Inquisition.

* J. T. van Braght, *Martyrology*, I, 151–153, quoted in R. J. Smithson, *The Anabaptists* (London, 1935), pp. 69–71.

It must not be concluded that all sectarians of the left were as violently nonviolent as Hutter. An even stronger and more longlasting note is that sounded by a man like the English John Bunyan (1628–1688), whose *Pilgrim's Progress* has long been read far beyond the circles of the Baptist sect of which he was a lay preacher. This book is an allegory of life seen as a pilgrimage toward a happy end, and the joys of Beulahland, a pilgrimage full of trials, but not by any means a series of horrors. It is written in simple language, and its view of life is quite untortured.

## IV The Catholic Response

The dominant early Catholic response to the challenge of the Protestant Reformation was to stand pat and try to suppress the rebels. Such, basically, was the papal policy toward Luther. Yet the fact remains that the religious ferment out of which Protestantism emerged was originally a ferment *within* the Catholic church. To that ferment many who remained within the Church had contributed. Erasmus and other Christian humanists greatly influenced the early stages of what has come to be called the Catholic Reformation. Particularly in Spain, as the next chapter will show, but spreading throughout the Catholic world, there was a revival of deep mystical impulses and a corresponding increase in popular participation in religion.

*The pope in Hell: an antipapal German woodcut, 1521.*

Within a long generation, the Catholic church was to rally its spiritual and material forces, achieve a large measure of reform from within, and, by winning back areas in Germany, Bohemia, Hungary, and Poland, establish the territorial limits of Protestantism in the West substantially where they now are. This Catholic Reformation, in Protestant historical writing usually called the Counter-Reformation, was no mere negative defense, but a positive spiritual renewal in its own right. It did not restore the medieval unity of Christendom, but it did preserve and reinvigorate fundamental Catholic beliefs and practice.

They were not preserved without the aid of the secular arm. Both the Catholic and the Protestant Reformations were inseparably tied up with domestic and international politics, as we shall see in detail in the next chapter. The powerful House of Hapsburg, both in its Spanish and its German branches, was the active head of political Catholicism in the next few generations. The French monarchs, though their support was perhaps rather more political than religious, none the less helped greatly to preserve France as a Catholic land. Moreover, in France itself the seventeenth century was to witness a many-sided Catholic revival. In many parts of Germany and its Slavic borderlands, and in Italy, the reigning princes and their nobilities were powerful influences behind the old religion.

Nor were Catholic fundamentals preserved without special organization. Once more, as with the Cluniacs, the Cistercians, the mendicant orders, this renewal of Catholic strength, this need to achieve in the name of the old something quite new, produced a series of new orders of the regular clergy, a revival of the old monastic ideals of austere simplicity and social service. The reforming current was already gathering strength when the papacy was still in the lax hands of Leo X, Luther's opponent. During Leo's pontificate an earnest group formed at Rome the Oratory of Divine Love, dedicated to the deepening of spiritual experience through special services and religious exercises. In the 1520's, the Oratory inspired the foundation of the Theatines, an order aimed particularly at the education of the secular clergy. In the 1520's also a new branch of the Franciscans appeared, the Capuchins, to lead the order back to Francis' own ideals of poverty and preaching to the poor. During the next decade or so, half a dozen other new orders were established, among them the Ursuline nuns, pioneers in the education of girls. The greatest of these by far was the Society of Jesus, founded in 1540.

*Ignatius Loyola: the only authentic portrait of the saint, by Coello.*

### The Jesuits

The founder of the Jesuits was the Spaniard, Ignatius Loyola (1491–1556), who had been a soldier and turned to religion after a painful wound received in battle. The Society of Jesus was from the beginning the soldiery of the Catholic church; its head bore the title of general. Loyola set the rules for his order in his *Spiritual Exercises*. The following extracts bring out admirably two major characteristics of the Jesuits: first, the absolute (for once the word must be taken literally) obedience to higher authority, to the Catholic church as embodied in its hierarchy; and second, the realistic, middle-of-the-road estimate of what can be expected of ordinary human beings in this world. Note the moderate position on predestination:

> 1. Always to be ready to obey with mind and heart, setting aside all judgment of one's own, the true spouse of Jesus Christ, our holy mother, our infallible and orthodox mistress, the Catholic Church, whose authority is exercised over us by the hierarchy.
>
> 13. That we may be altogether of the same mind and in conformity with the Church herself, if she shall have defined anything to be black which to our eyes appears to be white, we ought in like manner to pronounce it to be black. For we must undoubtedly believe, that the Spirit of our Lord Jesus Christ, and the Spirit of the Orthodox Church His Spouse, by which Spirit we are governed and directed to Salvation, is the same; . . . .
>
> 14. It must also be borne in mind, that although it be most true, that no one is saved but he that is predestinated, yet we must speak with circumspection concerning this matter, lest perchance, stressing too much the grace or predestination of God, we should seem to wish to shut out the force of free will and the merits of good works; or on the other hand, attributing to these latter more than belongs to them, we derogate meanwhile from the power of grace.*

Born in controversy, the Jesuits have always been a center of controversy. To their hostile critics, who have been numerous both within and without the Catholic church, the Jesuits have seemed unscrupulous soldiers of the pope. Though they have rarely been accused of the simpler vices common gossip has long alleged against the regular clergy—fondness for food and drink, laziness, laxity with women—they have

* *Documents,* ed. H. Bettenson, pp. 363, 364–365.

been accused of a subtler devotion to worldly power, to success in a quite unspiritual sense. They have been accused of preaching and practicing the doctrine that the end justifies the means, that as soldiers of the one true Church they may indulge in dirty fighting as long as such tactics seem likely to bring victory.

This is indeed a slander, for even at the purely worldly level, Jesuit devotion to Catholic tradition is too deep for them to make Machiavelli's mistake of underestimating the hold the moral decencies have on human beings. And the historical record leaves no doubt of Jesuit success in bolstering the spiritual as well as the material credit of Catholicism in these critical days of the sixteenth and seventeenth centuries. Jesuits were everywhere, in Hungary, in Poland, in England, in Holland, trying to win back lost lands and peoples from the Protestants. They were winning new lands and peoples on the expanding frontiers of the West, in India, in China, in Japan, in North America. They were martyrs, preachers, teachers, social workers, counselors of statesmen, always disciplined, never lapsing into the kind of fleshly worldliness that had been the fate of other monastic orders. As realists, they particularly sought to influence the politically powerful and to mold the young men who would later become leaders. Their schools rapidly acquired great fame for their humanistic classical teaching and their insistence on good manners and adequate food and exercise as well as for the soundness of their Catholic doctrines.

### The Inquisition

The Jesuits were the chief new instruments of the Catholic Reformation. An old instrument of the Church was also employed—the Inquisition, a special ecclesiastical court which in its papal form began in the thirteenth century as part of the effort to put down the Albigensian heresy and in its Spanish form began in the fifteenth century as part of the effort of the new Spanish monarchy to force religious uniformity on its subjects. Both papal and Spanish inquisitions were medieval courts, which used medieval methods of torture. Both were employed against the Protestants in the sixteenth century.

Protestant tradition sometimes makes both the Inquisition and the Jesuits appear as the promoters of a widespread and veritable reign of terror. Certainly the Jesuits and their allies made full use of the many pressures and persuasions any highly organized society can bring to bear on nonconformists. And the Inquisition did perpetrate horrors against former Muslims in Spain and against Catholics-turned-Protestants in the Low Countries. But the Inquisition does not appear to have been a really major force in stemming the Protestant tide. It was most active in countries of southern Europe—Italy, Spain, Portugal—where Protestantism was never a real threat. And in the regions where the Catholic Reformation was most successful in winning back large numbers to the Roman faith—the Germanies, the Slavic and Magyar marches of the East—sheer persecution was not a decisive factor.

### The Council of Trent

The Catholic Reformation was not a change of dogma, not a change of spiritual direction. If anything, revulsion against the Protestant tendency toward some form of the "priesthood of the believer" hardened Catholic doctrines into a firmer insistence on the miraculous power of the priesthood. Protestant variation promoted Catholic uniformity. Not even on indulgences did the Church yield; interpreted as a spiritual return for spiritual effort, not as a money transaction, indulgences were reaffirmed by the Council of Trent. The work of this council ties together the various measures of reform and illustrates clearly the fact that what the Catholic Reformation reformed was not doctrine but practice.

The council met in Trent, a small city in the Alpine borderlands of Austria and Italy, in 1545 at the call of Paul III (1534–1549), the first of a line of reforming popes. A member of the ambitious Farnese family, Paul was in many respects a secular Renaissance figure, but he also realized that reform of the Church was overdue and made it imperative to run the risk of convoking another general council. To liberals—including liberal Catholics—the Council of Trent has seemed no true general council, but an instrument in the hands of the popes and the Jesuits, a mere rubber stamp. Certainly in conception it was meant to provide at least a chance for reconciliation with the Protestants. Leading figures in the more con-

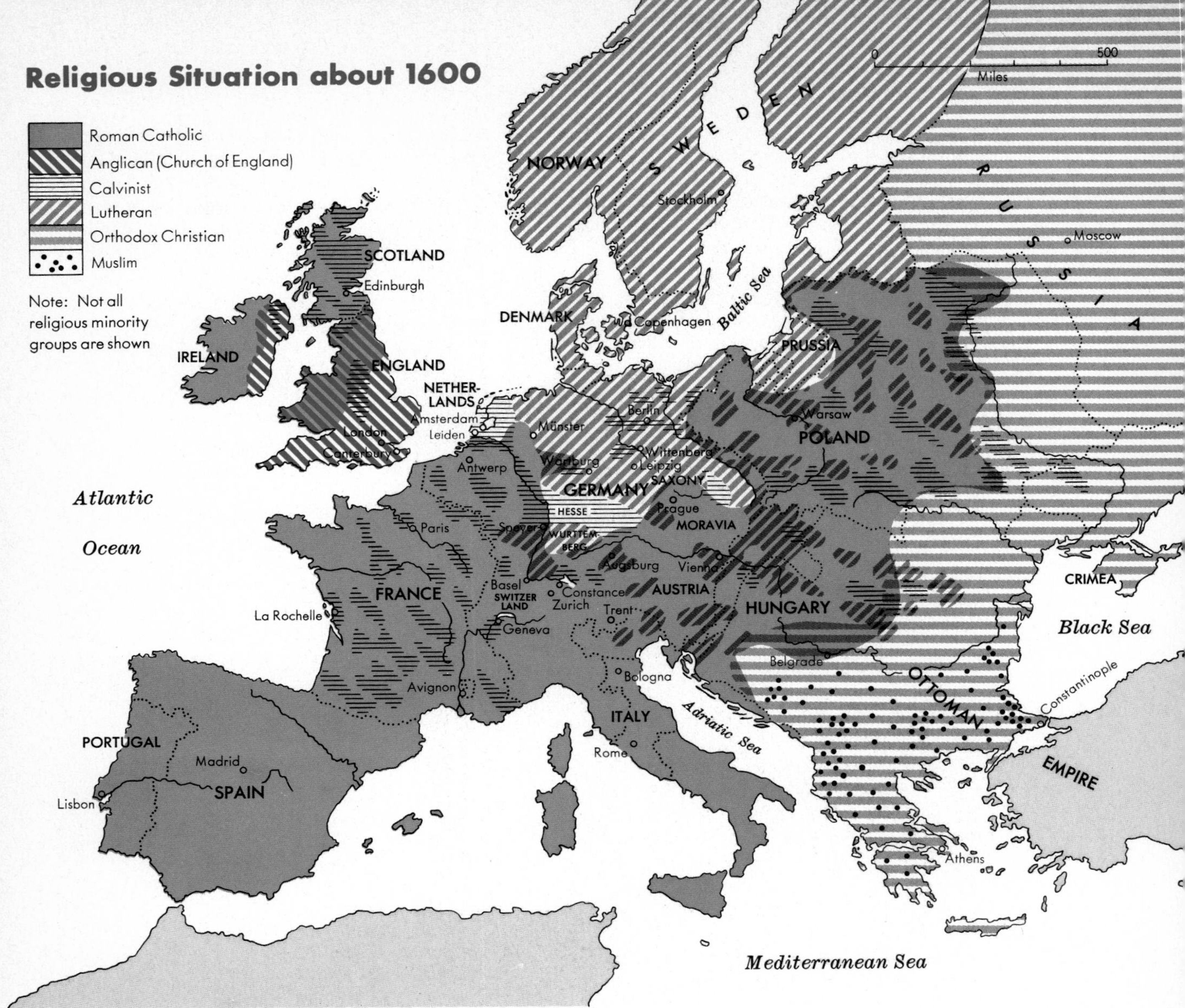


servative Protestant groups were invited, but they never attended. The French clergy, with their Gallican tradition, did not cooperate freely, and indeed part of the work of the Council of Trent was not accepted in France for some fifty years. The council was caught in the web of the religious wars and intrigues of high politics, and its work was several times interrupted. Nevertheless it continued to meet off and on for twenty years until it completed its work of reaffirming and codifying doctrine in 1564.

On matters of doctrine, the Council of Trent took a stand that ruled out all possibility of a compromise with the Protestants on the major issues separating them from Catholics. It reaffirmed the essential role of the priesthood, reaffirmed all seven sacraments, reaffirmed the great importance of both faith and works, reaffirmed that both the Scriptures and the spokesmen of the Church were authorities on theology. The uncompromisingly traditional stand taken by the council is evident in the *Professio Fidei Tridentina* (the Trent Profession of Faith), which for long was subscribed to by converts to Catholicism. It runs in part:

> I most firmly acknowledge and embrace the Apostolical and ecclesiastical traditions and other

observances and constitutions of the same Church. I acknowledge the sacred Scripture according to that sense which Holy Mother Church has held and holds, to whom it belongs to decide upon the true sense and interpretation of the holy Scriptures, nor will I ever receive and interpret the Scriptures except according to the unanimous consent of the Fathers.

. . . . .

I profess likewise that true God is offered in the Mass, a proper and propiatory sacrifice for the living and the dead, and that in the most Holy Eucharist there are truly, really and substantially the body and the blood, together with the soul and divinity of our Lord Jesus Christ, and that a conversion is made of the whole substance of bread into his body and of the whole substance of wine into his blood, which conversion the Catholic Church calls transubstantiation.*

The Council of Trent and the reforming popes of the later sixteenth century effected in Catholic practice the kind of change that had been achieved under Cluniac auspices five hundred years earlier. The Council insisted on the strict observance of clerical vows and on the ending of abuses. It took measures against the sale of church offices and against nonresidence of prelates. It called for the establishment of seminaries to give priests better training. To promote discipline among the laity, it imposed censorship on a large scale, issuing the *Index,* a list of books that Catholics were not to read because of the peril to their faith. The *Index* included not only the writings of heretics and Protestants but also the works of such anticlericals as Machiavelli and Boccaccio.

Under Pius V, pope from 1566 to 1572, a standard catechism, breviary, and missal were drawn up to embody for purposes of instruction the codifying work of the Council of Trent. In short, the whole structure of the Church, both for the training of the priesthood and for the training of the layman, was tightened up, given a new spirit. The papal court was no longer just another Italian Renaissance court. It is true that, especially among the upper clergy and in the monasteries, laxity had again crept in by the eighteenth century. That same century witnessed the inroads of excessive rationalism, especially in certain sections of the teaching clergy in France, Italy, and in the Hapsburg domains. But the widespread corruption against which Luther and his fellows inveighed never again prevailed in the West.

The strength of the Catholic Reformation is shown by the fact that, once it was well launched, the Protestants made few further territorial inroads. Within a century of Luther's revolt, the broad lines of the territorial division in the West between areas dominantly Catholic and areas dominantly Protestant were established much as they are today. England, Scotland, Holland, northern and eastern Germany (with a southward projection in Württemberg and Switzerland), and Scandinavia were predominantly Protestant. Ireland, Belgium, France, southern Germany (with a northern projection in the valley of the Rhine), the Hapsburg lands, Poland, Italy, and the Iberian peninsula were predominantly Catholic. But only predominantly. There were Catholic minorities in England, Scotland, and Holland, and the two faiths interpenetrated most confusedly in a greatly divided Germany; there were Protestant minorities in Ireland, France, and even in some of the Hapsburg lands the Jesuits had won back.

## V The Place of Protestantism in History

### Protestantism and Progress

The Reformation has often been interpreted, especially by Protestants, as something peculiarly "modern," something forward-looking and even "democratic" as distinguished from the stagnant and status-ridden Middle Ages. This view seems to gain support from the obvious fact that those parts of the West which in the last three centuries have been economically most prosperous, which have worked out most successfully democratic constitutional government, and which have made the most striking contributions to modern Western culture, especially in the sciences and technology, were predominantly Protestant. Moreover, the states which, since the decline of Spain after 1600, have risen to a prepon-

* Ibid., pp. 374–375.

derance of power and prestige in the West—namely France, the British Empire, Germany, and now the United States—have been with one exception predominantly Protestant. And the one exception, France, has had since the eighteenth century a strong, at times a leading, element among its people which, though not in the main Protestant, is strongly secularist and anticlerical. It looks as if the nations that went Protestant also went modern and progressive.

This notion that Protestantism is a cause or at least an accompaniment of political and cultural leadership in the modern West needs to be examined carefully. It has, of course, the kind of truth certain modern philosophers have called "the truth of the myth." That is, for a good many years a good many Protestants and secularists in these prosperous countries have believed that their Protestantism was a major part of what made them prosperous. To the average Victorian Englishman, for instance, at the height of British power and wealth, the fact that his country had gone Protestant in the sixteenth century was at least as important as Magna Carta—and the existence of good deposits of coal and iron—in producing the prosperous England of which he was so proud. The historian must record the acceptance of the myth; he must also attempt to go back to the events that were used to construct the myth.

We find that Protestantism in the sixteenth century looks in many ways quite different from Protestantism seen from the nineteenth and twentieth centuries, just as Magna Carta in the thirteenth century looks quite different from Magna Carta looked back at from the twentieth. First, sixteenth-century Protestants were not rationalists; they were almost as "superstitious" as the Catholics. Luther actually threw his ink bottle at the devil, or so they tell the tourists at the castle of the Wartburg where they point out the dark patch on the wall where the bottle struck; the Calvinists burned witches, or at any rate hanged them. To put the matter more positively, the Protestants for the most part shared with their Catholic opponents very fundamental Christian conceptions of original sin, the direct divine governance of the universe, the reality of heaven and hell, and—most important—they had no more than did the Catholics a general conception of life on this earth as improving, as progressing systematically and regularly to an even better life for coming generations.

Second, these early Protestants were by no means tolerant, by no means believers in the separation of church and state. When they were in a position to do so, they used governmental power to prevent public worship in any form other than their own. Many of them persecuted those who disagreed with them, both Protestants of other sects and Catholics—that is, they banished them or imprisoned them or even killed them.

Third, these early Protestants were hardly democratic, at least in most of the senses that loose (but indispensable) word has for twentieth-century Americans. Logically, the Protestant appeal from the authority of the pope backed by Catholic tradition to the conscience of the individual believer fits in with notions like "individualism," "rights of man," and "liberty." Some historians have even found a correlation between the Protestant appeal to the authority of the Bible and the later characteristic American appeal to the authority of a written constitution. But most of the early Protestant reformers certainly did not hold that all men are created equal; they were not social and economic equalitarians. Rather, they believed in an order of rank, in a society of status. Lutheranism and Anglicanism were clearly conservative in their political and social doctrines. Calvinism can be made to look very undemocratic indeed if we concentrate on its conception of an elect few chosen by God for salvation and an unregenerate majority condemned to eternal damnation. And in its early years in Geneva and in New England Calvinism came close to being a theocracy, an authoritarian rule of the "saints."

In the long run, however, Calvinism favored the domination of a fairly numerous middle class. As we shall see shortly, the most persuasive argument for a causal relation between Protestantism and modern Western democratic life does not proceed directly from the ideas of the early Protestants about men in society, but from the way Protestant moral ideals fitted in with the strengthening of a commercial and industrial middle class. Finally, among the Anabaptists and other radical sects, we do find even in the sixteenth century demands for political, social, and economic equality. But where these demands are made, they are cast in biblical language and rest on concepts of direct divine intervention quite strange to us. Moreover, many of these sects tended not so much toward active social revolt to improve earthly standards of living as toward a peculiarly Protestant form of withdrawal from things of this earth, toward a pacifism, a mysticism, and a spiritual exclusiveness quite compatible with leaving the unregenerate majority in possession of this unworthy sense-world.

The Protestant Reformation, then, did not create modern society single-handed. But it did challenge those in authority in many parts of Europe and did start all sorts of men, some of them in humble circumstances, thinking about fundamental problems of life in this world as well as in the next. Its educators and propagandists, using the new weapon of the printing press, began the drive toward universal literacy. It was one of the great destroyers of the medieval synthesis. Its most important positive action can best be traced through its part in forming the way of life of the middle classes who were to lay the foundations of modern Western democracy.

## The Weber Thesis

The German sociologist Max Weber explored this question in *The Protestant Ethic and the Spirit of Capitalism,* first published in 1904. The thesis that he advanced has aroused a storm of controversy, in part because he touched on the sensitive area of religion and in part because a mere sociologist dared to invade the even more sensitive province of the historian. Though many historians nowadays reject his conclusions, the Weber thesis remains a stimulating and suggestive contribution to the ventilation of an issue that can never be fully resolved.

What started Weber's exploration was evidence suggesting that in his own day German Protestants had a proportionately greater interest in the world of business, and German Catholics a proportionately smaller interest, than their ratio in the German population would lead one to expect. Why was this so? Weber's answer—his celebrated thesis—may be summarized as follows: The accumulation of capital requires some abstention from immediate consumption; the entrepreneur, if he is a true capitalist, must save some of his profits so that they may be "plowed back" into his enterprise to enable him to produce still more and make higher profits, with a higher potential for future capital. To achieve this a businessman must not only guard his expenditures but also work very hard; he must spend the bulk of his time "making money." In very simple terms, hard work and no play meant more production, more profits, more capital.

Weber argued that Protestantism, especially in its Calvinist form, encouraged this sort of life. It encouraged hard work because, as the maxim put it, "The devil lies in wait for idle hands." Work keeps a man from temptation to run after women, or play silly games, or drink, or do many other things unpleasing to the Calvinist God. More, work is positively a good thing, a kind of tribute we pay to the Lord. Luther, too, glorified work of all kinds and preached the doctrine of the dignity of the vocation a man is called to, be it ever so humble. In almost all forms of Protestantism we find this feeling, so contrary to the contempt for work of the field and counting-house evident in the tradition of chivalry.

So much for work, the positive side of the equation. But on the negative side, Protestantism, and in particular Calvinism, discouraged many kinds of consumption which took energies away from the large-scale production that is the essence of the modern economic system. The Calvinist, to put it mildly, discouraged the fine arts, the theater, the dance, expensive clothes, what the American economist Veblen called "conspicuous consumption" generally. But he did not discourage—in fact he encouraged by his own way of living—the satisfaction of the simpler, commoner, needs of solid, substantial food, shelter, clothing, and the like, all needs most readily supplied by large-scale industry serving a mass demand. The Calvinist represents a new development of the perennial Christian ascetic tradition.

A society with many Calvinists tended to produce much, to consume solidly but without "waste" (we are speaking here in terms of economics, not in terms of art or morals). Therefore, under competitive conditions, its business leaders accumulated the kind of surplus we call capital, which they could invest in the methods of production that have so enriched the West. All work and no play—well, not much—made the Calvinist society an economically prosperous one.

The Scots, the Dutch, the Swiss, the Yankees of New England—all of them markedly Calvinistic peoples—have long had a popular reputation for thrift, diligence, and driving a hard bargain. And it is surprising how many concrete bits of

*This panel painting by Hans Leu the Elder shows Zurich at the turn of the sixteenth century.*

evidence reinforce the Weber thesis. The Protestant societies at once cut down the number of holy days—holidays without work. They kept Sunday very rigorously as a day without work, but the other six were all work days. The Calvinists even eliminated Christmas, and, since there were as yet no national lay equivalents of the old religious festivals, no Fourth of July or Labor Day, the early modern period in most Protestant countries had a maximum of work days per year. This is a marginal matter, but it is in part by such margins that economic growth is won. Many Protestant theologians rejected the medieval Catholic doctrine that regarded interest on investments beyond a low, "just" rate as usury, an illegitimate and immoral thing. In general, they rejected most of the medieval doctrines suggested by the term "just price" in favor of something much closer to our modern notions of free competition in the market. In the market, God would certainly take care of his own.

Finally, the firm Calvinist retention of the other world as the supreme, but for the individual never certain, goal helped shield the wealthy from the temptation of the newly rich to adopt the standards of life of a loose-living, free-spending upper class. Prosperity might be a token that a man was predestined to election, but so, too, was the cautious way he husbanded his profits. Among Calvinists family fortunes founded by hard work and inconspicuous consumption tended to hold together for several generations at least.

Weber's thesis must not be taken as the sole explanation of the rise of capitalism in early modern times. It is but one of many variables in a complex situation. In the first place, the stirrings of modern economic life far antedated Luther and Calvin, and were clearest and most important in many regions—Italy, southern Germany, Belgium—which were not actually won over to Protestantism. Banking began in northern Italy under Catholic rule—in Florence, for instance—at the time when the theoretical official prohibition of usury still prevailed. Almost certainly relaxation of rules against usury would have received official Catholic sanction even had there been no Protestant Reformation. In the second place, there is no perfect coordination between Protestantism and industrial development on one hand and Catholicism and industrial backwardness (or notably slower development) on the other. Belgium, the German Rhineland, Piedmont, and Lombardy are striking examples of Catholic regions which on the whole have kept in modern times well up to the fore in general productiveness and prosperity. In the third place, no sensible explanation of the rise of modern industrial economy can neglect the simple facts of geography and natural resources. Suppose, contrary to all likelihood, Italy had turned solidly Calvinistic; this still would not give Italy the coal and iron that Calvinist, or at least Protestant, England had.

Yet the "Protestant ethic" remains an important element in the economic transformation of modern Europe. It gave perhaps the extra fillip, the margin that started the West on its modern path—along with that opening up of Europe overseas which helped the Atlantic nations over the Mediterranean nations, along with the natural resources of northern and western Europe, along with the damp, temperate climate that made hard work easier than in the Mediterranean, along with free enterprise, freedom for science and invention, relatively orderly and law-abiding societies, and whatever else goes to produce that still not fully understood phenomenon, economic growth.

### Protestantism and Nationalism

One final big generalization about the Protestant Reformation is much less disputable than attempts to tie that movement with modern individualism, democracy, and industrialism. After the great break of the sixteenth century, both Protestantism and Catholicism became important elements in the formation of modern nationalism. Here again we must not fall into the trap of one-way causation. The Protestants were not always patriots; French Huguenots sought help from the English enemy; French Catholics sought it from the Spanish enemy. Much besides the Reformation goes into the formation of the modern state system of the West and its cementing patriotism. "Frenchness" and modern "Germanness" perhaps began as far back as the Strasbourg oaths of the ninth century. But where a specific form of religion became identified with a given political unit, religious feeling and patriotic feeling each reinforced the other. This is most clear where a political unit had to struggle for its independence. Protestantism heightened Dutch resistance to the Spaniard; Catholicism heightened Irish resistance to the Englishman. But even in states already independent in the sixteenth century, religion came to strengthen patriotism. England from Elizabeth I on has, despite the existence of a Catholic minority, proudly held itself up as a Protestant nation. Spain has with at least equal pride identified itself as a Catholic nation. In the great wars to which we must now turn, religion and politics were inextricably mixed.

## Reading Suggestions on the Protestant Reformation

GENERAL ACCOUNTS

O. Chadwick, *The Reformation* (*Penguin). A comprehensive, up-to-date survey addressed to the general reader; Volume III in the series "The Pelican History of the Church."

R. H. Bainton, *The Reformation of the Sixteenth Century* (*Beacon). Excellent introduction by a scholarly Protestant historian, author of several more specialized works on the period.

E. H. Harbison, *The Age of Reformation* (*Cornell Univ. Press). A brief, perceptive introduction.

*The New Cambridge Modern History*. Vol. II: *The Reformation, 1520–1559* (Cambridge Univ. Press, 1958). Collaborative work, useful for reference, though without bibliographies. The editor, G. R. Elton, has summarized many of its conclusions in his lively *Reformation Europe, 1517–1559* (Meridian, 1964).

A. G. Dickens, *Reformation and Society in Sixteenth-Century Europe* (*Holt). Informative broad survey, with many illustrations; by a ranking English scholar.

H. G. Koenigsberger and G. L. Mosse, *Europe in the Sixteenth Century* (Holt, 1968.) Up-to-date scholarly survey, with excellent bibliographical material.

E. F. Rice, Jr., *The Foundations of Early Modern Europe, 1460–1559* (*Norton). Brief, up-to-date manual.

LUTHER

R. H. Bainton, *Here I Stand: A Life of Martin Luther* (*Mentor). Sympathetic, scholarly, readable.

E. H. Erikson, *Young Man Luther* (*Norton). Luther's "identity crisis" persuasively presented by the distinguished psychoanalyst and historian.

H. Grisar, *Martin Luther: His Life and Works* (Herder, 1930). From the Catholic point of view.

E. G. Schwiebert, *Luther and His Times* (Concordia, 1952). From the Lutheran point of view; particularly useful for the setting and the effects of Luther's revolt.

K. Brandi, *The Emperor Charles V* (*Humanities). Comprehensive study of Luther's antagonist.

H. Holborn, *A History of Modern Germany*. Vol. I: *The Reformation* (Knopf, 1959). Scholarly and readable.

THE OTHER FOUNDERS

J. Courvoisier, *Zwingli: A Reformed Theologian* (*John Knox). Good study of an important and often neglected figure.

F. Wendel, *Calvin: The Origins and Development of His Religious Thought* (Harper, 1963). Translation of a solid study by a French scholar.

G. Harkness, *John Calvin: The Man and His Ethics* (*Apex). A good short introduction.

J. Mackinnon, *Calvin and the Reformation* (Longmans, 1936). Substantial longer study.

J. J. Scarisbrick, *Henry VIII* (Univ. of California Press, 1968). The first full-dress scholarly biography in sixty-five years.

A. G. Dickens, *The English Reformation* (*Schocken). Detailed study down to 1559, with excellent scholarly references.

T. M. Parker, *The English Reformation to 1558,* 2nd ed. (*Oxford). Excellent short account.

G. H. Williams, *The Radical Reformation* (Westminster Press, 1962). Huge, encyclopedic, and indispensable study of the Anabaptists and other left-wing reformers.

F. H. Littell, *The Anabaptist View of the Church,* 2nd ed. (Starr King, 1958). Perceptive brief interpretation.

THE CATHOLIC RESPONSE

H. Daniel-Rops, *The Catholic Reformation,* 2 vols. (*Image). Translation of an admirable study by a French Catholic.

A. G. Dickens, *The Counter-Reformation* (*Holt). Recent comprehensive survey by an English Protestant.

B. J. Kidd, *The Counter-Reformation* (S. P. C. K., 1933). Scholarly account by an Anglican.

P. Janelle, *The Catholic Reformation* (Bruce, 1951). Scholarly account by a Catholic.

R. Fülop-Miller, *Jesuits: History of the Society of Jesus* (*Capricorn), and H. Boehmer, *The Jesuits* (Castle, 1928). Respectively, by a Catholic and Protestant.

THE PLACE OF PROTESTANTISM IN HISTORY

J. Huizinga, *Erasmus and the Age of Reformation* (*Torchbooks). By the great Dutch historian.

M. Weber, *The Protestant Ethic and the Spirit of Capitalism* (*Scribner). The famous controversial work on the interrelationship of religion and economics. Weber's thesis is turned around, to emphasize economic motivation, in the equally famous work of R. H. Tawney, *Religion and the Rise of Capitalism* (*Mentor).

L. W. Spitz, ed. *The Reformation: Material or Spiritual?* (*Heath). Samples from the diverse answers that scholars have given to the question; with a good critical bibliography.

E. Troeltsch, *Protestantism and Progress* (*Beacon). By one of the most important religious philosophers of modern times.

P. Tillich, *The Protestant Era* (*Phoenix). Abridged version of a study by an important German theologian.

R. H. Popkin, *A History of Skepticism from Erasmus to Descartes* (*Torchbooks). A useful reminder that there were nonreligious currents in the intellectual life of a very religious era.

SOURCES

H. S. Bettenson, *Documents of the Christian Church*, 2nd ed. (*Oxford). Admirably arranged compilation, particularly helpful for the Reformation.

H. J. Hillerbrand, *The Reformation in Its Own Words* (*Torchbooks). Also very useful.

Châteillon, *Concerning Heretics*, ed. R. H. Bainton (Columbia Univ. Press, 1935). One of earliest tracts to urge religious freedom, not just toleration.

# 13

# *Dynastic and Religious Warfare*

*Above: Marble bust of Philip II, from the workshop of Leone Leoni. Right: A Rembrandt self-portrait (1640).*

## I International Politics

Historians have chosen a number of different dates to mark the watershed between "medieval" and "modern." Americans, for understandable reasons, like to think of 1492 as the great year; Protestants naturally pick 1517 and the Ninety-Five Theses. For the kingdoms of western Europe historians single out the appearance of strong and ambitious monarchs—1461, Louis XI in France; 1469, the marriage of Ferdinand of Aragon and Isabella of Castile; 1485, Henry VII, the first Tudor, in England. For international relations they are likely to choose a date obscure to most of us—1494, when Charles VIII of France led his army over the Alps toward the conquest of Italy and began what has been called "the first modern war."

All such dates are of course arbitrary. As our discussion of the Renaissance has shown, the dividing line between medieval and modern

culture cannot be placed in a single country or a single year. Moreover, as we shall see later, it can be argued that what really makes the modern world different from preceding worlds is the combination of rationalism, natural science, technology, and economic organization which has given men a new power over natural resources. By this standard, the great change comes as late as the eighteenth century, and the sixteenth and seventeenth centuries are but preparation.

### The Modern State System

Still, for the historian of international relations, a difference between the medieval and the modern organization of the European state system is noticeable as early as the late fifteenth century. First of all, there *was* a state system, to which France, Spain, England, and most of the nations of Europe belonged. Western society in early modern times was a group of states, big, middle-sized, and little, each striving to grow, usually in a quite concrete way by annexing others in whole or in part, or at least by bringing them under some sort of control. In practice, at any given moment some states were on the offensive, trying to gain land, power, and wealth; others were on the defensive, trying to preserve what they had. Historically, some few of these units have been so small, so self-contained, that they have never tried to expand. Yet even the model small democracies of the twentieth century, like Sweden and Denmark, have taken the offensive at some time in the past five hundred years; and Sweden, briefly in the seventeenth century, was almost a great power.

The constituent units of this system of competing states are usually termed "sovereign" or "independent." We may roughly call a state sovereign if its rulers have an armed force they can use against others. In this sense, there has been since the height of feudal disintegration, perhaps in the tenth century, a continuous though irregular process of reducing the number of sovereign states, which lasted down to World War I. If a feudal lord with his own armed retainers is called "sovereign," since he could and did make war on his own initiative, then the tenth-century West had thousands of such units. By the end of the Middle Ages, however, over large areas of the West, with the partial exception of much-fragmented Germany, the little feudal units had been absorbed into much bigger states. Local wars had become impossible, or if they did occur, they were risings of dissident nobles against the monarch and were felt to be civil wars. The great but shadowy unity of Western Christendom was destroyed at the end of the Middle Ages; but so too was the real disunity of numerous local units capable of organized war among themselves.

As the modern state system began to shape up in the fifteenth and sixteenth centuries, the three well-organized monarchies of Spain, France, and England dominated the western part of Europe. The smaller states of Scotland, Portugal, and Scandinavia generally played a subordinate role. In central Europe, the Holy Roman Empire, with its many quasi-independent member states, did not have the kind of internal unity enjoyed by the Atlantic powers. Yet, under the leadership of the Austrian Hapsburgs, the empire proved capable of taking a leading part in international competition. Between the French and Hapsburg power centers lay the zone of fragmentation where the Burgundian dukes of the fifteenth century had tried to revive the middle kingdom. Out of this zone have come the modern small nations of Holland, Belgium, Luxembourg, Switzerland, and the larger (but never quite major) power, Italy. As we have seen, Renaissance Italy was divided into several "sovereign" states, which among themselves formed a state system with wars, diplomacy, and "balance of power." As early as the fourteenth century Italy anticipated on a small scale the international politics of Europe as a whole in later centuries. Modern formal diplomacy, in particular, is of Italian origin. To the southeast was a new factor in international relations, the Ottoman Empire, with European lands right up to and beyond the Danube. To the east, the great state of Muscovite Russia was beginning to be formed, and Poland was already great at least in size. But save for Ottoman Turkey, which sought to expand northwestward, and which was therefore actively anti-Hapsburg, the eastern and southeastern states of Europe were not yet really integrated into high politics.

Save for the overseas expansion of Europe, we have here a picture that is not worlds apart from the present one. Italy is today one political nation instead of a dozen, the German power unit was until 1945 one unified nation instead of the decentralized Holy Roman Empire, and on the east Russia is a very great power indeed, Poland a lesser one, while Turkey retains only a vestige of European territory. Still, on the whole, the European state system has the broad lines it had five centuries ago. Its units are still "sovereign."

This comparative stability has not been maintained without threats to destroy it. In succession, certain states have attempted to break it down—sixteenth-century Spain; the France of Louis XIV in the seventeenth century and of the Revolution and Napoleon at the turn from the eighteenth to the nineteenth; the Germany of the Kaiser and Hitler in the twentieth. They have tried to absorb the other states, or at the very least to control them to a point where they were scarcely sovereign. Each time, the threatened units sooner or later joined together in a coalition that was able to beat the armies of the aggressive power and maintain the system. Each time, England, which after the late medieval venture of the Hundred Years' War never attempted to absorb lands on the Continent of Europe (save for the few square miles of Gibraltar), sooner or later intervened to bolster, often to lead, the coalition against the aggressor—or, in more neutral terms, the "disturber." To use a time-honored phrase, the system was maintained through the workings of the "balance of power." This principle is not primarily a moral one, though some writers have defended it as basically moral in the sense that it tends to preserve the independence of organized states. Balance of power is, rather, a descriptive principle, a thread through the intricacies of international politics in the modern West. We must take up this thread in 1494.

## Dynastic State and Nation-State

First, however, we must examine briefly the nature of the political units that make up the competitive state system. It is the fashion to call them *dynastic* states up to about the end of the eighteenth century and *nation*-states thereafter. The distinction is a good rough working one, and some of its implications may be detected in the change of title imposed on Louis XVI by the Revolution—from king of France, which suggests that the kingdom was real estate belonging to the Bourbon dynasty, to king of the French, which suggests that he was the leader accepted by the French nation. In the early modern period many states were loose agglomerations of formerly independent units that were sometimes separated from each other by foreign territory, that sometimes spoke separate languages, and that were tied together almost solely by the ruling dynasty. The Hapsburg realm is a good example. In war and diplomacy the dynastic ruler and his circle of nobles and bureaucrats were a team imbued with team spirit, but the different peoples in the state had relatively little sense of patriotism, of common national effort and ambitions. Early modern wars were less than total wars. Except in their disastrous effects on government finances and on taxes, they scarcely touched the lives of common people who were not actually in the way of contending armies. In the peace settlements, no one talked about "national self-determination of peoples," or worried greatly about transferring areas and populations from one ruler to another.

The distinction between dynastic states and nation-states must not be exaggerated or oversimplified. Especially in the great monarchies of Spain, England, and France a degree of national patriotism existed as early as the sixteenth century. Many of the obvious signs of national feeling are clear, in spite of all the local variations common to these countries. The English had long known the French scornfully as "frogs," and the French had retaliated by calling the English *les godons,* the French mispronunciation of a familiar English blasphemy. In the great war between England and Spain which culminated in the defeat of the Armada, all the signs of intense popular patriotic feeling were clearly present in England. It is true that mingled with nationalist there were religious feelings; the Englishman hated and feared the Spaniard not only as a foreigner but as a Catholic. But this mingling of nationalism and religion was to last right down to our own time.

Even in divided Germany, Luther could count on Germans to dislike Italians. Hatred of the foreigner binds men together at least as effectively as love of one another. Nor does the custom, so strange to us, of transferring political units by marriage of ruling families really affect the basic similarity between the state system of early modern times and our own. Perhaps the accidents of marriage account for the unusual combination of Germany and Spain under Charles V; but for the most part the alliances and alignments of the sixteenth century conform extremely well to conditions of geography, resources, tradition, and culture.

The differences between the present-day state and the early modern state are generally exaggerated by most of us today. The differences are real, and they make these dynastic wars seem petty and confusing, but they are not in the main differences of kind. They are differences of degree of efficiency, centralization, ability to command vast numbers of men and great resources, and rapidity of movement. A study of the bewildering wars, big and little, of the early modern centuries, with their dubious diplomacy and their uncertain treaties of peace, can at least give us some perspective on our own international troubles. Politically and morally, if not technologically, they are much the same troubles that our forefathers have known for five hundred years.

By 1500, then, almost all the European sovereign states possessed in at least a rudimentary form most of the social and political organs of a modern state. They lacked only a large literate population brought up in the ritual and faith of national patriotism. Notably they had two essential organs, a diplomatic service and an army, both professional, both usually controlled from a common governmental center.

## Diplomacy

Some forms of diplomacy can be traced back into the Middle Ages, and indeed into ancient times. But the fifteenth and sixteenth centuries saw the steady development of modern diplomatic agencies and methods. Governments established central foreign offices and sent diplomats on regular missions to foreign courts. Espionage and the secret services developed under the cover of open diplomacy. Formal peace conferences were held, and formal treaties were signed, to the accompaniment of the ceremony and protocol we now associate with such occasions. Finally, a set of rules governing all these formal relations began to take shape, a set of rules that can be called international law.

The apparatus of international politics developed most fully and soonest in Renaissance Italy, and found its classic expression in the admirably organized diplomatic service of the Republic of Venice. The detailed reports Venetian ambassadors sent back to the Senate from abroad are among the first documents of intelligence work we have. They are careful political and social studies of the personalities and lands involved rather than mere gossipy cloak-and-dagger reports. Here is an excerpt from the report of the Venetian ambassador to England in the reign of the Catholic Mary Tudor. If its estimate of English political psychology seems strange, remember that in less than twenty-five years the English changed their religion officially three times.

> But as for religion, speaking generally, your Highness may be sure that the example and the authority of the prince can here achieve everything. For as the English think highly of religion, and are moved by it, so they satisfy their sense of duty towards the prince, living as he lives, believing as he believes, and finally doing all he tells them to. In all this the English rather conform externally, in order not to be in disfavor with their ruler than follow any inner light, for they would conform in the same way to the Mohammedan or Jewish faith were the king to adopt such a faith and want them to, and indeed they would accommodate themselves to anything, but the more readily to something that seemed to promise them more freedom of living—or more utility.*

In those days, the diplomat abroad was a most important maker of policy in his own right. With rapid travel impossible, his government could not communicate with him in time to prescribe his acts minutely, and he had often to make important decisions on his own. Good or bad diplomacy, good or bad intelligence about foreign lands, made a vital difference in a state's success or failure in the struggle for power.

## Armies and Navies

The armed forces made still more difference. These early modern centuries are the great days of the professional soldier, freed from the limitations of feudal warfare and not yet tied to the immense economic requirements and the inhuman scale of our modern warfare. The officer class in particular could plan, drill, and campaign on a fairly large but quite manageable scale; they could do more than the interminable jousting of late medieval times. They could, so to speak, handle warfare as an art and sometimes

* E. Alberi, *Relazione degli Ambasciatori veneti,* Series I (Florence, 1839 ff.), II, 362. Our translation.

as a pleasure. The common soldiers, too, for the most part were mercenaries; the word "soldier" in fact comes from *solidus,* the Latin for a "piece of money." Some of these mercenaries were recruited at home, usually among the poor and dispossessed, sometimes by impressment. Others were foreigners who made a profession of soldiering, particularly Swiss and Germans. Thousands of Swiss and German mercenaries served in the armies of Francis I of France together with Englishmen, Scots, Poles, Italians, Albanians, and Greeks.

These professional forces were often trained to parade, to dress ranks, to keep discipline. They were whipped if they broke discipline, although threats of punishment did not always prevent desertions when pay was late or rations inadequate. Each regiment, troop, or other unit commonly wore the same uniforms; whole armies, however, usually displayed such an extraordinary variety of costume that in battle recognition of friend and foe was not easy. Tactics and strategy in the field were under the control of a formal officer hierarchy that culminated in a general in command, who in turn was at least somewhat controlled by the central government through a ministry of war. In short, though these armies would look anarchic to a modern professional of the spit-and-polish school, they were far better organized and disciplined than feudal levies had been.

Yet the early modern armies also show many feudal survivals, many forms of entrenched privilege, many ways of twisting away from centralized control. The officer class continued to preserve many of its old habits of chivalry, such as the duel, which often seriously menaced internal discipline. If the feudal lord no longer brought his own knights for the forty days of allotted time, his descendant as regimental colonel often raised his own regiment and financed it himself. Weapons were of an extraordinary variety. Reminders of the old hand-to-hand fighting survived in the sword and in the pike, the long shaft used by foot soldiers against the armored knight and his mount. Hand firearms—arquebus, musket, pistol, and many others—were slow-loading and slow-firing, and usually not even capable of being aimed with any accuracy. The cannon, quite unstandardized as to parts and caliber, and heavy and hard to move, fired solid balls, rather than exploding shells.

Armies on the march lived mostly off the land, even when they were in home territory. But they were beginning to develop the elaborate modern organization of supply and the modern service of engineers. Both the growth of military technology and differences of national temperament were reflected in the shift of military predominance from Spain to France about 1600. Spain, the great fighting nation of the sixteenth century on land, excelled in infantry, where the pike was a major weapon. France, the great fighting nation of the seventeenth and early eighteenth centuries on land, excelled in artillery, engineering, and fortification, all services that were more plebeian, less suited to the former feudal nobility than infantry and cavalry.

Meanwhile, the first modern navies were also growing up. In the later Middle Ages, Venice, Genoa, and Pisa had all begun to assemble fleets of galleys disciplined both as ships and in fleet maneuvers. In the Renaissance, Venice took the lead with its arsenal and its detailed code of maritime regulations. Naval organization, naval supply, the dispatch and handling of ships, all required more orderly centralized methods than an army. They could not tolerate the survival of rugged feudal individualism, indiscipline, and lack of planning. The officer class, as in the armies, was predominantly aristocratic, but it came usually from the more adventurous, the less custom-ridden part of that class. During the sixteenth century, naval supremacy passed out of the Mediterranean to the Atlantic, where it rested briefly with Spain, and thence passed in the seventeenth century to the northern maritime powers of England, Holland, and France.

## II Hapsburg and Valois

### The Italian Wars of Charles VIII and Louis XII

Charles VIII of France (1483–1498) inherited from his parsimonious father Louis XI a well-filled treasury and a good army. He continued Louis's policy of extending the royal domain and added the Duchy of Brittany, which had long been largely independent of the French crown, by marrying its heiress. Apparently secure on the home front, Charles decided to expand abroad. As the remote heir of the Angevins who had seized the throne of Naples in the thirteenth century, Charles disputed the right of the Aragonese Ferrante to hold that throne. He chose to invade Italy, however, not only because he had this tenuous genealogical claim but also because Renaissance Italy was rich, held romantic attractions for the northerners, and was divided into small rival political units—it looked, in short, to be easy picking. So it was at first, for in the winter of 1494–1495 Charles paraded his army through to Naples in triumph. But his acquisition of Brittany had already disturbed his neighbors, and his possession of Naples threatened the balance of power in Italy. The French intrusion provoked the first of the great modern coalitions, the so-called Holy League composed of the papacy (which, remember, was also an Italian territorial state), the empire, Spain, Venice, Milan, and soon England. This coalition forced the French armies out of Italy without much trouble in 1495.

Charles was followed on the French throne by his cousin of the Orléans branch of the Valois family, Louis XII (1498–1515). Louis married Charles's widow to make sure of Brittany, and then tried again in Italy, reinforced by still another genealogical claim, this time to Milan. Since his grandmother came from the Visconti family, Louis regarded the Sforza dukes as simple usurpers; he proceeded to drive Il Moro from Milan in 1499. In this second French invasion, the play of alliances was much subtler and more complicated, quite worthy of the age of Machiavelli. Louis tried to insure himself from the isolation that had ruined Charles by allying in 1500 with Ferdinand of Aragon, with whom he agreed to partition Naples. Then, in 1508, Louis helped form one of those cynical coalitions that look on paper as though they could break the balance-of-power principle, because they are the union of the strong against a much weaker victim. This was the League of Cambray, in which Louis, Ferdinand, Pope Julius II, and the emperor Maximilian joined to divide up the lands held in the lower Po Valley by the rich but—on land at least—militarily weak Republic of Venice.

The practical trouble with such combinations is that the combiners do not really trust one another, and usually fall to quarreling over the pickings. All went well for the despoilers at first, though the Venetians rallied and retook their mainland stronghold of Padua. Then Ferdinand, having taken the Neopolitan towns he wanted, decided to desert Louis. The pope, frightened at the prospect that France and the empire might squeeze him out entirely, in 1511 formed another "Holy League" against France with Venice and Ferdinand, later joined by Henry VIII of England and the emperor Maximilian. Despite some early successes in the field, the French could not hold out against such a coalition, for they now had a war on two fronts. Henry VIII attacked the north of France and won at Guinegate in 1513 a battle that has always been a sore spot with Frenchmen. It was called (by the English) the "battle of the spurs" from the speed with which the French cavalry spurred their flight from the battlefield. In Italy too the French were defeated, and Louis XII, like Charles VIII, was checkmated.

### Charles V versus Francis I

These two French efforts were, however, merely preliminaries. The important phase of this first great modern test of the balance of power was to follow immediately, and to take a basically different form. For there were now really two aggressors: the French house of Valois, still bent on expansion, and the house of Hapsburg. When the Hapsburg Charles V succeeded his grandfather Maximilian as emperor in 1519, he was a disturber by the mere fact of his existence rather than by temperament or intent. He had inherited Spain, the Low Countries, the Hapsburg lands in central Europe as well as the headship of the Holy Roman Empire, and the preponderance in Italy. He apparently had France squeezed in a perfect vise.

The vise almost closed. Louis XII's successor on the French throne, Francis I (1515–1547), was badly defeated by the imperial—mostly Spanish—forces at Pavia in 1525. Francis himself was taken prisoner and held in Madrid until he signed a treaty giving up all his Italian claims, and ceding the Duchy of Burgundy. This treaty he repudiated the moment he was safely back on French soil. It is probable that Charles V would not have "eliminated" France entirely even had he been able to. These early modern wars were

*Francis I of France: portrait by Joos van Cleve.*

in no sense "total," and there were accepted limits to what might decently be done to the defeated. Certainly these people convey the impression of engaging in a kind of professional athleticism that was often bloody and unscrupulous but by no means without rules. The players sometimes changed sides; one of the imperial commanders at the battle of Pavia in which the French were so severely beaten was the Constable de Bourbon, a great French noble at odds with his king.

The same Bourbon commanded the Spanish and German mercenaries of the emperor at the time of the horrible sack of Rome in 1527. Pope

Clement VII (1523–1534), a Medici and a good Italian at heart, had first supported Charles V but then turned against him after his great success at Pavia. In the League of Cognac, 1526, he allied himself with the other main Italian powers and with Francis. In reply, Charles besieged Rome, but he did not plan the sack, which lay heavily on his conscience as a good Catholic. The sack took place when his mercenaries became infuriated by delays in pay and supplies. In all but the most hardened partisan circles it outraged public opinion as a needless atrocity.

Charles was now at the height of his power. By the end of the decade, he had made peace with the pope and with Francis. In 1530, he was crowned by the pope as emperor and as king of Italy, the last ruler to receive this double crown, this inheritance of Charlemagne and the ages, with the full formality of tradition. But the Western world over which he thus symbolically ruled was a very different world from Charlemagne's, and Charles was in fact no emperor, but a new dynast in a new conflict of power.

France was still in the vise between the Spanish and the German and Netherlandish holdings of Charles, and Francis I, a proud, consciously virile Renaissance prince, was not one to accept for long so precarious a position—above all, a position in which he lost face. He used the death of the Sforza ruler of Milan in 1535 to reopen the old claim to Milan and to begin the struggle once more. Neither Francis nor Charles lived to see the end of this particular phase of the Hapsburg–Valois rivalry. Neither side secured decisive military victory. In 1559 the important Treaty of Cateau-Cambrésis confirmed Hapsburg control of Milan and Naples. It marked the failure of France to acquire a real foothold in Italy, but it also marked the failure of the Hapsburgs to reduce the real strength of France, which retained the important bishoprics of Metz, Toul, and Verdun on her northeastern frontier, first occupied during the 1550's. The Hapsburg vise had not closed largely because France proved militarily, economically, and politically strong enough to resist the pressure. But the vise itself was a most imperfect instrument, and Charles was not so strong as he looked on the map to be. His German arm was paralyzed by the political consequences of the Reformation and the stubborn resistance of Protestant princes.

The last phase of the personal duel between the aging rivals, Charles and Francis, is a concrete example of how many variables enter the play of balance of power. Francis, to gain allies, did not hesitate to turn to Charles's rebellious German subjects. Although head of a Catholic state, a "most Christian" king, he allied himself with the Protestant duke of Cleves. He did not stop with Protestants, and concluded an alliance with the Muslim Ottoman emperor, Suleiman the Magnificent, who attacked Charles in the rear in Hungary. At the death of Francis in 1547, his son Henry II continued the Protestant alliance.

One other participant in the complex struggles of the first half of the sixteenth century was England. Though not yet a great power, she was already a major element in international politics. The men who guided English policy were probably not moved by a consciously held theory of the balance of power which told them to intervene in Europe always on behalf of the group that was being beaten, that seemed weaker at the time; but they often behaved as though they had arrived intuitively at some such conclusion. Other factors were also involved. For one thing, England after 1534 was deeply involved in her own religious troubles; moreover, she had on her northern border an independent Scotland, which tended to side with France. Finally, to English statesmen, with memories of the long medieval struggles with the French, the great hereditary enemy was always France. Yet in a pinch the English were quite capable of allying with the hereditary enemy if they thought Charles was too strong. This happened in 1527, after Charles had won at Pavia and had taken Rome. The English minister, Cardinal Wolsey, in that year worked out an alliance with France.

The English were also capable of reversing themselves. In 1543, when Charles was beset by Protestants and Turks, Henry VIII came to his aid against Francis. But not too vigorously. In the campaign of 1544, something like a Christion revulsion against the French alliance with the infidel Turk had brought the Germans together for the moment, and a German army was actually on its way to Paris along the Marne Valley route. The English had landed on the Channel coast; had they really pressed matters in co-operation with the Germans, Paris itself might have fallen. But they rather deliberately besieged the Channel port of Boulogne, and Francis escaped with his capital city intact.

## The Wars of Philip II

The first great Hapsburg effort to dominate Europe ended with the Treaty of Cateau-Cambrésis and the religious Peace of Augsburg, four years earlier, granting German Lutherans official recognition. The second effort at domination of Europe was less Hapsburg than Spanish. In 1556, Charles V abdicated both his Spanish and imperial crowns and retired to a monastery, where he died two years later. His brother, Ferdinand I (1556–1564), secured the Austrian Hapsburg complex of territories and, by election, the empire. His son, Philip II (1556–1598), got Spain and the overseas colonies, the Burgundian inheritance of the Netherlands, and the Italian holdings of Milan and Naples. Philip's realm was no mere national state; even without the Germanies, it was a supranational state threatening France, England, and the whole balance of power. Its rich possessions in the New World helped provide it with resources for war.

Like his father, Philip II found Protestantism and the concept of many separate Christian political units intolerable. He sought, if not world conquest, at least the forced unity of the West. Philip's attempt to invade England and restore Catholicism there has left him as one of the villains of Anglo-Saxon tradition. While he was no brilliant, jovial Renaissance monarch, he was hardly the cold-blooded "devil of the south" he appeared to be to Protestants and moderate Catholics. He was a serious, hard-working administrator, and certainly no lover of war for its own sake. Devout and dutiful, he saw Protestantism as an intolerable divisive force that must be wiped out by force if necessary. He was a doctrinaire chained to a past no one could restore, committed to a lost cause.

Philip's major points of involvement were: (1) Italy, which as long as it remained divided was to be a major source of difficulties in the play of balance of power or, put another way, a source of territory to be annexed by expansionist powers; (2) the Netherlands, where the revolt of his Dutch Protestant subjects was soon to involve Philip not only with them but with Protestant England; (3) France, where the second half of the century brought a series of civil wars of religion in which Philip was bound to appear as the Catholic champion; (4) the Mediterranean, where the Turks, now at the height of their naval power, threatened Spanish control; (5) the newly discovered Americas and Asia, where, as we shall see in the next chapter, England and France were beginning to challenge the monopoly Spain and Portugal had tried to set up. Since this New World as well as the Old World was at stake in Philip's wars, there is some justification for considering these as in fact the first "world wars."

## The Revolt of the Netherlands

The dramatic focal point of these struggles was the Netherlands. When the Burgundian inheritance had come to the Hapsburgs, Charles V had come to count heavily on their wealth (estimated to be the highest per capita in Europe) to finance his constant wars. But he had made no attempt to absorb the seventeen provinces into a unified superstate. They were essentially autonomous units of a great dynastic holding, with their own complex of feudal privileges confirmed by their new ruler. They had medieval estates or assemblies, dominated by the nobility and the wealthy merchants, which raised taxes and armies, but they had few effective institutions binding together the seventeen provinces. In the mid-sixteenth century the full force of Protestantism was only beginning to be felt in an area still overwhelmingly Catholic. There were small minorities of Lutherans and Anabaptists, and Calvinism was just starting to move northward across the French border.

Philip II was by nature and temperament bound to antagonize his subjects in the Low Countries. Charles V had liked the area and made Brussels his favorite place of residence, but Philip was thoroughly Spanish in outlook and never visited the area after the early years of his reign. For all his medievalism Philip had up-to-date ideas about centralized efficient rule and curtailed the political and economic liberties of the Netherlands. The inhabitants were a commercial and seafaring people, intent on conducting business without the jealous restrictions of Spanish regulations of trade and industry. Those who were Protestants resented and feared Philip's use of the Inquisition in the Netherlands.

Europe in 1555
Austrian
Spanish
Possessions of the House of Hapsburg
Boundary of the Empire
Battle sites
NORWAY
SCOTLAND
Edinburgh
North Sea
IRELAND
Dublin
ENGLAND
Bosworth Field
London
Canterbury
Calais
DENMARK
Copenhagen
Amsterdam
Leyden
NETHERLANDS
Antwerp
Cleves
Münster
Bremen
Elbe R.
BRANDENBURG
Berlin
Wittenberg
Torgau
Leipzig
Oder R.
Warburg
HESSE
Rhine R.
SAXONY
SILESIA
THE EMPIRE
Prague
BOHEMIA
Atlantic Ocean
BRITTANY
Ivry
Seine R.
Paris
Vervins
Verdun
LUXEMBOURG
Metz
Speyer
WÜRTTEMBERG
Danube R.
Toul
FRANCHE COMTÉ
Nantes
Loire R.
La Rochelle
FRANCE
BURGUNDY
Basel
Constance
Augsburg
BAVARIA
AUSTRIA
Vienna
Zurich
SWITZERLAND
TYROL
STYRIA
Cognac
AUVERGNE
Geneva
Trent
CARINTHIA
CARNIOLA
SAVOY
MILAN
Pavia
Padua
Venice
Bologna
Po R.
Rhône R.
Avignon (to the Papacy)
PROVENCE
Genoa
TUSCANY
PAPAL STATES
VENETIAN REPUBLIC
Adriatic Sea
BASQUE PROV.
NAVARRE
Valladolid
Tordesillas
Ebro R.
ARAGON
PORTUGAL
Lisbon
SPAIN
Madrid
Tagus R.
Toledo
CASTILE
Guadalquivir R.
Palos
Seville
Cadiz
CORSICA (to Genoa)
Rome
NAPLES
Naples
BALEARIC IS.
SARDINIA
Mediterranean Sea
SICILY
MALTA
(Tributary to Ottoman Empire)
B A R B A R Y S T A T E S
Stock
Balti

London
Amsterdam
Leyden
Utrecht
Armada sea fight
Calais
Boulogne
Bruges
Antwerp
FLANDERS
Scheldt R.
Guinegate
ARTOIS
NETHERLANDS
Cambray
Cateau-Cambrésis
FRANCE
0 100 Miles
TEUTONIC ORDER
PRUSSIA
LITHUANIA
W. Dvina R.
Moscow
Oka R.
Volga R.
RUSSIA
Ural R.
Don R.
Kiev
UKRAINE
Dnieper R.
KHANATE OF THE CRIMEA
Dniester R.
MOLDAVIA
TRANSYLVANIA
WALLACHIA
Belgrade
Danube R.
Black Sea
Caspian Sea
MONTE-NEGRO
OTTOMAN EMPIRE
Constantinople
Salonika
Aegean Sea
Lepanto
Athens
PELOPONNESUS
(to Venice)
RHODES
CRETE
CYPRUS
(to Venice)
Tigris R.
Euphrates R.
0 500
Miles

This explosive mixture of religion, politics, and economic interests produced the revolt. Philip sent Spanish garrisons to the Netherlands, and attempted to enforce edicts against heretics. Opposition, which centered at first in the privileged classes who had been most affected by Philip's political restrictions, soon spread to the common people. In 1566, when a group of 200 nobles petitioned Philip's regent to adopt a more moderate policy, an official sneeringly referred to "these beggars." The name stuck, proudly adopted by the rebels. The political restlessness, combined with an economic slump and the growing success of the Calvinists in winning converts, touched off riots in August 1566, which resulted in heavy destruction of Catholic churches in such major centers as Ghent, Antwerp, and Amsterdam. Philip responded to this "Calvinist fury" in 1567 by dispatching to the Netherlands an army of twenty thousand Spaniards headed by the unyielding, politically stupid duke of Alba.

In those days the Spanish infantry was the best in Europe, and the rebels were ill-armed and ill-prepared. Their eventual success was a heroic achievement against great odds, fully deserving the praise sympathetic historians have given it. It was, however, no extraordinary victory of weakness over strength, but rather a victory fully consonant with a fact of Western political life—that no thoroughly disaffected population can be long held down by force alone. Alba had the force, and he set up a Council of Troubles—later dubbed the "Council of Blood" —which resorted to executions, confiscations, and severe taxation on a large scale. The number of victims executed under the Council of Blood totaled about a thousand, yet all the repression accomplished was to heighten the opposition to Spanish policy. In 1573 Alba gave up in despair.

Meantime, the rebel "Beggars" turned to a kind of naval guerrilla warfare, gained control of the ports of the populous northern province of Holland, and then ended effective Spanish authority in Holland and adjacent areas. Large numbers of Protestant refugees, especially Calvinists, from other provinces resettled themselves in Holland as a result. The historical split was appearing between the largely Catholic southern Netherlands and the mainly Protestant north—to use popular terminology, between Belgium and Holland (the name of the province is often, though inaccurately, applied to all seven northern provinces). It was to be a religious, not a linguistic split, for Dutch was the language both of the north and of Flanders in the south; French was spoken only in the Walloon country of the southeast. North and south had much to unite them, and union of all seventeen provinces was the goal of the rebel leader, William of Orange, the Silent, prince in the 1570's. William, who got his nickname because his silences could be discreet or deceptive by turn, was a convivial nobleman with firm political convictions but few religious ones (he was, at different periods, a Lutheran, a Catholic, and a Calvinist).

William's goal of unity seemed almost assured in the wake of widespread revulsion at the "Spanish Fury" of 1576, when Spanish troops, desperate because their pay was two years in arrears, sacked the great Belgian port of Antwerp and massacred several thousand of its inhabitants. But in 1578, when the duke of Parma arrived to govern the Netherlands, Philip's policies at last showed signs of statesmanship, a willingness to compromise in the face of facts. By political concessions to old privileges of self-rule, Parma won back the southern provinces, which remained basically Catholic after the exodus of many Calvinists to the north. It was too late to win back the northern provinces, except perhaps by radical religious concessions which Philip was by temperament utterly unable to make. By the Union of Utrecht, the Dutch tightened their organization and in 1581 took the decisive step of declaring themselves independent of the Spanish Crown. They made good that declaration by their courageous use of their now much better-organized land forces. But they were greatly helped by three facts. First, Philip, like most of the great aggressors, had been drawn into fighting on more than one land front. He had to cope with Turks, the French Protestants, and the anti-Spanish moderate French Catholics, as well as with grave internal economic problems. Second, fate gave the Dutch that invaluable spiritual aid, a martyr. And last and most important, they acquired a major ally.

The martyr was William the Silent, who was assassinated in 1584 by an individual moved either by religious hatred or by the reward Philip had set upon the outlawed Dutchman's head, or by both. William's death deprived the Dutch of the first great leader in their national history, but

*The battle between the English fleet and the Spanish armada, 1588.*

the assassination did not profit the Spanish cause, since it made William a Protestant and Dutch hero. The ally was England, now under Elizabeth I firmly Protestant and from the start sympathetic with the Dutch cause. Elizabeth, however, was no crusader, and her kingdom appeared to be no match for powerful Spain. She had been hesitant to come out openly on the Dutch side, especially since in the uncertain condition of French politics in the midst of internal religious wars, a Franco-Spanish alliance against England and Holland seemed by no means impossible. Here too Philip showed himself incapable of diplomacy. He permitted France to maneuver into neutrality, and provoked England by fomenting Catholic plots against Elizabeth. The English in turn provoked Spain. For years they had been preying on Spanish commerce on the high seas, and Hawkins, Drake, and other English sailors had been raiding Spanish possessions in the New World. When an English army came to the aid of the Dutch in 1585, Philip decided to make formal war on England, though he still had the Dutch, the Turks, and other enemies on his hands. He, like all aggressors in the last few centuries overextended himself by taking on too many enemies at the same time.

## The End of Spanish Preponderance

The great Spanish Armada of unwieldly men-of-war which he sent out to invade England was defeated in the English Channel in July 1588 by a skillfully maneuvered lighter English fleet, and was utterly destroyed afterward by a great storm. The battle was the beginning of the end of Spanish preponderance, the beginning of English greatness in international politics, and the decisive step in the achievement of the independence of the Dutch Republic. These portentous results were not so evident in 1588 as they are now, but even at the time the defeat of the Armada was seen as a great event. Protestants everywhere were enormously heartened, and the storm that finished the destruction of the Spanish fleet was christened the "Protestant wind."

Philip II died in 1598 after a long and painful illness, in the great, severe palace of the Escorial he had built near Madrid. He had ordered an open coffin put beside his bed, and a skull with a crown of gold. Save for the seven northern provinces of the Netherlands—and even these he had never officially given up—the great possessions with which he had begun to reign were still his. Indeed, he had added Portugal in 1580 at the death of the Portuguese cardinal-king Henry and had made the whole Iberian peninsula formally if briefly one. Yet he knew almost as clearly as we know that his life had been a failure. He left his kingdom, as we shall see, worn out, drained of men and money. And, whatever his aims in international politics had been, whether a Spanish hegemony, a revived Western empire, or merely the extinction of the Protestant heresy, he had realized none of them. Under his illegitimate half-brother Don John of Austria, the Spanish fleet had indeed participated in the great naval victory over the Turkish fleet at Lepanto in 1571. But Lepanto was at most a checking of Ottoman expansion, not a great gain for the Spaniards. It was no balance for the loss of the great Armada.

## III The Catholic States: Spain and France

### The "Age of Absolutism"

The states that took part in these dynastic and religious wars experienced in their domestic development an uneven working out of the new political aims and methods of the Renaissance. They were all to a degree centralized states with paid professional armies and paid professional civilian bureaucrats. They had a central financial system with some control over even local taxation and the supply of money, a central legal system that made some attempt to apply the same kind of law to all individuals within the state, and a central authority—king, king and council, king and parliament, estates, Cortes, or other assembly—that could actually make new laws. Phrases like "Age of Absolutism" and "Divine Right of Kings" are frequently used of the early modern centuries, and not without reason. Over almost all of Europe, the control of central administration usually rested with a monarch who inherited his throne and claimed the right to make the kind of final decisions that modern democracies make by some sort of popular vote, or at least through legislatures.

But it is of major importance to note that everywhere in the sixteenth century there were strong survivals of the old medieval local privileges, of local ways of life quite different from the standards set by the court or the capital. While the greater nobility was losing power and influence at the center, the lesser nobles continued to dominate the countryside. The early modern governments were less "absolute," in at least one very significant sense of the term, than the government of a modern democracy like the United States. They could not possibly make and enforce the kind of regulation which federal and state agencies nowadays can make and enforce—public health regulations like pure food and drug acts, licensing the practice of medicine, setting of standards of measure, even the kind of standardization of higher education we have achieved in the training of teachers, for instance, by accreditation and other controls. This last instance suggests that standardization, the efficient application of general rules to large areas and large groups, is in the United States partly a matter of voluntary control from *below*. Generally speaking, such collaboration from below was not attained in these first modern centuries. The standardization came from *above*, from a small group that had been won over to these new methods of governing, which did increase their power. It is this active attempt of a minority to achieve "streamlining" that justifies our use of terms like absolutism for these centuries.

### Power and Limits of Spanish Absolutism

Spain provides a clear-cut example of the difference between the concepts of absolutism with which this minority worked and the varied and often successfully recalcitrant groups on which this minority sought to impose its standardized rules. The reigns of the two hard-working Spanish monarchs, Charles V (technically, Charles I of Spain, 1516–1556, and Charles V as Holy Roman emperor) and Philip II (1556–1598), span almost the whole sixteenth century. Charles was rather a medieval survival than a modern king. He did little to remodel the instruments of government he inherited from his grandparents, Ferdinand and Isabella. Brought up in the Low Countries, Charles came to Spain a stranger, with a Flemish following that already had the modern northern European contempt for "backward" Spain, and showed it. His election to the imperial throne made him further suspect in Spain. In 1520, a group of Spanish cities, led by Toledo, rose up in the revolt of the *comuneros*. This revolt, like most such uprisings, was compounded of many elements. The municipalities disliked the growth of central control; the aristocrats were restless in the face of the new monarchical dignity, no longer just like their own; the poor and the middling had class feelings and grievances. The comuneros were put down in 1521, but Charles had been frightened out of what reforming zeal he may have had, and did his best not to offend his Spanish subjects. His son, at least, grew up a Spaniard first of all.

Philip II was much more willing and able to build a new-model centralized state in Spain. He did devise a system of consultative councils, topped by a council of state, and manned by great nobles; but these councils could do no more than advise. Philip made the final decisions, and the details were worked out by a series of private secretaries and local organs of government, not manned by nobles. Furthermore, Philip reduced the representative assemblies, the Cortes, to practical impotence. In Castile, nobles and priests, because they did not pay direct taxes, no longer attended the sessions of the Cortes, and the delegates of the cities were left as a powerless rump. The Cortes of Aragon, while retaining more power, was seldom convoked by Philip. Above all, Philip had assured sources of income—his tax of a fifth of the value of the precious cargoes from America, direct taxes from the constituent states of his realm, revenues from the royal estates and from the sale of offices and patents of nobility, revenues from the authorized sale, at royal profit, of dispensations allowed by the pope (permission to eat meat on Fridays and in Lent, and even something very close to the very indulgences that had raised Germany against the pope). Philip, like most continental monarchs of his time, had no need to worry over representative bodies with control of the purse. Yet he was always heavily in debt, and on three occasions during his reign—at the beginning, in the middle, and near the end—suspended payments on his obligations; his bankruptcies triggered that of the famous Fugger firm in Augsburg.

Even in this matter of revenue, where Philip's power at first sight looks so complete and unchecked, the actual limitations of the absolute monarch of early modern times are clear. Except by borrowing and hand-to-mouth expedients like the sale of offices, he could not notably increase his income. He could not summon any representative group together and get them to vote new monies. In the first place, the constituent parts of his realm, Castile, Aragon, Navarre and the Basque provinces (both at the western end of the Pyrenees, adjoining France), the Italian lands, the Low Countries, the Americas, and the newest Spanish lands, named after the monarch himself, the Philippine Islands, had no common organs of consultation. Each had to be dealt with as a separate problem, and the slowness of communication with his far-flung domains further delayed the always deliberate process of decision-making. For the most part the nobility and clergy were tax exempt, and could not be called upon for unusual financial sacrifices. Add to all this the difficulty of collection, the opportunities for graft, and the lack of a long accumulated administrative and financial experience, and one can see why Philip could not have introduced a more systematic general taxation.

Outside the financial sphere, the obstacles to

*The Escorial, the combined palace, monastery, and mausoleum built by Philip II near Madrid.*

really effective centralization were even more serious. The union of the crowns of Aragon and Castile, achieved by the marriage of Ferdinand and Isabella, had by no means made a unified Spain. To this day, regionalism—to call it by a mild name—is perhaps more acute in Spain than in any other large European state. In those days, some of the provinces did not even have extradition arrangements for the surrender of common criminals within the peninsula. Many of them could and did levy customs dues on goods from the others. The old northern regions, which had never been well conquered by the Muslims, preserved all sorts of *fueros* or privileges. Aragon still preserved the office of *justicia mayor,* a judge nominated, it is true, by the Crown, but for life, and entrusted with an authority something remotely like that of the United States Supreme Court.

What the Hapsburgs might have accomplished in Spain had they been able to expend their full energies on the task of uniting and developing their lands can never be known. What they did do was exhaust the peninsula and weaken the lands overseas in their effort to secure hegemony over Europe and to subdue the Protestant heresy. This was indeed the great age of Spain, the age when both on land and on sea the Spanish were admired and envied as the best fighters, the age when Spain seemed destined to be mistress of both the Americas, the age when Spain seemed the richest of states, the age of Loyola and Cervantes, the golden age of Spanish religion, literature, and art. But it was a brief flowering, and Spanish greatness largely vanished in the seveteenth century.

### The Spanish Economy

Spain is a classical example of a great political unit that failed to maintain a sound economic underpinning for its greatness. The peninsula is mountainous, and its central tableland is subject to droughts, but its agricultural potentialities are greater, for example, than those of Italy as a whole, and it has mineral resources, notably in iron. Moreover, Spain was the first of the great European states to attain lands overseas, and a navy and merchant marine to integrate the great resources of the New World with an Old World base. Yet all this wealth slipped through Spain's fingers in a few generations. Certainly a major factor in this decline was the immense cost of the wars of Charles V and Philip II. The Low Countries, which had brought in a large revenue to Charles, were a pure drain on Philip's finances. The famous Spanish infantry had to be paid everywhere it went, and the money thus spent went out of Spain forever, with nothing in the long run to show for it. Philip took over from his father a heavy debt, which grew heavier through his long reign.

Now governmental expenditure on armed forces, though in itself unproductive, is not necessarily fatal to a national economy. If such expenditure stimulates even greater productivity within the nation and its dependencies, then the nation may even grow in wealth, as did imperial Germany after 1870. But this was not true of sixteenth-century Spain. She drew from the New World vast amounts of silver and many articles—sugar, indigo, tobacco, cocoa, hides—without which she could hardly have carried on her European wars at all. But it was not enough to pay for world dominion. The bullion passed through Spanish hands into those of bankers and merchants in other European countries, partly to pay for the Spanish armies and navies, partly to pay for the manufactured goods Spain had to send to the New World.

In accordance with an economic policy common to other colonial powers of the time, Spain forbade industrial production in her colonies and sought to supply them with manufactured goods. But she could not, or did not, develop her own industrial production to take care of this need. Her merchants had by royal decree a monopoly on trade with the Indies. But as the century wore on, they were more and more reduced to the role of mere middlemen, sending to the Indies goods increasingly imported from the rest of Europe—and paid for with the bullion of the Indies. The English, the Dutch, and other competitors smuggled goods into Spanish overseas territories on a large scale. To use a favorite modern term, Spain's governmental expenditures were not used to "prime the pump" for increased national productivity—or, more accurately, the pumps they primed were not Spanish, but foreign, pumps. By 1600, Spanish home industry was on the decline.

The free-trade economists of the nineteenth century offered a simple explanation for this failure of Spain to make good use of her economic opportunities—monopoly under government supervision. Sixteenth-century Spain was certainly moving toward that economic policy called *mercantilism,* which reached its fullest development in seventeenth-century France. Although Spain lacked the true mercantilist passion for building national wealth under government auspices, she used many mercantilist techniques, the endless regulation in general and the narrow channeling of colonial trade in particular. The Spanish system left little room for individual economic initiative. In Castile, a single institution, the famous *Casa de Contratación* (House of Trade), controlled every transaction with the Indies and licensed every export and import. The amount of sheer paperwork, in an age unblessed by typewriters and mimeographs, was enormous.

Yet bureaucratic methods and monopolies were not the sole source of difficulty. The whole direction of Spanish civilization turned Spanish creative energies into other channels than the industrial. Warfare, politics, religion, art, traditional farming, or simply living like a *hidalgo* (*hijo de algo,* "son of somebody," hence "nobleman," "gentleman") were respectable activities. What Americans broadly understand by "business" was, if not disgraceful, certainly not an activity on which society set a premium. Not that as a nation the Spanish were lazy; the lower classes especially had to work very hard. That epitome of so much we think of as Spanish, Don

Quixote, was hardly a lazy man, but his activity was not exactly productive of material wealth. If we take into consideration the numerous holidays, the habit of the siesta, the large numbers of beggars, soldiers, priests, monks, and hidalgos, as well as the lack of encouragement to new enterprises and techniques and the heavy hand of an inefficient bureaucracy—if we put all this together, it becomes clear that the total national effort was bound to be inadequate in competition with nations better organized for modern economic life. Spain, in short, presents almost the antithesis of the picture of what goes into the "capitalist spirit" drawn by Weber in his hypothesis on the Protestant ethic.

### The Spanish Style

Yet the Spanish supremacy, though short-lived, was real enough, and has helped make the world we live in. Half the Americas speak Spanish (or a rather similar tongue, Portuguese) and carry, however altered, a cultural inheritance from the Iberian peninsula. French, Dutch, and English national unity and national spirit were hardened in resistance to Spanish aggression. The Spanish character, the Spanish "style," was set—some may say hardened—in this Golden Age, which has left to the West some magnificent paintings and one of the few really universal books, the *Don Quixote* of Cervantes (1547–1616). This Spanish style is not at all like those of France and Italy, so often tied with Spain as "Latin"—a term that is very misleading if used in contrast to "Nordic" or "Germanic," and particularly so if the "Latin" lands and their peoples are grouped together as "sunny." For the Spanish spirit is among the most serious, most darkly passionate, most unsmiling in the West. It is a striving spirit, carrying to the extreme the chivalric "point of honor," the religious pain of living in this flesh, the desire for something more.

The Spanish spirit stands out in the paintings of an artist who was not a native Spaniard at all, but El Greco, "the Greek" (1541–1614). Born Domenico Theotokopouli on the island of Crete, trained both in the Byzantine tradition of the Aegean world and the newer manner of Renaissance Venice, he settled at Toledo, the religious capital of Castile. In quality and technique, El Greco's paintings contain elements of the Baroque, the dominant artistic style of the late sixteenth and seventeenth centuries. Named from the Portuguese word *barroco* describing a deformed or irregular pearl, the Baroque distorted and exaggerated the neoclassicism of the Renaissance, sometimes for decorative or dramatic effect, sometimes, as with El Greco, to convey tension or a yearning for something beyond the physical.

El Greco was the master painter of the Catholic Reformation; almost all his great works had religious themes. Perhaps the most celebrated, executed for a church in Toledo, concerns the burial of the Count of Orgaz. This fourteenth-century Castilian nobleman had built a church to honor Saint Augustine and Saint Stephen. When he died, the two saints miraculously appeared to bury his body. In the painting, the two saints gently lift the count, and the aristocratic mourners gravely witness the miracle as an angel conveys the count's soul to the Virgin, to Christ, Saint Peter, and the host of the blessed waiting above. The whole effect is heightened by El Greco's characteristic distortion of human figures, with their long, thin heads, their great eyes turned upward. The painting stretches toward heaven like the pinnacles of a Gothic cathedral; it is a most extraordinary effort to record the mystic's unrecordable experience.

Spain is indeed the land of passionate religious will to overcome this world in mystical union with Christ. Saint Teresa of Avila (1515–1582) and Saint John of the Cross (1542–1591) bring back the tortured ecstasies of the early Christian ascetics, and add a dark, rebellious note of their own. Theirs was no Eastern attempt to withdraw from the world of sense and common sense, but a heroic effort to combat this world of the sense and thus transcend it. They worked vigorously to reform Spanish monasticism, and Saint John, in particular, was harshly persecuted by established religious interests. They were both familiar figures to the Spanish common people, who in their own way identified themselves with these saints in their struggle. Here is a portion of a modern writer's account of the funeral of John of the Cross:

> Hardly had his breath ceased than, though it was an hour past midnight, cold and raining hard, crowds assembled in the street and poured into the convent. Pressing into the room where

*El Greco's portrait of Cardinal Don Fernando Niño de Guevara.*

he lay, they knelt to kiss his feet and hands. They cut off pieces from his clothes and bandages and even pulled out the swabs that had been placed on his sores. Others took snippings from his hair and tore off his nails, and would have cut pieces from his flesh had it not been forbidden. At his funeral these scenes were repeated. Forcing their way past the friars who guarded his body, the mob tore off his habit and even took parts of his ulcered flesh.*

The creations of Cervantes, in their very different way, carry the mark of the Spanish style. Spain is Don Quixote tilting with the windmills, aflame for the Dulcinea he has invented, quite mad. But it is also the knight's servant, Sancho Panza, conventional, earthy, unheroic, and sane enough, though his sanity protects him not at all from sharing his master's misadventures. Cervantes almost certainly meant no more than an amusing satire of popular tales of chivalry. But his story has got caught up in the web of symbolism we live by, and the Don and his reluctant follower are for us Spain forever racked between ambitious heroism and relucant common sense.

* Gerald Brenan, "A Short Life of St. John of the Cross," in *The Golden Horizon,* ed. Cyril Connolly (London, 1953), pp. 475–476.

This tension runs all through *Don Quixote.* Chivalry is indeed silly, and worth satire—gentle satire:

> "I would inform you, Sancho, that it is a point of honor with knights-errant to go for a month at a time without eating, and when they do eat, it is whatever may be at hand. You would certainly know that if you had read the histories as I have. There are many of them, and in none have I found any mention of knights eating unless it was by chance or at some sumptuous banquet that was tendered them; on other days they fasted. And even though it is well understood that, being men like us, they could not go without food entirely, any more than they could fail to satisfy the other necessities of nature, nevertheless, since they spent the greater part of their lives in forests and desert places without any cook to prepare their meals. . . ."
>
> "Pardon me, your Grace," said Sancho, "but seeing that, as I have told you, I do not know how to read or write, I am consequently not familiar with the rules of the knightly calling. Hereafter, I will stuff my saddlebags with all manner of dried fruit for your Grace, but inasmuch as I am not a knight, I shall lay in for myself a stock of fowls and other more substantial fare." *

The extreme of pride—pride of race, of faith, of nation—has seemed to the outside world the mark of Spain. Perhaps there is little to choose among the triumphant prides of nations in triumph. Yet as the "shot heard round the world" sounds very American, so the Cid, the legendary hero of the reconquest from the Muslims, is very Spanish in these verses as he goes off to his crusade:

*Por necesidad batallo*
*Y una vez puesto en la silla*
*Se va ensanchando Castilla*
*Delante de mi caballo.*

* *Don Quixote,* trans. Samuel Putnam (New York, 1949), I, 78–79.

*[I fight by necessity:*
*But once I am in the saddle,*
*Castile goes widening out*
*Ahead of my horse.]*

## The French Monarchy

North of the Pyrenees another of the new monarchies had emerged in the fifteenth century. Perhaps no province of France—not even Brittany with its Celtic language and autonomous traditions, not even Provence with its language of the troubadours, its ties with Italy, its long history as a separate unit—shows the intense awareness of its own separateness that is to be found in Catalonia or the Basque provinces of Spain. Moreover, unlike Greece, Italy, and the Iberian peninsula, France for the most part is not cut up by mountain ranges into relatively isolated regions; great barriers like the Alps and Pyrenees are on her borders. Even so, France was but imperfectly tied together under Francis I (1515–1547), contemporary of Charles V and Henry VIII. Provinces like Brittany, which had only recently come under the Valois crown, retained their own local representative bodies (estates), their own local courts (parlements), and many other privileges. The nobility held on to feudal memories and attitudes, though it had lost most of its old governmental functions to royal appointees. The national bureaucracy was most rudimentary, a patchwork that could hardly fit into a modern administrative chart, with its little boxes showing who consults with whom, who obeys whom in a chain of authority.

As we have seen, however, the kingdom of Francis I possessed strength enough to counter the threat of encirclement by Charles V. The king himself was not another Louis XI. Self-indulgence weakened his health and distracted him from the business of government; his extravagant court and, far more, his frequent wars nearly wrecked the finances of the state. Yet in many respects Francis was a good Renaissance despot, thoroughly at home in the age of Machiavelli. He was the first French king to be addressed as "Majesty," a title earlier reserved for the emperor, and one modern historian has pronounced him to be "the most absolute" king of France—a considerable compliment in the light of the splendor of Louis XIV. At the beginning of his reign Francis extended the royal gains made at papal expense in the Pragmatic Sanction of Bourges in 1438. In the Concordat of Bologna, 1516, the pope allowed the king a very great increase in control over the Gallican church, including the important right of choosing bishops and abbots. In the face of treason Francis responded by confiscating the estates of the Constable de Bourbon. In adversity he had courage: witness his successful recovery after the disaster at Pavia in 1525. In diplomacy he was unscrupulous and flexible: witness his alliance with the Turks and with the German Protes-

*The Château of Chambord, built by Francis I in the Loire Valley.*

tants. Good-looking (at least until his health broke down), amorous, courtly, lavish, Francis comported himself as many people expect royalty to behave. He did things on the grand scale; it is reported that it took 18,000 horses and pack animals to move the king and his court on their frequent journeys. Francis built the famous chateaux of Chambord and Fontainebleau, two of the masterpieces of French Renaissance architecture. In Paris he remodeled the great palace of the Louvre and founded the Collège de France, second only to the university (the Sorbonne) as an educational center. He patronized men of letters and artists, among them numerous Italians including Benvenuto Cellini and Leonardo da Vinci.

The artistic and humanist Renaissance spread gradually northward from Italy in the sixteenth century, taking on somewhat different characteristics in various countries. In France, the architecture of the Renaissance still bears the stamp of late Gothic, as at Chambord, or, as in the smaller chateaux like Chenonceaux and Azay-le-Rideau, is classically French in its restraint and graceful ornamentation. French humanists are scholarly indeed, French poets conscious adapters of Latin and Greek concepts and language. Two very great sixteen-century French writers point up this national stamp, which is by no means without paradoxical contrasts, on a classic Renaissance ground. Montaigne (1533-1592) was an essayist, a reasonable skeptic, a worried self-analyst, in his own way a seeker, and as a stylist one of the chief makers of the rigorously disciplined, orderly, conventional French literary language. Rabelais (1494-1553), once a monk, was exuberant, fleshly, optimistic, unreasonable, indecent, excited, undisciplined (but very learned), a perpetual reminder that not all French writers are logical, conventional adherents to literary standards of clarity and orderliness.

Francis was the last strong king of the house of Valois. After his death in 1547, his son Henry II and his grandsons were barely able to maintain the prestige of the Crown. Possibly not even a greatly gifted ruler could have prevented the disorders of the second half of the sixteenth century, disorders that seriously crippled France in the international rivalries of the day. These were the years of the French religious wars, the crisis that almost undid the centralizing work of Louis XI and his successors.

## Religious and Civil Strife, 1562-1598

In France, Protestantism scarcely touched the great peasant masses except for parts of the south, notably Languedoc. The Huguenots were strong among the nobility and among the new classes of capitalists and artisans. The religious map of France also showed a territorial as well as a class division, an exception to the rule that in Europe the north tends to be Protestant and the south Catholic. The northernmost sections of France, up against the Low Countries, though affected by Lutheranism at first, remained ardently Catholic, as did Brittany, most of Normandy, and the region of Paris. By the later sixteenth century the Protestants were strongest in south-central France, above all in the lands of the old Albigensian heresy and in the southwest. Even in these regions, however, the employer class was more likely to be Protestant, the workers to be Catholic. The French nobility took up with Protestantism partly in response to a missionary campaign directed toward them from Geneva itself and partly for political reasons. The old tradition of local feudal independence among the nobles encouraged resistance to the centralized Catholic monarchy and its agents. The German princes in revolt had everything to gain in a worldly way by confiscation of church property and establishment of an Erastian Lutheran church. But, after the Concordat of 1516, the French kings had everything to lose by a Protestant movement that strengthened their restive nobility and that in its Calvinist form was the very opposite of Erastian.

Sporadic warfare began soon after the death of Henry II in 1559 (ironically, he was fatally wounded in a tournament celebrating the Treaty of Cateau-Cambrésis). For the next generation the crown passed in succession to Henry's three sons—Francis II (1559-1560), Charles IX (1560-1574), and Henry III (1574-1589)—and France was torn by civil and religious strife. Since Charles IX was a boy of ten at his accession, authority was exercised by his mother, the famous Catherine de' Medici, who shared the humanistic and artistic tastes of her famous Florentine family and, contrary to Protestant prejudices, had no particular religious convictions. But Catherine did have intense maternal

*Portrait of Henry IV (Henry of Navarre).*

devotion and was determined to preserve intact the magnificent royal inheritance of her sons. This inheritance seemed to her jeopardized by the rapid growth of the Huguenots in numbers and importance, their increasing pressure for official recognition, and the increasing counter-pressure from Catholics against any concessions. What especially worried Catherine was the apparent polarization of the high nobility by the religious issue—the great family of Guise was zealously dedicated to the Catholic cause, and the powerful families of Bourbon and Montmorency to the Huguenot.

Success in sporadic fighting during the 1560's netted the Huguenots some concessions. Their ambitious leader, Coligny, who was linked to the Montmorencys, gained great influence over the unstable Charles IX and apparently seriously hoped to take over control of the government. Panicky at the danger to the prospects for her sons and to her own position, Catherine planned to have Coligny assassinated. When he was only wounded, she abruptly threw in her lot with the Guises and persuaded Charles to follow suit. The result was the massacre of Huguenots on Saint Bartholomew's Day (August 24, 1572). Three thousand victims fell in Paris, including Coligny, many of them dragged from their beds in the first hours of the morning according to a prearranged plan; thousands more perished in the provinces. In spite of Saint Bartholomew's Day and subsequent reverses in the field, the Huguenots remained strong. As the warfare continued, the Catholic nobles organized a threatening league headed by the Guises, and both sides took to negotiating with foreigners for help, the Catholics with Spain and the Protestants with England. Thus the French crown found itself pushed into opposition to both groups.

### Henry of Navarre Victorious

The French civil and religious strife culminated in the War of the Three Henrys (1585–1589)—named for Henry III, the Valois king and the last surviving grandson of Francis I; Henry, duke of Guise, head of the Catholic League; and the Bourbon Henry of Navarre, the Protestant cousin and heir-apparent of the childless king (his grandmother had been the sister of Francis I). The threat that a Protestant might succeed to the throne pushed the Catholic League to the extreme of proposing a deliberate violation of the rules of succession by making an uncle of Henry of Navarre, the Catholic cardinal of Bourbon, king. But in an established monarchy rules of succession are in fact what we call "constitutional" laws and have behind them the force of public opinion. Moderate French public opinion, already disturbed by the extremes of both Catholics and Protestants, now turned against the Catholic League.

Paris, however, was a strong Catholic city, and a popular insurrection there, the "Day of the Barricades" (May 12, 1588), frightened Henry III out of the city, which triumphantly acclaimed Guise as king. Henry III took the weak man's way out, and connived at—indeed almost certainly planned—the assassination of the two great men of the Catholic League, Henry of Guise and his brother Louis. Infuriated, the League rose in full revolt, and King Henry was forced to take refuge in the camp of Henry of Navarre, where he in turn was assassinated by a monk.

Henry of Navarre was now by law King Henry IV (1589–1610), first of the house of Bourbon. The Catholics set up the aged cardinal of Bourbon as "King Charles X," but in the decisive battle of Ivry in March 1590 Henry won a great victory and laid siege to Paris. Spanish troops, sent down from Flanders by Philip II, repeatedly forced him to lift the siege. As a matter of fact, Philip planned to have the French Estates-General put Henry aside and bestow the crown of France on the Spanish infanta Isabella, daughter of Philip II and his third wife, Elizabeth of Valois, who was the child of Henry II and Catherine de' Medici. In the face of this new threat, Henry was persuaded that if he would abjure his own Protestant faith he could rally the moderate Catholics and secure at least tolerated status for the Protestants. He turned Catholic in 1593 and Paris was surrendered, giving rise to the perhaps apocryphal tale that he had remarked "Paris is well worth a Mass." Henry now declared war against Spain and brought it to a successful conclusion with the Treaty of Vervins, 1598, which essentially confirmed the Cateau-Cambrésis settlement of 1559. Spain ended her intervention in France and restored all conquests to the French crown.

## The *Politiques* and the Edict of Nantes

Within France the Edict of Nantes, also in 1598, endeavored to achieve a lasting religious settlement. While it did not bring complete religious freedom, it did provide for a large measure of toleration. The Huguenots were granted substantial civil liberties and were allowed the exercise of their religion in certain areas, and their great nobles were permitted it in their own households. Public worship by Huguenots was forbidden in episcopal and archiepiscopal cities, and most particularly in Paris. Of the two hundred towns where Huguenots could worship, they were to fortify and garrison one hundred at government expense as symbols of safeguard.

The intellectual preparation for the Edict of Nantes and for the revival of the French monarchy under Henry IV had been in large part the work of a group of men known by the untranslatable French term *politiques,* which is nearer to "political moralist" than it is to our "politician." The greatest of them, Jean Bodin, who died in 1596, has been rather unfairly labeled a proponent of absolute monarchy. He did indeed hold that the sole possibility of order in a divided France lay in obedience to a king above petty civil strife. We have already noted that in the early modern world a pluralism of religious belief was not regarded as a good in itself. So too for the kind of political pluralism of parties, pressure groups, and the like we accept in a democracy as a positive good, so long as public order is not violated. Bodin and his colleagues emphasized the need for political unity to maintain law and order. But they were by no means what we now call totalitarians. Bodin was far from preaching that the king must be obeyed no matter what he did; he was a moderate who believed in acceptance of the limitations imposed by history and tradition on any practical program of politics. The politiques were convinced that under the supremacy of the French state Frenchmen could be allowed to practice different forms of the Christian religion.

Some of the politiques were unreligious persons; but the best of them, like Michel de l'Hospital, were Christians who held firmly to the belief that the basic aim of those who fought the religious wars—to put down by force those who disagreed with them in matters religious—was un-Christian. Here is l'Hospital addressing the Estates-General in 1560:

> If they are Christians, those who try to spread Christianity with arms, swords, and pistols do indeed go contrary to their professed faith, which is to suffer force, not to inflict it. . . . Nor is their argument, that they take arms in the cause of God, a valid one, for the cause of God is not one that can be so defended with such arms. . . . Our religion did not take its beginnings from force of arms, and is not to be kept and strengthened by force of arms.

Yet l'Hospital is a good child of his age, and he cannot conceive that men can really hold and practice different religious faiths in the same political society:

> It is folly to hope for peace, quiet and friendship, among persons of different religions. And there is no opinion so deeply planted in the hearts of men, as opinion in religion, and none which so separates one from another.

He can but hope that as good Frenchmen they will sink their quarrels in a common Frenchness and a common Christianity:

> Let us pray God for the heretics, and do all we can to reduce and convert them; gentleness will do more than harshness. Let us get rid of those devilish names of seditious factions, Lutherans, Huguenots, Papists: let us not change the name of Christian.*

### Henry IV and the Restoration of the French Monarchy

Henry IV, first Bourbon king of France, could hardly have succeeded in his work of pacification had not the nation been ready for it; he was particularly fortunate in coming on the scene when the passions of civil war were nearing exhaustion. The high degree of success he achieved, however, depended greatly on his own personal qualities. A realist rather than a cynic, as the remark about Paris being worth a Mass might suggest, Henry balanced concessions to the Huguenots with generous subsidies to the Catholic League for disbanding its troops, and he declined to summon the Estates-General because of its potential for proving troublesome.

Other kings in other days, like Louis XI of France and Henry VII of England, had accomplished the restoration of law and order, but only Henry of Navarre became a genuinely popular hero. Witty, dashing, with a pronounced taste for pretty women and bawdy stories, he was the most human king the French had had for a long time, and the best-liked monarch in their whole history. His court casually included his wife, his mistresses, and his children, legitimate and otherwise. He made jokes about his financial difficulties. And, most of all, he convinced his subjects that he was truly concerned for their welfare. Among ordinary Frenchmen, Henry IV is still remembered as the king who remarked that every peasant should have a chicken in his pot on Sunday.

Henry's economic experts reclaimed marshes for farm land, encouraged the luxury crafts in Paris, and planted thousands of mulberry trees to foster the culture and manufacture of silk. They extended canals and launched a program of building roads and bridges that eventually won France the reputation of maintaining the best highways in Europe. Faced with a heavy deficit when he took office, Henry's chief minister, the Huguenot Sully (1559–1641), systematically lowered it until he brought government income and expenditure into balance. His search for new revenues had some unhappy consequences, however. He not only continued the old custom of selling government offices but permitted the beneficiary to transmit the office to his heir on payment of an annual fee—a lucrative new source of royal income but an even greater source of future difficulty, since more and more officeholders were more concerned with enjoying and protecting their vested interests than with the faithful execution of their duties. For the rest, the incidence of taxation remained lopsided, with some provinces much more heavily burdened than others, and with the poor paying much more than their fair share. Collection remained in the hands of contractors called "farmers," and the treasury suffered loss of revenue from entrusting this public function to often unscrupulous private entrepreneurs. Fiscal weakness was to remain the Achilles' heel of the monarchy for the next two centuries.

## IV The Protestant States: England and the Dutch Republic

### Henry VIII, 1509–1547

In England Henry VII had already established the new Tudor monarchy on a firm footing. That Henry VIII did not run through his heritage and leave an exhausted treasury and discredited monarchy was not because he lacked the will to spend lavishly. As Martin Luther wrote of him, "Junker Heintz will be God and does whatever he lusts."* Henry loved display, elaborate palaces (Hampton Court, near London, is the best known), and all the trappings of Renaissance monarchy. His "summit conference"

* P. J. S. Dufey, ed., *Oeuvres complètes de Michel de l'Hospital* (Paris, 1824), I, 395–402. Our translation.

* Quoted in J. J. Scarisbrick, *Henry VIII* (Berkeley, 1968), p. 526.

with Francis I, a kindred luxurious spirit, near Calais in 1520 has gone down in tradition as "The Field of Cloth of Gold."

Henry, however, did not seriously undermine royal finances and otherwise added considerably to the luster of the English monarchy. There were many reasons for this. One may find in history a bankrupt government in a relatively prosperous society, as in the France of 1789; one may also find a prosperous, well-run government in a relatively poor society, as in eighteenth-century Prussia; Tudor England had the good fortune to enjoy both solvent government and a a prosperous society. No doubt the great enclosures of land for sheep-farming and other factors helped create a new poor; marginal farmers, for instance, who lost their right to pasture animals on the common lands now enclosed in private estates lost the margin that had permitted them to get by. But many Englishmen, and especially the new upper classes, continued on the whole to thrive. Moreover, this national material wealth was not unduly expended in foreign wars, the really major cause of disastrous financial difficulties of modern governments. Democratic critics have often accused European royalty of ruinous expenditures on palaces, retinues, pensions, mistresses, and high living of all sorts; yet the fact seems to be that such expenditures were usually a comparatively small part of the total outlay for purposes of government. Henry's wives—he had six—his court, his royal progresses, did not by any means beggar his country; the wars of Charles V and Philip II did beggar Spain.

Henry VIII made war in a gingerly manner, never really risking big English armies on the Continent, and contenting himself with playing a rather cautious game of balance of power. He made full use of the opportunities afforded him by the English Reformation to add to royal revenues by confiscation of monastic property, and, even more important, by rewarding his loyal followers with lands so confiscated. Henry thus followed in the footsteps of his father in helping create a new upper class, which was soon actually a titled or noble class. In these critical years of English development, the new class was, in contrast to France, on the whole loyal to the Crown and yet, in contrast to some of the German states, by no means subservient to the Crown, by no means a mere ennobled bureaucracy.

Henry, who did not have the patience to attend to the daily details of administration, relied heavily on members of the new class as his chief assistants—Wolsey in the early part of his reign, then Cranmer who as archbishop of Canterbury enabled Henry to marry Anne Boleyn, and, above all, Thomas Cromwell, later made earl of Essex, who superintended all the precarious political ramifications of the break with Rome. Cromwell exploited the potentialities of the printing press to achieve wide dissemination of propaganda favoring the royal point of view. He was, in fact, a master administrator, who endeavored to make the royal administration more loyal, professional, and efficient, less tied to the king's household and to special interests, in short, more modern in character. He achieved a great deal; but he was bound to have some failures and bound, also, to antagonize other ambitious royal servants. Discredited with the king by the action of his enemies, Cromwell was executed in 1540. Wolsey, too, had been disgraced and died awaiting execution. Henry could be ruthless, yet he could be tactful and diplomatic, as he was in the crucial matter of dealing with Parliament.

### Tudor Parliaments

Most important of all, Henry was able to get what he wanted from his Parliaments, including statutes that separated the English church from Rome, and grants for his wars and conferences. Henry's Parliaments were very far from being elected legislatures based on wide suffrage. The Tudor House of Lords had a safe majority of men—titled nobles and, after 1534, bishops of the Anglican church—who were in fact of Tudor creation or allegiance. The House of Commons was composed of the knights of the shire, chosen by the freeholders of the shires, and of the burgesses, representatives of incorporated towns or boroughs (not by any means all towns). In most boroughs, a very narrow electorate chose these members of Parliament. Since the majority of the people of the shires were agricultural workers or tenants, rather than freeholders of land, the county franchise, too, was limited. In fact, the knights of the shire were chosen from among, and largely by, the squires and the lesser country gentlemen. Royal favor and royal patronage, as well as the patronage of the great lords, could pretty well mold the shape of a House of Commons.

Still, even the Tudor Parliaments are nearer a modern legislative assembly than the parallel assemblies, or estates, of the Continent. The great point of difference lies in the composition of the House of Commons, which had emerged from the Middle Ages not as a body representing an urban bourgeoisie but as a composite of the rural landed gentry and the ruling groups in the towns, meeting in one body. On the Continent, the assemblies corresponding to the English Parliament were estates (*Stände* in German, *états* in French). They usually sat in three distinct houses—one representing the clergy, another all the nobles, great and small, and a third the lay commoners. Some countries, as for instance Sweden, had four estates—clergy, nobles, townsmen, and peasants.

Historians today emphasize the fact that the political differences between England and the Continent rest on a somewhat, though by no means totally, different social structure. There was certainly an English nobility or aristocracy ranging from barons through viscounts, earls, and marquises to dukes at the top. These nobles, plus Anglican bishops, composed the House of Lords. For those just below the nobles the use of the term "gentry" or "gentleman" is still much debated among social historians of early modern England. We may here content ourselves with noting, first, that younger sons of nobles in England were not themselves titled nobles, as they were on the Continent, but were members, usually top members, of a complex group for which there is no good single name, though Englishmen even today distinguish its members as "gentlemen"; and second, that this group, roughly divisible into the younger sons and descendents of nobles, the "squires" or "country gentlemen," the rich merchants and bankers (who almost always acquired landed estates and became squires), the leading lawyers, civil servants, Anglican clergy, dons at Oxford and Cambridge (who at first were usually in Anglican orders), officers in the army and navy, and a scattering of others in the liberal professions—this group was never a closed caste, but remained open to socially mobile individuals from the lower classes. The conventional term "middle class" certainly does not describe it in early modern times; the term "gentry" applies only to part of it; perhaps we can settle for "ruling class" or "establishment."

Finally, in England, Parliament came out of the Middle Ages with the power to make laws or statutes, including money laws. These laws did indeed require royal consent. But at the end of the fifteenth century Parliament had already obtained much more than the merely advisory powers which were all that the French Estates-General, for instance, really had. Moreover, the "Reformation Parliament," which passed the Act of Supremacy and other religious legislation, sat for the unprecedented span of seven years (1529–1536) and gave the institution of Parliament new self-confidence.

Purely in terms of constitutional structure, then, the Tudor Parliaments could have quarreled as violently with the Crown as did the Stuart Parliaments in the next century. Although the Tudor monarchs had their spats and difficulties with Parliament, on the whole they got what they wanted out of Parliament without serious constitutional crises. This was particularly true of Henry VIII and Elizabeth I. These monarchs succeeded in part, as we have noted, because their Parliaments, if not precisely packed, were generally recruited from men favorable to the Crown, to which they owed so much. But the Tudor monarchs succeeded because they were skillful rulers, willing to use their prestige and gifts of persuasion to win the consent of Parliament, careful to observe the constitutional and human decencies. Moreover, both Henry and Elizabeth were good hearty persons, sure of themselves and their dignity, immensely popular with all classes of their subjects. Both were fortunate enough to be able to incorporate in their persons strong national feelings of patriotic resistance to the two most hated foreign foes, the Roman church and the Spanish monarchy.

### Religious Flux

The course of Tudor domestic history, however, did not run with perfect smoothness. Henry VII had faced two pretenders; Henry VIII met opposition to his religious policy. A Catholic minority, strong in the north, continued throughout the sixteenth century to oppose the Protestant majority, sometimes in arms, sometimes in intrigues. The death of Henry VIII in 1547 marked the beginning of a period of really extraordinary religious oscillation.

Henry was succeeded by his only son, the ten-year-old Edward VI, borne by his third wife, Jane Seymour. Led by the young king's uncle, the Duke of Somerset, Edward's government pushed on into Protestant ways. The Six Articles, by which Henry had sought to preserve the essentials of Roman Catholic theology, worship, and even church organization, were repealed in 1547. The legal title of the statute commonly called the Six Articles had been "An Act for Abolishing Diversity in Opinion." The goal was still uniformity, and in the brief reign of Edward VI an effort was made to prescribe uniformity of religious worship through a prayerbook and articles of faith duly imposed by Parliament. Cranmer, archbishop of Canterbury, was a convinced Protestant much influenced by the ideas of Zwingli, and had committed himself by his marriage—as did Luther—to a clear, symbolic break with Roman Catholicism. Under his supervision, the patient bulk of the English people was pushed into Protestant worship.

Then, in 1553, the young king, Edward VI, always a frail boy, died. Protestant intriguers vainly attempted to secure the crown for a Protestant, Lady Jane Grey, a great-grandaughter of Henry VII and a quiet, scholarly young woman with no ambitions. But Edward VI was followed by his older sister Mary, daughter of the Catholic Catherine of Aragon whom Henry VIII had put aside. Mary had been brought up a Catholic, and at once began to restore the old ways. Of course there was a rebellion, which flared into the open when Mary announced a marriage treaty by which she was to wed Philip II of Spain. Yet Mary prevailed against the rebels, and Lady Jane Grey was executed for a plot she had never really shared in. The Catholic cardinal Pole was made archbishop of Canterbury, under Rome, and Cranmer was burned at the stake. Catholic forms of worship came back to the parishes, but significantly the church land settlement of Henry VIII remained undisturbed. The vigorous persecution of Protestants—most of the nearly three hundred people burnt were from the lower classes, and many were women—gave Mary her lasting epithet of "Bloody" and laid the foundations of the English Protestant hatred and suspicion of Catholicism, traces of which still survive today.

Mary, too, died after a short reign, in 1558. The last of Henry's children left was Elizabeth, daughter of Anne Boleyn. She had at her father's request been declared illegitimate by Parliament in 1536. Henry's last will, however, rehabilitated her, and she now succeeded as Elizabeth I (1558–1603). She had been brought up a Protestant, and once more the ordinary English churchgoer was required to switch religion. This time the Anglican church was firmly established; the prayerbook and Thirty-Nine Articles of 1563 issued under Elizabeth (and noted in the last chapter) have remained to this day the essential documents of the Anglican faith.

The Elizabethan settlement, moderate and permanent though it was did not fully solve the religious problem. England still had a Catholic party. Spain, especially after Elizabeth's repudiation of Catholicism, was a serious enemy; it seemed hardly likely that the heavy expenses of a real war could be long avoided. Moreover, independent Scotland could always be counted on in those days to take the anti-English side. The new queen of Scotland was Mary Stuart, granddaughter of Henry VIII's sister, Margaret, and therefore the heir to the English throne should Elizabeth I die without issue. Mary did not wait for Elizabeth's death, but on the ground that Elizabeth was in fact illegitimate, herself assumed the title of Queen of England and Scotland.

Finally, the English Catholics were by no means the most serious of Elizabeth's religious critics; numerous Protestant groups not satisfied with the Thirty-Nine Articles were coming to the fore. Broadly, these people are called Puritans, since they wished to "purify" the Anglican church of what they considered papist survivals in belief, ritual, and church government. Actually, the Puritans ranged from moderates to radicals. The moderates would be content with a simpler ritual but would retain bishops. The Presbyterians were Calvinists who would substitute councils (synods) of elders, or presbyters, for bishops, and would adopt the full Calvinist theology. The Brownists, named for their leader

*Portrait of Queen Elizabeth by an unknown artist. The map of England is at her feet.*

Robert Browne, were the radical wing of Puritanism; they were Calvinists who wanted to have each congregation an independent body.

### Elizabeth the Queen

Thus Elizabeth faced a decidedly grim prospect during the early years of her reign. The troubles of the reigns of Edward and Mary had undone some of the work of the two Henrys; dissension seemed all around her. Yet she was to reign for nearly fifty years and to give her name to one of the greatest ages of English culture.

The personality of Elizabeth is hardly heartwarming. She was vain (or simply proud), not altogether proof against flattery, but too intelligent to be led astray by it in great matters. She was a good Renaissance realist (a better one than Machiavelli himself), somewhat too overpowering and impressive for a woman, but very effective in the pageantry and posing of public life. She was loved by her people if not by her intimates. She never married, but in the early years of her reign she played off foreign and domestic suitors one against another with excellent results for her foreign policy, in which she was always trying to avoid the expenses and dangers of war, trying to get something for nothing. One may believe that her spinsterhood settled on her at first as no more than a policy of state, and later as a convenient habit. She had male favorites, but probably not lovers.

Mistrusting the great aristocrats, Elizabeth picked her ministers from the ranks just below the nobility, talented men like Burleigh and Walsingham who put her government in splendid order. Thanks to skillful diplomacy, which made full use of the French and Dutch opposition to Spain, the showdown with Philip was postponed until 1588, when the kingdom was ready for it. Mary Queen of Scots proved no match at all for her gifted cousin, not merely because she was not a good politician, but even more because she had no sure Scottish base to work from. Mary was a Catholic, and Scotland under the leadership of John Knox was on its way to becoming one of the great centers of Calvinism. Mary managed everything wrong, including, and perhaps most important in a puritanical land, her love affairs. Her subjects revolted against her, and she was forced in 1568 to take refuge in England, where Elizabeth had her put in confinement. Mary alive was at the very least a constant temptation to all who wanted to overthrow Elizabeth. Letters, which Mary declared were forged, and over which historians still debate, involved her in what was certainly a very real conspiracy against Elizabeth, and she was tried, convicted, and executed in 1587, to become a romantic legend.

The dramatic crisis of Elizabeth's reign was the war with Spain, resolved in the defeat of the great Spanish Armada in 1588. But her old age was not to be altogether quiet. Her relations with Parliament became increasingly strained. Forced to turn frequently to Parliament for approval of financial measures, she met mounting criticism of her religious policy from Puritan members of the Commons. She got her money not by making concessions to the Puritans but by grudgingly conceding more rights to the Commons. The Commons responded not with expressions of gratitude but with bolder criticism of the queen's policy, and at what proved to be the last meeting of Parliament Elizabeth attended, failed to salute her appearance with the usual salvo of applause. The stage was being set for the great seventeenth-century confrontation between the Crown and Parliament.

During Elizabeth's final years the stage was also being set for a drama that was to have an even longer run—the Irish question. The ruling Anglo-Irish landed class was out of touch with the native masses. In 1542, the country had been made a kingdom, but by no means an independent one, since the crowns of England and Ireland were held by the same person. An earlier act, the Statute of Drogheda (Poynings' Act), in 1495 had put the Irish Parliament firmly under English control and had made laws enacted in the English Parliament applicable to Ireland. Attempts to enforce Protestant laws passed by the English Parliament outraged the native Irish, who had remained faithfully Catholic.

In 1597, the Irish rose under the leadership of Hugh O'Neill, earl of Tyrone. The revolt was temporarily successful but was put down bloodily in 1601 after the favorite of Elizabeth's old age, the Earl of Essex, had failed dismally to cope with it. Essex, too, involved himself in a plot against his mistress, and was executed after its discovery and suppression. But the Elizabethan settlement of the Irish question was to prove only a stopgap.

## The Elizabethan Age

The Age of Elizabeth, then, was a time of wars, rebellions, personal and party strife, and intense competition. Yet there was a solid foundation under the state and society that produced the literature, music, architecture, science, and wealth and victories of the Elizabethan Age. That foundation was in part a good administrative system, itself based on a substantial degree of national unity, or, negatively, on the absence of the extreme local differences and conflicts of the Continent. It was in part general economic prosperity, based on individual enterprise in many fields—enterprise often unscrupulous and, as far as raids on the commerce of foreigners like the Spaniards went, piratical. It was certainly something not simply material, a common sentiment that kept Englishmen together and that traced for most of them limits beyond which they would not carry disagreement. Elizabeth herself played a large part in holding her subjects together; her religious policy, for example, was directed at stretching the already broad principles and practices of the Church of England so that they would cover near-Catholicism and near-Congregationalism. But there was a limit to this stretching, and Elizabeth "persecuted" Catholics on the Right and Brownists on the Left—that is, she did not grant to them the right to practice their religion publicly. But in contrast to Mary's severity, Elizabeth's response was largely a matter of fining offenders.

The Age of Elizabeth I was marked by a great flowering of culture that extended beyond the chronological limits of her reign, 1558 to 1603, back into the reign of Henry VIII and forward into that of her successor, James I. This is the English Renaissance, tardiest of the great classical Renaissances. It has the range and variety we have found in other lands and the same dependence on the old Greeks and Romans we have found elsewhere. It is hard to pick up a poem, an essay, a play, any piece of writing not purely religious, without coming very soon upon a classical allusion. Yet the English Renaissance also holds on to much that could be grown only in the climate of the island. Tudor and early Stuart architecture is a case in point. The new palaces and manor houses are no longer much like the medieval castles; they are more open, more elegant. But they preserve all sorts of Gothic habits, mullioned windows, tracery and carving, traditional woodwork.

The ladies and gentlemen who lived in these houses cultivated all the muses, played the lute, sang madrigals, admired contemporary paintings, and dressed as did ladies and gentlemen in the pacesetter of European style, Italy. Yet the commonplace is still true: England was not a land of great original creation in music and the plastic arts; Holbein, the superb portraitist of Tudor personages, was a German. The greatness of Elizabethan England, when it is not in the deeds of Drake, Hawkins, Thomas Cromwell, Burleigh, the Tudors themselves, lies in the words of Thomas More, Shakespeare, Francis Bacon, Spenser, Ben Jonson, and many others who are part of the formal higher education of English-speaking people all over the world.

Their writings have suffered popular admiration and neglect as well as the thorough academic working-over that goes with the status of established classics. They belong to a culture now four hundred years past, and their authors wrote English before its structure and its word order were tamed, partly by the influence of French prose, into their present straightforward simplicity. For most of us, they are much easier to read about than to read. Yet on the whole they have survived intact as classics. Shakespeare, notably, continues even outside the English-speaking world to be a kind of George Washington of letters, above reproach. He is the necessary great writer of a great people, as is Dante for the Italians, Goethe for the Germans, Pascal or Molière or Racine for the French, Cervantes for the Spanish, Tolstoy or Dostoevsky for the Russians.

These Elizabethans are overwhelmingly exuberant. They are exuberant even in refinement, full-blooded even in erudition. Above all, they are anxious to get in that something more, that transcending something that makes words more than words, and occasionally more than sense. To a later generation, the tame, orderly admirers of measure and sense in the late seventeenth and eighteenth centuries, these Elizabethans were uncouth, undisciplined. To the nineteenth-century Romantics, they were brothers in romance. This love of the excessive is obvious in much Elizabethan writing, in the interminable, allusion-packed, allegory-mad stanzas of Spenser's *Faerie Queene,* in the piling up of quotations from the ancient Greeks and Romans, in Shakespeare's love of puns and all kinds of rhetorical devices, in the extraordinarily bloody nature of their tragedies—remember, for example, the stage littered with corpses at the end of *Hamlet*.

The Elizabethans were also exuberant patriots, lovers of their country in the first flush of its worldly success. Here is one of the most famous speeches in Shakespeare, that of the dying John of Gaunt in *Richard II,* in itself an admirable sample of the English Renaissance, right down to the inevitable allusion to Greco-Roman mythology:

*This royal throne of kings, this scepter'd isle,*
*This earth of majesty, this seat of Mars,*
*This other Eden, demi-paradise,*
*This fortress built by Nature for herself*
*Against infection and the hand of war,*
*This happy breed of men, this little world,*
*This precious stone set in the silver sea,*
*Which serves it in the office of a wall*
*Or as a moat defensive to a house,*
*Against the envy of less happier lands,*
*This blessed plot, this earth, this realm, this England.*

## The Dutch Republic

Almost contemporaneous with the Elizabethan Age was the great age of the Dutch, which extended from the late sixteenth century through the first three quarters of the seventeenth. The United Provinces of the Northern Netherlands, as we have seen, gained effective independence from Spain before the death of Philip II, though formal international recognition of their status was delayed until the Peace of Westphalia in 1648. The Dutch state was a republic in the midst of monarchies, but it was an aristocratic merchant society, far from being a popular democracy. Despite its small size (approximately that of the state of Maryland), it was a great power, colonizing in Asia, Africa, and the Americas, trading everywhere, supporting an active and efficient navy.

In economic life, the Dutch were the pacesetters of seventeenth-century Europe, and Amsterdam succeeded Antwerp (as Antwerp had earlier succeeded Bruges) as the major trading center of northwestern Europe. Dutch ships played a predominant role in the international carrying trade: in the mid-seventeenth century it is estimated that the Dutch operated between half and three-quarters of the world's merchant vessels. The Dutch also controlled the very lucrative North Sea herring fisheries. Their East India Company, founded in 1602, assembled and exploited a commercial empire. It paid large

*Pieter de Hooch's "Dutch Courtyard."*

and regular dividends and served as a pioneer in the institution of the joint-stock company, sponsored by the state and pooling the resources of many businessmen, who could never have risked such a formidable undertaking on an individual basis. The Bank of Amsterdam (founded in 1609) was also a model, minting its own florins, and offering its depositors so many useful services that it made Amsterdam the financial capital of Europe. The Dutch invented life insurance and perfected the actuarial calculations on which successful insurance is based. Specialized industries grew up in the cities and towns of Holland—diamond-cutting, printing, and bookbinding at Amsterdam; shipbuilding at Zaandam; gin-distilling at Schiedam; woolens at Leiden and linens at Haarlem. The Dutch, together with their Catholic cousins under Spanish rule in Flanders, were in the van of European agricultural progress; they created new farm plots called polders by diking and draining lands formerly under the sea, and they experimented with new techniques and new crops. The growing of tulip bulbs in the fields around Haarlem set off a wild financial speculation in the 1630's.

In government, by contrast, the Dutch Republic was no model of up-to-date efficiency, for the United Provinces were united in name only, fragmented by Dutch deference to traditional local self-government. The seven provinces sent delegates (*Hooge Moogende,* High Mightinesses) to the Estates General, which functioned like a diplomatic congress rather than a central legislature. Each province did have a chief executive, the *stadholder,* originally the local lieutenant of the Spanish king in the days of Spanish rule, and the fact that most of the provinces chose as stadholder the incumbent prince of the House of Orange made him a symbol of national unity. Twice in the seventeenth century, however, the preponderance of the Orange stadholder was successfully challenged by the most important official of the most important province, the grand pensionary of Holland. In the first quarter of the century Jan van Olden Barneveldt, organizer of the East India Company, dominated Dutch political life until he was executed because of his support of the Arminian doctrine of free will against Calvinist predestination; in the third quarter, Jan De Witt, an expert in actuarial mathematics, also "ran" the republic until he was killed by a lynch mob when the soldiers of Louis XIV overran an ill-prepared Holland in the 1670's.

In religion, Dutch practicality resulted in a wide toleration. The beneficiaries were the substantial minority of Catholics, Protestant dissidents from Calvinist orthodoxy—Lutherans, Anabaptists, and even eventually Arminians—and Jewish refugees from persecution in Spain and Portugal, Poland and Lithuania. While the Jews made a considerable contribution to Dutch prosperity, an even greater one came from another set of refugees, Calvinists from the southern Netherlands. The freedom of the Dutch placed their universities, especially that of Leiden, at the top of the European learned world and made Holland a publishing center for works in French and English as well as in Dutch.

The Dutch of the seventeenth century also made major contributions to Western culture. In painting, Rembrandt (1606–1669) was at the summit of a group of artists, including Frans

Hals and Vermeer, who painted outstanding scenes of everyday life for the homes of prosperous businessmen. In science, Christian Huygens (1629–1695), son of a distinguished poet, was a major figure in the advance of mathematics and physics; in biological studies, Jan Swammerdam (1637–1680) pioneered in the use of the microscope and probably discovered the red corpuscles in the blood; and Anton van Leeuwenhoek (1632–1723), with a microscope of his own making, first described protozoa and bacteria. In philosophy, Baruch (or Benedict) Spinoza (1632–1677), a Jew rejected by his fellow religionists as unorthodox, laid the basis for much modern philosophical thought by his self-conscious, high-minded, rigorous rationalism. Indeed, one of his books has the remarkable title *Ethics Mathematically Demonstrated.*

The style of Dutch civilization in this great age is solid, reasonable, sober but far from colorless, by no means puritanical in any ascetic sense. Yet it is also a persuasive exhibit in support of Weber's thesis on the Protestant ethic. Certainly this little nation, through intelligence, hard work, adventurous exploration, and hard trading, and, as we shall see in the next chapter, some rather unscrupulous exploitation of non-European peoples, made for itself a great place in the world. But by 1700 the great days of Holland were coming to an end. The Dutch Republic declined, not absolutely, but relatively to the great powers around it—Britain, France, and Prussia. The Dutch, like the Swedes who reached a peak of power a bit later, simply did not have a home base extensive enough to support the status of a great power.

## V Germany and the Thirty Years' War

Like the great wars of the sixteenth century, the Thirty Years' War, 1618–1648, was in part a conflict over religion, and like them it had a Hapsburg focus. This time, however, the focus was more on the Austrian than the Spanish Hapsburgs, and so the bulk of the fighting took place in Germany. While the Hapsburg emperor, Ferdinand II (1619–1637), did not aspire to universal rule, he did make the last serious political and military effort to unify Germany under Catholic rule. The Thirty Years' War began as a conflict between Catholics and Protestants; it ended as an almost purely political struggle to reduce the power of the Hapsburgs in favor of France and a newcomer to high international politics, Sweden.

The Augsburg Peace of 1555 did not bring complete religious peace to Germany. It did not recognize Calvinism, to say nothing of the more radical Protestant sects, and it left unsettled the problem of ecclesiastical reservation. On this latter issue, an imperial decree provided that if a Catholic prelate were converted to Protestantism the property formerly under his control should remain in Catholic hands. But this was a one-sided proclamation; it had not been formally negotiated with the Protestants, who greatly resented it.

By the opening of the seventeenth century, the religious situation in Germany was becoming increasingly unsettled. In spite of the Augsburg peace, Calvinism had spread rapidly since 1555. Calvinist princes ignored the provision in the settlement against proselytizing, and proved equally vigorous in Lutheran and in Catholic regions. The consequences were riots and disorder, followed by the formation of the Calvinist Protestant Union (1608), which in turn prompted the creation of a Catholic League in 1609. Thus Germany was split into rival camps a decade before the outbreak of war. From the start, moreover, both the Protestant Union and the Catholic League had political as well as religious ambitions. Both really represented the interests of German particularism—that is, of the individual German states—against those of the empire, even though the Catholic League and its leader, Maximilian of Bavaria, were to ally with the emperor Ferdinand.

The German religious situation concerned the Spanish Hapsburgs as well as their Austrian cousins. After the Dutch revolt, the Spaniards wanted to stabilize a line of communications between their Italian and Belgian lands, so that men and money could move over the Alps and down the Rhine, which flowed through the lands of some rulers who were friendly to the Hapsburgs and others who were hostile. Chief among

*Vermeer's "View of Delft," painted ca. 1658.*

the latter was the Calvinist elector of the Palatinate, with his capital at Heidelberg; his lands, in a rich vineyard area along the Rhine, constituted a major obstacle to Spanish communications. Both the Dutch and the French were also involved, for they wanted to thwart Spanish plans of securing the overland route from Italy to Belgium. The Bourbon monarchs of France did not relish the idea of being encircled by Hapsburg territory any more than the Valois had done.

### The Bohemian Period, 1618-1625

In 1618 the head of the Protestant Union was the Calvinist elector of the Palatinate, Frederick, who was married to the daughter of James I of England. Frederick hoped to break the Catholic hold on the empire upon the death of the emperor Matthias (reigned 1612–1619), who was old and childless. The electors of Saxony, Brandenburg, and the Palatinate were Protestants; if there could be four Protestant electors instead of three when Matthias died, the majority could then install a Protestant emperor. Because three electors were Catholic archbishops, the only way to get an additional Protestant was to oust the one lay Catholic elector, the king of Bohemia. The king-elect of Bohemia, Ferdinand, was a strongly Catholic Hapsburg prince, already chosen by Matthias to be his heir.

Bohemia, today a part of Czechoslovakia, was then a Hapsburg crown land; its Czech nationalists wanted local independence from the rule of Germans and of Vienna. The Czechs expressed

*The hanging of thieves during the Thirty Years' War: a contemporary engraving.*

their national defiance of the Germans in part by following the faith that John Hus had taught them, the chief feature of which was Utraquism (from the Latin for "both"), the practice of giving the laity communion in wine as well as in bread. While Lutherans, Calvinists, and Utraquists were tolerated, Catholicism remained the state religion. Though Ferdinand guaranteed freedom of Protestant worship, the prospect of his becoming king of Bohemia and then emperor alarmed the Protestants. The arrest of some Protestants who had lost two legal cases touched off a revolt, which began with the famous Defenestration of Prague (May 23, 1618), when the angry rebels actually threw two Catholic imperial governors out of a window into a courtyard 70 feet below. They landed on a pile of dung, and escaped with their lives.

The Czech rebels set up their own government and offered the crown of Bohemia to the elector Frederick of the Palatinate. The inept Frederick went off to Prague, leaving badly defended his Rhineland territories, which the Spaniards occupied in 1620. Meantime, Catholics in Bohemia, Spain, and Flanders rallied against the rebels with money and men. After the emperor Matthias died in 1619, the electors chose the Hapsburg Ferdinand to be emperor (Ferdinand II, reigned 1619–1637). Maximilian of Bavaria, head of the Catholic League, joined Ferdinand, in return for a promise of Frederick's electoral post; even the Lutheran elector of Saxony joined the Catholic Ferdinand, who also secured the neutrality of the Protestant Union. England also remained neutral, even though, as a Protestant, Frederick was very popular in his father-in-law's kingdom. In Bohemia, Maximilian and the Catholic forces won the Battle of the White Mountain (November 8, 1620). Derisively nicknamed "the Winter King" because of his short tenure, Frederick fled, and Ferdinand made the Bohemian throne hereditary in his own family. With the aid of the Jesuits, he enforced Catholicism and abolished toleration for Utraquists and Calvinists, but granted it temporarily to Lutherans because of his obligations to the elector of Saxony. He executed the Czech leaders of the rebellion, confiscated their lands, and permitted terrible destruction in Bohemia.

The continued presence of Spanish forces in the Palatinate posed a threat to others. The Protestant king Christian IV of Denmark (1588–1648) feared the Hapsburgs would move northward to the Baltic; the French faced a new Hapsburg encirclement; and the Dutch were menaced by an immediate Spanish attack. The Dutch made an alliance with Christian IV, and another with the fugitive Frederick of the Palatinate, agreeing to subsidize his reconquest of his Rhenish lands. Had Frederick accepted a proposal of the Spanish to return to the Palatinate under their auspices, there might have been no Thirty Years' War; but he turned it down. When fighting resumed, Frederick was routed again, whereupon Ferdinand transferred the Palatine electorate to Maximilian (1625).

In France, meantime, Cardinal Richelieu, who was emerging as chief minister of Louis

XIII (reigned 1610–1643), fully recognized the Hapsburg danger. Richelieu was ready to arrange a dynastic marriage between the future Charles I of England and Louis XIII's sister, Henrietta Maria, and to make an alliance with other Protestants—Frederick, the Dutch, Christian IV of Denmark, and also Gustavus Adolphus, the Lutheran king of Sweden. Richelieu could count on the understanding of Pope Urban VIII, who felt that the fulfillment of Hapsburg ambitions would be bad for the interests of the Church. By the summer of 1624 the new coalition was in being. But Spanish victories in Holland (1625) and the unwillingness of Gustavus Adolphus to serve under the Danes spoiled the plan. Christian IV now had to fight for the Protestants alone, thus inaugurating the Danish phase of the war.

### The Danish Period, 1625-1629

A vigorous and ambitious monarch, King Christian IV (1588–1648) had increased his royal power by taking full advantage of the increased authority that Lutheranism gave to the king. When he intervened in the war, he sought not only to defend his coreligionists but also to extend Danish political and economic hegemony over northern Germany. Still another factor now entered the struggle, the famous—and infamous—private army of Wallenstein (1583–1634). This general, though born of a German Protestant family in Bohemia, was reared a Catholic and fought on the imperial side. His army was recruited and paid by himself, and lived off the land by requisitions and plunderings, sometimes at the expense of imperial and Catholic sympathizers. Wallenstein, who had bought up huge tracts of Bohemian real estate confiscated from Czech rebels, was in fact a German condottiere, a private citizen seeking to become a ruling prince, perhaps even dreaming of a united German empire, no longer the old medieval successor to Charlemagne's empire, but a fine, new-model of monarchy. He never came close to success, but his army was a major factor in the war at its most critical period. Together with the forces of the Catholic League under the command of Count Tilly, Wallenstein's armies defeated the Danes and moved northward into Danish territory.

Then, at the height of the imperial and Catholic success, Ferdinand and his advisers overreached themselves. By the Edict of Restitution and the Treaty of Lübeck in 1629, they sought to take the fullest advantage of their victories. The Edict of Restitution not only reaffirmed the Augsburg exclusion of the Calvinists and Protestant radicals from toleration but also demanded the restoration of all ecclesiastical estates that had passed from Catholic to Lutheran hands since 1551, *three generations before*. The Treaty of Lübeck allowed Christian IV to recover his lands, but it exacted from him a promise not to intervene in Germany. This seemed to the outside world a sign that Hapsburg power was actually spreading to the Baltic, a region thoroughly Protestant and hitherto only on the margin of imperial control. The old pattern was then repeated. The Hapsburgs on the wave of success went outside the bounds of their customary spheres of influence; those upon whose spheres they thus encroached fought back against the trespass; the trespasser was finally forced to withdraw.

More and more the Emperor Ferdinand became indebted to the ambitious Wallenstein, and less and less could he control him. Wallenstein planned to found a new Baltic trading company with the remains of the Hanseatic League, and by opening the Baltic to the Spaniards make possible a complete victory over the Dutch. When Ferdinand asked him for troops to use in Italy against the French, Wallenstein, intent on his northern plans, refused to send them because Gustavus Adolphus of Sweden had decided to attack the imperial forces in Germany. Soon Ferdinand dismissed Wallenstein, leaving Maximilian of Bavaria, who was placated by Wallenstein's departure, and Count Tilly in command of the imperial forces. If Ferdinand had next placated the Protestants as well by revoking the Edict of Restitution, peace might have been possible. But he refused to do so, and the war entered its Swedish phase.

### The Swedish Period, 1630-1635

Called "the Lion" or "the Hurricane" of the north, Gustavus Adolphus (reigned 1611–1632) was a much stronger Protestant champion than

Christian had been. Like Christian, Gustavus had ambitions for political control over northern Germany, and he hoped, too, that Sweden might assume the old Hanseatic economic leadership. He had tamed the unruly Swedish nobility, given his country an efficient government and a sound economy, taken lessons from the Dutch in military tactics, and proved himself and his armies against Russians and Poles by establishing a Swedish foothold on the south shores of the Baltic. A Lutheran, tolerant of Calvinists, he brought a large, well-disciplined army of Swedes, Finns, and Lapps, equipped with hymnbooks, and added to them all the recruits, even prisoners, that he could induce to join his forces. Sharing their hardships, he usually restrained them from plunder. Richelieu agreed to subsidize his forces, and Gustavus agreed not to fight against Maximilian and to guarantee freedom of worship for Catholics. The Protestant electors of Saxony and Brandenburg denounced the Edict of Restitution, and mobilized, in part to revive the Protestant cause, but also to protect the Germans against the Swedes.

German Protestant hesitation ended after a Catholic victory that probably did more to harm the Catholic cause than a defeat. The fall and sack of Magdeburg, the "Maiden City" of the Protestants and a great symbol of their cause, is one of those events that should warn the student of international politics that he must not leave moral forces out of his calculations. Magdeburg was taken by storm by the imperialists in May 1631, and was almost wholly destroyed by fire and pillage. The imperial general Pappenheim, who commanded at the storming of the walls, estimated that twenty thousand people were killed. Each side sought to blame the sack on the other and to enlist in its cause public opinion all over Europe. A volume issued in 1931 on the three-hundredth anniversary of the sack of Magdeburg takes forty-six pages to list contemporary accounts in European newspapers (then in their infancy), pamphlets, broadsides, popular songs, and cartoons. The Protestants accused the imperial commander-in-chief, Tilly, of actually planning the destruction of the city and the killing of its inhabitants, an accusation from which most historians absolve him, for the imperial troops clearly got out of hand. The Catholics countered by accusing the Protestants of setting the fires themselves as a deliberate "scorched-earth" policy. But the Protestants were the sufferers, and in the long run, as the

*The siege of Magdeburg, 1631.*

outpourings of the press took effect, their cause was strengthened.

Now the Protestant elector of Brandenburg had to ally himself with Gustavus, and so did the Protestant elector of Saxony, threatened by Tilly's starving troops. At Breitenfeld in September 1631, Gustavus defeated Tilly; combined with a defeat of the Spaniards off the Dutch coast, this turned the tide against the Hapsburgs. The Saxons invaded Bohemia and recaptured Prague in the name of Frederick of the Palatinate, while Gustavus invaded the Catholic lands of south-central Germany, taking Frankfurt and Mainz, and obtaining the alliance of many princes and free cities. In the crisis, Ferdinand turned back to Wallenstein, who consented to return to his command.

Gustavus had been more successful than Richelieu, his sponsor, had expected; indeed, too successful, since not only the Hapsburgs but Maximilian and the Catholic League, still friends of France, were suffering from the Swedes. Gustavus was planning to reorganize all Germany, to unite Lutheran and Calvinist churches, and even to become emperor—aims opposed by all the German princes, Catholic and Protestant alike. But the strength of Gustavus' position declined: his allies were untrustworthy and his enemies, Maximilian and Wallenstein, drew together. In November 1632 the Swedes won the battle of Lützen, defeating Wallenstein; Gustavus Adolphus, however, was killed.

Once more a moment had arrived when peace might have been possible, yet the fighting, and the plague, famine, and death accompanying it, continued. The pope, suspect among the cardinals as hostile to the Catholic cause, wanted peace. Richelieu preferred war, in order to further French aims in the Rhineland; the Swedes needed to protect their heavy investment and come out of the fighting with some territory; the Spaniards hoped that Gustavus' death meant that the Hapsburg cause could be saved and the Dutch defeated. Gustavus' chancellor, Oxenstierna, an able diplomat, was recognized by the German Protestants in 1633 as chief of the Protestant cause.

Wallenstein negotiated with the enemies of the empire (he wanted the French to recognize him as king of Bohemia); his army began to dribble away and he was again dismissed by the emperor Ferdinand, who suspected him of treachery. On February 24, 1634, an English mercenary in the imperial service murdered Wallenstein and won an imperial reward. At Nordlingen, in September 1634, the forces of Ferdinand defeated the Protestants, thereby lessening the influence of Sweden and making Cardinal Richelieu the chief strategist for the Protestant cause, which now became the Bourbon cause.

## The Swedish and French Period, 1635-1648

The remaining years of the Thirty Years' War were years of Hapsburg-Bourbon conflict, a sequel to the Hapsburg–Valois wars. The Protestant commander had to promise future toleration for Catholicism in Germany, and undertake to keep on fighting indefinitely in exchange for French men and money. More and more the original religious character of the war became transformed into a purely dynastic and political struggle. The armies themselves on both sides were made up of a mixture of men from just about every nationality in Europe; they fought as professional soldiers, changing sides frequently, and taking their women and children with them everywhere. On the imperial side camp followers were kept in some kind of order by officials known informally as "provosts of the harlots."

In 1635 the emperor Ferdinand at last relinquished the Edict of Restitution and made a compromise peace with the elector of Saxony. Most of the other Lutheran princes signed also. Alarmed by the imperial gains and by the renewed activity of the Spaniards in the Low Countries, Richelieu made new arrangements with Oxenstierna in Germany and a new alliance with the Dutch. No longer confining himself to the role of subsidizer, he declared war on Spain. The war would go on, though the only German allies the French and Swedes still had were a few Calvinist princes.

A great Dutch naval victory over Spain (1639) put an end to the power of the Spanish navy, which had been declining for some years. The power of Spain was further sapped by unrest in Catalonia and by the revolt (1640) of Portugal, which Philip II had annexed in 1580 and which now proceeded to reestablish its independence. The death of Richelieu (1642) and of Louis XIII

*Etching by Jacques Callot depicting the return home of mercenaries from the Thirty Years' War.*

(1643) did not alter French policy. Within a few days after the death of Louis, the French defeated the Spaniards at Rocroy so thoroughly that Spain was knocked out of the war, and in fact out of the competition for European hegemony. The dreams of Charles V and Philip II ended here.

Two peace conferences now opened in the northwestern area of Germany called Westphalia: between Hapsburgs and Swedes at Osnabrück, and between Hapsburgs and French not far away at Münster. At Osnabrück proceedings were delayed by the sudden Swedish invasion of Denmark, where Christian IV had shown his jealousy of rising Swedish power. At Münster, the French refused to treat with a Spanish delegate: they wished to make peace only with the Austrian Hapsburgs. The Baltic quarrel petered out when Christina, Gustavus Adolphus' daughter, who greatly wanted peace, became queen of Sweden in 1644.

The problems for settlement were many and delicate, the negotiations complex; differences between the allies that had been unimportant during open warfare proved critical when it came to a religious settlement. The meetings dragged on for several years while the fighting and destruction continued. The Dutch made a separate peace with the Spaniards, and pulled out of the French alliance after they learned of secret French negotiations with Spain hostile to their interests. French victories forced the wavering emperor Ferdinand III (reigned 1637–1657) to agree to the terms that had been so painstakingly hammered out, and on October 24, 1648, the Peace of Westphalia put an end to the Thirty Years' War.

## The Peace of Westphalia

In religion the terms of the peace extended the *cuius regio eius religio* principle of the Augsburg settlement to Calvinists as well as to Lutherans and Catholics. Princes could still "determine" the faith of their territories, but the right of dissidents to emigrate was recognized. In most of Protestant Germany multiplicity of sects was in fact accepted. On the vexing question of ecclesiastical reservation the year 1624 was designated by compromise as the normal year for establishing the status of Church property; for the Protestants this was a great improvement over the Edict of Restitution. States forcibly converted to Catholicism during the war won the right to revert to Protestantism; for Protestants in Hapsburg territories, however, there was no toleration.

Territorially, though some of the separate German states came out well, Germany herself was a victim. France secured part of Alsace and sovereignty over the long-occupied bishoprics of Metz, Toul, and Verdun. Sweden received most of Pomerania, along the Baltic shore of Germany, a large cash indemnity with which to pay the huge armies still mobilized, and three votes in the German Diet. As recompense for the loss of Pomerania, Brandenburg received the Archbishopric of Magdeburg and several other bishoprics. The family of Maximilian of Bavaria kept the electorate of the Palatinate and a part of its territory; the rest was returned to the son of Frederick who was restored as an elector, thus raising the total number of electors to eight. German particularism gained, as the individual German states secured the right to conduct their own foreign affairs, making treaties among themselves and with foreign powers if these were not directed against the emperor. This last was a face-saving for the Hapsburgs, but the fact that the constituent states now had their own foreign services, their own armies, their own finances—three obvious earmarks of "independence" in our state system—is clear evidence that the Holy Roman Empire of the German nation was no longer a viable political entity. The Westphalian settlement also formally recognized the independence of two smaller states, the Swiss Confederation, the nucleus of which had first broken away from Hapsburg control during the later Middle Ages, and the United Netherlands of the Dutch, already independent in fact for more than half a century.

Despite the peace, the danger was great that fighting would resume. Sweden had 100,000 soldiers in arms in Germany, of whom only a few were Swedes; the rest were professional fighting men whose whole life was war. A similar problem of demobilization and resettlement faced the imperial authorities. Many soldiers engaged themselves as mercenaries to any ruler who would hire them, and some simply became brigands. Moreover, since the treaty did not provide a means for enforcing the religious property settlement, any attempt to recover lost property might provoke a new fight. The huge amount of money to be paid the Swedes gave rise to bitterness that itself endangered the peace.

For more than two centuries after 1648, the Thirty Years' War was blamed for everything that later went wrong in Germany. We now know that the figures given in contemporary sources are inflated and unreliable; sometimes the number of villages allegedly destroyed in a given district was larger than the whole number of villages that had ever existed there. Also scholars traditionally failed to note that the economic decline in Germany had begun well before the war opened in 1618. Yet, even when we make allowances for these early exaggerations, we must note that contemporaries everywhere in Germany felt the catastrophe to have been overwhelming. The over-all diminution in population was from about 21 million in 1618 to less than 13½ million in 1648; the suffering of individuals was indeed extreme.

In assessing intangible damages some historians trace to this disastrous war aspects of modern Germany that have made her a disturbing influence in the modern world. They point to a national sense of inferiority heightened by her delayed achievement of national unity, a lack of the slow ripening in self-government that a more orderly growth in early modern times might have encouraged, a too strong need for authority and obedience brought out in response to the anarchic conditions of the seventeenth century. These are dangerously big generalizations that are at most suggestive; they can by no means be proved.

It is true, however, that the final outcome of the war raised almost as many problems as it solved. Neither the pope, who denounced the Peace of Westphalia, nor many Protestants, who felt betrayed by it, were satisfied. Despite the great loss of life, the war made little change in the social hierarchy of Germany; once the fighting was over, the nobility often succeeded in forcing the peasants back onto the soil by denying them the right to leave the village or to engage in home industry. Politically the main change was probably the further shrinkage in the power of the empire. The recognition that individual German states could conduct their own foreign policies was a triumph for German particularism, the culmination of three centuries of particularist gains since the Golden

Europe in 1648
Brandenburg-Prussia
Austrian Hapsburg Lands
Spanish Hapsburg Lands
Swedish possessions
Venetian possessions
Ottoman Empire
Boundary of the Holy Roman Empire
Battle sites
Approximate division line between Puritans and Cavaliers in England, May, 1643
NORWAY
Oslo
SCOTLAND
Edinburgh
Dunbar
Berwick
North Sea
ULSTER
Drogheda
IRELAND
Dublin
Wexford
Preston
Marston Moor
ENGLAND
Nottingham
Worcester
Naseby
London
DENMARK
Copenhagen
Lübeck
Hamburg
Texel
Bremen
UNITED NETHERLANDS
Osnabruck
Münster
WEST-PHALIA
THE
EMPIRE
Magdeburg
Lützen
SAXONY
POMERANIA
BRANDENBURG
Berlin
Elbe R.
Oder R.
SPANISH NETHERLANDS
Rhine R.
Atlantic Ocean
Seine R.
Paris
Verdun
PALATINATE
Heidelberg
Metz
Toul
ALSACE
Strasbourg
Prague
BOHEMIA
Nantes
Orléans
Loire R.
FRANCE
FRANCHE COMTÉ
BAVARIA
Danube R.
AUSTRIA
Vienna
STYRIA
SWITZERLAND
VALTELLINE
Geneva
TYROL
CARINTHIA
CARNIOLA
Bordeaux
SAVOY
PIEDMONT
MILAN
Rhône R.
Po R.
Venice
Avignon (to the Papacy)
Genoa
Marseilles
Florence
PAPAL STATES
VENETIAN REPUBLIC
PORTUGAL
Burgos
Ebro R.
Lisbon
Tagus R.
SPAIN
Madrid
Barcelona
CORSICA (to Genoa)
Rome
BALEARIC IS.
Valencia
Guadalquivir R.
Seville
Granada
SARDINIA
NAPLES
Naples
Mediterranean Sea
Palermo
SICILY
ALGIERS (Tributary to Ottoman Empire)
TUNIS
MALTA
0
500
Miles

FINLAND
L. Onega
L. Ladoga
Gulf of Finland
INGRIA
ESTONIA
LIVONIA
Novgorod
Pskov
COURLAND
LITHUANIA
W. Dvina R.
Vilna
Smolensk
PRUSSIA
POLAND
Warsaw
Vistula R.
Kiev
Dnieper R.
Dniester R.
RUSSIA
Moscow
Volga R.
Oka R.
Ural R.
Don R.
Caspian Sea
CRIMEA
MOLDAVIA
TRANSYLVANIA
WALLACHIA
Belgrade
Danube R.
Morava R.
Black Sea
Constantinople
Vardar R.
Salonika
OTTOMAN EMPIRE
Tigris R.
Euphrates R.
Aegean Sea
Athens
RHODES
CYPRUS
(to Venice)
CRETE

Bull of 1356. Now direct Hapsburg power was limited to Hapsburg lands, and such states as Bavaria, Saxony, and, above all, Brandenburg-Prussia could move to the fore in German affairs. Finally, non-Austrian Germans harbored bitter resentment against the Hapsburgs for having fought this most terrible of dynastic and religious wars simply to protect family interests.

## Reading Suggestions on Dynastic and Religious Warfare


GENERAL ACCOUNTS

*The New Cambridge Modern History* (Cambridge University Press). The first four volumes of this lengthy collaborative project, still in the process of publication, contain much information on the topics covered in this chapter; the bibliographies are not yet available.

H. G. Koenigsberger and G. L. Mosse, *Europe in the Sixteenth Century* (Holt, 1968). An excellent up-to-date survey, with useful bibliographical footnotes.

C. J. Friedrich, *The Age of the Baroque, 1610–1660* (*Torchbooks). Firm and provocative volume in the "Rise of Modern Europe" series, with a very full bibliography.

J. H. Elliott, *Europe Divided, 1559–1598* (*Torchbooks). Useful recent survey.

H. Trevor-Roper, ed., *The Age of Expansion* (McGraw-Hill, 1968). Sumptuously illustrated collaborative volume touching on many topics in European and world history from the mid-sixteenth to mid-seventeenth century.

D. Ogg, *Europe in the Seventeenth Century,* 8th ed. (*Collier), and G. N. Clark, *The Seventeenth Century,* 2nd ed. (*Oxford Univ. Press). Two good general histories, very different from one another in focus and organization.

*The Cambridge Economic History of Europe.* Vol. IV: *The Economy of Expanding Europe in the Sixteenth and Seventeenth Centuries* (Cambridge Univ. Press, 1967). Expert chapters on selected aspects of the economy rather than an overall survey.

E. F. Rice, Jr., *The Foundations of Early Modern Europe, 1460–1559,* and R. S. Dunn, *The Age of Religious Wars, 1559–1689* (*Norton). Very recent and very good introductory sketches.

WAR AND DIPLOMACY, 1494–1598

L. Dehio, *The Precarious Balance: Four Centuries of the European Power Struggle* (*Vintage). A German historian interprets the shifting balance of power, beginning with the sixteenth century.

G. Mattingly, *Renaissance Diplomacy* (*Penguin). A stimulating and indispensable introduction.

C. Petrie, *Earlier Diplomatic History, 1492–1713* (Macmillan, 1949). A useful manual.

C. H. Carter, *The Secret Diplomacy of the Habsburgs, 1598–1625* (Columbia Univ. Press, 1964.) An instructive case study in diplomatic history.

C. W. C. Oman, *A History of the Art of War in the Sixteenth Century* (Dutton, 1937). Highly interesting study of a neglected aspect of history.

J. F. C. Fuller, *A Military History of the Western World,* 3 vols. (*Funk & Wagnalls). By an informative and somewhat unorthodox general; the first two volumes contain material relevant to this chapter.

SPAIN

J. Lynch, *Spain under the Habsburgs*, 2 vols. (Oxford Univ. Press, 1964, 1969). A thorough, up-to-date, scholarly study; the first volume treats the sixteenth century, and the second the seventeenth.

J. H. Elliott, *Imperial Spain, 1469–1716* (*Mentor). Another useful recent account.

R. B. Merriman, *The Rise of the Spanish Empire in the Old World and the New*, 4 vols. (Macmillan, 1918–1934). Volume III of this older standard work deals with Charles V, and Vol. IV with Philip II.

R. T. Davies, *The Golden Century of Spain, 1501–1621* (*Torchbooks) and *Spain in Decline, 1621–1700* (*Papermac). Readable general accounts.

K. Brandi, *The Emperor Charles V* (*Humanities). A very complete study of the ruler of a trouble-ridden dynastic conglomerate.

C. Petrie, *Philip II of Spain* (Norton, 1963). An interesting and, for an Englishman, impartial biography.

J. H. Elliott, *The River of Catalans: A Study in the Decline of Spain, 1598–1640* (Cambridge Univ. Press, 1963). An important monograph.

FRANCE

J. E. Neale, *The Age of Catherine de' Medici* (*Torchbooks). Excellent introduction to the French civil and religious wars.

A. Guérard, *France in the Classical Age: The Life and Death of an Ideal* (*Torchbooks). Lively and highly personal interpretation.

A. J. Grant, *The Huguenots* (Butterworth, 1934). Brief and reasonably dispassionate.

J. W. Thompson, *The Wars of Religion in France, 1559–1576* (Univ. of Chicago Press, 1909). Detailed narrative.

J. R. Major, *The Estates General of 1560* (Princeton Univ. Press, 1951). An important monograph by a scholar who has published other studies on French representative institutions.

W. J. Stankiewicz, *Politics and Religion in Seventeenth Century France* (Univ. of California Press, 1960). Goes back to the *politiques* of the late sixteenth century.

Q. Hurst, *Henry of Navarre* (Appleton, 1938). Standard biography.

N. L. Roelker, ed., *The Paris of Henry of Navarre* (Harvard Univ. Press, 1958). Selections from the informative *Mémoires-Journaux* of Pierre de l'Estoile, a rich source of social history.

ENGLAND

C. Read, *The Tudors* (*Norton). Highly readable introduction to the interrelations of personalities and politics.

S. T. Bindoff, *Tudor England* (*Pelican). Sound, scholarly introduction.

J. D. Mackie, *The Earlier Tudors, 1485–1558* (Clarendon, 1952), and J. B. Black, *The Reign of Elizabeth, 1558–1603*, 2nd ed. (Clarendon, 1960). Comprehensive, scholarly volumes in the "Oxford History of England."

G. R. Elton, *The Tudor Revolution in Government* (*Cambridge Univ. Press). Important study of the shift to a bureaucratic state.

D. L. Keir, *Constitutional History of Modern Britain since 1485* (*Norton). A good introduction to a difficult topic.

J. J. Scarisbrick, *Henry VIII* (Univ. of California, 1968). The first new scholarly biography in over half a century.

J. E. Neale, *Queen Elizabeth I: A Biography* (*Anchor); *Elizabeth I and Her Parliaments,* 2 vols. (*Norton); *The Elizabethan House of Commons,* rev ed. (*Penguin). By a ranking expert on Elizabethan politics.

C. Read, *Government of England under Elizabeth* (*University Press of Virginia); *Mr. Secretary Walsingham and the Policy of Queen Elizabeth* (Harvard Univ. Press, 1925). By another ranking expert on the Elizabethan field.

E. Jenkins, *Elizabeth the Great* (*Capricorn). Sound biography focusing on the queen as a person.

J. M. Levine, ed., *Elizabeth I* (*Spectrum). Appraisals of the great queen.

W. P. Haugaard, *Elizabeth and the English Reformation* (Cambridge Univ. Press, 1968). Recent scholarly evaluation.

G. Mattingly, *The Armada* (*Houghton). A truly great history.

A. L. Rowse, *The England of Elizabeth: The Structure of Society* (*Macmillan) and *The Expansion of Elizabethan England* (St. Martin's, 1955). Complementary studies by a maverick English scholar rebelling against academic caution.

A. Fraser, *Mary, Queen of Scots* (Delacorte, 1969). Sound recent biography of Elizabeth's impulsive antagonist.

K. R. Andrews, *Elizabethan Privateering during the Spanish War* (Cambridge Univ. Press, 1964). Very readable scholarly monograph.

H. Haydn, ed., *Portable Elizabethan Reader* (*Viking). A good anthology.

L. B. Wright and V. A. LaMar, eds., *Life and Letters in Tudor and Stuart England* (Cornell Univ. Press, 1962). A miscellany addressed to the general reader with much interesting material.

THE DUTCH REPUBLIC

C. J. Cadoux, *Philip of Spain and the Netherlands* (Butterworth, 1947). A moderate restatement of the Protestant and liberal position.

P. Geyl, *The Revolt of the Netherlands, 1555–1609* (*Barnes and Noble) and *The Netherlands in the Seventeenth Century,* 2 vols. (Barnes and Noble, 1961, 1964). Detailed studies by a distinguished Dutch historian who regrets the disruption of the unity of the Low Countries. A briefer statement may be found in his *History of the Low Countries* (St. Martin's, 1964).

C. V. Wedgwood, *William the Silent* (*Norton). Sound biography of the Dutch national hero.

V. Barbour, *Capitalism in Amsterdam in the Seventeenth Century* (*Ann Arbor). Illuminating study of an important factor in Dutch success.

GERMANY AND THE THIRTY YEARS' WAR

H. Holborn, *A History of Modern Germany*. Vol. 1: *The Reformation* (Knopf, 1959). This authoritative study goes down to 1648.

C. V. Wedgwood, *The Thirty Years' War* (*Anchor). Full and generally well-balanced narrative.

S. H. Steinberg, *The "Thirty Years' War" and the Conflict for European Hegemony, 1600–1660* (*Norton). Briefer, more recent account.

T. K. Rabb, ed., *The Thirty Years' War: Problems of Motive, Extent, and Effect* (*Heath). Differing views on these controversial questions.

M. Roberts, *Gustavus Adolphus: A History of Sweden, 1611–1632,* 2 vols. (Longmans, 1953, 1958). Sympathetic detailed biography.

HISTORICAL FICTION

S. Putnam, ed., *The Portable Cervantes* (*Viking). Selections from *Don Quixote* in the best available translation.

H. J. C. von Grimmelshausen, *Simplicius Simplicissimus* (*Liberal Arts). Picaresque novel written in the seventeenth century and set against the background of the Thirty Years' War, which is realistically depicted.

W. Scott, *Kenilworth* (*Airmont). By the famous Romantic novelist. The setting is Elizabethan England.

# 14

# *The Expansion of Europe*

## Fifteenth Through Seventeenth Centuries

*Above: Early sixteenth-century stone carving of the Aztec god Zipe Totec. Above right: Santo Domingo in 1590. Right: The Great Wall of China, built in the third centry B.C. to guarantee an isolation that proved elusive.*

### I Introduction

Many atlases provide a series of maps showing the "known world" at certain periods—starting usually from the known world of Homer, little more than the eastern Mediterranean and its fringes. Next come the known worlds of Alexander the Great and the Romans, centered still on the Mediterranean, hazy or blank for much of interior Europe and Africa, with only the western fringes of Asia known, and with the Americas still unsuspected. Then from late medieval explorations through the great modern discoveries, the series goes on to the full fruition of geographical knowledge, which happened only yesterday. There is a revealing symbolism in that phrase "known world," for we really mean "known to interested members of Greco-Roman society and its Christian successor states of the West." The Chinese, too, had a "known world," as did the Red Indians.

CIVITAS S. DOMI
NICI IN HISPANI
OLA SITA
NEC SPE NEC METV

### Ancient and Modern Expansion Contrasted

In the prehistoric ages of movement and migration, which included such daring feats as the Polynesian settlement of the Pacific islands, the movers kept no written records and no concrete ties with their place of origins. They were not societies in expansion, but groups of individuals on the move. The expansion of the West was a very different thing. From the very start in ancient Greece and Rome, records were kept, indeed maps were made, and the nucleus always remained in touch with its offshoots. Western society has expanded *as a society*, often as a group of states.

The modern Western expansion, which began in the mid-fifteenth century, however, differed in important ways from the expansion that had carried the cultures of the ancient Near East as far as western and northern Europe. In the first place, this modern expansion was much faster and covered more ground. Although some secrets of the Arctic and the Antarctic, some details of the wilder interiors of the world, were not known to us until the twentieth century, it is broadly true that the whole world was revealed to Europeans within the two and a half or three centuries after 1450—within four long lifetimes. In the second place, this modern expansion was the first time our Western society crossed great oceans. Ancient and medieval Western navigation had clung to the narrow seas and the shorelines. The ancients had even commonly drawn up their boats on land to spend the night. Now Westerners crossed the Atlantic and the Pacific, far from the protecting land. In the third place, this expansion carried Westerners well outside the orbit of relations with Byzantines and Muslims, who were also successors to the cultures of Socrates and Christ, into relations with a bewildering variety of races, creeds, and cultures, from naked savages to cultivated Chinese. Not since the Germanic peoples had been tamed and converted in the early Middle Ages had Westerners come into close contact with primitive peoples. Finally, and of very great importance, expanding Europe possessed a margin of superior material and technological strength that lasted up to our own time, and enabled Western society to do what no society had ever done before—extend its influence around the world.

An important element of that margin was the possession of firearms; yet firearms could be legally or illegally acquired by non-Europeans, and very soon were. The strength by which Europeans overcame the world was not quite so simple as the possession of firearms. It was a compound of technological and economic superiority and of superior political and social organization, which in turn permitted superior military organization. This superiority was not applied from a common Western center, but rather by half a dozen competing Western nations, each anxious to cut the others' throats, and quite willing to arm and organize natives against its Western competitors. Frenchmen in North America armed the Indians against the British and the British armed them against the French. Yet not even the Iroquois were able to maintain themselves against white society. French, British, Portuguese, Dutch, Spanish, and later German and American peoples intrigued against one another in the Far East, and yet not until the mid-twentieth century did any Asian nation (save only Japan, and Japan not until about 1900) really compete successfully in war and politics with a Western land. So great was Western superiority that the rivalries of competing powers did not delay the process of expansion but probably stimulated and hastened it.

How far this physical superiority in the expansion of the West throughout the world was—and is—also a spiritual and moral superiority is a problem we in the West today cannot answer as firmly as did our fathers. But you will not understand the successful expansion of Europe if you do not realize that those who carried out the expansion, though moved often by greed, by sheer despair over their lot at home, by the Renaissance enthusiasm for new things, and by many other motives, were also moved by the conviction that they were doing God's work, the work of civilization, that they were carrying with them a better way of life. They were confident and energetic people, capable of great endurance and courage, and they have made over the face of the globe.

### The Motives and Nature of Early Modern Expansion

Why did men living on the Atlantic coasts of Europe in the second half of the fifteenth century venture out on an ocean that ancient and medieval mariners had not seriously tried to penetrate? While we cannot answer the question with finality, so small a thing as the magnetic compass helped make ocean voyages possible. Without the compass, earlier mariners had been helpless, except when clear weather gave them sun or stars as guides. The actual origins of the compass are obscure, but we know that by the beginning of the fifteenth century it was familiar to European sailors and that it was a normal part of navigation by the time of Columbus. Better instruments and better methods of determining a ship's position at sea were also fully in hand by the late fifteenth century. Shipbuilders were getting away from older types of traditional Mediterranean ships, building somewhat longer and narrower vessels that could stand the long swells of the ocean, deliberately trying to find the kind of ship that could be handled in these unknown waters. Technologically, the way was ready for the great explorations.

Politically, the control of the usual trade routes in the Near East by the new Ottoman Turkish power turned men's minds to the search for another way to India and China. Yet the Italians, especially the Venetians and Genoese, who were already installed in the Near East, were making arrangements with the Turks. More important, actually, was the fact that Spain, Portugal, France, and England were all rising in political and economic activity, all on the way up that had been shown them by the Italians. Blocked in the Near East, in part by Italians, they eyed the unoccupied and nearby Atlantic. To those who interpret everything in terms of economics, Renaissance men discovered new worlds because the aggressive drives natural to nascent capitalism sent them on their way.

Yet technology and the politics of the trade routes had to be taken advantage of by men, men in the state of mind that sent Columbus out across the unknown ocean—to see with his own eyes what was there, to test his theory that because the earth is round one can travel from Europe westward and reach Asia. The explorations of Europeans were guided in part by the new spirit of empirical science, the spirit that impelled men, if for instance they heard about the existence of unicorns, to go out and try to find some. Their medieval predecessors did not need to see a unicorn to believe in its existence. This new scientific spirit, however, did not immediately banish unicorns, mermaids, and sea serpents from men's minds. In fact, the first news of these strange worlds resulted in a whole new set of wonders, some real or merely exaggerated, which the publishing of accounts of travel brought to all Europe.

Nothing makes more clear the consecutive, planned, deliberately scientific nature of these early modern explorations and settlements than the contrast with the sporadic, unplanned, and perhaps wholly mythical earlier oceanic navigation. Tradition is full of these early voyages, and of Atlantis, a lost continent now sunk beneath the waves but once inhabited, which Plato and later commentators tell about. Irishmen, Norsemen, Breton fishermen, and others have all been credited with the "discovery" of America, a discovery that was never widely reported in the medieval West. Of all these tales of pre-Columbian discovery, that of the Vikings' reaching the North American continent about the end of the tenth century is most likely. There is not the slightest doubt that Norsemen reached Iceland and settled it, and that they had outposts in Greenland. Their traditional literature, the heroic poems known as sagas, credit Leif Ericson with reaching a Wineland (or Vineland), which most experts believe to have been some part of the New England or Canadian coast. It is quite possible that all during the Middle Ages, more probably toward their close, fishermen from northwest Europe fished the Grand Banks off the coast of Newfoundland. Yet even if hundreds of Europeans reached the New World before Columbus, they did not establish a permanent link between the two worlds; they were not explorers of the kind we are about to discuss, and they were, above all, not supported by an organized social purpose.

## II East by Sea to the Indies

### Prince Henry and the Portuguese

The first of the great names in modern expansion is not that of a bold explorer or conquistador, but that of an organizing genius who directed the work of others—in modern terms, a "planner." Prince Henry of Portugal, known as "the Navigator," lived from 1394 to 1460. He was a deeply religious man, and he may well have been moved above all by a desire to convert the populations of India and the Far East, whose existence had been well known to Westerners since the travels of Marco Polo in the thirteenth century. Indeed, there was a widespread conviction in the West that these distant peoples were in fact already Christian and for true salvation needed only to be brought in direct contact with the Roman Catholic church. One of the great medieval legends was that of Prester (that is, Priest) John, a powerful Christian ruler somewhere out in the East. Prester John was never found, and the Portuguese in India were soon disabused of their first notion that the Hindus—since they were not Muslims—must be Christians.

Prince Henry and his associates presumably also wanted to promote Portuguese commerce and national power as well as the Christian faith. They hoped to break the monopoly over the trade in gold from sub-Saharan Africa held by Arab merchants from North Africa. They went about their work carefully, sending out frequent well-equipped expeditions. In the Atlantic, their vessels discovered Madeira and the Azores, uninhabited islands where the Portuguese and other Europeans then began to settle. The main thrust southward gradually crept along the harsh desert coast of Africa where the Sahara meets the Atlantic, until in 1445 the Portuguese passed Cape Verde, where the land began to grow greener and to trend hopefully eastward. Whether Henry himself believed that Africa could be circumnavigated is not absolutely certain, but according to tradition the Phoenicians had done it, and Greco-Roman geographers had believed that Africa was surrounded by the ocean.

By 1472, after Prince Henry's death, the Portuguese reached the end of the bulge of West Africa at the Cameroons, and faced the disheartening fact that the coast was once more trending southward, not eastward. But they kept on, stimulated by royal patronage, and in the next generation two great explorers finished the job. In 1488, Bartholomeu Dias, blown far south by a great storm, turned northeast and found that he had rounded the great cape later called Good Hope. He was followed by Vasco da Gama, who set out in 1497 with four ships to reach India and worked northward along the east coast of Africa, coming soon to an area of Arab trading where the route to India was well known. Despite Arab jealousy of the intruder, da Gama secured a pilot and reached the Malabar coast of India at Calicut ten months and fourteen days out from Lisbon. The Portuguese now had an ocean route to the East.

On the next great voyage toward India, the Portuguese made a lucky strike that was to break the Spanish monopoly in South America and ensure that one of the great Latin-American states would be Portuguese in language and culture. Pedro Cabral, in 1500, started out to repeat da Gama's voyage to India. But by now the Portuguese were used to long voyages on the open ocean, far from sight of land, and they no longer needed to creep around the coast of Africa. Cabral kept boldly southward from the bulge of Africa, and was apparently blown somewhat westward of his course so that he made a landfall on the bulge of the South American continent in what is now Brazil. He at once detached a ship and sent it home to announce his discovery. Since the voyages of Columbus were well known to navigators by this time, some geographers think that Cabral set out deliberately to see what he could find south of the westward route Columbus had taken. Six years previously, in 1494, Spain and Portugal had by the Treaty of Tordesillas agreed to partition these new lands along a north-south line three hundred and seventy leagues (about a thousand miles) west of the Azores, so that Brazil fell quite definitely into the Portuguese sphere.

The main Portuguese push, however, was toward India and the Far East. The explorer was succeeded by that other characteristic agent of European expansion, the trader. But the trader by no means worked alone. He was aided and protected by the power of his state, which aimed to set up for its nationals a monopoly of trade with the newly discovered lands. The great figure of early Portuguese imperialism is Affonso de Albuquerque, governor of the Indies from 1509 to 1515, under whom the Portuguese founded their capital at Goa in India and from that base organized regular trade routes toward southeast Asia and China. By 1557 they had established a base at Macao on the China coast near Canton, and they had begun trade with the Japanese.

## Africa

The two new worlds thus opened to Europeans were very different both from Europe and

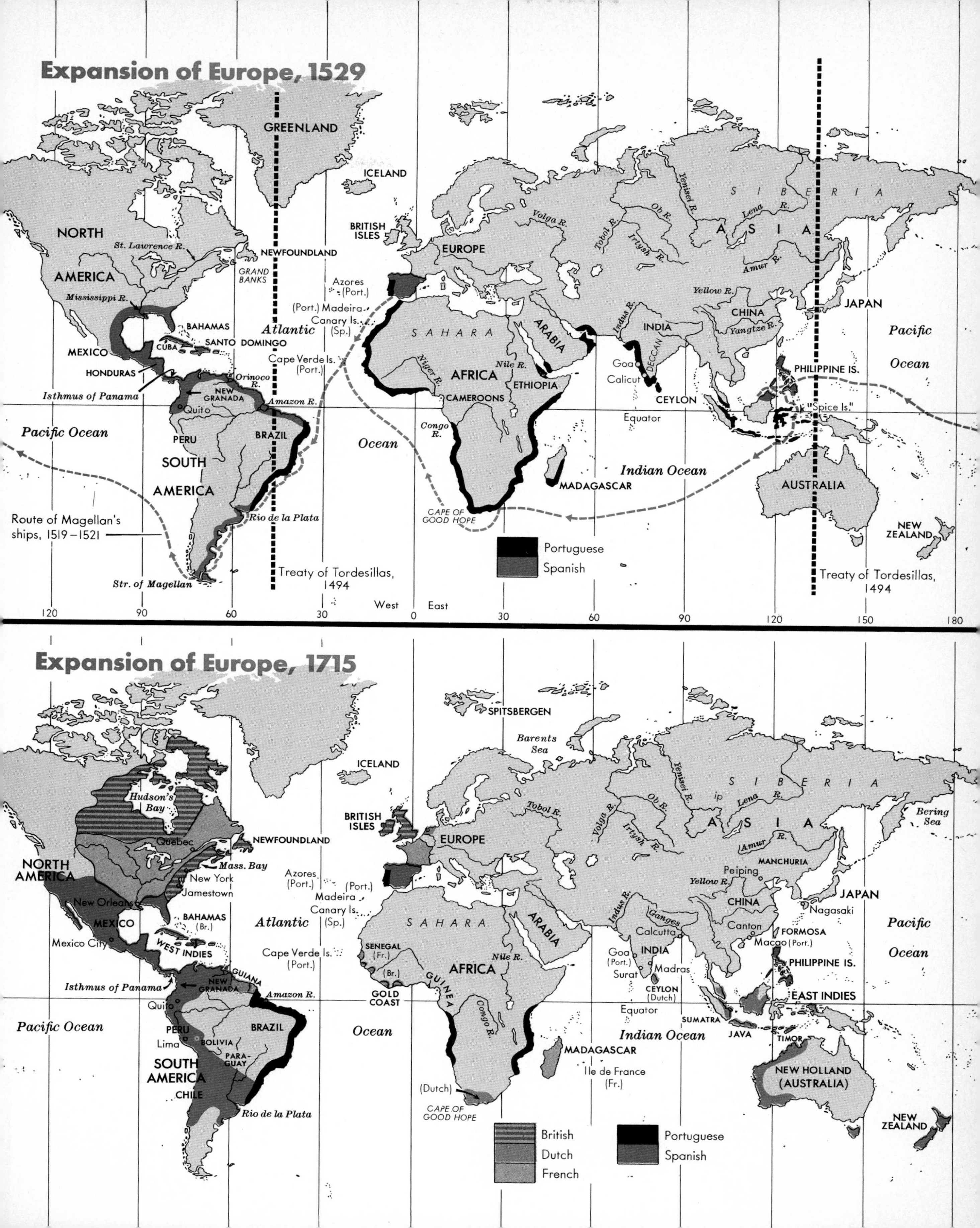
Expansion of Europe, 1529
GREENLAND
ICELAND
BRITISH ISLES
NEWFOUNDLAND
GRAND BANKS
NORTH AMERICA
St. Lawrence R.
Mississippi R.
Azores (Port.)
(Port.) Madeira
Canary Is. (Sp.)
Atlantic
BAHAMAS
CUBA
SANTO DOMINGO
MEXICO
HONDURAS
Cape Verde Is. (Port.)
Isthmus of Panama
Orinoco R.
NEW GRANADA
Quito
Amazon R.
Pacific Ocean
PERU
BRAZIL
SOUTH AMERICA
Ocean
Route of Magellan's ships, 1519–1521
Rio de la Plata
Str. of Magellan
Treaty of Tordesillas, 1494
EUROPE
SAHARA
AFRICA
Niger R.
Nile R.
ETHIOPIA
CAMEROONS
Congo R.
CAPE OF GOOD HOPE
MADAGASCAR
ARABIA
Volga R.
Tobol R.
Ob R.
Irtysh R.
Yenisei R.
Lena R.
SIBERIA
ASIA
Amur R.
Yellow R.
CHINA
Yangtze R.
JAPAN
Indus R.
INDIA
DECCAN
Goa
Calicut
CEYLON
Equator
Indian Ocean
PHILIPPINE IS.
"Spice Is."
Pacific
Ocean
AUSTRALIA
NEW ZEALAND
Portuguese
Spanish
Treaty of Tordesillas, 1494
120
90
60
30
West
0
East
30
60
90
120
150
180
Expansion of Europe, 1715
SPITSBERGEN
Barents Sea
ICELAND
Hudson's Bay
Quebec
NEWFOUNDLAND
BRITISH ISLES
EUROPE
NORTH AMERICA
Mass. Bay
New York
Jamestown
Azores (Port.)
(Port.) Madeira
Canary Is. (Sp.)
New Orleans
MEXICO
BAHAMAS (Br.)
Atlantic
Mexico City
WEST INDIES
Cape Verde Is. (Port.)
Isthmus of Panama
GUIANA
NEW GRANADA
Amazon R.
Quito
Pacific Ocean
PERU
Lima
BOLIVIA
BRAZIL
PARA-GUAY
SOUTH AMERICA
CHILE
Rio de la Plata
Ocean
SAHARA
SENEGAL (Fr.)
(Br.)
GOLD COAST
GUINEA
AFRICA
Nile R.
Congo R.
(Dutch)
CAPE OF GOOD HOPE
ARABIA
MADAGASCAR
Ile de France (Fr.)
Tobol R.
Volga R.
Ob R.
Irtysh R.
Yenisei R.
SIBERIA
Lena R.
ASIA
Amur R.
Bering Sea
MANCHURIA
Peiping
Yellow R.
CHINA
JAPAN
Nagasaki
Indus R.
Ganges
Calcutta
Goa (Port.)
INDIA
Surat
Madras
CEYLON (Dutch)
Equator
Indian Ocean
Canton
FORMOSA
Macao (Port.)
PHILIPPINE IS.
EAST INDIES
SUMATRA
JAVA
TIMOR
Pacific
Ocean
NEW HOLLAND (AUSTRALIA)
NEW ZEALAND
British
Dutch
French
Portuguese
Spanish

*A view of Macao, the Portuguese outpost in China, in 1598, by Theodore de Bry.*

from each other. Africa—excluding North Africa, from Morocco to Egypt, which had long been part of the Mediterranean world—was hot, relatively thinly populated, poor by current European standards. India, China, and much of southeast Asia were even then thickly populated, with great wealth accumulated in a few hands, with much that Europeans wanted in the way of spices, silks, and other luxuries. Africa was in a sense bypassed, though the many coastal stations that the Europeans founded soon carried on a flourishing trade in slaves. The African tribes on the great westward bulge of the continent had not been wholly out of touch with the more efficient societies to the north. Caravans organized by North African traders came across the Sahara to Timbuktu, on the upper Niger River, for gold and slaves and brought with them Islam and some of the wares of civilization. The present-day states of Mali and Ghana have taken the names of black empires which ruled over this area in the Middle Ages.

In central and southern Africa, the tribes were not far from the Stone Age. They were men without cities and states, men with cultures so different from those of Europe that few Europeans made any effort to understand them. Nor did the Europeans, at least in these centuries, do much to undermine these primitive cultures. Save for the enforced mass migration of blacks as slaves, most of them to the Americas, save for some trade in ivory and other tropical goods, Africa had for years little effect on Europe, and Europe had little effect on Africa. Except for South Africa, where the Dutch began settlement in the seventeenth century, Africa was not to be subject to colonialism until the partitions of the nineteenth century.

## India

The India that Europeans reached around Africa had been marginally in touch with Europe for several thousand years. Alexander the Great had campaigned in northern India, and throughout the Middle Ages the Arabs had served as a link in trade and in the transmission of such Indian inventions as Arabic numerals, which are actually Hindu in origin. Now a direct link was forged between the West and India, never to be loosened. The link did not take the form of union or assimilation, for West and East hardly communicated at the higher levels of cultural interchange. The Portuguese were contemptuous of the Indians once they discovered that they were not the Christians of Prester John. Among the Dutch, French, and British who followed the Portuguese to India, this attitude of contempt became set in the conventional idea of white superiority. While this feeling of European superiority has probably been exaggerated both in Western literary tradition and in the minds of educated Indians quick to take offense, still it was always present, most clearly reflected centuries later in Kipling's famous *Ballad of East and West:*

*Oh, East is East, and West is West, and never the twain shall meet,*
*Till Earth and Sky stand presently at God's great Judgment Seat. . . .*

Western superiority was at bottom a superiority on the battlefield. Long after the initial European monopoly of firearms had ended, a European or European-trained and commanded native army or navy could always subdue a native Asian army or navy. In India, at least, European domination was greatly helped by the political and military disunity of the subcontinent. When the Portuguese reached India, Muslim invaders were consolidating foreign rule of the sort that for thousands of years had periodically brought comparative order to northern India. The Muslim empire was misleadingly called Mogul (Mughal or Mongol), for its rulers were Turks from central Asia and its founder was a descendant of Tamerlane. It had little hold over the regions of southern India where Europeans established their footholds. Local Indian rulers, whether they were Muslim or Hindu in faith, were in intense rivalry and were a ready prey to European promises of aid. All the European powers found it easy, not merely to win Indian princes to their side, but to raise and train on their own responsibility native armies to fight under Portuguese, French, Dutch, or British flags.

Perhaps the lack of political and social integration in India is the basic reason why a few handfuls of Europeans were able to dominate the country until 1945. China, too, saw her armed forces beaten whenever they came into formal military conflict with European or European-trained armies or fleets; China, too, was forced to make to European nations all sorts of concessions—treaty ports, and above all extraterritoriality, that is, the right of Europeans to be tried in their own national courts for offenses committed on Chinese soil. Yet China, unlike India, was never "annexed" by a European power, never lost its "sovereignty." For China preserved a fairly strong central government, and had many strands of ethical and political unity that India lacked.

The variety and range of Indian life are extraordinary. Some of the more isolated parts of India in the Deccan or southern peninsula were inhabited by tribesmen of no higher level than many African tribesmen. Some, on the northern edges, were warrior tribesmen much like those of the highlands of Central Asia. In the great valleys of the Indus and the Ganges, and in the richer parts of the Deccan, there was a wealthy, populous society basically Hindu in culture, though when the Europeans arrived, it was dominated in many areas by invaders of Muslim faith and culture. Hindu society itself was the result of an amalgamation between earlier native stocks and invaders from the north who certainly spoke a language closely related to Greek, Latin, and indeed our own, and who probably were white "Indo-Europeans" or "Aryans." The early history of India, however, is most confusing, and we cannot tell how many these invaders were, or just where they came from, though the invasion apparently had taken place between 2000 and 1200 B.C. It seems almost certain that the white invaders' consciousness of differing from the natives is responsible basically for the characteristic Indian institution of *caste*.

According to the laws of caste, men and women were by the fact of birth settled for life in a closed group which pursued a given occupation and occupied a fixed position in society. When the Europeans reached India, there were apparently something over a thousand castes, including a group at the bottom without caste, the "untouchables." The ruling groups were of two main castes, the Brahmins or priests, and the Kshatriya or warriors. The great multiplicity of castes lay in the third group, the Vaisya or commonalty, and was based largely on vocation or trade. In theory, marriage between members of different castes was forbidden, as was change of caste through social mobility. In fact, in the centuries since the invasion by the "Indo-Europeans" considerable human intermixture had undoubtedly occurred. Yet even today the upper classes in most of India are of a lighter color than the lower.

The most striking thing about Indian culture was the high place occupied by the priestly caste, the Brahmins. The Brahmin faith has strains of a most otherworldly belief in the evils of the life of the flesh and the attainment of salvation by a mystic transcendence of the flesh in ascetic denial. With this is a doctrine of the transmigration of souls, in which sinful life leads to reincarnation in lower animal life, and virtuous life leads, at least in some forms of Hindu belief, to ultimate freedom from flesh of any sort and reunion with the perfect, the ineffable. But official Brahminism became a series of rigid and complicated rituals, and the religion of the common people retained from earlier times an elaborate polytheism lush with gods and goddesses who were by no means ethereal, but fleshly indeed. Against all this worldliness there rose in the sixth century B.C. a great religious leader, Gautama Buddha, himself of noble stock. Buddhism accepts the basic Brahminical concept of the evil of this world of the flesh, but it finds salvation, the *nirvana* of peaceful release from the chain of earthly birth and rebirth, in a life ascetic but not withdrawn, a life of charity and good works. Buddhism died out in the land of its birth, but it spread to China, Japan, and southeastern Asia.

In these lands it took two forms, still existing. In the northern lands of Tibet, China, Japan, the Mahayana (Great Vehicle) continued in theology to emphasize Buddha's strong ethical desire to make nirvana available to all. In southeastern Asia and Ceylon, the Hinayana (Lesser Vehicle) prevailed. In theory, the Hinayana relies more on ritual, and its monks are wholly detached from the world. Buddhism remains one of the great higher religions of the world. It has made some converts among Western intellectuals, especially in an altered form known as Zen Buddhism, originally a kind of Japanese stoicism.

The religious thought of India has left a residue of greater otherworldliness, of greater emphasis on a mystical subduing of the flesh, of a revulsion from struggle for wealth, satisfaction of the common human appetites, worldly place and power, than has Christianity or Islam. In practice, Indian life, even before the Europeans came, displayed plenty of violence, plenty of greed, cruelty, and self-indulgence. Except as superstition and taboo and ritual, little of the higher religions had seeped down to the masses. To some Western minds, the educated classes of India have seemed to take refuge in otherworldly doctrines as a psychological defense against the worldly superiority of the West and the poverty and superstition of their own masses. But the fact remains that for three hundred years educated Indians have insisted that they feel differently about the universe and man's place in it than do we, that theirs is a higher spirituality.

## China

China, too, resisted the West, and in many ways more successfully than did India. A very old civilization that goes back several thousand years before Christ was established in the valleys of the Yangtze and the Yellow rivers. Like the other civilizations bordering the great nomadic reservoir of the Eurasian heartland—the Mesopotamian, the Indian, the European—it was subject to periodical incursions of the Eurasian tribesmen. It was against such incursions that the famous Great Wall of China was built in the third century B.C. On the whole, the Chinese protected their basic institutions against the victorious nomads, whom they absorbed after a few generations. At just about the time when the first Europeans were setting up permanent trade relations with China, the last of these "barbarian" conquests occurred. Early in the seventeenth century, Mongolian tribes established a state of their own in eastern Manchuria, to the north of China proper. In 1644, they seized the Chinese capital of Peking and established a dynasty that lasted until 1911. But the Manchus, like other outsiders before them, left Chinese institutions almost untouched.

Chinese history is by no means the uneventful record of a "frozen" and unchanging society that some Westerners have thought. It is filled with the rise and fall of the dynasties, with wars and plagues and famines, with the gradual spread of Chinese culture southward and eastward, to the region of Canton, to Vietnam, to Korea, to Japan. It has periods of effective governmental centralization, and periods of "feudal" disintegration; its arts and techniques passed through the cycle of flourishing, decadence, and renewal. Many elements of continuity, however, existed under the flux.

First of all, at the base of Chinese social life was a communal village organization, held together by very strong family ties, a cult of ancestor worship, and hard work guided by traditional farming methods. The Chinese village, basically unchanged until the communist reforms of our own day, was one of the oldest socio-economic organizations in the civilized world. Second, at the top of this society was an emperor, Son of Heaven, the "natural" ruler of a great

*A mandarin: engraving from John Ogilby's "Atlas Chinensis," 1671.*

*"Sage under a Pine Tree": a Chinese painting from the Sung dynasty (960–1279).*

state. The Chinese were conditioned to at least formal imperial unity in somewhat the same way early medieval Westerners were conditioned to the unity of Roman Catholic Christendom. Third, the business of running this vast empire was entrusted to one of the most remarkable ruling classes history has ever recorded, the *mandarins*, a bureaucracy of intellectuals, or at any rate of men who could pass literary and philosophical examinations in classics, examinations requiring a rigorously trained memory.

The mandarin class proved not very resilient in the face of new European ideas, and it was by no means immune to graft and to nepotism. But it had served the state for several millennia, and its existence is one of the reasons for the extraordinary stability of Chinese society. Although in theory the class was one open to talents, the necessary education was too expensive and too hard to acquire for any but a very few gifted, lucky, and persistent poor boys.

Just as in India, China had an immense population at the very margin of existence, and a small upper class that enjoyed gracious living of a kind hardly available to the medieval Western upper classes. The Chinese millions had their superstitions, their demons, their otherworld. The earlier periods of Chinese cultural flowering show traces of mystical beliefs among the educated, traces of the eternal Platonism of the human spirit. Still, everyone who has known the Chinese, even the casual traveler who makes some effort to appreciate what is going on about him, finds in the educated Chinese a lack of mysticism and otherworldliness. Or, in positive terms, he finds a sense of worldly realism, an acceptance of the universe as it appears to common sense, a concern with human relations, with politeness, decorum, and the like, and an absence of the theology, sacraments, and faith in a supranatural god which we in the West expect in a higher religion.

It has been commonly said that China never had a religion, in the sense that Buddhism, Christianity, and Islam are religions with a firm doctrine of salvation. The conventional Confucianism of the upper classes is indeed a code of manners and morals, not a sacramental religion, not a religion in which the faithful undergo the miracle of sharing in something ineffable. Confucius, a sage who flourished early in the fifth century B.C., was no mystic, no prophet, but a moralist who taught an ethical system of temperance, decorum, obedience to the wisdom of the wise and the good. This lack of commitment to an otherworldly religion, however, has by no means made the Chinese more receptive to Western ideas. At least until our own times, China has resisted westernization more effectively than has any other great culture.

## The Portuguese Empire

The empire that the Portuguese founded in Asia and Africa was a trading empire, not an empire of settlement. They established along the coasts of Africa, India, and China a series of posts, or "factories," over which they hoisted the Portuguese flag as a sign that they had annexed these bits of territory to the Portuguese crown. From these posts they traded with the natives. As all the European colonial powers did later, they offered relatively cheap and relatively mass-produced articles—guns, knives, cheap cloth, and gadgets of all sorts. In return, they got gold and silver (when they could), slaves, pepper and other spices, still essential especially for meats in those days without refrigeration, silks and other luxuries, and, finally, raw materials such as cotton and, in the New World, tobacco and sugar.

Two guiding principles of this trade were accepted by almost all contemporaries, whether in the mother country or in the colonies, as simple facts of life. First, in this trade the mother country was the determining element, and would naturally provide manufactured goods and services while the colony produced raw materials. Second, foreigners, nationals of other European lands, were excluded from this trade; they could not deal directly with the colony or take part in the commerce between mother country and colony. The Portuguese, in sum, followed a policy of mercantilism, symbolized by the virtual monopoly Lisbon exercised over European imports of pepper and cinnamon during the sixteenth century.

Armed forces were essential to the establishment and maintenance of this colonial system. Relatively small land forces proved sufficient both to keep the natives under control and to ward off rival European powers from the trading posts. A large and efficient navy was also necessary, for the easiest way to raid a rival's trade was to wait until its fruits were neatly concentrated in the hold of a merchant vessel, and then take it at sea as a prize. Such deeds are now known as piracy, a very common activity in these early modern centuries. Sometimes, especially in the eighteenth century, the pirates became in fact outlaws, men of no nation, willing to rob nationals of any country. In these earlier centuries, they were often openly an unofficial adjunct of a given navy, called privateers and operating only against enemies or neutrals, never against their own nationals. A navy was, then, essential to protect the sea routes of a colonial power. The Portuguese fleet was not only a merchant fleet; under the command of governors like Albuquerque, it was a great military fleet that brushed aside Arab opposition and for a few decades ruled the oceans of the Old World.

The Portuguese made no serious attempt to settle large numbers of their own people either in the hot coastlands of Africa or in the already densely populated lands of India and the Far East. Nor, save in the single respect we are about to encounter, did they attempt to make over these natives into pseudo-Portuguese. There were of course useful places for Portuguese in the colonial services, both civilian and military; many of the natives were enlisted in the armed forces or used as domestic help and in subordinate posts such as clerks. These natives inevitably picked up, however imperfectly, the language and culture of the colonial power. But neither among the primitive tribes of Africa nor among the Indian and Chinese masses did this process of europeanization go very fast or far.

Nor did the Portuguese attempt to rule directly, to alter the political, social, or economic structure of native life. They left the old ruling chiefs and the old ruling classes pretty much as they had found them. In the total lives of these millions, the imported European wares played extremely little part in these early days. The native upper classes monopolized most of them, and Europe could not yet flood non-European markets wth cheap manufactured goods made by power-driven machinery. Nothing Western touched these masses of natives in the sixteenth century, nothing tempted them away from their millennial ways of life, in anything like the degree our twentieth-century West attracts and tempts the East.

There is one exception. The Portuguese and the Spanish, and even their relatively secular-minded rivals, the English, Dutch, and French, did attempt to Christianize the natives. Some of these attempts were coercive, as at Goa where the Portuguese pulled down all the native temples and made it impossible to practice traditional religion. From the first, however, much sincerity, devotion, and hard work also went into the missionary movement.

The earliest missionaries underestimated the obstacles they were to encounter. Many of them were in a sense partly converted themselves; that is, they came to be very fond of their charges, and convinced that these were in fact almost Christians already. Some of the Jesuits in China, the first European intellectuals to live in this very civilized country, seriously believed that with just a bit more effort the full reconciliation between Christianity and Confucianism could be achieved.

From the start, difficulties arose between the missionaries, anxious to protect their charges, and the traders and colonial officials, driven by their very place in the system to try to exploit the natives. Local chiefs and monarchs regarded converts as potential traitors, more loyal to their Western faith than to their Eastern rulers.

Finances and manpower were always a serious problem, with so many tens of millions to convert and tend, and with so few men and so little money to do the work.

Measured in statistical terms, the effort to convert India and the Far East to Christianity did not make a serious impression on the masses —something under a million converts by 1600. The greatest missionary successes tended to occur in areas of Buddhism, then in a state of decay comparable to that of Catholicism on the eve of the Reformation, and the greatest failures in areas of Islam, for Muslims have very seldom abandoned their faith for any other. Yet the influence of Christianity cannot be measured in terms of actual church memberships in the East; it has been far greater on the upper and intellectual classes than on the masses and is an important part of the whole Western impact on the East.

The Portuguese, though first in the field in the East, very soon had to yield to newer rivals. Like the Spaniards, they suffered from an inadequate, or at any rate inadequately run, home industry; their banking, their business methods, their initiative—if not their scruples—were not up to competition with the aggressive expanding powers of northwest Europe. Though monopolizing the import of pepper from the East, they sought the assistance of the more knowledgeable merchant community of Antwerp in distributing the pepper to European markets. The cloth and other wares they traded in the East they often had to import from countries with more developed industries. After the sixteenth century, they ceased to add to their empire and their wealth, and sank back to a decidedly secondary place in international politics. A great poem, the *Lusiads* (1572) of Camões, is their monument.

The sixty years of union between the Spanish and Portuguese monarchies, 1580–1640, accelerated the decline of Portugal's imperial fortunes by involving her in prolonged worldwide warfare with Spain's great adversary, the Dutch Republic. Better-equipped and better-disciplined Dutch forces drove the Portuguese from most of their posts in Indonesia and from Ceylon and parts of the Indian coast. Yet a Portuguese empire did survive along the old route around Africa to Goa, on the island of Timor in Indonesia, and in Macao in China. And it still survives as of 1971—notably some 800,000 square miles of African territory in Angola and Portuguese Guinea on the west coast, and Mozambique on the east. The first European colonial empire in Africa has become the last. It has endured so long in part because the Portuguese never voluntarily relinquished any territories; the Republic of India had to seize Goa by force in 1961. Another reason for the longevity of the empire in the face of such active and hungry rivals as the French, Dutch, and British is the existence of a force in history difficult for modern Americans to recognize—that of inertia. It has been very hard to destroy outright any going territorial concern. Portugal's more successful rivals took away Portuguese leadership, but left her a participant in the competition. Finally, the survival of the Portuguese Empire was greatly aided by the fact that the greatest of the European imperial powers, England, remained through modern times in alliance with Portugal. The complete victory of France or Holland in the colonial scramble might possibly have brought an end to the Portuguese Empire.

## III West by Sea to the Indies

### Columbus

In the earliest days of concerted effort to explore the oceans, the rulers of Spain had been too busy disposing of the last Muslim state in the peninsula, Granada, and uniting the disparate parts of Spain to patronize scientific exploration as the Portuguese had done. But individual Spanish traders were active, and Spain was growing in prosperity. When Portuguese mariners found the three groups of Atlantic islands—Azores, Madeira, and Canaries—a papal decree assigned the Canaries to the crown of Castile and the others to Portugal. Once the marriage of Ferdinand and Isabella had united Aragon and Castile, Queen Isabella wanted to catch up with the Portuguese. So in 1491, when the fall of Granada seemed imminent, she commissioned

Columbus to try out his plan to reach India by going west.

Columbus (1451–1506) was an Italian, born in Genoa. He was essentially self-educated but, at least in navigation and geography, had educated himself very well. His central conception, that it would be possible to reach the Far East—"the Indies"—by sailing westward from Spain, was certainly not uniquely his. That the earth is a globe was a notion entertained by ancient Greek geographers, and revived with the renaissance of the classics. Toscanelli at Florence in 1474, Behaim at Nuremberg in the very year of Columbus' voyage, published maps that showed the earth as a globe—but without the Americas, and with the combined Atlantic and Pacific much narrower than they are in fact. The growth of oceanic navigation had made it possible to act on this notion by deliberately sailing west on the Atlantic. But it was still a strikingly novel idea, and a persistent, innovating personality was needed to win support for such an expedition.

Columbus met with many rebuffs, but finally, with the support of the wealthy Spanish trading family of Pinzon, was able to get the help of Queen Isabella. With the sole aim of reaching the Indies he might not have been able to set out. But, as his commission shows, he was also charged to discover and secure for the Spanish crown new islands and territories, a mission that probably reflects the importance of ancient and medieval legends about Atlantis, St. Brendan's isle, and other lands beyond the Azores. Even if he did not reach the Indies, there seemed a chance that he would reach something new.

He reached a New World. Setting out from Palos near Cadiz on August 3, 1492, in three ships so small that they could all be propped up comfortably on the deck of a modern aircraft carrier, he made a landfall on a Bahaman island on October 12 of the same year, and eventually went on to discover the large islands we know as Cuba and Santo Domingo (Haiti). On a second voyage, in 1493, he went out with seventeen ships and some fifteen hundred colonists, explored further in the Caribbean, and laid the foundations of the Spanish Empire in America. On his third voyage in 1498–1500, he reached the mouth of the Orinoco in South America but encountered difficulties among his colonists and was sent home in irons by the royal governor Bobadilla, who took over the administration of the Indies for the Crown. He was released on his return to Spain, and in 1502–1504 made a fourth and final voyage, in which he reached the mainland at Honduras. He died in comparative obscurity at Valladolid in Spain in 1506, totally unaware that he had reached, not Asia, but a new continent.

That continent was, by a caprice of history, not destined to bear his name, though it is now liberally sprinkled with other placenames in his honor. News of Columbus' voyage soon spread by word of mouth in Europe. But printing was still in its infancy; there were no newspapers or geographical institutes; the international learned class—the humanists—were more interested in Greek manuscripts than in strange lands; and, from early Portuguese days on, governments had done their best to keep their discoveries as secret as possible. The most effective spreading of the work in print about the New World was done by another Italian in the Spanish service, Amerigo Vespucci, who wrote copiously about his alleged explorations in the immediate footsteps of Columbus. Scholars doubt that Vespucci really made all the discoveries, from the southeastern United States to the tip of South America, that he claimed to have made. But his letters came to the attention of a German theoretical geographer, Martin Waldseemüller, who in 1507 published a map blocking out a landmass in the southern part of the New World which he labeled, from the latinized form of Vespucci's first name, America. The map was read and copied, and though Waldseemüller in a new map of 1531 removed it in favor of a noncommittal "Terra Incognita" (unknown land), two new continents had been christened.

### Later Explorers

From now on, the roster of discovery grows rapidly. Ponce de León reached Florida in 1512, and Balboa in 1513 crossed the Isthmus of Panama and saw a limitless ocean, on the other side of which the Indies did indeed lie, for it was the Pacific. Many other Spaniards and Portuguese in these first two decades of the sixteenth century explored in detail the coasts of what was to be Latin America. It was now quite clear that an immense landmass lay athwart the westward route from Europe to Asia, and that even the narrow Isthmus of Panama was an obstacle not readily to be overcome by a canal. Maritime exploration then turned to the problem of getting around the Americas by sea and into the Pacific. North America proved an obstacle indeed, for none of the great estuaries—Chesapeake, Delaware, Hudson—promising though they looked to the first explorers, did more than dent the great continent, the breadth of which was totally unknown. The St. Lawrence looked even better, for to its first French explorers it seemed like the sought-for strait. But even the St. Lawrence gave out, and the rapids near Montreal, which showed it was only another river after all, received the ironic name of Lachine (China) Rapids, for this was not the way to China. Not until the mid-nineteenth century was the usually icechoked "Northwest Passage" discovered by the Englishman Sir John Franklin, who died in the Arctic wastes before he could return to civilization.

The "Southwest Passage" was found only a generation after Columbus, in the course of an expedition that is the most extraordinary of all the great voyages of discovery. Ferdinand Magellan, a Portuguese in the Spanish service, set out in 1519 with a royal commission bidding him to find a way westward to the Spice Islands of Asia. Skirting the coast of South America, he found and guided his ships through the difficult fogbound passage that bears his name, the Straits of Magellan, reached the Pacific, and crossed it in a voyage of incredible hardship. Scurvy alone, a disease we now know to be caused by lack of vitamin C, and a standard risk in those early days, meant that he and his men had to surmount torturing illness. After he had reached the islands now known as the Philippines, Magellan was killed in a skirmish with the natives. One of his captains, however, kept on along the known route by the Indian Ocean and the coast of Africa. On September 8, 1522, the *Victoria* and her crew of eighteen men—out of five ships and 243 men that had sailed in 1519—landed at Cadiz. For the first time, men had circumnavigated the earth and had proved empirically that the world is round.

What these explorations cost in terms of human suffering, what courage and resolution were needed to carry them through, is very hard for our easy-traveling generation to imagine. Here, from the bare report the sailor Pigafetta gives of Magellan's expedition, is a firsthand account of one of the crises:

> Wednesday, the twenty-eight of November, 1520, we came forth out of the said strait, and entered into the Pacific sea, where we remained three months and twenty days without taking in provisions or other refreshments, and we only ate old biscuit reduced to powder, and full of grubs, and stinking from the dirt which the rats had made on it when eating the good biscuit, and we drank water that was yellow and stinking. We also ate the ox hides which were under the mainyard. . . . Besides the above-named evils, this misfortune which I will mention was the worst, it was that the upper and lower gums of most of our men grew so much that they could not eat, and in this way so many suffered, that nineteen died.*

Such accounts could be multiplied for every part of the newly discovered world and for every nation taking part in the expansion of the West.

## Foundation of the Spanish Empire

As a by-product of Magellan's voyage, the Spaniards who had sponsored him got a foothold in the Far East, which they had reached by sailing west. As we have seen, by the Treaty of Tordesillas in 1494 Spain and Portugal had divided the world—the world open to trade and empire—along a line that cut through the Atlantic in such a way that Brazil became Portuguese. This same line, extended round the world, cut the Pacific so that some of the islands Magellan discovered came into the Spanish half. Spain conveniently treated the Philippines as if they also came in the Spanish half of the globe, though they are just outside it, and colonized them from Mexico.

Up to now, we have concerned ourselves mostly with maritime explorations and the founding of coastal trading stations. The Spaniards in the New World, however, very soon explored by land, and acquired thousands of square miles of territory. To the explorer by sea there succeeded the conquistador, often of the

* Lord Stanley of Alderly, *The First Voyage Round the World by Magellan, translated from the accounts of Pigafetta, and other contemporary writers* (London, 1874), pp. 64–65.

impoverished, noble hidalgo class, half explorer, half soldier and administrator, and all adventurer. Of the conquistadors, two, Hernando Cortés and Francisco Pizarro, have come down in history with a special aura of tough romance. With a handful of men they conquered the only two civilized regions of the New World: the Aztec Empire of Mexico, conquered by Cortés with 600 soldiers in 1519, and the Inca Empire of Peru, conquered by Pizarro with 180 soldiers in 1531–1533. The narrative of these conquests, whether in the classic nineteenth-century histories of the American William Prescott or in the narratives of actual participants, remains among the most fascinating if not among the most edifying chapters of Western history. A book of this scope cannot possibly do justice to the drama of the conquerors of Mexico and Peru, nor to the many other Spaniards who in search of glory, salvation, gold, and excitement toiled up and down these strange new lands—Quesada in New Granada (later Colombia); Coronado, de Soto, and Cabeza de Vaca in the southwest of what became the United States; Mendoza in La Plata (the lands around the river Plate—today Uruguay and Argentina); Valdivia in Chile; Alvarado in Guatemala; and many others, not least Ponce de León hunting for the fountain of eternal youth in Florida.

Unlike the great cultures of India and the Far East, the pre-Columbian cultures of the Americas crumbled under the impact of the Europeans. From Mexico to Bolivia, Paraguay, and Patagonia (in southern Argentina), millions of people survive who are of Red Indian stock, and a full understanding of Latin America requires some knowledge of their folkways and traditions. Mexican artists and intellectuals in our day proudly hold up their Indian heritage against the Yankees, and against their own europeanized

*Machu Picchu, ancient Inca city in the Andes of Peru. Corn and potatoes were grown on the terraces.*

nineteenth-century rulers. But the structure of the Aztec and the Inca empires has simply not survived. The sun-god in whose name the Inca ruled, the bloody Aztec god of war, Huitzilopochtli, are no longer a part of the lives of men, as are Confucius and Buddha. Today the old civilizations of Peru and Central America are of interest chiefly as fascinating examples of the endless variety of human life on this earth. But the fact that they once existed as large territorial states, and made high achievements in art and science, is further evidence against naïve Western notions of white superiority.

Well before the end of the sixteenth century, the work of the conquistadores had been done, and in Latin America the first of the true colonial empires of Europe—in contrast to the trading empires in Africa and Asia—had been founded. Nowhere, save in the region of the La Plata and in central Chile, was the native Red Indian stock eliminated and replaced by a population almost entirely of Old World stock—something that has happened in the United States and Canada save for a tiny Indian minority. Over vast reaches of Mexico and Central and South America, a crust of Spanish or Portuguese formed at the top of society and made Spanish or Portuguese the language of culture; a class of mixed blood, the *mestizos,* was gradually formed from the union, formal or informal, of Europeans and natives; and in many regions the Indians continued to maintain their stock and their old ways of life almost untouched. Finally, wherever, as in the Caribbean, the Indians were exterminated under the pressure of civilization, or, as in Brazil, they proved inadequate as a labor force, the importation of slaves from Africa added another ingredient to the racial mixture.

Moreover, geography and the circumstances of settlement by separate groups of adventurers in each region combined to create a number of separate units of settlement tied together only by their dependence on the Crown and destined to become the independent nation-states of Latin America today. Geography alone was perhaps a fatal obstacle to any subsequent union of the colonies, such as was achieved by the English colonies that became the United States of America. Between such apparently close neighbors as the present Argentine and Chile, for instance, lay the great chain of the Andes, crossed only with great difficulty by high mountain passes. Also, between the colonies of the La Plata and the colonies of Peru and New Granada lay the Andes and the vast tropical rain forests of the Amazon Basin, still essentially unconquered today. The highlands of Mexico and Central America are as much invitations to local independence as were the mountains of Hellas to the ancient Greeks. Cuba and the other Caribbean islands have the natural independence of islands. And even had the coastal fringes of Brazil not been settled by Portuguese, men of a different language from the Spaniards, these regions have for the most part no easy land connections with the rest of Latin America. Geography alone would probably have kept Brazil separate.

## The Balance Sheet of Latin American Empire

The Spaniards transported to the New World the centralized administrative institutions of Castile. At the top of the hierarchy were two vice-royalties, that of Peru with its capital at Lima and that of New Spain with its capital at Mexico City. From Lima the viceroy ruled for the Crown over the Spanish part of South America, save for Venezuela. From Mexico City the viceroy ruled over the mainland north of Panama, the West Indies, Venezuela, and the Philippines. Each capital had an *audiencia,* a powerful body staffed by professional lawyers and operating both as a court of law and as an advisory council. During the sixteenth century audiencias were also established in Santo Domingo, Guatemala, Panama, New Granada, Quito, Manila, and other major centers. In Madrid, a special Council of the Indies formulated colonial policy and supervised its execution.

This was certainly a centralized, paternalistic system of government, which has rightly enough been contrasted with the "salutary neglect" in which the North American colonies were generally left by the home government until the crisis that led to the American Revolution. But it was not—given the vast areas and the varied peoples under its control, it could not be—as rigid in practice as it was in theory. The rudiments of popular consultation of the Spanish colonists existed in the *cabildos abiertos* or assemblies of citizens in the towns. Moreover, as time went on the bureaucracy itself came to be filled largely with colonials, men who had never been in the home country, and who developed a sense of local patriotism and independence. Madrid and Seville were simply too far away to enforce all their decisions. Notably in the matter of trade, it proved impossible to maintain the rigid monopolies of mercantilistic theory, which sought to confine trade wholly to the mother country, and to prohibit, or severely limit, domestic industry in the colonies. Local officials connived at a smuggling trade with the English, Dutch, French, and North Americans, which in the eighteenth century reached large proportions.

The hand of Spain was heaviest in the initial period of exploitation, when the rich and easily mined deposits of the precious metals in Mexico and Peru were skimmed off for the benefit both of the Spanish crown, which always got its *quinto,* or fifth, and of the conquistadores and their successors, Spaniards all. This gold and silver did the natives no good, but in the long run it did no good to Spain, since it went to finance a vain bid for European supremacy and to pay for wares needed by the colonies that the mother country did not produce. By the early seventeenth century the output of precious metals was declining, and the Spanish American colonial economy and society had settled down

*Castrovirreina: a Peruvian mining town in 1613. Llamas are being led toward the town from the works.*

in a rough equilibrium. It was not a progressive economy, but neither was it a hopelessly backward one. Colonial wares—sugar, tobacco, chocolate, cotton, hides, and much else—flowed out of Latin America in exchange for manufactured goods and for services. Creoles (American-born of pure European stock) and mestizos were the chief beneficiaries of this trade. Above the African slaves in the social pyramid, but well below the mestizos, were the native Indians. This, then, was a system of social caste based on color, one that never became so rigid as that in North America but that still damaged native pride and self-respect.

Especially in the Caribbean, but to a degree everywhere, the whites tried to use native labor on farms, in the mines, and in transport. The results were disastrous, for epidemics of smallpox and other new diseases introduced by the Europeans decimated the ranks of the native population. In the West Indies the Carib Indians were wiped out, and in central Mexico, it has been estimated by scholars that the total population fell from about nineteen million when Cortés arrived to only some two and a half million at the end of the century, eighty years later. Here, as with the gold and silver, some ironic spirit of history seems to have taken revenge on the whites: though the question of the origin of syphilis is still disputed, many historians of medicine believe that it was brought from the West Indies, where it was mild, to Western civilization, where it became virulent. The attempt to regiment native labor in a plantation system or to put it on a semimanorial system of forced labor, known as the *encomienda,* proved almost as disastrous. The encomiendas, which had been developed in Spain itself for lands reconquered from the Muslims, grouped farming villages whose inhabitants were "commended" to the protection of a conquistador or colonist. The "protector" thereby acquired both a source of income without engaging in demeaning labor and an economic base for a potential defiance of central authority. The shortage of native labor made recourse to black slaves inevitable. A final element in the social and racial situation was the character of the colonial whites, who tended to be aggressive and insensitive; by and large, except for some clerics, the gentler souls stayed home.

Yet against all these forces making for harshness and cruelty, there were counteracting forces.

Spanish imperial policy toward the natives was in aim by no means ungenerous, and even in execution holds up well in the long and harsh record of intercourse between whites and non-whites all over the globe. The New Laws of 1542 forbade the transmission of encomiendas by inheritance, thereby striking a blow against feudal decentralization. The New Laws also forbade the enslavement of native Indians, who were regarded as wards of the Crown. The central government in Spain passed many laws to protect the Indians, and though these were often flouted in the colonies—a phenomenon not unknown in the English colonies—they put a limit to wholesale exploitation of the natives. Their cause was championed by men of great distinction, and notably by Bartolomé de las Casas (1474–1566), "Father of the Indians," bishop of Chiapas in Mexico.

Unlike their counterparts in Africa and Asia, the Indian masses were converted to Christianity. More than Spanish pride was involved in the grandiose religious edifices constructed by the colonists and in their elaborate services. Many priests seemed to realize the need to fill the void left in the lives of the Indians by the destruction of old temples and the suppression of complex pagan rituals. Church and state in the Spanish and Portuguese colonies in the New World worked hand in hand, undisturbed for generations by the troubles roused in Europe by the Protestant Reformation and the rise of a secular anti-Christian movement. The Jesuits in Paraguay set up among the Guarani Indians a remarkable society, a benevolent despotism, a utopia of good order, good habits, and eternal childhood for the Guarani. On the northern fringes of the Spanish world, where it was to meet the Anglo-Saxons, a long line of missions in California and the Southwest held the frontier. Everywhere save in wildest Amazonia and other untamed areas the Christianity of the Roman Catholic church brought to the natives a veneer of Western tradition, and made them in some sense part of this strange new society of the white men.

In their close union of church and state, in their very close ties with the home country, in their mercantilist economics, and in still other respects, the Portuguese settlements in Brazil resembled those of the Spaniards elsewhere in Latin America. Yet there were significant dif-

*A reconstruction of the Great Temple at Tenochtitlán, capital of the Aztec Empire.*

ferences. The Portuguese settlements were almost entirely rural: Brazil had nothing to compare with the urban splendor of Mexico City or Lima. A large number of black slaves were imported into the tropical areas of Brazil, and, because the white males drew no sexual color line, the races became more thoroughly mixed in colonial times than they did in most Spanish colonies except Cuba. Finally, perhaps because of the relative proximity of Brazil to European waters, the Portuguese had more troubles with rival nations than the Spaniards did. The existence on today's map of those fragments of imperial hopes—French Guiana (Cayenne), Dutch Guiana (Surinam), and Guyana (a British colony to 1966)—is a witness to the fact that the northern maritime nations made a serious effort to settle in what became Brazil.

## IV The North Atlantic Powers and Russia

Spain and Portugal enjoyed a generation's head start in exploration and one of nearly a century in founding empires of settlement. Without this head start, which they owed in part to their position as heirs of the Mediterranean trade, Spain and Portugal could scarcely have made the great mark in the world that they did. For the northern Atlantic states soon made up for their late start. As early as 1497 the Cabots, father and son, Italians in the English service, saw something of the North American coast, and gave the English territorial claims based on their explorations. In the first half of the sixteenth century the explorations of another Italian, Verrazzano, and the Frenchman Jacques Cartier gave France competing claims, which were reinforced in the early seventeenth century by the detailed explorations of Champlain. Dutch claims began with the voyages of Henry Hudson, an Englishman who entered their service in 1609.

### English, Dutch, and Swedes in North America

The English did not immediately follow up the work of the Cabots. Instead, they put their energies in the mid-sixteenth century into the profitable business of interloping, that is, of breaking into the Spanish trading monopoly. John Hawkins, in 1562, started the English slave trade, and his nephew, Francis Drake, penetrated to the Pacific, reached California, which he claimed for England under the name of New Albion, and returned to England by the Pacific and Indian oceans, completing the first English circumnavigation of the globe. By the end of the century, the great fishing grounds off northeastern North America had become an important prize, and under Sir Humphrey Gilbert in 1583 the English staked out a claim to Newfoundland which gave them and their later colonists a firm place in these valuable fisheries.

In 1584, Sir Walter Raleigh attempted to found a settlement on Roanoke Island (in present-day North Carolina) in a land the English named, from their Virgin Queen Elizabeth, Virginia. Neither this, nor a colony sent out in 1587, managed to survive. But early in the next century the English established two permanent footholds, at Jamestown in Virginia, 1607, and at Plymouth in New England, 1620. Both were to become colonies of settlement, regions in which the sparse native population was exterminated and replaced by men and women for the most part of British stock. But in their inception both were nearer the pattern of trading posts set by the Spanish and Portuguese. Both were established by chartered trading companies with headquarters in England; both, and especially the Virginian, cherished at first high hopes that they would find, as the Spaniards had, great stores of precious metals. Both were disappointed in these hopes, and managed to survive the first terrible years of hardship by the skin of their teeth. Tobacco, first cultivated in 1612, and the almost legendary Captain John Smith, explorer and man of resourcefulness, saved the Virginia colony; and furs (notably beaver), codfish, and Calvinist toughness saved Plymouth. Both colonies gradually built up an agricultural economy, supplemented by trade with the mother country and interloping trade with the

West Indies. Neither received more than a few tens of thousands of immigrants from abroad. Yet both these and the later colonies expanded by natural increase in a country of abundant land for the taking. The thirteen colonies by 1776 were a substantial series of settlements with almost three million inhabitants.

Before these English colonies were completed, one important and one very minor foreign group had to be pushed out. The Dutch, after their successful resistance to Spain, had entered the competition for commerce and empire. They had founded a trading colony at New Amsterdam at the mouth of the Hudson and had begun to push into the fur trade. This made them rivals of both the English and the French, further north in Canada. They lacked an adequate home base to be a great power, however, and in a war with England in the 1660's they lost New Amsterdam, which was annexed by the English in 1664 and became New York. The Dutch, though very few in number, were destined to supply some important families to the future United States, as names like Stuyvesant, Schuyler, and Roosevelt suggest.

The Swedes, too, were now making a bid for greatness, and in 1638 they founded Fort Christiana on the Delaware near present-day Wilmington. But New Sweden was never a serious competitor, and in 1655 Fort Christiana was taken over by the Dutch, who in turn were ousted by the English. Pennsylvania, chartered to the wealthy English Quaker William Penn in 1681, filled the vacuum left by the expulsion of the Swedes and the Dutch from the Delaware. It was to be the keystone colony before it became the keystone state.

## The Thirteen Colonies

By the early eighteenth century, the English settlements formed a continuous string from Maine to Georgia, grouped into thirteen colonies, each founded separately and each with its own charter. Perhaps American popular tradition exaggerates the differences between the southern and the northern group. Massachusetts was not settled wholly by democratic plain people, "Roundheads," nor was Virginia settled wholly by great English landowners, gentlemen or "Cavaliers." Both colonies—and all the others—were settled by a varied human lot, which covered most of the range of social and economic status in the mother country, save for the very top. Dukes and earls did not emigrate. But the poorest could and did, as indentured servants or as impressed seamen who deserted ship.

Still, it is true that New England was for the most part settled by Calvinist Independents (Congregationalists), already committed to wide local self-government and to a distrust of a landowning aristocracy; and it is true that the southern colonies, especially tidewater Virginia, were settled for the most part by Anglicans used to the existence of frank social distinctions and to large landholdings. In Virginia, the Church of England became the established church; in Massachusetts, the Puritan Congregationalists, nonconformists in the homeland, almost automatically became conformists in their new home, and set up their own variety of state church. Geography, climate, and a complex of social and economic factors drove the South to plantation monoculture of tobacco, rice, indigo, or cotton even in colonial days, and drove New England and the Middle Colonies to small farming by independent farmer-owners and to small-scale industry and commerce. Yet in the Piedmont sections of Virginia and the Carolinas, there were small farmers, Presbyterians, Scotch-Irish, Germans from Pennsylvania, a very northern mixture. Some historians hold that the natural environment, and not any original difference of social structure and beliefs, accounts for the diverging growths of North and South and their eventual armed conflict.

To us who are their heirs, it has seemed that these English colonists brought with them the religious freedom, the government by discussion, and the democratic society of which we are so proud. So they did, though they brought the seeds, the potentialities, rather than the fully developed institutions. These colonists came from an England where the concept of freedom of religion was only beginning to emerge from the long struggles of the sects. It was quite natural for the Virginians and the New Englanders to set up state churches. Yet, just as in contemporaneous England, these immigrants represented too many conflicting religious groups to enforce anything like the religious uniformity that prevailed to the south among the Spanish colonists and to the north among the French. Even in Calvinist New England, "heresy" appeared from the start, with Baptists and Quakers, and even Anglicans, who seeped into New

Hampshire and eventually even into Boston. Moreover, some of the colonies were founded by groups which from the first practiced religious freedom and separated church and state. In Pennsylvania, founded by Quakers who believed firmly in such separation; in Maryland, founded in part to give refuge to the most distrusted of groups at home, the Catholics; in Rhode Island, founded by Roger Williams and others unwilling to conform to the orthodoxy of Massachusetts Bay—in all these colonies there was something like the complete religious freedom that was later embodied in the Constitution of the United States.

The seeds of democracy, too, existed, although the early settlers, not only in Virginia but even in the North, accepted class distinctions more readily than we now do. No formal colonial nobility ever arose, however, and the early tendency to develop a privileged gentry or squirearchy in the coastal regions was balanced by the equalitarianism of the frontier and by careers open to talent in the towns. Government by discussion was firmly planted in the colonies from the start. All of them, even the so-called proprietary colonies like Pennsylvania, which were granted to a "proprietor," had some kind of colonial legislative body.

Here we come to the critical point of difference between the English and the Spanish and French governments in the New World. The Spanish and French governments were already centralized bureaucratic monarchies; their representative assemblies were no more than consultative and had no power over taxation. Royal governors in Latin America and in New France could really run their provinces, leaning on men they appointed and recalled, and raising funds by their own authority. England, while also a monarchy, was a parliamentary monarchy, torn by two revolutions in the seventeenth century. Though the Crown was represented in most colonies by a royal governor, the English government had no such bureaucracy as the Spanish and French had. Royal governors in the English colonies had hardly even a clerical staff and met with great difficulty in raising money from their legislative assemblies. The history of the colonies is full of bickerings between governors and colonial assemblies, in which the governor, with little local support, and with but sporadic backing from the home government, was often stalemated. Moreover, in all the colonies the established landowners, merchants, and professional men, though not everywhere all the people, could and did participate not only in colonial assemblies but also in local units of government—towns in New England, counties in the rest of the colonies. Locally, too, there was nothing like an authoritative bureaucracy. Finally, the settlers brought with them the common law of England, with its trial by jury and its absence of bureaucratic administrative law.

In sum, not only the opportunities of an almost empty land—the frontier—but also English traditions and ideas and the weakness of the central government were major factors in the growth of American democracy. Frenchmen and Spaniards did not bring to their colonies what the English brought to theirs. Their "frontier" was a very different one.

## New France

To the north, in the region about the Bay of Fundy and in the St. Lawrence Basin, the French built on the work of Cartier and Champlain. New France was to be for a century and a half a serious threat to the English North American colonies. The St. Lawrence and the Great Lakes gave the French easy access to the heart of the continent, in marked contrast to the Appalachians which stood between the English and the Mississippi. The French were also impelled westward by the fact that the fur trade was by all odds their major economic interest, and furs are goods of very great value and comparatively little bulk, easily carried in canoes and small boats. Moreover, led by the Jesuits, the Catholic French gave proof of a far greater missionary zeal than did the Protestant English. The priest, as well as the *coureur des bois* (trapper), led the push westward. Finally, the French in North America were guided in their expansion by a conscious imperial policy directed from the France of the Bourbon monarchs, *la grande nation* at the height of its prestige and power.

Accordingly, it was the French, not the English, who explored the interior of the continent. By 1712 they had built up a line of settlements—or rather, isolated trading posts, with miles of empty space between, thinly populated by Indians—which completely encircled the English colonies on the Atlantic coast. The story of these French explorers, missionaries, and traders, admirably told by the American historian Francis Parkman, is one of the most fascinating pages of history. The names of many of them—La Salle, Père Marquette, Joliet, Frontenac, Cadillac, Iberville—are a part of our American heritage. Lines of outposts led westward from Quebec to the Great Lakes, and other lines moved northward up the Mississippi from Mobile and New Orleans (where a colony named Louisiana after Louis XIV had been founded at the beginning of the eighteenth century) to join them.

Yet, impressive though this French imperial thrust looks on the map, it was far too lightly held to be equal to the task of pushing the English into the sea. It was a trading empire with military ambitions, and except in Quebec it never became a true colony of settlement. And even there it never grew in the critical eighteenth century beyond a few thousand inhabitants. Frenchmen simply did not come over in sufficient numbers, and those who did come spread themselves out over vast distances as traders and simple adventurers. Frenchmen who might have come, the Huguenots who might have settled down as did the Yankee Puritans, were excluded by a royal policy bent on maintaining the Catholic faith in New France.

## The Indies, West and East

The northwestern European maritime powers intruded upon the pioneer Spanish and Portuguese both in the New World and in the Old. The French, Dutch, and English all sought to gain footholds in South America, but had to settle for the unimportant Guianas. They broke up thoroughly the Spanish hold on the Caribbean, however, and ultimately made that sea of many islands a kaleidoscope of colonial jurisdictions and a center of constant naval wars and piracy. Today, these West Indian islands are for the most part a seriously depressed area, with the growth of the tourist industry their main hope; in early modern times, however, they were one of the great prizes of imperialism. The cheap slave labor that had replaced the exterminated Carib Indians raised for their masters on the plantations the great staple tropical crops, tobacco, fruits, coffee, and, most basic of all, cane sugar, which had as yet no rival in beet sugar, a crop that flourishes today in northern climates.

The French, Dutch, and English began as well to raid the trading empires the Iberian powers had set up in the Old World; they also raided one another, both in times of official peace and in wartime. By 1715, the bases of their trading and colonial empires had been firmly laid in Asia and Africa. India proved to be the richest prize, and the most ardently fought for. The Mogul Empire was not strong enough in southern India to keep the Europeans out, but it did prove strong enough to confine them on the whole to the coastal fringes. Gradually, in the course of the seventeenth century both the French and the English established themselves in India on the heels of decaying Portuguese power and wealth. The English defeated a Portuguese fleet in 1612 and immediately thereafter got trading rights at Surat on the western coast. Although the able and active Mogul emperor Aurangzeb tried to revoke their rights in 1685, he soon found their naval and mercantile power too much to withstand. In 1690, the English founded in Bengal in eastern India the city they were to make famous, Calcutta. Meanwhile, the French had got footholds on the south coast near Madras, at a place called Pondichéry, and soon had established other stations. By the beginning of the eighteenth century, the stage was set in India as in North America for the decisive struggle for overseas empire between France and Britain.

Both countries operated in India, as they had initially in North America, by means of chartered trading companies, the English East India Company and the French Compagnie des Indes Orientales. In their trading activities the companies were backed up by their governments when it was clear that bits of land around the trading posts had to be held, and that the whole relation with India could not be a purely commercial one. Gradually, both countries became involved in support of their companies in Indian politics and wars. But neither country made an effort to found a New England or a New France in the East.

The Dutch entered even more vigorously into the competition, founding their own East India (1602) and West India (1621) companies. In sharp contrast to the close government supervision exerted by Spain and Portugal over colonial activities every step of the way, the Dutch granted these private business ventures full sovereign powers. They had the right to maintain their own fighting fleets and armies, declare war and wage it, negotiate peace, and govern dependent territories. The Netherlands East India Company succeeded in pushing the Portuguese out of Ceylon and then, bypassing India proper, concentrated on southeastern Asia, especially the East Indies. Here again they pushed the Portuguese out, save for part of the island of Timor, and they also discouraged English interlopers. And through it all the company paid an annual dividend averaging 18 percent. In spite of their rapid decline as a great power in the eighteenth century, the Dutch got so firm a hold in Java and Sumatra that their empire in Indonesia was to last until the mid-twentieth century.

### Africa

All three of the northern maritime powers needed to use the same basic ocean route around Africa that the Portuguese had pioneered in the fifteenth century. All three got African posts. The Dutch put themselves in a good strategic situation by occupying the southern tip of Africa, the Cape of Good Hope, in 1652. The cape was for them essentially a fitting station for their ships on the long voyage to Indonesia and the Far East, but it was empty except for primitive tribes, and its climate was suitable for Europeans. Though immigration was never heavy, a colony of settlement did grow up, the nucleus of the Afrikaners of South Africa today. Here, notably, the French Huguenots were welcomed. In West Africa, the Dutch took from the Portuguese some posts on the Gold and Guinea coasts, and got a share of the increasingly lucrative slave trade.

The French also worked down the African coast, which was not held in the blocks of territory seen on the map today, but in separate posts which gave ample room for interlopers. In 1626, the French were in Senegal in West Africa. In the Indian Ocean they were on the island of Madagascar, formally annexed by Louis XIV in 1686; in 1715 they took the island of Mauritius from the Dutch, rechristening it the Isle de France. The British broke into the competition by securing a foothold at the mouth of the Gambia River in West Africa (1662), later followed by other acquisitions at French and Dutch expense. Thus a map of Africa and adjacent waters in the eighteenth century shows a series of coastal stations controlled by the various European imperial powers. But the interior remained untouched, save by the slavers and native traders, and was to all intents and purposes unexplored. Only in the nineteenth century was the "Dark Continent" opened up to European expansion.

### The Far East

China, long established as a great empire, was better able to withstand European pressure for territory. Somehow, even in the decay of their imperial power, the Portuguese were able to cling to Macao, and the Dutch, on their heels as always, obtained a station on Formosa in 1624. The Jesuits, bringing with them European instruments and learning that interested the Chinese, were able in the seventeenth century to get tolerated positions in China, but they made little real headway against rooted Chinese ways of life. Indeed, the Chinese, convinced that their own land was the Middle Kingdom—that is, central in a spiritual and cultural sense—of the whole world, regarded the Europeans as ignorant barbarians who should be paying them tribute. They kept open only the slender privileged trade from Canton and Macao. This trade was indeed enough to keep Chinese and Europeans in firm contact, but the real opening of China was not yet.

In Japan, the European penetration started much as in China. In 1549, the great Jesuit missionary Saint Francis Xavier had begun work with the Japanese. In the sixteenth century the Portuguese, and in 1609 the Dutch, won trading footholds. General trade with the Europeans was carried on from Nagasaki. But the Japanese reacted even more strongly than did the Chinese. Though Christianity did not make wholesale conversions, it did make considerable headway. The Tokugawa family, the feudal military rulers of Japan from 1600 to 1868, feared Christianity not only as a threat to national traditions but also as a threat to their own rule, because of the opportunities it might give European powers to intervene in Japanese politics and intrigue with their enemies. They therefore decided to close their land entirely to foreign dangers. In the early seventeenth century, they suppressed Christianity by force and sealed off Japan. Foreigners were refused entry, and Japanese were refused exit; even the building of large ships capable of sailing the ocean was forbidden. The

*The Dutch island in Nagasaki harbor, 1699.*

Dutch, who had persuaded the Japanese that Protestants were less subversive than the Catholic Portuguese, were allowed, under strict supervision, to cling to an island in Nagasaki harbor, where after 1715 they were limited to two ships a year. Not until the American Commodore Perry came to Japan in 1853 was this amazing self-blockade really broken and Japan thrown open to the rest of the world.

## East by Land: The Russian Thrust to the Pacific

The expansion of Europe in these early modern centuries was not restricted to the Atlantic maritime powers. Although our own American tradition naturally centers on the Columbuses, the Magellans, the Captain John Smiths, general history must find a place for the extraordinary Russian exploration and conquest of Siberia. It offers all sorts of parallels with European expansion in the New World, from the chronological (the Russians crossed the Urals from Europe into Asia in 1483) to the political, for the expanding Muscovite state of Russia was a "new" monarchy, newer in some ways than the Spain of Charles V and Philip II or the England of Elizabeth I. This Russian movement has also been likened to the American expansion from the Atlantic seaboard to the Pacific. Compared with the Russian advance to the Pacific, the American westward movement was relatively slow, however: the Russians covered some 5,000 miles in about forty years; we took longer to go a shorter distance. But the Russian advance left vast areas "behind the lines" unsettled and unabsorbed at each stage, whereas our own more gradual movement tended to consolidate each stage rather more than the Russians did.

Then, too, the American pioneer faced formidable geographic barriers of mountain and desert, whereas the Russian had easier going on the enormous Siberian flatlands, where the river basins—the Ob, the Yenisei, the Lena, and their tributaries—facilitated rapid progress. For the Americans too, the Indians often posed serious military and political problems, whereas the Siberian tribesmen, widely scattered across the area, seem on the whole to have helped the Russians rather than to have opposed them. Though enormous in extent, Siberia continued to be very sparsely inhabited.

It was the victories of Ivan the Terrible over the Kazan Tatars that led to the first major advances in the sixteenth century. Private enterprise led the way: the Stroganov family obtained huge concessions in the Ural area, where they made great fortunes in the fur trade, and discovered and began to exploit the first iron mines known in Russia. The Stroganovs hired bands of Cossack explorers, who led the eastward movement. The government followed at some distance behind with administrators and tax collectors, soldiers and priests, as each new area was opened up. At a suitable point on a river basin, the spearhead of the advance party would build a wooden palisade and begin to collect furs from the surrounding countryside. Almost before the defenses of each new position had been consolidated, the restless advance guard would have moved some hundreds of miles further eastward to repeat the process. The Daniel Boone of the Siberian adventure was surely the famous Cossack leader Yermak, whose exploits in his own lifetime took on legendary proportions.

Tobolsk, the first major Siberian center founded by the Russians, remained a major seat of administration; but Irkutsk and finally Okhotsk on the Pacific were reached by the 1640's. A Siberian bureau in Moscow had nominal responsibility for the government of the huge area, but decisions had to be made on the spot because of the communications problem, although the Russians had an efficient postal service working quite early. Thus the Siberians always tended to have the independence traditionally associated with men of the wide open spaces, and reinforced by the Cossack and outlaw traditions from which many of them sprang. Because Okhotsk and its neighborhood along the Pacific were intensely cold, and the ocean frozen for a good many months in the year, the Russians were soon looking enviously southward toward the valley of the Amur, which flowed into the Pacific at a point where the harbors were open all the year round.

Explorations in this area brought the Russians into contact with the Chinese, whose lands they were now casually invading. But the Chinese government of the period did not care very much about these regions, which, from its own point of view, were far-northerly outposts. In 1689 the Chinese signed a treaty with Moscow, the first they had concluded with any European state. This treaty stabilized the frontier, demilitarized the Amur Valley, and kept the Russians out of Manchuria, the home territory of the ruling Chinese dynasty. It also provided the two powers with a buffer region of Mongolian-inhabited territory, which acknowledged Chinese overlordship. Incidentally, it also recognized the Russian advances to the north. With almost incredible speed, the Russians had acquired an empire whose riches are even today by no means fully exploited. Russia's future as an Asian power with a vital interest in Pacific affairs was established at just about the time the English took New Amsterdam from the Dutch.

## North by Sea to the Arctic

By 1715, the expansion of Europe was beginning to affect almost every part of the globe. European explorers, missionaries, traders, proconsuls of empire, had spread out in all directions. Even Arctic exploration, stimulated by the hope of finding a Northwest or a Northeast Passage that would shorten the route to the Far East, had already gone a long way by the beginning of the eighteenth century. Henry Hudson had found not only the Hudson River but also Hudson's Bay in the far north of Canada. In the late seventeenth century, English adventurers and investors formed an enterprise that still flourishes in Canada today—the Hudson's Bay Company, originally set up for fur trading along the great bay to the northwest of the French settlement in Quebec. In the late sixteenth century, the Dutch under Barents had penetrated far into the European Arctic, had discovered the island of Spitsbergen to the north of Norway, and had ranged across the sea named after their leader, the Barents Sea. Finally, the Russians under government patronage explored most of the long Arctic coasts of their empire early in the eighteenth century.

# V The Impact of Expansion

## The Black Side of the Record

The record of European expansion contains pages as grim as any in history. The African slave trade, begun by the Portuguese and entered by other peoples for its financial gains, is a series of horrors, from the rounding up of the slaves by native chieftains in Africa through their transportation across the Atlantic to their sale in the Indies. What strikes a modern most of all is the matter-of-fact acceptance of this trade, as if the blacks were literally so much livestock. The Dutch slave trader *St. Jan* (note the irony of the saint's name) started off for Curaçao in the West Indies in 1659. Her log recorded every day or so deaths of slaves aboard, in parallel columns for men, women, and children, until between June 30 and October 29 a total of 59 men, 47 women, and 4 children had died. But there were still 95 slaves aboard when disaster struck, thus simply and unmovingly recorded:

> *Nov. 1.* Lost our ship on the Reef of Rocus, and all hands immediately took to the boat, as there was no prospect of saving the slaves, for we must abandon the ship in consequence of the heavy surf.
>
> *Nov. 4.* Arrived with the boat at the island of Curaçao; the Hon'ble Governor Beck ordered two sloops to take the slaves off the wreck, one of which sloops with eighty four slaves on board was captured by a privateer.*

And here is the Hon'ble Governor Beck's report to his Board of Directors in Holland:

> What causes us most grief here is, that your honors have thereby lost such a fine lot of negroes and such a fast sailing bark which has been our right arm here.
>
> Although I have strained every nerve to overtake the robbers of the negroes and bark, as stated in my last, yet have I not been as successful as I wished. . . .
>
> We regret exceedingly that such rovers should have been the cause of the ill success of the zeal we feel to attract the Spanish traders hither for your honors' benefit, by previous notices and otherwise, for the augmentation of commerce and the sale of the negroes which are to come here more and more in your honors' ships and for your account. . . .
>
> I have witnessed with pleasure your honors' diligence in providing us here from time to time with negroes. That will be the only bait to allure hither the Spanish nation, as well from the Main as from other parts, to carry on trade of any importance. But the more subtly and quietly the trade to and on this island can be carried on, the better will it be for this place and yours.*

Americans need hardly be reminded of the fact that we virtually exterminated the native Indian population east of the Mississippi, and that if they massacred us when they could, we replied in kind often enough, and with superior means. There were, of course, exceptions to this bloody rule. In New England, missionaries like John Eliot did set up little bands of "praying Indians," and in Pennsylvania, the record of the relations between the Quakers and the Indians was excellent. The white man's diseases, which in those days could hardly have been controlled, and the white man's alcoholic drinks, which were surely quite as hard to control, did more to exterminate the red men than did fire and sword.

## The Economic Record

Seen in terms of economics, however, the expansion of Europe in early modern times was by no means the pure "exploitation" and "plundering" it sometimes appears to be in the rhetoric of anti-imperialists. There was robbery, just as there was murder or enslavement. There was, in dealing with the natives, even more giving of slight or nominal value in exchange for land and goods of great value. Just as all Americans are familiar with the slogan "The only good Indian is a dead Indian," so they know for how little the Indians sold the island of Manhattan. Finally, the almost universally applied mercantilist policy kept money and manufacturing in the hands of the home country. It relegated the colonies to the

**Documents Illustrative of the History of the Slave Trade to America,* ed. Elizabeth Donnan (Washington, D. C., 1930), I, 143.

*Ibid., pp. 150, 151.

production of raw materials, a role not so well rewarded, generally speaking, as other economic roles, and one that tended to keep even colonies of settlement in a relatively primitive and certainly economically dependent condition.

Still, with all these limitations granted, the expansion of Europe was in economic terms an expansion of the total wealth produced here on earth. Although Europeans certainly took the lion's share in these early days, the expansion added to the goods available to non-Europeans. Not many European mercantilist monopolies were so watertight in practice that they prevented enterprising natives from sharing in the new trade and its profits. Although few Europeans settled in India or in Africa, their wares, and especially their weapons, began gradually the process of europeanizing, or westernizing, or modernizing the rest of the world. By the eighteenth century this process was only beginning, and in particular few of the improvements in public health and sanitation that Europeans were to bring to the East had yet come about; nor had any greater public order come to India and Africa. But over the whole world, in the New World especially, there were signs of the material progress that was to result in the worldwide "revolution of rising expectations" of our own time.

## Effects of Expansion on the West

The West has in its turn been greatly affected by its relations with other peoples. The list of items that have come into Western life since Marco Polo and Columbus is long. It includes foodstuffs above all; utensils and gadgets, pipes for smoking, hammocks and pajamas; styles of architecture and painting, bungalows and Japanese prints; and much else. Some of the novelties caught on more quickly than others. Tobacco, brought into Spain in the mid-sixteenth century as a soothing drug, had established itself by the seventeenth century as essential to the peace of mind of many European males. Maize or Indian corn (in Europe, "corn" refers to cereal grains in general) was imported from the New World and widely cultivated in well-watered areas of Spain and Italy. Potatoes, on the other hand, though their calorie content is high and though they are cheaper to grow in most climates than the staple breadstuffs, did not immediately catch on in Europe. In France, they had to be popularized in a regular campaign which took generations to be effective. Tomatoes, the "love-apples" of our great-grandfathers, were long believed to be poisonous and were cultivated only for their looks. Tea and coffee, which Europeans and North Americans now take for granted as imports everyone uses, were just beginning to become available in large quantities by 1700.

Among Westerners, knowledge of non-European beliefs and institutions eventually penetrated to the level of popular culture, where it is marked by a host of words—"powwow," "kowtow," "taboo," "totem," for instance. At the highest level of cultural interchange, that of religion and ethical ideas, however, the West took little from the new worlds opened after Columbus. The first impression of Westerners, not only when they met the relatively primitive cultures of the New World, but even when they met the old cultures of the East, was that they had nothing to learn from them. Once the process of interchange had gone far enough, some individuals were impressed with the mysticism and otherworldliness of Hindu philosophy and religion, and with the high but quite this-worldly ethics of Chinese Confucianism. Others came to admire the dignity and simplicity of the lives of many primitive peoples. But for the most part what struck the Europeans—when they bothered at all to think about anything more than money-making and empire-building—was the poverty, dirt, and superstition they found among the masses in India and China, the low material standards of primitive peoples everywhere, the heathenness of the heathens.

Yet certainly exposure to these very different cultures acted as a stimulus in the West and broadened our horizons. The mere accumulation of so much new information gave the Western mind something new to occupy itself with. Perhaps the first effect was no more than to increase the fund of the marvelous, the incredible. The early accounts of the New World are full of giants and pygmies, El Dorados where the streets are paved with gold, fountains of eternal youth, wonderful plants and animals. All this was a great stimulus to the literary and artistic imagination, from the island of Shakespeare's *Tempest* to the Xanadu of Coleridge's *Kubla Khan*.

But science, too, was encouraged. A dip into any of the early collections of voyages, say the famous and easily available record of voyages edited in English by Richard Hakluyt in 1582, gives an impression more of the realistic sense and careful observation of these travelers than of their credulity and exaggerations. Here is modern geography already well on the way to maturity, and here too is the foundation of the modern social sciences of anthropology, comparative government, even of economics. Here, as well as in the work of a Bacon or a Galileo, you will find the origins of that important modern Western contribution to the culture of our world, natural science. A good example is the following attempt to report on the puzzling Hindu institution of caste. It is from the travels of Pietro della Valle, an early seventeenth-century Italian:

> The whole Gentile-people of *India* is divided into many sects or parties of men, known and distinguisht by descent or pedigree, as the Tribes of the Jews sometimes were; yet they inhabit the Country promiscuously mingled together, in every City and Land several Races one with another. 'Tis reckon'd that they are in all eighty four; some say more, making a more exact and subtle division. Every one of these hath a particular name, and also a special office and Employment in the Commonwealth, from which none of the descendants of that Race ever swerve; they never rise nor fall, nor change condition: whence some are Husbandmen, others Mechanicks, as Taylers, Shoemakers and the like; other Factors or Merchants, such as they whom we call *Banians,* but they in their Language more correctly *Vania;* others, Souldiers, as the *Ragiaputi;* . . . so many Races which they reckon are reduc'd to four principal, which, if I mistake not, are the Brachmans, the Souldiers, the Merchants and the Artificers; from whom by more minute subdivision all the rest are deriv'd, in such number as in the whole people there are various professions of men.*

It may well be that the intellectual effects of the great discoveries were on the whole unsettling, disturbing. They helped, along with the new astronomy, the new mechanics, the Protestant Reformation, and much else, to break the medieval "cake of custom." They helped, literally, to make a New World of ideas and ideals. Such changes are always hard on ordinary human beings, for they demand that men change their minds, something which most of us, in spite of current American belief to the contrary, find very hard to do.

* *The Travels of Pietro della Valle in India,* ed. Edward Grey (London, 1892), I, 78–79.

## The Revolution in Prices

One great effect of the discoveries had repercussions that are still evident. The great new supplies of gold and silver from the Americas set in motion a long-term trend toward rising prices. By the middle of the seventeenth century, Spain is estimated to have imported 18,000 tons of bullion—enough to increase the gold supply of Europe by 20 percent and the silver supply by 300 percent. Everywhere new coins were circulated, and everywhere prices rose—by some 400 percent in Spain during the sixteenth century, by less dramatic but still substantial amounts elsewhere. This escalation of prices accompanied and helped to cause a general economic expansion that ultimately produced the Industrial Revolution.

In the long process of inflation and expansion, which has continued with ups and downs to the present, some groups gained and others lost. In general, the merchants, financiers, "businessmen" in the broadest sense, enjoyed a rising standard of living. Those on relatively fixed incomes suffered, including landed proprietors, unless they turned to large-scale capitalist farming, and including also governments, unless they were able to cultivate new sources of income. Wage earners, artisans, peasants, and the mass of people generally did not receive additional income as fast as prices rose until very recent years. In short, here as elsewhere, the effects of expansion were unsettling, often indeed harsh, as well as stimulating.

A distinguished American historian, Walter P. Webb, made a still more sweeping generalization about the effects of these extraordinary discoveries. The vast new lands of the "frontier" in the New World were, he maintained, a bonanza or windfall, and supplied the real force behind the great increase in man's power to get more out of his natural environment with less sacrifice, the real force behind the great novelty of modern Western civilization—its wealth and power.*

Here it must be noted again that the attempt to find a single, one-way causative factor in the great movements of history is a dangerous one. The great opportunities for expansion that the

*Walter P. Webb, *The Great Frontier* (Boston, 1952).

discoveries of the explorers gave to Europeans were certainly a factor in the rapid growth of productivity, population, and technical skills that characterizes the modern world. The great and easily acquired supplies of gold and silver from the New World were in the late sixteenth century a specific and useful "pump-priming" that furthered the growth of modern capitalism in northwest Europe. But the "frontier theory" of modern Western capitalist society is no more to be taken as a sole explanation than, say, the Marxist theory of economic determinism or the Weber theory of the spirit of Protestant ethics. Most obviously, the roots of the discoveries themselves, like the roots of Protestantism and modern science, lie deep in the Middle Ages. Before the new worlds could be available to Europeans at all, trade, navigation, government organization—all had to arrive at the point where Henry the Navigator, Columbus, da Gama, and the others could proceed methodically to the discoveries and conquests that after all had been there for the Greeks, the Phoenicians, the Romans, or the Vikings to make, had they been able and willing.

### Toward One World

By the beginning of the eighteenth century, there were still blank spots on the map of the world, especially in the interior of Africa and in our Pacific Northwest. Yet, in spite of this and in spite of the fact that Japan and, to a lesser extent, China tried to exclude European influence, it was already clear that only one system of international politics existed in the world. From now on, all general European wars tended to be world wars. They were fought, if only by privateers, on all the seven seas, and, if only by savages and frontiersmen, on all the continents. Sooner or later, any considerable transfer of territory anywhere, any great accession of strength or wealth anywhere, had its effect on the precarious international equilibrium that we call the balance of power. From the eighteenth century on, there was One World.

This was certainly not One World of the spirit. There was no common authority of any kind that could reach all men. There were pockets of isolated peoples. And the masses of the world, even at its center in Europe, were ignorant enough of what really went on in the hearts and heads of men elsewhere. But already Western goods penetrated almost everywhere, led by firearms, but followed by a great many other commodities, not all of them "cheap and nasty," as later critics of imperialism complained. Already an educated minority was growing up all over the world from professional geographers to journalists, diplomatists, and men of business, who had to deal with what are now for the first time quite literally the affairs of the whole world and its peoples.

## Reading Suggestions on the Expansion of Europe

BACKGROUND AND GENERAL ACCOUNTS

J. H. Parry, *The Age of Reconnaissance* (*Mentor) and *The Establishment of the European Hegemony, 1415–1715: Trade and Exploration in the Age of the Renaissance* (*Torchbooks). Excellent introductions by a ranking expert in the field.

C. E. Nowell, *The. Great Discoveries and the First Colonial Empires* (*Cornell Univ. Press). Handy brief introduction.

B. Penrose, *Travel and Discovery in the Renaissance, 1420–1620* (*Atheneum). Very informative survey with accounts of voyages not easily available elsewhere.

J. N. L. Baker, *A History of Geographical Discovery and Exploration,* rev. ed. (Barnes and Noble, 1963). A standard work.

P. Sykes, *A History of Exploration from the Earliest Times to the Present* (Routledge, 1934). A comprehensive treatment of the subject.

C. R. Beazley, *The Dawn of Modern Geography,* 3 vols. (John Murray, 1897–1906). An authoritative account; stops in 1420 but useful for the background of this chapter.

G. Jones, *The Norse Atlantic Saga* (Oxford Univ. Press, 1964). A recent summary of what we know, not exaggerated.

H. Trevor-Roper, ed., *The Age of Expansion: Europe and the World, 1559–1660* (McGraw-Hill, 1968). By no means so comprehensive in treatment as the title suggests, but with enlightening chapters on the Spaniards, the Dutch, and the Far East.

THE PORTUGUESE

C. R. Boxer, *The Portuguese Seaborne Empire, 1415–1825* (Knopf, 1969). Admirable study by a leading expert in the series "History of Human Society." Boxer has also written a succinct survey covering the same period: *Four Centuries of Portuguese Expansion* (*Univ. of California Press).

E. Sanceau, *Henry the Navigator* (Norton, 1947). A good biography of the Portuguese sponsor of exploration.

H. H. Hart, *Sea Road to the Indies* (Macmillan, 1950). Deals with da Gama and other Portuguese explorers.

C. McK. Parr, *So Noble a Captain* (Crowell, 1953). A very scholarly treatment of Magellan and his circumnavigation.

THE SPANIARDS

J. H. Parry, *The Spanish Seaborne Empire* (Knopf, 1966). Excellent up-to-date account; in the useful series "History of Human Society."

S. E. Morison, *Admiral of the Ocean Sea,* 2 vols. (Little, Brown, 1942). The best book on Columbus; by a historian who retraced Columbus' route in a small ship. He has also published the briefer *Christopher Columbus, Mariner* (*Mentor).

C. H. Haring, *The Spanish Empire in America* (Oxford Univ. Press, 1947). Long a standard treatment of the subject.

W. H. Prescott, *The Conquest of Mexico* and *The Conquest of Peru* (many editions). Celebrated narratives written more than a century ago; may be sampled in various abridgments, among them *The Portable Prescott* (*Viking).

L. B. Hanke, *The Spanish Struggle for Justice in the Conquest of America* (*Little, Brown). Study of an important and often neglected side of the Spanish record.

THE DUTCH

C. R. Boxer, *The Dutch Seaborne Empire, 1600–1800* (Hutchinson, 1965). Full up-to-date survey by a capable scholar: another volume in the "History of Human Society."

A. Hyma, *The Dutch in the Far East* (Wahr, 1942). Stressing social and economic developments.

B. H. M. Vlekke, *Nusantara: A History of Indonesia,* rev. ed. (Lorenz, 1959). Introduction to the most important region of Dutch imperial activity.

THE FRENCH AND THE BRITISH

J. B. Brebner, *The Explorers of North America, 1492–1806* (*Meridian). Good brief survey.

G. Lanctot, *History of Canada,* 2 vols. (Harvard, 1963–1964). Detailed study to 1713; by a French Canadian scholar.

G. M. Wrong, *The Rise and Fall of New France,* 2 vols. (Macmillan, 1928). Sound study by an English Canadian scholar.

S. E. Morison, ed., *The Parkman Reader* (*Little, Brown). Selections from the celebrated multivolumed *France and England in North America* by the famous nineteenth-century historian Francis Parkman.

J. H. Rose, ed., *The Cambridge History of the British Empire,* Vol. I (Cambridge Univ. Press, 1929). Detailed survey to 1783.

AFRICA, ASIA, AND THE PACIFIC

H. Labouret, *Africa before the White Man* (Walker, 1963); B. Davidson, *Africa in History* (Macmillan, 1969); R. Oliver and J. D. Fage, *A Short History of Africa* (*Penguin). Three helpful introductions.

D. F. Lach and C. Flamenhauf, eds., *Asia on the Eve of Europe's Expansion* (*Spectrum). Introductory survey.

R. Grousset, *The Civilizations of the East,* 4 vols. (Knopf, 1931–1934). Vol. III is particularly enlightening on Chinese culture; other volumes deal with the Middle East, India, and Japan.

A. L. Basham, *The Wonder That Was India* (*Evergreen). A more careful survey of Indian history up to the Muslim invasions than the title might suggest.

E. D. Reischauer and J. K. Fairbank, *East Asia: The Great Tradition* (Houghton, 1960). An expert survey of China, Japan, and Korea from the beginnings.

K. S. Latourette, *China* (*Spectrum). Excellent introduction.

G. B. Sansom, *Japan: A Short Cultural History,* rev. ed. (Appleton, 1962). Perceptive study by a leading British expert who has also written more detailed works.

C. Lloyd, *Pacific Horizons* (Allen & Unwin, 1946), and *Captain Cook* (Faber & Faber, 1952). Readable modern reviews of early Pacific exploration.

THE AMERICAS

J. Soustelle, *Daily Life of the Aztecs on the Eve of the Spanish Conquest* (Weidenfeld & Nicolson, 1961). Instructive study by an anthropologist.

S. J. and B. Stein, *Colonial Heritage of Latin America* (*Oxford Univ. Press). Essays stressing economic dependence.

H. Robinson, *Latin America* (*Praeger). Informative geographical survey.

A. P. Newton, *The European Nations in the West Indies, 1493–1688* (Black, 1933). Excellent study of a great arena of colonial rivalry.

C. M. Andrews, *The Colonial Period of American History* (*Yale Univ. Press). Volumes 1–3 of this detailed study treat the settlements.

D. J. Boorstin, *Americans: The Colonial Experience* (*Vintage). A provocative briefer treatment.

L. B. Wright, *Cultural Life of the American Colonies, 1607–1763* (*Torchbooks). An especially good volume in the series "New American Nation."

THE IMPACT OF EXPANSION

B. Davidson, *African Slave Trade* (*Atlantic Monthly Press). By a prolific writer on African history.

D. Lach, *China in the Eyes of Europe* (*Phoenix). The view in the sixteenth century; Lach has also published companion volumes on India, Japan, and Southeast Asia (all *Phoenix).

*The Cambridge Economic History,* Vol. IV (Cambridge Univ. Press, 1967). Scholarly essays on expanding Europe in the sixteenth and seventeenth centuries.

E. J. Hamilton, *American Treasure and the Price Revolution in Spain,1501–1650* (Harvard Univ. Press, 1934). Long a standard study, but its conclusions are now being reappraised.

HISTORICAL FICTION

N. Shute [pseud.], *An Old Captivity* (*Lancer). On the Viking explorer Leif Ericson.

L. Wallace, *The Fair God* (*Popular Library). A real thriller, a century old, on the Aztecs of Mexico; by the author of *Ben Hur.*

C. S. Forester, *To the Indies* (Little, Brown, 1940). Fine novel on Columbus.

R. Sabatini, *The Sea Hawk* (Houghton, 1923). A good melodramatic novel of adventures on the sea in the late sixteenth century.

W. Cather, *Shadows on the Rock* (Knopf, 1931). Sensitive recreation of life in New France by a distinguished modern American novelist.

# 15

# *Divine-Right Monarchy—and Revolution*

*Above: Bernini's lifesize marble sculpture "The Ecstasy of St. Teresa," 1645–1652.*
*Above right: Painting of a Molière farce, with Molière himself at the far left.*
*Right: St. Paul's Cathedral, London, begun in 1675.*

## I Introduction

The Peace of Westphalia in 1648 brought to a close not only the Thirty Years' War but also a whole epoch in European history. It ended the age of the Reformation and Counter-Reformation, when wars were both religious and dynastic in motivation and the chief threats to a stable international balance came from the Catholic Hapsburgs and from the militant Protestants of Germany and the Netherlands. After 1648 religion, though continuing to be a major source of friction in France and the British Isles, ceased to be a significant international issue. The main force jeopardizing the European balance was the entirely secular ambitions of Bourbon France, for seventy-two years—from 1643 to 1715—under a single monarch, Louis XIV, who inherited the throne at the age of four and a half. Louis was the very embodiment of the characteristic early modern form of royal absolutism, monarchy by

FARCEVRS FRANÇOIS ET ITALIENS
DEPVIS 60 ANS ET PLVS
EN 1670

*An illustration from Abraham Bosse's "Le Palais Royal" (1640) gives a good picture of French fashions and taste.*

divine right, and he was the very personification of royal pride, elegance, and luxury. To the French Louis XIV was the *grand monarque*, and his long, long reign marked the culmination of their *grand siècle*, the great century that had begun under Cardinal Richelieu in the twenty years before Louis's accession and that was marked by the international triumph of French arms and French diplomacy and still more, French ways of writing, building, dressing, and eating, the whole style of life of the upper classes in *la grande nation*.

While the culture of *la grande nation* went from one triumph to another, Louis XIV's bid for political hegemony was ultimately checked. His most resolute opponent was England, still in the throes of the greatest political upheaval in her history. The upheaval resulted from the collision between the forces of the Stuart monarchy and High Church Anglicanism, on the one hand, and those of Parliament and the Puritans, on the other. The final settlement was a compromise weighted in favor of the parliamentary side, but still a compromise and therefore compatible with the modern image of England as the country of gradual, peaceful, orderly change. This was not the image prevailing in the seventeenth century, after decades of violence and flux, with one English king executed and another obliged to go into exile. In those days, understandably, England was synonymous with revolution.

The English political turmoil was not the only seventeenth-century revolution. Alfred North Whitehead, the eminent English mathematician and philosopher of the early twentieth century, called the 1600's "the century of genius." It was the century of Galileo and Francis Bacon, of Descartes and Pascal, of Newton and Locke, and of many others who helped to build the foundations of modern science, to provide it with indispensable tools, and to establish patterns of thought and procedures that are variously known as rational, empirical, and inductive. This intellectual and scientific revolution had repercussions more far-reaching than those emanating from the court or the culture of Louis XIV's France or even from the England of the Puritan revolution. The "century of genius" was the necessary prelude to what has been termed "the great modern revolution," the practical applications of the new science and technology, above all the radical transformation in the techniques of producing goods. The results have been dazzling technical feats and the provision of plenty and comfort on an unprecedented scale—but also materialism of unprecedented dimensions, and bitterness and hostility on the part of disadvantaged groups, classes, and nations.

## II Bourbon France

### Louis XIII and Richelieu

France's *grand siècle* was almost blighted in the bud when, in 1610, the capable and popular Henry IV was assassinated by a madman in the prime of his career. The new king, Louis XIII (1610–1643), was only nine years old; the queen-mother, Marie de' Medici, served as regent but showed little of her famous family's political skill. Her Italian favorites and French nobles, Catholic and Huguenot both, carried on a hectic competition which threatened to undo all that Henry IV had accomplished. In the course of these troubles the French representative body, the Estates General, met at Blois in 1614 for what was destined to be its last meeting until 1789 on the eve of the great French Revolution. Significantly, the meeting was paralyzed by tensions between the noble deputies of the second estate and the bourgeois of the third. Meanwhile, Louis XIII, though barely in his teens, was attempting to assert authority personally and reduce the role of his mother. Poorly educated, sickly, nervous, and subject to spells of depression, Louis needed expert help; he was fortunate in securing that of a remarkably talented assistant, Richelieu (1585–1642).

Efficient and ambitious, a sincere but not an ardent Catholic, Richelieu had proved his administrative capacity as bishop of Luçon. Tiring of life in a remote bishopric, he moved to Paris and showed great skill and considerable unscrupulousness in political maneuvering during the confused days of Marie de' Medici's regency. He emerged as the conciliator between the king and his mother, and was rewarded with election to the College of Cardinals and then, in 1624, with selection by Louis as his chief minister. While the king maintained a lively interest in affairs of state and was by no means a "do-nothing" king, Richelieu was the virtual ruler of France for the next eighteen years. He proved to be a good Machiavellian and a good *politique*, subordinating religion and every nonpolitical consideration to *raison d'état* (reason of state), a phrase that he probably coined himself.

When Richelieu entered the king's service, he claimed to have promised Louis that he would "ruin the Huguenot party, humble the pride of the great nobles, recall all his subjects to their duty, and raise his name among foreign nations to the level where it ought to be."* The promise proved to be a largely accurate forecast of Richelieu's program and accomplishments. *Raison d'état* made the "ruin" of the Huguenot party his first priority, for the political privileges the Huguenots had received by the Edict of Nantes made them a major obstacle to the creation of a centralized state. The hundred fortified towns they governed, chiefly in southwestern France, constituted a state within the state, a hundred

*As quoted in C. J. Friedrich, *The Age of the Baroque, 1610–1660* (New York, 1952), p. 198 n. Our translation.

*Triple portrait of Richelieu, by Champaigne.*

centers of potential rebellion that Richelieu was determined to bring under control. Alarmed, the Huguenots did in fact rebel. It took the royal forces fourteen months to besiege and take their chief stronghold, the Atlantic port of La Rochelle. It finally fell in 1628 after the besiegers constructed a great jetty to seal off the access of its harbor to the sea (Louis XIII, incidentally, was so excited by the project that he wanted to lend the masons a hand in the work). Richelieu thereupon canceled the political and military clauses of the Edict of Nantes but left its religious provisions intact.

The siege of La Rochelle lasted so long because France scarcely possessed a navy worth the name. In the next ten years, Richelieu created a fleet of thirty-eight warships for the Atlantic and a dozen galleys, manned by slaves (an exception to the rule that white men were never enslaved in the modern Western world), for the Mediterranean. Meanwhile, he skillfully guided France through the Thirty Years' War, his eye always on the greatness of France, husbanding French resources carefully, committing them only when concrete gains for France seemed possible, and ensuring favorable publicity by supplying exaggerated accounts of French victories for the *Gazette de France*. In every way Richelieu was one of the great practitioners of realistic power politics in international relations.

*Raison d'état*, indeed, motivated all his policies. He lived in elaborate style, accompanied on his travels by his private choir and corps of musicians, not just because he was fond of music but because he believed such a retinue befitted the chief minister of a great and splendid kingdom. In 1635, he founded the famous French Academy, to compile a dictionary of the French language and to set the standards and style of the national culture. He tried to humble the factious nobles, though with only middling success, by ordering the destruction of some of their châteaux and forbidding the favorite aristocratic indulgence of private duels. More effective was his transfer of supervision over the local administration from the nobles and from officeholders of dubious loyalty who had purchased their posts to the more reliable *intendants*. These royal officials had existed earlier but with only minor functions, as vaguely defined as their name, which means "superintendents." Now they were given greatly increased powers over justice and the police and especially over the vital work of apportioning and collecting taxes.

Richelieu was unquestionably a great statesman, a man largely responsible for building *la grande nation* of Louis XIV. Historians have always differed in their estimates of how good for France in the long run his work was to prove. For royalists generally, his work was sound, an efficient, centralized state. For others, he built in a sense too well, made the French government so centralized, so professionally bureaucratic, that it had no place for the give and take of politics, for government by discussion. Except for attempting to equalize the incidence of taxes among the provinces of France, Richelieu did little to remedy the chronic fiscal weakness of the government, particularly corruption in tax collection and the piling up of deficits. His concentration on *raison d'état* led him to take an extraordinarily callous view of the subjects on whose loyal performance of their duties the welfare of the state depended. He once wrote:

> All politicians agree that when the people are too comfortable it is impossible to keep them within the bounds of their duty . . . they must be compared to mules which, being used to burdens, are spoiled more by rest than by labour.*

*Quoted by C. V. Wedgwood, *Richelieu and the French Monarchy* (New York, 1950), p. 137.

## Mazarin and the Fronde

The deaths of Richelieu and Louis XIII in successive years (1642, 1643), the accession of a child king, and the regency of the hated Hapsburg queen-mother, Anne of Austria (she was a Hapsburg from Spain, where the dynasty was called "the house of Austria")—all seemed to threaten a repetition of the crisis that had overcome France after the death of Henry IV. The crisis was averted, or, rather, delayed by the new chief minister, Mazarin (1602–1661). Picked and schooled by Richelieu himself, Mazarin, too, was a cardinal (though not a priest, as his predecessor had been) and a past master of *raison d'état*. He, too, was careless about the finances of the French state, but, unlike Richelieu, he amassed an immense personal fortune during his public career, bestowing lavish gifts on his five Italian nieces, who married into the high French nobility, and collecting a magnificent library, which he willed to the French state. He antagonized both branches of the French nobility—the *noblesse de l'épée* (nobility of the sword), descendants of the feudal aristocracy, and the *noblesse de la robe* (nobility of the gown, from the robes worn by judges and other officials), descendants of commoners who had bought their way into government office. The former resented being excluded from the regency by a foreigner; the latter, who had invested heavily in government securities, particularly disliked Mazarin's casual way of borrowing money to meet war expenses and then letting the interest payments on government borrowings fall into arrears.

The discontent boiled over in the uprising of the Fronde, 1648–1653, named for the slingshot used by Parisian children to hurl pellets at passers-by. The peasantry and the common people of Paris, both impoverished by an economic depression accompanying the last campaigns of the Thirty Years' War, participated in some of the rioting. But the Fronde was essentially a noble revolt, led first by the judges of the Paris Parlement, a high court, and then, after the Peace of Westphalia, by aristocratic officers returned home from the Thirty Years' War. Various "princes of the blood" (relatives of the Bourbon royal family) intervened with their private armies. Though Mazarin twice had to flee Paris and go into exile in Germany, the upshot of the

*Paris barricades during the uprising of the Fronde, 1648.*

Fronde was to confirm him in power and to pave the way for the personal rule of Louis XIV. The youthful king got a bad fright when the frondeurs actually broke into the room where he was feigning sleep, and he resolved to hold firmly to the reins of state. The Fronde failed essentially because it had no real roots in the country, not even in the rising middle classes. It was a struggle for power between Mazarin and his new bureaucracy, and two privileged noble groups. Each of the two groups distrusted the other, and the *noblesse de l'épée* was split by personal feuds and factions; all Mazarin had to do was apply the old Roman maxim: divide and rule.

## Le Grand Monarque

When Mazarin died in 1661, Louis XIV began to rule as well as to reign. At the age of twenty-two the king already demonstrated an impressive royal presence, as evidenced by this report from Madame de Motteville, a seasoned observer of the French court:

As the single desire for glory and to fulfill all the duties of a great king occupied his whole heart, by applying himself to toil he began to like it; and the eagerness he had to learn all the things that were necessary to him soon made him full of that knowledge. His great good sense and his good intentions now made visible in him the rudiments of general knowledge which had been hidden from all who did not see him in private. . . .

He was agreeable personally, civil and easy of access to every one; but with a lofty and serious air which impressed the public with respect and awe . . . , though he was familiar and gay with ladies.*

Louis continued to be "familiar and gay" with the ladies until finally, after the death of his Spanish queen, he settled down in the 1680's to a proper middle-aged marriage with Madame de Maintenon, a Huguenot turned devout Catholic who had been the governess of his illegitimate children.

Louis XIV succeeded so well as the *grand monarque* because by education, temperament, and physique he was ideally suited to the role. Though he had received from Mazarin little instruction in the arts and sciences, he had received full tutelage in diplomacy and in military administration. It has been remarked that Louis had just enough education to be guided always by *raison d'état*, though not by reason itself. Endowed with excellent manners—"civil and easy of access to everyone," as Mme de Motteville observed—he also had admirable self-discipline, patience, and staying power. He never lost his temper in public and went through long daily hours in council meetings and elaborate ceremonial with unwearied attention and even enjoyment; in this respect, his conspicuous lack of a sense of humor may have been a positive asset. An indispensable asset was his iron physical constitution, which enabled him to withstand his rigorous schedule, made his indifferent to heat and to cold, and allowed him to survive both a lifetime of gross overeating (his stomach is reported to have been twice the normal size) and the crude medical practice of the day.

He was five feet five inches tall—a fairly impressive height in those days—and increased his stature by wearing shoes with high red heels. To provide a suitable setting for the monarch who considered himself the Sun King, to neutralize the high nobility politically by isolating it in the ceaseless ceremonies and petty intrigues of artificial court life, and also to avoid a repetition of the mob's intrusion that had so disturbed the young Louis during the Fronde, he moved the capital from Paris to Versailles a dozen miles away. There on sandy wasteland he built his celebrated palace more than a third of a mile long, flanked by elaborate stables and other outbuildings, approached from Paris by a majestic avenue, and set in an immense formal garden with 1,400 fountains, the water for which had to be pumped up from the River Seine at staggering expense. Versailles housed, mainly in cramped uncomfortable quarters, a court of ten thousand, including dependents and servants of all sorts.

* *Memoirs of Madame de Motteville,* trans. K. P. Wormeley, (Boston, 1902), III, 243.

## Divine-Right Monarchy

The admired and imitated French state, of which Versailles was the symbol and Louis XIV the embodiment, can also stand as the best historical example of divine-right monarchy. We have for the France of Louis's prime one of those convenient but oversimplified tags that history furnishes so abundantly. Perhaps Louis never actually said "L'Etat, c'est moi" (I am the State), but the phrase has stuck, and it is certainly not altogether misleading as an attempt to summarize a state of mind and an ideal. In theory, Louis was for his subjects no mere man but the earthly representative of God on earth—or at least, in France. He held this position by the divinely ordained workings of the principle of primogeniture; he was not elected by his subjects, nor did he acquire his throne by force of arms. He was born to a position God had planned for the legitimate male heir of the tenth-century Hugh Capet. As God's agent, his word was final, for to challenge it would be to challenge the whole structure of God's universe. Disobedience was both a political and a religious offense.

Now though Louis has been dead less than three centuries, the ideas and sentiments centered on this divine-right monarchy are so utterly alien to contemporary Americans that it takes an effort of the historical imagination not to dismiss them as nonsense. Two clues may help us understand why they were once held so widely and so firmly. The first clue is the survival of the char-

*The Palace of Versailles: an engraving by P. Menant.*

acteristic medieval view that right decisions in government are not arrived at by experiment and discussion, but by "finding" the authoritative answer provided for in God's scheme of things. In the days of Louis XIV many men still believed that God through his chosen agents directly managed the state. While other men were beginning to question this idea, especially in England, the full force of their questioning was not to come for another generation or two on the continent of Europe.

A second clue lies in the deliberate effort by Henry IV, Richelieu, Louis XIV and other makers of the new Bourbon monarchy to cope with specific problems. Their central problem was how to bring men together into those larger political units necessitated by the course of technological and economic growth, the overseas discoveries, and the pressure of a slow but steady increase of population. In 1600 France had a population estimated at sixteen million, the largest of any state in Europe. The problem was to make these millions who were used to thinking, feeling, and behaving as Normans, Bretons, Flemings, Alsatians, Burgundians, Provençaux, Gascons, Basques—even just as villagers or members of a medieval "corporative" society—think, feel, and behave as Frenchmen. The makers of the Bourbon monarchy could not rely on a common language, for only a minority spoke standard French; the millions who had to get along together as Frenchmen spoke several dozen mutually incomprehensible languages or at least dialects. And of course they could not rely on a common educational system, a common press, common participation in political life; all that lay in the future. They could, and did, attempt to set up at least a symbol of common Frenchness, a king of France who was king for Celtic-speaking Bretons as for Catalan-speaking southerners. That king collected taxes, raised armies, touched in a hundred ways the lives of ordinary men who had to feel that the king had a right to do all this, that he was doing it *for* them, rather than *to* them. A king who was, if not like the old Roman emperors a god himself, at least the agent of God, was the kind of king they could understand and accept.

Divine-right monarchy, with its corollary of obedience on the part of subjects, is thus one phase of the growth of the modern centralized nation-state. It was an institution that appealed to very old theological ideas, such as the biblical admonition to obey the powers that be, for "the powers that be are ordained of God." But it was an institution that was also inspired by the newer ideas of binding men together in a productive, efficient state. In practice, naturally, the institution did not wholly correspond to theories about it. Louis XIV was not the French state, and his rule was not absolute in any full, logical sense of that word. He simply did not have the physical means for controlling in detail what his subjects did. Such control is actually much more completely possible under modern techniques of communication, propaganda, and administration than it ever was in days of "absolute" monarchy.

The early modern monarchy in France and throughout the West was subject to many limitations besides those set by the physical possibilities of supervision. Medieval survivals made for diversities of many sorts, in laws, customs, weights and measures, as well as language. All stood in the way of the uniformity, the administrative neatness and exactness, that are essential to the smooth working of a chain of command. Important groups still clung to medieval privileges—that is, to rights, immunities, a status, which they felt did not depend on the king's will, which were, certainly in the minds of those who enjoyed them, legal limitations on the power of the king. Many of these groups were corporations —municipal councils, judicial boards like the Parlement of Paris, economic groups such as guilds—which usually possessed written charters and traditional privileges difficult for the government to override. Particularly troublesome were the aristocratic and religious forces, both Catholic and Huguenot, that had been involved in the civil strife of the late sixteenth century.

## The Nobility

In all the important countries of Europe the feudal nobility maintained themselves into early modern times; the degree to which they were integrated into the new machinery of state was of crucial importance in the development of modern Europe. In Hapsburg Spain, as indeed in the Hapsburg lands of central Europe, the old nobility generally accepted the new strength of the Crown, but maintained much of their privilege and all their old pride of status. In Prussia, as a later chapter will show, they were most success-

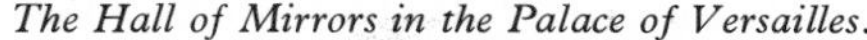

*The Hall of Mirrors in the Palace of Versailles.*

*The noblesse de la robe: Municipal councillors of Toulouse.*

fully integrated into the new order, becoming on the whole faithful servants or soldiers of the Crown, but with a social status that set them well above mere bourgeois bureaucrats. In England, as we shall shortly see, the nobility achieved a unique compromise with the Crown. In France, the feudal "nobility of the sword" were in effect shoved aside by the Crown and deprived for the most part of major political functions, but they were allowed to retain social and economic privileges and important roles as officers in the king's army.

This process of reducing the old French nobility to relative powerlessness at least in national political life had begun during the fifteenth century, and had been hastened by the religious and civil wars of the next century. An important part of the nobility, perhaps nearly half, had espoused the Protestant cause, in large part from sheer opposition to the Crown. The victory of Henry IV, purchased by his conversion to Catholicism, was a defeat for the nobility. The process was completed by the increasing use under Richelieu and Louis XIV of commoners in the task of running the government, from the great ministers of state, through the intendants, down to local administrators and judges. These commoners were usually elevated to the *noblesse de la robe* but did not have at first the social prestige of the *noblesse de l'épée*. The Fronde demonstrated that these new nobles could not be counted upon as loyal supporters of the Crown. Among the old nobles they aroused a contemptuous envy, summed up in the famous complaint of the ultra-aristocratic duc de Saint-Simon that only "vile bourgeois" had the confidence of the king; the nobles of the sword knew they were shelved. By the end of Louis's reign, however, the two kinds of nobility had become much better amalgamated, giving the whole order a new lease on life.

## Gallican and Huguenot

In medieval times, the clergy had been a separate order, backed by the supranational power and prestige of the papacy and possessing privileges not wholly in the control of the Crown. Even under Louis XIV the French clergy continued to possess important corporate privileges. They were not subject to royal taxation; they contributed of their own free will a gift of money which they voted in their own assembly. In the centralized France that emerged from the Hundred Years' War the Crown had fostered the evolution of Catholicism in France into a national Gallican church, firmly Catholic but also under good control by the monarchy, and friendly to new ideas, political, social, and economic. Under Louis XIV the Gallican union of throne and altar reached a high point in 1682 when a great assembly of French clerics drew up the Declaration of Gallican Liberties, asserting in effect that the "rules and customs admitted by France and the Gallican church" were just as important as the traditional authority of the papacy. "Ocean itself, immense though it is, has its limits," pronounced Bishop Bossuet, a great defender of Louis's monarchy by divine right. In practice, however, the flamboyant new Gallican claims for French royal authority did not prove to be very important.

Louis XIV took as the goal of his religious policy the application of a traditional French motto—*un roi, une loi, foi* (one king, one law, one faith). Whereas Richelieu had attacked only the political privileges of the Huguenots, Louis attacked their fundamental right of toleration and finally abolished it. He began by pulling down Huguenot churches not specifically authorized by the Edict of Nantes, then put restrictions on Huguenots' education, their admission to the professions, and their right to marry outside their faith. A campaign for converting Protestants to the Roman faith assumed a coercive aspect through the notorious *dragonnades*, the billeting of dragoons in Huguenot households as a persuasive measure. Misled by exaggerated reports of the success achieved, and pressed by the fanatically anti-Huguenot lower Catholic clergy, Louis revoked the Edict of Nantes in 1685. After the revocation, fifty thousand Huguenot families fled abroad, notably to Prussia, Belgium, Holland and the Dutch colony in South Africa, England (where they were given a chapel in Canterbury cathedral itself), and the colonies of British North America, as the name of New Rochelle, New York, reminds us. The practical skills and the intellectual gifts of the refugees strengthened the lands that received them, and the departure of industrious workmen and of thousands of veteran sailors, soldiers, and officers weakened the mother country. Some Huguenots remained in France, worshipping underground in spite of persecution.

### Quietism and Jansenism

Within the Catholic church itself, Louis had to contend with two important elements that refused to accept his Gallicanism. The Quietists, a group of religious enthusiasts led by Madame Guyon, sought for a more mystical and emotional faith. Their tendency to exhibitionism and self-righteousness combined with their zeal for publicity belied their name of Quietist and offended the king's sense of propriety. The Jansenists, sometimes called the Puritans of the Catholic church, were a high-minded group whose most distinguished spokesman was the scientist and philosopher Pascal. Named for Cornelius Jansen, bishop of Ypres in the early seventeenth century, the Jansenists took an almost Calvinistic stand on the issue of predestination. They stressed the need to obey the authority of God rather than that of man, no matter how exalted the position of the particular man might be. They therefore questioned both the authority of the pope (and of his agents, the Jesuits) and that of the king. On the surface, Louis was successful in repressing both Quietists and Jansenists, but the latter in particular survived to trouble his successors in the eighteenth century.

### The Royal Administration

Just as Louis XIV was never wholly master of the religious beliefs and practices of his subjects, he never quite succeeded in building up an administrative machine wholly under royal control. At Versailles he had three long conferences weekly with his ministers, who headed departments essentially like those of any modern state—War, Finance, Foreign Affairs, Interior. The king kept this top administrative level on an intimate scale; he usually had only four ministers at one time, and gave them virtually permanent tenure. Colbert served as controller general for eighteen years, and Le Tellier for thirty-four as secretary of state for the Army, a portfolio then entrusted to his son, who had been ennobled as the marquis de Louvois. All told only sixteen ministers held office during the fifty-four years of his personal reign.

The ministers were responsible directly to Louis XIV, and not to any legislative body. The Estates General never met during his lifetime. From the top, a reasonably clear chain of command proceeded down through the intendants, whose number was fixed at thirty, with each at the head of a *généralité,* a big administrative unit roughly corresponding to the older provinces. Below the intendants were their subordinates, the *subdélégués,* and at the bottom were the towns and villages of France, which sometimes defied or ignored the royal command. Even the indefatigable Louis could do no more than exercise general supervision over the affairs of his large and complex kingdom. And he probably could not have achieved even partial success without the invention of printing. For the familiar government printed forms to be filled out were already in existence. And they are still there, duly filled out and filed in their hundreds of thousands in the local historical archives of France.

In practice, naturally, the royal administration was full of difficulties and contradictions. There were many superimposed and often conflicting jurisdictions, survivals of feudalism and the medieval struggle to control feudalism. The officials of Louis XIV, by the very fact of being nobles of the gown, possessed a privileged status which they could hand down to their heirs. They, too, tended to form a "corporation," tended even as individuals to be more their own masters in their own bailiwicks than the theory of royal absolutism would allow. The key provincial administrators, the intendants, may seem to have been no more than agents of the Crown. Yet anyone who pursues in local history the detailed records of what they actually did finds that many of them exercised considerable initiative and were by no means rubber-stamp officials. Nor was the old administrative device of moving the intendants about from one généralité to another sufficient to overcome this centrifugal tendency.

A particularly important potential for trouble existed in the parlements, the supreme courts of appeal in the various provinces, of which one, the Parlement of Paris, enjoyed special prestige and power from its place at the capital and from the size of its territorial jurisdiction, almost half of the kingdom. The judges who staffed the courts headed the nobility of the gown, owned their offices, and were not removable at the will of the king. In addition to the usual work of a court of appeals, the parlements claimed through their function of registering royal edicts something very close to what in American usage is called the right of judicial review. That is, they claimed to be able to refuse to register an edict if they thought it "unconstitutional," not in accord with the higher law of the land. The claim, of course, negated theoretical royal absolutism.

Actually, Louis got around the difficulty in his own lifetime. The Parlement of Paris had already lost a round in its struggle with the royal power by entering the lists against Mazarin in the Fronde. Now Louis successfully utilized another old institution, the *lit de justice* (literally, "bed of justice"), in which he summoned the Parlement of Paris before him in a formal session and ordered the justices to register a royal edict. In this way, for instance, he enforced measures against Jansenism, which was strong among the judges. But the parlements, too, were to plague his eighteenth-century successors.

## Mercantilism and Colbert

Just as divine-right monarchy was not peculiarly French, so the mercantilism identified with the France of Louis XIV was common to many other Western states in the early modern period. But, like divine-right rule, mercantilism flourished most characteristically under the Sun King. It most famous exponent was Colbert (1619–1683), who had served his apprenticeship under Mazarin and advanced rapidly to become controller general early in the personal reign of Louis.

Mercantilism was part and parcel of the early modern effort to construct strong, efficient political units. The mercantilists quite frankly aimed to make a given nation as self-sustaining as possible, as independent as possible of the need to import from other nations, which were its rivals and its potential enemies. Within a given nation, the mercantilists held that national production should provide the necessities of life for a hard-working population, and the necessities of power for a nation able to fight and win wars. These goals they believed, demanded planning and control from above. They did not think that the old traditional ways of manor and guild, the old standard of the "just price," brought out the energies and abilities needed in an expanding economy. They were all for sweeping away these remnants of medieval controls. But they did not believe, as the free-trade economists after them were to believe, that all that was necessary was to destroy these controls and leave individual businessmen free to do whatever they thought would enrich them most as individuals. Instead, the mercantilists would channel the national economic effort by government subsidies, by grants of monopolies, by direct production in government-run industries, by encouraging scientific and technological research, and of course by protective tariffs.

The mercantilist viewed France overseas as a special part of France, a part that should be run from the homeland by a strong government. Already in the seventeenth century many foodstuffs and raw materials were more easily available overseas than in Europe. Colonies, therefore, should be encouraged to provide necessities so that the mother country need not import them from her competitors. In return, the mother country would supply industrial goods to the colonies and have a monopoly over colonial trade. This mercantilistic attitude toward colonies was held not only by absolutist France and Spain, but by the more limited governments of England and Holland.

The great practitioner of mercantilism, Colbert, never quite attained the supremacy reached by Richelieu and Mazarin; he was the collaborator, never the master, of Louis XIV. Other great ministers, Louvois for military affairs especially, stood in the way of his supremacy. Yet Colbert was influential in all matters affecting the French economy, most interested in foreign trade and in the colonies, and therefore in the merchant marine and in the navy. His hand was in everything, in invention, in technological education, in attracting enterprising foreigners to settle in France, in designing and building ships.

Among the industries he fostered were the processing of sugar, chocolate, and tobacco from the colonies; the production of military goods by iron foundries and textile mills, one of which had more than a thousand workers; and the luxuries for which the French have been famous ever since. The Gobelins tapestry enterprise in Paris was taken over by the state and its output expanded to include elegant furniture, for which the king was a major customer. Glassblowers and lacemakers were lured away from Venice, despite strenuous efforts by the Venetian Republic, including the use of poison, to keep their valuable techniques secret. In a blow against French competitors Colbert imposed heavy tariffs on some Dutch and English products. To promote trade with the colonies and also with the Baltic and the Mediterranean he financed a battery of trading companies, of which only the French East India Company eventually succeeded.

At home, Colbert encouraged reforestation, so that iron foundries could have abundant supplies of charcoal (then essential for smelting); he also promoted the planting of mulberry trees to nourish the silkworms vital to textile output. He even attempted—vainly, as it turned out—to impose what we could call "quality control" by ordering that defective goods should be prominently exhibited in public, along with the name of the offending producer, and that for a third offense the culprit himself was to be exhibited. He also endeavored, again for the most part in vain, to break down the barriers to internal free trade, like provincial and municipal tariffs or local restrictions on the shipment of grain to other parts of France. He did, however, sponsor the construction of important roads and canals; the Canal du Midi (Southern Canal) linking the Atlantic port of Bordeaux and the Mediterranean port of Narbonne reduced transport charges between the two seas by three-fourths and was described as the greatest engineering feat since Roman days.

Whether the great prosperity France achieved in the first thirty years of Louis's reign came about because of, or in spite of, the mercantilist policies of Colbert is a question difficult to answer. The convinced adherent of laissez-faire doctrines will argue that France would have done even better had her businessmen been left alone. But this was not the seventeenth-century way, not even in England and Holland. Under the mercantilist regime, France did attain an undoubted leadership in European industry and commerce. That lead she lost, in part because the last two wars of Louis XIV were ruinously expensive, in part because from the eighteenth century on France's rival, England, took to the new methods of power machinery and concentrated on large-scale production of inexpensive goods. France remained largely true to the policies set by Colbert—relatively small-scale production of a variety of goods, often luxuries, and predominantly consumer goods. But the difference between French and English industry was also a difference in the focus of national energies. France in early modern times, like Spain before her, spent an undue proportion of her national product in the ultimately unfruitful effort to achieve the political domination of both Europe and the overseas world by force of arms.

## III The Wars of Louis XIV

### The Goals of Expansion

France was the real victor in the Thirty Years' War, acquiring lands on her northeastern frontier. In a postscript to the main conflict, she continued fighting with Spain for another decade until at the Peace of the Pyrenees, 1659, Mazarin secured additional territories, Artois, in the north adjoining Flanders, and Roussillon, at the Catalan-speaking Mediterranean end of the Pyrenees. Well recovered from the wounds of her own religious wars and prospering economically, France was ready for further expansion when the young and ambitious monarch began his personal rule in 1661.

What were the goals of that expansion? To complete the gains of 1648 and 1659 and secure the kingdom's "natural frontiers" along the Rhine and the Alps? To wage a mercantilist war and bring to book France's major economic competitors, Holland and England? Or to revive the multinational empire that Charlemagne had ruled nine hundred years earlier? Historians today tend to believe that Louis pursued each of these goals in sequence, as he became more and more powerful and more and more convinced that the proper occupation of a king was the aggrandizement of his kingdom. In addition, Louis was keenly aware of the potentialities of French cultural imperialism, and wanted French culture, French tastes in the arts, and French social ways to spread their influence all over Europe.

While French cultural imperialism went from triumph to triumph, his political and military designs won some successes but met ultimate failure. In North America, in India, in Holland, and on the Rhine, and in dozens of other places, the agents of Louis were working to increase their master's power and prestige. Other peoples became convinced that France was threatening things that they held dear—life, property, independence, self-respect. Under this threat, most of the European states allied themselves against the French aggressor and beat him.

### The Instruments of Expansion

Louis XIV and his talented experts fashioned splendid instruments to support an aggressive foreign policy. In 1661 half a dozen men made up the whole Ministry of Foreign Affairs; half a century later, it had a huge staff of clerks, archivists, coders (and decoders) of secret messages, renegade priests and ladies of easy virtue who operated as clandestine agents, great lords and prelates who lent their dignity to important missions, and professional assistants who did most of their work. The growth of the French army was still more impressive, from a peacetime force of 20,000 to a wartime one almost twenty times larger. In size, the armies of Louis XIV were beginning to assume a truly modern look.

In quality, however, French forces were rather less modern. The ranks were filled not with citizen soldiers raised by some kind of universal conscription but with mercenaries and the victims of the press gang. Leadership may be described as semiprofessional. Both the basic larger unit, the regiment, and the basic smaller one, the company, were not only led but also recruited and paid by their commanders—colonel and captain, respectively. These men were usually nobles, who purchased their commissions and behaved as though they were a combination of condottieri and of feudal lords bringing their private forces to do battle for their overlord.

Despite these inherent limitations, Louis and his lieutenants almost revolutionized the character of France's fighting forces. At the Ministry of War the father-and-son team of Le Tellier

*Mignard's equestrian portrait of Louis XIV.*

and Louvois arranged the grouping of regiments in a brigade under a general to bring them under closer control. They also introduced two new ranks of officer, major and lieutenant-colonel, to give more opportunities to talented commoners; these new commissions were awarded only for merit and were not available for purchase, like the colonelcies and captaincies. Supplies were made more abundant, pay was made more regular, and a real effort was launched to weed out the "deadbeats" who appeared only on regimental paydays. The inspector-general, Martinet, made his name a byword for the enforcement of rigorous drilling and discipline.

In the field, particularly during Louis's early wars, the king had the invaluable help of two senior commanders, Condé and Turenne, both veterans of the Thirty Years' War. French armies showed particular strength in artillery, engineering and siege techniques, all particularly important in those days before "lightning warfare," when armies moved ponderously and did much of their fighting in the waterlogged Low Countries. Louis XIV also relished the opportunity to make a grand entry into a newly captured town. The French boasted a siege engineer of genius, Vauban, of whom it was said that a town he beleaguered was indefensible and one he defended was impregnable (and in fact the little city of Belfort, in Alsace, which he had fortified, resisted a long Prussian siege two centuries later in the war of 1870). Finally, while military medical services remained crude and sketchy, a large veterans' hospital was built in Paris, the Hôtel des Invalides, one of the most splendid monuments of the *grand siècle.*

## The Successes of Louis XIV

The main thrust of Louis XIV, unlike that of the Valois, which had been toward Italy, was northeast, toward the Low Countries and Germany. He sought also to secure Spain, if not quite as a direct annexation, at least as a French satellite with a French ruler. Finally, French commitments overseas in North America and in India drove him to attempt, against English and Dutch rivals, the establishment of a great French empire outside Europe.

The first actual war of Louis XIV was a minor affair, but it showed how he was going to move. When he married the daughter of Philip IV of Spain, his bride had renounced her rights of inheritance. Now Louis claimed that, since her dowry had never been paid, her renunciation was invalid. His lawyers dug up an old family rule, the *right of devolution,* which Louis claimed gave his wife lands in Belgium, then the Spanish Netherlands. In the ensuing War of Devolution with Spain, 1667–1668, Turenne won various victories, but Louis did not press them. The Dutch, just north of Belgium, felt alarmed for their independence and also for their prosperity because of the discriminatory tariff against their

*Hotel des Invalides from the south.*

goods introduced by Colbert in 1667. They entered into a Triple Alliance with England and Sweden to prevent Louis's upsetting the balance of power. A compromise peace at Aix-la-Chapelle, 1668, awarded Louis only Lille and other towns on the Franco-Belgian border.

Furious at the Dutch because of their economic ascendancy, their Calvinism, and, most of all, their republicanism, Louis resolved to teach them a lesson. He isolated them diplomatically by buying the alliance of Sweden and England, their former partners in the Triple Alliance. In 1672 French forces invaded Holland. The terrified Dutch lynched their bourgeois leader, Jan de Witt, whom they blamed for their military unpreparedness, and turned to the youthful stadholder of Holland (and of several other provinces), William III of Orange, the great-grandson of the martyred hero of Dutch independence, William the Silent. The French advance was halted by the desperate expedient of opening the dikes and flooding polders with the sea waters from which they had been reclaimed. Even without the strong leadership of William of Orange, Europe would probably have responded to the threat of French domination by forming an anti-French alliance. As it was, Spain, the empire, and a still rather minor German state, Brandenburg-Prussia, joined against France and her allies. The anti-French coalition was not very effective, and French diplomacy separated the allies at the treaties of Nijmegen (Nimwegen) in 1678–1679. Holland was left intact at the cost of promising neutrality, and the French gave up their high tariff on Dutch goods; Spain yielded to France the Franche Comté (County of Burgundy) and some towns in the Spanish Netherlands; Prussia, which had won a crucial battle against Sweden at Fehrbellin in 1675, was obliged by French pressure to give the Swedes back their Baltic German lands.

The power and prestige of France were now at their peak. Louis's place in Europe rested by no means solely on his armed forces; he also enjoyed to an unusual degree the position of leader and exemplar of culture and taste. Rulers all over Europe, and in particular the host of princes and princelets in the Germanies, aped the standards of Versailles. The prestige of France was not diminished by those who hated while they envied, admired, and imitated her. She was now *la grande nation,* adding to material power the very great power of cultural prestige.

### The Failures of Louis

Yet in the last three decades of Louis's reign most of these assets were dissipated, especially the concrete ones of wealth and efficient organization. Not content with the prestige he had won in his first two wars, Louis embroiled himself with most of the Western world in what looked to that world like an effort to destroy the independence of Holland and most of western Germany, and to bring the great Iberian peninsula under a French ruler. The prelude to new military aggression was the juridical aggression of the "chambers of reunion," special courts set up by the French, in the early 1680's, to tidy up the loose ends of the peace settlements of the past generation. There were loose ends aplenty on the northern and eastern frontiers of France, a zone of fragmentation and confused feudal remnants, many of which were ultimately under the suzerainty of the Holy Roman emperor. After examining the documents in disputed cases the chambers of reunion "reunited" many strategic bits of land to territories acquired earlier by France. The French did not hesitate to threaten force to back up these awards, as they did in the case of the former free city of Strasbourg, the chief town of Alsace.

Continued French nibbling at lands in western Germany set off the third of Louis's wars, the War of the League of Augsburg (1688–1697). Louis's assertion of a dynastic claim to most of the lands of the German elector Palatine was the last straw. The league against him was largely put together by his old foe, William of Orange, who after 1688 shared the throne of England with his wife Mary, daughter of James II of England. Thenceforth, England was thoroughly committed to take sides against Louis. The League of Augsburg also included Spain, the empire, and the Alpine state of Savoy, which was also threatened by Louis's tactic of "reunions." The great sea victory of the English over the French at Cape La Hogue in 1692 showed that England, not France, was to be mistress of the seas. But on land the honors were more nearly even. William was beaten in battle in the Low Countries time and again, but he was never decisively crushed. In Ireland, French attempts to intervene on behalf of the deposed English king, James II, were foiled at the Battle of the Boyne in 1690. France and England also exchanged blows in India, the West Indies and North America, where the colonists called it "King William's War."

Louis was growing old, and perhaps for the moment he had had enough. The Peace of Ryswick, concluded in 1697, was one of those comparatively rare peaces without victory, a general agreement to keep things as they were. It lasted barely four years, for in 1701 Louis, after much personal soul-searching, took a step that led to the great world war over the Spanish succession. His brother-in-law, the Hapsburg king of Spain, Charles II, died in 1700 without a direct heir. For several years the diplomatists of Europe had been striving to arrange by general consent a succession that would avoid putting on the Spanish throne either a French Bourbon or an Austrian Hapsburg. They had agreed on a Bavarian prince; but he had died in 1699, and the whole question was reopened. New plans were made, partitioning the Spanish inheritance between Hapsburgs and Bourbon. But Charles II of Spain made a new will, giving his lands intact to Philip of Anjou, the grandson of Louis XIV, and then died. Louis could not withstand the temptation. He accepted on behalf of Philip, despite the fact that he had signed the treaty of partition. The threat to the balance of power was neatly summarized in the remark a gloating Frenchman is supposed to have made, "There are no longer any Pyrenees" (the great mountain chain that separates France and Spain). England, Holland, Savoy, the empire, and many German states formed the Grand Alliance to preserve the Pyrenees.

In the bloody war that followed, the French were gradually worn down in defeat. Their North American possession of Acadia (Nova Scotia) was taken by the English. In four major European battles Blenheim (1704), Ramillies (1706), Oudenarde (1708), and Malplaquet (1709), the French were beaten by the Allies under two great generals, the English John Churchill, Duke of Marlborough, ancestor of Winston Churchill, and the Savoyard prince Eugene. But the French were not annihilated. The last of the Allies' victories, Malplaquet, had cost them twenty thousand casualties, at least as many as the French suffered. Somehow, by scraping the bottom of the barrel for men and money, the French managed even after Malplaquet to keep armies in the field.

Moreover, the Grand Alliance was weakening. The English, now following their famous policy of keeping any single continental power from attaining too strong a position, were almost as anxious to prevent the union of the Austrian and Spanish inheritances under a Hapsburg as to prevent the union of the French and the Spanish inheritance under a Bourbon. At home, they faced a possible disputed succession to the throne, and some of the mercantile classes were sick of a war that was injuring trade, and that seemed unlikely to bring any compensating gains. In 1710, the Tory party, inclined toward peace, won a parliamentary majority and began negotiations that culminated in a series of treaties at Utrecht in 1713.

## The Utrecht Settlement

Utrecht was a typical balance-of-power peace. France was contained but by no means humiliated. She lost to England Newfoundland, Nova Scotia, and the Hudson's Bay territories, but she preserved Quebec and Louisiana, as well as her Caribbean islands. Louis gained in a sense what he had gone to war over, for Philip of Anjou was formally recognized as King Philip V of Spain and secured the Spanish lands overseas. The French and Spanish crowns were however, by specific provision, never to be held by the same person, so the Allies, too, had won a point. Furthermore, England took from Spain the Mediterranean island of Minorca, which she handed back later in the century, and the great Rock of Gibraltar guarding the Atlantic entrance to the Mediterranean. The English also gained, by what was called the Asiento, the right to supply Negro slaves to the Spanish colonies, a right that gave them a chance also at interloping trade or just plain smuggling.

The Austrian Hapsburgs, denied the main Spanish succession, were compensated with the former Spanish possessions in Italy, Milan and Naples, and the former Spanish Netherlands. Holland was granted the right to maintain garrisons in certain fortified towns in these now "Austrian" Netherlands, the "barrier fortresses," for better defense against possible French aggression. Savoy, an Italian state that had been true to the Grand Alliance, was rewarded with Sicily; though diplomatic jockeying substituted for this prize in 1720 the lesser island of Sardinia, the duke of Savoy was able to call himself king of Sardinia and thus started the long process that united Italy under the crown of Savoy in the nineteenth century. The elector of Brandenburg-Prussia, too, was rewarded with a royal title, King *in* Prussia (not *of,* for Prussia was outside the Holy Roman Empire).

In all the general European settlements of modern times—Westphalia, Utrecht, Vienna, Versailles—historians discern the elements, the imperfections, that led to subsequent unsettlement and another general war. Utrecht is no exception, even though of all the great modern settlements it is the one in which victors and vanquished seem closest. First of all, the rivalry between France and England for empire overseas was not at all settled. In India, as in North America, each nation was to continue after Utrecht as before the effort to oust the other from land and trade. In Europe, the Dutch were not really protected from French expansion by the right to the barrier fortresses in the Austrian Netherlands. The Austrian Hapsburg leader, now the emperor Charles VI, never forgot that he had wanted to be "Charles III" of Spain and never quite gave up hope that somehow he could upset the decisions made at Utrecht. The distribution of Italian lands satisfied nobody, Italian or outsider, and the next two decades were filled with acrimonious negotiations over Italy. In short, no one seemed to have quite what he wanted, which is one of the difficulties of working out reasonable compromise solutions.

## French Aggression in Review

In retrospect, this first period of French aggression seems one of the less violent and critical tests of the European state system. True, these wars caused horrors enough, especially in the deliberate French devastation of the German Palatinate during the War of the League of Augsburg. Their total cost in human lives and in economic resources was very great. The battle of Malplaquet, which left forty thousand men wounded, dying, or dead in an area of ten square miles, was not surpassed in bloodshed until Borodino in Napoleon's Russian campaign a century later. The year of Malplaquet, 1709, was one of the grimmest in modern French history, when bitter cold, crop failures, famine, and relentless government efforts to stave off bankruptcy by collecting more taxes caused almost universal suffering. The Parisians complained bitterly in this parody of the Lord's Prayer: "Our Father which art at Versailles, thy name is hallowed no more, thy Kingdom is great no more, thy will is no longer done on earth or on the waters. Give us this day thy bread which on all sides we lack. . . ."* These wars were not simply struggles among professional armies directed by professional politicians; they were wars among peoples, wars that brought out feelings of patriotism and hatred for the foreigner and the aggressor.

Yet in comparison with the wars of religion that had preceded them, and with the wars of nationalism and revolution that were to follow, the wars of Louis XIV seem to have lacked the all-out qualities of human drives toward both good and evil. Louis set himself up as a champion of Catholicism, especially after the revocation of the Edict of Nantes in 1685, and much was made of William of Orange as a Protestant champion. In the end, however, the coalition against Louis was a complete mixture of Catholic and Protestant, in which religion played a comparatively minor role. There were of course many elements of religious concern that entered into the struggle. Both in England and in New England the French were dreaded as Catholics. Yet in all these matters of public attitudes toward the enemy, simple dislike of the "foreigner" is conspicuous. Louis XIV, unlike his predecessor in aggression, Philip II of Spain, did not entertain any real hope of stamping out Protestantism among the Dutch.

Yet no lay substitute for the crusading religious spirit had emerged. Unlike Napoleon, Louis XIV was not the product of the stimulating force of a revolution; unlike Hitler, he was not the product of a humiliating national defeat. He was indeed the Sun King, a great and admired ruler, but he was also the legitimate, even conventional, ruler of a land long used to prominence in Europe. The aggression of Louis XIV was, like the culture of his France, a moderate, measured, "classical" aggression, lacking the heaven-storming fervor of aggressions born of revolution.

## IV Stuart England

### A Head Start in Representative Government

English-speaking people throughout the world have come to believe that England has always had a representative and constitutional government; or, put negatively, that England never went through the stage of divine-right absolute monarchy most of the continental states went through. This belief is largely correct, but it would be better stated as follows: To the extent that English government utilized the new methods of professional administration developed in the fifteenth and sixteenth centuries, it may be considered potentially just as absolute as any divine-right monarchy. But representative government has grown in the West under historical conditions that have provided a check on this potential. The check is the concept of a "constitution," a set of rules, written down or simply traditional, not to be altered by the ordinary processes of government. These rules are in the modern Western tradition felt to be limitations on the authority even of a government elected by the majority of the people, a guarantee to the individuals and to groups that they may do certain things even though men in governmental posts of authority do not want them to. Without these rules and habits of constitutionalism, or "civil rights"—and without powerful and widespread human sentiments backing them up—the machinery of parliamentary government could be as ruthlessly absolute as any totalitarian government.

In seventeenth century England the development of potentially absolute institutions was checked and modified by the continued growth of

*Quoted in G. R. R. Treasure, *Seventeenth Century France* (Rivingtons, 1966), p. 413.

representative institutions at both the local and the national level. In France, for instance, cardinal-ministers and kings were able to raise money and govern without the Estates General. In England, Parliament met in 1629 and quarreled violently with King Charles I. For eleven long years, until 1640, Charles too governed without calling Parliament. But in 1640 he felt obliged to call Parliament and, though he dismissed it at once when it proved recalcitrant, he had to call another in that same year. This was the famous Long Parliament, which sat—with changes of personnel and with interruptions—for twenty years, and which made the revolution that ended the threat of absolute divine-right monarchy in England. If we understand why Charles, unlike his French counterpart, was obliged to call Parliament, we have gone a long way toward understanding why England had a head start in modern representative government.

Two very basic reasons go back to medieval history. First, as we have already seen, in the English Parliament the House of Commons represented two different social groups not brought together in one house on the Continent, the aristocratic "knights of the shire" and the "burgesses" of the towns and cities. The strength of the Commons lay in the practical working together of both groups, which intermarried quite freely and, in spite of some economic and social tensions, tended to form a single ruling class with membership open to talented and energetic men from the lower classes.

Second, local government continued to be run by magistrates who were not directly dependent on the Crown. We must not exaggerate: England, too, had its bureaucrats, its clerks and officials in the royal pay. But whereas in France and in other continental countries the new bureaucracy tended to take over almost all governmental business, especially financial and judicial affairs, in England the gentry and the higher nobility continued to do important local work. The Elizabethan Poor Law of 1601 put the care of the needy not under any national ministry but squarely on the smallest local units, the parishes, where decisions lay ultimately with the amateur, unpaid justices of the peace, recruited from the gentry. In short, the privileged classes were not, as in France, shelved, thrust aside by paid agents of the central government; nor did they, as in Prussia, become themselves mere agents of the Crown. Instead, they preserved a firm base in local government and an equally firm base in the House of Commons. When Charles I tried to govern without the consent of these privileged classes, when he tried to raise from them and their dependents money to run a bureaucratic government without these privileged amateurs, they had a solid institutional basis from which to resist.

## The Role of Royal Personalities

But they had to struggle. They had to fight a civil war. No matter how much emphasis the historian may put on the social and institutional side, he cannot ignore what looks like the sheer accident of human personality. The Tudors from Henry VII to Elizabeth I, with some faltering under Edward VI and Mary, had been strong personalities and had been firmly—quite as firmly as any Valois or Hapsburg—convinced that they were called to absolute monarchy. They had slowly built up a very strong personal rule, handling their Parliaments skillfully, giving in occasionally in detail, but holding the reins firmly. Henry VIII and his daughter Elizabeth both commanded the kind of devotion from their subjects that can be built in time into formidable personal rule; they could hold the emotional loyalty of the English. Their successors could not. Elizabeth I was childless, and in 1603 she was succeeded by the son of her old rival and cousin, Mary Queen of Scots. James Stuart, already king of Scotland as James VI, became James I of England (1603–1625), thus bringing the two countries, still legally separate, under the same personal rule. James was a pedant by temperament, very sure of himself, and above all sure that he was as much a divine-right monarch as his French cousins. He was a Scot, and therefore a foreigner and an object of distrust to his English subjects. He lacked entirely the Tudor heartiness and tact, the gift of winning people to him.

His son Charles I (1625–1649), under whom the divine-right monarchy came to an end, was by no means as unattractive a monarch and, partly because of his martyrdom, has had his ardent partisans among historians. But if he had many of the graces of a monarch, it is still true that Charles I was no man to continue the work of the Tudors. He was quite as sure as his father had been that God had called him to rule England, and he could never make the happy compromises the Tudors made or repeat their popular appeals.

### Issues between Crown and Parliament

The fundamental fact about the actual break between the first two Stuarts and their parliamentary opponents is that both were in a sense revolutionaries. Both were seeking to bend the line of English constitutional growth away from the Tudor compromise of a strong Crown working with and through a late medieval Parliament based on the alliance of nobility, gentry, and commercial classes. James and Charles were seeking to bend the line toward divine-right monarchy of the continental type; the parliamentarians were seeking to bend it toward something even newer, the establishment of a legislative body possessing the final authority in the making and carrying out of law and policy.

Behind this struggle lay the fact that the business of state was gradually growing in scope and therefore in money cost. Foreign relations had by the end of the sixteenth century begun to take on modern forms, with a central foreign office, ambassadors, clerks, travel expenses and the like, all involving more money and personnel. The money required by Stuarts—and indeed by Bourbons, Hapsburgs, and the rest of the continental monarchs—did not simply go for high living by royalty and the support of parasitic nobles. It went to run a government that was beginning to assume many new functions. Basically, James I and Charles I failed to get the money they needed because those from whom they sought it, the ruling classes, succeeded in placing the raising and spending of it in their own hands through parliamentary supremacy. The Parliament that won that supremacy was in fact a committee—a big one, but still a committee—of the ruling classes. It was not a democratic legislature.

One final fact in the background of this struggle between Crown and Parliament: Religion played a major part in welding both sides into cohesive fighting groups. The struggle for power in England was in part a struggle to impose a uniform worship on Englishmen. The royalist cause was identified with High Church Anglicanism, that is, with an episcopalian church government and a liturgy and theology that made it a sacramental religion relatively free from left-wing Protestant austerities. The parliamentary cause, at first supported by many moderate Low Church Anglicans, also attracted a strong Puritan or Calvinist element. Later, it came under the control of the Presbyterians and then of the extreme Puritans, the Independents or Congregationalists.

The term "Puritanism" in seventeenth-century English history is a confusing one, and must remain so to those who demand simple, clear-cut definitions. For it was used as a blanket term to cover a wide variety of religious experience, from that of moderate evangelical Anglicans to that of the radical splinter sects of the 1640's and 50's. Its core went back to Zwingli and Calvin, to the repudiation of Catholic sacramental religion and the rejection of music and the adornment of the church. It placed a positive emphasis on sermons, on simplicity in church and out, and on "purifying" the tie between the worshiper and his God of what the Puritans considered Catholic "superstitions" and "corruptions."

### The Reign of James I

In the troubled reign of James I (1603–1625), we may distinguish three major threads of the struggle in which his son was to go under—money, foreign policy, and religion. In all three issues, the Crown and its opposition each tried to bend the line of constitutional development in its own direction. In raising money, James sought to make the most of revenues which he did not need to ask Parliament to grant. Parliament sought to make the most of its own control over the purse strings by insisting on the principle that any new revenue-raising had to be approved by Parliament. On the whole, James got along, though he levied some taxes without parliamentary grant. One of these, on the somewhat insignificant commodity of imported dried currants, was refused by an importer named Bate. Bate's case was decided in favor of the Crown by the Court of Exchequer, and the decision attracted much attention because the judges held the king's powers in general to be absolute. Then a royal "benevolence"—a euphemism for a direct imposition on an individual—was resisted by a certain St. John, and his appeal was sustained by the chief justice,

*Portrait of James I by Daniel Mytens, 1621.*

Sir Edward Coke. James then summarily dismissed Coke from office and thereby once again focused the attention of his subjects on his broad use of the royal prerogative.

Foreign affairs had been regarded by the Tudors as strictly a matter of royal prerogative. The delicate problem of marriage for Elizabeth I, for instance, had naturally concerned her Parliaments and the public. But Parliament made no attempt to dictate a marriage, and Elizabeth was most careful not to offend her subjects in her own tentative negotiations. On the other hand, when James I openly sought a princess of hated Spain as a wife for his son Charles, his subjects did more than grumble. The Commons in 1621 made public petition against the Spanish marriage. When James rebuked them for what he considered meddling, the House drew up the Great Protestation, the first of the great documents of the English Revolution, in which they used what they claimed were the historic privileges of Parliament to assert what was in fact a new claim for parliamentary control of foreign affairs. James responded by dissolving Parliament and imprisoning four of its leaders. The Spanish marriage fell through, but the betrothal of Charles in 1624 to a French princess, also a Catholic, was hardly more popular with the English people.

In religion, the policy of Elizabeth I had been broad and moderate. Though she persecuted—that is, refused to permit open religious services of—both extremes of Catholics and Puritans, she allowed much variety of actual practice within the Anglican church. James summed up his religious policy in the phrase "No bishop, no king" —which meant that he believed the enforcement of the bishops' monarchical power in religion was essential to the maintenance of his own monarchical power. James at once took steps against what he held to be Puritan nonconformity. He called a conference of Anglican bishops and leading Puritans at Hampton Court in 1604, at which he presided in person and used the full force of his pedantic scholarship against the Puritans. The conference dissolved with no real meeting of minds, and royal policy continued to favor the High Church, anti-Puritan party. In spite of James's failure to achieve anything like religious agreement among his subjects, his reign is a landmark in the history of Christianity among English-speaking peoples. In 1611, after seven years' labor, a committee of forty-seven ministers authorized by him achieved the English translation of the Bible that is still widely used. The King James Version remains a masterpiece of Elizabethan prose, perhaps the most remarkable literary achievement a committee has ever made.

## The Troubles of Charles I

Under Charles I, all his father's difficulties came to a head very quickly. England had been maneuvered into war against Catholic Spain, always a popular kind of war among Englishmen of the time. Though English forces were small, all wars cost money; Charles found Parliament most reluctant to grant him funds, even though the members hated Spain. Meanwhile, in spite of his French queen, Charles got involved in a war against France. This he financed in part by a forced loan from his wealthier subjects and by quartering his troops in private houses at the householders' expense. Consequently, Parliament in 1628 passed the Petition of Right, in which some of the most basic rules of modern constitutional government are first explicitly stated: No taxation without the consent of Parliament; no billeting of soldiers in private houses; no martial law in time of peace; no one to be imprisoned except on a specific charge and subject to the protection of regular legal procedure. Note that all the principles set forth in this Stuart Magna Carta are limitations on the Crown.

Charles, to get money in new subsidies from Parliament, consented to the Petition of Right. But he also collected duties not authorized by Parliament. Parliament protested by resolutions, not only against his unauthorized taxes but also against his High Church policy. The King now veered from conciliation to firmness; he dissolved Parliament in 1629 and then had Sir John Eliot, mover of the resolutions, and eight other members arrested. Eliot died in prison in the Tower of London, the first martyr on the parliamentary side.

For the next eleven years (1629–1640), Charles governed without a Parliament. He squeezed every penny he could get out of the customary royal revenues, never quite breaking with precedent by imposing a wholly new tax, but stretching precedent beyond what his opponents thought reasonable. Ship money illustrates how Charles worked. It had been levied by the Crown before, but only on coastal towns for naval expenditures in wartime; Charles now imposed ship money on inland areas, and in peacetime. A very rich gentleman named John Hampden from inland Buckinghamshire refused to pay it. In 1637, he lost his case in court by a narrow margin, but he had directed public attention to the new expedient.

In religious matters, Charles was under the sympathetic guidance of a very High Church archbishop of Canterbury, William Laud, who systematically enforced Anglican conformity and deprived even moderate Puritans of their pulpits. Puritans were sometimes brought before the Star Chamber, long a highly respected administrative court but now gaining a reputation for high-handed one-sided justice because it denied the accused the safeguards of the common law. In civil matters, Charles made use of an opportunist conservative, Thomas Wentworth, earl of Strafford, who had deserted the parliamentary side and went on to become lord lieutenant of Ireland.

England was seething with repressed political and religious passions underneath the outward calm of these years of personal rule. Yet England was certainly as prosperous as she had been under Tudor rule. The relative weight of the taxation that offended so many Englishmen was, so far as one can tell from the imperfect statistics of early modern times, less than on the Continent and far less than taxation in any modern nation in the Western world. The Englishmen who resisted the Crown by taking arms against it were clearly not downtrodden, poverty-stricken people revolting from despair, but self-assertive, hopeful people out to get the things they wanted —power, wealth, their own form of religious worship, their own newly conceived rights.

The attempts of twentieth-century historians to isolate the economic motives of seventeenth-century English revolutionaries have stirred up a great storm of controversy. The storm has centered on the role of the gentry, that numerous

*Van Dyck's portrait of Charles I hunting, ca. 1635.*

group of landed aristocrats just under the high nobility, who did much of the fighting in the civil wars. The Labour party intellectual R. H. Tawney claimed that the more enterprising, more capitalistically minded gentleman farmers, rather like rural bourgeois, supported the Puritans. His antagonist, Hugh Trevor-Roper, a professor at Oxford, asserted that on the contrary the gentry backing the Puritans were those who were barely holding their own or sinking down the economic scale in the face of inflation, the enclosure of lands for sheep farming, the competition coming from the secular owners of former monastic lands, and other unsettling forces. Neutral historians tend to conclude that these are over-abstract attempts to define the indefinable, the role of an amorphous social class whose economic status varied but whose political decisions were by no means taken on economic grounds.

## The Road to Civil War, 1638-1642

The English Revolution actually began in Scotland. If Charles I had not had to contend with his fellow Scots, he could perhaps have weathered his financial difficulties for a long time. But in Scotland Laud's attempt to enforce the English High Church ritual and organization came up against the three-generations-old Scots Presbyterianism. In 1638, a Solemn League and Covenant banded the Presbyterians of the Scottish kirk to resist Charles by force if need be. Charles marched north against the Scots but concluded a temporizing pacification in 1639. Even this mild campaign had been too much for the treasury, and Charles, facing an empty one, called an English Parliament in 1640. This Short Parliament, firmly denying any money until the piled-up grievances of nearly forty years were settled, was dissolved at once. Then the Scots went to war again, and Charles, defeated in a skirmish, bought them off by promising the Scottish army £850 per day until peace was made. Since he could not raise £850 a day, he had to call another Parliament, which became the famous Long Parliament of the revolution.

Holding the unpaid Scots army as a club over Charles's head, the Long Parliament put through a great series of reforms that struck at the royal power. It abolished ship money and other disputed taxes. It disbanded the unpopular royal administrative courts, like the Star Chamber, which had become symbols of Stuart absolutism. Up to now, Parliament had been called and dismissed at the pleasure of the Crown; the Triennial Act of 1640 made obligatory the summoning of future Parliaments every three years, even if the Crown did not wish to do so. Parliament also attacked the royal favorites, whom Charles reluctantly abandoned. Archbishop Laud was removed, and Strafford, declared guilty of treason, was executed in May 1641.

Meanwhile, Strafford's unfeeling policy toward the Irish had borne fruit in a rebellion that amounted to an abortive war for national independence by Irish Catholics. Parliament, unwilling to trust Charles with an army to put down this rebellion, drew up in 1641 the Grand Remonstrance summarizing all its complaints. Charles now made a final attempt to repeat the tactics that had worked in 1629. Early in 1642, he ordered the arrest of five of his leading opponents in the House of Commons, including Hampden of the ship-money case. The five took refuge in the privileged political sanctuary of the City of London, where the king could not reach them. Charles I left for the north and in the summer of 1642 rallied an army at Nottingham; Parliament simply took over the central government. The Civil War had begun.

Signs were already evident during these first years of political jockeying that strong groups in England and in Parliament wanted something more than a return to the Tudor balance between Crown and Parliament, and between religious conservatives and religious radicals. In politics, the Nineteen Propositions that Parliament submitted to the king in June 1642, and that he of course rejected, would have firmly established parliamentary supremacy and left Charles a rather weak "constitutional" monarch, much like the present English queen. In religion, the Root and Branch Bill, introduced in 1641 but not enacted, would have radically reformed the whole Church of England, destroying, "root and branch," the bishops and much of what had already become traditional in Anglican religious practices. The moderates in politics and religion were plainly going to have trouble defending their middle-of-the-road policies among the extremists of a nation split by civil war.

## The Civil War, 1642-1649

England split along lines partly territorial, partly social and economic, and partly religious. The royalist strength lay largely in the north and west, relatively less urban and less prosperous than other parts and largely controlled by country gentlemen loyal to throne and altar. Parliamentary strength lay largely in the south and east, especially in the great city of London and in East Anglia, where the gentry were firm Puritans. The Scots were always in the offing, distrustful of an English Parliament but quite as distrustful of a king who had sought to foist episcopacy on their kirk.

In the field, the struggle was at first indecisive. The royalists, or Cavaliers, recruited from gentlemen used to riding, had at first the important advantage of superior cavalry. What swung the balance to the side of Parliament was the development under a Puritan gentleman named Oliver Cromwell (1599–1658) of a special force, recruited from ardent Puritans of the eastern counties, and gradually forged under strict discipline into the famous "Ironsides." At Marston Moor in 1644, Cromwell won a crucial battle. The parliamentary army, now reorganized into the New Model Army, staffed by radicals in religion and politics, stood as Roundheads (from their short-cropped hair, something like a crew-cut) against the cavaliers. At the battle of Naseby in 1645, the New Model was completely victorious over the king, and Charles in desperation took refuge with the Scots army, who turned him over to the English Parliament in return for £400,000 back pay.

Now a situation arose that was to be repeated, with variations for time and place, in the French Revolution in 1792 and the Russian Revolution in 1917. The group of moderates who had begun the revolution and who still controlled the Long Parliament were confronted by the much more radical group who controlled the New Model Army. In religion, the moderates, seeking to retain some ecclesiastical discipline and formality, were Presbyterians or Low Church Anglicans; in politics, they were constitutional monarchists. The radicals, who were opposed to churches disciplined from a central organization, were Independents or Congregationalists, and they already so distrusted Charles that they were able at least to contemplate that extraordinary possibility, an England under a republican form of government. The situation was complicated by the Scots, firmly Presbyterian and hostile to the radical Roundheads, whom they regarded as religious anarchists.

The years after 1645 were filled with difficult negotiations, during which Charles stalled for time to gain Scots help. In 1648, Cromwell beat the invading and now royalist Scots at Preston, and his army seized the king. Parliament, with the moderates still in control, now refused to do what the army wanted, to dethrone Charles. The Roundhead leaders then ordered Colonel Pride to exclude by force from the Commons ninety-six Presbyterian members. This the Colonel did in December 1648, in true military fashion, with no pretense of legality. After "Pride's Purge" only some sixty radicals remained of the more than five hundred members originally composing the Long Parliament; they were known henceforth as the Rump Parliament. The Rump brought Charles to trial before a special high court of trustworthy radicals, who condemned him to death. On January 30, 1649, Charles I was beheaded.

*The House of Commons as shown on the Great Seal of England used by the Commonwealth, 1651.*

## Cromwell and the Interregnum, 1649-1660

England was now a republic, under the government known as the Commonwealth. But the radicals did not dare call a free election, which would almost certainly have gone against them. (A similar phenomenon is not uncommon in other revolutions—witness Lenin's arbitrary dissolution in January 1918 of the constituent assembly elected by universal suffrage). From the start, the Commonwealth was in fact the dictatorship of a radical minority come to power through the tight organization of the New Model Army. From the start, too, Cromwell was the dominating personality of the new government. He was, in a sense, an unwilling dictator. In religion an earnest and sincere Independent, but no fanatic, a patriotic Englishman, strong-minded, stubborn, but no pathological luster after power, by no means unwilling to compromise, he was nevertheless a prisoner of his position.

Cromwell faced a divided England, where the majority were no doubt royalist at heart and certainly sick of the fighting, the confiscations, the endless changes of the last decade. He faced a hostile Scotland and an even more hostile Ireland. The disorders in England had encouraged the Catholic Irish to rebel once more against the Protestant English "garrison." Finally, Cromwell faced a war with Holland, brought on largely by the Navigation Act of 1651, a typically mercantilist measure. By forbidding the importation of goods into England and the colonies except in English ships or in ships of the country producing the imported goods, the Navigation Act deliberately struck at the Dutch carrying trade.

Charles II, eldest son of the martyred Charles I, landed in Scotland, accepted the Covenant—that is, guaranteed the Presbyterian faith as the established Scottish kirk—and led a Scots army once more against the English. Once more the English army proved unbeatable, and at the battle of Worcester in September 1651 the hope of the Stuarts went down for the time. Charles took refuge on the Continent, after a romantic escape in disguise. The Dutch War, 1652-1654, was almost wholly a naval one, and ended victoriously for the English.

By 1654, Cromwell had mastered all his foes. He himself went to Ireland and suppressed the rebellion with bloodshed that is still not forgotten. In the so-called Cromwellian Settlement, he dispossessed native Irish landholders in favor of Protestants; he achieved order in Ireland, but not peace. Cromwell also waged an aggressive war against Spain, from whom the English acquired the rich Caribbean sugar island of Jamaica. Even in this time of troubles, the British Empire kept growing.

Cromwell, however, could not master the Rump Parliament, which brushed aside his suggestions for an increase of its membership and a reform of its procedures. In April 1653 he forced its dissolution by appearing in Parliament with a body of soldiers. In December 1653 he took the decisive step of setting himself up as lord protector of the Commonwealth of England, Scotland, and Ireland, with a written constitution—the only one England has ever had—known as the Instrument of Government. Under this constitution an elected Parliament of 460 members was provided for. It was in fact chosen by Puritan sympathizers, for no royalist dared vote. Even so, the Lord Protector had constant troubles with his parliaments and in 1657 yielded to pressure and accepted some modifications in his dictatorship. Meanwhile, to maintain order, he had divided the country into twelve military districts, each with a major general commanding a military force. Oliver Cromwell died in 1658, and was succeeded as lord protector by his son Richard. But Richard Cromwell was a nonentity, and the army soon seized control. By now some army leaders saw in the restoration of the Stuarts the best hope of putting an end to the chronic political turbulence. To ensure the legality of the move, General Monk, commander of the Protectorate's forces in Scotland, summoned back the Rump and readmitted the living members excluded by Pride's Purge. This partially reconstituted Long Parliament enacted the formalities of restoration, and in 1660 Charles Stuart came back from exile to reign as Charles II.

## The Revolution in Review

It is no doubt misleading to say that there was a Reign of Terror in the English Revolution. Much of the bloodshed was the respectable bloodshed of formal battle between organized armies, not the revolutionary bloodshed of guillotine, lynching, and judicial murder. Still, Charles I was beheaded; Strafford, Laud, and others suffered the death penalty; royalists had their properties confiscated. Above all, the Puritans at the height of their rule in the early 1650's attempted to enforce on the whole population the difficult, austere life of the Puritan ideal. This enforcement took the familiar form of "blue laws," of prohibitions on horse-racing, gambling, cock-fighting, bear-baiting, dancing on the green, fancy dress, the theater, on a whole host of ordinary phases of daily living.

This English Reign of Terror and Virtue, coming too early for modern techniques of propaganda and control over the masses, was not entirely effective. Many an Anglican clergyman, though officially "plundered"—that is, deprived of his living—kept up his worship in private houses; many a cock fight went on in secluded spots. Nevertheless, the strict code was there, with earnest persons to try to enforce it, and with implacable enemies to oppose it. The famous remark of the historian Macaulay—that the Puritans prohibited bear-baiting, not because it gave pain to the bear, but because it gave pleasure to the spectators—is a sample of the deep hostility that still survives in England toward the reign of the Puritan "saints." So too is the popular doggerel of the time:

*To Banbury came I, O profane one,*
*Where I saw a Puritane-one,*
*Hanging of his cat on Monday*
*For killing of a mouse on Sunday.**

Many Englishmen have seemed rather ashamed of their great revolution, preferring to call it the Civil War or the Great Rebellion, and recalling instead as their Glorious Revolution the decorous movement of 1688–1689, to which we shall come in a moment. Yet the events of 1640–1660 are of major importance, not only in the history of England, but in the history of the West. Here for the first time the monarchy was firmly challenged in a major revolt and a constitutional and representative government was set up, based on a legislature backed by politically active private citizens. Though the Stuarts were restored, no English king ever again could hope to rule without a Parliament, or restore the Court of Star Chamber, or take ship money, benevolences, and other controversial taxes. Parliament thenceforward retained that critical weapon of the legislative body in a limited monarchy, ultimate control of the public purse by periodic grants of taxes.

Moreover, minority groups had gone much further, and in their extraordinary fermentations had foreshadowed much modern social thought and action. One such group, the Levelers, though they never attained power, won considerable sympathy from the revolutionary army. They put forward a program later carried by emigrants to the American colonies. The Levelers anticipated much of what we now call political democracy—universal suffrage, regularly summoned Parliaments, progressive taxation, separation of church and state, protection of the individual against arbitrary arrest, and the like. There are even hints of the socialistic drive toward economic equality, though in those days collectivist programs were tied up closely with biblical ideas. The Diggers, for example, were a small sect that preached the sharing of earthly goods in a kind of communism. They actually dug up public lands in Surrey near London and began planting vegetables. They were driven off, but not before they had got their ideas into circulation. The Fifth Monarchy men, the Millennarians, and a dozen other radical sects preached the Second Coming of Christ and the achievement of some kind of utopia on earth.

Still more important, there emerged from these English struggles, even more clearly than from the religious wars on the Continent, the conception of religious toleration. The Independents, while they were in opposition, stood firmly on the right of religious groups to worship God as they wished. Though in their brief tenure of power they showed a willingness to persecute, they were never firmly enough in the saddle to make of England another seventeenth century Geneva or Boston. Moreover, many of the Puritans sincerely believed that compulsion should not be exercised to secure conformity.

At least one of the sects held to the idea and practice of religious toleration as a positive good. The Quakers, led by George Fox (1624–1691), were Puritans of the Puritans. They themselves eschewed all worldly show, finding even buttons ostentatious, the names of days and months indecently pagan, the polite form "you" in the singular a piece of social hypocrisy, and legal oaths

*Richard Brathwaite, *Barnabee's Journal* (London, 1774), Pt. I.

or oathtaking most impious. Hence they met for worship not on the day of the pagan sungod, but on First Day; they addressed any man as "thou"; and they took so seriously the basic Protestant doctrine of the priesthood of the believer that they did entirely without a formal ordained ministry. In the Religious Society of Friends, as they are properly known, any worshiper who felt the spirit move might testify in what in other sects would be a sermon. But Quakers felt too deeply the impossibility of forcing the inner light in any man, were too sure that conversion is the work of God alone, to try to *make* men Quakers. They would abstain entirely from force, particularly from that shocking kind of force we call war, and would go their own Christian way in peace, in the hope that in God's good time men would freely come to God's way—and their way.

Still another of our basic freedoms owes much to this English experience. Freedom of speech was a fundamental tenet of the Puritans, though again at the height of their power they by no means lived up to it. The pamphlet literature of the early years of the great turmoil is a lively manifestation of free speech in practice. And it received a classic statement in the *Areopagitica* of the poet John Milton, who was the secretary of the Commonwealth.*

## The Restoration, 1660-1688

The Restoration of 1660 kept Parliament essentially supreme but attempted to undo some of the work of the Revolution. Episcopacy was restored in England and Ireland, though not as a state church in Scotland. Against the "dissenters," as Protestants who would not accept the Church of England were then termed, the so-called Clarendon Code set up all sorts of civil liabilities and obstructions. For instance, by the Five Mile Act all Protestant ministers who refused to subscribe to Anglican orthodoxy were forbidden to come within five miles of any town where they had previously preached. Yet the dissenters continued to dissent without heroic sufferings. In characteristically English fashion, the Test Act of 1672, which prescribed communion according to the Church of England on all officeholders, local as well as national, was simply got around in various ways, though it was not actually repealed until 1828. One way was "occasional conformity," by which a dissenter of not too strict conscience might worship as a Congregationalist, say, all year, but might once or twice take Anglican communion. Another, developed in the eighteenth century, was to permit dissenters to hold office, and then pass annually a bill of indemnity legalizing their illegal acts. Dissenters remained numerous, especially among the artisans and middle-class merchants, and as time went on they grew powerful, so that the "nonconformist conscience" was a major factor in English public life. Indeed, the three-century progression of names by which these non-Anglican Protestants were called is a neat summary of their rise in status—the hostile term "dissenter" became "nonconformist" in the nineteenth century and "Free Churchman" in the twentieth.

The Restoration was also a revulsion against Puritan ways. The reign of Charles II (1660-1685) was a period of moral looseness, of gay court life, of the Restoration drama with its ribald wit (the Puritans in power had closed the theaters), of the public pursuit of pleasure, at least among the upper classes. But the new Stuarts had not acquired political wisdom. Charles II dissipated some of the fund of good will with which he started by following a foreign policy that seemed to patriotic Englishmen too subservient to the wicked French king Louis XIV. The cynic is tempted to point out that, if Charles's alliance with Louis in 1670 was most un-English, it did result in the final extinction of any Dutch threat to English seapower. And it sealed a very important English acquisition, that of New Amsterdam, now New York, first taken in the Anglo-Dutch War of 1664-1667.

What really undid the later Stuarts and revealed their political ineptitude was the Catholic problem. Charles II had come under Catholic influence through his French mother and very possibly embraced the Roman religion before he died in 1685. Since he left no legitimate children, the crown passed to his brother, James II (1685-1688), who was already a declared Catholic. In the hope of enlisting the support of the dissenters for the toleration of Catholics, James II issued in 1687 a Declaration of Indulgence, granting freedom of worship to *all* denominations, Protestant dissenters as well as Catholics,

* The reference is to the Council of the Areopagus, the supreme judicial and political authority in ancient Athens.

in England and Scotland. This was in the abstract an admirable step toward full religious liberty.

But to the great majority of Englishmen, Catholicism still seemed what it had seemed in the time of Elizabeth I, the great menace to the English nation. Actually, by the end of the seventeenth century the few remaining Catholics in England were glad to be left in something like the status of the dissenters and were no real danger to a country overwhelmingly Protestant. But they were an unappeased majority in Ireland, and it was always possible to stir Englishmen to an irrational pitch by an appeal to their fear and hatred of "popery."

The political situation, moreover, was much like that under Charles I; the Crown wanted one thing, Parliament wanted another. Although James II made no attempt to dissolve Parliament or to arrest members, he simply went over Parliament's head by issuing decrees, like the Declaration of Indulgence granting full religious toleration, in accordance with what he called the "power of dispensation." Early in his reign, he had made a piddling rebellion by the duke of Monmouth, a bastard son of Charles II, the excuse for two ominous policies. First, his judges organized the "bloody assizes" which punished suspected rebel sympathizers with a severity that seemed out of all proportion to the extent of the rebellion. Second, he created a standing army of thirty thousand men, part of whom he stationed near London in what appeared an attempt to intimidate the capital. To contemporaries it looked as though James were plotting to force both Catholicism and divine-right monarchy on an unwilling England. The result was the Glorious Revolution.

## The Glorious Revolution of 1688-1689

The actual revolution was in fact a coup d'état engineered at first by a group of James' parliamentary opponents who were called *Whigs*, in contrast to the *Tories* who tended to support at least the more moderate measures of the later Stuart monarchs. The Whigs were the direct heirs of the moderates of the Long Parliament, and they represented an alliance of the great lords and the prosperous London merchants.

James II married twice. By his first marriage he had two daughters, both Protestant—Mary, who had married William of Orange, the great Dutch opponent of Louis XIV, and Anne. Then in 1688 a son was born to James and his second wife, who was Catholic, thus apparently making the passage of the crown to a Catholic heir inevitable. The Whig leaders responded with a great barrage of propaganda, including a whispering campaign to the effect that the queen had not even been pregnant, but a new-born babe had been smuggled into her chamber in a warming pan, so that there might be a Catholic heir. Then the Whigs and some Tories negotiated with William of Orange, who could hardly turn down a proposition that would give him the solid assets of English power in his struggle with Louis XIV. He accepted the offer of the English crown, which he was to share with his wife, the couple reigning as William III (1689–1702) and Mary II (1689–1694). On November 5, 1688, William landed at Tor Bay on the Devon coast with some fourteen thousand soldiers. When James heard the news, he tried to rally support, but everywhere the great lords and even the normally conservative country gentlemen were on the side of the Protestant hero. James fled from London to France in December 1688, giving William an almost bloodless victory.

Early in 1689 Parliament formally offered the crown to William on terms that were soon enacted into law as the Bill of Rights. This famous document, summing up the constitutional practices that Parliament had been working for since the Petition of Right in 1628, is in fact almost a succinct form of written constitution. It lays down the essential principles of parliamentary supremacy—control of the purse, prohibition of dispensation power to the Crown, regular and frequent meetings of Parliament. Three major steps were necessary after 1689 to convert the British Constitution into a parliamentary democracy in which the Crown has purely symbolic functions as the focus of patriotic loyalty. These were, first, the concentration of executive direction in the hands of a committee of the party in majority in a given Parliament—that is, the Cabinet headed by a prime minister, the work of the eighteenth and early nineteenth centuries; second, the establishment of universal suffrage and payment of members of the Commons, the work of the nineteenth century, completed in the twentieth; and third, the abolition of the power of the House of Lords to veto legislation passed by the Commons, the work of the early twentieth century. Thus we can see that full democracy was still a long way off in 1689. William III and Mary were real rulers, who did not think of themselves as purely ornamental monarchs, without power over policy.

Childless, they were succeeded by Mary's younger sister, Anne (1702–1714). Anne and her nonentity of a husband strove hard to leave an heir to the throne, but all their many children, perhaps merely because of the inadequacies of medical science of the day, were still-born or died in childhood. The exiled Catholic Stuarts, however, did better. The little boy born to James II in 1688, and brought up at the court of St. Germain near Paris, grew up to be known as the "Old Pretender." But in 1701 Parliament passed the Act of Settlement, which settled the crown, in default of heirs to Anne, the heir apparent to the sick William III, not on the Catholic pretender but on the Protestant Sophia of Hanover or her issue. The line to her went back to her grandfather, James I. On Anne's death in 1714, the crown therefore passed to Sophia's son, George, first king of the House of Hanover. It need hardly be pointed out that this settlement had clearly established the fact that Parliament, and not the divinely ordained succession of the eldest male in direct descent, made the king of England.

One more act of Queen Anne's reign helped settle for good an old problem. This was the formal union of the kingdoms of England and Scotland under the name of Great Britain in 1707. Scotland was to send sixteen peers to the Lords and forty-five members to the Commons of the Parliament of the United Kingdom. One flag, the Union Jack, with the superimposed crosses of St. George for England and St. Andrew for Scotland, was henceforth to be the national flag of Great Britain. The union, most necessary to ensure the carrying out of the Hanoverian succession in both kingdoms, met with some opposition in both. But on the whole it went through with surprising ease, so great was Protestant fear of a possible return of the Catholic Stuarts. And, in spite of occasional sentimental outbreaks of Scottish nationalism even in our own day, the union has worked very well. With the whole of England and the colonies open to Scots politicians and businessmen, the nation famed for its thrifty and canny citizens achieved a prosperity it had never known before.

The Glorious Revolution did not, however, settle one other perennial problem—Ireland. The Catholic Irish rose in support of the exiled James II and were put down at the battle of the Boyne in 1690. William then attempted to apply moderation in his dealings with Ireland, but the Protestant "garrison" there soon forced him to return to the severe spirit of Cromwellian policy. Although Catholic worship was not actually forbidden, all sorts of galling restrictions were imposed on the Catholic Irish, including the prohibition of Catholic schools. Moreover, economic persecution was added to the religious, as Irish trade came under stringent mercantilist regulation. This was the Ireland whose misery inspired Jonathan Swift to make his "modest proposal" that the impoverished Irish solve their economic problems by selling their babies as articles of food.

## V The Century of Genius

In the seventeenth century the cultural, as well as the political, hegemony of Europe passed from Italy and Spain to France, England, and Holland. Especially in literature, the France of Corneille, Racine, Molière, Boileau, Bossuet, and a host of others set the imprint of a style on the West. Yet the men who achieved the abiding effect of the seventeenth century on our culture were truly international in origin and outlook, and were rather philosophers and scientists than men of letters. Men like Galileo, Descartes, Pascal, and Newton launched the great modern scientific revolution and prompted Whitehead to claim that ever since their day we "have been living upon the accumulated capital of ideas provided . . . by the genius of the seventeenth century."*

* A. N. Whitehead, *Science and the Modern World* (New York, 1948), p. 58.

## Natural Science

A major role in the cultivation of the scientific attitude was taken by the Englishman Francis Bacon (1561–1626). Though not himself a successful practitioner of science, he was the tireless proponent of the necessity for the observation of phenomena and the patient accumulation of data. If you observe enough facts, he seems to say, they will somehow make sense of themselves by the process of *induction,* in contrast with the medieval *deduction* he was attacking:

> There are and can be only two ways of searching into and discovering truth. The one [deduction] flies from the senses and particulars to the most general axioms, and from these principles, the truth of which it takes for settled and immovable, proceeds to judgment and to the discovery of middle axioms. And this way is now in fashion. The other [induction] derives axioms from the senses and particulars, rising by a gradual and unbroken ascent, so that it arrives at the most general axioms last of all. This is the true way, but as yet untried.*

While both deduction and induction are essential in science, Bacon's emphasis on induction was a necessary corrective in his time and helped to set modern science on its way.

Progress along that way was facilitated by the invention of new instruments, by the establishment of scientific societies, and by the advance of mathematics. Both the great figures of the "century of genius" and scores of unknown or now forgotten individuals contributed to the new instruments that permitted more exact measurements and more detailed observations. For instance, Dutch glassmakers probably first put two lenses together and discovered that they could thus obtain a greater magnification. By 1610, the Italian Galileo (1564–1642) was using the new device in the form of a telescope to observe the heavens, and by about 1680 the Dutchman Van Leeuwenhoek was using it in the form of a microscope to discover tiny creatures—protozoa—hitherto unknown. Working from a discovery made by Galileo, another Italian, Torricelli, invented the barometer. The Frenchman Pascal (1623–1662), using Torricelli's invention, proved by measuring the height of a column of mercury at the base and then at the top of a mountain that what we call air pressure diminishes with altitude, and went on to show that a vacuum is possible, in spite of the old adage "Nature abhors a vacuum."

Two important organizations promoting scientific investigation were the Royal Society for Improving Natural Knowledge, founded in 1662, and the Académie des Sciences, founded in 1666. The one, in characteristic English fashion, was a private undertaking; the other, sponsored by Colbert for the greater glory of Louis XIV and the French state, was a government institution, whose fellows received salaries and also instructions to avoid discussing religion and politics. Both financed experiments and both published scientific articles in their "house organs," the *Philosophical Transactions* and the *Journal des Sçavans* (savants). Scoffers sometimes mocked their activities; Charles II roared with laughter at the news that the Royal Society was weighing the air. But ultimately the scientific societies exerted a strong affirmative influence, at least on the community of learned men. It would be hard to improve on the Royal Society's statement of purpose, in which it promised "to examine all systems, theories, principles, hypotheses, elements, histories and experiments" and "to question and canvass all opinions, adopting nor adhering to none, till by mature debate and clear arguments, chiefly such as are deduced from legitimate experiments, the truth of such experiments be demonstrated invincibly."

Meanwhile mathematics, the language of science, took a great leap forward. In 1585, Stevin, a Fleming, published *The Decimal, Teaching with Unheard-of Ease How to Perform All Calculations Necessary among Men by Whole Numbers without Fractions*. Another great time-saver was devised by Napier, a Scot, who offered *The Marvelous Rule of Logarithms* (1616) which introduced the principle of the slide rule and shortened the laborious processes of multiplying, dividing, and taking square root. Next, the Frenchman Descartes (1596–1650) worked out analytical geometry, which brings geometry and algebra together, as in the plotting of an algebraic equation on a graph. The mathematical achievements of the century culminated in the perfection of a method of dealing with variables and

* Bacon, *The Great Instauration.*

probabilities. Pascal had made a beginning with his studies of games of chance, and Dutch insurance actuaries had devised tables to show the life expectancy of their clients. Then Newton and the German Leibniz, apparently quite independently of one another, invented the calculus. The detailed description of the new invention must be left to the experts, but its practical value is indicated by the fact that without the calculus, and without Cartesian geometry, Newton could never have made the calculations supporting his revolutionary hypotheses in astronomy and physics.

The Englishman Isaac Newton (1642–1727), building on the work of earlier astronomers, especially Copernicus, Kepler, and Galileo, made the great theoretical generalization that is now part of every schoolboy's picture of the astronomical universe. This is the law of gravitation. The sun, the planets, and their satellites are, according to this theory, held in their orbits by the force of mutual attraction. Newton stated the formula that this force is proportional to the product of the masses of two bodies attracted one to the other, and inversely proportional to the square of the distance between them.

The law of gravitation is a part of physics as well as of astronomy. Physics too came of age in the seventeenth century, and like astronomy is capped by the work of Newton. Here too Galileo is of importance, though recent research has shown that a devoted follower may have invented the story of how by dropping balls of different weights from the Leaning Tower of Pisa he disproved Aristotle's theory that objects fall with velocities proportional to their weight. Galileo's studies of projectiles, pendulums, and falling and rolling bodies helped to establish modern ideas of acceleration.

Newton also contributed to optics, using a prism to separate sunlight into the colors of the spectrum. He demonstrated that objects only appear to be colored, that their color is not intrinsic but depends on their reflection and absorption of light. Newton first hit on some of his great discoveries when he was an undergraduate at Cambridge, but published them only many years later in the *Principia Mathematica*, 1687. ("The Mathematical Principles of Natural Philosophy" is the English translation of the title.) He won fame early and held it long, gaining successively a professorship at Cambridge, a knighthood, the presidency of the Royal Society, and a well-paid government post as Master of the Mint.

Meanwhile, the mechanistic views of the physicists were invading geology and physiology. In 1600, the Englishman Gilbert, in a study of magnetism, suggested that the earth itself was a giant magnet. In 1628, Harvey, the physician of Charles I, published his demonstration that the human heart is in fact a pump, and that the human blood is driven by the heart along a system of circulation. And in 1679 the Italian Borelli showed that the human arm is a lever, and that the muscles do mechanical "work."

### World-Machine and Rationalism

All these investigations in the various sciences tended to undermine the older Aristotelian concept of something "perfect." Instead of perfect circles, Keplerian and Newtonian astronomy posited ellipses. Instead of bodies moving in straightforward fashion of themselves, Newton's laws of motion pictured bodies responding only to forces impressed upon them. All these investigations, in short, suggested a new major scientific generalization, a law of uniformity that simplified and explained, that coordinated many separate laws into one general law summing up millions of man-hours of investigation. Galileo almost made this achievement, but he got into trouble with the Church for suggesting that the earth was not stationary, as had always been thought, but moved. Forced to recant, he managed to have the last word, "And yet it does move!" A dozen other major figures made essential contributions to the overall generalization. It was Newton who drew everything together into that grand mechanical conception that has been called the "Newtonian world-machine."

The Newtonian world-machine and, indeed, the whole of the new science had very important theological and philosophical implications. Natural science, strictly speaking, does not deal with the great problems of theology and philosophy. It does not give men ends, purposes, but rather means, and the theories it provides are always explanations, not moral justifications. Yet, historically speaking, the rise of modern science has been associated with a very definite world-view and system of values, for which the best name is perhaps rationalism. This is a wide term, and it is possible to be at the same time a rationalist and a believer in a supernatural God. Historically, however, the balance of the influence of rationalism in the West has been to banish God entirely, or at any rate reduce him to a First Cause that started this Newtonian world-machine going, but does not—indeed cannot—interfere with its working.

For the rationalist took as his model the neatly integrated mathematical universe that the scientists had worked out. He would not start with the revealed truths of Christianity, as the Schoolmen had done, but would question all formulations until he had something to start with as clear and as certain as the axioms of Euclidean geometry. Here is how the most influential of these philosophers, Descartes, began to put himself straight:

> I thought . . . that I ought to reject as downright false all opinions which I could imagine to be in the least degree open to doubt—my purpose being to discover whether, after so doing, there might not remain, as still calling for belief, something entirely indubitable. Thus, on the ground that our senses sometimes deceive us, I was prepared to propose that no existing thing is such as the senses make us image [*sic*] it to be; and because in respect even of the very simplest geometrical questions some men err in reasoning . . . , I therefore rejected as false (recognising myself to be no less fallible than others) all the reasonings I have previously accepted as demonstrations; and, finally, when I considered that all the thoughts we have when awake can come to us in sleep (none of the latter being then true), I resolved to feign that all the things which had entered my mind were no more true than the illusions of my dreams. But I immediately became aware that while I was thus disposed to think that all was false, it was absolutely necessary that I who thus thought should be somewhat; and noting that this truth *I think, therefore I am,* was so steadfast and so assured that the suppositions of the sceptics, to whatever extreme they might all be carried, could not avail to shake it, I concluded that I might without scruple accept it as being the first principle of the philosophy I was seeking.*

From this start, Descartes finally arrived at God—but a God who in his mathematical orderliness and remoteness from this confusing world must seem like a supreme geometer and therefore quite unreal to believers in a personal God. We are encountering the famous Cartesian dualism—mind and soul, on the one hand, body and matter, on the other, each pair apparently existing and functioning in its own separate world.

Scientist and rationalist helped greatly to establish in the minds of educated men throughout the West two complementary concepts that were to give the Enlightenment of the eighteenth century a pattern of action toward social change, a pattern still of driving force in our world. These were, first, the concept of a regular "natural" order underlying the irregularity and confusion of the universe as it appears to unreflecting man in his daily experience; and, second, the concept of a human faculty, best called "reason," obscured in most men by their faulty traditional upbringing, but capable of being brought into effective play by good—that is, rational—upbringing. Both these concepts can be found in some form in our Western tradition at least as far back as the Greeks. What gives them novelty and force at the end of the seventeenth century is their being welded into the doctrine of progress—the belief that all human beings can attain here on earth a state of happiness, of perfection, hitherto in the West thought to be possible only for Christians in a state of grace, and for them only in a heaven after death.

### The Classical Spirit

Art and letters as well as science and philosophy had a part in setting the pattern of the Enlightenment. The characteristic literary attitude of the seventeenth century, which flowered in the France of Louis XIV, is often known as *l'esprit classique*. The classical spirit leans toward measure, toward discipline, toward conformity with "those rules of old discover'd, not deviz'd," toward a dignified eloquence and an aristocratic refinement. The best writers of the age, however, found in their classical models not a confirmation of existing standards but a better, simpler set of standards that the eighteenth century could later easily express in terms of nature and reason. Boileau (1636–1711), the chief literary critic of the day, who set the rules for writing poetry, issued the pronouncement "Que toujours le bon sens s'accorde avec le rhyme" ("Always have good sense agree with the rhyme").

The great French dramatists, in particular, were trying to find in the infinite variety of men and manners something universal, something typical of all men and all times. Molière (1622–

* *Discourse on Method,* Part IV, in *Descartes' Philosophical Writings,* trans. N. K. Smith (London, 1952), pp. 140–141.

*Portrait of Descartes by Frans Hals.*

1673) made the main characters of his satirical comedies not only individuals but also social types—the miser in *L'Avare,* the hypocrite in *Tartuffe,* the boastful and ignorant newly rich man in *Le Bourgeois Gentilhomme.* Corneille (1606–1684) and Racine (1639–1699) followed the classical canons of tragedy; they took subjects from mythology and wrote in the rhymed couplets of Alexandrine verse (so called because its iambic hexameters had been used for a poem about Alexander the Great). To observe the rigid rules governing time, place, and action—the "unities" derived from Aristotle's *Poetics*—they pruned the dramatic action of irrelevance and restricted it to one place and a time span of twenty-four hours. But within this rigid form Corneille and Racine created moving portraits of human beings seeking exalted ideals of honor or crushed by overwhelming emotions. The French tragedies of the seventeenth century may be ranked next to the Greek tragedies of antiquity, not so much because of their classical form, but rather because of their psychological insight and emotional power.

Even in its broadest sense, the term "classical spirit" does not do justice to the full range of seventeenth-century literature. La Rochefoucauld (1613–1680) mastered an epigrammatic prose of classic simplicity but used it for devastatingly realistic or cynical maxims far removed from the lofty teachings of the classics:

> We all have enough strength to bear the misfortunes of others. . . . We generally give praise only in order to gain it for ourselves. . . . Virtue in woman is often the result of love of reputation and ease. . . . We always find something not altogether displeasing in the misfortunes of our friends.*

With the seventeenth century, the business of printing, as distinguished from the art of printing, began to take on some of the attributes of bigness. The number of people who could read increased all through the West, though most strikingly in northwestern Europe. From now on, there is a printed literature in all the main languages of the West, and a full history of ideas in the West would not neglect any of them. Yet seen in broad outline, German literature, though in bulk sufficient to occupy plenty of modern scholars, had not attained greatness or wide influence, and Spanish and Italian literature had passed their Renaissance peaks. The seventeenth was the great century of French literary flowering. As yet, English remained a tongue peripheral to European culture, and English writers, even Shakespeare, were not generally known abroad. England by her political example, by her great contributions to natural science, and at the end of the century by her political and philosophical writers, Locke above all, had indeed entered fully into the current of the common culture of the West. But the most important work of the two great English scientists, Newton and Harvey, as well as the most important theorizing of Francis Bacon, was first published in Latin.

Yet to all of us to whom English is a mother tongue the seventeenth century produced one of the great classics, Milton's *Paradise Lost,* the only epic written in English in the grand style that still finds readers, not all of them compelled by academic requirements. Milton was a Christian humanist, a classical scholar of staggering erudition, who needs copious footnoting for the twentieth-century reader. He was very active on the Puritan side of the Civil War, serving, as we have seen, as secretary of Oliver Cromwell and

* *The Maxims of La Rochefoucauld,* trans. F. G. Stevens (London, 1939), pp. 9, 49, 65, 173.

of the Commonwealth. In addition to other poems, he has left many incidental writings cast in a rather difficult prose style.

To the historian of culture, the major fact of English writing in the seventeenth century is not Milton, classic though he is, nor the comedies of the Restoration stage, but the simplification, the clarification, the modernization of English prose style that was achieved in the last half of the century. In formal writing, perhaps above all under the influence of the poet Dryden (1631–1700), English began to model itself on French, on its straightforward word order, on its comparatively brief sentences, free from long periodic clauses, and on its polish, neatness, and clarity. English began to simplify itself also at a popular level, exemplified in the prose of John Bunyan (1628–1688) of *The Pilgrim's Progress,* in that of Daniel Defoe (ca. 1660–1731) of *Robinson Crusoe.* Even a modern American can read a piece of English prose picked at random from writings of 1700 and not feel he is reading something strange; this would hardly be true of a random choice from fifty years earlier.

## The Arts

The term "classical spirit" hardly expresses the full achievement of the fine arts in the seventeenth century. The France of Louis XIV did produce neoclassical monuments like the symmetrical columned exterior of Versailles and the wings of the Louvre. But the interior of Versailles is another matter, with its dramatic Hall of Mirrors and Staircase of the Ambassadors and its acres of ceiling painted with smirking cherubs. Theatrically and lavish embellishment are two of the hallmarks of Baroque, the characteristic artistic style of the century. A very moderate Baroque building, chastened by neoclassical restraints, is St. Paul's Cathedral in London. It is, incidentally, the only major church structure ever designed and brought to completion by a single architect, in this case Christopher Wren, who also rebuilt fifty-one London parish churches gutted by the great fire of 1666. More exuberant examples of Baroque may be found in churches as far apart as Mexico and Austria. The city of Rome is a great museum of Baroque monuments, many of them the work of Bernini (1598–1680), architect and sculptor. They include the great open spaces and curved colonnades of St. Peter's Square; the *baldacchino,* the canopy on twisted bronze columns rising eight stories above the main altar in St. Peter's; fountains with fantastic mythological figures, including that of the Tritons where tourists throw their coins; and a sculpture attempting to portray the inexpressible ecstasy of Saint Teresa of Avila when she felt her heart pierced by the golden arrow of divine love.

In painting, the late sixteenth-century master El Greco had achieved a Baroque union of distortion and mysticism. Velázquez (1599–1660), the outstanding painter of seventeenth-century Spain, followed more faithfully the secular and realistic traditions of Renaissance art. A court painter, he did forty portraits of the Hapsburg King Philip IV, not all of them flattering by any means, and some marvelous pictures of the royal children and the court dwarves. Velázquez had the gift of achieving what one critic has called "optical" realism as opposed to "photographic" realism, depicting what the eye sees at a glance rather than all the details that are present.

In the Low Countries, the chief center of northern European painting, some artists also attained a kind of "optical realism" in their treatment of everyday subjects—the artist at work in his studio, worthy businessmen, the well-to-do

*Vermeer's "The Artist in His Studio," ca. 1665–1670.*

*Bernini's baldacchino above the main altar at St. Peter's, Rome.*

*Diego Velazquez' "The Surrender of Breda."*

*Nicholas Largeilliere's "Louis XIV and His Heirs."*

*Diego Velazquez' "The Maids of Honor," 1656.*

household. The Fleming Rubens (1577–1640) not only received commissions from French and English royalty but also made a fortune from his art and established a studio with two hundred students, a veritable factory of painting. The rosy, fleshy nudes for which Rubens is famous have the exuberance of Baroque, and he himself worked on the grand scale, contributing, it has been estimated, at least in part to more than two thousand pictures. Rembrandt (1609–1669), the Dutch genius, sometimes strove to involve the viewer directly in the action depicted, a very Baroque quality. In successive sketches for *Ecco Homo,* when Pilate allows the crowd to choose between Christ and Barabbas, Rembrandt progressively eliminated the crowd, and the beholder of the final version comes to realize that he is part of the multitude choosing Barabbas over Christ. A devout Mennonite, Rembrandt chose religious themes for almost half his works; he is the only great Protestant religious painter, a rare exception to the rule that Protestant tradition has not welcomed the visual arts.

In music, the term "Baroque" may serve to convey much of the accomplishment of the century of genius. Here Italy took the lead, following in the paths laid out by the musicians of the Renaissance. In Rome, Frescobaldi (1583–1644) released the dramatic potentialities of the pipe organ, and attracted thousands to his recitals at St. Peter's. In Venice, Monteverdi (1567–1643), contending that "speech should be the master of music, not its servant," backed his contention in practice by writing the first important operas. This Baroque compound of music and the theater gained immediate popularity. Venice soon had no fewer than sixteen opera houses, which were already establishing the tradition of slighting the chorus and orchestra to pay for the "stars." The star system reached its height at Naples, the operatic capital of the later 1600's. There conservatories (originally institutions for "conserving" orphans) stressed voice training; composers provided operatic vehicles that were little more than loose collections of arias; and the crowning touch of unreality came with the Neapolitan custom of having the male roles sung by women and the female by *castrati,* male sopranos.

Seventeenth-century opera at its best rose above the level of stilted artificiality. Purcell (1658–1695), the organist of Westminster Abbey and virtually the only significant native composer of opera in English musical history, produced a masterpiece for the graduation exercises at a girl's school. This was the beautiful and moving *Dido and Aeneas.* In France, Louis XIV realized the potentiality of opera for enhancing the resplendence of the Sun King, and from Italy imported Lully (1632–1687), musician, dancer, speculator, and politician extraordinary, who vied with Molière for the post of "cultural director" at court. Lully's operatic exercises on mythological themes are for the most part now forgotten, but the overtures and dances that he wrote for them live on as a prelude to the great eighteenth-century achievement in instrumental music.

## A Legacy of Contrasts

The seventeenth century bequeathed a rich and diverse legacy, at once scientific, classical, Baroque, and much else besides. Its complexity may be underscored by noting the contrasts between the two greatest political writings issuing from England's century of revolution, and finally by noting the contrasts in the career and ideas of a single individual, Pascal.

Thomas Hobbes' *Leviathan*, published in 1651 and much influenced by the disorders caused by the Civil War, was steeped in Machiavellian pessimism about the inherent sinfulness of man. The state of nature, that is, when men live without government, is a state of war, where men prey upon their fellows and human life becomes, in Hobbes' famous description, "solitary, poor, nasty, brutish, short." Men's only recourse is to agree among themselves to submit absolutely to an all-powerful state, the Leviathan, which will enforce peace. John Locke's *Two Treatises of Government*, published in 1689 to defend the Glorious Revolution, accepts neither the divine-right theory of absolutism nor the Hobbesian justification of absolutism out of desperation. Locke paints a generally cheerful picture of the state of nature, which suffers only from the "inconvenience" (note the mild terminology) of lacking an impartial judicial authority. To secure such an authority men contract among themselves to accept a government, not the omnipotent Leviathan, but a government that respects a man's life, liberty, and property. Should the king seize property by imposing unauthorized taxes or should he follow policies like those of James II, then his subjects are justified in overthrowing their monarch. Locke's relative optimism and his enthusiasm for constitutional government nourished the major current of political thought in the next century, culminating in the American and French revolutions. But events after 1789 brought Hobbesian despair and authoritarianism to the surface once more.

*Rubens' "Marie de' Medici Landing in Marseilles."*

In some ways the man who best symbolized the fecund "century of genius" was the many-sided Pascal. As a mathematician and physicist, he won an important place in the history of science, with his demonstration of air pressure and of the possibility of a vacuum. He also invented a calculating machine and tried to market it, though not very successfully, and he started the first horse-drawn bus line in Paris. Yet, with all his this-worldly modernity, Pascal was also a profoundly other-worldly man, who spent the last years of his life in religious meditation, defended the Jansenists against the Jesuits—incidentally in lively, epigrammatic modern French, with the skill, fervor, and one-sidedness of the born pamphleteer—and left unfinished at his death one of the most remarkable works of Christian apologetics in existence, the fragments known as the *Pensées* (thoughts). Here he wrote:

> Man is but a being filled with error. This error is natural, and, without grace, ineffaceable. Nothing shows him the truth: everything deceives him. These two principles of truth, reason and the senses, besides lacking sincerity, reciprocally deceive each other. The senses deceive reason by false appearances: and just as they cheat reason

they are cheated by her in turn: she has her revenge. Passions of the soul trouble the senses, and give them false impressions. They emulously lie and deceive each other.*

These are hardly the words of a typical rationalist; nor is one of his best-known aphorisms: "Cleopatra's nose: if it had been shorter, the whole face of the earth would have been changed."

The seventeenth century, and not the sixteenth, is the age when the "modern" comes fully into existence. In this century the new science, the new technology, the new economic life finally made possible a belief in progress, in steadily increasing human command over material resources, in steadily increasing possibilities of happiness for most men and women right here on earth. In this century Christianity met in this new spirit of belief in progress the sternest challenge to new adaptations it had met in nearly two millenia. And yet, as we see with much of its classical literature, with much Baroque art, with the new religious movements, the seventeenth century was keenly aware of mystery, of horror, of emotion, of the apparently insoluble paradoxes faced by man, whom Pascal called "a reed, but a thinking reed."

* Pascal, *Thoughts, Letters, and Opuscules,* trans. O. W. Wright (Boston, 1882), p. 192.

## Reading Suggestions on Divine-Right Monarchy and Revolution

EUROPE IN GENERAL

R. S. Dunn, *The Age of Religious Wars, 1559–1689* (*Norton). Crisp, comprehensive, and up-to-date survey.

M. Ashley, *The Golden Century* (Praeger, 1969). Another valuable recent introduction to seventeenth-century Europe.

C. J. Friedrich, *The Age of the Baroque, 1610–1660;* F. L. Nussbaum, *The Triumph of Science and Reason, 1660–1685;* J. B. Wolf, *The Emergence of the Great Powers, 1685–1715* (*Torchbooks). In the series "The Rise of Modern Europe," with full, up-to-date bibliographies.

G. N. Clark, *The Seventeenth Century* (*Galaxy), and D. Ogg, *Europe in the Seventeenth Century* (*Collier). Older, briefer, and still useful surveys.

E. F. Heckscher, *Mercantilism,* rev. ed. 2 vols., (Macmillan, 1955). A famous and controversial work.

A. Vagts, *A History of Militarism* (*Free Press), and E. M. Earle, ed., *Makers of Modern Strategy* (*Atheneum). Both are helpful on seventeenth-century warfare.

E. Barker, *The Development of Public Services in Western Europe, 1660–1930* (Oxford Univ. Press, 1944). Treats an important topic usually totally neglected.

F. L. Nussbaum, *A History of Economic Institutions of Modern Europe* (Crofts, 1933). An abridgment of Sombart's *Moderne Kapitalismus,* with its argument that war is economically creative.

J. U. Nef, *War and Human Progress* (Harvard Univ. Press, 1950). An answer to Sombart, arguing that war is economically destructive.

H. Kamen, *The War of Succession in Spain, 1700–1715* (Indiana Univ. Press, 1969). Focused more on Spain than on the war.

A. T. Mahan, *The Influence of Sea Power on History, 1660–1783* (*Hill and Wang). A most influential but badly outdated book.

T. Aston, ed., *Crisis in Europe, 1560–1660* (Basic Books, 1965). Essays on the controversial thesis that upheavals like the Fronde and the English Civil War were part of a wider crisis attending the shift from a feudal to a capitalist economy and society.

FRANCE

G. R. R. Treasure, *Seventeenth Century France* (Rivingtons, 1966). Full and lucid survey.

J. D. Lough, *An Introduction to Seventeenth Century France* (McKay, 1961). Designed for the student of literature, but useful for anyone interested in the subject.

W. J. Stankiewicz, *Politics and Religion in Seventeenth Century France* (Univ. of California Press, 1960). Good special study.

J. B. Wolf, *Louis XIV* (*Norton). Recent scholarly political biography.

A. Guérard, *France in the Classical Age: The Life and Death of an Ideal* (*Torchbooks). Stimulating interpretation of early modern France.

W. H. Lewis, *The Splendid Century* (*Anchor). Emphasizing society under Louis XIV.

C. V. Wedgwood, *Richelieu and the French Monarchy* (*Collier). and M. Ashley, *Louis XIV and the Greatness of France* (*Free Press). Good short introductions.

O. Ranum, *Richelieu and the Councillors of Louis XIII* (Oxford Univ. Press, 1963). An important monograph on administration.

C. W. Cole, *Colbert and a Century of French Mercantilism*, 2 vols. (Columbia Univ. Press, 1939). A solid, detailed study.

J. E. King, *Science and Rationalism in the Administration of Louis XIV* (Johns Hopkins Univ. Press, 1949). Monograph showing the relations between intellectual and political history.

W. F. Church, ed., *The Impact of Absolutism in France* (*Wiley). Useful selections from source materials and commentaries on the era of Richelieu and Louis XIV.

ENGLAND

M. Ashley, *England in the Seventeenth Century* (*Penguin), and C. Hill, *The Century of Revolution, 1603–1714* (*Norton). Two sound surveys by experts.

G. Davies, *The Early Stuarts, 1603–1660*, and G. N. Clark, *The Later Stuarts, 1660–1714*, rev. eds. (Clarendon, 1949). More detailed scholarly treatments, in the Oxford History of England.

W. Notestein, *The English People on the Eve of Colonization, 1603–1630* (*Torchbooks). Admirable social history.

C. V. Wedgwood, *The King's Peace, 1637–1641; The King's War, 1641–1647; A Coffin for King Charles* (Macmillan, 1955–1964). A recent detailed study of the Great Rebellion by a ranking expert.

S. R. Gardiner, *History of England, 1603–1642*, 10 vols.; *History of the Great Civil War, 1642–1649*, 4 vols.; and *History of the Commonwealth and Protectorate, 1649–1656* (Longmans, 1904–1913). An older major work of detailed history. Gardiner's views may be sampled in his brief textbook, *The First Two Stuarts and the Puritan Revolution, 1603–1660*, first published in 1876 and recently reprinted (*Apollo).

D. H. Willson, *King James VI and I* (Holt, 1956). Sound appraisal.

P. Zagorin, *The Court and the Country* (Routledge, 1969). A fresh study of the origins of the English Revolution.

L. Stone, *Social Change and Revolution in England, 1540–1640* (*Barnes & Noble). A good introduction to the controversy over the gentry, which is also summarized in "Storm over the Gentry," an essay in J. H. Hexter, *Reappraisals in History* (*Torchbooks).

M. Ashley, *Oliver Cromwell and the Puritan Revolution* (*Collier). Recent evaluation of a still controversial figure.

C. H. Firth, *Oliver Cromwell and the Rule of the Puritans in England* (Putnam's 1900). Often considered the best of the very many books on Cromwell.

E. Bernstein, *Cromwell and Communism: Socialism and Democracy in the Great English Revolution* (Allen & Unwin, 1930). The second part of the title of this significant study is the more accurate.

G. Davies, *The Restoration of Charles II, 1658–1660* (Huntington Library, 1955). An authoritative monograph completing the work of Gardiner and Firth.

A. Bryant, *King Charles II* (Longmans, 1931). Unusually sympathetic in tone.

F. C. Turner, *James II* (Macmillan, 1948). Balanced treatment of a ruler generally subject to partisan interpretation.

S. B. Baxter, *William III and the Defense of European Liberty* (Harcourt, 1966). Recent and sympathetic.

J. R. Tanner, *English Constitutional Conflicts of the Seventeenth Century* (*Cambridge Univ. Press). Full and scholarly.

G. P. Gooch, *English Democratic Ideas in the Seventeenth Century* (*Torchbooks). An older work, still worth reading.

C. Brinton, *The Anatomy of Revolution,* rev. ed. (*Vintage). Generalizations based on England's seventeenth-century revolution, France's eighteenth-century one, and Russia's twentieth-century one. Selected bibliographies for each revolution.

*Everybody's Pepys,* ed. O. F. Morshead (Harcourt, 1926). A useful abridgment of the famous diary kept during the 1660's; a fascinating document of social history.

THE CENTURY OF GENIUS

P. Smith, *A History of Modern Culture,* 2 vols. (*Collier). An older work, and a mine of information on aspects of culture often neglected in intellectual histories.

C. Brinton, *The Shaping of Modern Thought* (*Spectrum). A survey of intellectual history from the Renaissance on.

H. F. Kearney, *Origins of the Scientific Revolution* (*Barnes & Noble). A many-sided introduction to this controversial topic.

H. Butterfield, *The Origins of Modern Science, 1300–1800* (*Free Press). A lively and controversial survey, minimizing the contribution of scientists before Galileo.

A. N. Whitehead, *Science and the Modern World* (*Free Press). An incisive and influential critique of what modern science really means and implies; rather difficult but well worth the effort.

A. R. Hall, *The Scientific Revolution, 1500–1800* (*Beacon). A solid account, written from the standpoint of the historian.

L. S. Feuer, *The Scientific Intellectual: The Psychological and Sociological Origins of Modern Science* (Basic Books, 1963). A stimulating interpretation from a more controversial point of view.

A. Wolf, *A History of Science, Technology, and Philosophy in the Sixteenth and Seventeenth Centuries* (*Torchbooks). A standard account.

P. Hazard, *The European Mind, 1680–1715* (*Meridian). Especially dramatic study as indicated by its original French title: *La Crise de la conscience européenne.*

B. Willey, *The Seventeenth Century Background* (*Anchor). Essays on Descartes, Hobbes, Milton, and other figures in the intellectual and religious life of the century.

Ernest Mortimer, *Blaise Pascal* (Harper, 1959). A sympathetic study, admirably written.

F. H. Anderson, *Francis Bacon: His Career and His Thought* (Univ. of Southern California Press, 1962). The best recent treatment.

S. E. Bethell, *The Cultural Revolution of the Seventeenth Century* (Roy, 1951). A literary study with fruitful suggestions for the historian of ideas.

M. R. Bukofzer, *Music in the Baroque Era* (Norton, 1947); H. Leichtentritt, *Music, History, and Ideas* (Harvard, 1938); P. H. Láng, *Music in Western Civilization* (Norton, 1941). Three works helpful for the interpretation of music and history.

G. Bazin, *The Baroque* (New York Graphic Society, 1968). Lavishly illustrated survey of art.

V.-L. Tapié, *The Age of Grandeur* (Weidenfield & Nicolson, 1960). Comprehensive and informative evaluation of neoclassicism and Baroque.

HISTORICAL FICTION

A. Dumas, *The Three Musketeers; Twenty Years After; The Vicomte de Bragelonne* (many editions). The famous "D'Artagnan" trilogy, set in seventeenth-century France; properly swashbuckling, yet based on sound research.

T. Gautier, *Captain Fracasse* (*National Textbook). A good picaresque tale, based on conscientious research; set in the France of Louis XIII.

A. Manzoni, *The Betrothed,* trans. A . Colquhoun (*Dutton). Milan about 1630; a famous Italian novel.

N. Hawthorne, *The Scarlet Letter* (*many editions). The best introduction to the Puritan spirit through fiction.

R. Graves, *Wife to Mr. Milton* (*Noonday). A good novel; not kind to Milton.

W. M. Thackeray, *Henry Esmond* (*many editions). Set in England about 1700.

# 1715 to 1815

# 16

# *The Old Regime and the International Balance*

## I Introduction: The Prospect in 1715

Long years of peace and quiet appeared to be in prospect for Europe in 1715. In the West, the Utrecht settlement of 1713 had ended Louis XIV's prolonged threat to the balance of power, and in the Baltic the protracted Great Northern War between Russia and Sweden was nearing a settlement. The death of Louis XIV himself in 1715 gave fresh promise of international stability, for the crown of France passed to his great-grandson, Louis XV, a boy of five. During a long regency France would probably be too preoccupied with internal matters to attempt adventures abroad. Finally, the last war of Louis XIV had exhausted his own state and had also brought his victorious opponents to the edge of bankruptcy. Europe needed an extended period of convalescence.

Historians use the term "Old Regime" to describe the institutions prevailing in Europe, es-

*Above: A contemporary caricature of Peter the Great cutting the beard of a boyar as part of his campaign to modernize Russia. Right: An eighteenth-century French aristocrat: portrait by Jacques Louis David.*

Europe in 1715
Brandenburg-Prussia
Austrian Hapsburg Lands
Swedish possessions
Venetian possessions
Ottoman Empire
Boundary of the Holy Roman Empire
Battle sites
NORWAY
Oslo
SCOTLAND
Edinburgh
Berwick
North Sea
ULSTER
IRELAND
Drogheda
Boyne R.
Dublin
Limerick
DENMARK
Copenhagen
KINGDOM OF GREAT BRITAIN
SWEDISH POMERANIA
ENGLAND
Hamburg
UNITED NETHERLANDS
Bremen
Elbe R.
Fehrbellin
BRANDENBURG
Berlin
London
Ryswick
Utrecht
Nimwegen
THE
Dover
Tor Bay
Oudenarde
Ramillies
WEST-PHALIA
Oder R.
C. La Hogue
AUSTRIAN NETHERLANDS
Aachen
SAXONY
Atlantic Ocean
Malplaquet
EMPIRE
Rhine R.
Seine R.
Paris
Verdun
Metz
Prague
BOHEMIA
Versailles
LORRAINE
Rastadt
Toul
ALSACE
Blenheim
Nantes
Blois
Orléans
Strasbourg
Augsburg
AUSTRIA
Loire R.
FRANCHE COMTÉ
BAVARIA
Vienna
FRANCE
STYRIA
SWITZERLAND
CARINTHIA
Geneva
TYROL
Bordeaux
CARNIOLA
SAVOY
MILAN
Rhône R.
Venice
Avignon (to the Papacy)
Genoa
Po R.
VENETIAN REPUBLIC
Burgos
PORTUGAL
Ebro R.
Marseilles
Florence
PAPAL STATES
SPAIN
Adriatic Sea
Lisbon
Tagus R.
Madrid
Barcelona
CORSICA (to Genoa)
Rome
BALEARIC IS.
Valencia
NAPLES
Guadalquivir R.
MINORCA (Br.)
Naples
Seville
SARDINIA (to Austria, 1714; to Savoy, 1720)
Granada
Mediterranean Sea
Gibraltar (Br.)
Palermo
SICILY
ALGERIA
TUNIS
MALTA
0
500
Miles

FINLAND
L. Onega
L. Ladoga
Nystadt
Gulf of Finland
St. Petersburg
Narva
INGRIA
ESTONIA
LIVONIA
Novgorod
Pskov
COURLAND
W. Dvina R.
Volga R.
Moscow
Oka R.
Smolensk
Vilna
LITHUANIA
PRUSSIA
R U S S I A
Warsaw
POLAND
Vistula R.
Kiev
Dnieper R.
Poltava
Don R.
Volga R.
Dniester R.
TRANSYLVANIA
MOLDAVIA
NGARY
CRIMEA
Caspian Sea
WALLACHIA
Black Sea
Passarovitz
Danube R.
ONTE-
NEGRO
O T T O M A N
E M P I R E
Constantinople
Vardar R.
Salonika
Tigris R.
Aegean Sea
Athens
Euphrates R.
RHODES
CYPRUS
CRETE
ENGLAND
Calais
ALSACE
1648–1681
THE EMPIRE
ARTOIS
1659
Paris
LORRAINE
1766
FRANCHE COMTÉ
1678
FRANCE
1601
Rhône R.
Avignon
ROUSSILLON
1659
CORSICA
1768
Growth of France
1559-1769
Boundary of the Empire, 1559

pecially France, before 1789: It was the Old Regime of the eighteenth century in contrast to the "new" regime of the French Revolution. On the surface, the Old Regime resembled the still older regime of the Middle Ages, though the forces that were to accomplish the economic and social transformation of modern Europe were already at work beneath the surface. The economy remained largely agrarian, for most Europeans lived in farming villages and retained the parochial outlook of the peasant. In western Europe—particularly in Britain, France, the Low Countries, and Germany west of the Elbe River—the great majority of peasants had long been free of the bonds of serfdom. In eastern Europe, however—notably in Germany beyond the Elbe, and in Hungary, Poland, and Russia—the majority were still serfs.

The social foundations of the Old Regime rested on the medieval division of society into the first estate of the clergy, the second estate of the nobility, and the third estate of commoners, who included the urban bourgeoisie as well as the peasantry. Within the third estate, only the men at the top exerted much political influence—well-to-do businessmen in England and Holland, French lawyers or merchants wealthy enough to purchase government office. Generally, bourgeois influence diminished as one moved eastward. Almost everywhere the titled nobles and the landed gentry of the second estate still wielded substantial power and wanted to regain some of that assumed by the "vile bourgeois," in the phrase of the disgruntled Duc de Saint-Simon. Every government in Europe tended to represent the interests of the few, whether it was an absolute monarchy, like France or Prussia, a constitutional monarchy, like Britain, or a republic, like the Dutch United Provinces.

Europe had long been oligarchical, agrarian, and parochial, and in 1715 it looked as though it would remain so forever. The Old Regime, however, did not last forever; its apparent stability was deceptive. Its social and economic foundations were beginning to crumble under the pressure of revolutionary economic changes, while leaders of the intellectual movement called the Enlightenment were voicing the demands for political and social reform that culminated in the revolution of 1789.

The international stability promised by the Utrecht settlement also faded relatively soon. The defeat and death of Louis XIV did not end the worldwide rivalry of Britain and France, who began another round of their long conflict in 1740. Meanwhile, the rapid emergence of two new states caused shifts in the balance of power. Russia was moving out of semi-isolation to take an active and often aggressive part in international affairs, and the German electorate of Brandenburg-Prussia was emerging from obscurity as a first-class military power, intent on expansion.

## II The Western Powers

The changes in commerce, agriculture, and industry that helped to undermine the Old Regime were most evident in western Europe, especially in France, the Low Countries, and, above all, Britain. They were in fact economic revolutions, though some historians shy away from the term because it may suggest a more sudden discharge of economic energy or technological inventiveness than actually occurred. The commercial, agricultural, and industrial revolutions, while slower and less dramatic than political upheavals, were in the long run perhaps even more dramatic and radical in their consequences. They were a central part of the great modern revolution that transformed the world during the last two centuries.

### The Commercial Revolution

In the eighteenth century, the commercial revolution was more advanced than the other two. Its basic institutions had been developed before 1715, banks and insurance firms in the Renaissance, for example, and chartered trading companies in the sixteenth century. Mercantilism, the rather ill-defined set of principles determining governmental policies toward commerce, had matured in the Spain of Philip II and the France of Louis XIV and Colbert. In the eighteenth century, the steady growth of seaborne trade, stimulated by an increasing population and a rising demand for food and goods, quickened the pace of the commercial revolution. Many ports were enjoying a great boom—in England, London, Bristol, and Liverpool; in France, Nantes and Bordeaux, on the Atlantic coast, nourished by the colonial trade, and Marseille, on the Mediterranean, nourished by the Levant trade; in Italy, Leghorn, established as an admirably run free port by the Grand Duchy of Tuscany; and in Germany, Hamburg, on the lower Elbe, which signified the shift in economic focus from the Baltic to the North Sea.

The burgeoning maritime trade increased the demand for insurance on ships and cargoes. Early in the century the insurance brokers of London often gathered in coffee houses to discuss business, news, and politics. Specialists in marine insurance gravitated to Edward Lloyd's coffee house in Lombard Street and continued to meet there after Lloyd died in 1713. Thus was born Lloyd's of London, the firm that developed the standard form of policy for marine insurance and published *Lloyd's List,* the first detailed and accurate shipping newspaper. Another great London institution to emerge from the informal atmosphere of the coffee house was the stock exchange. As the buying and selling of shares in joint-stock companies increased, traders began to gather at Jonathan's; in 1773 the name was changed from Jonathan's to the Stock Exchange Coffee House.

Marine insurance prospered in part because improved charts and the installation of lighthouses and buoys made navigation safer. At sea, captains could determine their geographical position by using two new instruments, the sextant and the chronometer. The sextant, an elaboration of the telescope, showed the altitude of the sun at noon and thus indicated the ship's latitude. The chronometer, a clock unaffected by the motion of the ship, was kept on Greenwich Mean Time (the time at the meridian running through Greenwich near London). The two new instruments made it possible to calculate the ship's longitude, which represented the difference between Greenwich Mean Time and the local time aboard ship as calculated with the sextant.

On land, the improvements in communication and transport came much more slowly. Except for the good highways of France, European roads were scarcely better than paths or trails. The shipment of goods overland remained slow, unsafe, and expensive until after 1750, when the construction of turnpikes and canals gradually eased the situation. The pioneer English canal, built in 1759–1761 by the duke of Bridgewater, cut in half the cost of moving coal from the mines on his estate to the new factory town of Manchester.

Businessmen also faced the handicaps imposed by restrictive guild regulations and by the abundance of coins, weights, measures, and local tolls. Sweden, for example, minted only copper money, including a monstrosity weighing 43 pounds. Baden, one of the smaller German states, had 112 separate measures for length, 65 for dry goods, 123 for liquids, and 163 for cereals, not to mention 80 different pound weights! A German merchant who shipped timber down the Elbe from Dresden in Saxony to Hamburg had to pay so many tolls to the towns and principalities along the way that of 60 planks floated at Dresden only six would reach Hamburg. Even in France, supposedly the land of uniformity and centralization, all sorts of local taxes and other obstacles to internal trade persisted.

The survival of local vested interests showed the limitations of the power of the mercantilist state. Mercantilism required the regulation of trade on the national, rather than the local, level. But no eighteenth-century government possessed the staff of officials needed to make national regulation effective. Austria, Prussia, and some other German states endeavored to assimilate mercantilism into the more systematized policy called *cameralism* (from *camera,* the council or chamber dealing with expenditures and income). Though the cameralists took a broad view both of economic activities and of governmental responsibilities, their main effort bore upon the planning and administration of state budgets, especially the increase of revenues. Other European states relied heavily on private companies and individuals to execute most of their policies. Thus the English and Dutch East India Companies exercised not only a trading monopoly in their colonial preserves but also virtual sovereign powers, including the right to maintain soldiers and conduct diplomacy. Inventors worked on their own, not in government laboratories, although the state occasionally offered prizes on matters of critical importance to the business community. Although the English Parliament promised £20,000 for the invention of a reliable "seagoing" clock, the inventor of the chronometer had to wait twenty-five years to collect his prize money. On the whole, private initiative did more than sluggish governments to advance the commercial revolution. The fact was underlined by two speculative booms that occurred early in the century—the Mississippi Bubble in France and the South Sea Bubble in England.

### The Mississippi and South Sea Bubbles

In 1715, hardly a state in Europe could manage the large debts that had piled up during the recent wars. Yet all of them had to find some way of meeting at least part of the large annual interest on bonds and other obligations, or else go bankrupt. The governments of France and England chose the way of experiment. They transferred the management of state debts to joint-stock companies, which they rewarded with trading concessions. The commerce of the companies, it was hoped, would prove so lucrative that their profits would easily cover the interest charges on government bonds.

John Law (1671-1729), a Scottish mathematician wizard and an inveterate gambler, presided over the experiment in France. He studied monetary problems and banking methods in Amsterdam, at that time the economic school of Europe. Law was a mercantilist, but with a difference. He agreed with the mercantilist doctrine that the strength of a state depended upon the quantity of money it possessed. But, he asserted, the limited supply of silver and gold made it difficult to increase the amount of specie circulating in any country and therefore difficult to promote business. Paper money, Law concluded, was the solution—paper money backed by a nation's wealth in land and in trade. The quantity of paper money in circulation could easily be raised or lowered in accordance with the needs of business. Trading companies would prosper as never before, the whole country would prosper, and, in the general prosperity, government debts would be paid off.

The death of Louis XIV gave Law the opportunity to try his "system." The regent for Louis XV, the duke of Orléans, who was a gambling crony of Law, permitted him to set up a central bank in Paris. Whereas the value of French money had been sinking lower and lower as the government progressively debased the coinage, Law's bank, following the practice of the Bank of Amsterdam, issued paper notes of stable value. Business activity at once increased. Next, Law set up the Mississippi Company, which received a monopoly of commerce with the Louisiana colony and soon absorbed the other French colonial trading companies.

Law's system now reached to almost every corner of the French economy, and Law himself, appointed controller general, became the economic dictator of the kingdom. His company took over the government debt and agreed to accept government bonds in partial payment for shares of Mississippi stock. Many bondholders responded enthusiastically to Law's offer, because the bonds had depreciated to twenty percent or less of their face value. Law, however, had to sell additional shares of Mississippi stock in order to obtain sufficient working capital for his company. To attract cash purchasers, Law promoted a boom in Mississippi stock, painting the company's prospects in brightest colors. Investors, large and small, caught the fever of speculation, and by the close of 1719 Mississippi stock was selling at forty times its par value.

The Mississippi Bubble soon burst, for Law's paper money could not stand the pressure. As the price of Mississippi shares rose higher and higher, cautious investors decided to cash in. They sold their shares, received payment in banknotes, then took the notes to Law's bank and demanded their redemption in specie. The bank exhausted its reserves of gold and silver and suspended specie payments in February 1720. Law was forced to relinquish the post of controller general in May 1720; he fled France shortly thereafter.

The explosion of the Mississippi Bubble had international repercussions, for within a few weeks of Law's resignation the South Sea Bubble burst in London. It might have been expected that management of the English government's debt would devolve upon the Bank of England. Founded in 1694 as a private institution (it was fully nationalized only after World War II), the Bank of England issued banknotes and rendered other valuable services to the government during the last wars against Louis XIV. But, in negotiations for the right to manage the debt, the bank was outbid by the new South Sea Company, which paid the government the exorbitant sum of more than seven and a half million pounds. The resources of the South Sea Company were slim, consisting largely of the

*London during the South Sea Bubble: a Hogarth engraving. The sign above the door at the upper left says "Raffleing for Husbands with Lottery Fortunes—in Here."*

right to exploit the trading concessions that Britain obtained under the Asiento agreement at the end of the War of the Spanish Succession. These privileges were limited to furnishing Spain's American colonies with 4,800 slaves annually and to sending one ship a year to Panama for general trade.

The South Sea Company, like the Mississippi Company, invited government creditors to transfer their bonds into company stock. The directors of the company bought and sold shares in secret to create a more lively market for them, encouraged purchases of stock with a down payment of only ten percent in cash, and spread reports of forthcoming sailings by the company's ships on voyages of unparalleled promise. In short, like Law, they created a speculative boom. South Sea shares, with a par value of £100, sold for £129 in January of 1720, and for £1050 in June. Dozens of other promoters sprang into action, advertising schemes for wheels of perpetual motion, for making salt water fresh, "for carrying on an undertaking of great advantage, but nobody to know what it is." The gullibility of the investing public was remarkable, but it was not inexhaustible. South Sea shares fell to £880 in August 1720, and to £150 in September. Parliament ordered an investigation and, to protect the company's creditors, seized the estates of its directors, who had meantime destroyed the company's books and fled the country.

The two bubbles produced some unfortunate results. The collapse of the Mississippi scheme ruined Law, whose talents, if used more discreetly, might have revitalized the French economy. In England, the South Sea fiasco long impeded the development of new stock companies, which were henceforth required to buy costly charters. It tarnished the reputations of many in high places. The royal mistresses and King George I himself had been "let in on the ground floor" in return for endorsing the venture enthusiastically, and more than a hundred members of Parliament had borrowed money from the company in order to buy its shares on the installment plan.

The bubbles were by no means total misfortunes. They were an acute instance of the economic growing pains suffered as the states of Europe groped for solutions to baffling financial problems. Voltaire later correctly observed that Law's "imaginary system gave birth to a real commerce," and released French business from the torpor induced by the defeats of Louis XIV. The Mississippi Company, reorganized after 1720, consistently made a handsome profit. In England, the strongest institutions rode out the bursting of the South Sea Bubble; the East India Company continued to pay an annual dividend of five to ten percent, and the Bank of England, no longer in competition for government favor, became once more the financial mainstay of the realm. In the political shake-up following the Bubble, the Whig statesman Robert Walpole came to power with a program of honoring the debt as a *national* debt. This was a novel concept and a great step forward in fiscal morality in an age when most states still treated their debts as the monarch's personal obligation, to be acknowledged or repudiated as he saw fit.

## The Agricultural Revolution

The agricultural revolution, the second of the forces transforming the modern economy, centered on improvements that enabled fewer farmers to produce more crops. The application of technological discoveries to agriculture was an old story, as old as the irrigation ditches of ancient Mesopotamia and the improved plows and horse-collars of the Middle Ages. What was new and revolutionary in the eighteenth century was the accelerating tempo of the advance in farming techniques. The Netherlands, both Dutch and Austrian, continued in the van, producing the highest yields per acre planted and pioneering in the culture of new crops, like the potato, the turnip, and clover. Turnips furnished feed for livestock until the spring pasturing season began, thus eliminating the necessity for massive slaughtering of stock at the onset of winter. Clover, by fixing nitrogen in the soil, increased the fertility of the land and ended the necessity for having fields lie fallow every third year. In England, the new crops were taken up by "Turnip" Townshend (Viscount Townshend, 1674–1738), whose plan for four-year rotation—planting a field in turnips, barley, clover, and wheat in successive years—soon became standard on many English estates.

Townshend and other "improving landlords" in England were the great publicists of the new agriculture. Jethro Tull (1674–1741) studied French truck-gardens and vineyards, where farmers obtained heavy yields from small plots by planting seeds individually and by carefully hoeing the soil around each plant and vine. Tull adapted French methods to the much larger grain fields of England. In place of the inefficient custom of scattering seed broadcast, he planted it deep in regular rows with a horse-drawn "drilling machine," and he cultivated his crops with a horse-drawn hoe. The improvements of Tull and Townshend won enthusiastic praise from Arthur Young (1741–1820), the articulate publicist of the new agriculture, who published lengthy reports on his frequent trips throughout the farming districts of the British Isles and part of the Continent. Young won an international following that included George III, George Washington, the Marquis de Lafayette, and Catherine the Great. Before 1789, however, the new agriculture gained the support of only the most enterprising landlords, and even in Britain it appealed chiefly to the holders of large estates.

The agricultural revolution of the eighteenth century, uneven though it was, marked an important stage in the long, gradual shift from the largely self-sufficient manor of the Middle Ages to the modern capitalist farm producing specialized crops. The improving landlords needed large amounts of capital, and they also needed large plots of land that were not subdivided into long narrow strips for individual cultivators or otherwise used in common by many individuals. Since these old ways hampered the new agriculture, there was a mounting demand that common fields be fenced off as the private lands of single proprietors. Enclosures, which in Tudor days were introduced to extend sheep pastures, were now sought in order to increase cropland. The new enclosure movement reached its peak in the last decades of the eighteenth century and the first decades of the nineteenth, when Parliament passed hundreds of separate enclosure acts affecting several million acres. Rural England was assuming its modern aspect of large fields fenced by hedgerows.

Enclosures, then, created large farms well suited to the application of drill-planting, horse-hoeing, and crop rotation. They enabled Britain to feed her growing population by increasing her agricultural output. But they also created widespread social misery. In Georgian England, as in ancient Greece and Rome, the development of capitalistic estates ruined many small farmers, or yeomen, who could not get along without their rights to use common lands and who could not afford to buy tools, install fences, and become improving landlords themselves. Many of them became hired hands on big farms or sought work in the expanding towns.

### The Beginnings of the Industrial Revolution

By increasing productivity and at the same time releasing part of the agricultural labor force for jobs off the farm, the agricultural revolution was assisting the Industrial Revolution. Industry also required raw materials, markets for its manufactures, and capital to finance the building and equipping of factories. The raw materials and the markets were supplied in part by the colonies overseas, and the capital in part by merchants. Thus the commercial revolution, too, assisted the Industrial Revolution.

In textiles, the making of yarn and cloth had long been organized under the "domestic system." Spinners and weavers worked at home on simple wheels and looms; often they did not buy their own raw materials or market their finished products but worked as wage-laborers for an entrepreneur who furnished the raw materials and sold the finished yarn and cloth. In some industries, however, production was organized not under the domestic system but in primitive factories, which assembled many laborers in a large workshop, though still relying on hand processes rather than on machines. These early factories were particularly common in enterprises utilizing expensive materials, like gold or silver threads for luxury cloth, or requiring close supervision for reasons of state, like cannon foundries.

The Industrial Revolution made the domestic system obsolete and transformed the factory system. Machines superseded simple hand tools like the spinning wheel and the home loom, and water or steam replaced human muscles and animal energy as the source of power. Because power-driven machines were often big and complicated, larger factories were needed to house them. By 1789, these revolutionary changes had affected only a few industries, but they were key industries—mining, metallurgy, munitions, and textiles.

Coal-mining was becoming a big business, largely because of the increased demand for coke by iron smelters. Smelters had always used charcoal to make iron from ore, and they continued to do so in countries like Sweden that had abundant wood for charcoal. But in England, where most of the great forests had been cut down, the price of charcoal rose so high that it constituted eighty percent of the cost of producing iron. By 1750, despite the abundant native supply of ore, the output of English smelters was declining rapidly, and the country was using more and more imported iron. Ordinary coal could not replace charcoal as smelter fuel because the chemicals in coal made the iron too brittle. Here necessity mothered invention, as the Darby family of Shropshire discovered how to remove the chemical impurities from coal by an oven process that converted it into coke.

In England, the Darbys and other private firms were the pioneers in metallurgy. On the Continent, governments took the lead—a significant exception to the rule about the inability of states to solve economic problems. Warfare required weapons and munitions in large quantities; France and Prussia met the demand by setting up state-financed and state-operated foundries and arms factories.

The revolution in textiles was focused on the cheaper production of cotton cloth. The flying shuttle, a technical device first applied to the hand loom in England (1733), enabled a single weaver to do work that had previously required the services of two. Looms equipped with the flying shuttle used up the supply of hand-spun thread so rapidly that the London Society for the Encouragement of Arts, Manufactures, and Commerce offered a prize for improvement of the spinning process. James Hargreaves won the prize in 1764 with his spinning jenny, a series of spinning wheels geared together which made eight threads simultaneously. Soon the jenny was adapted to water power, and its output was increased to a hundred or more threads at once. The eventual emancipation of industry from dependence on unreliable water power was foreshadowed in the 1760's when the Scotsman James Watt introduced the steam engine.

Although Britain had nearly 150 cotton mills in 1789, woolens and dozens of other basic commodities were still made by hand. Full industrial development would not take place until the canal and railroad permitted cheap transport of heavy freight and until the shortages of capital and skilled labor were overcome. A Swedish inventor of the early 1700's designed excellent machines for cutting wheels and files but could not raise the money to put them into operation. And in Britain the difficulty of making precise parts for Watt's engine delayed its production in large quantities. While the eighteenth century had taken many of the initial steps in the Industrial Revolution, it remained for the next century to apply them on a truly revolutionary scale.

## The Assets of Britain

Leadership in the economic revolutions was making Britain the wealthiest nation in the world. British bankers, buttressed by the Bank of England and by the careful management of the national debt, extended credit to business enterprises at the relatively low interest rate of five percent. The City, the square mile comprising the City of London proper and including the financial district, recovered quickly from the South Sea Bubble and challenged Amsterdam's position as the international capital of trade and finance. In the course of the eighteenth century, British merchants outdistanced their old trading rivals, the Dutch, and gradually took the lead over their new competitors, the French. Judged by the three touchstones of mercantilism—commerce, colonies, and sea power—Britain was the strongest state in Europe.

The British colonial empire, however, was not a mercantilist undertaking in the full sense. Supervision of the colonies rested with a government department, the Board of Trade, which followed an easygoing policy of "salutary neglect" contrasting with the rigid controls exerted by other colonial powers over their possessions. In the long run, as the American Revolution was to show, "salutary neglect" did not satisfy the colonists, but in the short run it worked reasonably well by promoting the colonists' prosperity and self-reliance.

The Royal Navy enjoyed the assets of a superior officer corps and greater size. Future captains went to sea at the age of sixteen or even younger, and passed through long practical training before receiving commissions. The ships they commanded in the mid-century wars were inferior in design to those of France and Spain; but there were more of them. Britain had a 2-to-1 advantage over France in number of warships, a 6-to-1 lead in merchant ships, and a 10-to-1 lead in total number of experienced seamen, merchant and naval. In wartime, the fleet could draw on the merchant marine for additional sailors and auxiliary vessels. Service in the Royal Navy had its grim aspects. Food was monotonous and unhealthy, and punishments included flogging and keel-hauling, in which the victim was dragged the length of the barnacle-encrusted keel. Since these were the common afflictions of all sailors in the eighteenth century, however, they did not put the British navy at a comparative disadvantage.

The British army, by contrast, was neither large nor impressive. Its offices were reputed to be the poorest in Europe, and its soldiers were in part mercenaries from the German state of Hesse-Cassel, the Hessians of the American Revolutionary War. Neglect of the army was a deliberate policy. The British Isles were relatively safe from invasion; moreover, the English people feared a standing army as an instrument of potential absolutism, for they remembered the uses that Cromwell and James II had made of this weapon.

The Glorious Revolution, which in its preliminary stage had done so much to confirm distrust of the army, had also confirmed Britain's unique and greatest asset—the supremacy of Parliament. Parliament had approved the accession of William and Mary in place of James II. When Anne, Mary's sister and the last Stuart monarch, died in 1714, Parliament had already arranged for the succession of the House of Hanover. Under the first kings of the new house—George I (1714–1727) and George II (1727–1760)—the institution that was to assure the everyday assertion of parliamentary supremacy was undergoing steady development. This was the cabinet.

## Cabinet Government

Today the British cabinet is a committee of the majority party of the House of Commons, headed by the prime minister, and it remains in office as long as it can continue to enlist the support of a majority in Commons. It is "Her Majesty's Government," while the chief minority party forms "Her Majesty's Opposition," a loyal opposition whose leader receives an official salary. The cabinet rules because it controls the executive branch of the government; the monarch merely reigns.

Under the first two Hanoverian kings the cabinet was only starting to accumulate this immense authority. George I and George II by no means abdicated all the old royal prerogatives. They took a direct interest in the South Sea Bubble and other financial matters, and they intervened in the conduct of war and diplomacy to a degree that would be regarded as highly improper today. George II was the last English monarch to command troops in person on the battlefield—in 1743 during the War of the Austrian Succession. The two Georges chose their cabinet ministers from the Whig party, then in control of the Commons. They did so, however, not because they were required to, but because it suited their convenience, and because they thoroughly distrusted the Tories, some of whom were involved in futile Jacobite plots to restore to the throne the descendants of James II (Jacobite from *Jacobus,* Latin for James). The Whigs, on the other hand, had engineered the Glorious Revolution and had arranged the Hanoverian succession.

For two decades after the collapse of the South Sea Bubble, from 1721 to 1742, Robert Walpole, who led the Whigs in the Commons, headed the

*A political campaign in England: Hogarth's "Canvassing for Votes" (1757).*

cabinet; he was in fact prime minister, although the title was not yet official. Walpole was a master politician who maintained his majority in the Commons by skillful manipulation of the Whigs. The task was not easy, for party discipline of the modern kind did not exist; the terms "Whig" and "Tory" referred to informal and shifting interest groups, not to parties in our sense. In 1733, when Walpole forced the resignation of ministers opposed to his plan for radical fiscal reform, he took a major step toward establishing the principle of cabinet unanimity on a crucial issue.

Under the first two Georges the Whigs were a coalition of landed gentry and "funded" gentry; that is, of nobles and squires from the country and of business and professional men from London and provincial towns. Thus the Whigs renewed a political alliance that had first appeared in the later Middle Ages when the knights of the shire had joined the burgesses to form the Commons. In the Whig parliaments the country gentlemen predominated by sheer numbers; in 1754, for instance, they outnumbered by 5 to 1 the merchants and lawyers sitting in the House of Commons. Family ties, common political aims, and a common reverence for property bound together the rural and urban Whigs. In order to consolidate the gains of the Glorious Revolution, the Whigs opposed Jacobite schemes and supported the unprepossessing Hanoverians. To protect property, they passed legislation making death the penalty for stealing livestock, for cutting down cherry trees, and for other relatively minor offenses.

What did terms like "gentry," "gentleman," and "squire" connote about social class in the eighteenth century? Historians are still debating the question, but it is generally agreed that they referred to a class just below the titled nobility. The ranks of the gentry included the younger sons of nobles, technically not nobles themselves since the title and a seat in the House of Lords passed only to the eldest son. They also included other owners of landed estates, all of whom were addressed verbally as "sir" and in writing as "Esquire," (originally a shieldbearer, the lieutenant of the feudal knight). Historically, the gentry lived off the revenues of landed property, but by the eighteenth century many of them also had a stake in the commercial revolution. Indeed, successful businessmen sometimes bought country estates, set themselves up as gentlemen, and were accepted as such by the local gentry. The intermingling of country gentlemen with men of business and intermarriage of the two classes demonstrated that Britain enjoyed more social mobility than did the states of the Old Regime on the Continent.

Robert Walpole himself exemplified the Whig fusion of landed and funded elements. He inherited his manners and his tastes from his father, a country squire. A heavy drinker and a devotee of bawdy stories, he established the English politician's tradition of the long country weekend in order to indulge his passion for hunting. Like many Whig squires, Walpole married into the aristocracy of trade; his wife was the daughter of a timber merchant and former Lord Mayor of London. As prime minister, Walpole, the country gentleman, promoted the interests of the City by ensuring political stability through Whig cabinets and financial stability through the gradual retirement of the national debt.

In social and political structure, the Britain of Walpole was, of course, oligarchic rather than democratic. Only gentlemen could hope to rise in the professions, to become army and navy officers, lawyers, clergymen, and physicians. In local affairs, the landed gentry alone supplied the justices of the peace, who not only presided over courts, but also fixed wage scales, superintended the relief of the poor, provided for the maintenance of bridges and highways, and were fanatic defenders of the propertied classes. Their stringent enforcement of the laws against theft accounts for the saying "As well be hanged for a sheep as for a lamb."

In the main, only gentlemen had the right to vote for members of Parliament. The small number of voters in many constituencies encouraged corruption, particularly in the "rotten" or "pocket" boroughs, which had such a tiny electorate that control of their vote reposed in the pocket of some wealthy lord. Politicians often bribed voters outright or else promised them places on the government payroll. An immensely rich Whig, the duke of Newcastle, controlled the outcome of elections in four counties and in seven pocket boroughs.

Thus in Britain, as on the Continent, the ruling classes governed the voteless masses. And the masses were sometimes in material terms worse off than their continental counterparts, as in the case of the landless agricultural workers whose numbers mounted with the enclosure movement. London was already big enough to have incipiently, at least, all the troubles of a modern metropolis—slums, slum dwellers, crimes of violence, even traffic jams—and an almost complete lack of police and fire protection. (Of juvenile delinquency we do not hear much, partly because it melted indistinguishably into the very considerable adult delinquency, and partly because in those days of universal child labor among the lower classes there were not many idle children.)

Yet the British ruling classes, selfish and narrow-minded though they often were, had at their best a sense of noblesse oblige, of public spirit and civic-mindedness. Within the aristocracy of land and trade there were fewer social barriers than on the Continent, and the English gentry were on the whole more responsive than their continental counterparts to the need for changes and reform. Disraeli, the great nineteenth-century Tory, dubbed the Whig cabinets of the first two Georges a "Venetian oligarchy," by which he meant that the wealthy ran the country for their private benefit, like the merchants of Renaissance Venice. And so they did; yet the Whigs, for all their oligarchy and their corruption, provided the most enlightened government in eighteenth-century Europe.

### The Liabilities of France

Where Britain was strong, France was weak. In the France of Louis XV (1715–1774), barriers to social mobility were more difficult to surmount, though commoners who were rich or aggressive enough did overcome them. France suffered particularly from the rigidity of its colonial system, the inferiority of its navy, and the very mediocre abilities of most of its statesmen. The Ministry of the Navy, which ruled the overseas empire, regarded these possessions as so many warships permanently at anchor. It refused to sanction steps toward self-government and applied the same regulations to colonies as different as the sugar islands of the West Indies and the wilderness of Canada. The plethora of controls stifled the initiative of the colonists, and the French imperial system lacked the elasticity to meet the test of war. The mother country, however, prospered, as commercial activity doubled in Nantes, Bordeaux, and other ports, and refineries were set up to process the raw sugar imported from the plantations of Guadeloupe and Martinique.

The French navy needed greater resources and better leadership. Its warships, though admirably designed, were inadequate in number. Since Dutch and British vessels carried much of French commerce, the merchant marine was too small to supplement the fleet. French naval officers, though rigorously trained in the classroom, lacked the experience gained by British captains in a lifetime at sea. Moreover, in a fashion characteristic of the Old Regime at its worst, officers from the aristocracy devoted much of their energies to thwarting the rise of those from the middle class.

French rulers were almost bound to neglect the navy in favor of the army, since France was above all a land power, and its vulnerable northeastern frontier, lying across the Flemish plain, invited invasion. Except in size, however, the army of Louis XV scarcely lived up to the great traditions of Louis XIV. The troops were poorly trained, and the organization was top-heavy. There was one officer to fifteen men, as compared with one to thirty-five in the more efficient Prussian army. Many aristocratic officers regarded a commission simply as a convenient way of increasing their personal wealth.

Both the navy and the army underwent important reforms later in the century after the defeats suffered by France in the Seven Years' War (1756–1763). The number of warships was increased, the officer corps of the army was cleared of much deadwood, and more aggressive military tactics were introduced. These improvements accounted in part for the excellent showing made by France in the American Revolutionary War and in the military campaigns resulting from her own revolution. They came too late, however, to save the vanishing prestige of the Old Regime.

The Old Regime was weakest at its head, the monarchy itself. There were no sun kings in France after the death of Louis XIV, and few ministers who approached the caliber of Richelieu or Colbert. The duke of Orléans, regent from 1715 to 1723, was a gambler, drunkard, and pervert, who popularized the word "roué" by remarking that his lecherous friends deserved to be broken on the wheel (*roue* is French for "wheel"). The regent, however, did attempt two important experiments. He allowed John Law to

*Making bread—the staple food for most of the population—in an eighteenth-century French bakery. The dough is kneaded (Fig. 1) in a wooden trough, formed into loaves (Figs. 3 and 4), and baked in an oven (Fig. 5). The illustration is from Diderot's "Encyclopédie."*

try out his "system," as we have seen, and, in place of Louis XIV's method of ruling through individual bourgeois ministers, he set up a series of ministerial councils staffed by men from distinguished noble families. Although the first experiment produced some beneficial results, the second failed, after a three-year trial, in part because of the endless squabbles among the noble councillors, particularly between the nobles of the robe and the nobles of the sword, "between the grandnephews of lawyers and the ever-so-great-grandsons of feudal lords." The French second estate had outlived its usefulness. The regency proved that the nobles were no longer able to govern; the mid-century wars proved that they were no longer able to lead French armies to victory.

They were, however, still capable of causing trouble. The strongholds of the nobles of the robe were the important courts known as parlements, in Paris and in some provincial capitals. The parlements took advantage of the regency to extend their long-standing claim to register government edicts before they were published and enforced. A papal bull condemned the doctrines of the influential French Catholic minority of Jansenists, who had family ties with the judges of the parlements, and whose differences with the Crown were now more a matter of politics than of religion. When the Parlement of Paris refused to register the bull, the regent held a *lit de justice,* a special royal session obliging the Parlement to follow the royal command. But the judges of the parlements in Paris and elsewhere retaliated by going on strike, refusing to carry on their normal court business. The cold war between parlement and king continued for half a century. It was marked by repeated strikes on the part of the judges, by the exiling of recalcitrant judges from the capital by the king, and, in the 1760's, by the suppression, at the behest of the parlements, of the Jesuits, the great foe of the Jansenists. In the last years of his reign Louis XV tried to end the problem once and for all by suppressing the parlements and substituting new courts more under royal control. But the parlements returned, more arrogant than ever, under his successor.

Meantime, soon after the end of Orléans' regency, power passed to one of the few statesmen of prerevolutionary France, Cardinal Fleury, the tutor of Louis XV and the chief minister from 1726 until his death in 1743 in his ninetieth year. Without attempting basic reforms, the aged cardinal, in the words of Voltaire, "treated the state as a powerful and robust body which could cure itself." Fleury did not remedy the chronic and deep-seated injustice and inefficiency of French fiscal methods, but he did stabilize the coinage, and he put the farming of taxes on a more businesslike basis by restricting tax-farmers to the comparatively modest profit of seven and a half percent. To make loans more readily available, he established state pawnshops in the chief cities of France. Fleury's success impressed Lady Mary Montagu, the observant wife of an English diplomat, who wrote in 1739:

> France is so much improved, it is not . . . the same country we passed through twenty years ago. Everything I see speaks in praise of Cardinal Fleury; the roads are all mended . . . and such good care taken against robbers, that you may cross the country with your purse in your hand. . . . The French are more changed than their roads; instead of pale, yellow faces, wrapped up in blankets, as we saw them, the villages are filled with fresh-coloured lusty peasants, in good cloth and clean linen. It is incredible the air of plenty and content that is over the whole country.*

The administrative stability achieved by Fleury soon vanished after Louis XV began his personal rule in 1743. Intelligent but timid, lazy, and debauched, Louis XV did not have the interest or the patience to supervise the details of government in the manner of Louis XIV. He appointed and dismissed ministers on a personal whim or at the bidding of his mistresses and favorites. In thirty years he had eighteen different foreign secretaries and fourteen different controllers general (the chief fiscal officer). Each change in personnel meant a shift in policy, and Louis aggravated the instability by conspiring against his own appointees. France had two conflicting foreign policies: that of the diplomatic corps; and the "King's Secret," conducted by royal agents who operated at cross purposes with the regular diplomats. Yet, while allowing the reins of government to go slack, Louis refused to give them over to firmer hands.

Nevertheless, France remained a great power. Still the most populous country in Europe, she possessed almost inexhaustible reserves of strength. Her army, though enfeebled, was the largest in the world, and her navy was the second largest. She led the world in overseas trade until Britain forged ahead of her in the last quarter of the eighteenth century. French tastes, French thought, and the French language retained the international preeminence they had won in the age of Louis XIV. The misgovernment and the other weaknesses of the Old Regime were relative rather than absolute.

* *Letters*, Everyman edition (New York, 1906), pp. 271–272.

### The Other Western States

Spain was the only other state in western Europe with a claim to great-power status. Sweden and the Dutch Republic no longer filled the major international roles they had played during the seventeenth century. During the first two decades of the new century, the Great Northern War killed off the flower of Swedish manhood and withered the Baltic empire of Sweden. The Dutch, exhausted by their wars against Louis XIV, could no longer afford a large navy or an energetic foreign policy. There was considerable justification for Frederick the Great's gibe that Holland "was a cockboat in the tow of the English frigate." When William III of Orange (and England) died in 1702, many of the Dutch provinces permitted his quasi-monarchical office of stadholder to stand vacant, and dominance passed to the merchant oligarchy. Dutch seaborne trade, though no longer the greatest in Europe, continued to be substantial, and the republic settled down to a life of prosperous and relative obscurity.

Spain suffered comparatively little damage from the great war over the succession to her throne that was fought in the early 1700's. The loss of Belgium and parts of Italy at the Utrecht settlement of 1713 reduced the unwieldy Spanish domains to more manageable size. The new Bourbon kings were a marked improvement over the last Spanish Hapsburgs. Philip V (1700–1746), the first of the Spanish Bourbons, infused fresh life into the country's fossilized institutions by importing French advisers schooled in the system of Louis XIV. He also enlisted the aid of two able adventurers, Alberoni and Ripperda, whose fantastic careers almost outdid John Law's. Alberoni, the son of an Italian gardener, was successively a cook, a diplomat, the chief minister of Spain, and a cardinal. Ripperda, a Dutch business expert and diplomat, ultimately lost the favor of Philip, entered the service of the sultan of Morocco, and, after a lifelong alternation between the Protestant and Catholic faiths, died a Muslim. Philip and his remarkable advisers cut down the excessive formalities and endless delays of Spanish administration. They reasserted the authority of the monarchy over the traditionally powerful nobility and clergy.

They improved the tax system, encouraged industry, built up the navy, and fortified strategic points in the Spanish empire in America.

The new dispensation, however, did not strike at the root causes of Spanish decline. The greed of governors and the restrictions of mercantilism still checked the progress of the colonies. The mother country remained impoverished, burdened with reactionary noble and clerical castes, and hampered by inadequate resources. Philip V himself was neurotic, refusing, for instance, to cut his toenails, which grew so long that he limped. He was dominated by his strong-willed second wife, Elizabeth Farnese, the patroness of Alberoni. Since Philip's son by his first marriage would inherit Spain, Elizabeth was determined to find thrones for her own two sons. Her persistent attempts to secure the succession of Italian states for them repeatedly threatened the peace of Europe.

## III Italy and Germany

### Disunited Italy

By 1715, the Italian states had lost much of the political and economic power they had enjoyed during the Renaissance. It is easy to see why. The opening of new worlds overseas and the rise of Spain, England, and the other Atlantic powers had diminished the importance of the Mediterranean. In the Mediterranean itself, the Ottoman Turks and their satellites in North Africa long menaced Italian shipping and trade. Moreover, beginning with the French invasion of 1494, Italy had been threatened with conquest by one of the new national monarchies.

The Spanish Hapsburgs made the conquest. For almost two centuries Spain ruled Milan, Naples, and Sicily directly, and dominated the rest of the peninsula. In the readjustment of the European balance in 1713, Italy exchanged one foreign master for another, as the Austrian Hapsburgs took over the Italian possessions of their Spanish cousins. On the completion of the readjustment in 1720, the political map of the peninsula showed Austria established in Lombardy, flanked by the decaying commercial republics of Venice and Genoa. In the mountainous northwest was the small but rising state of Piedmont-Savoy, technically the Kingdom of Sardinia after its acquisition of that island in 1720. Farther down the peninsula were the Grand Duchy of Tuscany (formerly the Republic of Florence), the Papal States, and the Austrian Two Sicilies. None of these states was more than a minor power.

Yet Italy could not be written off as a negligible quantity in the eighteenth century. Rome remained the capital of Catholicism, Venice still produced fine painters, and Naples was the schoolmaster of European musicians. Lombardy, Tuscany, and Naples all contributed to the economic and intellectual advances of the century. Meantime, Italy was a major stake in balance-of-power politics, a perennial source of dissension and spoils. In 1720, to counter the ambitions of the Spanish queen, Elizabeth Farnese, the Austrian Hapsburgs took over the island of Sicily, which had gone to Piedmont in the Utrecht settlement; in return, Piedmont secured Sardinia, originally assigned to Austria. In the 1730's, a series of exchanges gave the Two Sicilies to Elizabeth's elder son, "Baby Carlos," while the Austrians gained some minor bits of territory and the succession of Tuscany. In 1768, Genoa sold the island of Corsica to France. Italy was, in the old phrase, merely "a geographical expression," not a political whole but a series of parts to be shifted and exchanged by ambitious dynasts and empire builders from outside the peninsula.

### Divided Germany

In some ways Germany deserved even more to be called a geographical expression, for it was divided into three hundred states, large, small, and minute. The Thirty Years' War had caused wide devastation, and the Peace of Westphalia ending the war in 1648 had enhanced the sovereign rights of the particular German states and reduced virtually to zero the authority of their nominal overlord, the Holy Roman emperor. Unlike Italy, however, Germany did include two considerable powers, Austria and Prussia.

The Austrian Hapsburgs won a series of military and diplomatic victories in the two decades before 1715. In 1699, by the peace of Karlovitz, they recovered Hungary from the Ottoman Turks, thereby advancing their own *Drang nach Osten.* In 1713, though they failed to keep the old Hapsburg crown of Spain from going to the Bourbon Philip V, they were compensated with Spain's Belgian and Italian territories. Yet these last acquisitions were distant from the main bloc of Hapsburg lands in central Europe.

Charles VI (1711–1740), aware that his title of Holy Roman emperor conferred little real authority, concentrated on the Hapsburg family possessions. He spent much of his reign persuading his own noble subjects to ratify the Pragmatic Sanction, a constitutional agreement whereby, in the absence of sons, his daughter Maria Theresa would succeed him in all his lands. A good deal of scorn has been directed at Charles for devoting so much time and energy to a scrap of paper, but recent historians have noted that the Pragmatic Sanction did indeed establish the principle of linking together the scattered family territories. Much, however, remained to be done to consolidate Hapsburg rule over an assemblage of lands which represented many different nations and could never be forged into a single national monarchy. In three key national areas—German Austria, Czech Bohemia, and Magyar Hungary—the nobles still kept most of their medieval prerogatives and, by controlling local estates and diets, controlled grants of taxes and the appointment of officials. The financial and military weakness of the Hapsburg regime was underlined by the fact that when Charles VI died, in 1740, the exchequer was nearly empty and the pay of the army and of the civil service was more than two years in arrears. The army was well short of its paper strength of 100,000 men as it faced the great test of strength with Prussia that came in 1740.

### The Rise of Prussia

Whereas Austria enjoyed the appearances rather than the realities of great-power status, Prussia possessed few of the appearances but a great many of the realities. Its territories were scattered across north Germany from the Rhine on the west to the Vistula and beyond on the east; consisting largely of sand and swamp, these lands had meager natural resources and carried on relatively little trade. With fewer than three million inhabitants in 1715, Prussia ranked only twelfth among the European states in population. Her capital city, Berlin, located on the unimportant river Spree, had few of the obvious geographical advantages enjoyed by Constantinople, Paris, London, and the other great capitals. A wise prophet in 1600 might well have foreseen that Catholic Austria would never unite a Germany in which Protestantism was so strong. But he would probably have predicted that a new Germany would center in Frankfurt in the heart of the Rhine country, or in Saxon Leipzig or Dresden; he would hardly have chosen the unpromising town of Berlin and the minor house of Hohenzollern.

The Hohenzollerns had been established since the fifteenth century as electors of Brandenburg, which lay between the Elbe and Oder rivers. A Hohenzollern was the last master of the Teutonic Knights, a crusading order which in the thirteenth century had pushed the Germanic frontier beyond the Vistula to a land called Prussia at the southeast corner of the Baltic Sea. In 1618, when East Prussia fell to the Hohenzollerns, it was separated from Brandenburg by Polish West Prussia and was still nominally a fief held from the Polish king. In western Germany meantime (1614), the Hohenzollerns acquired Cleves, Mark, and some other parcels in the lower Rhine valley and Westphalia. Thus, when Frederick William, the Great Elector (1640–1688), succeeded to the Hohenzollern inheritance as the Thirty Years' War was drawing to a close, his lands consisted of a nucleus in Brandenburg with separate outlying regions to east and west. With extraordinary persistence, the rulers of Brandenburg-Prussia for the next two hundred years devoted themselves to the task of making a solid block of territory out of these bits and pieces.

The Great Elector was the first in a line of able Hohenzollern rulers. In foreign policy, he won recognition from Poland as the full sovereign of Prussia, no longer subject to Polish overlordship. He also tried, with less success, to dislodge the Swedes from the Pomeranian territories, between Brandenburg and the Baltic, which they had acquired in 1648. Though he won military renown by defeating the Swedes at Fehrbellin in 1675, he made few practical gains because of his own tortuous diplomacy. In the wars against Louis XIV, he shifted repeatedly from the French to the anti-French side and back.

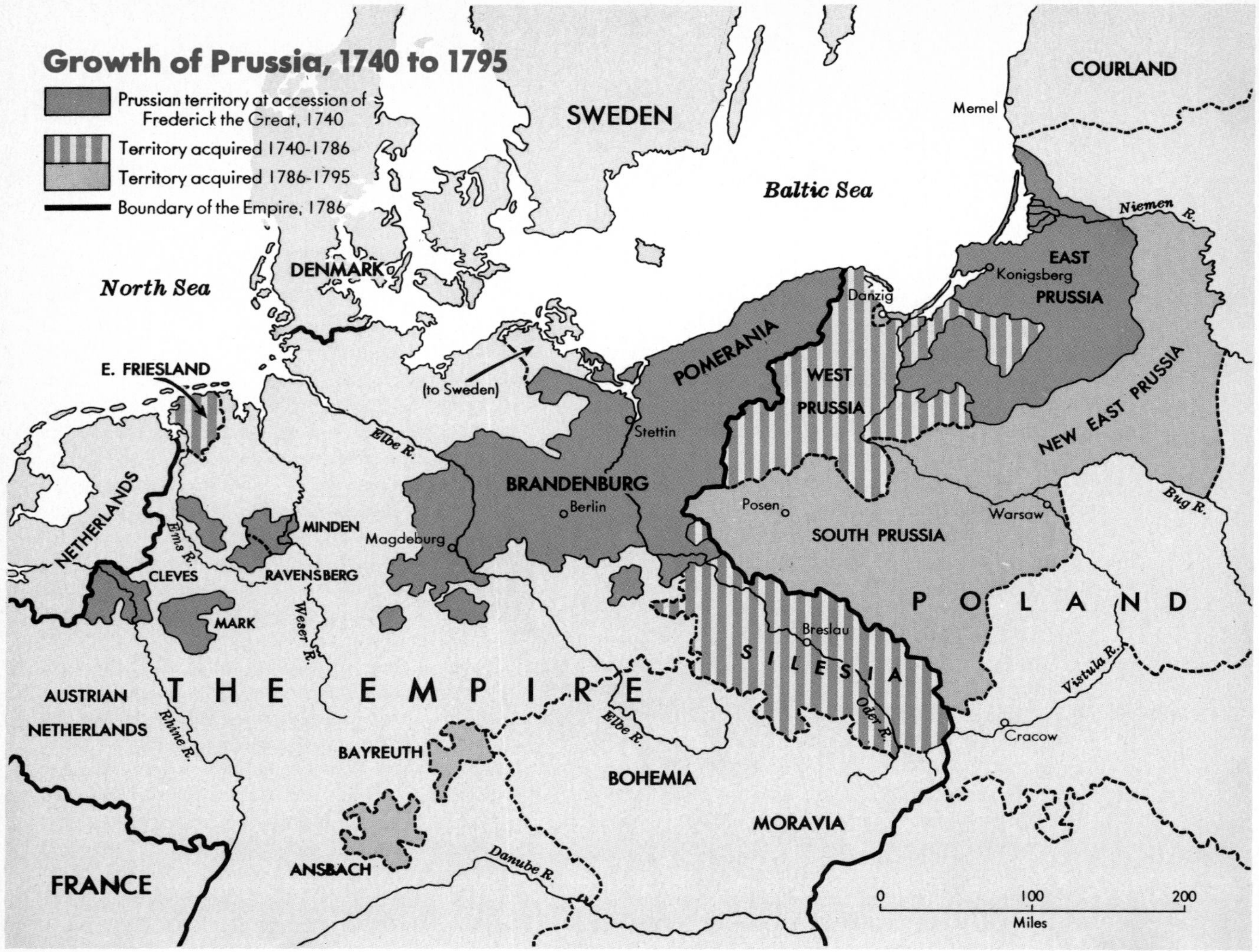


In domestic policy, his accomplishments were more substantial. He had found his domains largely ruined by war, the farms wasted, the population cut in half, the army reduced to a disorderly rabble of a few thousand men. The Great Elector repaired the damage thoroughly. To augment the population, he encouraged the immigration of Polish Jews and other refugees from religious persecution, notably twenty thousand French Huguenots to whom he gave partial exemption from taxation. He built a small but efficient standing army that enabled Prussia to command large foreign subsidies for participating in the campaigns for or against Louis XIV. In peacetime, he assigned the soldiers to the construction of public works like the canal between the Elbe and the Oder.

In administration, the Great Elector fixed the Hohenzollern pattern of militarized absolutism, a policy in which he was assisted by an educational tradition and a Lutheran state church that taught the virtues of obedience and discipline. On his accession, he found that in all three territories—Prussia, Brandenburg, and Cleves-Mark—the authority of the ruler was limited by estates, medieval assemblies representing the landed nobles and the townspeople. In all three territories he battled the estates for supremacy and won, thereby delaying for two centuries the introduction of representative government into the Hohenzollern realm. He gradually gathered into his own hands the crucial power of levying taxes. Much of the actual work of collecting taxes and performing other administrative functions was done by the War Office and the army; policing, too, was done by the military. Like

Louis XIV, the Great Elector reduced the independence of the aristocracy; unlike Louis, however, he relied not on bourgeois officials but on a working alliance with the landed gentry, particularly the celebrated *Junkers* of East Prussia. He confirmed the Junkers' absolute authority over the serfs on their estates and their ascendancy over the towns, and he encouraged them to serve the state, especially as army officers. In contrast to other monarchies, the absolutism of the Hohenzollerns rested on the cooperation of the sovereign and the aristocracy, not on their mutual antagonism.

Under the Great Elector's son, Frederick I (1688–1713), Prussia played only a minor role in the last two wars against Louis XIV and made few territorial gains in the Utrecht settlement. But in 1701 the elector Frederick made a significant gain in prestige by assuming the title "King in Prussia" and insisting on international recognition of his new status as the price for his entry into the War of the Spanish Succession. Though technically Frederick was king only in East Prussia, which lay outside the boundaries of the Holy Roman Empire, even a limited royal title conferred new dignity on the Hohenzollerns. In living up to his new eminence, however, King Frederick I nearly bankrupted his state by lavish expenditures on the trappings of monarchy. Since he thought that a suggestion of marital infidelity enhanced the majesty of a king, he maintained an official mistress with whom he took decorous afternoon promenades. Actually, he was happily married, and his talented queen enlivened the provincial Hohenzollern court by inviting intellectuals and artists to Berlin. As Frederick the Great later remarked, under Frederick I Berlin was the "Athens of the north."

*Berlin in the late eighteenth century.*

### Frederick William I

But as Frederick the Great also remarked, under the next king, Frederick William I (1713–1740), Berlin became the "Sparta of the north." The flirtation with luxury and the finer things of life proved to be a passing exception to the usual Hohenzollern rule of austerity. Frederick William I returned with a vengeance to the policies of the Great Elector and devoted himself entirely to economy, absolutism, and the army. As soon as he had given his father a lavish funeral, he dismissed most of the officials of the court, converted a large portion of the royal palace into offices, and reduced governmental expenses to a fraction of what they had been. He reiterated the order "Ein Plus machen" ("Make a surplus"), and he bequeathed a full treasury to his son. His frugality enabled him to undertake the occasional project that he thought really worth while. Thus he financed the immigration of 12,000 South German Protestants to open up new farmlands in eastern Prussia.

To strengthen royal control over the apparatus of state, Frederick William I instituted a small board of experts, with the wonderfully Germanic title of Generaloberfinanzkriegsunddomänendirektorium (General Superior Finance, War, and Domain Directory). Individual members of the General Directory were charged both with administering departments of the central government and with supervising provinces. The arrangement, while cumbersome, did detach provincial administration from local interests and bring it under closer royal control. The king insisted on hard work and punctuality. He treated the experts of the General Directory as he treated lesser officials, paying them meanly and belaboring them with his cane for slovenly performance of their duties. A late arrival at one of the daily sessions of the General Directory paid a severe fine; an unexcused absentee faced six months in jail.

Frederick William I doubled the size of the standing army, but he maintained the strength of the laboring force of his underpopulated state by furloughing troops for nine months a year to work on farms. To secure guns and uniforms, he established state factories. The army also prompted his sole extravagance—a regiment of grenadiers, all six feet tall or over, who wore special caps more than a foot high to increase the impression of size. In recruiting his beloved "giants," the king threw economy to the winds, employing scores of scouts in other German states, paying exorbitant prices, and even trading royal musicians and prize stallions for especially tall specimens. Frederick William cherished his army too much to undertake an adventurous foreign policy. His only significant military campaign was against Sweden in the last phase of the Great Northern War, whereby Prussia obtained in 1720 part of Swedish Pomerania and also the important Baltic port of Stettin at the mouth of the Oder River. Thus Frederick William advanced the Great Elector's old aim of liquidating the Swedish possessions in Germany.

Eighteenth-century observers rightly called the Prussia of Frederick William an armed camp and berated its army for being a "gigantic penal institution" in which minor infractions of regulations entailed the death penalty. The king himself, obsessed with military matters, showed scant concern for culture, neglected the education of his subjects, and despised everything French. He carried parsimony to the extreme of refusing pensions to soldiers' widows. The inadequate fees of judges and lawyers encouraged the corruption and lethargy that obstructed the course of justice in Prussia. Yet this regime worked, and, in terms of power, worked extremely well, despite its glaring shortcomings. The Junkers, although feudal in outlook, were intensely loyal to the Hohenzollerns and made splendid officers. The army, though smaller than those of France, Russia, and Austria, was the best drilled and disciplined in Europe. When Frederick William I died in 1740, the Prussian David was ready to fight the Austrian Goliath.

## IV The Eastern Powers

### The Early Years of Peter the Great

Even more spectacular than the rise of Prussia was the emergence of Russia as a major power during the era of Peter the Great (1682–1725). In 1682, at the death of Czar Fëdor Romanov, Russia was still a backward eastern European country, with few diplomatic links with the West, and very little knowledge of the outside world. Contemporaries, Russians as well as foreigners, report on the brutality, immorality, drunkenness, illiteracy, and filth prevalent among all classes of society. Even the clergy, most of whom could not read, set no shining example by their mode of life. It is little wonder that students familiar with conditions in Russia before the advent of Peter have saluted him as the great revolutionary who altered the face of his country. Yet the changes he made were neither so numerous nor so drastic as his admirers have often claimed. Moreover, the foundations for most of them were already present in the society he inherited, and Russia would no doubt eventually have become a power of international importance without Peter, although it would have taken longer. Even if we accept all these dilutions of the usual estimate of his contribution, however, the fact remains that Peter was an awe-inspiring—and terror-inspiring—figure.

Czar Fëdor died childless in 1682, leaving a fifteen-year old brother, Ivan, who was partly blind and almost an idiot, and an ugly but capable sister, Sophia, both children of Czar Alexis (1645–1676) by his first wife. The ten-year-old Peter was the half-brother of Ivan and Sophia, the son of Alexis by his second wife, and as bright and vigorous as Ivan was debilitated. A major court feud developed between the partisans of the family of Alexis' first wife and those of the family of the second. At first the old Russian representative assembly, the *zemski sobor,* elected Peter as czar. But Sophia, as leader of the opposing faction, won the support of the *streltsy,* or musketeers, a special branch of the military, many of whom belonged to the conservative religious schismatics known as the Old Believers. Undisciplined, and angry with their

*The Western view of Russia: "Five Standing Muscovites," by Hogarth.*

officers, some of whom had been cheating them, the streltsy were a menace to orderly government.

Sophia and her supporters encouraged the streltsy to attack the Kremlin, and the youthful Peter saw the infuriated troops murdering some of his mother's family and racing through the palace in pursuit of the rest, stabbing the furniture with swords and spears. For good measure, they killed many of the nobles living in Moscow and pillaged the archives where the records of serfdom were kept. Though their movement obviously had some social content, it was primarily a successful effort by Sophia to gain power. Sophia now became regent for both Ivan and Peter, who were hailed as joint czars.

But before her power was stabilized, she had to deal with the ungovernable streltsy, who terrorized the capital until threatened with open war by the regular army. Once the streltsy were calmed, Sophia moved to punish the Old Believers and any revolting serfs that could be captured. The first woman to govern Russia since Kievan times, Sophia was bound to face severe opposition. Even her supporters would not allow her to proclaim herself autocrat. And the maturing Peter, though out of favor and away from court, posed a threat to her position; in the end, the streltsy let her down. In 1689, Sophia was shut up in a convent, and Peter and Ivan ruled together until Ivan's death in 1696, although in practice Ivan never counted for anything.

The young Peter was almost seven feet tall, and extremely lively. Highly intelligent, he had learned to read and write (but never to spell) from a drunken tutor who was the only academic instructor the troubled times afforded. Even in his early years, Peter was fascinated by war and military games. He set up a play-regiment, staffed it with full-grown men, enlisted as a common soldier in its ranks (promoting himself from time to time), ordered equipment for it from the Moscow arsenals, and drilled it in war games with unflagging vigor, himself firing off cannon or pounding on a drum with equal enjoyment. He discovered a broken-down boat in a barn and unraveled the mysteries of rigging and sail with the help of Dutch sailors settled in the foreigners' suburb of Moscow. Sailing remained one of his keenest passions. Though he married at the age of sixteen, Peter neglected his wife and preferred working on his military maneuvers, sailing his boats, and relaxing with his peculiar circle of cronies.

This rowdy lot smoked huge quantities of tobacco (horrifying the conservative Muscovites, who believed that smoking was specifically forbidden by the biblical text which says that what cometh out of the mouth defileth a man), and regularly got completely drunk. They would engage in obscene parodies of church services, or play elaborate and highly dangerous practical jokes on the unoffending citizenry, roaring about Moscow in winter late at night on sleighs and treating the sleeping populace to shrieking serenades. Masquerades and parties lasted for days; staid Moscow ladies, accustomed to almost haremlike seclusion, were commanded to put on low-necked evening dresses in the Western style, and dance and engage in social chitchat. They were literally forced to drink with the czar and his friends: If a lady refused, Peter simply held her nose and poured the wine down her throat. Peter spent enormous sums of state revenue on this sort of party and richly endowed his boon companion Lefort, a young Swiss soldier of fortune who became field marshal, grand admiral, and "chief diplomat."

The almost frantic energy that Peter devoted to pleasure reflected only part of his appetite for new experience. At various times he took up carpentry, shoemaking, cooking, clockmaking, ivory-carving, etching, and—worst of all—dentistry. Once he had acquired a set of dentist's tools, nobody was safe, since Peter did not care whether the intended victim had a toothache or not; whenever he felt the need to practice, he practiced—and those were the days before anesthetics. Preferring to wear shabby workclothes, driving his own horses, neglecting formal obligations and paying little attention to court and church ceremony, Peter in his own person was a shock to the Muscovites, and not in the least in keeping with their idea of a proper czar.

After Lefort died in 1700, Peter's favorite was Menshikov, a man of low birth, who received high offices, the title of prince, and a huge fortune. Like many of the public servants of the period, he was an unscrupulous grafter. Peter wrote to Menshikov as "my brother," and, though he came to distrust him, he never ruined him as he did many other favorites. Meantime, Peter had his first wife shut up in a convent and made a nun. He later took on as mistress a girl from the Baltic region, who had already passed through the hands of Menshikov and others, and after some years of liaison with her, during which she gave birth to two of his children, he finally married her in 1712. This was the empress Catherine, a simple, hearty, affectionate woman, long devoted to her difficult husband, and able to control him as no other human being could. But again, one can understand the horrified reaction of the old-fashioned Russian noble.

### The Western Trip

In 1695, anxious to try his hand at war, Peter led a campaign against the Turks at Azov in the area of the Black Sea. He failed, but in the next year, with the help of Dutch experts, he assembled a fleet of riverboats on the Don, sailed them downriver, and defeated the Turks at Azov. Since the Hapsburgs were also at war with the Turks, this rather surprising Russian contribution aroused much curiosity. The project of forming a league against the Turks with the states of western Europe now gave Peter the pretext for a trip outside Russia, the first undertaken by a Russian sovereign since the Kievan period.

*Peter the Great at Zaandam during his European tour.*

Though ostensibly traveling incognito as a noncommissioned officer, Peter naturally failed to conceal his identity; there were no other authoritarian seven-footers in the party. What fascinated him was Western technology, especially naval. He planned to go to Holland, England, and Venice, where the best ships (in his opinion) were built, find out how they were made, and bring the knowledge back to Russia for the advancement of Russian aims. He hired several hundred technicians to work in Russia, raised money by selling to an English peer the monopoly of tobacco sales in Russia, and visited every sort of factory or museum or printing press he could find. The huge Russian czar in all his vigor and crudity, emerging into the air of western Europe from his antiquated and stagnant country, made an unforgettable impression.

From this celebrated trip many well-known pictures emerge: Peter laboring as a common hand on the docks in Holland; Peter and his suite, drunk and dirty, wrecking the handsome house and garden of the English diarist John Evelyn near London: "There is a house full of people," wrote Evelyn's harassed servant, "and that right nasty." Less well known perhaps are the spectacles of Peter dancing with a German princess, mistaking her whalebone corsets for her ribs, and commenting loudly that German girls have devilish hard bones; of Peter receiving an honorary degree at Oxford; of Peter deep in conversation (Dutch) with William Penn about the Quaker faith; of Peter gobbling his food without benefit of knife or fork, or asleep with a dozen followers on the floor of a tiny room in a London inn with no windows open.

Before Peter could get to Venice, the Western trip was interrupted by news that the streltsy had revolted again (1698). Peter rushed home and personally participated in the punishment of the alleged plotters; he and Menshikov rather enjoyed chopping off the heads of the victims. Though many innocent men suffered torture and death, Peter had broken the streltsy as a power in Russian domestic life.

From the West, Peter had returned more determined than ever to modernize his country and

*Peter the Great cutting the long sleeves of the boyars.*

his countrymen. The very day of his return he summoned the court jester, and with his assistance went about with a great pair of shears, stopping his courtiers and clipping off their beards. It was an action full of symbolism, for the tradition of the Orthodox church held that God was bearded; if man was made in the image of God, man must also have a beard. Deprived of his beard, man was no longer made in God's image, and was a natural candidate for damnation. This was the way the Muscovite nobles and churchmen felt. Peter now decreed that Russian nobles must shave, or else pay a substantial tax for the privilege of wearing their beards. Bronze beard-tokens worn around the neck certified that the tax had been properly paid; without such a token a bearded man ran the risk of being clipped on sight.

Presently, Peter issued an edict commanding that all boyars, members of the gentry class, and the city population generally must abandon long robes with flowing sleeves and tall bonnets, and adopt Western-style costume. The manufacture of the traditional clothes was made illegal, and Peter added point to his decree by taking up his shears again and cutting off the sleeves of people wearing them. The enactments on the beards and on dress were regarded by the victims as an assault on precious customs and a forcible introduction of hated foreign ways.

### Peter's Wars

War was Peter's greatest interest. We can understand his policies at home only after we realize how closely related they were to the virtually constant warfare of his reign, and to the ever-mounting need for money for fighting. On his way back to Russia in 1698, he discovered that the Austrians, instead of being eager to join him in a full-scale crusade against the Turks, were anxious to end their Turkish war. Irritated by the Austro-Turkish Peace of Karlovitz in 1699, which he felt to be a betrayal of Russia, Peter made a separate peace with the sultan in 1700. By this time, his plans for new aggression were already formed.

The victim was to be Sweden. Peter's allies were Denmark and Poland, the latter under its elected king, Augustus the Strong, who was also elector of Saxony and who had become an intimate of Peter after their first meeting in 1698. The real engineer of the alliance and moving spirit of the war against Sweden was a nobleman named Patkul from the Baltic shore, deeply resentful of measures taken by the Swedes against the feudal proprietors of that area. Patkul went from interview to interview holding out to Augustus and Peter the prospect that after they had defeated Sweden they might divide her Baltic territories. In 1697, the Swedish throne had descended to a youth of fifteen, King Charles XII, whom Peter, Augustus, and Patkul hoped they might easily overcome. They might have reconsidered had they seen Charles strengthening his sword arm by beheading at a single stroke apiece whole flocks of sheep driven down his palace corridors in single file.

The fact was that Peter the Great characteristically rushed unprepared into the Great Northern War (1700–1721). Charles knocked Denmark out of the war before Russia even got in. He then frustrated Augustus' efforts to take the Baltic port of Riga and completely defeated a vastly larger Russian force at Narva (1700), capturing the entire supply of modern cannon of which Peter was so proud. Instead of taking advantage of Peter's helplessness, however, and marching into Russia, Charles detoured into

Poland, where he spent seven years pursuing Augustus, sponsoring his own king of Poland, a noble named Stanislas Leszczyński, and eventually forcing Augustus to abandon the Polish crown to Leszczyński and to give up the Russian alliance. Charles then seized and executed Patkul.

In the interim, Peter had been busy rebuilding the Russian armies and had conquered from the Swedes the two Baltic provinces nearest to Russia, Ingria and Livonia. In the first he founded in 1703 a new city, St. Petersburg, soon to be the capital of Russia. In 1708, Charles made the mistake of sweeping far to the south and east into the Ukraine in an effort to join forces with the Cossacks, whose leader Mazepa was an ally. Exhausted by the severe winter, the Swedish forces were finally defeated by the Russians in the decisive battle of Poltava (June 27, 1709). Charles managed to flee safely westward across the Dniester River and onto Turkish territory.

Peter was able to reinstate Augustus as King of Poland, but he was not able to force the Turks to surrender to him the refugee king of Sweden. To avenge his defeat, Charles engineered a war between Turkey and Peter (1710–1711). For the first time the Russians made an appeal to the Balkan Christian subjects of the Turks on the ground of their common Orthodox faith. Bearing banners modeled on those of Constantine, first emperor of Byzantium, and promising liberation from the Muslims, the Russian forces entered Turkish territory by crossing the river Pruth westward into the Danubian province of Moldavia (now a part of Romania). Here the Turkish armies trapped Peter and forced him to surrender (1711).

The Turks could have dragged Peter off in captivity to Istanbul had they wanted, but they proved unexpectedly lenient. They required the surrender of Azov and the creation of an unfortified "no-man's land" between Russian and Ottoman territory. Furious with the Turks for not taking full advantage of Peter's discomfiture, Charles worked to bring about still another Russo-Turkish war. Although he came very close to success, the Turks eventually expelled their firebrand visitor, and Charles went sadly home (1714).

The Great Northern War dragged on for seven more years, involving the Prussians and affecting the interests of all the western European powers. As Russian forces seized Finland, inflicted naval defeats on the Swedes in the Baltic, and occupied islands only a few miles from the Swedish coast, the Swedish empire was obviously dissolving. To the last years of the Great Northern War belong a whole series of matrimonial and other alliances between Russia and the petty German courts, bringing the Russians deep into central Europe and embroiling them in questions in which Russia really had no national interest. From a remote and little-known state somewhere behind Poland, Russia had emerged as a major military power—with enough might to affect the destiny of the western European states themselves.

## Russian Expansion in Europe, 1689-1796

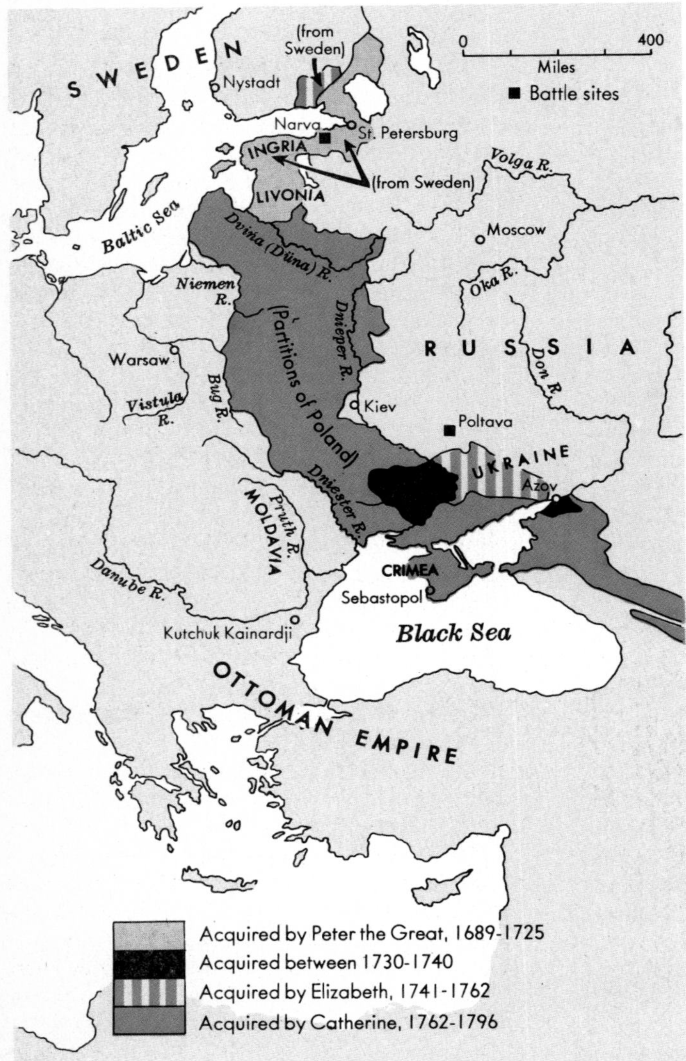

The death of Charles XII in 1718 cleared the way for peace negotiations, but it took a Russian landing in Sweden proper (1719) to force a decision. At Nystadt (1721), Russia returned Finland to Sweden and agreed to pay a substantial sum for all the former possessions of Sweden along the eastern shore of the Baltic. These Baltic lands were Peter's famous "window on the west," putting Russia into immediate contact with Europe; no longer did all seaborne traffic to Russia have to sail around the northern edge of Europe and into the White Sea. Next, Peter undertook a brief campaign (1722–1723) against the Persians. At his death in 1725, Russia had been at war for almost the entirety of his thirty-five year reign.

### Peter's Government

Constant warfare requires constant supplies of men and money. Peter's government developed a crude form of draft system according to which a given number of households had to supply a given number of recruits. More men died of disease, hunger, and cold than at the hands of the enemy, and desertion was commonplace. But the very length of the Great Northern War meant that survivors served as a tough nucleus for a regular army. Though Peter built a Baltic fleet at the first opportunity, Russian naval tradition failed to strike deep roots. From 800 ships (mostly very small) at the moment of his death, the fleet declined to fewer than twenty a decade later. There was no merchant marine whatever. The apprehensions of the English and the Dutch that Russian emergence on the Baltic would create a new maritime nation proved unfounded.

To staff the military forces and the administration, Peter rigorously enforced the rule by which all landowners owed service to the state. He eventually decreed "civil death" for those who failed to register; this put them outside the protection of the law, and anyone could attack or kill them without fear of the consequences. State service became compulsory for life; at the age of fifteen, every male child of the service class was assigned to his future post, in the army, in the civil service, or at court. Peter often forced the gentry to do jobs they considered beneath them; he did not care whether they were interested in their work or even very much whether they had been trained for it. He filled their ranks with newcomers, who obtained grants of land, rank, and title. And he required that when a member of this class died he must leave his estate intact to one of his sons, not necessarily the eldest, so that it would not be divided anew in every generation.

Thus the class of service nobility—which now substantially included the survivors of the nobility of ancient birth, the old boyars—was brought into complete dependence upon the czar. The system threw open the possibility of a splendid career to men with talent. A person without estates or rank who reached a certain level in any branch of the service (for example, major in the army) automatically received lands and a title of nobility. The nobility of ancient birth viewed this as a cheapening of their position and hated to see new recruits come into their own social order. But under Peter there was little they could do about it.

To raise cash, Peter tried all kinds of measures. He debased the currency; he taxed virtually everything—sales, rents, real estate, tanneries, baths, and beehives—and appointed special "revenue-finders" to think up new levies. The government held a monopoly over a bewildering variety of important products, including salt and oil, coffins and caviar. The basic tax on each individual household was not producing enough revenue, partly because the number of households had declined as a result of war and misery, and partly because households were combining in order to evade payment. Peter's government therefore substituted a head tax on every male—the "soul tax," as the Russians called it—making it useless for individuals to conceal themselves in households. This innovation required a new census, which produced a most important, and unintended, social result: The census takers now classified as serfs a large number of floaters on the edge between freedom and serfdom, who thus found themselves and their children eternally labeled as unfree. At the cost of human exploitation, Peter's government managed in its later years to balance the budget.

In the administration, new ministries (*prikazy*) were first set up to centralize the handling of funds received from various sources. A system of army districts adopted for reasons of military efficiency led to the creation of the first provinces, eight, then nine, then twelve, embracing all Russia. Each province had its own governor, and many of the functions previously carried on inefficiently by the central government were thus decentralized. With the czar often away from the capital, and many of the former prikazy abolished, decentralization had gone so far that Russia seemed at times to have little central government. But when Peter set out for the Pruth campaign in 1711, he created a nine-man "governing Senate" to exercise power in his absence. Later, Peter copied the Swedish system of central ministries to supersede the old prikazy and created nine "colleges" —for foreign affairs, army, navy, commerce, mines and manufactures, justice, income, expenditure, and control. Each "college" was administered not by a single minister but by a majority vote of an eleven-man board of directors or *collegium*. Corruption now became more difficult, because the conduct of any one member of a college could be checked by his colleagues. But the lengthy deliberations of so many directors often delayed final decisions.

The total picture of Peter's efforts to increase the efficiency of government is one of mixed success at best. Attempts to model Russian local government on Swedish practice broke down because of the enormous difference between the two countries in literacy, size, tradition, and attitude toward civic responsibility. Corruption still continued in high places; savage punishments were inflicted on some of those who were caught, while others, like Menshikov, were apparently immune. Yet the cumbrous machinery that Peter established, hit or miss, to meet the immediate needs of his wars was superior to any that Russia had previously known.

### Other Innovations

Ever since 1703, Peter had been building a great city in the swamps he had seized from the Swedes. Thousands of men died in the effort to drain the marshes and create a seaport and a capital worthy of its imperial resident. Remote from the rest of Russia, St. Petersburg was frightfully expensive, because all food and building materials had to be transported great distances. It was also dangerous. When floods poured through the streets, Peter roared with laughter at the sight of furniture and household effects floating away. Wolves prowled the broad new boulevards and devoured a lady in front of Prince Menshikov's own house one fine day in June. But Peter made St. Petersburg his capital and commanded all members of the nobility to make it their home. Although palaces sprang up at the czar's command, the nobles complained bitterly about abandoning their beloved Moscow for this uncomfortable and costly town. Thus St. Petersburg became the symbol of Peter's war against his own gentry.

Peter also determined to disarm future threats to his power from the Church. Knowing how the clergy loathed the new regime he was trying to impose, he simply failed to appoint a successor when the patriarch of Moscow died in 1700. Eventually, in 1721, he extended the collegiate system of administration to the Church itself. He put it under an agency first called the "spiritual college," and later the Holy Directing Synod, headed by a procurator who was a layman. Thus the Church became more than ever a department of state. Peter's own statement of his purpose is remarkably frank:

> From the collegiate government of the church there is not so much danger to the country of disturbances and troubles as may be produced by one spiritual ruler. For the common people do not understand the difference between the spiritual power and that of the autocrat; but, dazzled by the splendor and glory of the highest pastor, they think that he is a second sovereign of like power with the autocrat or with even more, and that the spiritual power is that of another and better realm. If then there should be any difference of opinion between the Patriarch and the Tzar, it might easily happen that the people, perhaps misled by designing persons, should take the part of the Patriarch, in the mistaken belief that they were fighting for God's cause.*

The educational advances of the period reflected Peter's technological and military interests. Naval, military, and artillery academies were established to educate future officers and also many civil servants. When the government tried to institute compulsory education by requiring the establishment of two schools in each province, it stressed mathematics and navigation, and the attempt failed. Part of the difficulty came from the reluctance of parents to see their children "waste time" in school, and part from the government's inexperience and its unwillingness to begin with primary education, which was

* Quoted by E. Schuyler, *Peter the Great* (New York, 1884), II, 389.

left to inadequate church schools. At all levels, foreigners had to be summoned to provide Russia with scholars. An Academy of Sciences founded just before Peter's death began with seventeen imported fellows, and eight students, also imported. Probably the mere presence in the new capital of these exotic academies helped to stimulate the native intellectual developments that would characterize the next generation. Such tokens as the first Russian newspaper (1703) and the printing of occasional textbooks also augured well for the future.

Peter continued the practice, begun long before him, of importing foreign technicians and artisans to practice their crafts and teach them to Russians. Quite aware of the mercantilist ideas of the age, he offered such inducements as freedom from taxation and from government service, and all sorts of tariff protection, to develop manufacturing. Though sometimes employing a substantial number of laborers, industrial enterprise in Russia, chiefly textiles and iron, continued to be backward. The labor force was recruited among unwilling and badly treated serfs and criminals. Factory owners were permitted to buy and sell serfs (otherwise a privilege restricted to the gentry), provided they were always bought or sold as a body together with the factory itself. This "possessional" industrial serfdom hardly provided much incentive for good work, and Russian produce continued inferior to comparable goods manufactured abroad. In the commercial field, Peter's heavy protective tariffs discriminated against foreign goods, encouraging smuggling and false registration of foreign agents as Russian nationals. The effort to make Russia a manufacturing nation exporting its own produce was a failure. But Peter's conquests in the Baltic did give Russia the great port of Riga, and he succesfully bent every effort to make St. Petersburg into a great trading center.

## Peter Evaluated

The records of Peter's secret police are full of the complaints his agents heard as they moved about listening for subversive remarks. The wives and children of the peasantry found themselves deserted by their men, who were snatched away to fight on distant battlefields or to labor in the swamps to build a city that nobody but Peter wanted. The number of serfs increased with the imposition of the new soul tax and the multiplication of land grants to service men. The tax burden was backbreaking. Service men found themselves in a kind of bondage of their own, condemned to work for the czar during the whole of their lives and seldom able to visit their estates. Nobles of ancient birth found themselves treated no differently from the upstarts who were flooding into their class from below. Churchmen of the conservative school were more and more convinced that Peter was the Antichrist himself, as they beheld the increase of foreigners in high places and saw the many innovations imported into the government and social life from the hated West. Rumors circulated that this was not the true czar at all, but a changeling somehow substituted for the real Peter by foreigners during the trip abroad, and sent back to persecute Russians and to ruin Russia.

Among the lower orders of society resistance took the usual form: peasant uprisings, punished with fantastic brutality. The usual allies of the peasant rebels, the Cossacks, suffered mass executions and sharp curtailment of their traditional independence. The leaders of the noble and clerical opposition focussed their hopes on Peter's son by his first wife, the young heir to the throne, Alexis, who, they believed, would stop the expensive and (they felt) needless foreign wars, and move back to Moscow and comfortable Russian conservatism. Alexis, an alcoholic, was afraid of his father and was early estranged from him. Though not stable enough to lead a true conspiracy against Peter, he fanned the hopes of the opposition by letting them know he shared their views. Eventually he caused a scandal by fleeing abroad and asking asylum from his brother-in-law, the Austrian emperor Charles VI. Promising him fair treatment and forgiveness, Peter lured Alexis back to Russia and made him the showpiece of one of those horrible Russian investigations of nonexistent plots. Many were tortured, killed, and exiled; Alexis himself was tortured to death in his father's presence.

In the early nineteenth century, when the first self-conscious group of Russian intellectuals developed a keen interest in the past history of their country, they made a central figure of Peter. He had, they felt, intensified Western influences on Russian society and had thus turned his back on Russia's peculiarly Slavic character and her

Byzantine heritage. One group hailed these actions as necessary to put Russia on her proper course. Its opponents damned Peter for having forced an unnatural development upon his country, and for having warped its social and political life by imposing an alien pattern. But both his friends and enemies among these later intellectuals believed, as most scholars have since argued, that what he did was drastic and revolutionary.

Yet we can see that Peter simply intensified the chief characteristics of Russian society. He made a strong autocracy even stronger, a universal service law for service men even more stringent, a serf more of a serf. His trip abroad, his fondness for foreign ways, his worship of advanced technology, his mercantilism, his wars, all had their precedents in the period of his forerunners. The Church, which he attacked, had already been weakened by the schism of the Old Believers, itself the result of Western influences. Peter's true radicalism was in the field of everyday manners and behavior. The attack on the beards, the dress, the calendar (he adopted the Western dating from the birth of Christ and abandoned the traditional dating from a hypothetical year of the Creation), his hatred of ceremony and fondness for manual labor—these things were indeed new. So too were the vigor and passion with which he acted. They were decisive in winning a revolutionary reputation for a monarch who in the major aspects of his reign was carrying out policies long since established.

## Poland and the Ottoman Empire

By the early eighteenth century, Russia was the only great power in eastern Europe. Poland and the Ottoman Empire still bulked large on the map, but their territories included lands they were soon to lose. Both states suffered from incompetent government, from a backward economy, and from the presence of large national and religious minorities. The Orthodox in Cath-

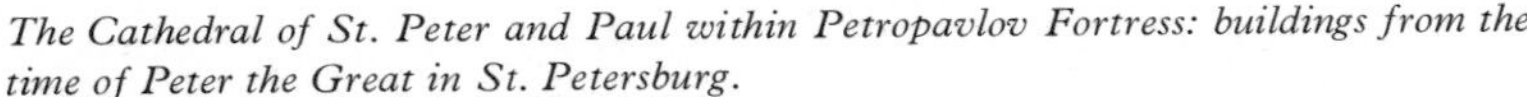

*The Cathedral of St. Peter and Paul within Petropavlov Fortress: buildings from the time of Peter the Great in St. Petersburg.*

olic Poland and Muslim Turkey were beginning to look to Russia for protection. In addition, the evident decay of both states stimulated the aggressive appetites of their stronger neighbors. Poland, consequently, was doomed to disappear as an independent power before the end of the century, the victim of partition by Russia, Austria, and Prussia. Turkey held on, but only just, and was already beginning to acquire the perilous reputation of being "the Sick Man of Europe."

The Polish government was a political curiosity shop. The monarchy was elective; each time the throne fell vacant, the Diet chose a successor, usually the candidate who had offered the biggest bribes, and sometimes a foreigner. Once elected, the king was nearly powerless, since he was obliged to transfer the royal prerogatives to the Diet when he accepted the crown. The Diet was dominated by the nobility and was celebrated for its *liberum veto,* whereby any one of its members could block any proposal by shouting "I do not wish it!" and then galloping off before his colleagues could catch up with him to make him change his mind. The Diet was not a parliament in the Western sense of the term, but an assembly of aristocrats, each of whom thought of himself as a power unto himself; unanimity was therefore necessary for all decisions. This loosely knit Polish national state had no regular army or diplomatic corps or central bureaucracy. Unlike the English gentry or Prussian Junkers, the dominant nobles had no concept of service to the Crown or indeed any sense of loyalty except to their own social class. They helped destroy a once-flourishing urban middle class by persecuting Jewish shopkeepers and foreign merchants. On their estates, the lot of the serfs was harsher than it was in Russia.

Compared with Poland, the Ottoman Empire was still a functioning state, yet it was falling farther and farther behind the major European powers, particularly in economics and technology. Not until the nineteenth century did it produce an emperor who would attempt the kind of massive assault on traditional ways that Peter the Great had mounted. In the eighteenth century, with rare exceptions, the sultans were captives of harem intrigue and could do little to discipline such powerful groups as the Janissaries, who exploited their privileges and neglected their soldierly duties. This retrograde and corrupt government did at least govern, however, and showed considerable staying power in war. The Sick Man was to linger on throughout the century, kept alive in part by Ottoman vitality, and in part by the rivalry between the two would-be heirs of the Turkish inheritance, Russia and Austria.

## V War and Diplomacy, 1713-1763

### Main Characteristics

From the survey just concluded of the European states in the early eighteenth century, it is evident that the international balance was both fluid and precarious. Should the strong states decide to prey upon the weak, the balance was certain to be upset. One such upset resulted from the Great Northern War, which enabled Russia to replace Sweden as the dominant power in the Baltic. The expansion of Russia continued to threaten the balance during most of the eighteenth century; the chief victims, in addition to Sweden, were Poland and Turkey. A second major threat to the balance came from the expansion of Prussia at the expense of Austria, Poland, and Sweden. A third involved the colonial and commercial rivalry between Britain and the Bourbon monarchies of France and Spain.

These were not the only international issues of the day. The old competition between Austria and France, which dated back to the Hapsburg-Valois wars of the 1500's, remained lively. It was complicated by the already mentioned ambitions of Elizabeth Farnese, second wife of Philip V of Spain, who won the support of France and threatened the Austrian hegemony in Italy. The Austrian Hapsburgs themselves were vigorous expansionists, aiming to drive the Turks from the Danube and extend their own domains southeast to the Black Sea.

While the interplay of all these rivalries led to frequent shifts in the international balance, the idea that there should be a balance of power was generally maintained. Indeed, eighteenth-century war and diplomacy are often cited as the classic case history of balance-of-power politics in operation. The limited financial resources of the governments of the Old Regime allowed only limited warfare; nobody could as yet afford the enormous armies or navies required for total war. On the battlefield, generals were reluctant to risk losing soldiers who represented a costly investment in training, they favored sieges and other formal maneuvers executed according to conventions well understood by all belligerents. At the peace table, diplomats were reluctant to destroy an opponent; according to another well-understood convention, they generally sought to award him a bit of territory or a minor throne as compensation for a greater loss. Like "total war," "unconditional surrender" was not an eighteenth-century concept.

The manner in which the century conducted war and diplomacy has often been likened to an elaborate game. It was a serious and sometimes a bloody game, but it was governed by extensive rules generally observed by the players and designed to minimize their losses and to keep any of them from being eliminated entirely from the play. The principal players—the monarchs, diplomats, generals, admirals—were for the most part aristocrats, who accepted a uniform code of behavior. Whatever their nationality, they usually understood and respected one another far more than they understood or respected the lower social classes in their own countries.

In practice, some of the most successful players—notably Frederick the Great of Prussia and Pitt of England—did not always play the game according to the rules. The custom of compensating the loser was forgotten in the case of Poland, which was partitioned out of existence late in the century. Earlier in the century, however, the way the powers handled the Polish and the Turkish questions afforded most instructive insights into the game of international politics.

### The Turkish and Polish Questions, 1716-1739

The Ottoman Empire suffered heavy losses in the Austro-Turkish War of 1716–1718. By the Treaty of Passarowitz (1718), the Hapsburg emperor, Charles VI, recovered the portion of Hungary still under Ottoman rule and secured other Danubian lands that form part of present-day Romania and Yugoslavia. A second Turkish war, 1735–1739, reversed the outcome of the first and disclosed the growing infirmity of the Hapsburg army. In this second war Austria was allied with Russia, but, in a fashion foreshadowing the later struggles of the two powers for control of the Balkans, they fell to quarreling over division of the prospective spoils. In the end there was little to divide, and Charles VI had to hand back to Turkey the Danubian lands annexed at Passarowitz. During the negotiations leading to the Austro-Turkish settlement of 1739, France gave the Ottoman Empire powerful support in order to redress the balance of power. This was one of many occasions on which the French sought to check Hapsburg expansion by utilizing their 200-year-old Turkish alliance.

In the early 1730's, Bourbon and Hapsburg were on opposing sides in a crisis over the kingship of Poland. During the Great Northern War, as we have seen, Stanislas Leszczynski, the protege of Charles XII of Sweden, had temporarily replaced Augustus the Strong as king of Poland. While Augustus recovered the Polish crown, thanks to the support of Peter the Great, Leszczyński had by no means completed his historical role, for he gave his daughter, Marie, in marriage to Louis XV of France. When Augustus died in 1733, French diplomats engineered the election of Stanislas to succeed him. But both Austria and Russia disliked the prospect of a French puppet on the Polish throne, and Russia sent 30,000 troops into Poland and convoked a rump session of the Diet which elected a rival king, Augustus III, son of Augustus the Strong. The stage was set for the War of the Polish Succession, 1733–1735—Stanislas, France, and Spain versus Augustus III, Russia, and Austria.

After French and Austrian armies had fired away at each other for a while in the Rhine Valley and in northern Italy, hundreds of miles from Poland, the diplomats worked out a compromise settlement. To the satisfaction of Austria and Russia, Augustus III secured the Polish throne. From the French standpoint, Stanislas Leszczyński was well compensated for his loss. He acquired the duchy of Lorraine, on the northeastern border of France, with the provision that when he died Lorraine would go to his daughter, Marie, and thence to the French crown. France would thus move one step closer toward filling out her "natural" frontiers. To be sure, Lorraine already had a duke, Francis, husband of the Hapsburg heiress, Maria Theresa, who moved to the Italian Grand Duchy of Tuscany, where the old line of rulers conveniently died out in 1737. Finally, as a by-product of the settlement, Elizabeth Farnese of Spain capped twenty years of maternal perseverance by procuring the Kingdom of Naples for "Baby Carlos," her elder and now grown-up son.

The War of the Polish Succession may well seem futile and trivial, much ado about a kingship possessing no real power. And the postwar settlement, which affected chiefly Italy and Lorraine, may seem to be a striking case of diplomatic irrelevance. Yet the whole Polish crisis neatly illustrates the workings of dynastic politics and the balance of power. Certainly no great national issues were at stake, except for the rather nebulous ones of French, Russian, and Austrian prestige. The statesmen regarded thrones as the pawns of diplomacy, to be assigned without reference to the wishes of the populations. No politician of the Old Regime would have contemplated canvassing Neapolitan sentiment on Carlos or holding a referendum to see whether the Poles preferred Stanislas or Augustus.

The complicated arrangements of the 1730's preserved the balance of power by giving something to almost everybody involved. Although the diplomats could not prevent a little war over Poland, they did keep it from becoming a big one. The achievement showed the old international system at its best. Throughout the period from 1713 to 1739 the force of diplomacy operated to avert or at least to localize wars. Britain and France took the lead in the campaign to keep any one power from upsetting the international applecart. To frustrate Elizabeth Farnese's attempts to oust the Hapsburgs from Italy in the late 1710's, the French dispatched an army and the British deployed a fleet. The British also sent a squadron to the Baltic during the last part of the Great Northern War so that Czar Peter's gains would not be too great. To prevent the dismemberment of Ottoman territories in Europe, Britain intervened in the negotiations between Turkey and Austria at Passarowitz in 1718, and the French revived their Ottoman alliance in the 1730's.

## The War of Jenkins' Ear

The diplomatic partnership of Britain and France in the 1720's and 1730's reflected the basic policies of Walpole and Fleury, both of whom sought stability abroad to promote economic recovery at home. The partnership, however, collapsed in the face of the competition between the two Atlantic powers for commerce and empire. Neither Walpole nor Fleury could prevent the worldwide war between Britain and the Bourbon monarchies that broke out in 1739 and that lasted, with many intervals of peace, until the final defeat of Napoleon in 1815. This "Second Hundred Years' War" had, in fact, already begun half a century before 1739, in the days of Louis XIV. The Utrecht settlement of 1713 had not fully settled the rivalry between Britain and France (and France's Bourbon partner, Spain). Thus the war of 1739 was as much the renewal of an old struggle as the onset of a new one.

The specific issue behind the crisis of 1739 was the comparatively minor question of British chagrin at the disappointing results of the Asiento privilege. As the South Sea Company discovered, the Asiento gave Britain little more than a token share in the trade of the Spanish American colonies. What British captains could not get legitimately they got by smuggling. Spain retaliated by establishing a coast-guard patrol in American waters to ward off smugglers. British merchants complained of the rough treatment handed out by the Spanish guards, and in 1738 they exhibited to Parliament Captain Jenkins, who claimed that Spanish brutality had cost him an ear, which he duly produced, preserved in salt and cotton batting. Asked to state his reaction on losing the ear, he replied, "I commended my soul to God and my cause to my country." Walpole retorted that the protection of British smugglers against legitimate Spanish patrols did not give the government a very strong case. But Walpole could restrain neither the anti-Spanish fever sweeping the country to which Jenkins had commended his cause, nor the bellicose faction of "Boy Patriots" that had arisen within Walpole's own Whig party.

In October 1739, to the joyful pealing of churchbells, Britain began the War of Jenkins' Ear against Spain. "They are ringing their bells now," Walpole observed tartly. "They will be wringing their hands soon." As if to vindicate his prophecy, the British fleet lost the opening campaign in the Caribbean, and France showed every sign of coming to Spain's assistance. Dynastic ties had already brought the two Bourbon monarchies into alliance during the Polish war;

now French economic interests were at stake, for France supplied the bulk of the wares which Spanish galleons carried to America, and which cheaper British contraband was driving out of the Spanish colonial market.

## The War of the Austrian Succession, 1740-1748

In 1740, a chain of events linked the colonial war to a great continental conflict, the War of the Austrian Succession. On the death of the emperor Charles VI in 1740, the Hapsburg domains passed to his daughter, Maria Theresa, who was only twenty-three years old. Expecting to outwit Maria Theresa because of her youth, her sex, and her political inexperience, the German princes ignored the Pragmatic Sanction guaranteeing her succession and looked forward to the possible partition of the Hapsburg lands. In addition, the elector of Bavaria, a cousin of the Hapsburgs, hoped to become Holy Roman emperor, defeating Maria Theresa's husband, Francis of Lorraine and Tuscany. The first of the German princes to strike, however, was Frederick the Great (1740–1786), who had just inherited the Prussian throne from Frederick William I. In December 1740 Frederick suddenly invaded Silesia, a Hapsburg province located in the upper Oder valley to the southeast of Brandenburg. Though Frederick advanced a flimsy family claim to Silesia, Europe generally regarded his invasion as an act of simple aggression.

In the ensuing War of the Austrian Succession, England and Austria were ranged against France, Spain, Prussia, and Bavaria. Frederick won an emphatic victory in the campaigns on the Continent. The Prussian army astounded Europe by its long night marches, sudden flank attacks, and other tactics of surprise quite different from the usual deliberate warfare of sieges. Frederick, however, deeply antagonized his allies by repeatedly deserting them to make secret peace arrangements with Austria. And he did little to support the imperial aspirations of the Bavarian elector, who enjoyed only a brief tenure as "Emperor Charles VII."

The Anglo-Austrian alliance worked no better than the Franco-Prussian one. Many Englishmen felt that George II was betraying their true interests overseas by entangling them in German politics and the defense of Hanover. Nevertheless, the British preference for the Hanoverians over the Stuarts was evident when "Bonnie Prince Charles," the grandson of the deposed James II, secured French backing and landed in Britain (1745). He won significant recruits only among the chronically discontented Scottish highlanders, and in 1746 he was thoroughly defeated at Culloden. Jacobitism, never a very important political threat, was dead.

Outside Europe, the fighting of the 1740's was indecisive. The New England colonists took Louisburg, the French naval base on Cape Breton Island commanding the approach to the St. Lawrence. On the other side of the world, the French took the port of Madras from the English East India Company. The Treaty of Aix-la-Chapelle (1748) restored both Louisburg and Madras to their former owners, and Britain later agreed to give up the troublesome Asiento privilege. In central Europe, on the other hand, the war was a decisive step in the rise of Prussia to the first rank of powers. The new province of Silesia brought not only a large increase in the Prussian population but also an important textile industry and large deposits of coal and iron. Maria Theresa got scant compensation for the loss of Silesia. Although her husband, Francis, won recognition as Holy Roman emperor, she had to surrender Parma and some other territorial crumbs in northern Italy to Philip, the second son of Elizabeth Farnese.

## The Uneasy Peace, 1748-1756

The peace made in 1748 lasted only eight years. Then another and greater conflict, the Seven Years' War of 1756–1763, broke out, caused partly by old issues left unsettled at Aix-la-Chapelle and partly by new grievances arising from the War of the Austrian Succession. The world struggle between Britain and the Bourbons kept right on in the undeclared warfare waged during the years of nominal peace after 1748. In Asia, the English and French East India companies fought each other once removed, so to speak, by taking sides in the rivalries of native princes in southern India. By 1751, the energetic

*Maria Theresa with Francis I and their children.*

French administrator Dupleix had won the initial round of this indirect fight. Then the English, led by the equally energetic Clive, seized the initiative, and in 1754 Dupleix was called back home by the directors of the French company, who were unwilling to back his aggressive policy. In North America, English colonists from the Atlantic seaboard had already staked out claims to the rich wilderness between the Appalachians and the Mississippi. But the French, equally intent on appropriating the area, stole a march on them and established a string of forts in western Pennsylvania from Presqu'Isle (later Erie) south to Fort Duquesne (later Pittsburgh). In 1754, a force of Virginians under the youthful George Washington tried unsuccessfully to dislodge the French from Fort Duquesne.

In Europe, the dramatic shift of alliances called the Diplomatic Revolution immediately preceded the outbreak of the Seven Years' War. In the new war the fundamental antagonisms were the same as in the old—Britain versus France, Prussia versus Austria—but the powers reversed their alliances. Britain, which had joined Austria against Prussia in the 1740's, now paired off with Frederick the Great. And, in the most revolutionary move of the Diplomatic Revolution, France, which had sided with Frederick before, not only stood against him but also joined with her hereditary enemy, Hapsburg Austria. The Diplomatic Revolution reflected the resentment of the powers at the disloyal behavior of their old partners in the War of the Austrian Succession. The French had bitter memories of Frederick's repeated desertions and secret peace arrangements. Britain deplored Austrian reluctance to defend English continental interests, which included maintaining the territorial integrity of Hanover and excluding the French from the Austrian Netherlands. Austria, in turn, regarded Hanover and Belgium as peripheral to her main concern, the recovery of Silesia.

In 1755, the British almost unwittingly touched off the Diplomatic Revolution. In order to enlist a second power in the task of defending Hanover, they concluded a treaty with Russia, which had taken a minor part in the War of the Austrian Succession as an ally of England. The Anglo-Russian treaty alarmed Frederick the Great, who feared an eventual conflict between Prussia and Russia for control of the Baltic and Poland. In January 1756 the Prussian king concluded an alliance with Britain which detached her from Russia. The alliance between England and Prussia isolated France and gave the Austrian chancellor, Kaunitz, the opportunity he had been waiting for. What Austria needed in order to avenge herself on Frederick and to regain Silesia was an ally with a large army; what Austria needed was the alliance of France, not Britain. Using the Anglo-Prussian alliance as an argument, Kaunitz convinced Louis XV and his mistress, Madame de Pompadour, to drop the traditional Bourbon-Hapsburg feud in favor of a working partnership. The last act of the Diplomatic Revolution occurred when Russia joined the Franco-Austrian alliance. The Russian empress Elizabeth (1741–1762) hated Frederick the Great and feared his aggression all the more now that he had deprived her of her English ally.

## The Seven Years' War, 1756-1763

The new war, like its predecessor, was really two separate wars—one continental, the other naval and colonial. In the European campaigns of the Seven Years' War, Frederick the Great faced a formidable test. Prussia confronted the forces of Austria, France, and Russia, whose combined population was more than fifteen times larger than her own. She had almost no allies except for Britain, which supplied financial subsidies but little actual military assistance. The Spartan traditions of the Hohenzollerns enabled Prussia to survive. The king himself set the example; in 1757, he wrote to one of his French friends:

> I am assaulted from every side. Domestic trials, secret afflictions, public misfortunes, approaching calamities—such is my daily bread. But do not imagine I am weakening. If everything collapses I should calmly bury myself beneath the ruins. In these disastrous times one must fortify oneself with iron resolutions and a heart of brass. It is a time for stoicism: the disciples of Epicurus would find nothing to say. . . .*

* Quoted in G. P. Gooch, *Frederick the Great* (London, 1947), p. 41.

*Frederick the Great on the terrace of Sans Souci, his palace near Potsdam.*

Frederick's "iron resolution" and "heart of brass" led him to adopt any expedient to gain his ends. To fill up the depleted ranks of his army, he violated international law by impressing soldiers from Prussia's smaller neighbors, Mecklenburg and Saxony. Since British subsidies covered only a fraction of his war expenses, he seized Saxon, Polish, and Russian coins and melted them down for Prussian use.

A final factor in saving Prussia, perhaps the most important one of all, was the shakiness of the apparently formidable coalition arrayed against her. Most fortunately for Frederick, his enemies were never capable of exploiting their military success to deliver a knockout blow. Russia's generals were timid, and those of France and Austria were sometimes downright incompetent. Moreover, the French, the strongest of the allies, had to fight a two-front war, in Europe and overseas, but did not have the financial resources to do both. The grand alliance created by Kaunitz suffered to an unusual extent from the frictions, mistrust, and cross-purposes that customarily beset wartime coalitions. Indeed, the coalition did not last out the war. When Elizabeth of Russia died in January 1762, she was succeeded by Czar Peter III, a passionate admirer of Frederick the Great, who at once deserted Elizabeth's allies and placed Russia's forces at Frederick's disposal. Although he occupied the Russian throne for only a few months, Peter's brief rule marked a decisive turning in the Seven Years' War. In 1763 Prussia won her war, and Austria agreed to the Peace of Hubertusburg confirming the Hohenzollern retention of Silesia.

Meanwhile, Frederick's British partner was gaining a smashing victory abroad. During the first year and a half of the fighting, the British suffered setbacks on almost every front. At sea, they lost the important Mediterranean base of Minorca in the Balearic Islands, a disaster to which the home government contributed by sending (too late) reinforcements (too few) under Admiral Byng (a poor choice). Byng was unfairly saddled with the whole blame and was executed—"in order to encourage the others," Voltaire observed ironically. In North America, the British lost the outpost of Oswego on Lake Ontario and fumbled an attack on Louisburg, the key to French Canada. The most dramatic of Britain's misfortunes occurred in India. In June 1756, the nawab of Bengal, a native ally of the French, crowded 146 British prisoners into one small room with only two windows. The result was the atrocious "Black Hole" of Calcutta, thus described by an officer of the English East India Company:

> It was the hottest season of the year, and the night uncommonly sultry. . . . The excessive pressure of their bodies against one another, and the intolerable heat which prevailed as soon as the door was shut, convinced the prisoners that it was impossible to live through the night in this horrible confinement; and violent attempts were immediately made to force the door, but without effect for it opened inward.
>
> At two o'clock not more than fifty remained alive. But even this number were too many to partake of the saving air, the contest for which and for life continued until the morn. . . .
>
> An officer, sent by the nawab, came . . . with an order to open the prison. The dead were so thronged, and the survivors had so little strength remaining, that they were employed near half an hour in removing the bodies which lay against the door before they could clear a passage to go out one at a time; when of one hundred and forty-six who went in no more than twenty-three came out alive. . . .*

William Pitt turned the tide in favor of Britain. This famous representative of the Whig oligarchy sat in Parliament for Old Sarum, a notorious rotten borough. The grandson of "Diamond" Pitt, a merchant prince who had made a fortune in India, he consistently supported the interests of the City. In the late 1730's he had led the Whig rebels, the Boy Patriots who forced Britain into the War of Jenkins' Ear against Walpole's pacifistic policy. Now Pitt's great war ministry (1757–1761) at last ended the shilly-shallying policies of the cabinets that had held office since Walpole's downfall in 1742. When deficits rose higher and higher, Pitt used his personal and business connections with the City to assist the successful placement of government loans. He strengthened the Anglo-Prussian alliance by sending Frederick substantial subsidies and placing English forces in Hanover under an able Prussian commander in place of the bungling duke of Cumberland, a son of George II. Everywhere Pitt replaced blundering generals and admirals; everywhere his energetic measures transformed the character of the naval and colonial war. In 1759, the Royal Navy defeated both the Atlantic and Mediterranean squadrons of the French fleet.

Britain's command of the seas enabled her to continue trading abroad at a prosperous pace, while French overseas trade rapidly sank to one-sixth of the pre-war rate. Cut off from supplies and reinforcements from home and faced by generally superior British forces, the French colonies fell in quick succession. In Africa, Britain's capture of the chief French slaving station ruined the slavers of Nantes in the mother country. In India, Clive and others avenged the Black Hole by punishing the nawab of Bengal and capturing the key French posts. In the West Indies, the French lost all their sugar islands, except for Santo Domingo. In North America, the 65,000 French, poorly supplied and poorly led, were helpless against the million British colonists, fully supported by their mother country. Fort Duquesne was taken at last, and renamed after Pitt, and the British went on to other triumphs in the war that the colonists called "French and Indian." In Canada, the English general Wolfe took Louisburg (1758) and in the next year, 1759, lost his life but won immortal fame in a great victory on the Plains of Abraham outside Quebec. When the remaining French stronghold, Montreal, fell in 1760, the doom of France's American empire was sealed.

This rain of victories led the British to expect sweeping gains in the postwar settlement; their expectation was soon disappointed. Pitt had won the war, but he did not make the peace: the accession of the obstinate and ambitious George III in 1760 led to the dismissal of the prime minister the next year. In the Peace of Paris, 1763, the successors of Pitt allowed the French to recover their islands in the West Indies, then highly prized as a major source of sugar. British planters in the Caribbean were much relieved, for their markets had been flooded by sugar from captured French islands during the war. But to outraged patriots it seemed as though Britain had let the grand prize slip through her fingers.

France, however, lost all her possessions on the mainland of North America. Britain secured both Canada and the vast disputed territories between the Appalachians and the Mississippi. Moreover, Spain, which had joined France in

* R. Orme, *A History of the Transactions of the British Nation in Indostan* (London, 1778), II, sec. 1, 74 ff.

1762 when the war was already lost, ceded to Britain the territories of Florida, including both the peninsula and the coast of the Gulf of Mexico over to the Mississippi. In compensation, France gave Spain the city of New Orleans and the vast Louisiana territories west of the Mississippi. In India, though Britain permitted France to retain a few trading stations, the French were not allowed to fortify their posts or to continue their old policy of manipulating the politics and rivalries of native states. For Britain, the Seven Years' War marked the beginning of a virtually complete ascendancy in India; for France it marked the virtual end of her "old Empire."

## North America and the Caribbean, 1763

**Situation after the Seven Years' War**

### The International Balance in Review

The peace settlements of Hubertusburg and Paris ended the greatest international crisis that was to occur between the death of Louis XIV and the outbreak of the French Revolution. New crises were to arise soon after 1763, as the next chapter will show in detail—in 1768, a Russo-Turkish war (which Russia won); in 1772, the first partition of Poland; in 1775, the American War of Independence. The new crises in the East did not fundamentally alter the international balance; they accentuated shifts that had long been underway. And, although American independence cost Britain the thirteen colonies, the maritime and imperial supremacy she had gained in 1763 was not otherwise seriously affected.

The international balance established in 1763, then, remained largely unchanged down to 1789. In the incessant struggle for power during the eighteenth century, the victorious states were the strongest states—Britain, Prussia, and Russia. The states that were less fit—France, Spain, Austria, Turkey—survived, though they sometimes suffered serious losses. The weakest units, Poland and Italy—as a Spanish diplomat observed early in the century—were being "pared and sliced up like so many Dutch cheeses."

The duke of Choiseul, the foreign minister of Louis XV during the Seven Years' War, remarked that the "true balance of power resides in commerce." Choiseul's remark held a large measure of truth, but not the whole truth. The world struggle between Britain and the Bourbon empires did much to justify the mercantilist view that conceived of international relations in terms of incessant competition and strife. According to the mercantilist doctrine of the fixed amount of trade, a state could enlarge its share of the existing supply only if it reduced the shares held by rival states, either through war or, in time of peace, through smuggling and retaliatory legislation. All this was borne out by the War of Jenkins' Ear and by British success, and French failure, in maintaining overseas trade during the course of the Seven Years' War. Yet the modern concept of economic warfare was only beginning to take shape. During the War of the Austrian Succession English visitors continued to arrive in Paris, and London brokers supplied both insurance and information on naval movements to French shipowners.

Moreover, economic factors did not wholly explain all the changes in the international balance during the century. For example, efficient utilization of Prussian resources played its part in the victories of Frederick the Great. But his success depended still more on qualities that had little to do with economics—his own brilliant and ruthless leadership, and the discipline of the society that he headed. The case of Britain seemingly offers the most compelling evidence to support Choiseul's contention, as Pitt turned her formidable financial and commercial assets to practical advantage. Yet Pitt himself is not to be explained in simple economic terms. His accession as prime minister in the dark days of 1757, like that of Churchill in the dark days of 1940, was made possible by a political system that enabled the right man to come forward at the right time.

Finally, the eighteenth century, despite its wars, was an interlude of comparative calm between the age of religious strife that had preceded it and the storms of liberalism and nationalism that were to be loosed by the French Revolution. The prospect in 1715, the prospect of long years of peace and quiet, had not, after all, been wholly deceptive. The Seven Years' War of the eighteenth century, for example, did not begin to equal in destructive force the Thirty Years' War of the seventeenth. Much more was involved here than the relative shortness of the Seven Years' War. Few of the combatants had the feeling of fighting for a great cause, like Catholicism or Protestantism or national independence. The fighting itself was conducted in a more orderly fashion than it had been a hundred years before; soldiers were better disciplined, and armies were better supplied; troops lived off the land less often and no longer constituted such a menace to the lives and property of civilians. Eighteenth-century warfare reflected the order and reason characteristic of the Age of the Enlightenment.

## Reading Suggestions on the Old Regime and the International Balance

GENERAL ACCOUNTS

The following volumes in the series "The Rise of Modern Europe" (*Torchbooks) provide a detailed introduction to eighteenth-century war and politics and have extensive and up-to-date bibliographies: P. Roberts, *The Quest for Security, 1715–1740;* W. L. Dorn, *Competition for Empire, 1740–1763;* and L. Gershoy, *From Despotism to Revolution, 1763–1789.*

M. S. Anderson, *Europe in the Eighteenth Century, 1713–1783* (Holt, 1961). A very good introductory volume by a British scholar.

R. J. White, *Europe in the Eighteenth Century* (*St. Martin's). Another good introduction, also by a British scholar, at a less advanced level.

*The New Cambridge Modern History* (Cambridge Univ. Press). Two volumes of this ambitious but uneven series, still in the course of publication, contain materials useful for the present chapter. VI: *The Rise of Great Britain and Russia, 1688–1725* (1970); VII: *The Old Regime, 1713–1763* (1957).

ECONOMICS AND SOCIETY

H. J. Habakkuk and M. Postan, eds., *The Cambridge Economic History of Europe,* Vol. VI, Parts 1 and 2 (Cambridge Univ. Press, 1965). Scholarly essays on the economic revolutions by many writers.

E. F. Heckscher, *Mercantilism,* rev. ed., 2 vols. (Macmillan, 1955). A famous and controversial work; a mine of information on eighteenth-century economic developments.

J. Carswell, *The South Sea Bubble* (Stanford Univ. Press, 1960). Excellent monograph.

T. S. Ashton, *The Industrial Revolution, 1760–1830* (*Galaxy). Clear and informative introduction.

P. Mantoux, *The Industrial Revolution in the Eighteenth Century* (*Torchbooks). Classic study of the factory system in England.

P. Deane, *The First Industrial Revolution* (Cambridge Univ. Press, 1965). Up-to-date study of the British economy, 1750–1850; based on lectures to undergraduates at Cambridge University.

A. Goodwin, ed., *The European Nobility in the Eighteenth Century* (Black, 1953). Very helpful essays arranged country by country.

D. Ogg, *Europe of the Ancien Régime* (*Torchbooks). A social study, focused on Britain.

WESTERN EUROPE

W. E. H. Lecky, *A History of England in the Eighteenth Century,* 8 vols. (Longmans, 1883–1890). A celebrated detailed study.

B. Williams, *The Whig Supremacy, 1714–1760,* 2nd ed., rev. C. H. Stuart (Clarendon, 1962). A competent modern survey.

J. Plumb, *England in the Eighteenth Century* (*Penguin). A good brief account by a scholar who has also written studies of Walpole, the elder Pitt, and the first four Georges.

L. B. Namier, *The Structure of Politics at the Accession of George III* (*St. Martin's) and *England in the Age of the American Revolution* (*St. Martin's). Detailed and controversial studies, revising traditional concepts of eighteenth-century English political institutions.

C. G. Robertson, *Chatham and the British Empire* (*Collier). Brief, popular introduction to the achievements of the elder Pitt.

L. Kronenberger, *Kings and Desperate Men* (*Vintage). Lively essays on eighteenth-century English society and personalities.

A. Cobban, *A History of Modern France.* Vol. I: *1715–1799* (*Penguin). Good general survey by a British scholar.

J. Lough, *An Introduction to Eighteenth-Century France* (McKay, 1961). Clear and enlightening discussion of the Old Regime.

C. B. A. Behrens, *The Ancien Régime* (*Harcourt). Readable and generously illustrated study stressing French society.

A. M. Wilson, *French Foreign Policy during the Administration of Cardinal Fleury* (Harvard Univ. Press, 1936). A sound monograph, and one of the relatively few good books in English on the France of Louis XV.

G. P. Gooch, *Louis XV* (Longmans, 1956), and Nancy Mitford, *Madame de Pompadour* (*Pyramid). Entertaining and rather old-fashioned biographical studies.

F. Ford, *Robe and Sword* (*Torchbooks). An instructive study of the French aristocracy in the eighteenth century.

H. Kamen, *The War of Succession in Spain, 1700–1715* (Univ. of Indiana Press, 1969). Detailed study of the Bourbon impact upon Spain.

CENTRAL AND EASTERN EUROPE

H. Holborn, *A History of Modern Germany,* Vol. II (Knopf, 1964). Succinct scholarly survey of the period from 1648 to 1840.

H. Rosenberg, *Bureaucracy, Aristocracy, Autocracy* (*Beacon). A somewhat opinionated analysis of Prussian history, 1660–1815.

S. B. Fay, *The Rise of Brandenburg-Prussia to 1786,* rev. K. Epstein (*Holt). A lucid little volume, packed with information.

F. L. Carsten, *The Origins of Prussia* (*Oxford Univ. Press). Excellent monograph that carries the story through the reign of the Great Elector.

F. Schevill, *The Great Elector* (Univ. of Chicago Press, 1947). A helpful study of the founder of the Hohenzollern despotism.

R. R. Ergang, *The Potsdam Führer* (Columbia Univ. Press, 1941). A splendid study of Frederick William I of Prussia.

E. Schuyler, *Peter the Great,* 2 vols. (Scribner's, 1884). An old but excellent account by an American diplomat and scholar.

V. Klyuchevsky, *Peter the Great and the Emergence of Russia* (*Collier). A very good introductory account.

M. Raeff, ed., *Peter the Great: Reformer or Revolutionary?* (*Heath). Good cross section of judgments on the controversial czar.

THE INTERNATIONAL BALANCE

A. Sorel, *Europe Under the Old Régime* (*Torchbooks). A famous little essay on the eighteenth-century balance by a French expert.

L. Dehio, *The Precarious Balance* (*Vintage). Reflections on the shifts in the balance of power by a German scholar.

J. F. C. Fuller, *A Military History of the Western World,* 3 vols. (*Minerva). The second volume of this stimulating survey covers the seventeenth and eighteenth centuries.

C. T. Atkinson, *A History of Germany, 1715–1815* (Methuen, 1908). An older account, particularly full on war and diplomacy.

B. H. Sumner, *Peter the Great and the Ottoman Empire* (Blackwell, 1949). A short and meaty monograph.

H. Dodwell, *Dupleix and Clive* (Methuen, 1920). A balanced treatment of the imperial antogonists in India.

SOURCES

Arthur Young, *Tours in England and Wales* (London School of Economics and Political Science, 1932). A good selection from the reports of this prolific and perceptive agricultural expert.

Lady Mary W. Montagu, *Letters* (Everyman). By perhaps the best of the century's excellent letter writers; particularly valuable on the Hapsburg and Ottoman empires.

C. A. Macartney, ed., *The Hapsburg and Hohenzollern Dynasties in the Seventeenth and Eighteenth Centuries* (*Torchbooks). Helpful collection of documentary materials on Austrian and Prussian history.

G. P. Gooch, *Courts and Cabinets* (Knopf, 1946). A graceful introduction to the memoirs of some of the great personages of the era.

HISTORICAL FICTION

H. Fielding, *Tom Jones* (*several editions). The greatest of social novels on eighteenth-century England.

T. Smollett, *The Adventures of Roderick Random* (*Signet). A novel that provides a good contemporary account of life in His Majesty's Navy in the reign of George II.

D. Merezhkovsky, *Peter and Alexis* (Putnam, 1905). Novel dramatizing the conflict between the great czar and his son.

# 17

# *The Enlightenment*

## I Basic Principles and Traits

Reason, natural law, progress—these were key words in the vocabulary of the eighteenth century. It was the Age of the Enlightenment, when the belief became widespread that human reason could cure men of past ills and help them to achieve utopian governments, perpetual peace, and a perfect society. Reason would enable men to discover the natural laws regulating existence, and the progress of the human race would thereby be assured.

The intellectuals who professed this optimistic creed were known by the French name of *philosophes,* though some of them were not French and few of them were philosophers in the strict sense. The philosophes were critics, publicists, economists, political scientists, and social reformers. By no means all of them expressed their views in the naïvely simple and cheerful way formulated at the end of the last

*Above: Houdon's bust of Voltaire, 1781.*
*Above right: Fragonard's "The New Model."*
*Right: Frederick the Great leading a chamber concert at Sans Souci.*

paragraph. The most famous philosophe, Voltaire, in his most famous tale, *Candide,* ridiculed the optimists who thought that all was for the best in the best of all possible worlds. Many intellectuals followed Voltaire in stressing the unreasonable aspects of human behavior and the unnatural character of human institutions. Nevertheless, though many pessimistic cross-currents eddied beneath the gleaming surface of the Enlightenment, the main current of the age was optimistic. Voltaire himself, for all his skepticism, carried on a lifelong crusade against the unnatural and the unreasonable. On the whole, the Enlightenment believed men capable of correcting the errors of their ways, once they had been pointed out to them, and of moving on to a better and brighter future. A perfect instance was the American Declaration of Independence, which listed the pursuit of happiness as a fundamental human right along with life and liberty. The idea that men could pursue happiness and that they might even attain it was indeed new and revolutionary, a profound departure from the traditional Christian belief that such joy could never be expected on earth.

### The Inheritance from Locke and Newton

The philosophes of the eighteenth century derived their basic principles from the men of the preceding "century of genius." Their faith in natural law came from Newton; their confidence in the powers of human reason in part from Descartes, who had deduced a whole philosophy from the fact that he reasoned at all, and still more from John Locke (1632–1704). In his celebrated defense of England's Glorious Revolution, the *Second Treatise of Government,* Locke contended that men are "by nature all free, equal, and independent," and submit to government because they find it convenient to do so, not because they acknowledged any divine right on the part of the monarchy.

The new psychology that Locke advanced in the *Essay Concerning Human Understanding* (1690) strengthened his case against absolute monarchy. Defenders of political and religious absolutism contended that the inclination to submit to authority was present in men's minds when they were born. Locke's *Essay* denied the existence of such innate ideas. He called the new-born mind a *tabula rasa,* a blank slate:

> Let us then suppose the mind to be . . . white paper, void of all characters, without any ideas. How comes it to be furnished? . . . To this I answer, in one word, from EXPERIENCE. . . . Our observation employed either about *external sensible objects, or about the internal operations of our minds perceived and reflected on by ourselves, is that which supplies our understandings with all the materials of thinking*. These two are the fountains of knowledge, from whence all the ideas we have, or can naturally have, do spring.*

In other words, the two "fountains of knowledge" were environment, rather than heredity, and reason, rather than faith. Locke's matter-of-fact outlook and his empiricism (reliance on experience) place him among the rationalists. He believed that human reason, though unable to account for everything in the universe, explains all that men need to know. "The candle that is set up in us," he wrote, "shines bright enough for all our purposes."

Locke pointed the way to a critical examination of the Old Regime. The philosophes read and admired both his political writings and the *Essay Concerning Human Understanding*. They submitted existing social and economic institutions to the judgment of common sense and discovered many to be unreasonable and unnecessarily complex. Locke's psychology suggested to them that teachers might improve human institutions by improving the thinking of the rising generation. The philosophes sought what was in effect the right kind of chalk to use on the blank slates of impressionable young minds; their search brought them to accept the view of the universe that has been aptly termed the "Newtonian world-machine."

The Enlightenment seized on Newton's discoveries as revelations of ultimate truth. Newton had disclosed the natural force, gravitation, that held the universe together; he made the universe make sense. The philosophes believed that comparable laws could be found governing and explaining all phases of human activity. They pictured themselves as the Newtons of statecraft, justice, and economics who would reduce the most intricate institutions to formulas as neat as Sir Isaac's own mathematical

* *Essay Concerning Human Understanding,* Book II, Chap. I.

laws and principles. The world, they argued, resembled a giant machine. Hitherto, men had hampered its operations because they did not understand the machinery; once they grasped the basic laws by which it ran, the "world-machine" at last would function as it should.

The optimistic implications of this credo were expressed most completely in *The Progress of the Human Mind* (1794) by the philosophe Condorcet, written, ironically enough, when he was in hiding as a victim of political persecution during the French revolutionary Reign of Terror. Condorcet asked:

> If men can predict, with almost complete assurance, the phenomena whose laws are known to them . . . why should it be regarded as a vain enterprise to chart, with some degree of probability, the course of the future destiny of mankind by studying the results of human history? Since the only basis of belief in the natural sciences is the idea that the general laws, known or unknown, regulating the phenomena of the universe are regular and constant, why should this principle be any less true for the development of the intellectual and moral faculties of man than for the other operations of nature?*

"Nature has placed no bounds on the perfecting of the human faculties," Condorcet concluded, "and the progress of this perfectibility is limited only by the duration of the globe on which nature has placed us." †

## The Advance of Science

The technological and scientific advances of the eighteenth century further buttressed the faith in natural law and progress. The philosophes hailed both the improvements in industry and agriculture and the rapid expansion of the pure sciences. Biology and chemistry were now beginning to assume a modern look. Linnaeus (1707–1778), a Swede, demonstrated the natural laws of family relationships in biology. He proposed a system for classifying all known plants and animals by genus and species, and thus established the foundation for the system of binomial nomenclature that biologists still follow.

Modern chemical analysis started with Black and Lavoisier. Joseph Black (1728–1799), a Scottish professor, exploded the old theory that air was composed of a single element by proving the existence of several discrete gases. Black's French contemporary Lavoisier (1743–1794) continued his study of gases and demonstrated that water was made up of hydrogen and oxygen (this last a name that he invented from a Greek root meaning "acid" because the element was thought to be present in all acids). Lavoisier asserted that all substances were composed of a relatively few basic chemical elements, of which he identified twenty-three. During the Revolution Lavoisier served on the commission of experts preparing the metric system; he was executed because he had been one of the hated tax farmers of the Old Regime.

In the eighteenth century astronomy and physics consolidated the great advances they had made in the seventeenth. Another member of the metric commission, Laplace (1749–1827), "the Newton of France," rounded out Sir Isaac's investigation of celestial mechanics and explained the movement of the solar system in a series of mathematical formulas and theorems. In the American colonies the versatile Benjamin Franklin (1706–1790) showed that electricity and lightning were really the same thing. He obtained an electrical charge in a key attached to the string of a kite flown during a thunderstorm in Philadelphia. This experiment, which aroused a lively interest across the Atlantic, was repeated at Versailles for the French royal family.

Almost everybody who was anybody in the eighteenth century attempted experiments. Voltaire made a serious hobby of chemistry; Montesquieu studied physics; and a noble French lady reportedly kept a cadaver in her carriage so that she might employ her travels profitably in dissection and the study of anatomy. Almost every state in Europe had its philosophes and its royal society or learned society to promote the progress of knowledge. Intellectual life was by no means limited to the capitals and big cities; by the middle of the eighteenth century, for example, many provincial towns in France possessed academies, well equipped with reading rooms and lending libraries. In addition, intellectuals paid scant attention to national frontiers and, even in wartime, continued to visit enemy

* Condorcet, *Esquisse d'un tableau historique des progrès de l'esprit humain* (Paris, n.d.), p. 203. Our translation.

† Ibid., p. 5.

countries and correspond with their citizens. It was a striking example of the eighteenth century's disposition to keep warfare within strict limits and maintain business as usual.

### French Leadership

Thus cosmopolitan qualities of the century appeared at their best in the Enlightenment, which had its roots in France and England and extended its branches to Scotland, Germany, Italy, Spain, and the New World. Yet this Age of Reason also marked the high point of French cultural hegemony, when, as the American philosophe Thomas Jefferson put it, every man had two homelands, his own and France. The French language endowed the Enlightenment with its medium of communication; the salons of Paris helped to set the tone of enlightened writing; the great *Encyclopédie,* edited and published in France, provided a vehicle for enlightened thought.

By the eighteenth century, French was the accepted international language. Louis XIV had raised it to supremacy in diplomacy; the great writers of his age, like Boileau, La Rochefoucauld, Racine, and Molière, had made it preeminent in literature and on the stage. There was much justice in the claim that "a dangerous work written in French is a declaration of war on the whole of Europe." Almost everywhere, even in distant Russia, rulers, aristocrats, and intellectuals preferred French to their native tongues. In 1783, it was the Academy of Berlin that conducted a competition for the best reply to the question "What has made the French language universal?" According to the prize-winning essay, "Precise, popular, and reasonable, it is no longer just French; it is the language of humanity."

The Parisian salons taught writers precision, reasonableness, and the popular touch. The salon was the reception room of a large private home where guests assembled for an afternoon or evening of conversation under the guidance of the hostess, usually a wealthy woman from the nobility or the upper bourgeoisie. Here is a contemporary report of the way in which one of them conducted her salon:

> This circle was formed of people who were not linked together. She had taken them from here and there, but chosen so well that when they were together they harmonised like the strings of an instrument tuned by a cunning hand. . . . She played on this instrument with an art that was almost genius; she seemed to know what sound the string she was going to touch would give: I mean that so well were our characters and minds known to her, that she had only to say one word to bring them into play. Nowhere was conversation livelier, or more brilliant, or better controlled. . . . The minds she worked upon were neither shallow nor weak. . . . Her gift for throwing out an idea, and giving it to men of this type to discuss; her gift for discussing it herself, like them, with precision, and sometimes with eloquence; her gift for bringing in new ideas and varying the conversation . . .; these gifts, I say, are not those of an ordinary woman. It was not with fashionable trifles or self-conceit that, every day for four hours' conversation without weariness or emptiness, she knew how to make herself interesting to these brilliant minds.*

Although some salons were snobbish and superficial, most of them gave young philosophes the opportunity to receive a hearing—and to obtain a square meal; they welcomed and, if the need arose, protected new men and new ideas. Pressure from the salons determined the outcome of elections to the French Academy, which passed under the control of the philosophes in the 1760's.

The great organ of the philosophes was the *Encyclopédie,* which published its first volume in 1751 and, when it was completed a generation later, totaled twenty-two folio volumes of text and eleven of plates. Its roster of 160 contributors included Voltaire, Montesquieu, Rousseau, Condorcet, Quesnay, and Turgot. For years the editor-in-chief, Denis Diderot (1713–1784), put in a fourteen-hour working day to advance his crusade for reason and progress. He commissioned the drawing of superb plates showing the details of the new industrial machines and even learned to operate some of the machines himself. Diderot and his fellow encyclopedists did not intend to compile an objective compendium of information. Rather, as Diderot explained in the

* *Memoirs of Marmontel,* trans. Brigit Patmore (London, 1930), p. 270.

article on the word "encyclopedia," they aimed to assemble knowledge "in order that the labors of past centuries should not prove useless for succeeding centuries; that our descendants, by becoming better informed, will at the same time *become happier and more virtuous*" (our italics).

The purposes of the *Encyclopédie* were subversive and didactic: to expose and thereby ultimately to destroy the superstition, the intolerance, and the gross inequalities of the Old Regime and instruct the public in the virtues of natural law and the wonders of science. It accomplished its purposes, antagonizing many defenders of the Old Regime but gaining enough subscribers to prove a profitable business venture. Louis XV tried to prevent its being printed or circulated, the Church condemned it for its materialism and for its skepticism, and the publishers, without consulting Diderot, ordered the printers to cut out many passages likely to cause offense. But to no avail. The indignation of Diderot, the ridicule leveled by the philosophes at their enemies, the loyalty of the subscribers to the *Encyclopédie,* and the help given the editors by Choiseul, the foreign minister, and Madame de Pompadour, the king's mistress and herself an enlightened spirit—all frustrated the censors. In the small provincial city of Dijon, for example, there were sixty copies of the *Encyclopédie* in 1768.

## II The Reform Program of the Philosophes

### Laissez-Faire Economics

Since the philosophes passed severe judgments on almost every facet of the Old Regime, the major reforms they proposed encompassed economic behavior, standards of justice, and quality of education, as well as religious and political practices. Their economic program was introduced in the articles written for the *Encylopédie* by the versatile François Quesnay (1694–1774), biologist, surgeon, and personal physician to Louis XV and Madame de Pompadour. Quesnay headed a group of thinkers and publicists who adopted the name of Physiocrats, believers in the rule of nature. The name revealed the basic outlook of the school. The Physiocrats expected that they would, as Quesnay claimed, discover natural economic laws "susceptible" of a demonstration as severe and incontestable as those of geometry and algebra." And to arrive at such laws, the "sovereign and the nation should never lose sight of the fact that land is the only source of wealth, and that agriculture increases wealth."*

This new Physiocratic concept of natural wealth clashed with the mercantilist doctrine of equating money and wealth. "The riches which men need for their livelihood do not consist of money," Quesnay argued; "they are rather the goods necessary both for life and for the annual production of these goods." Mercantilist states, therefore, committed a whole series of errors by placing excessive emphasis on the accumulation of specie. They tried to regulate commerce, when they should have freed it from controls. They made goods more expensive by levying tariffs and other indirect taxes, whereas they should have collected only a single, direct tax on the net income from land. "Laissez faire, laissez passer," the Physiocrats urged—live and let live, let nature take its course. They repudiated the controlled economy of mercantilism and enunciated the "classical" or 'liberal" doctrine of the free economy. The state ought not to disturb the free play of natural economic forces. Most of all, it ought not to interfere with private property, so necessary for the production of agricultural wealth.

The classic formulation of laissez-faire economics was made by the Scotsman Adam Smith (1727–1790) in his *Inquiry into the Nature and Causes of the Wealth of Nations* (1776). Smith, too, leveled a vigorous attack on mercantilism. It was wrong to restrict imports by tariffs for the protection of home industries:

It is the maxim of every prudent master of a family never to attempt to make at home what it will

* Quesnay, "Maximes Générales du Gouvernement Economique d'un Royaume Agricole," in E. Daire, ed., *Physiocrates* (Paris, 1846), I, 82. Our translation.

*Adam Smith.*

cost him more to make than to buy. The tailor does not attempt to make his own shoes, but buys them of the shoemaker. The shoemaker does not attempt to make his own clothes, but employs a tailor. . . .

What is prudence in the conduct of every private family, can scarce be folly in that of a great kingdom. If a foreign country can supply us with a commodity cheaper than we ourselves can make it, better buy it of them with some part of the produce of our industry. . . .*

Like the Physiocrats, Adam Smith attributed the wealth of nations to the production of goods; but, as befitted a resident of Britain, the leading commercial and industrial state of the day, he took a less agrarian view of the matter. For Adam Smith, production depended less on the soil (the Physiocratic view) than on the labor of farmers, craftsmen, and millhands. Again like the Physiocrats, he minimized the role of the state, claiming that men who were freely competing to seek their own wealth would be led to enrich their whole society, as if they were being guided by "an invisible hand"—that is, by nature. Thus, Smith claimed, government should merely be a passive policeman:

According to the system of natural liberty, the sovereign has only three duties to attend to; . . . first, the duty of protecting the society from the violence and invasion of other independent societies; secondly, the duty of protecting, as far as possible, every member of the society from the injustice and oppression of every other member of it, or the duty of establishing an exact administration of justice; and thirdly, the duty of erecting and maintaining certain public works and certain public institutions, which it can never be for the interest of any individual, or small number of individuals, to erect and maintain.*

The mercantilists had raised the state over the individual and had declared a ceaseless trade warfare among nations. Adam Smith and the Physiocrats, reversing the emphasis, proclaimed both the economic liberty of the individual and free trade among nations to be natural laws. The laissez-faire program of the Enlightenment marked a revolutionary change in economic thought and was later used to justify the rugged individualism of nineteenth-century industrial barons. It did not, however, revolutionize the economic policies of the great powers, who long remained stubbornly mercantilist. As the next chapter will show, Turgot, the chief practical exponent of Physiocratic doctrine, tried in vain to emancipate French agriculture and French business from traditional restrictions during his brief tenure as chief minister of Louis XVI in the 1770's. The Physiocrats neglected what so many philosophes neglected. They overlooked the difficulty of accommodating the simple and reasonable dictates of natural law to the complexity of politics and the irrationality of human nature.

### Justice

The disposition to let nature take its course, so evident in laissez-faire economics, also characterized the outlook of the philosophes on ques-

* Book IV, Chap. 2.

* Book IV, Chap. 9.

tions of justice. They believed that manmade legislation prevented the application of the natural laws of justice. They were horrified by the cumbersome judicial procedures of the Old Regime and by its unjust and antiquated statutes. New lawgivers were needed to humanize and simplify legal codes, and a new science was needed to make the punishment of crime both humane and effective.

The new science, which laid the foundations of modern sociology, was promoted by Cesare Beccaria (1738–1794), a north Italian philosophe and the author of *Essay on Crimes and Punishments* (1764). Beccaria formulated three natural laws of justice, which are excellent examples of the Enlightenment's confident belief that common sense would enable men to formulate nature's truths. First, punishments should aim to

> prevent the criminal from doing further injury to society, and to prevent others from committing the like offense. Such punishments, therefore, . . . ought to be chosen, as will make the strongest and most lasting impressions on the minds of others, with the least torment to the body of the criminal.

Second, justice should act speedily,

> because the smaller the interval of time between the punishment and the crime, the stronger and more lasting will be the association of the two ideas of *Crime* and *Punishment*.

And last:

> Crimes are more effectively prevented by the *certainty* than by the *severity* of the punishment. . . . The certainty of a small punishment will make a stronger impression than the fear of one more severe. . . .*

Beccaria attacked both torture and capital punishment because they deviated so sharply from these natural laws. Torture, he claimed, falsely assumed that "pain should be the test of truth, as if truth resided in the muscles and fibres of a wretch in torture." Jail sentences, not execution, should be imposed as punishments. Like many later reformers, Beccaria asserted that punishment alone was not enough. The best method of prventing crime was to "let liberty be attended with knowledge," to "perfect the system of education."

* *Essay on Crimes and Punishments,* Chaps. 12, 19, and 27.

## Education

In education, too, the Old Regime failed to pass the tests of reason and natural law. The philosophes deplored both the almost universal ecclesiastical control of education and the heavy emphasis on theology, Greek and Latin, and ancient history. They demanded more consideration of science, modern languages, and modern history. A few universities responded, but most did not, so that the academic world contributed little to the Enlightenment. While prestigious old institutions like Oxford, Cambridge, and the Sorbonne were stagnating, the liveliest universities were two new German ones. Halle, founded in Brandenburg in 1694, was renowned for its tolerance of both free philosophical inquiry and of pietist rebellion against Lutheran orthodoxy. Göttingen, founded in the electorate of Hanover in 1737, possessed an exceptionally comprehensive library, open to faculty and students alike. In addition, the medical schools at Leiden in Holland and, later in the century, at Vienna and at Edinburgh in Scotland gave their respective universities a certain distinction in science.

The most sweeping revisions in primary education were proposed by the great nonconformist of the Enlightenment, Jean-Jacques Rousseau (1712–1778). Rousseau rebelled against the strict and disciplined society of his birthplace, Calvinist Geneva. He rebelled against the intensive bookish studies he had been forced to pursue as a young boy, and against the polite conventions he later encountered in the Paris salons. The result was *Emile* (1762), half treatise and half romance, a long and fervent plea for progressive education. *Emile* had two heroes—Emile, the student, and Rousseau himself, the teacher. The training that Rousseau prescribed for his pupil departed in every particular from eighteenth-century practice: "Life is the trade I would teach him. When he leaves me, I grant you, he will be neither a magistrate, a soldier, nor a priest; he will be a man."* Rousseau followed a laissez-faire policy toward his pupil. He did not argue with Emile, or discipline him, or force him to learn reading at any early age. Emile observed the world of nature from firsthand experience, not in books. He learned geography by finding his own way in the woods (with his tutor's help),

* *Emile,* Everyman ed. (New York, 1911), p. 9.

and agriculture by working in the fields. And when in his teens he was finally taught to read, his first assignment was Defoe's *Robinson Crusoe,* "the best treatise on an education according to nature."

Rousseau's educational program had many faults. It was impractical, for it assumed that every child should have the undivided attention of a tutor twenty-four hours a day. And it fostered the permanent dependence of pupil upon teacher; when Emile married and became a father, he implored his tutor to remain at his post: "I need you more than ever now that I am taking up the duties of manhood." And yet *Emile* was a most important book. Rousseau returned to some of the great ideas of the past—to the Renaissance concept of the universal man and to the ancient Greek ideal of the sound mind in the sound body. His theoretical program was adapted to the practical requirements of the classroom by the Swiss educator Pestalozzi (1746–1827), who set an influential example by teaching geography, drawing, and other novelties in his experimental school. Still more influential was the reaction of Pestalozzi against the barracks tradition of drilling lessons into the pupil through a combination of endless repetition and bodily punishment. Students of the twentieth century may thank the educational reformers of the eighteenth for having discovered the natural law that children should be treated as children, not as miniature adults.

## Anticlericalism and Deism

Attacks on clerical teaching formed part of a vigorous and growing body of criticism against the role of the clergy in the Old Regime. In denouncing fanaticism and superstition, the philosophes singled out the Society of Jesus, the symbol and the instrument of militant Catholicism. Pressure for the dissolution of the Jesuits gained the support of Catholic rulers, who had long been annoyed by Jesuit intervention in politics. In the 1760's the Jesuits were expelled from several leading Catholic countries, including Portugal, France (at the instance of the parlements rather than that of the monarch), and the homeland of Loyola himself, Spain. Pope Clement XIV dissolved the Society in 1773; it was revived half a century later, when the political and intellectual climate had become less hostile.

As champions of tolerance, the philosophes showed a particular affinity for the religious attitude called deism (from the Latin *deus,* "god"). Deist doctrines arose in seventeenth-century England, the England of the civil war and Newtonian science, where the deists sought settlement of religious strife by the use of reason rather than by resort to arms. All men, they asserted, could agree on a few broad religious principles. Since the Newtonian world-machine implied the existence of a mechanic, the deists accepted God as the creator of the universe; some of them also believed that he would preside over the Last Judgment. But they limited his role to the distant past and the remote future, and they doubted that he had any concern with day-to-day human activities or would answer prayer and bestow grace. The deists particularly denounced as superstitions Christian beliefs and practices hinging on mysteries and miracles, like the Trinity, the Virgin Birth, and the Eucharist.

## Voltaire

The chief exponent of deism in France was Voltaire (1694–1778), a veritable one-man Enlightenment who poured forth a prodigious quantity of letters, plays, tales, epics, histories, and essays. Clear, witty, and often bitingly satirical, his writings were enormously popular, not least when they were printed under an assumed name or outside France to evade the censorship. It was Voltaire who made Frenchmen aware of great Englishmen like Locke, Newton, and Shakespeare (though Shakespeare's exuberance suggested the Renaissance far more than it did the Enlightenment). And it was Voltaire who broadened the writing of history to include economics and culture as well as war and politics, thus foreshadowing the "new history" and "surveys of civilization" of the twentieth century. He was himself a highly successful, and sometimes unscrupulous, businessman, who made a fortune out of speculations.

Voltaire coined the anticlerical watchword "Ecrasez l'infâme"—crush the infamous thing, crush bigotry, superstition, perhaps the Church itself. He had experienced political intolerance at first hand. As a young man he had spent a year as a prisoner in the gloomy Paris Bastille and three years of exile in England because he had criticized the French government and had offended a member of the privileged nobility. The religious and political freedom of Britain made an immense impression on the refugee:

> If there were just one religion in England, despotism would threaten; if there were two religions, they would cut each other's throats; but there are thirty religions, and they live together peacefully and happily.*

Back home, Voltaire carried on a life long crusade for tolerance. In 1762, a Protestant merchant of Toulouse, Jean Calas, was accused of having murdered his son to prevent his conversion to Catholicism. Calas died in agony, his body broken on the wheel. Voltaire discovered that the accusation against Calas was based on rumor and that the court condemning him had acted out of anti-Protestant hysteria. He campaigned for three years until the original verdict was reversed, and the name of Calas was cleared.

The existence of evil—of injustices like that which broke Calas—confronted the Age of Reason with a major problem. Few of the philosophes accepted the traditional Christian teaching that evil arose from original sin, from the fall of Adam and Eve. If God were purely benevolent, they asked, why then had he created a world in which evil so often prevailed? Could a perfect God produce an imperfect creation? Alexander Pope, Voltaire's English contemporary, contended that this was the best of all possible worlds:

*All Nature is but Art, unknown to thee;*
*All chance, direction which thou canst not see;*
*All discord, harmony not understood;*
*All partial evil, universal good:*
*And, spite of Pride, in erring Reason's spite,*
*One truth is clear,* Whatever is, is right.

Voltaire took his stand in *Candide,* which satirized the disasters abounding in the best of all possible worlds. A real disaster had inspired the writing of *Candide*—the great earthquake, tidal wave, and fire that engulfed the city of Lisbon on November 1, 1755, and killed upwards of 10,000 people.

Deism enabled Voltaire to effect a kind of reconciliation between a perfect God and the imperfect world. Voltaire believed that God was indeed the Creator:

> When I see a watch . . . , I conclude that an intelligent being arranged the springs of this mechanism so that the hand should tell the time. Similarly, when I see the springs of the human body, I conclude that an intelligent being has arranged these organs to be kept and nourished in the womb for nine months; that the eyes have been given for seeing, the hands for grasping, etc.*

But, Voltaire concluded, there was no way to determine whether or not God would attempt to perfect his creation. On one point Voltaire had no doubts: He never questioned the usefulness of religion for the masses. "Man," he stated, "has always needed a brake." He practiced what he preached by building a church for the tenants on his country estate at Ferney on the French-Swiss frontier.

### Materialism and Atheism

Not all philosophes were prepared to make even this concession to religion. La Mettrie (1709–1751) eliminated any need for religion by propounding a totally materialistic philosophy in a work entitled *Man a Machine*. The world and all its inhabitants, human as well as animal, he argued, are self-regulating mechanisms made out of one universal substance and behaving as their natures compel them to behave. Helvétius (1715–1771), whose wife ran a salon, carried these ideas a step further and scandalized France by claiming that "personal interest is the only and universal estimator of the merit of human actions."† Because self-interest could act as a kind of inner brake, men did not require the external brake on their actions that was thought to be provided by religion.

The most outspoken atheist of the Enlightenment was D'Holbach (1723–1789), a German baron living in Paris who presided over a salon. Like Helvétius he regarded self-interest as the mainspring of morality:

* *Lettres Philosophiques,* No. 6. Our translation.

* *Le Traité de Métaphysique,* Chapter II. Our translation.

† Helvétius, *On the Mind,* as quoted in L. G. Crocker, ed., *The Age of Enlightenment* (New York, 1969), p. 149.

> Since we must judge men's actions according to their effects on us, we approve the self-interest which motivates them whenever an advantage for mankind results from it. . . . But in this judgment we are not ourselves disinterested. Experience, reflection, habit, reason have given us a moral taste, and we find as much pleasure in being the witnesses of a great and generous act as a man of good taste experiences on seeing a beautiful painting of which he is not the owner. . . . The virtuous man is one who has been taught by correct ideas that his self-interest or happiness lies in acting in a way that others are forced to love and to approve out of their own self-interest.*

Holbach's claim that the virtuous man is "taught by correct ideas" reflects the influence of Lockean psychology and has been viewed sometimes with rather exaggerated alarm as a forecast of totalitarian indoctrination.

Holbach denounced churches as sinister institutions thwarting the benevolent operation of reason and of natural law. He dismissed God as a "phantom of the imagination," whose existence was denied by the evils and imperfections of the world that he was alleged to have created. A wealthy man, Holbach extended the hospitality of his salon to all, even to Jesuit refugees from anticlerical persecution. His tolerance impressed his contemporaries more favorably than his atheism did; most philosophes continued to profess deism, which was halfway between belief and disbelief.

### Political Thought: Montesquieu

"In politics as in religion toleration is a necessity," decreed Voltaire. To him, therefore, tolerant Britain seemed utopia, and he paid the British constitution the most flattering compliment at the command of his age when he claimed that it "might have been invented by Locke, Newton, or Archimedes." Montesquieu (1689–1755), an aristocratic French lawyer and philosophe, set out to analyze the political virtues of Britain. In his major work, *The Spirit of the Laws* (1748), Montesquieu laid down the premise that no one system of government suited all countries. Laws, he wrote,

> should be in relation to the climate of each country, to the quality of its soil, to its situation and extent, to the principal occupation of the natives, whether husbandmen, huntsmen, or shepherds: they should have relation to the degree of liberty which the constitution will bear; to the religion of the inhabitants, to their inclinations, riches, numbers, commerce, manners, and customs.*

Montesquieu cautioned against supposing that old customs could simply be decreed out of existence, citing the telling example of Peter the Great's failure to impose Western ways on Russia.

In spelling out the influence of tradition and environment upon forms of government, Montesquieu concluded that republics were best suited to the small and barren countries, limited monarchies to the middle-sized and more prosperous, and despotisms to vast empires. Britain, being middle-sized and prosperous, was quite properly a monarchy limited by aristocracy. The hereditary nobility sat in the House of Lords; a kind of nobility of talent, the elected representatives, composed the Commons. All this was admirable in Montesquieu's view, for he pronounced the mass of people "extremely unfit" for government. If only the French monarchy had let the aristocracy retain its old political functions, France would never have sunk to her present low state.

Montesquieu found another key to the political superiority of Britain in the famous concept of checks and balances. In Parliament, Lords and Commons checked each other; in the government as a whole, the balance was maintained by means of the separation of powers:

> When the legislative and executive powers are united in the same person, or in the same body of magistrates, there can be no liberty; because apprehensions may arise, lest the same monarch or senate should enact tyrannical laws, to execute them in a tyrannical manner.
>
> Again, there is no liberty, if the judiciary power be not separated from the legislative and executive. Were it joined with the legislative the life and liberty of the subject would be exposed to arbitrary control; for the judge would be then the legislator. Were it joined to the executive power, the judge might behave with violence and oppression.†

* *Système de la Nature,* trans. L. G. Crocker, ed., in *The Age of Enlightenment,* pp. 160–161.

* Thomas Nugent, trans. (New York, 1949), Bk. I, ch. 3.

† Ibid., Book XXI, chap. 6.

Here Montesquieu failed to take into account a development that was not exactly obvious in the mid-eighteenth century, when *The Spirit of the Laws* appeared. He failed to see that the British constitution was moving, not toward a greater separation of powers, but toward their concentration in the House of Commons; the cabinet was becoming the instrument for the assertion of legislative supremacy over the executive.

Montesquieu likewise ran into trouble when he tried to derive specific corollaries from his general theorem about the influence of climate and geography on human institutions. Autocracy and Catholicism, he asserted, flourished in the Mediterranean states where the climate is warm and natural resources are abundant. Moderate government and Protestantism, conversely, are at home in the colder and harsher environment of northern Europe. The facts did not always confirm this rule about north and south. Freedom-loving Protestant Britain and Holland behaved in good northern fashion; but if Montesquieu were correct, barren, northern, Protestant Prussia should have been a citadel of liberty, not the stronghold of Hohenzollern absolutism. By jumping to conclusions from insufficient evidence, Montesquieu committed a fault common among the philosophes. But, unlike some of them, he had too firm a grasp on political realities to assume that governments either were or should be the same everywhere. Later political thinkers made good use of the comparative methods introduced by *The Spirit of the Laws* and refined Montesquieu's judgments on the interrelationship of geography, religion, and politics.

### Rousseau

From the standpoint of American history, as we shall see, Montesquieu and Locke proved to be the most influential political thinkers of the Enlightenment. From the standpoint of European history, the most important was Jean-Jacques Rousseau, who inspired the radicals of the French Revolution. Rousseau's ideas proceeded from a sweeping generalization very typical of the Enlightenment. Whereas nature dignifies man, he contended, civilization corrupts him; man would be corrupted less if civilized institutions followed nature more closely. This theme ran through many of Rousseau's principal writings. In *Emile,* it was at the heart of his program for educational reform; earlier, it was enunciated in the *Discourse on the Moral Effects of the Arts and Sciences* (1750), which won a competition set by the Academy of Dijon. The Academy asked: Has the restoration of the arts and sciences had a purifying effect upon morals? Certainly not, the prizewinner answered; it has nearly ruined them.

In a second discourse, *On the Origin of the Inequality of Mankind* (1755), Rousseau blamed the vices of civilization on private property:

> The first man who, having enclosed a piece of ground, bethought himself of saying, "This is mine," and found people simple enough to believe him, was the real founder of civil society. From how many crimes, wars, and murders, from how many horrors and misfortunes might not any one have saved mankind, by pulling up the stakes, or filling up the ditch, and crying to his fellows: "Beware of listening to this imposter; you are undone if you once forget that the fruits of the earth belong to us all, and the earth itself to nobody."

Men accepted laws and governors in order to protect their property:

> They had too many disputes among themselves to do without arbitrators, and too much ambition and avarice to go long without masters. All ran headlong to their chains, in hopes of securing their liberty; for they had just wit enough to perceive the advantages of political institutions, without experience enough to enable them to foresee their danger.

Government was evil, Rousseau concluded, but a necessary evil. "What, then, is to be done? Must societies be totally abolished? . . . Must we return again to the forest to live among bears?" No, civilized men could not return to a primitive existence, could "no longer subsist on plants or acorns, or live without laws and magistrates." *

Rousseau's major political work, *The Social Contract* (1762), attempted to reconcile the liberty of the individual and the institution of

* In *The Social Contract and Discourses,* Everyman ed. (New York, 1913), pp. 192, 205, 228.

government through a new and revolutionary version of the contract theory of government. Earlier theories of contract, from the Middle Ages to John Locke, had hinged on the agreement between the people to be governed, on the one hand, and a single governor or small group of governors, on the other. Earlier theories postulated a political contract; Rousseau's contract was social in that a whole society agreed to be ruled by its general will:

> Each of us puts his person and all his power in common under the supreme direction of the general will, and, in our corporate capacity, we receive each member as an indivisible part of the whole.

"Each individual," Rousseau continued "may have a particular will contrary or dissimilar to the general will which he has as a citizen." If the individual insists on putting self-interest above community interest, he should be obliged to observe the general will. "This means nothing less than that he will be forced to be free." Thus, the general will was moral as well as political in nature, for it represented what was *best* for the whole community, what the community *ought* to do.

Formulating the general will, Rousseau believed, was the business of the whole people. The power of legislation, he argued, could never be properly transferred to an elected body:

> The deputies of the people . . . are not and cannot be its representatives; they are merely its stewards, and can carry through no definitive acts. Every law the people has not ratified in person is null and void—is, in fact, not a law. The people of England regards itself as free; but it is grossly mistaken; it is free only during the election of members of Parliament.*

Executing the general will, however, could legitimately be the business of a smaller group. Like Montesquieu, Rousseau believed that the number of governors should vary inversely with the size and resources of the state—monarchy for the wealthy, aristocracy for the state of middling size and wealth, and democracy for the small and poor. Rousseau doubted, however, that any state was ready for the absolute form of democracy in which the people themselves actually executed the laws. "Were there a people of gods, their government would be democratic. So perfect a government is not for men." *

Rousseau was quite aware that *The Social Contract* was not a manual of practical politics. On another occasion, when he made suggestions for the reform of the Polish government, his counsels were decidedly more cautious. He admonished the Poles to renew their national spirit through education and patriotic festivals. While favoring the abolition of the *liberum veto,* he recommended that the elective monarchy be retained, that the nobles keep many of their privileges but acquire a new sense of duty, and that the serfs be liberated but only after they had been taught responsibility.

Although these suggestions were moderate enough, the influence of Rousseau has not been exerted on the side of moderation. Almost every radical political doctrine in the past two centuries has owed something to Rousseau. Socialists justify collectivism on the basis of his attacks on private property and of his insistence that "the fruits of the earth belong to us all." Patriots and nationalists hail him as an early prophet of the creed that nations do—and should—differ. Throughout his writings as well as in his advice to the Poles, he referred to "the dear love of country." *The Social Contract* concluded with a plea for the establishment of a "civil religion," which would displace the traditional faith. The moral code of early Christianity might be retained, Rousseau allowed, but the state should no longer have to compete with the church for the allegiance of citizens.

Rousseau's concept of the general will has aroused conflicting interpretations. Because it is ethical in character, it seems to represent something more than the sum of individual wills—the whole appears to be more than the sum of its parts. Many, therefore, see in Rousseau a man who exalted the welfare of the nation over that of the citizens composing it, a man who indeed worshiped the state and proposed the "civil religion" of *The Social Contract* so that everyone would have to follow suit. Dictators have justified their totalitarianism by asserting that they have a special insight into the general will; Hitler's celebrated "intuition" is an example. The police state can be justified on the grounds that it is doing its subjects a favor by "forcing them to be free."

* Everyman ed. (New York, 1913), pp. 13, 15, 78.

* Ibid., p. 56.

The authoritarian interpretation indicates some of the possible consequences of Rousseau's ideas, but it overlooks both the strongly idealistic and democratic tone of his writings and his personal hostility toward the absolutism of the Old Regime. It seems plausible that by the general will Rousseau was describing the acceptance of democratically achieved decisions by the good citizen—something like the Friends' "sense of the meeting" or the more recent idea of consensus. In short, the concept of the general will is an attempt to understand the psychology of obedience to manmade laws, but it does not take care of the difficulty created when there is no "sense of the meeting." Yet Rousseau's declaration—"Were there a people of gods, their government would be democratic"—has stirred democratic disciples from the French Revolution on down to the present. The people are not gods? Then they must be trained in godliness, and Rousseau himself pointed the way. *Emile* showed how education could help, and *The Social Contract* at least implied that men might one day become so virtuous that they would follow the general will naturally and would no longer have to be "forced to be free."

## III Enlightened Despotism

Some philosophes sought a short cut to utopia, a political prescription that was more practicable than *The Social Contract* and that could operate within the framework of existing monarchical institutions. They found the answer in enlightened despotism. The Physiocrats, the chief theorists of enlightened despotism, had little sympathy with the concern of Montesquieu and Rousseau over the status of the legislative power. In the Physiocratic view, God was the legislator, nature preserved the divine legislation, and the sole duty of government was to administer these natural laws. Democracy and aristocracy alike had the fatal weakness of delegating administrative authority to individuals whose transient selfish aims clashed with the permanent welfare of the nation. By contrast, the Physiocrats explained, the personal interests of a hereditary monarch coincided with national interests through his "co-ownership" of the territories under his rule. Because the king was best qualified to work for the national interest, he should be a despot, not in any sinister sense but on the model of the tyrants of ancient Greece or the best of the Renaissance despots. Like a new Solon, the enlightened despot should unearth the natural laws decreed by God and clear away the accumulation of artificial, manmade law that was choking progress.

In the eighteenth century, "enlightened" or "benevolent" despots occupied many thrones—in Prussia, Frederick the Great; in Austria, Joseph II; in Russia, Catherine the Great; in Spain, Charles III; in Sweden, Gustavus III; and still others. The program of enlightened despotism won such wide endorsement from European monarchs and their apologists because it gave them the opportunity to pose as the champions of reason and progress while pressing their age-old fight to make royal authority more absolute. Their mixture of reason and *raison d'état* made their kingdoms at best uncertain proving grounds both for the theory of enlightened despotism and for the practicality of the whole reform program of the Enlightenment.

### Frederick the Great

Of all the monarchs of eighteenth-century Europe, Frederick II, the Great, of Prussia (1740–1786), appeared best attuned to the Enlightenment. As a youth, he rebelled against the drill-sergeant methods of his father, Frederick William I. He delighted in music, and played the flute, which he took with him even on military campaigns. An attentive reader of the philosophes, he exchanged letters with them and brought Voltaire to live for a time as his pensioner in his palace at Potsdam near Berlin. He wrote a pamphlet, *Anti-Machiavel,* denouncing the immorality of *The Prince*. And he himself laid down the fundamental requirements for an enlightened despot, as we can see in the following:

> Princes, sovereigns, kings are not clothed with supreme authority to plunge with impunity into debauchery and luxury. . . . [The prince] should often remind himself that he is a man just as the least of his subjects. If he is the first judge, the first general, the first financier, the first minister of the nation, . . . it is in order to fulfill the duties which these titles impose upon him. He is only the first servant of the state, obliged to act with fairness, wisdom, and unselfishness, as if at every instant he would have to render an account of his administration to his citizens.*

Frederick was indeed "the first servant of the state," shunning luxury, wearing stained and shabby clothing, and toiling long and hard at his desk. But did he also act with "fairness, wisdom, and unselfishness"? Despite his *Anti-Machiavel,* Frederick conducted foreign and military affairs in true Machiavellian style. "The principle of aggrandizement is the fundamental law of every government,"† he wrote, and the way he managed his invasion of Silesia in 1740 would have aroused the envy of Caesar Borgia. At home, closeted in his Potsdam palace where he conducted the business of state by correspondence, he drove his subordinates like slaves. Viewed as a general, diplomat, and the master mechanic of Prussian administration, Frederick the Great was efficient and successful, but he was scarcely enlightened. His claim to be a benevolent despot must rise or fall on the record of his social and economic reforms.

No Physiocrat could have done more than Frederick to improve Prussian agriculture. From western Europe he imported clover, potatoes, crop rotation, and the iron plow, which turned up the soil more effectively than the old wooden share. He drained the swamps of the lower Oder Valley, opened up farms in Silesia and elsewhere, and brought in 300,000 immigrants, mainly from other areas of Germany, to settle the new lands and augment the sparse population of East Prussia. This revival of the historic German "push to the East" meant that by the time he died one family out of five in his domains came from recent immigrant stock. After the ravages of the Seven Years' War, Frederick gave the peasants tools, stock, and seed to repair their ruined farms. He nursed along the admirable German tradition of scientific forestry, which was then only in its infancy.

Frederick, however, was hostile to the doctrine of laissez-faire and cut imports to the bone in order to save money for support of the army. His mercantilism stimulated the growth of Prussian industry, particularly the textiles and metals needed by the army. But it also placed a staggering burden of taxation on his subjects and produced several economic absurdities. For instance, Frederick tried to make Prussia grow its own tobacco, for which the climate was not suited. And, since the German taste for coffee required a large outlay of money abroad, he laid a heavy duty on imported coffee beans, and even established a special corps of French "coffee smellers" to trap smugglers.

The religious and social policies of Frederick the Great likewise combined the Age of Reason at its most reasonable with the Old Regime at its least enlightened. A deist, Frederick prided himself on religious tolerance. When the Jesuits were expelled from Catholic states, he invited them to seek refuge in predominantly Lutheran Prussia; he gave the minority of Catholics, particularly important in Silesia, virtually full equality, urging them to build their church steeples as high as they liked, and set the example by constructing a large new Catholic church in the center of Berlin. He even boasted that he would build a mosque in his capital if Muslims wanted to settle there. Yet the same Frederick alleged that Jews were "useless to the state," levied special heavy taxes on his Jewish subjects, and tried to exclude them from the professions and from the civil service.

Frederick rendered Prussians a great service by his judicial reforms, which freed the courts from political pressures. He ordered a reduction in the use of torture, and he put an end to the curious custom of taking appeals from the ordinary courts to university faculties; he instituted a regular system of appellate courts. He mitigated the venal practice of bribing judges by insisting that "tips" received from litigants be placed in a common pool from which each judge should draw only his fair share.

Yet the same Frederick took a positively medieval view of the merits of social caste, in part because of his own firmly held stoical convictions about the patriotic duties required of both ruler and subjects. He did nothing to loosen

* "Essai sur les Formes de Gouvernement et sur les Devoirs des Souverains," *Oeuvres Posthumes* (Berlin, 1788), VI, 64, 83–84. Our translation.

† Quoted by G. Ritter, *Frederick the Great: A Historical Profile* (Berkeley, 1968), p. 7.

the bonds of serfdom that still shackled much of the Prussian peasantry. When he gave the peasants material assistance and urged them to learn the three R's, his aims were severely utilitarian. Peasants were to learn nothing beyond the rudiments of reading and writing; otherwise, they might become discontented with their station in life, which was, in his view, that of "beast of burden." Regarding the middle class, too, with disdain, Frederick respected only the landed nobility and gentry. At the close of the Seven Years' War he forced all bourgeois officers in the army to resign their commissions; business and professional men were to be exempt from military service but subject to heavy taxation. He opposed membership in the Academy of Berlin for the leading German writer of his age, Lessing, because his dramas defended middle-class values of social and political freedom and were written in German, not French. Even the favored Junkers did not escape Frederick's penny-pinching. Although he appointed only Junkers as army officers, he discouraged their marrying to reduce the number of potential widows to whom the state would owe a pension.

While Frederick indulged his favorite dogs and horses, giving them special house privileges, he was temperamentally incapable of getting along with people. He despised and neglected his wife. Voltaire, that great French champion of toleration, could not tolerate the strain of prolonged daily association with Frederick. When the king requested him to edit his rather feeble French verses, Voltaire made a cutting remark about washing the dirty linen of royalty; Frederick retorted by comparing his guest to an orange, to be sucked dry and thrown away. The two men eventually renewed their friendship through the less demanding medium of correspondence.

Frederick's will directed that he be buried beside his pet dogs—"Such," remarked a French observer, "is the last mark of contempt he thought proper to cast upon mankind." The verdict has been sustained by many liberal historians, who pronounce Frederick's supposed enlightenment a mere device of propaganda, an attempt to clothe the nakedness of his absolutism with the decent intellectual garments of the age. This is, however, rather too harsh and one-sided, an attempt perhaps to fix on Frederick part of the guilt for the atrocities committed by Hitler and the Nazis almost two centuries after him. It would be fairer to argue that Frederick espoused two often conflicting philosophies—the Spartan traditions of the Hohenzollerns and the humane principles of the Enlightenment. The former, with its strong Protestant convictions of man's sinfulness, kept him from sharing the latter's optimistic estimate of human nature and potentiality. Frederick was an enlightened despot only so far as he could reconcile the precepts of the Age of Reason with the imperatives of Prussian kingship. He was a Hohenzollern, first and always.

### Maria Theresa and Joseph II

Frederick's decisive victory in the War of the Austrian Succession laid bare the basic weaknesses of the Hapsburgs' dynastic empire. The empress Maria Theresa (1740–1780) saw the need for reform and often took as her model the institutions of her hated but successful Hohenzollern rival. She had the advice of capable ministers, some of them schooled in cameralism, the new "science" taught at Halle and other German universities, which combined the study of mercantilism, finance, and public administration. The empress and her experts increased taxes, especially on the nobility, and strengthened the central government at the expense of local aristocratic assemblies, building up the still rather sketchy departments of central administration. They obliged the non-German provinces to accept the hegemony of the German officials and German language of Vienna. Unlike Frederick the Great, Maria Theresa also took the first steps toward the abolition of serfdom. While personally very devout, she extended her policies to the Church, subjecting it to heavier taxation, confiscating some monastic property, and expelling the Jesuits. The pope declared himself deeply offended by this Hapsburg adaptation of the Gallicanism long practiced by the French monarchy in asserting the subordination of church to state.

Maria Theresa employed both force and charm to get her way. The nobles of Hungary momentarily forgot their anti-German tradition when the beautiful and spirited empress, her infant son in her arms, personally appealed to their chivalry in the crisis of the War of the Austrian Succession. She was the first housewife of

*Emperor Joseph II working a plow.*

the realm as well as the first servant of the state. She was the mother of sixteen children, and she adored and respected Francis, her grasping, fickle husband. Francis' will provided a large bequest for his mistress; his widow executed its terms to the letter.

Maria Theresa was fundamentally out of sympathy with the Age of Reason. "Lady Prayerful," as Catherine the Great called her, banned the works of Rousseau and Voltaire and even forbade the circulation of the Catholic *Index,* lest that list of forbidden books pique the curiosity of her subjects. History, therefore, has denied her the title of enlightened despot and chosen instead Joseph II, her eldest son, who became emperor after the death of Francis in 1765 and was coregent with his mother until her death in 1780. Frederick the Great wrote Voltaire a glowing estimate of the new emperor:

> Born in a bigoted court, he has cast off its superstition; raised in magnificence, he has assumed simple manners; nourished on incense, he is modest; burning with a thirst for glory, he sacrifices his ambition to the filial duty which he executes scrupulously; and, having had only pedantic teachers, he still has enough taste to read Voltaire and to appreciate his merits.*

* "Correspondance avec les Souverains," *Oeuvres Complètes de Voltaire* (Paris, 1828), LXXIV, 37. Our translation.

Frederick exaggerated only a little. Earnest, industrious, and puritanical in temperament, Joseph promised to make "philosophy the legislator of my empire." Thwarted and restrained by Maria Theresa in her lifetime, seeking solace in work for the grief caused by the death of his young wife, the impatient emperor plunged into activity after his mother died. During his ten years as sole ruler, 1780–1790, eleven thousand laws and six thousand decrees issued from Vienna. This frenzied pace gave the misleading impression that the son's policies always ran counter to the mother's; actually, their goals were often identical, but Joseph's methods of achieving them were more abrupt and less cautious and conciliatory than Maria Theresa's.

In religious policy, Joseph did make a genuine innovation when, for the first time in the history of Catholic Austria, Calvinists, Lutherans, and Orthodox Christians gained full toleration. And, with a generosity unparalleled in Hapsburg annals, the emperor took measures to end the ghetto existence of the Jews, exempting them from special taxes and from the requirement of wearing a yellow patch as a badge of inferiority. On the other hand, Joseph continued his mother's moves to increase state control over the church in Austrian lands, a control that now went by the name of Josephism because of the emperor's insistence that he and not the pope was the supreme arbiter of ecclesiastical matters in Hapsburg territories. He encouraged what he considered socially useful in Catholicism and dealt ruthlessly with what he judged superfluous and harmful. Thus he established hundreds of new churches and at the same time reduced the number of religious holidays. He called monks "the most dangerous and useless subjects in every state" and promised to convert "the monk of mere show into a useful citizen." He cut in half the number of monks and nuns and, of 2,100 monasteries and nunneries, he suppressed 700, chiefly those run by the contemplative orders. Houses actively engaged in educational or charitable work were generally spared. The government sold or leased the lands of the suppressed establishments, applying the revenue to the support of the hospitals that were beginning to earn Vienna its reputation as a great medical center.

Unlike Frederick the Great, Joseph really believed in popular education and social equality. His government provided the teachers and textbooks for primary schools. More than a quarter of the school-age children in Austria actually attended school—the best record of any country in late eighteenth-century Europe. Everyone in Vienna, high and low, was invited to visit the Prater, the great public park of the capital, the entrance to which bore the inscription, "A place of pleasure for all men, prepared for them by their friend." The new Austrian legal code followed the recommendations of Beccaria in abolishing capital punishment and most tortures and in prescribing equality before the law. Aristocratic offenders, like commoners, were sentenced to stand in the pillory and to sweep the streets of Vienna. Joseph's peasant policy marked the climax of his equalitarianism. He freed the serfs, abolished most of their obligations to manorial lords, and deprived the lords of their traditional right of administering justice to the peasantry. He also experimented with the collection of a single tax on land as recommended by the Physiocrats, a revolutionary innovation from the social as well as the economic point of view, because the estates of the aristocracy were to be taxed on the same basis as the farms of the peasantry.

Joseph's economic policies, however, often followed the traditions of mercantilism and cameralism, notably in the erection of high protective tariffs and in the government's close supervision of economic life. In politics Joseph continued his mother's Germanizing program. He customarily spoke German, patronized German writers, and made the French playhouse in Vienna a German-language theater. He attempted to terminate the autonomous rights of his non-German possessions, such as Bohemia, Hungary, and Belgium.

Both Joseph's enlightened reforms and his Germanizing measures aroused mounting opposition. Devout peasants, almost oblivious of his well-meaning attempts to improve their social and economic status, keenly resented his meddling with old religious customs. The nobility clamored against his equalitarian legislation; in the case of the single-tax experiment their opposition was so violent that he had to revoke the decree a month after it was issued. Hungary and Belgium rose in open rebellion against his centralizing efforts and forced him to confirm their autonomous liberties.

In foreign policy, too, his ambitious projects miscarried. By supporting Russian plans for the dismemberment of Turkey, Austria gained only a narrow strip of Balkan territory. Joseph also attempted to annex lands belonging to the neighboring south German state of Bavaria, where the death of the ruler opened another of those succession quarrels so common in the eighteenth century. But Frederick the Great was determined to check any advance of Hapsburg power in Germany. In the half-hearted "Potato War" of the late 1770's, Austrian and Prussian troops spent most of their time foraging for food, and Joseph secured only a tiny fragment of the Bavarian inheritance.

Joseph II worked himself to death, as one of his friends observed, "by governing too much and reigning too little." Where his mother had often sought to flatter or charm her opponents out of their opposition, Joseph simply laid down the law. He defended his habit of interfering personally in almost every detail of government:

> What else can I do in this country devoid of mind, without soul, without zeal, without heart in the work? I am killing myself because I cannot rouse up those whom I want to make work; but I hope I shall not die until I have so wound up the machine that others cannot put it out of order, even if they try to do so.*

* Quoted in Prince de Ligne, *His Memoirs, Letters, and Miscellaneous Papers* (Boston, 1902), II, 132.

*Batoni's painting of Joseph II with the future emperor Leopold II.*

Joseph never got the machine properly wound up; he could not implant in the Austrian bureaucracy the almost inhuman Prussian discipline that was needed to serve his purposes. Joseph II died unshaken in the conviction that he had pursued the proper course, yet believing that he had accomplished nothing. In the judgment of posterity, however, Joseph appears as the most truly enlightened despot. In ten years he attempted more than Frederick attempted in almost half a century. Though some of his major reforms, like the abolition of serfdom, were repealed soon after his death, others survived him, helping to transform the Hapsburg lands into a more modern centralized state.

### Leopold II and Gustavus III

Outside Germany enlightened despots guided governments in Italy, the Iberian peninsula, and Sweden. Prominent among them was Joseph II's younger brother Leopold, grand duke of Tuscany from 1765 until he became emperor in 1790. Leopold tidied up the administration of his Italian duchy, which included the busy port of Leghorn in addition to the city of Florence. He introduced economic reforms along Physiocratic lines and judicial reforms in line with the recommendations of Beccaria on the abolition of torture and of the death penalty. Unlike his brother, Leopold actively enlisted the participation of his subjects in affairs of state, and, unlike any other enlightened despot, he contemplated establishing a representative assembly and studied the constitution of Virginia for guidance.

Sweden's benevolent despot, King Gustavus III (1771–1792), was the most theatrical monarch of the century. Like his uncle, Frederick the Great, Gustavus admired the French and French ideas, and, when he inherited the Swedish crown, he proclaimed in ringing speeches his devotion to the Age of Reason. He also resolved not to be cramped by the oligarchical factions that had run the country since the death of the warrior king, Charles XII, early in the century. While he distracted Swedish party leaders at the opera one evening, his soldiers staged a coup that enabled him to revive the royal authority and to dissolve the factions. In economics and religion, his enlightenment outdistanced that of his uncle in Prussia, for he removed obstacles to both domestic and foreign trade and extended toleration to Jews as well as to the non-Lutheran Christian sects. Success, however, turned the head of Gustavus III. As he became more and more arbitrary, the nobles determined to recover their old power; in 1792, he was assassinated at a masquerade in Stockholm, and oligarchy resumed its sway.

### Pombal and Charles III

One of the most remarkable features of enlightened despotism was its emergence in the Iberian peninsula, so long the preserve of aristocratic and clerical influence. Its representative in Portugal was not a monarch but the marquis of Pombal, the first minister of King Joseph I (1750–1777). Pombal secured his reputation by the speed and good taste he demonstrated in rebuilding Lisbon after the earthquake of 1755. The Portuguese economy depended heavily on income from the colonies, on the sale of port wine to Britain, and on the purchase of manufactured goods from Britain. Pombal tried to enlarge its base by fostering local industries and encouraging the growth of grain in addition to grapes. To weaken the grip of clericalism on Portuguese life, he ousted the Jesuits, advanced religious toleration, and modernized the curriculum of the national University of Coimbra. To weaken that of the nobles, he attacked their rights of inheritance. Pombal's methods were in every instance high-handed, and when he fell from power in 1777 the prisons released thousands of men whom he had confined years earlier for their alleged involvement in aristocratic plots.

The Spanish enlightened despot was Charles III (1759–1788), Elizabeth Farnese's "Baby Carlos." When he inherited the crown on the death of his half-brother, he had already been seasoned in the struggle against feudalism and clericalism by a long and successful apprenticeship as king of Naples. With the assistance of advisers whom he brought from Naples and of lawyers from the lower ranks of the Spanish nobility, Charles III energetically advanced the progressive policies begun under his father, Philip V. Though a pious Catholic, he objected strongly to the political activities of the Church and forced the Jesuits out of Spain. He reduced the authority of the aristocracy, extended that of the Crown, and made Spain more nearly a centralized national state. He curbed the privileges of the great sheep ranchers, whose almost unlimited grazing rights blighted Spanish agriculture. To revivify the torpid economy, he undertook irrigation projects, reclaimed waste lands, and established new roads, canals, banks, and textile mills. The results were astonishing: Spain's foreign commerce increased fivefold during the reign of Charles III. His successors, however, abandoned many of his forward-looking policies, and Spain soon began to slip back into her old ways, though the influence of the Enlightenment at least remained alive.

### Limitations of Enlightened Despotism

The question of succession, in fact, vitiated the whole structure of enlightened despotism. So long as monarchs came to the throne by the accident of birth, there was nothing to prevent the unenlightened or incapable mediocrity from succeeding the enlightened despot. This happened in Spain, where the well-meaning but feeble Charles IV (1788–1808), succeeded Charles III; it happened in Sweden, where the weak Gustavus IV (1792–1809), succeeded Gustavus III; and it happened in Prussia under Frederick the Great's unenlightened nephew, Frederick William II (1786–1797). The principal exception to the rule occurred in Austria, where Emperor Leopold II (1790–1792), with his long experience in Tuscany, managed to salvage some of the reforms of Joseph II.

Even the least of the enlightened despots deserve the credit for having improved a few of the bad features of the Old Regime. But not even the best of them could strike a happy balance between enlightenment and despotism. Joseph II was too doctrinaire, too inflexible in his determination to apply the full reform program of the Age of Reason. Pombal and Gustavus III, in particular, were too arbitrary. Frederick the Great, obsessed with strengthening the crown, entrenched the power of the Junkers, who were hostile to the whole Enlightenment. Finally, in Russia, events during the century after the death of Peter the Great furnished another lesson in the difficulty of adjusting rational principles to political realities.

## IV Russia, 1725-1825

### The Fate of the Autocracy, 1725-1762

When Peter the Great died, he left a tangled family situation in which nobody could truly decide who was his legitimate successor. Over the course of the next thirty-seven years, the throne changed hands seven times. The succession zigzagged across the family tree of the Romanovs: first to Peter's widow, who ruled as Empress Catherine I (1725–1727); then to Peter's young grandson, son of the murdered Alexis, who became Peter II (1727–1730); then to Peter's niece, who reigned as Empress Anne (1730–1740); then to Anne's great-nephew, Ivan VI, only eight weeks old when he began his one-year reign (1740–1741); then to Peter's own daughter by Catherine I, the empress Elizabeth (1741–1762); then to Elizabeth's nephew, Peter III, who reigned only for six months in 1762; and finally to Peter III's brilliant young widow, who became Catherine II, the Great (1762–1796), and dominated Russia as Peter I himself had done. More important than the individuals who governed Russia between Peter and Catherine the Great were the social forces contending for power, and the social processes at work in an autocracy suddenly deprived of its autocrat and for so long unable to produce a new one. In the series of palace overturns, the guards' regiments founded by Peter exercised a decisive influence. The service nobility, no longer restrained by the Czar, now entered into its era of dominance.

On the death of Peter the Great, his immediate circle, particularly Menshikov, had every reason to fear the passage of the throne to the nine-year-old Peter, son of Alexis, and possible heir to the loyalties of the old nobility who had hated Peter the Great. Menshikov therefore strongly supported his one-time mistress, the empress Catherine I, and succeeded in rallying to her side members of the guards who had come to like her while on campaigns. Since Catherine herself took little interest in affairs of state, Menshikov ran Russia during the two years of her reign. He tried to make himself secure by appointing a six-man "Supreme Privy Council" at the top of the administration, and to perpetuate his power he even planned to marry his daughter to the young heir, the future Peter II. On the death of Catherine I in 1727, he took the eleven-year-old boy into his house, where he proceeded to make him an alcoholic, as his father had been.

But Menshikov's arrogance had alienated even his followers; he was exiled after the old boyars, led by the families of Dolgoruky and Galitsyn, had gained supremacy. Two Dolgoruky princes put themselves on the Supreme Privy Council, and the young Peter was engaged to a member of their family. The ascendancy of boyar families marked the return to supreme influence of a group that had been losing power ever since the days of Ivan the Terrible. Their plans were brought into crisis by the sudden death of Peter II on the very day scheduled for his coronation (January 19, 1730).

Their program can be studied in the conditions they submitted to the new candidate for the throne, Anne, the widow of the duke of Courland. Summoning her from her petty Baltic principality, the Dolgoruky and the Galitsyns demanded that she sign these Articles before taking the throne. By their terms, she undertook never to marry or name an heir, and to continue the Supreme Privy Council, which by now had eight members, including four Dolgoruky and two Galitsyns. She further swore not to make peace or war, levy taxes, confer ranks in the army above that of colonel, or spend state funds without the specific consent of the Council. Moreover, the Councillors claimed for themselves supervision over the guards' regiments. This insistence on limiting the power of the new empress reflected the outraged feelings of the old boyars, who had long been claiming the right to be consulted on all matters of state. The entire program was the most explicit constitutional destruction of all that Peter the Great had striven for. Anne signed the Articles. Had she kept to their provisions, Russia would have embarked on an era of boyar oligarchy.

But the military-service nobility looked with horror at the prospect of taking orders indefinitely from the small group of old boyars. And the service gentry had a powerful lever in the guards' regiments. What its members wanted was an autocrat who would loosen the bonds that Peter the Great had forged for them. And so, when one of the Supreme Privy Councillors, the clever German Ostermann, convinced Anne that she need not abide by the Articles, the gentry in its armed might supported him. Anne simply tore up the Articles; thus, the attempt to create an oligarchy of the two great families failed. The gentry now had the real power in Russia.

Anne allowed her lover, the German adventurer Biren, and a flock of Germans to obtain the most influential positions in the state. The secret police, abolished after the death of Peter the Great, was now revived, and many thousands suffered torture, exile, and death at its hands. When Anne died, the German favorites fell out among themselves, with Ostermann, a man of real ability, the eventual winner. Meanwhile, the czar was the infant Ivan VI, whose mother, a German princess, acted as regent, and was so lazy that she lounged in her bedroom without the energy even to put on her clothes. Foreign intrigue produced the next shift in the imperial title. The French were anxious to terminate the power of Ostermann, who had been instrumental in cementing an alliance between Russia and France's traditional enemy, Austria. A clever French ambassador played on the patriotic feelings of the guardsmen, disgusted with the behavior of the Germans at court. In 1741 a guard's coup brought to the throne the daughter of Peter the Great, Elizabeth. The infant Ivan VI vanished into a prison cell with his indolent mother.

Elizabeth inherited her father's lust for life but not his brains or interest in matters of state. A succession of lovers had kept her busy all her life, and her habits did not change when she came to the throne. Though owning thousands of splendid dresses, she lived rather sluttishly in grubby palaces and enjoyed most of all a rousing peasant banquet with plenty to drink and lots of rustic music. Important state papers languished for days because the empress could not be bothered to read them, much less sign them. Though she proclaimed her intention of restoring her father's methods of rule, she had no clear conception of what these had been. In an autocracy the autocrat has to assume responsibility for affairs of state; this Elizabeth did not do, and Russia drifted.

Soon after her accession, Elizabeth proclaimed her nephew, the half-mad Peter, heir to the throne. In 1745 he married a clever little German princess, the future Catherine II. Peter III, as he became after his succession in January 1762, has had a bad press; he surely was not unusually intelligent, but was hardly the utter lunatic portrayed in the memoirs of his celebrated wife, who loathed him. The chief trouble with Peter seems to have been his great admiration for Prussia and his dislike of Russia. His effort to introduce rigid discipline on the Prussian model into the Russian army and his hatred for the influential guards' regiments cost him the friends he needed most. He could have played his war games with his toy soldiers, held courts-martial on rats whom he convicted of gnawing cardboard fortresses, and swilled his favorite English beer with impunity, and he would not have been any worse than many another czar. But to drill the guards in the Prussian manner was unforgivable. So a new palace revolution took place, and Peter was eventually murdered by one of Catherine's lovers. The Empress' own role in his overthrow is still obscure.

## Nobles and Serfs, 1730-1762

A deeply dissatisfied social group that had the power to make and unmake autocrats naturally had a program for the redress of its own grievances. Once the gentry had enabled Anne to tear up the Articles in 1730, it began strenuous efforts to emancipate itself from the servitude riveted upon it by Peter. Anne repealed the law requiring the noble to leave his estate intact to one of his sons. She founded a military school for noblemen's sons, graduation from which entitled one to a commission; no longer did young gentlemen have to start their careers in the ranks, as under Peter. Anne shortened the terms of service from life to twenty-five years, and exempted one son of every family with at least two sons, so that there would be one member of each generation to look after the estate.

Simultaneously came a deepening of the authority of the nobles over the serfs. The proprietors became the government's agents for the collection of the poll tax. Serfs could no longer obtain their freedom by enlisting in the army and could not engage in trade or purchase land without written permission from their masters. Masters could deport their serfs to Siberia and might punish them physically in any way they wished. Moreover, under Elizabeth, a series of laws restricted the right of owning serfs to those who were already nobles. Thus. the class that had been open to new recruits under Peter was closed by his daughter.

In 1762, finally, Peter III decreed that the nobles no longer need serve at all unless they wished to do so; except in the midst of a war, they might resign any time they chose. It was little wonder that some of the nobles proposed to erect a solid gold statue of Peter III. To understand the revolutionary nature of this liberation of the nobles from a duty to serve, we must remember that they had historically obtained their lands and serfs only on condition that they would serve. Now they kept their lands and serfs but had no obligations. Yet the service that had been hated when it was compulsory became fashionable now that it was optional; there was really little else for a Russian noble to do except serve the state. In contemplating all this, a great Russian historian remarked that the logic of history would have properly required that all serfs be liberated the day after the nobles were released from their duty to serve. But nothing could have been further from the thoughts of Peter III or of any other Russian leader.

In these middle decades of the eighteenth century, successive waves of foreign influence affected the Russian nobility. It was not only the influx of foreigners that brought in Western habits; it was also the involvement of Russia in the European wars of the period, and the increased travel abroad by Russians. Under Elizabeth, when the hated Germans disappeared from court, the way was clear for the French to exert their influence. With the French language came the literature, and many a Russian noble bought French books by the yard for his library because it was the thing to do. The champagne business boomed (the Russians liked the sweet kind that most Frenchmen despised); French styles of dress were copied by both men and women. Francomania took its extreme form among those Russians who were ashamed of being Russian and who would not fall in love with any girl unable to speak French. Indeed, the noble and the peasant no longer spoke the same language. This deep rift between the Frenchified nobles and the Russian people was to prove of critical importance for later Russian history.

## Catherine the Great (1762-1796)

With the advent of Catherine II, we come to the most arresting personality to occupy the Russian throne since the death of Peter. Brought up in a petty German court, she found herself transplanted to St. Petersburg as a mere girl, living with a husband she detested, and forced to pick her way through the intrigues that flourished around the empress Elizabeth. She managed to steer clear of trouble only by using her keen wits. Catherine fancied herself as an intellectual; she wrote plays, edited a satirical journal, and steeped herself in the literature of the Enlightenment. Both before and after ascending the throne she maintained a goodly supply of lovers, several of whom had important roles in affairs of state.

Catherine had a truly twentieth-century feeling for the importance of public relations, and cared deeply that leading spirits in the West should think well of her and of the state of Russia under her rule. Hence her voluminous correspondence with Westerners. She invited Diderot to take up in Russia the task of editing the *Encyclopédie;* then she bought his library, but he kept his books and received a pension—very favorable publicity for Russia and the Russian empress. Diderot himself visited Russia in 1773; though he came back entranced with Catherine, who, he said, had the soul of Brutus and the charms of Cleopatra, the visit was not entirely a success. Catherine complained that in the excitement of conversation he pinched her legs until they were black and blue. Voltaire, though he judiciously stayed away from Russia, accepted Catherine's bounty, and in return poured out the praises that she yearned for, calling her "the north star" and "the benefactress of Europe."

Catherine would perhaps have liked to reform conditions in Russia; there was something of the enlightened despot about her "style." But as a woman and a foreigner and a usurper, owing the throne to a conspiracy, she could not act upon her inclinations. Depending as she did upon the good will of the nobility, she could not lay a finger on the institution of serfdom. She had to reward her supporters with vast grants of state land, inhabited by hundreds of thousands of state peasants, who once could not be sold but now became privately owned serfs who could be sold. Even in theory, Catherine felt, Russia was so large that the only possible form of government was an autocracy. As an autocrat she was as arbitrary as any of her predecessors.

Once firmly established on the throne, however, Catherine decided to convoke a commission to codify the laws of Russia, a task that had not been accomplished since 1649. Catherine herself, with the help of advisers, spent three years composing the *Instruction* to the delegates, a long, rather windy document, full of abstract argument drawn from Montesquieu's *Spirit of the Laws* and Beccaria's *Crimes and Punishments* but altered to conform with the empress's own beliefs. Here one can discern no intention to meddle with the fundamental institutions of Russia, but some concern for eliminating their worst abuses. The 564 delegates to the commission were elected by organs of the central government and by every social class in Russia except the serf peasants. Each delegate—noble, townsman, crown peasant, Cossack—was charged to bring with him a collection of written documents from his neighbors presenting their grievances and demands for change.

Many of these survive and teach us a great deal about the state of public opinion in Catherine's Russia. Nobody seems to have been dissatisfied with the autocracy; at least we find no requests that it modify its power or consult its subjects. People did seek more rights and duties for local government and wanted their own obligations more clearly defined. Each class of representatives was eager to extend the rights of that class: The free peasants wanted to own serfs; the townsmen wanted to own serfs and be the only class allowed to engage in trade; the nobles wanted to engage in trade, and to have their exclusive right to own serfs confirmed. After 203 sessions lasting over a year and a half, devoted to inconclusive and sometimes heated debate, Catherine put an end to the labors of the commission in 1768. It had not codified the laws, but from Catherine's own point of view it had been a success; she knew that most of her subjects supported her as absolute autocrat. It is important to remember that the commission, with all its imperfections, was the last effort by the czardom to consult the Russian people as a whole for 138 years—until revolution summoned the first duma into existence in 1906.

Catherine turned the spadework of the legislative commission to good advantage in her later reforms, which resulted from the great rebellion of the Cossacks under the leadership of Pugachev, 1773–1775. Pugachev roused the frontiersmen to revolt against Catherine's cancellation of their special privileges. Pretending to be Czar Peter III, and promising liberty and land to the serfs who joined his forces, Pugachev swept over a wide area of southeastern Russia and finally marched toward Moscow. Like the disturbances of the seventeenth century, Pugachev's revolt revealed the existence of bitter discontent in Russia, a discontent directed not at the supreme autocrat but at the landlords and local officials.

The ramshackle provincial administration almost collapsed under the strain of Pugachev's rebellion. Orders filtered down slowly to local officials, and the soldiers defending the government moved almost as slowly. When the rebels were finally suppressed, and Pugachev was traveling northward in an iron cage before being drawn and quartered, Catherine took action. Her reorganization of local government (1775) created fifty provinces where there had been twenty before. She thus replaced a small number of unwieldy units with a larger number of small provinces, each containing roughly 300,000 to 400,000 inhabitants. The reform of 1775 gave the nobles the lion's share of provincial offices but subjected them to the close direction of the central government, which had its own administrative, financial, and legal representatives in each province.

In the charter of 1785 the nobles received exemption from military service and taxation and secured absolute mastery over the fate of their serfs and their estates. A charter to the towns in the same year (1785) disclosed Catherine's sympathy with the tiny but growing middle class. It established the principle of municipal self-government, but the principle remained a dead letter because of the rigorous class distinctions maintained in the backward urban centers of Russia. For the serfs, needless to say, there was no charter. Indeed, besides adding almost a million to their number by the gifts of state lands to private persons, Catherine increased still further the power of the proprietors. Long accustomed to selling the serfs without their land, the landlords now received the right to make such sales legally. Serf families were broken up, violent punishments and even torture employed (one notorious lady tortured seventy-five of her own serfs to death, but she was imprisoned for it), serfs were gambled away at cards, given as presents, and mortgaged for loans. All serfowners were not cruel any more than all slaveowners in our own slave states, but both institutions tended to degrade both master and man. As in the American South, there was a distinction in Russia between fieldhands and household servants. Great landowners often had hundreds of the latter, some of whom were formed into orchestras, gave dramatic performances, tutored the sons of the family, or acted as household poets and scientists.

The contrast between the climate of the Enlightenment which surrounded the court and the actual conditions in Russia was keenly felt by sensitive men. Foremost among them was a young noble, Alexander Radishchev, educated abroad and widely traveled. In his *Journey from St. Petersburg to Moscow,* Radishchev included vivid and horrifying vignettes of serfdom and the abuses of the administration. Moreover, Radishchev's poetry praised Cromwell, the regicide. It is possible that the author's truly Western culture might have enabled him to get away with this in the early days of Catherine's reign. But by 1790 the French Revolution was under way, and Catherine had begun to hate the French and "their abominable bonfire" as much as she had formerly loved them. Proposing to burn the dangerous books of the Enlightenment, she could hardly overlook the subversive character of Radishchev's writings. Off he went into exile in Siberia. Similarly, the humanitarian Freemason Nicholas Novikov, manager of the newly active Moscow University Press, editor of newspapers, and sponsor of campaigns to raise money and food for famine-stricken peasants, was also jailed on flimsy charges. Though Novikov had done nothing against the regime, it could not tolerate the continuance of any enterprise it did not dominate. The two enlightened intellectuals, Radishchev and Novikov, not only serve as an illustration of the contrast between Catherine's professed principles and her actual conduct but also provide the first real examples of thoroughly westernized individual Russians.

### Paul (1796-1801)

Catherine's son Paul (who may or may not have been the son of Catherine's husband, Peter III) succeeded her in 1796 as a man of forty-two. All his life his mother had distrusted him, fearing that there might be a conspiracy to oust her and install Paul, ostensibly a legitimate Romanov. The best-educated Russian royal personage to date, active and eager to serve the state, Paul found himself given no duties, kept in the dark about the secrets of state, and even deprived of his two eldest children, Alexander and Constantine, whom Catherine insisted on educating herself.

Consequently, when Paul finally did succeed to the throne, he appeared to be motivated chiefly by a wish to undo his mother's work and act in every possible way contrary to the precedents she had set. He exiled some of Catherine's favorites, and released many of her prisoners, including Radishchev and Novikov. Paul believed in legality and system, and hoped to install a great deal more of both in Russia. He tried to restore more power and order to the central administration by putting the colleges under single ministers in place of the former boards of directors. Paul's behavior, however, was spasmodic and eccentric. He forbade the importation of sheetmusic because he feared that all music would be as revolutionary as the *Marseillaise*. He imposed a strict curfew on the capital. He issued a manifesto limiting to three the number of days per week a serf might be required to work on his master's land, but it is not clear whether this was a binding law or only a recommendation. In any case, he continued to give away state lands, and transformed some half a million state peasants into privately owned chattels.

What was probably fatal to Paul was his policy of toughness toward the nobility. A noble, he is said to have remarked, is the man I am talking to at the moment, and he ceases to be a noble when I stop talking to him. This definition could hardly be expected to appeal to the privileged masters of Russia. Paul exacted compulsory service again, and in the provinces he curtailed the powers of the nobility. Nobles found themselves forced to meet the bills for public buildings, paying new taxes on their lands, and subjected to corporal punishments for crimes. Paul, like Peter III, wanted to prussianize the army, and especially to inculcate in the officers a sense of responsibility for the men. In the guards' regiments such programs were detested, and a conspiracy of guardsmen ended in 1801 with Paul's murder and Alexander's succession. The forces behind the coup were the same as those that had engineered so many shifts of power during the preceding century. The precise degree to which Alexander was informed of the coup in advance is sometimes debated, but he knew at least that the conspirators intended to force his father's abdication.

### Alexander I (1801-1825)

In Alexander I there came to the throne an emperor whom historians usually call enigmatic. Educated by a liberal Swiss tutor, he absorbed so much of the new eighteenth-century doctrines that he actually blossomed out with a red-white-and-blue ribbon, the colors of revolutionary France, on hearing of the fall of the Bastille to the Paris mob. Yet the application of liberal principles in Russia would involve a direct challenge to the most powerful forces in society. So, although Alexander would occasionally say to his intimates that some day he would grant Russia a constitution and himself retire to a castle on the Rhine, in fact this was little but romantic twaddle. Tall and handsome, utterly devastating to the ladies, charming and cultivated, Alexander liked to please everybody; he vacillated, compromised, and in the end accomplished very little. Moreover, he loved power dearly, and always shied away from proposals to limit it.

The quarter-century of his reign was twice interrupted by major wars against Napoleon, in 1805–1807 and in 1812–1815. In the first period of relative peace, 1801–1805, Alexander gathered round him a small group of young men which he called "the unofficial committee." One of the members, Stroganov, had been an active member of the Jacobin Club in Paris during the revolution; two others greatly admired the English system of government. Meeting regularly after dinner over coffee and brandy, the unofficial committee had as its self-appointed task the preparation of a constitution for Russia, after due study of all known constitutions. But its discussions were little more than the unsystematic talk of pleasant, well-born young men who had dined well. A decree sponsored by the committee did abolish the administrative colleges and created eight new ministries to take their place; but this in fact had largely been accomplished by Paul. When the committee stopped meeting in 1803, it had done nothing with regard to serfdom. The czar himself in these years passed two laws, whose very mildness shows how little he intended to disturb existing institutions. One of them forbade the public advertisement of sales of serfs without land, but the law was easily circumvented. The other created a new category of "free farmers," serfs who had been freed by their masters, and prescribed that if a proprietor freed an entire village of serfs he must confer their land upon them at the same time. Since this left the initiative for liberation entirely in the hands of the proprietor, fewer than 40,000 among all the millions of serfs in Russia actually received their freedom.

In the second period of peace, 1807–1811, Alexander had as his chief mentor a remarkable figure, Michael Speransky, son of a Russian priest, intelligent, well educated, and conscientious. Utilizing Montesquieu's principle of the separation of powers, Speransky drafted for Alexander a constitutional project that would have made Russia a limited monarchy. A series of elected assemblies, beginning at the lowest level of administrative subdivision and continuing on up through district and province, would culminate in a great national assembly, the duma. A similar pyramid of courts and a new set of executive institutions were also planned. The duma would have to approve any law promulgated by the czar and would have been a genuine Russian parliament. It is true that the franchise Speransky proposed would have enormously favored the nobility, while the serfs of course would not have participated in government. It is also true that Speransky did not include emancipation of the serfs in his proposal. None the less, the plan was decidedly advanced; Speransky knew that not everything could be accomplished at once. Indeed, as it turned out, Alexander balked at executing the plan that he himself had commissioned Speransky to draw up.

This is one of the most critical moments in all Russian history. Why did Speransky fail? He instituted a reform of the civil service, requiring examinations and a system of promotion by merit, which disturbed many of the almost illiterate and thoroughly incompetent men in high office. He even proposed that the nobility pay an income tax. Friends and intimates of the czar spread slander about Speransky, but at bottom Alexander himself was at fault and unwilling to act on his own alleged beliefs. Speransky's scheme was shelved, except for two elements that in no way diminished the power of the czar. A Council of State, which could advise the czar, was created, but he was not obliged to take its advice. Since he appointed and dismissed all members, the effect was simply to increase imperial efficiency, not to limit imperial authority. Further administrative efficiency was obtained through the reorganization of the ministries, whose duties were set out clearly for the first time, eliminating overlapping.

During the second war against Napoleon (1812–1815) Alexander fell under the influence of a Baltic baroness named Madame de Krüdener, a mystical lady now repenting an ill-spent youth. She convinced the czar that he was a "man from the North" designed by destiny to overthrow Napoleon and institute a new order. At the Russian court an atmosphere of pious mysticism and conservatism replaced the earlier flashes of liberal views. Although the leading spirits of the new religiosity were all nominally Orthodox, its character was rather Protestant. It was based upon assiduous reading of the Bible, and it also included a mixture of elements from Freemasonry, Pietism, and the more eccentric Russian sects. It aimed at the union of all Christendom in one faith and thus aroused the fear and opposition of many Orthodox clerics. Its real importance lay in its impact on Alexander, who was now convinced that as the bearer of a sacred mission all he needed to do was follow the promptings of his inmost feelings.

During the last decade of Alexander's reign, 1815–1825, the most important figure at court was Count Arakcheev, a competent but brutal officer, who once bit off the ear of one of his men as a punishment. The chief innovation of the decade, accomplished under Arakcheev's direction, was the hated system of "military colonies," the drafting of the population of whole districts to serve in the regiments quartered there. When not drilling or fighting, the soldiers were to work their farms, and their entire lives were subject to the whims of their officers. Far from being model communities, the military colonies were virtual concentration camps. By the end of Alexander's reign, almost 400,000 soldiers were living in them.

Though Alexander gave Russia no important reforms, he did act on liberal principles outside Russia, in Poland and in Finland. Made king of Poland by the Vienna settlement of 1815, Alexander gave the Poles an advanced constitution, with their own army, their own Polish officialdom, and the free use of their own language. He allowed the Finns, after their annexation by Russia in 1809, to preserve their own law codes and the system of local government introduced during the long preceding Swedish rule. But the "liberal czar" was liberal only outside his Russian dominions.

### Russian Foreign Policy, 1725–1796

The motives of Russian foreign policy in the century between the death of Peter the Great and that of Alexander I were still the ancient ones of expansion against Sweden, Poland, and Turkey. But as a new member of the European power constellation, Russia found that pursuit of these old aims was now involving her in matters that had primary significance for western Europe. In 1726 Ostermann concluded an alliance with the Hapsburg Empire which was to be a cornerstone of Russian foreign policy. Yet, especially in joint undertakings against the Turks, the Russians and Austrians found, as early as the 1730's, that they had conflicting ambitions in southeast Europe. This early conflict of interests was a cloud, still no larger than a man's hand, but destined to swell into the colossal thunderhead that exploded in the World War of 1914–1918. To the eighteenth century also belong the first regular Russian diplomatic service, the first Russian participation in international espionage and intrigue, and the first real Russian foreign ministers: Ostermann and his Russian successor Bestuzhev-Ryumin, men of enormous personal influence on the course of Russian diplomacy.

In the War of the Polish Succession (1733–1735) Russian forces took part in alliance with Austria in supporting Augustus III and helped to force the abdication of Stanislas Leszczyński. Immediately, the Russians and Austrians became allies in a new war against the Turks, 1735–1739. Though the Russians successfully invaded the Crimea, their gains at the Treaty of Belgrade in 1739 were limited to Azov. The Austrians failed to cooperate satisfactorily in an invasion of the Danubian principalities and made it clear that they did not relish a Russian advance into the principalities and thus to the Hapsburg frontiers.

At the opening of the War of the Austrian Succession in 1740, the Russians were preoccupied with the dynastic problem. We have already seen how the French ambassador worked to put Elizabeth on the throne and to bring about the downfall of the pro-Austrian Ostermann. But, since Bestuzhev-Ryumin continued Ostermann's policies, French hopes were largely disappointed. Prussian (and therefore anti-Austrian) influence manifested itself with the appearance of Peter III as heir, and with the choice of the future Catherine II as his bride. Thus, during the War of the Austrian Succession, there was a good deal of jockeying for Russian assistance. The advance of Frederick the Great along the Baltic shore alarmed the Russians, and so, as the war ended, a Russian corps was leisurely pushing westward, intending to join the fighting.

Anti-Prussian sentiment crystallized during the interval of peace before the outbreak of the Seven Years' War. Bestuzhev labored mightily to obtain an alliance with England, which he managed in 1755, the Russians accepting a large subsidy in exchange for a promise to keep troops in readiness against the Prussians. But the Diplomatic Revolution of 1756, making Prussia and England allies, negated this arrangement. The Russians thus remained loyal to Austria and fought the Prussians in the Seven Years' War. Once more Russian forces marched west, so slowly that there was suspicion of treason and the commander was removed. In 1758 the invasion of East Prussia began; and eventually in 1760 Russian forces entered Berlin. Elizabeth's death and the succession of the pro-Prussian Peter III led the Russians to change sides and join the Prussians briefly against the Austrians and French. Catherine, on her succession, withdrew the Russian forces, but did not again attack the Prussians. Thus Russia found herself excluded from the peace conferences that took place in 1763.

In foreign policy, Catherine the Great was as vigorous and unscrupulous as she was at home. She concentrated on the traditional anti-Polish and anti-Turkish aims of Russia. In 1763, only a year after she became empress, the throne of Poland fell vacant, and Catherine secured the election of her former lover, a pro-Russian Pole, Stanislas Poniatowski. Frederick the Great joined with Catherine in a campaign to win rights for the persecuted Lutheran and Orthodox minorities in Catholic Poland. One party of Polish nobles, their national pride offended at foreign intervention, resisted, and secured the aid of France and Austria, which adopted the stratagem of pressing Turkey into war with Russia to distract Catherine from Poland.

In the first Russo-Turkish War (1768–1774), Catherine's forces won a series of victories. A Russian Baltic fleet, sent all the way around Europe and into the Mediterranean through the Straits of Gibraltar, destroyed the Turkish fleet in the Aegean (1770), largely owing to the superior seamanship of a few English officers who were advising the Russians. But the Russians failed to follow up their initial advantage by storming the Straits and attacking Istanbul, and operations shifted to the Crimea and the Danubian principalities. While the Russians and Turks were discussing peace terms, Frederick the Great had concluded that Russia had been too successful against the Turks and might seize most of Poland for herself unless he acted quickly.

So Frederick took the leading part in arranging the first partition of Poland (1772). Poland lost to Russia, Prussia, and Austria almost one-third of her territory and one-half of her population. Frederick's share of the loot—the lands immediately to the west of East Prussia—was the smallest but included the strategic region that had previously separated Brandenburg from East Prussia. Maria Theresa, the empress of Austria, abandoned her Turkish and Polish allies to participate. She did seem somewhat reluctant, yet, as Frederick the Great observed, "She wept, but she kept on taking." Russia received a substantial area of what is now known as Belorussia, or White Russia.

Two years later, the Russians imposed upon the Turks a most humiliating peace treaty, at Kutchuk Kainardji (1774). Catherine annexed much of the formerly Turkish stretch of Black Sea coast and two places in the Crimea; the rest of the Crimea was separated from the Ottoman Empire as an independent Tatar state. She also obtained something the Russians had long coveted: freedom of navigation on the Black Sea and the right of passage through the Bosporus and the Dardanelles. A vaguely worded clause gave her various rights to protect the Christian subjects of the sultan, thus providing a convenient excuse for Russian intervention in Turkish affairs later on.

Catherine now began to dream of expelling the Turks from Europe and reviving the Byzantine Empire under Russian protection. She saw to it that her younger grandson was christened Constantine and imported Greek-speaking nurses to train him in the language. She also proposed to set up a kingdom of Dacia (the Roman name for the area) in the Danubian principalities to be ruled by her lover and general, Potemkin. By way of preparation, in 1783, Catherine annexed the Tatar state of the Crimea, where she built a naval base at Sebastopol. To achieve these grandiose designs, Catherine sought the consent of Austria and invited Joseph II on a famous tour by riverboat of the newly developed and annexed territories of the Russian southwest. On this tour, the Austrian emperor was allegedly shown the famous "Potemkin villages," mere cardboard façades facing the river to look like settlements but with nothing behind them; like so many other good stories, this one is untrue. At Sebastopol, however, signs pointed across the Black Sea, saying "This way to Byzantium." In the second Russo-Turkish war (1787–

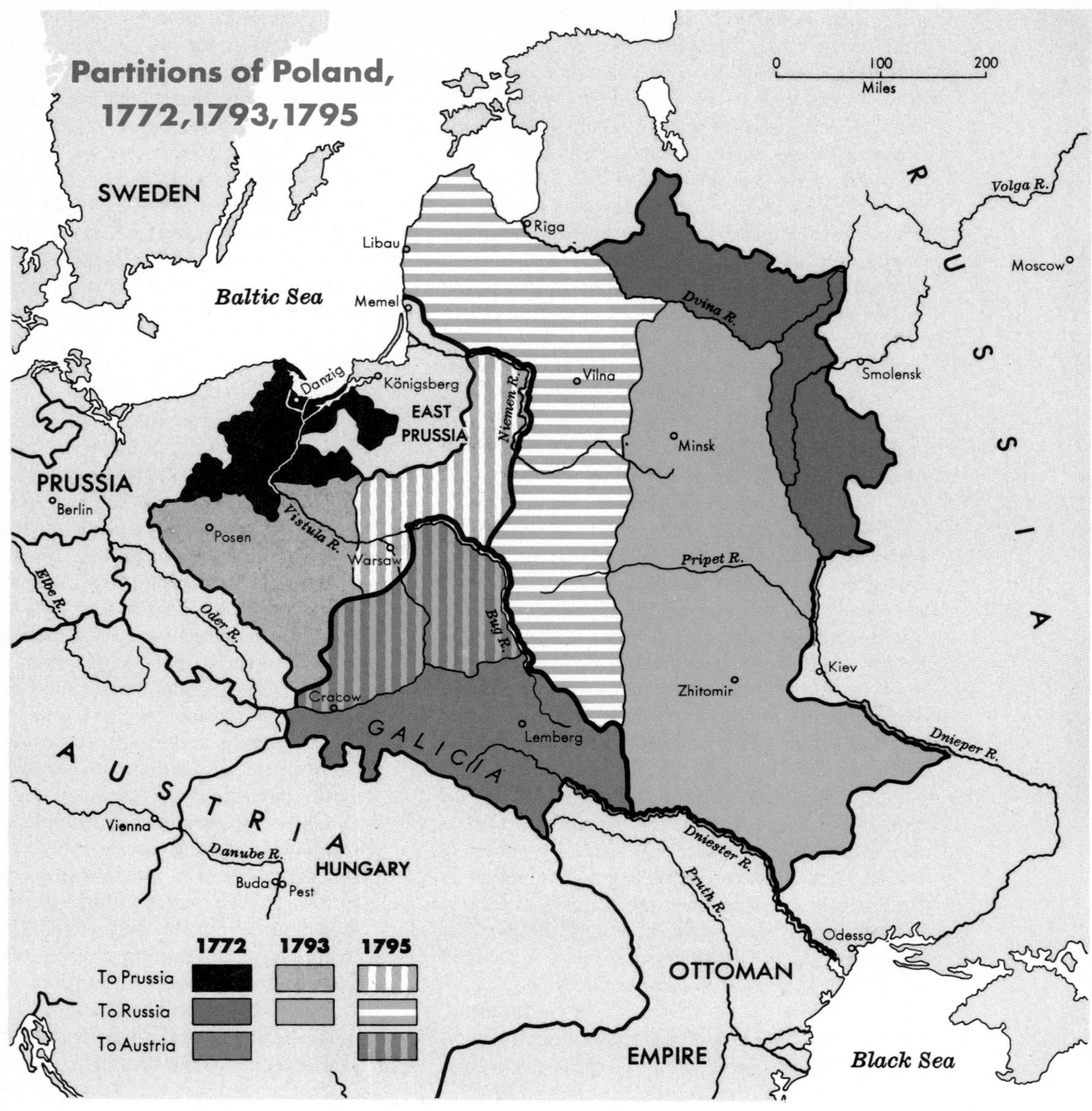


1791), Catherine's allies, the Austrians, once again provided feeble assistance and made a separate peace. Again, a conflict of interests over the European lands of the sultan precipitated Austro-Russian disagreement. In the end, Catherine had to abandon her Greek project and content herself with annexing the remaining Turkish lands along the northern coast of the Black Sea and securing recognition of Russian sovereignty over the Crimea.

Before her death, Catherine participated in two more partitions of Poland. The second partition came as the result of a Polish constitutional movement, supported by the Prussians in opposition to Russian interest. Catherine intervened on the pretext of defending the established order in Poland and fighting the virus of revolution. In 1793, both the Russians and Prussians took large new slices of Polish territory; the Austrians did not participate in this second partition of Poland.

An attempted Polish revolution against the reduction of their state to a wretched remnant dominated by foreigners was followed by the third and final partition of 1795, by which Poland disappeared from the map. This time Austria joined the other two powers and obtained Cracow; Prussia got Warsaw, and Russia secured Lithuania and other Baltic and east Polish lands.

The spectacular successes of Catherine meant the transfer to Russia of millions of human beings—Poles, Lithuanians, Belorussians—who loathed the Russians, and left a legacy of trouble. It also meant that Russia had destroyed useful buffers in the shape of the Polish and Tatar states, and now had common frontiers with her potential enemies, Prussia and Austria. The last two partitions of Poland had been made possible by the preoccupation of the Western powers with their war against revolutionary France; the story of Russian foreign policy after Catherine the Great forms part of the larger story of this great war.

## V George III and American Independence

### George III

Though Catherine the Great failed to apply the ideas of the Age of Reason, her name usually appears on lists of enlightened despots. Another name might possibly be added to the list—George III, king of Great Britain (1760–1820). "Farmer George" showed very little personal enlightenment beyond taking an interest in the agrarian revolution and writing articles on turnips for Arthur Young's *Annals of Agriculture*. In politics, however, he did attempt a course that may be termed a dilute form of enlightened despotism, or, more exactly, a reassertion of the monarch's authority. The first of the Hanoverian monarchs born and bred in England, George III proposed to reassert some of the royal prerogatives that had lapsed under the first two Georges. He tried to wrest control of the House of Commons from the long-dominant Whig oligarchy and retain it by the Whig devices of patronage and bribery. He endeavored to beat the Whigs at their own parliamentary game.

Virtuous as a person and devoted to his family, George as a monarch was stubborn, shortsighted, and in the long run unsuccessful. It was easy for him at first to exploit the factional strife among the Whigs, maneuver Pitt out of office in 1761, and make his friend and tutor, Lord Bute, the head of the cabinet. Bute and the king, however, found it hard to justify their failure to deprive France of the sugar-rich West Indies in the Peace of Paris, which brought the Seven Years' War to a conclusion. The Commons ratified the treaty, but George dismissed Bute to appease the critics of British diplomacy.

The harshest criticism came from John Wilkes, a member of Commons, who dubbed the Peace of Paris "the peace of God, for it passeth all understanding." Wilkes' attack on the treaty in his paper, the *North Briton*, infuriated the king; bowing to the royal anger, the Commons ordered the offending issue of the *North Briton* to be burnt. Later, Wilkes ran for Parliament three separate times, and three times the Commons, under royal pressure, threw out his election. When Wilkes finally took his seat again in 1774, he was a popular hero, and riots had occurred in defense of "Wilkes and Liberty." A wise king would have reconsidered his course, but George III did not relax his determination to manage both Parliament and cabinet. After seven years of short-lived, unstable ministries (1763–1770), George finally found a man to fill Bute's old role and do the king's bidding—Lord North, who headed the cabinet for a dozen years (1770–1782). Under North, royal intervention in politics at first stiffened, then wavered, and at length collapsed in the face of the revolt by the thirteen North American colonies.

### Background of the Revolt

The breach between colonies and mother country first became serious at the close of the Seven Years' War when Britain began to retreat from the old policy of "salutary neglect" and to interfere more directly and more frequently in colonial matters. But, by 1763, the colonies had acquired the habit of regulating their own affairs, though the acts of their assemblies remained subject to the veto of royally appointed governors or of the king himself. The vast territories in Canada and west of the Allegheny Mountains acquired in 1763 brought Britain added opportunities for profitable exploitation and added responsibilities for government and defense. When an uprising of Indians under Pontiac threatened frontier posts in the area of the Ohio Valley and the Great Lakes, colonial militias failed to take effective action, and British regulars were brought in. The continuing threat from the Indians prompted the royal proclamation of October 1763, forbidding "all our loving subjects" to settle west of a line running along the summit of the Alleghenies. To His Majesty's "loving subjects" in the seaboard colonies, however, the proclamation seemed deliberately designed to exclude them from the riches of the West.

The colonies resented still more keenly the attempt by Parliament to raise more revenue in North America. The British government had very strong arguments for increasing colonial taxes. The national debt had almost doubled during the Seven Years' War; the colonies' reluctance to recruit soldiers and raise taxes themselves had increased the cost of the war to British taxpayers; now the mother country faced continued expense in protecting the frontier. Surely the Americans would admit the reasonableness of the case for higher taxes.

That, however, was precisely what the Americans did *not* admit. The first of the new revenue measures, the Sugar Act of 1764, alarmed the merchants of the eastern seaboard because the customs officers actually undertook to collect duties on molasses, sugar, and other imports. Here was a departure from the comfortable laxity of salutary neglect. And here was a threat to the colonial economy, for the import duties had to be paid out of the colonies' meager supply of specie (metal coin). The second revenue measure, the Stamp Act of 1765, imposed levies on a wide variety of items, including legal and commercial papers, liquor licenses, playing cards, dice, newspapers, calendars, and academic degrees. These duties, too, drained the supply of specie, which sank so low that some merchants faced bankruptcy.

The revenue measures touched off a major controversy. Indignant merchants in the New World boycotted all imports rather than pay the duties, and in October 1765 delegates from nine of the thirteen colonies met in New York City as the Stamp Act Congress. The Congress complained that the new duties had "a manifest tendency to subvert the rights and liberties of the colonists."

That His Majesty's liege subjects in these colonies are entitled to all the inherent rights and liberties of his natural born subjects within the kingdom of Great Britain.

That it is inseparably essential to the freedom of a people, and the undoubted right of Englishmen, that no taxes be imposed on them but with their own consent, given personally or by their own representatives.

That the people of these colonies are not, and from their local circumstances cannot be, represented in the House of Commons in Great Britain.

That the only representatives of these colonies are persons chosen therein by themselves, and that no taxes ever have been, or can be constitutionally imposed on them, but by their respective legislatures.*

The Stamp Act Congress thus proclaimed the celebrated principle of no taxation without representation. Britain surrendered on the practical issue, but did not yield on the principle. The appeals of London merchants, nearly ruined by the American boycott against British goods, brought the repeal of the Stamp Act in 1765. In 1766, however, Parliament passed the Declaratory Act asserting that the king and Parliament could indeed make laws affecting the colonies.

For the next decade, Britain adhered firmly to the principles of the Declaratory Act, and colonial radicals just as firmly repeated their opposition to taxation without representation. Parliament again tried to raise revenue, this time by the Townshend duties (1767) on colonial imports of tea, paper, paint, and lead. Again the merchants of Philadelphia, New York, and Boston organized boycotts. In 1770, Lord North's cabinet withdrew the Townshend duties except for the three-penny tariff on a pound of tea, retained as a symbol of parliamentary authority over the colonies. Three years later, the English East India Company attempted the sale of surplus tea in North America, hoping to overcome

* *Documents of American History,* ed. H. S. Commager (New York, 1940), p. 58.

American opposition to the hated duty by making the retail price of East India tea, duty included, far cheaper than that of Dutch tea smuggled by the colonists. The result was the Boston Tea Party. On December 16, 1773, to the cheers of spectators lining the waterfront, a group of Bostonians who had a large financial stake in smuggled tea disguised themselves as Indians, boarded three East India ships, and dumped into the harbor chests of tea worth thousands of pounds.

Britain answered defiance with coercion, and the colonists met coercion with resistance. The Quebec Act (1774), incorporating the lands beyond the Alleghenies into Canada, bolted the door to the westward expansion of colonial frontiers. The "Intolerable Acts" (1774) closed the port of Boston to trade and suspended elections in Massachusets. At Lexington and Concord in April 1775, the "embattled farmers" of Massachusetts fired the opening shots of the War of Independence. At Philadelphia on July 4, 1776, the delegates to the Continental Congress formally declared the American colonies independent of Great Britain.

### Implications of the Revolution

For the mother country, the American Revolution implied more than the secession of thirteen colonies. It involved Britain in a minor world war that jeopardized her dominance abroad and weakened the power and prestige of King George III at home. The most crucial battle in North America came early in the war—the surrender at Saratoga in 1777 of the British forces under Burgoyne, who had been marching south from Montreal with the aim of driving a wedge between New England and the other rebellious colonies. Burgoyne's surrender convinced the French that support of the American colonists would give them an excellent chance to renew their worldwide struggle with Britain and avenge the humiliation of 1763. Entering the war in 1778, France soon gained the alliance of Spain and eventually secured the help, or at least the friendly neutrality, of most other European states. French intervention prepared the way for the victory of George Washington's forces and the final British surrender at Yorktown in 1781. In the peace signed at Paris in 1783, Britain recognized the independence of her former colonies. To Spain she handed back Florida, which she had taken in 1763, and the strategic Mediterranean island of Minorca. But she kept Gibraltar, which the Spanish had also hoped to recover, and she ceded only minor territories to France.

During the early years of the war, the British public had been inclined to agree with Dr. Samuel Johnson that the Americans were "a race of convicts" and "ought to be thankful for anything we allow them short of hanging." But the temper of opinion changed as the strength of American resistance became evident, as instances of British mismanagement piled up, and as most of Europe rallied to the rebellious colonies. By 1780, George III and his policies were so unpopular that the House of Commons passed a resolution declaring that "the influence of the crown has increased, is increasing, and ought to be diminished."

The influence of the Crown *was* diminished. In 1782, Lord North, who had been imploring the king for three years to accept his resignation, finally stepped down. In the next year, the post of prime minister fell to William Pitt the Younger, son of the heroic Pitt of the Seven Years' War. Though only twenty-five years old, he was a seasoned parliamentarian who was to head the cabinet for the next eighteen years. With the advent of Pitt, control of British politics shifted away from the king and back to the professional politicians. George III briefly contemplated abdication and then gradually resigned himself to the passive role of constitutional monarch. The British flirtation (it was really no more than that) with enlightened despotism had come to an end.

While American independence was a nationalist rather than a social revolution, the movement that produced it did have social implications. In the colonies, opinion was by no means unanimous in support of the revolution. Many well-to-do colonists, including southern planters and Pennsylvania Quakers, either backed the mother country or took a neutral position in the struggle; New York supplied more recruits to George III than to George Washington. Some of these "Loyalists" or "Tories" were to flee to Canada when independence became a fact. Scholars, however, now find that the traditional estimate—that only one-third of the colonists actively backed the Revolution—is too low. Revolutionary sentiment ran particularly high in Virginia and New England and among social groups who had the habit of questioning established authority—the pioneers living on the frontier, and the numerous Presbyterians, Congregationalists, and members of other strongminded Protestant sects. Like adolescents everywhere, the colonists resented parental tutelage yet appealed to family precedent. They claimed that they were only following the example set by Englishmen in 1688 and defended by John Locke.

The ideas of Locke and Newton were as well known and as much respected in North America as they were in Europe. They underlay the Declaration of Independence:

> When in the course of human events, it becomes necessary for one people to dissolve the political bands which have connected them with another, and to assume among the Powers of the earth, the separate and equal station to which the Laws of Nature and of Nature's God entitle them, a decent respect to the opinions of mankind requires that they should declare the causes which impel them to the separation.

The opening paragraph of the Declaration thus expressed the concept of a world-machine ruled by the Laws of Nature. The next paragraph applied to the colonies Locke's theory of contract and his justification of revolution:

> We hold these truths to be self-evident, that all men are created equal, that they are endowed by their Creator with certain unalienable Rights, that among these are Life, Liberty and the pursuit of Happiness. That to secure these rights, Governments are instituted among Men, deriving their just power from the consent of the governed. That whenever any Form of Government becomes destructive of these ends, it is the Right of the People to alter or to abolish it, and to institute new Government. . . .

Another political idea of the Enlightenment congenial to the revolutionaries was the separation of powers proposed by Locke and by Montesquieu as a guarantee against tyranny. At the heart of the draft drawn up by the delegates to the constitutional convention at Philadelphia in 1787 was the separation of the executive, legislative, and judicial arms of government. Each of the branches had the power to check the other two. The president, for instance, could check the Congress by applying a veto; Congress could check the executive and the judiciary through impeachment and the right of confirming appointments; and one house of Congress exercised a check on the other since the consent of both houses was required for legislation. Since these balancing devices were in part derived from Montesquieu, it may be argued that the recurrent tensions between president and Congress originated in the American adaptation of an eighteenth-century French misreading of British constitutional practice. The Founding Fathers of the American republic sought guidance not only from *The Spirit of the Laws* but also from the constitutions of the thirteen original states and from English precedents. The first ten amendments to the United States Constitution (1791), guaranteeing freedom of religion, freedom of the press, and other basic liberties, were taken mainly from the English Bill of Rights of 1689.

The Constitution abounded in compromises. It attempted a balance between states' rights and the central power of the federal government, and between the democratic principle of a directly elected House of Representatives and the aristocratic principle of an indirectly elected and conservative Senate. (Senators were chosen by state governments until 1913, when the Seventeenth Amendment provided for their direct election.) It was a compromise designed to win support from both rich and poor and from both the Tory opponents and the democratic supporters of the recent revolution. Like any compromise, it did not at first please all parties. Its democracy was watered down by legal existence of slavery in many states and by the fact that the states themselves determined requirements for voting, with a majority imposing significant property qualifications for the suffrage which were not lifted for a generation or more.

Yet the constitution worked well enough to make the new American republic a going concern and to arouse enthusiastic approval and envy among liberals in Europe and in the colonial society of Latin America. The Founding Fathers of the United States had succeeded perhaps better than any other statesmen of the eighteenth century in adjusting the ideals of the philosophes to the realities of practical politics.

## VI Challenges to the Enlightenment

### The Limitations of Reason

The Enlightenment, however, seldom produced such happy political results as it did in the United States. On the whole, the philosophes expected men to see reason when it was pointed out to them, to abandon the habits of centuries, and to revise their behavior in accordance with natural law. But men would not always see reason; as Joseph II discovered to his sorrow, they *would* cling perversely to irrational customs and unnatural traditions. The rationalism of the Enlightenment tended to omit from its calculations the complexities of human nature.

Responsibility for this major shortcoming lay partly with the classical spirit of the seventeenth century, inherited by the Enlightenment of the eighteenth. The writers of the Age of Louis XIV had found in their classical models, not a confirmation of existing standards, but a better, simpler set of standards that the eighteenth-century philosophes easily adapted to the concept of "nature's simple plan." The great writers achieve the miracle of giving life to these abstractions. But the lesser ones make only bloodless types, and encourage in their hearers and readers —the men and women who finally do work out social change—the belief that these easy mental images are somehow more real, and certainly more desirable, than the bewildering complexity of their concrete experiences. Like the classical spirit, the spirit of natural science went too far when it was applied uncritically to problems of human relations. It gave men the illusion that what was going on in their minds would shortly go on in reality.

A minor philosophe, the Abbé Mably, got at this central problem when he asked: "Is society, then, a branch of physics?" Most of the philosophes and their followers believed that it was. They applied to the unpredictable activities of man the mathematical methods used in the physical sciences. The Physiocrats, for example, tried to reduce the complexities of human economic activities to a few simple agricultural laws. Like the stars in their courses, men were thought to fit neatly into the Newtonian world-machine.

A few eighteenth-century minds disagreed. David Hume (1711–1776), the skeptical Scottish philosopher, insisted on submitting principles to the test of factual observation. The philosophes, he said, failed to do this and thus deduced untested conclusions from two great abstract principles—faith in natural law, belief in reason. Hume made short work of the philosophes' appeals to nature. The laws of justice, he argued, were not absolute and inflexible natural laws:

> Suppose a society to fall into such want of all common necessaries, that the utmost frugality and industry cannot preserve the greater number from perishing, and the whole from extreme misery; it will readily, I believe, be admitted, that the strict laws of justice are suspended, in such a pressing emergence, and give place to the stronger motives of necessity and self-preservation. Is it any crime, after a shipwreck, to seize whatever means or instrument of safety one can lay hold of, without regard to former limitations of property?

Nor, Hume argued, could human conduct be analyzed "in the same manner that we discover by reason the truths of geometry or algebra."

> It appears evident that the ultimate ends of human actions can never, in any case, be accounted for by *reason,* but recommend themselves entirely to the sentiments and affections of mankind, without any dependance on the intellectual faculties. Ask a man *why he uses exercise:* he will answer, *because he desires to keep his health,* If you then enquire, *why he desires health,* he will readily reply, *because sickness is painful.* If you push your enquiries farther, and desire a reason *why he hates pain,* it is impossible he can ever give any. . . .*

David Hume was among the first and most profound critics of the Age of Reason. The Ro-

* *An Enquiry Concerning the Principles of Morals,* ed. L. A. Selby-Bigge (Oxford, 1902), pp. 186, 293.

mantics of the next generation would repeat his warnings against reason and his pleas on behalf of the "sentiments and affections of mankind." In Hume's own day, Rousseau and Kant were also worried by rather similar problems. Rousseau both represented the Enlightenment and foreshadowed the revolt against it. No philosophe defended natural law more ardently, yet no Romantic argued more powerfully on behalf of the irrational faculties of man. "Too often does reason deceive us," Rousseau wrote in *Emile*. "We have only too good a right to doubt her; but conscience never deceives us; she is the true guide of man; . . . he who obeys his conscience is following nature and he need not fear that he will go astray."*

Immanuel Kant (1724–1804), who taught philosophy at the University of Königsberg in East Prussia, raised Rousseau's argument to the level of metaphysics. While advocating many of the doctrines of the Enlightenment, Kant also believed in a higher reality reaching ultimately to God. He called the eternal verities of the higher world *noumena,* in contrast to the phenomena of the material world. Knowledge of the noumenal realm, Kant believed, reached men through reason—reason, however, not as the Enlightenment used the term, not as common sense, but as intuition. The highest expression of the Kantian reason was the *categorical imperative*. This was the moral law within, the conscience implanted in man by God. It was the inescapable realization by the individual that, when confronted with an ethical choice, he must choose the good and avoid the evil, must follow the course that he would want to have become a universal precedent, not simply the most expedient solution to his own dilemma. Kant's redefinition of reason and his rehabilitation of conscience exemplified the philosophical reaction against the dominant rationalism of the Enlightenment. The popular reaction came in the challenge to enlightened assumptions from the evangelical revival.

### The Evangelical Revival

The evangelical revival began with the German Pietists, who were the spiritual heirs of the sixteenth-century Anabaptists and found a congenial academic base at the University of Halle. Deploring alike the growing Lutheran concern with the formalities of religion and the deists' emphasis on natural law, the Pietists asserted that religion came from the heart, not the head. For the Pietists God was far more than the watchmaker, the remote creator of the world-machine. One of the chief leaders of Pietism was a German nobleman, Count Zinzendorf (1700–1760), founder of the Moravian Brethren, who set up a model community based on Christian principles. Moravian emigrants to America planned a colony at Bethlehem, Pennsylvania, helping to give the "Pennsylvania Dutch" their reputation for thrift, hard work, and strict living. In England, meanwhile, the example of Zinzendorf and other Pietists inspired Wesley.

Ordained a priest of the Church of England, John Wesley (1703–1791) at first stressed the ritualistic aspects of religion. But after the failure of his two-year ministry to the backward colony of Georgia (1736–1737), he felt his own faith evaporating: "I went to America, to convert the Indians: but Oh! who shall convert me! Who, what is he that will deliver me from this evil heart of unbelief?" * Pietism converted Wesley and taught him that he would find faith through inner conviction. For more than fifty years, Wesley labored tirelessly to share his discovery, traveling throughout the British Isles, and preaching in churches, in the fields, at the pitheads of coal mines, and even in jails. Angry crowds came to scoff but remained to pray. When Wesley died in 1791, his movement had already attracted more than a hundred thousand adherents. They were called Methodists, because of their methodical devotion to piety and to plain dressing and plain living. Though Wesley always considered himself a good Anglican, the Methodists eventually set up a separate organization—their nonconformist "Chapel" in contrast to the established Church of England. The new sect won its following almost entirely among the lower and middle classes, among people who sought the religious excitement and consolation that they did not find in deism or in the austere formalism of the Church of England.

Although the beliefs of the Methodists diverged entirely from those of the enlightened rationalists, both groups worked in their different

* Everyman ed. (New York, 1911), pp. 249–250.

* *Journal,* Everyman ed. (New York, 1907), I, 74.

*John Wesley in 1788.*

ways to improve the condition of society. Where the philosophes advised public reform, the Methodists favored private charity; and where the philosophes attacked the *causes* of social evils, the Methodists accepted these evils as part of God's plan and sought to mitigate their *symptoms*. They had in full measure the Puritan conscience of the nonconformists. They began agitation against drunkenness, the trade in slaves, and the barbarous treatment of prisoners, the insane, and the sick. John Wesley established schools for coalminers' children and opened dispensaries for the poor in London and Bristol. The Methodists' success derived in part from their social activities; it also came from the magnetism of John Wesley and his talented associates. His brother Charles composed more than 6,500 hymns, and in America Methodist missionaries flourished under the dynamic leadership of Francis Asbury (1745–1816). The number of colleges called Wesleyan and the number of churches and streets called Asbury testify to the significance of Methodism in American social history.

### Literature

The middle-class public so strongly attracted to Methodism welcomed the novels of the Englishman Samuel Richardson (1689–1761), who made a significant contribution to this emerging literary form. A printer by trade, Richardson turned to writing late in life and produced three gigantic novels in the form of letters by the chief characters. In *Clarissa Harlowe* (1748), for example, Richardson devoted 2,400 pages of small print to the misfortunes of Clarissa, whose lover was a scoundrel, and whose relatives were a greedy pack, scheming to secure her considerable property. Whatever her plight, Clarissa never lost the capacity to pour out her miseries on paper. Her effusions were read aloud at family gatherings, it is said, and whenever some new disaster overwhelmed her, the family withdrew to its various rooms for solitary weeping. In spite of Richardson's sentimentality, his descriptions of the struggles of passion and the conscience carried conviction. But they were scarcely compatible with the ideas and goals of the Enlightenment.

Other masters of English fiction fitted somewhat more easily into the pattern of the Age of Reason. Tobias Smollett, in *Roderick Random* (1748), drew an authentic picture of life in the navy, with all its cruelty and hardship. Henry Fielding introduced a strong leaven of statire and burlesqued the excesses of Richardson. Fielding covered a broad social scene in his masterpiece, *Tom Jones* (1749), depicting both the hard-riding country squires and the low characters of the city slums. Richardson gave the English novel emotional and moral earnestness; Smollet and Fielding gave it vigorous realism.

In Germany the real force in literature was exerted not by the frenchified writers patronized by Frederick the Great but by the dramas of Lessing and the outpourings of the *Sturm und Drang* ("storm and stress"). Lessing (1729–1781) rather combined the middle-class appeal of Richardson and the enlightened devotion to toleration. In his romantic comedy *Minna von Barnhelm,* the lively heroine pits her feminine values against a Prussian officer in a fashion hardly acceptable to Frederick the Great. In *Nathan the Wise* Lessing dramatizes the deistic belief that Judaism, Christianity, and Islam are all manifestations of a universal religion.

A play of a very different kind gave its name to a whole movement by young German writers in the 1770's. The hero of *Sturm und Drang,* finding himself quite incapable of settling down, flees Europe to fight in the American Revolution:

> Have been everything. Became a day-labourer to be something. Lived on the Alps, pastured goats, lay day and night under the boundless vault of the heavens, cooled by the winds, burning with an inner fire. Nowhere rest, nowhere repose. See, thus I am glutted by impulse and power, and work it out of me. I am going to take part in this campaign as a volunteer; there I can expand my soul, and if they do me the favour to shoot me down,—all the better.*

Yearning, frustration, and despair were also dominant emotions in the most popular work of the Sturm und Drang period, *The Sorrows of Young Werther,* a lugubrious short novel by the youthful Goethe (1749–1832). Napoleon claimed to have read it seven times over, weeping copiously each time as the hero shoots himself to death because the woman he loves is already married. The self-pity and self-destruction, so at odds with the cheerful enlightened belief in progress, were to continue in the romantic movement which would sweep over Europe at the end of the eighteenth century.

On the whole, the eighteenth century was an age of prose and produced few poets of stature. Its literary monuments were the novels of Richardson and Fielding, the tales and essays of Voltaire, the plays of Lessing, Gibbon's *History of the Decline and Fall of the Roman Empire* (1788), and Dr. Johnson's *Dictionary* (1755). Edward Gibbon utilized history for a sustained Voltairian attack on Christian fanaticism and employed a Ciceronian prose style which, with its balance and discipline, perfectly suited the classical temper of the Enlightenment. Dr. Samuel Johnson's dictionary also expressed the style of the age. He declared in the preface:

> When I took the first survey of my undertaking, I found our speech copious without order and energetick without rules: wherever I turned my view, there was perplexity to be disentangled, and confusion to be regulated; choice was to be made out of a boundless variety, without any established principle of selection; adulterations were to be detected, without a settled test of purity; and modes of expression to be rejected or received, without the suffrages of any writers of classical reputation or acknowledged authority.

* Klinger, *Sturm und Drang,* quoted in Kuno Francke, *A History of German Literature as Determined by Social Forces,* 4th ed. (New York, 1931), p. 309.

*Dr. Johnson and James Boswell talking "till near two in the morning." Satirical etching by Thomas Rowlandson.*

Pedantry and prejudice sometimes overcame the autocratic doctor. His definition of a cough—"a convulsion of the lungs, vellicated by some sharp serosity"—revealed the dangers of employing little-known Latinisms. Whenever he could, he aimed a volley at his favorite target, the Scots. Thus he defined oats as "a grain, which in England is generally given horses, but in Scotland supports the people." In the main, however, Dr. Johnson succeeded admirably in his aim of becoming a kind of Newton of the English language.

### The Arts

The classicism of the century strongly affected its art. Gibbon's history, the researches of scholars and archaeologists, and the discovery in 1748 of the ruins of Roman Pompeii, well preserved under lava from Vesuvius, raised the interest in antiquity to a high pitch. For the men of the

Enlightenment, the balance and symmetry of Greek and Roman temples represented, in effect, the natural laws of building. Architects retreated somewhat from the theatricalism of the Baroque style and adapted classical models with great artistry and variety. We owe to them the elegance of the London townhouse, the monumental magnificence of the buildings flanking the Place de la Concorde in Paris, and the country-manor charm of Washington's Mount Vernon. The twentieth-century vogue of the "colonial" and the "Georgian" testifies to the lasting influence of this neoclassical architecture.

In painting, neoclassicism had an eminent spokesman in Sir Joshua Reynolds (1723–1792), the president of the Royal Academy and the artistic czar of Georgian England. Beauty, Sir Joshua told the academy, rested "on the uniform, eternal, and immutable laws of nature," which could be "investigated by reason, and known by study." Sir Joshua and his contemporaries, though preaching a coldly reasoned aesthetic, gave warmth to the portraits that they painted of wealthy English aristocrats. This was the golden age of English portraiture, the age of Reynolds, Lawrence, Gainsborough, and Romney. But it was also the age of William Hogarth (1697–1764), who cast aside the academic restraints of neoclassicism to do in art what Fielding did in the novel. Instead of catering to a few wealthy patrons, Hogarth created a mass market for the engravings that he turned out in thousands of copies, graphic sermons on the vices of London—*Marriage à la Mode, The Rake's Progress, The Harlot's Progress,* and *Gin Lane.*

The realism of Hogarth was not the only exception to the prevailing neoclassicism. In France, the style called rococo prevailed during the reign of Louis XV. It was even more fantastic than the baroque, but lighter, airier, more delicate and graceful, much addicted to the use of motifs from bizarre rock formations and from shells. In painting the rococo was a return to Rubens' concern for flesh tones, combined with a light quick touch that suggested improvisation; it may be sensed in the works of Watteau (1684–1721) and of Fragonard (1732–1806).

Meanwhile, three artistic fashions that were to figure significantly in forthcoming age of Romanticism were already catching on—the taste for the oriental, for the natural, and for the Gothic. Rococo interest in the exotic created a great vogue for things Chinese—Chinese wallpaper, the "Chinese" furniture of Thomas Chippendale, and all the delicate work in porcelain or painted scrolls that goes by the name of chinoiserie. Eighteenth-century gardens were bestrewn with pagodas and minarets, and gardeners abandoned Louis XIV's geometrical landscaping for the natural English garden. Even the dominance of neoclassical architecture was challenged. At Strawberry Hill near London, Horace Walpole, the son of the great Robert, endowed his house with an abundance of Gothic "gloomth"—battlements in the medieval style, and "lean windows fattened with rich saints in painted glass."

### Music

Music was perhaps the queen of the arts in the eighteenth century, and music, too, transcended the boundaries of narrow classicism or rationalism. Early in the century Johann Sebastian Bach (1685–1750) brought to perfection the Baroque techniques of seventeenth-century composers. He mastered the difficult art of the fugue, an intricate version of the round in which each voice begins the theme in turn while the other voices repeat and elaborate it. Bach also composed a wealth of material for the organ, the most baroque and the most religious of instruments. His sacred works included many cantatas, the Mass in B minor, and the two gigantic choral settings of the Passion of Christ according to Saint John and according to Saint Matthew. The religious music of Bach, dramatic and deeply felt, was a world apart from the anticlericalism of the Enlightenment.

In contrast to Bach's quiet career as composer and conductor in Germany was the stormy international experience of his contemporary Handel (1685–1759). Born in Germany, Handel studied in Italy, then spent most of his adult years in England trying to run an opera company in the face of the intrigues, clashes of temperament, and fiscal headaches inevitable in artistic enterprise. Handel wrote more than forty operas, including *Xerxes,* famous for "Handel's Largo." He used themes from the Bible for *The Messiah* and other vigorous oratorios directed at a mass audience and arranged for large choruses. These elaborate works differed greatly from the original oratorios of seventeenth-century Italy, which had

*Strawberry Hill, the residence of Horace Walpole.*

been written for the tiny prayer chapels called oratories.

While Bach and Handel composed many instrumental suites and concertos, it was not until the second half of the century that orchestral music really came to the fore. New instruments appeared, notably the piano, which greatly extended the limited range of the older keyboard instrument, the harpsichord. New forms of instrumental music also appeared, the sonata and the symphony, developed largely by Haydn (1732–1809). Haydn wrote more than fifty piano pieces in the form of the sonata, in which two contrasting themes are stated in turn, developed, interwoven, repeated, and finally resolved in a *coda* (the Italian for "tail"). Haydn then arranged the sonata for the orchestra, grafting it onto the Italian operatic overture to create the first movement of the symphony.

The operatic landmark of the early century was John Gay's *Beggar's Opera* (1728), a tuneful work caricaturing English society and politics in Hogarthian vein. Later, Gluck (1714–1787) revolutionized the technique of the tragic opera. "I have striven," he said,

> to restrict music to its true office of serving poetry by means of expression and by following the situations of the story, without interrupting the action or stifling it with a useless superfluity of ornaments. . . . I did not wish to arrest an actor in the greatest heat of dialogue . . . to hold him up in the middle of a word on a vowel favorable to his voice, nor to make display of the agility of his fine voice in some long-drawn passage, nor to wait while the orchestra gives him time to recover his breath for a cadenza.*

Accordingly, Gluck's operas were well-constructed musical dramas, not just vehicles for the display of vocal pyrotechnics. He kept to the old custom of taking heroes and heroines from classical mythology, but he tried to invest shadowy figures like Orpheus, Eurydice, and Iphigenia with new vitality.

Opera, symphony, and chamber music all reached a climax in the works of Mozart (1756–1791). As a boy, Mozart was exploited by his father, who carted him all over Europe to show

* Preface to *Alcestis,* as translated by Eric Blom and quoted in Curt Sachs, *Our Musical Heritage* (New York, 1948), p. 287.

off his virtuosity on the harpsichord and his amazing talent for composition. Overworked throughout his life, and in his later years overburdened with debts, Mozart died a pauper at the age of thirty-five. Yet his youthful precociousness ripened steadily into mature genius, and his facility and versatility grew ever more prodigious. He tossed off the sprightly overture to *The Marriage of Figaro* in the course of an evening. In two months during the summer of 1788, he produced the three great symphonies familiar to concert audiences as No. 39 (E flat major), No. 40 (G minor), and No. 41 ("The Jupiter"). Mozart's orchestral works also included a long list of concertos, with the solo parts sometimes for piano or violin and sometimes, just to show that it could be done, for bassoon or French horn. In chamber music, Mozart experimented with almost every possible combination of instruments.

Three of Mozart's great operas were in the comic Italian vein—the rococo *Così Fan Tutte* ("Thus Do All Women"); *The Marriage of Figaro* based on Beaumarchais's famous satire of the caste system of the Old Regime, in which Figaro the valet outwits and outsings his noble employers; and, finally, *Don Giovanni,* depicting the havoc wrought by Don Juan on earth before his eventual punishment in hell. Mozart composed with equal skill mournful and romantic arias for the Don's victims, elegantly seductive ballads for the Don himself, and a catalog of the Don's conquests for his valet ("A thousand and three in Spain alone"). The instruments in the pit dotted the *i*'s and crossed the *t*'s of the plot—scurrying violins to accompany characters dashing about the stage, portentous trombones to announce the entrance of the Devil. For the ballroom scene of *Don Giovanni,* Mozart employed three orchestras, playing simultaneously three different tunes for three different dances—a minuet for the aristocracy, a country dance for the middle class, a waltz for the lower orders. In his last opera, *The Magic Flute,* Mozart tried to create a consciously German work; but only the vaguest political significance emerged from the fantastic libretto, which apparently sought to vindicate the enlightened ideas of Joseph II and to decry the conservatism of Maria Theresa.

*The Magic Flute* was a rare exception to the cosmopolitanism of eighteenth-century music. The great composers with the German names had very little national feeling. Almost all of them felt equally at home in Vienna, Prague, Milan, Paris, and London, and they gratefully accepted patrons in any country. The fortunate Haydn moved from the princely estate of the Hungarian Esterhazy family to score an equal success with the paying public of the London concert-halls. Italian music was never totally eclipsed; Vivaldi, Scarlatti (father and son), and Boccherini were talented composers. Bach patterned his concertos on Italian models, Haydn borrowed Italian operatic overtures for his symphonies, and every operatic composer of the century profited from the labors of his Italian predecessors. The great musicians also borrowed freely from folk tunes and ballads, the popular music of their day, and were rewarded by having their themes whistled in the streets. Mozart's operas, Haydn's symphonies, and the choral masterpieces of Bach and Handel retained the capacity to engage the listener's emotions.

Of all the arts, music probably came closest to resolving the great conflict in eighteenth-century culture, the tension between reason and emotion, between the abstractions of the Enlightenment and the flesh-and-blood realities of human existence. In other realms, however, as the century drew toward its close, the lines were drawn for the vigorous prosecution of the conflict. In thought, the ideas of Kant and Hume were challenging the optimistic rationalism of the philosophes. Romantic artists and writers were beginning to defy the defenders of classicism. And in politics, as the century ended, the European powers sought to thwart the supreme effort to realize on earth the Enlightenment's dream of reason, natural law, and progress—the French Revolution.

## Reading Suggestions on the Enlightenment

IN GENERAL

W. L. Dorn, *Competition for Empire, 1740–1763,* and L. Gershoy, *From Despotism to Revolution, 1763–1789* (*Torchbooks). These two informative volumes in the series "Rise of Modern Europe" have very full bibliographies.

R. R. Palmer, *The Age of the Democratic Revolution,* Vol. I (*Princeton Univ. Press). A political history of Europe and America at the close of the Old Regime.

L. Krieger, *Kings and Philosophers, 1689–1789* (*Norton). Comprehensive survey, with a succinct up-to-date bibliography.

THE IDEAS OF THE ENLIGHTENMENT

Peter Gay, *The Enlightenment*, 2 vols. (Knopf, 1966, 1969; Vol. I also *Vintage). Comprehensive survey by a leading expert in the field; with extensive bibliographies.

G. R. Havens, *The Age of Ideas: From Reaction to Revolution in Eighteenth-Century France* (*Free Press). Most useful biographical sketches of the philosophes.

E. Cassirer, *The Philosophy of the Enlightenment* (*Beacon, 1955). An important and lucid study of the great principles of eighteenth-century thought.

K. Martin, *French Liberal Thought in the Eighteenth Century* (*Torchbooks). A brilliant and opinionated survey of the philosophes.

C. Becker, *The Heavenly City of the Eighteenth-Century Philosophers* (*Yale Univ. Press). A delightful essay, much influenced by A. N. Whitehead.

J. B. Bury, *The Idea of Progress* (*Dover, 1955). A famous old pioneering study.

L. I. Bredvold, *The Brave New World of the Enlightenment* (Univ. of Michigan Press, 1961). Controversial, basically hostile, but deserving attention.

L. G. Crocker, *An Age of Crisis* and *Nature and Culture* (Johns Hopkins Univ., Press, 1959, 1963). Penetrating criticisms of the implications of the Enlightenment.

SOME INDIVIDUAL THINKERS

A. Wilson, *Diderot: The Testing Years, 1713–1759* (Oxford Univ. Press, 1957). The first part of a definitive biography.

N. L. Torrey, *The Spirit of Voltaire* (Columbia Univ. Press, 1938), and Peter Gay, *Voltaire's Politics: The Poet as Realist* (*Vintage). Thoughtful studies.

A. Cobban, *Rousseau and the Modern State* (Allen & Unwin, 1934). A good introduction to the implications of Rousseau's thought.

J. L. Talmon, *The Origins of Totalitarian Democracy* (*Praeger). Highly critical interpretation of Rousseau and the whole Enlightenment.

F. Manuel, *The Prophets of Paris* (Harvard Univ. Press, 1962). Turgot and Condorcet are among those considered.

THE ENLIGHTENED DESPOTS

J. G. Gagliardo, *Enlightened Despotism* (*Crowell). Recent brief appraisal.

G. Bruun, *The Enlightened Despots,* rev. ed. (*Holt). Lively introductory sketch.

S. Andrews, ed., *Enlightened Despotism* (*Barnes & Noble). Brief excerpts from writings of the despots as well as from modern interpreters of the age.

G. Ritter, *Frederick the Great: A Historical Profile* (Univ. of California Press, 1968). Translation of well-balanced lectures by a German scholar.

L. Reniers, *Frederick the Great* (Oswald Wolff Ltd., 1960). A critical estimate.

W. H. Bruford, *Germany in the Eighteenth Century* (*Cambridge Univ. Press). A descriptive study, stressing social and intellectual history.

R. Pick, *Empress Maria Theresa* (Harper, 1966). Biography of her early years, down to 1757, written in an old-fashioned leisurely way.

S. K. Padover, *The Revolutionary Emperor* (Ballou, 1934). Warmly favorable account of Joseph II; highly critical of Maria Theresa.

R. Herr, *The Eighteenth-Century Revolution in Spain* (Princeton Univ. Press, 1958). Important reappraisal of the impact of the Enlightenment on Spain.

G. Scott Thomson, *Catherine the Great and the Expansion of Russia* (*Collier). A sound short introduction. Perhaps the best biography of Catherine is still K. Walizewski, *The Romance of an Empress* (Appleton, 1894).

GEORGE III

J. S. Watson, *The Reign of George III, 1760–1815* (Clarendon, 1960), Volume XII of "*The Oxford History of England.*" An up-to-date general account.

L. B. Namier, *The Structure of Politics at the Accession of George III* (*St. Martin's), and *England in the Age of the American Revolution* (*St. Martin's). Detailed and controversial studies of politics in the 1760's.

G. Rudé, *Wilkes and Liberty* (*Oxford). Analysis of the unrest in Britain early in George's reign.

AMERICAN INDEPENDENCE

E. S. Morgan, *The Birth of the Republic, 1763–1789* (*Phoenix); L. H. Gipson, *The Coming of the Revolution, 1763–1775,* and R. Alden, *The American Revolution, 1775–1783* (*Torchbooks). Standard accounts.

J. C. Miller, *Origins of the American Revolution* (*Stanford University), and B. Bailyn, *Ideological Origins of the American Revolution* (Harvard, 1967). Illuminating studies of the background.

C. Becker, *The Declaration of Independence* (*Vintage). A detailed analysis, emphasizing the influence of the Enlightenment.

THE ARTS

G. Bazin, *Baroque and Rococo Art* (*Praeger). Comprehensive and concise manual.

M. Bukofzer, *Music in the Baroque Era* (Norton, 1947). Survey down to 1750.

E. M. and S. Grew, *Bach* (*Collier); A. Einstein, *Mozart* (*Galaxy); E. J. Dent, *Mozart's Operas* (*Oxford). Informative works on individual musicians.

SOURCES

C. Brinton, ed., *The Portable Age of Reason Reader* (*Viking); I. Berlin, ed., *The Age of Enlightenment: The Eighteenth-Century Philosophers* (*Mentor). Two valuable anthologies.

B. R. Redman, ed., *The Portable Voltaire* (*Viking, 1949). A well-edited selection.

L. G. Crocker, ed., *The Age of Enlightenment* (Walker, 1969), and C. Macartney, ed., *The Habsburg and Hohenzollern Dynasties in the Seventeenth and Eighteenth Centuries* (Walker, 1970). Volumes in the "Documentary History of Western Civilization."

M. Beloff, ed., *The Debate on the American Revolution, 1761–1783* (*Torchbooks). Handy compilation of British speeches and writings for and against the rebels.

# 18

# *The French Revolution and Napoleon*

## I Causes of the Revolution

In France, as in the thirteen North American colonies, a financial crisis produced a revolution. There was not only a parallel but also a direct connection between the revolution of 1776 and that of 1789. French participation in the War of American Independence increased an already excessive governmental debt by more than 1,500,000,000 livres,* and the example of America fired the imagination of discontented Frenchmen. To them, Benjamin Franklin, the immensely popular American envoy to France, was the very embodiment of the Enlightenment, and the new republic overseas promised to be-

* It is impossible to set a very meaningful value on the prerevolutionary livre in terms of present-day money. It has been estimated that the livre was worth somewhat more than $1.00 in terms of the 1971 dollar, but the estimate is misleading because of the enormous increase in prices and the shifts in the proportionate cost of basic necessities during the two centuries since the Old Regime.

*Above: Jacques Louis David's "Napoleon in His Study" portrays the mature Napoleon as law-giver and administrator of empire. Above right: David's famous painting "The Death of Marat," 1793. Right: Jean-Francois Bosio's "A Parisian Salon in 1801" depicts the new aristocracy created by the Revolution.*

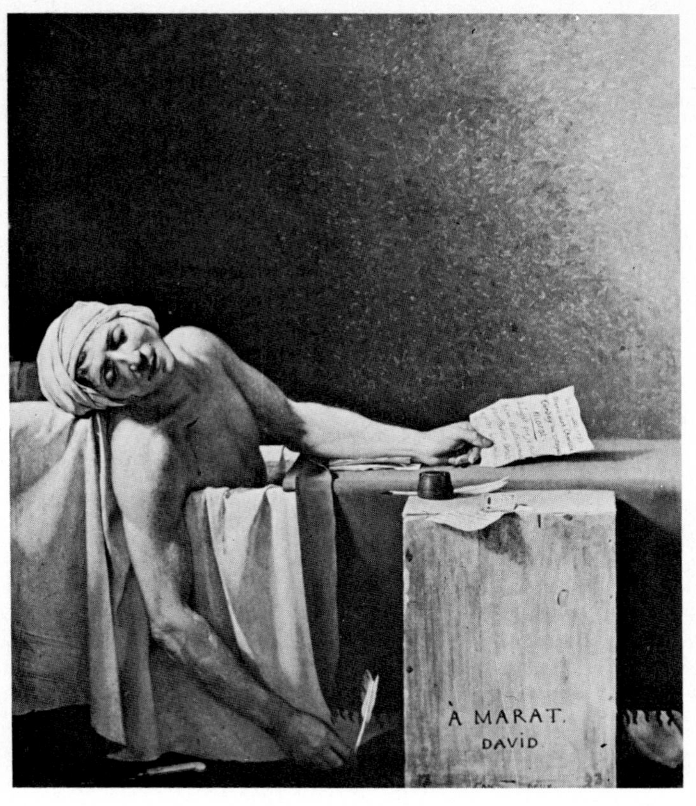
À MARAT.
DAVID

come the utopia of the philosophes. Yet it would be going too far to claim that the American Revolution actually caused the French Revolution; rather, it speeded up developments in France that had long been under way. The forces causing the upheaval of 1789 were almost fully matured in 1776. And, just as the reasons for revolution were more deeply rooted and more complicated in France than in America, so the revolution itself was to be more violent and more sweeping.

The immediate cause of the great French Revolution, then, was financial. King Louis XVI vainly tried one expedient after another to avert bankruptcy and finally summoned the Estates General, the central representative assembly that had last met 175 years earlier. Once assembled, the deputies of the nation initiated the reforms that were to destroy the Old Regime in France. The basic causes of the Revolution, however, reached deep into France's society and economy and into her political and intellectual history. Behind the financial crisis of the 1780's lay many decades of fiscal mismanagement; the government had been courting insolvency since the last years of Louis XIV. The nobles and clergy, jealously guarding their traditional privileges, refused to pay a fair share of the taxes. Resentment against inequitable taxation and inefficient government built up among the unprivileged—the peasantry, the workers, and, above all, the bourgeoisie.

What translated bourgeois resentment into demands for reform and potential revolution was the program of ideas put forward by the philosophes. Conservative apologists of the Old Regime have argued that the revolution was essentially a subversive plot hatched by a small minority of men who had been corrupted by the destructive ideas of the Enlightenment. Their center of operations was the network of six hundred Masonic lodges which had grown up in France since Freemasonry was first imported from England in the early eighteenth century. Modern scholarship has demonstrated the falseness of this conspiracy thesis. The Masons did number many influential men from the bourgeoisie and the nobility among their twenty to thirty thousand members, and their lodges were important disseminators of enlightened ideas, together with provincial academies, the *Encyclopédie,* and other writings of the philosophes. But some lodges actually forbade political discussions, and in general the Masons limited their political activity to relatively innocuous general statements in favor of equality and toleration. It seems clear beyond any doubt that what happened in 1789 and subsequent years was not the result of a plot but rather the denouement of a long drama in which every element in French society—king and noble, philosophe and Freemason, and on down the scale—played an important role.

## The Monarchy

France, the home of the Enlightenment, was never ruled by an enlightened despot until the advent of Napoleon. King Louis XV had refused to take decisive steps to remedy the abuses of the Old Regime. What Louis XV would not do, his grandson and successor, Louis XVI (1774–1792) could not do. When the new king, aged nineteen, learned that his grandfather had died of smallpox, he is said to have exclaimed: "What a burden! At my age! And I have been taught nothing!" The emperor Joseph II, his brother-in-law, later commented that Louis treated petty intrigues with the greatest attention and neglected important affairs of state. Honest, earnest, and pious, but also clumsy, irresolute, and stubborn, Louis XVI was most at home hunting, eating, or tinkering at locksmithing. He also labored under the severe handicap of a politically unfortunate marriage to a Hapsburg. Marie Antoinette, the youngest of the empress Maria Theresa's sixteen children, was badly educated, extravagant, and completely isolated in the artificial little world of Versailles. To patriotic Frenchmen she was a constant reminder of the ill-fated Franco-Austrian alliance during the Seven Years' War.

For want of a good mechanic, the machinery of centralized royal absolutism was gradually falling apart. The fact that it functioned at all could be credited to a relatively few capable administrators, notably the intendants who ran so much of provincial France. The best of the intendants, like the Physiocrat Turgot at Limoges, provided a welcome touch of enlightened despotism, but they could do little to stay the slow disintegration of the central government.

The whole legal and judicial system required reform. The law needed to be codified to eliminate obsolete medieval survivals and to end the overlapping of the two legal systems—Roman and feudal—that prevailed in France. The courts

*Left: Marie Antoinette and her children, painted by Le Brun. Right: David's sketch of the queen on her way to the guillotine.*

needed a thorough overhaul to make them swift, fair, and inexpensive. Many judges and lawyers purchased or inherited their offices and regarded them not as a public trust but as a means to private enrichment and elevation to the nobility of the robe. Louis XV had permitted his ministers to attack the strongholds of these vested interests, the parlements which existed in Paris and in a dozen provincial centers. One of the last acts of his reign had been the suppression of these high courts; one of the first moves taken by Louis XVI was their restoration. Many Frenchmen viewed the parlements favorably as a constitutional check on the absolutism of the monarchy, but they often failed to see that the parlements were also a formidable obstacle to social and economic reform.

### The First and Second Estates

Like the monarchy itself, the social and economic foundations of the Old Regime were beginning to crumble by the middle of the eighteenth century. The first estate, the clergy, occupied a position of conspicuous importance in France. Though forming less than one percent of the total population, the clergy controlled extensive and lucrative properties and performed many functions that are normally undertaken by the state today. They ran schools, kept records of vital statistics, and dispensed relief to the poor. The Gallican church, however, was a house divided. The lower clergy came almost entirely from the third estate; humble, poorly paid, and generally hardworking, the priests resented the wealth and the arrogance of their ecclesiastical superiors. The bishops and abbots maintained the outlook of the noble class into which they had been born. Although some of them took their duties seriously, others regarded the Church as a convenient way of securing a large income. Dozens of prelates turned the administration of their bishoprics or monasteries over to subordinates, kept most of the revenue themselves, and took up residence in Paris or Versailles.

The wealth and the lax discipline of the Church aroused criticism and envy. Good Catholics deplored the dwindling number of monks and nuns and their growing tendency to stress the exploitation of their properties. Well-to-do peasants and townspeople coveted these rich ecclesiastical estates. Taxpayers hated the tithe levied by the Church, even though the full ten percent implied by the word "tithe" was seldom demanded. They also complained about the Church's exemption from taxation and about the meager size of the "free gift" voted by the clergy to the government in lieu of taxes. The peasants on the whole remained moderately faithful Catholics and regarded the village priest, if not the bishop, with esteem and affection. The bourgeois, however, more and more accepted the anticlerical views of the philosophes. They interpreted Voltaire's plea to "crush the infamous thing" as a mandate to strip the Church of wealth and power.

Like the higher clergy, the nobles of the Old Regime, the second estate, enjoyed privilege, wealth—and unpopularity. Although forming less than two percent of the population, they held about twenty percent of the land. They had virtual exemption from taxation; they monopolized army commissions and appointments to high ecclesiastical office. The French aristocracy, however, comprised not a single social unit but a series of differing groups. At the top were the hereditary nobles, a few of them descended from royalty or from feudal lords of the Middle Ages, but more from families ennobled within the past two or three centuries. These "nobles of the sword" tended to view most of their countrymen, including the lesser nobility, as vulgar upstarts. In spite of their failure during the regency of Orléans, they dreamed of the day when they might rule France again, as the feudal nobles had ruled in the Middle Ages. Many of them, clustered at Versailles, neglected their duties as the first landlords of the realm.

Below the nobility of the sword came the "nobility of the robe," including the justices of the parlements and other courts and a host of other officials. The nobles of the robe, or their ancestors, had originally secured aristocratic status by buying their offices. But, since these dignities were then handed down from father to son, the mercenary origins of their status had become somewhat obscured with the passage of time. By the late eighteenth century, there was often little practical distinction between the gentry of the robe and their brethren of the sword; marriages between members of the two groups were common. On the whole, the nobles of the robe were richer than the nobles of the sword, and they exerted more power and influence by virtue of their firm hold on key governmental positions. The ablest and most tenacious defenders of special privilege in the dying years of the Old Regime were the rich judges of parlement, not the elegant but ineffectual courtiers of Versailles.

Many noblemen, however, had little wealth, power, or glamor. They belonged to the lowest level of French aristocracy—the *hobereaux,* the "little falcons" or "sparrowhawks." Hard pinched by rising prices, they vegetated on their country estates, since they could not afford the expensive pleasures of the court. In the effort to conserve at least part of their traditional status, almost all the hobereaux insisted on the meticulous collection of the surviving feudal and manorial dues from the peasantry. Their exhumation of old documents to justify levies sometimes long forgotten earned them the aoiding hatred of the peasants and prepared the way for the document-burning that occurred during the Revolution.

Not every noble was a snobbish courtier or a selfish defender of the status quo. Some hobereaux drifted down the social ladder to become simple farmers. Some nobles of the robe, attracted by the opportunities for profit, took part in business ventures—the Anzin coal mines and the Baccarat glassworks, for example. Even the loftiest noble families produced enlightened spirits, like the Marquis de Lafayette, who returned from the American War of Independence to champion reform at home, or like the young bloods who applauded the ingenious valet, Figaro, when he outwitted his social superiors in Beaumarchais's satire on aristocracy, *The Marriage of Figaro,* first staged in 1784.

## The Third Estate

The first two estates included only a small fraction of the French nation; 98 percent of Frenchmen fell within the third estate in 1789. The great majority of these commoners were peasants. In some respects, the status of the peasantry was more favorable in France than it was anywhere in Europe. Serfdom, which was still prevalent in central and eastern Europe, had disappeared almost entirely except in Lorraine and the Franche-Comté, both relatively recent annexations. While enclosures were gradually pushing small farmers off the land in England, small peasant holdings existed by the millions in France. Three out of every four adult peasants, it is estimated, held some land. Nevertheless, Arthur Young, the English agricultural expert, noted many signs of rural misery in his tour of France in the late 1780's. In southwestern France, for example:

> Pass Payrac, and meet many beggars, which we had not done before. All the country, girls and women, are without shoes or stockings; and the ploughmen at their work have neither sabots nor feet to their stockings. This is a poverty, that strikes at the root of national prosperity. . . . It reminded me of the misery of Ireland.*

Although the degree of agrarian distress varied greatly from province to province, the total picture was far from bright. The trouble came in part from three factors—backward methods of farming, the shortage of land, and overpopulation. The efficient techniques of the agricultural revolution made little headway in France before 1789. Vast areas were not cultivated at all or lay fallow every second or third year in accordance with medieval practice. The constantly increasing rural population simply could not find steady employment or a decent livelihood. Primitive farming required large tracts of land, but the property-holding three-quarters of the French peasantry controlled less than one-third of the land. The average holding was so small that even a propertied peasant might face starvation in poor crop years. Restrictions on the free movement of grain within France, traditionally imposed to keep local flour for local consumption, promoted hoarding and speculation and increased the danger of local famines if a crop failed. Landless peasants drifted to the cities or turned to brigandage.

Rising prices and heavy taxes also oppressed the peasants. The upward trend of prices in France throughout the eighteenth century brought prosperity to many towns, but to the backward rural economy it brought the hardship of inflation. The price of the products sold by the farmer rose less swiftly than that of the goods which the farmer had to buy. To the Church the peasants paid the tithe, and to the nobility they paid feudal and manorial dues. To the state they owed a land tax, an income tax, a poll tax, and a variety of other duties, of which the most widely detested was the *gabelle,* the obligatory purchase of salt from government agents, usually at an exorbitant price.

France had a long history of agrarian unrest, going back to the *jacquerie,* the savage peasant uprising during the Hundred Years' War. In the decades before 1789 there was no new jacquerie, but unemployment and poverty had created a revolutionary temper among the peasants. They did not want a change in the form of government; they were ignorant of the reform program of the Enlightenment. But they most emphatically wanted more land, if need be at the expense of the clergy and the nobility; they wanted an end to obsolete manorial dues; and they wanted relief from a system of taxation that bore hardest upon those who could least afford to pay.

The other members of the third estate, the urban workers and the bourgeoisie, had little reason to cherish the Old Regime. "Labor," in our modern sense of a large, self-conscious body of factory workers, hardly existed in prerevolutionary France, where few large factories as yet existed. Almost every good-sized town, however, had its wage earners and apprentices employed chiefly in small businesses or workshops. These urban laborers felt with particular sharpness the pinch of rising prices. They were not, however, to take the commanding role in the Revolution itself; geographically scattered, lacking in class cohesiveness, they were ready to follow the lead of the bourgeoisie.

The bourgeoisie included Frenchmen of very divergent resources and interests—rich merchants and bankers in the cities, storekeepers and lawyers in country towns and villages, doctors and other professional men, and thousands upon thousands of craftsmen running their own little businesses. Implacable hostility to the privileged estates and warm receptiveness to the propaganda of the philosophes cemented this sprawling middle class into a political force. The bourgeoisie suffered fewer hardships than the peasants and workers did, but they resented the abuses of the Old Regime perhaps even more

***Travels in France,* ed. Constantia Maxwell (Cambridge, England, 1929), pp. 23–24.

keenly. Though they paid a smaller proportion of their incomes in taxes, they violently denounced the inequality of assessments. While profiting by the rise in prices and able to buy up landed estates, the wealthier and more enterprising businessmen complained of guild regulations and other restrictions on free commercial activity. They found it galling to be snubbed by the nobility, treated as second-class subjects by the monarchy, and excluded from posts of power in government, Church, and army.

In sum, the men of the middle class fully realized their own growing economic importance, and they wanted social and political rights to match. Because they were wealthier, better educated, and more articulate than the peasants and wage earners, they took the leading part in formulating the grievances of the entire third estate. These grievances were compiled in statements called *cahiers* and submitted to the Estates General in 1789.

The cahier of the third estate of the Longuyon district in Lorraine may serve as a sample of bourgeois attitudes toward reform.* While it dealt in part with purely local problems, like the destruction of the woods to supply fuel for iron smelters, other portions showed a sharp awareness of the great issues of the day. The cahier pronounced the freedom of the press the "surest means of maintaining the freedom of the nation." It deplored the harshness of the criminal laws; they should conform to "the customs and the character of the French nation, the kindest people in the universe." It recommended "a social contract or act between the sovereign and his people," to safeguard "the personal freedom of all citizens" and "prevent the recurrence of those disastrous events which at present oppress the king and the nation." While insisting upon the sanctity of private property, the third estate of Longuyon advocated a large measure of equality. It proposed that "all Frenchmen should have the right and the hope of securing any state office, of whatever grade, and all military and ecclesiastical dignities." Existing taxes should be swept away, to be replaced by levies on "all property without distinction as to owners, and on all persons without distinction of order and rank."

* The full text of this *cahier* is printed in B. F. Hyslop, *A Guide to the General Cahiers of 1789* (New York, 1936), pp. 318–326. The quotations that follow are in our translation.

### The Financial Crisis

The chronic financial difficulties of the French monarchy strengthened the hand of the middle-class reformers. The government debt, already large at the accession of Louis XVI, tripled between 1774 and 1789; about half the increase resulted from French participation in the American War of Independence. In 1789, the debt stood at 4,500,000,000 livres. The budget for 1788, the only one computed for the Old Regime, made alarming reading:

| Estimated expenses | (in livres) |
|---|---|
| For debt service | 318,000,000 |
| For the court | 35,000,000 |
| For other purposes | 276,000,000 |
| Total | 629,000,000 |
| Estimated revenues | 503,000,000 |
| Estimated deficit | 126,000,000 |

Especially disturbing was the very high proportion of revenues consumed by interest payments on debts already contracted.

Louis XVI, in his feeble way, tried to cope with the growing emergency. On coming to the throne in 1774, he named as chief minister Turgot, who sympathized with the Physiocrats and had made a brilliant record as intendant of Limoges. Turgot temporarily reduced the deficit by imposing strict economies, particularly on the expenditures of the court. To promote the welfare of the third estate, he curtailed ancient guild monopolies, lifted restrictions on internal shipments of grain, and replaced the *corvée,* the work on highways demanded of peasants, with a tax affecting nobles and commoners alike. He even contemplated restoring the Edict of Nantes to bring the Huguenots back into French life and setting up a series of representative assemblies to meet demands for liberalization of the monarchy. Dismayed, the vested interests of the Old Regime rebelled and, seconded by Marie Antoinette, secured Turgot's dismissal in 1776. The ousted minister admonished Louis XVI: "Remember, sire, that it was weakness which brought the head of Charles I to the block."

Louis ignored Turgot's warning. The government continued to raise new loans—653,000,000 livres between 1783 and 1786 alone. Then in 1786 the bankers refused to make new advances. The French government was caught between the irresistible force of the third estate's demands for tax relief and the immovable object of the other estates' refusal to yield their fiscal exemptions. The monarchy had temporized and borrowed until it could afford neither fresh delays nor new loans. Calonne, the finance minister in 1786, proposed to meet the crisis by reviving Turgot's reforms. In the hope of persuading the first two estates to consent to heavier taxation, he convoked the Assembly of Notables, which included the chief aristocratic and ecclesiastical dignitaries of the kingdom. But the Notables declined to be persuaded.

Louis XVI dissolved the Notables and dismissed Calonne. Then, with unaccustomed firmness, he decided to levy a uniform tax on all landed property without regard to the social status of the holder. The clergy replied by reducing their "free gift" for 1788 to one-sixth of what it had previously been. The Parlement of Paris declared the new tax law illegal and asserted that only the nation as a whole assembled in the Estates General could make so sweeping a change. The king retreated and in the summer of 1788 announced that the Estates General would meet the following spring.

## The Estates General

In summoning the Estates General Louis XVI revived a half-forgotten institution which did not seem likely to initiate drastic social and economic reforms. The three estates, despite their immense variation in size, had customarily received equal representation and equal voting power, so that the two privileged orders could outvote the commoners. The Estates General of 1789, however, met under unique circumstances.

Its election and subsequent meeting took place during an economic crisis that heightened chronic social and financial tensions. One difficulty was the continued gravitation of unemployed peasants to the cities, especially Paris, in search of work. Another was the continued inflation, with prices rising at twice the rate of wages. A third was the treaty of 1786 with Eng-

*The opening of the Estates General, 1789: the last formal gathering of Old Regime France.*

land, which increased the importation of French wines and brandies into Britain in return for elimination of French barriers to importation of cheaper English textiles and hats. By 1788, in the face of English competition, severe unemployment was developing in some French textile centers. A final difficulty was the weather. Hail and drought had reduced the wheat harvest in 1788, and the winter of 1788–1789 was so bitter that the Seine froze over at Paris, blocking shipments of grain or flour by water. Half-starved and half-frozen, Parisians huddled around bonfires provided by the municipal government. By the spring of 1789 the price of bread had almost doubled—a very serious matter in an age when bread was the mainstay of the diet. It has been estimated that the average workingman normally spent almost half his wages on bread for his family; now he was obliged to spend a higher proportion.

France had survived bad weather and poor harvests many times in the past without experiencing revolution. This time, however, the economic hardships were the last straw. Starving peasants begged, borrowed, and stole, poaching on the hunting preserves of the great lords and attacking their game wardens. The turbulence in Paris boiled over in a riot (April 1789), witnessed by Thomas Jefferson, then the American minister to France:

> The Fauxbourg St. Antoine is a quarter of the city inhabited entirely by the class of day-laborers and journeymen in every line. A rumor was spread among them that a great paper manufacturer . . . had proposed . . . that their wages should be lowered to 15 sous a day [three-quarters of a livre]. . . . They flew to his house in vast numbers, destroyed everything in it, and in his magazines and work shops, without secreting however a pin's worth to themselves, and were continuing this work of devastation when the regular troops were called in. Admonitions being disregarded, they were of necessity fired on, and a regular action ensued, in which about 100 of them were killed, before the rest would disperse.*

These disturbances increased the sense of critical urgency pressing on the deputies to the Estates General.

* *Autobiography of Thomas Jefferson*, ed. P. L. Ford (New York, 1914), pp. 133–134.

The methods followed in electing the deputies aided the champions of reform. The suffrage was wide, especially in rural areas, where almost all adult males met the qualifications for voting. Indeed, it is probable that more Frenchmen actually voted in 1789 than in any subsequent election or referendum during the revolutionary era. In each district of France the third estate made its choice not directly by secret ballot but indirectly by choosing at a public meeting electors who later selected a deputy. Since this procedure greatly favored bourgeois orators over inarticulate farmers, middle-class lawyers and government administrators won control of the commoners' deputation. The reforming deputies of the third estate found some sympathizers in the second estate and many more in the first estate, where the discontented lower clergy had a large delegation. Moreover, in a departure from precedent, the king had agreed to "double the third," giving it as many deputies as the other two estates combined. Altogether, a majority of the deputies were prepared to make drastic changes in the Old Regime.

In all past meetings of the Estates General each estate, or order, had deliberated separately, with the consent of two estates and of the Crown required for the passage of a measure. In 1789, the king and the privileged orders favored retaining this "vote by order." The third estate, on the contrary, demanded "vote by head," with the deputies from all the orders deliberating together, each deputy having a single vote. Pamphleteers invoked Rousseau's concept of the general will. "What is the third estate?" wrote the abbé Siéyès in an influential broadside of the same name. "Everything."

> If votes were taken by order, five million citizens will not be able to decide anything for the general interest, because it will not please a couple of hundred thousand privileged individuals. The will of a single individual will veto and destroy the will of more than a hundred people.*

The question of procedure became crucial soon after the Estates General convened on May 5, 1789, at Versailles. Siéyès, a priest, and Mirabeau, a renegade nobleman, both of them sitting in the third estate, led the campaign for vote by head. On June 17, the third estate cut the Gor-

*Emmanuel Siéyès, *Qu'est-ce Que le Tiers Etat?*, ed. E. Champion (Paris, 1888), p. 82. Our translation.

dian knot of procedure by accepting Siéyès' invitation to proclaim itself the National Assembly. It also invited the deputies of the other two estates to join its sessions. A majority of the clerical deputies, chiefly parish priests, accepted; the nobility refused.

The king then barred the commoners from their usual meeting place, whereupon they assembled at an indoor tennis court on June 20 and solemnly swore never to disband until they had given France a constitution. To the "Tennis-Court Oath" Louis replied by a kind of *lit de justice,* commanding each estate to resume its separate deliberations. The third estate and some deputies of the first disobeyed. Louis, vacillating as ever, now gave in and on June 27 directed the noble and clerical deputies to join the National Assembly. The nation, through its representatives, had successfully challenged the king and the vested interests. The Estates General was dead, and in its place sat the National Assembly, pledged to reform French society and give the nation a constitution. The revolution had begun.

## II The Dissolution of the Monarchy

### Popular Uprisings, July-October 1789

The National Assembly had barely settled down to work when a new wave of rioting swept over France, undermining further the position of the king. Economic difficulties grew more severe during the summer of 1789. Unemployment increased, and bread seemed likely to remain scarce and expensive, at least until after the harvest. Meanwhile, the commoners feared that the king and the privileged orders might attempt a counterrevolution. Large concentrations of troops appeared in the Paris area early in July —to preserve order and protect the National Assembly, the king asserted. But the Parisians suspected that Louis was planning the forcible dissolution of the Assembly. Suspicion deepened into conviction after Louis dismissed Necker, the popular Swiss financier who had been serving as the chief royal adviser.

The reaction to Necker's dismissal was immediate. On July 12 and 13, the men who had elected the Paris deputies of the third estate formed a new municipal government and a new militia, the National Guard, both loyal to the National Assembly. Paris was forging the weapons that made it the leader of the Revolution. Crowds were roaming the streets, demanding cheaper bread and parading busts of Necker draped in black. On July 14 they broke into government buildings in search of arms. They found one arsenal in the Invalides, the great military hospital, and they hoped to find another in the Bastille, a fortress in the eastern part of the city. An armed group, several hundred strong, stormed the Bastille, killing part of the garrison and suffering many casualties themselves. The legend, cherished by defenders of the Old Regime, that participants in the assault were in the main simply "rabble" or "brigands" or a "mob" has been exploded by the facts. An official list of "Vainqueurs de la Bastille" (conquerors of the Bastille) carefully compiled some time after the event showed that the great majority of the accredited vainqueurs were craftsmen and tradesmen from the district of the city close to the Bastille. Of 662 names, 97 were those of joiners and cabinetmakers (woodworking was a specialty of the district); there were 41 locksmiths, 28 cobblers, 21 shopkeepers, 11 winesellers, a scattered representation of stonemasons, hatters, tailors, hairdressers, jewelers, goldsmiths, upholsterers and other skilled artisans, a dozen or so well-to-do bourgeois, and one woman (a laundress).

What the vainqueurs accomplished, though of little practical value, was of enormous symbolic significance. There were only seven prisoners to be released, all of whom had merited incarceration. Yet an aroused people had demonstrated what it could accomplish: the capture and subsequent demolition of the Bastille did much to insure the destruction of the Old Regime. It is no wonder the Fourteenth of July became the great national holiday of Frenchmen, their counterpart of the American Fourth of July.

Rioting spread over much of France late in July 1789, as the provincial population responded to the news from Paris or acted on its own. In town after town, mobs attacked the local version of the Bastille. Arthur Young, who was surveying the agriculture of Alsace, witnessed the scene at Strasbourg:

> The Parisian spirit of commotion spreads quickly; it is here; the troops . . . are employed to keep an eye on the people who shew signs of an intended revolt. They have broken the windows of some magistrates that are no favourites; and a great mob of them is at this moment assembled, demanding clamourously to have meat at 5 sous a pound.*

The countryside, in the meantime, was experiencing the "Great Fear," one of the most extraordinary attacks of mass delusion on record. From village to village word spread that "brigands" were coming, aristocratic hirelings who would destroy crops and villages and force the National Assembly to preserve the status quo. There were in fact no bands of brigands, only an occasional starving farmhand trying to steal food. But the peasants in many districts went berserk, grabbing hoes and pitchforks, anything resembling a weapon. When the brigands did not materialize, they attacked châteaux and broke into other buildings that might house a hoard of grain or the hated documents justifying collection of manorial dues. Some nobles voluntarily gave the peasants what they wanted; others saw their barns and archives burnt, and a few were lynched. The Great Fear, beginning as a psychological aberration, ended as an uprising of the peasantry against its traditional oppressors.

By the end of July 1789, then, four distinct sets of revolutionary events had taken place in France: (1) the constitutional revolution of June, resulting in the creation of the National Assembly; (2) the Paris revolution and the taking of the Bastille; (3) the comparable outbreaks in provincial cities and towns; and (4) the Great Fear. Each of the four drove another nail into the coffin of the Old Regime. The transformation of the Estates General into the National Assembly and the creation of new local governments undermined the traditional political advantages of the first two estates. The Great Fear began the destruction of their social and economic privileges. Everywhere, legally constituted officials were turned out, taxes went unpaid, and valuable records were destroyed.

* *Travels in France,* p. 181.

The "October Days," the last crisis of a momentous year, demonstrated anew the impotence of Louis XVI and the power of his aroused subjects. The harvest of 1789 had been good, but a drought crippled the operation of watermills for grinding flour from the wheat. Thus, as autumn drew on, Parisians still queued for bread and still looked suspiciously at the royal troops stationed in the neighborhood of their city. Rumors of the queen's behavior at Versailles further incensed them. Marie Antoinette made a dramatic appearance at a banquet of royal officers, clutching the dauphin (the heir to the throne) in her arms, striking the very pose that her mother, Maria Theresa, had employed so effectively to win the support of the Hungarians in the 1740's. And, on hearing that the people had no bread, she was said to have remarked callously: "Let them eat cake." This story was false, but it echoed and re-echoed in the lively new Paris papers that delighted in denouncing "l'Autrichienne" ("the Austrian hussy").

The climax came on October 5, 1789, when an array of determined women—rough market-women and fishwives, neatly dressed milliners, even middle-class "ladies with hats"—marched the dozen miles from Paris to Versailles in the rain. They disrupted the National Assembly, extracted kisses from Louis XVI, and later penetrated the palace, where they might have lynched Marie Antoinette if she had not taken refuge with the king. Although historians have not yet discovered who planned and organized this bizarre demonstration, it had very significant political consequences. On October 6, the women marched back to Paris, escorting "the baker, the baker's wife, and the baker's boy"—in other words, the royal family—who took up residence in the Tuileries Palace. More important, the National Assembly, too, moved to Paris. The most revolutionary place in France had captured both the head of the Old Regime and the herald of the new.

### Forging a New Regime

The outlines of the new regime were already starting to take shape before the October Days. The Great Fear prompted the National Assembly to abolish in law what the peasants were destroying in fact. On the evening of August 4,

*The march of the women to Versailles, 1789.*

1789, the Viscount de Noailles, a liberal nobleman, addressed the deputies:

> The kingdom at this moment hangs between the alternative of the destruction of society, and that of a government which will be the admiration and the exemplar of Europe.
>
> How is this government to be established? By public tranquility. . . . And to secure this necessary tranquility, I propose:
>
> (1) . . . That taxation will be paid by all the individuals of the kingdom, in proportion to their revenues;
>
> (2) That all public expenses will in the future be borne equally by all.*

The deputies voted the proposals of Noailles. In addition, the clergy gave up its tithes, and the liberal minority of the second estate surrendered the nobility's game preserves, manorial dues, and other medieval rights. The assembly made it a clean sweep by abolishing serfdom, forbidding the sale of justice or of judicial office, and decreeing that "all citizens, without distinction of birth, can be admitted to all ecclesiastical, civil, and military posts and dignities." When the memorable session inaugurated by Noailles' speech ended at two o'clock on the morning of August 5, the Old Regime was dead. It remained dead even after the deputies had second thoughts and awarded the nobles compensation for their losses.

Three weeks later, on August 26, 1789, the National Assembly formulated the Declaration of the Rights of Man. "Men are born and remain free and equal in rights," it asserted. "These rights are liberty, property, security and resistance to oppression." Property it called "an inviolable and sacred right," and liberty "the exercise of the natural rights of each man" within the limits "determined by law." "Law," the Declaration stated, "is the expression of the general will. All citizens have the right to take part, in person or by their representatives, in its formation." Further, "Any society in which the guarantee of rights is not assured or the separation of powers not determined has no constitution."*

The Declaration of the Rights of Man mirrored the economic and political attitudes of the middle class. It insisted on the sanctity of property, and it proclaimed that "social distinctions may be based only on usefulness," thus implying that some social distinctions were to be expected. It committed the French to the creed of constitutional liberalism already affirmed by the English in 1688–1689 and by the Americans in 1776, and it incorporated the key phrases of the philosophes: natural rights, general will, and separation of powers. The National Assembly made a resounding statement of the ideals of the Enlightenment. Yet, as the subsequent history of the Revolution soon demonstrated, the Assembly found no magic formula by which to translate these ideals into practice.

The economic legislation of the National Assembly provided a case in point. Belief in the theory of the equal taxation of all Frenchmen did not solve urgent financial problems. The new and just land tax imposed by the deputies simply could not be collected. Tax collectors had vanished in the general liquidation of the Old Regime, and naïve peasants now thought that they owed the government nothing. Once again,

* *Archives Parlementaires,* Series 1, VIII, 343. Our translation.

* G. Lefebvre, *The Coming of the French Revolution* (Princeton, 1947), Appendix.

the French state borrowed until its credit was exhausted, and then, in desperation, the National Assembly ordered the confiscation of Church lands (November 1789). "The wealth of the clergy is at the disposition of the nation," it declared, explaining that ecclesiastical lands fell outside the bounds of "inviolable" property as defined in the Declaration of the Rights of Man because they belonged to an institution and not to private individuals.

The government thus acquired an asset worth at least two billion livres. On the basis of this collateral it issued *assignats,* paper notes used to pay the government's debts. So far, so good: The assignats had adequate security behind them and temporarily eased the financial crisis. Unfortunately, the Revolution repeated the mistake of John Law at the time of the Mississippi Bubble. It did not know when to stop. As the state sold parcels of confiscated land—that is, as it reduced the collateral securing its paper money—it should have destroyed assignats to the same amount. The temptation not to reduce the number of assignats proved too great to resist. Inflation resulted: The assignats, progressively losing their solid backing, depreciated until in 1795 they were worth less than five percent of their face value.

The state sold at auction the property seized from the Church and from aristocratic émigrés. Well-to-do peasants profited by the opportunity to enlarge their holdings, and many bourgeois also bought up land, sometimes as a short-term speculation, sometimes as a long-term investment. The poor and landless peasants, however, gained nothing, since they did not have the money with which to buy. True to the doctrine of laissez-faire, the National Assembly made no move to help these marginal farmers. Following the same doctrine, it abolished the guilds and the irksome tariffs and tolls on trade within France. And deeming the few primitive organizations of labor unnatural restrictions on economic freedom, it abolished them too. In June 1791, after an outbreak of strikes, it passed the Le Chapelier Law banning both strikes and labor unions.

## The Civil Constitution of the Clergy

Since the suppression of tithes and the seizure of ecclesiastical property deprived the Church of its revenue, the National Assembly agreed to finance ecclesiastical salaries. The new arrangement virtually nationalized the Gallican church and made it subject to constant government regulation. The Assembly's decision to restrict monasteries and convents caused little difficulty; many of these establishments were already far gone in decay. But an uproar arose over the legislation altering the status of the secular clergy.

The Civil Constitution of the Clergy (June 1790) redrew the ecclesiastical map of France. It reduced the number of bishoprics by more than a third, making the remaining dioceses correspond to the new civil administrative units known as departments. It transformed bishops and priests into civil officials, paid by the state and elected by the population of the diocese or parish; both Catholics and non-Catholics (the latter usually a small minority) could vote in these elections. A new bishop was required to take an oath of loyalty to the state, and the Civil Constitution stipulated that he might not apply to the pope for confirmation, though he might write to him as the "Visible Head of the Universal Church."

These provisions stripped the "Visible Head of the Universal Church" of effective authority over the Gallican clergy and ran counter to the whole tradition of the Roman church as an independent ecclesiastical monarchy. Naturally the pope denounced the Civil Constitution. The National Assembly then required that every member of the French clergy take a special oath supporting the Civil Constitution, but only seven bishops and fewer than half of the priests complied. Thus a breach was opened between the Revolution and a large segment of the population. Good Catholics, from Louis XVI down to humble peasants, rallied to the non-juring clergy, as those who refused the special oath were termed. The Civil Constitution of the Clergy, supplying an issue for rebellion, was the first great blunder of the Revolution.

## The Constitution of 1791

The major undertaking of the National Assembly was the Constitution of 1791. To replace the bewildering complex of provincial units that had accumulated under the Old Regime the Assembly devised a neat and orderly system of local government very much in the spirit of the Enlightenment. It divided the territory of France into eighty-three departments of approximately equal size. Each department was small enough for its chief town to be within a day's journey of the outlying towns; each bore the name of a river, a mountain range, or some other natural landmark. The departments were subdivided into *arrondissements* or districts, and the districts into communes—that is, municipalities. The commune-district-department arrangement resembled, on a reduced scale, the American hierarchy of town-county-state. In the communes and departments, elected councils and officials enjoyed considerable rights of self-government. The administration of the new France, on paper anyhow, was to be far more decentralized than that of the Old Regime.

The principle of the separation of powers guided the reconstruction of the central government. The Constitution of 1791 established an independent hierarchy of courts staffed by elected judges to replace the parlements and other tribunals of the Old Regime. It vested legislative authority in a single elected chamber. Although the king still headed the executive branch, his actions now required approval by his ministers, who were responsible only to him and not to the legislature, as they generally are in a "parliamentary" or "cabinet" government. The king did receive the power of veto, but it was only a suspensive veto, which could block legislation for a maximum of four years. Louis XVI, no longer the absolute "king of France," acquired the new constitutional title "king of the French."

The new constitution subscribed to many other principles issuing straight from the Enlightenment. It mitigated the severity of punishments, undertook to give France a new uniform code of law (an undertaking executed by Napoleon), and it declared marriage a civil contract, not a religious sacrament. The state took over the old ecclesiastical functions of keeping records of vital statistics and providing charity and education. Indeed, the Constitution promised a system of free public education. It also promised that the foreign policy of revolutionary France would be more virtuous than that of autocratic France: "The French nation renounces the undertaking of any war with a view of making conquests, and it will never use its forces against the liberty of any people." *

* J. H. Stewart, *A Documentary Survey of the French Revolution* (New York, 1951), p. 260.

The Constitution of 1791 went a long way toward instituting popular government, but it stopped well short of full democracy. It divided Frenchmen into two classes of citizens, "active" and "passive," and limited the right of voting to "active" citizens, who paid annually in taxes an amount equal to at least three days' wages for unskilled labor in the locality. The "passive" citizens, numbering about a third of the male population, enjoyed the full protection of the law but did not receive the franchise. Moreover, the new legislature was chosen by a process of indirect election. "Active" citizens did not vote for their deputies but for a series of electors, who were required to be men of substantial wealth, and who ultimately elected the deputies. It was evidently assumed that the amount of worldly goods a man possessed determined the degree of his political wisdom.

The decentralized and limited monarchy established by the Constitution of 1791 was doomed to fail. It was too radical to suit the king and most of the aristocracy, and not radical enough for the many bourgeois who were veering toward republicanism. The majority in the National Assembly supporting the Constitution suffered the fate commonly experienced by the politically moderate in a revolution: they were squeezed out by the extremists. Despite their moderate intentions, they were driven to enact some drastic legislation, notably the Civil Constiution of the Clergy, which weakened their own position. And they failed to develop an effective party organization at a time when the deputies of the radical minority were consolidating their strength.

These radicals were the Jacobins, so named because they belonged to the "Society of the Friends of the Constitution," which maintained its Paris headquarters in a former Jacobin (Dominican) monastery. The Jacobins were no true friends of the Constitution of 1791. They accepted it only as a stopgap until they might end the monarchy and set up a republic based on universal suffrage. To prepare for the millennium, the Jacobins used all the techniques of a political pressure group. They planted rabble-rousing articles in the press and manipulated the crowds of noisy and volatile spectators at the sessions of the National Assembly. Their network of political clubs extended throughout the provinces, providing the only nationwide party organization in France. Almost everywhere, Jacobins captured control of the new department and commune councils. In local elections, as in the elections of the Estates General, an able and determined minority prevailed over a largely illiterate and politically inexperienced majority.

The defenders of the Old Regime played into the hands of the Jacobins. From the summer of 1789 on, alarmed prelates and nobles, including the king's own brothers, fled France, leaving behind more rich estates to be confiscated and giving Jacobin orators and editors a splendid opportunity to denounce the rats leaving a sinking ship. Many of these émigrés gathered in the German Rhineland to intrigue for Austrian and Russian support of a counterrevolution. The king's grave misgivings about the Civil Constitution of the Clergy prompted his disastrous attempt to join the émigrés on the Franco-German frontier. In June 1791, three months before the completion of the new constitution, Louis and Marie Antoinette left the Tuileries disguised as a valet and governess. But Louis unwisely showed his face in public, and a local official along the route recognized the royal profile from the portrait on the assignats. The alarm was sent ahead, and at Varennes in northeastern France a detachment of troops forced the royal party to make a hot, dusty, dispirited journey back to Paris. After the abortive flight to Varennes, the revolutionaries viewed Louis XVI as a potential traitor and kept him closely guarded in the Tuileries. The experiment in constitutional monarchy began under most unfavorable auspices.

### The Legislative Assembly, October 1791-September 1792

On October 1, 1791, the first and the only legislative assembly elected under the new constitution commenced its deliberations. No one faction commanded a numerical majority in the new assembly. The seats were held as follows:*

| | |
|---|---|
| Right (Constitutional Monarchists) | 265 |
| Center (Plain) | 345 |
| Left (Jacobins) | 130 |

* In the practice followed by most continental European assemblies, the Right sat to the right of the presiding officer as he faced the assembly, the Left to his left, and the Center in between.

The balance of political power rested with the timid and irresolute deputies of the Center, who were neither strong defenders of the Constitution nor yet convinced republicans. Since they occupied the lowest seats in the assembly hall, they received the derogatory nickname of the Plain or Marsh. The capable politicians of the Left soon captured the votes of the Plain, to demonstrate anew the power of a determined minority.

Leadership of this minority came from a loose grouping of Jacobins known as Girondins, because some of them came from Bordeaux, in the department of Gironde. Their chief spokesman was Brissot (1754–1793), an ambitious lawyer and journalist, a mediocre politician, and an inveterate champion of worthy causes, including emancipation of the blacks. Other leading Girondins were Condorcet, the distinguished philosophe and prophet of progress; Dumouriez, who later commanded the victorious French forces at Valmy; and Roland, a rather obscure civil servant with a very ambitious wife who ran a Girondin salon. The Girondins were much too loosely articulated to be compared to a political party in the modern sense; what held them together was largely their patriotic alarm over France's situation at home and abroad.

The Girondins specialized in fervent nationalist oratory. They pictured revolutionary France as the intended victim of a reactionary conspiracy, engineered by the émigrés, aided at home by the non-juring clergy and the royal family, and abetted abroad by a league of monarchs under Leopold II, the Austrian emperor and the brother of Marie Antoinette. But Louis XVI, despite the flight to Varennes, was no traitor, and Leopold II cautiously limited his aid to the émigrés. The sudden death of Leopold in March 1792, and the accession of his inexperienced and less cautious son, Francis II, at once increased the Austrian threat. At the same time, the mounting war fever in France convinced Louis XVI he should name Girondin ministers, including Roland to the Interior and Dumouriez to Foreign Affairs. On April 20, 1792, the Legislative Assembly declared war on Austria; the war was to continue, with a few brief intervals of peace, for the next twenty-three years. In the eyes of Frenchmen the war was defensive, not the campaign of conquest that the nation had forsworn in the fine phrases of its constitution.

Partly because the emigration of many nobles had depleted the corps of French officers, the war went badly for France at the outset. Prussia soon joined Austria, and morale sagged on the home front in June, when Louis XVI dismissed the Girondin ministers because they had proposed to banish non-juring priests, and appointed more conservative replacements. Spirits began to rise in July, especially with a great celebration of the third anniversary of the assault on the Bastille on the fourteenth. Paris was thronged with national guardsmen from the provinces on the way to the front, and the contingent from Marseilles introduced to the capital the patriotic hymn which became the national anthem of republican France. It was not only the Marseillaise that improved morale. On July 25 the Prussian commander, the Duke of Brunswick, issued a manifesto drafted by an émigré stating the war aims of the allies:

> To put a stop to the anarchy within France, to check the attacks delivered against throne and altar, to reestablish legal authority, to restore to the king the security and freedom of which he has been deprived, and to place him in a position where he may exercise the legitimate authority which is his due.

A threat followed. "If the Tuileries is attacked, by deed or word, if the slightest outrage or violence is perpetrated against the royal family, and if immediate measures are not taken for their safety, maintenance and liberty"—then Paris would witness "a model vengeance, never to be forgotten." *

The duke of Brunswick's manifesto did not frighten the French, as it was intended to do. On the contrary, it stiffened the already firm determination of republicans to do away with the monarchy. All through the early summer of 1792 the Jacobins of Paris had been plotting an insurrection. They won the support of a formidable following—army recruits, national guardsmen, and the rank and file of Parisians, who were angered by the depreciation of the assignats and by the high price and short supply of food and other necessities. One by one, the forty-eight *sections* or wards into which the city was divided came under the control of Jacobins, who advertised their democratic sympathies by inviting passive citizens to take part in political activity. The climax came on the night of August 9–10, when leaders of the sections ousted the regular municipal authorities from the Paris city hall and installed a new and illegal Jacobin commune.

The municipal revolution had immediate and momentous results. On the morning of August 10, the forces of the new commune, joined by national guardsmen, attacked the Tuileries and massacred the king's Swiss guards, while the royal family took refuge with the Legislative Assembly. The uprising of August 10 sealed the doom of the monarchy and made the Assembly little more than the errand boy of the new Paris commune. With most of the deputies of the Right and the Plain absent, the Assembly voted to suspend the king from office, to imprison the royal family, and to order the election of a constitutional convention. Until this new body should meet, the government was to be run by an interim ministry staffed in part by Roland and other Girondins, but in which the strongman was the minister of justice, Danton (1759–1794), a more radical and opportunistic politician. The birth of the First Republic was at hand.

## III The First Republic

### The September Massacres, 1792

The weeks between August 10 and the meeting of the Convention on September 21 were weeks of crisis and tension. The value of the assignats depreciated by forty percent during August alone. Jacobin propagandists, led by Marat (1743–1793), a frustrated and embittered physician turned journalist, continually excited the people of Paris, who were already stirred up by the economic difficulties and by the capture of the Tuileries. Excitement mounted still higher when the news arrived that Prussian troops had invaded northeastern France. In the emergency, Danton, the interim minister of justice, won immortality by urging patriots to employ "de l'audace, encore de l'audace, toujours de l'au-

* *Le Moniteur Universel,* August 3, 1792. Our translation.

dace"—boldness, more boldness, always boldness.

In Paris, boldness took the form of the September Massacres, lynchings of supposed traitors and enemy agents made possible by the collapse of normal police authority. For five days, beginning on September 2, blood-thirsty mobs moved from prison to prison. At each stop they held impromptu courts and summary executions. Neither the Paris commune nor the interim national ministry could check the hysterical wave of lynchings, though Roland did try. The number of victims exceeded one thousand and included ordinary criminals and prostitutes as well as aristocrats and non-juring priests, who were often innocent of the treason charged against them. The crowning horror was the mutilation of the princesse de Lamballe, the queen's maid of honor, whose severed head was paraded on a pike before the window of the royal prison so that Marie Antoinette might see "how the people take vengeance on their tyrants." The September Massacres foreshadowed the terror in store for France.

Later in the month (September 20, 1792), a rather minor French victory, grandly styled "the miracle of Valmy," turned the duke of Brunswick's forces back from the road to Paris; more solid French successes in Belgium, Savoy, and the Rhineland followed during the final months of 1792. Then the tide turned again, washing away the conquests of the autumn. By the summer of 1793 half-defeated France faced a hostile coalition including almost every major power in Europe. An atmosphere of perpetual emergency surrounded the Convention.

## Gironde and Mountain

In theory, the election of deputies to the National Convention (August-September 1792) marked the beginning of true political democracy in France. Both active and passive citizens were invited to the polls. Yet only ten percent of the potential electorate of seven million actually voted; the others abstained or were turned away from the polls by the watchdogs of the Jacobin clubs, ever on the alert against "counterrevolutionaries." The result was a landslide for the republicans:

| | |
|---|---|
| Right (Gironde) | 165 |
| Center (Plain) | 435 |
| Left (Mountain) | 150 |

The radicalism of the Convention was underlined by the Jacobin antecedents both of its Right and its Left. Many ties in common existed between the Gironde and the Mountain (so named because its deputies sat high up in the meeting hall). Deputies from both factions came mainly from middle-class professions like the law, were steeped in the ideas of the philosophes, and usually regarded with some distrust the masses of people who were now acquiring the name of *sans-culottes* (literally, "without knee-breeches"). They were the workingmen, both poor day laborers and lower-middle class artisans and craftsmen, all who proudly wore the long baggy trousers of the worker rather than the elegant breeches of the well-to-do. The term "sans-culottes," while always carrying social and economic implications, came to refer politically to any ardent supporter of the revolution, particularly a political activist in the Paris sections.

When the Convention met, Gironde and Mountain united to declare France a republic (September 21, 1792) but were soon wrangling over other questions. The Girondins favored a breathing spell in revolutionary legislation, and they also defended provincial interests against possible encroachments by Paris. As one of their deputies told the Convention (and his allusion to classical antiquity was most characteristic of the Revolution):

> I fear the despotism of Paris. . . . I do not want a Paris guided by intriguers to become to the French Empire what Rome was to the Roman Empire. Paris must be reduced to its proper one-eighty-third of influence, like the other departments.*

The Gironde, therefore, favored a large measure of federalism, which meant decentralization in the Revolutionary vocabulary, and a national government limited by many checks and balances. The details were set forth in a draft constitution completed early in 1793 by Condorcet. The executive and the legislature would be independent of each other and separately elected,

* Lasource, September 25, 1792. *Archives Parlementaires,* Series 1, LII, 130. Our translation.

the results of elections would be adjusted according to proportional representation, projected laws would be submitted to a popular referendum, and voters would have the right to recall unworthy elected officials. Condorcet's draft, though a wellspring of ideas for later political reformers, was not a practical blueprint for the emergency confronting the First Republic.

The leaders of the Mountain denounced federalism and advocated an all-powerful central government. Their chief spokesman was Maximilien Robespierre (1758–1794). This earnest young lawyer did not look like a revolutionary: He powdered his hair neatly and wore the light-blue coat and knee-breeches of the Old Regime. Yet Robespierre was a political fanatic whose speeches were lay sermons couched in the solemn language of a new revelation. He put his creed most forcefully in February 1794:

> What is the goal toward which we are striving? The peaceful enjoyment of liberty and equality: the rule of that eternal justice whose laws have been engraved . . . upon the hearts of men, even upon the heart of the slave who ignores them and of the tyrant who denies them.
>
> We desire an order of things . . . where our country assures the welfare of each individual and where each individual enjoys with pride the prosperity and the glory of our country; where the souls of all grow through the constant expression of republican sentiments; where the arts are the ornament of the freedom which in turn ennobles them; and where commerce is the source of public wealth, not just of the monstrous opulence of a few houses.*

Apparently Robespierre truly believed that he could translate the ideas of Rousseau's *Social Contract* into a practical political program. Like Rousseau, he had faith in the natural goodness of humanity, in "the laws engraved upon the hearts of men." He was sure that he knew the general will, and that the general will demanded a Republic of Virtue. If Frenchmen would not be free and virtuous voluntarily, then, as Rousseau had recommended, they would be "forced to be free."

Robespierre and the Republic of Virtue triumphed. The Mountain won out over the Gironde in the competition for the votes of the relatively uncommitted deputies of the Plain in the Convention. The first step came when, after one hundred hours of continuous voting, the Convention declared "Citizen Louis Capet" guilty of treason and by a narrow margin sentenced him to the guillotine without delay. Louis XVI died bravely on January 21, 1793. Although the majority of the French population disapproved of the king's execution, the majority did not control the Convention. The Girondin deputies split their votes on the issue. Those who voted against the death penalty took a courageous stand in defense of the humanitarian principles of the Enlightenment, but they also exposed themselves to the charge of being counterrevolutionaries.

A combination of events at home and abroad soon destroyed the Gironde. In February 1793 the Convention rejected Condorcet's draft constitution, and in the same month it declared war on Britain, Spain, and the Netherlands. France now faced a formidable coalition of opponents, since Austria and Prussia remained at war with her. In March, the army under the Girondin Dumouriez suffered a series of defeats in the Low Countries, and in April Dumouriez deserted to the enemy. Marat now loudly denounced all associates of Dumouriez as traitors; the Girondin deputies countered by calling for the impeachment of Marat, who was brought before a special tribunal and triumphantly acquitted. In July 1793 he was assassinated in his bath by Charlotte Corday, a young woman wielding a butcher's knife and convinced that she was a new Joan of Arc called to deliver France from Jacobin radicalism.

By then, the Girondins had been completely vanquished. In the face of unemployment, high prices, and shortages of food, soap, and other necessities, they had little to prescribe except more laissez-faire. The sections of Paris demanded price controls and food requisitioning; they also pressed for the expulsion of Girondins from the Jacobin clubs and the Convention. Finally, on June 2, 1793, a vast crowd of armed sans-culottes from the sections, following the precedent of August 1792, invaded the Convention and forced the arrest of twenty-nine Girondin deputies. Backed by these armed Parisians, the Mountain intimidated the Plain, and the Convention consigned the arrested Girondins to the guillotine. The Reign of Terror had begun.

* *Le Moniteur Universel,* February 7, 1794. Our translation.

## The Reign of Terror, June 1793-July 1794

How was it that the advocates of democracy now imposed a dictatorship on France? Here is Robespierre's explanation:

To establish and consolidate democracy, to achieve the peaceful rule of constitutional laws, we must first finish the war of liberty against tyranny. . . . We must annihilate the enemies of the republic at home and abroad, or else we shall perish.

If virtue is the mainstay of a democratic government in time of peace, then in time of revolution a democratic government must rely on *virtue* and *terror*. . . . Terror is nothing but justice, swift, severe, and inflexible; it is an emanation of virtue. . . . It has been said that terror is the mainstay of a despotic government. . . . The government of the revolution is the despotism of liberty against tyranny.*

The Convention duly voted a democratic constitution, drawn up by the Mountain, granting universal manhood suffrage and giving supreme power, unhampered by Girondin checks and balances, to a single legislative chamber. The Constitution of 1793 was approved by a large majority in a referendum attracting double the participation of the election of 1792, though still representing only a minority of potential voters. Operation of the constitution was then deferred, and it never came into force. As Robespierre explained, "To establish and consolidate democracy, we must first finish the war of liberty against tyranny."

The actual government of the Terror centered on a twelve-man Committee of Public Safety, composed of Robespierre and other stalwarts from the Mountain. Though nominally responsible to the Convention, the Committee of Public Safety exercised a large measure of independent authority and acted as a kind of war cabinet. Never under the dominance of a single individual, not even Robespierre, it really functioned as a committee—"The Twelve Who Ruled" is an appropriate description. A second committee, that of General Security, supervised police activities and turned suspected enemies of the Republic over to the new Revolutionary Tribunal. To speed the work of repression, the sixteen judges and sixty jurors of the Tribunal were eventually divided into several courts.

The Mountain scrapped much of the local self-government inaugurated under the Constitution of 1791. It also whittled steadily away at the prerogatives assumed by the Paris sections, which have been likened to forty-eight independent republics or town meetings in continuous session. Local Jacobin clubs purged department and commune administrations of political unreliables, while special local courts supplemented the grim labors of the Revolutionary Tribunal. To make sure that provincial France toed the line, the Mountain sent out trusted members of the Convention as its agents, the "deputies on mission." From the standpoint of administration, the Terror marked both an anticipation of twentieth-century dictatorship and a return to the age-old French principle of centralization. The deputies on mission were the successors of the intendants of Richelieu, the enquêteurs of Saint Louis, and the missi dominici of Charlemagne. "The Twelve Who Ruled" were more effective absolutists than Louis XIV himself.

*Ibid.

## The Record of the Terror

The "swift, severe, and inflexible justice" described by Robespierre took the lives of nearly twenty thousand Frenchmen. Although the Terror claimed such social outcasts as criminals and prostitutes, its main purpose was military and political—to clear France of suspected traitors, including Marie Antoinette, and to purge the Jacobins of dissidents. It fell with the greatest severity on the clergy, the aristocracy, and the Girondins, by no means always in Paris. Many of its victims came from the Vendée, a strongly Catholic and royalist area in western France which had risen in revolt. Prisoners from the Vendée were among the two thousand victims of the *noyades* (drownings) at Nantes, where the accused were set adrift on the River Loire in leaky barges. Equally grisly was the repression of an uprising of Girondin sympathizers at Lyons, which also claimed two thousand victims.

The wartime hysteria that helped to account for the excesses of the Terror also inspired a very practical patriotism. On August 23, 1793, the Convention issued a decree epitomizing the democratic nationalism of the Jacobins:

> From this moment, until the time when the enemy shall have been driven from the territory of the Republic, all Frenchmen are permanently requisitioned for the service of the armies.
>
> Young men will go into combat; married men will manufacture arms and transport supplies; women will make tents and uniforms and will serve in the hospitals; children will make old linen into bandages; old men will be carried into the public squares to arouse the courage of the soldiers, excite hatred for kings and inspire the unity of the republic.*

In an early application of universal conscription, the army drafted all bachelors and widowers between the ages of eighteen and twenty-five. Hundreds of open-air forges were installed in Paris to manufacture weapons. Since the war prevented the importation of the saltpeter needed for gunpowder, the government sponsored a great campaign to scrape patches of saltpeter from cellars and stables.

By the close of 1793, the forces of the republic had driven foreign troops from French soil. Credit for this new shift in the tide of battle did not rest solely with the Jacobins. The military successes of the republic reflected in part the improvements made in the army during the dying years of the Old Regime; they resulted still more from the weaknesses of the coalition aligned against France. Yet they could scarcely have been achieved without the new democratic spirit that allowed men of the third estate to become officers and that made the French army the most determined, the most enterprising—and perhaps, the most idealistic—in Europe.

Total mobilization demanded an equality of economic sacrifice. To exorcise the twin devils of inflation and scarcity, the Terror issued the "maximum" legislation, placing ceilings on prices and wages. In theory, at least, wages were checked at a maximum fifty percent above the wage rate of 1790, and prices were halted at thirty-three percent above the price level of 1790. The government rationed bread and meat, forbade the use of white flour, and directed all patriots to eat *pain d'égalité*—"equality bread," a loaf utilizing almost the whole of the wheat. Finally, early in 1794, the Convention passed the "Laws of Ventôse," named for a month in the new revolutionary calendar. These laws authorized seizure of the remaining properties of the émigrés and other opponents of the republic and recommended their distribution to landless Frenchmen.

Socialist historians have sometimes found in the "maximum" and the Laws of Ventôse evidence that the Terror was moving from political to social democracy, that the Republic of Virtue was indeed beginning the socialist revolution. Actually the "maximum" regulations did not prove very effective. Attempts by the government to enforce wage ceilings made Parisian workingmen indignant. And, though the "maximum" on prices temporarily checked the depreciation of the assignats, many price-controlled articles were available only on the black market, which even the government had to patronize.

Moreover, the redistribution of property permitted by the Laws of Ventôse was never implemented. When the laws were proposed, a spokesman for the Committee of Public Safety explained that no general assault on property was intended:

> The revolution leads us to recognize the principle that he who has shown himself the enemy of his country cannot own property. The properties of patriots are sacred, but the goods of conspirators are there for the unfortunate.*

To the thoroughgoing socialist not even the properties of patriots are sacred. The middle-class leaders of the Terror were not genuine socialists; only the emergencies of the Revolution forced them to abandon laissez-faire. They had to make food cheaper for townspeople—whence the "maximum"; and they had to promise men some hope of future well-being—whence the Laws of Ventôse.

The Terror presented its most revolutionary aspect in its drastic social and cultural reforms. The Convention abolished slavery in the French colonies; at home, according to Robespierre, "we desire to substitute all the virtues and all the miracles of the Republic for all the vices and all the nonsense of monarchy." When Robespierre

*Le Moniteur Universel*, August 24, 1793. Our translation.

* Saint-Just, February 26, 1794, in *Le Moniteur Universel* the next day. Our translation.

said all, he meant all—clothing, the arts, amusements, the calendar, religion. The Republic of Virtue could tolerate nothing that smelled of the Old Regime. Even the traditional forms of address, "Monsieur" and "Madame," gave way to "Citoyen" and "Citoyenne".

Ever since 1789, revolutionists had discarded elaborate gowns and knee-breeches as symbols of idleness and privilege. With the exception of Robespierre, good republican men were sansculottes and women affected simple, high-waisted dresses, copied from the costumes of the ancient Romans. Rome became the model for behavior—the virtuous Rome of the republic, of course, not the sordid empire. Parents named their children Brutus or Cato or Gracchus, and the theater shelved the masterpieces of Racine and Corneille for stilted dramas glorifying Roman heroes. Cabinetmakers, deserting the graceful style of Louis XV, produced sturdy neoclassical furniture decorated with Roman symbols. "The arts," said Robespierre, "are the ornament of the freedom which in turn ennobles them." Playwrights, authors, and editors who failed to ornament freedom properly experienced censorship or even the guillotine. The Jacobins reduced the lively newspapers of the early revolution to dull semiofficial organs.

They also instituted a sweeping reform of the calendar (October 1793). The first day of the republic, September 22, 1792, was designated the initial day of Year I, Roman numerals were assigned to the years, and the months received new and more "natural" names:

| | |
|---|---|
| Fall: | Vendémiaire (Grape harvest) |
| | Brumaire (Misty) |
| | Frimaire (Frosty) |
| Winter: | Nivôse (Snowy) |
| | Pluviôse (Rainy) |
| | Ventôse (Windy) |
| Spring: | Germinal (Sprouting) |
| | Floréal (Flowering) |
| | Prairial (Meadow) |
| Summer: | Messidor (Wheat harvest) |
| | Thermidor (Heat) |
| | Fructidor (Ripening) |

Each month had thirty days, divided into three ten-day weeks. Every tenth day was set aside for rest and for the celebration of one of the virtues so admired by Robespierre—Hatred of Tyrants and Traitors, Heroism, Frugality, Stoicism, not to mention two anticipations of Mother's Day (Filial Piety and Maternal Tenderness). The five days left over at the end of the year were dedicated to Genius, Labor, Noble Actions, Awards, and Opinion. The revolutionary calendar, for all its sanctimonious touches, was worthy of the Enlightenment. But it antagonized workmen, who disliked laboring nine days out of ten instead of six out of seven. It never really took root, and Napoleon scrapped it a decade later.

The Convention had better luck with another reform close to the spirit of the Age of Reason—the metric system. A special committee, including Condorcet, Laplace, Lavoisier, and other distinguished intellectuals, devised new weights and measures based on the uniform use of the decimal system rather than on the haphazard accumulations of custom. In August 1793 a decree made the meter the standard unit of length, and supplementary legislation in 1795 estab-

*Robespierre, having ordered the execution of all the rest of France, now guillotines the executioner: a contemporary cartoon.*

lished the liter as the measure of volume and the gram as the unit of weight. Although the Convention could do little to implement the ambitious revolutionary ideal of universal education, it did convert establishments of the Old Regime into the nuclei of such great Parisian institutions as the Louvre Museum, the National Archives, and the Bibliothèque Nationale (one of the world's major libraries).

Sometimes the forces of tradition resisted even the Terror, which tried to destroy the old religion but never succeeded in legislating a new faith. Many churches were closed and turned into barracks or administrative offices; often their medieval glass and sculpture were destroyed. Some of the Jacobins launched a "de-Christianization" campaign to make Catholics into philosophes and their churches into "temples of Reason." Robespierre, however, disliked the cult of Reason; the Republic of Virtue, he believed, should acknowledge an ultimate author of morality. The Convention therefore decreed (May 1794) that "the French people recognize the existence of the Supreme Being and the immortality of the soul." At the festival of the Supreme Being, June 8, 1794, Robespierre set fire to figures representing Vice, Folly, and Atheism, and from the embers a statue of Wisdom emerged, but smudged with smoke because of a mechanical slip-up. The audience laughed. The deistic concept of the supreme being was too remote and the mechanics of the new worship were too artificial to appeal to the religious emotions of Frenchmen.

Indeed, the Republic of Virtue was too abstract in ideals, and too violent in practice, to retain popular support. Like the Geneva of Calvin, the France of Robespierre demanded superhuman devotion to duty and inhuman indifference to hardships and bloodshed. During the first half of 1794, Robespierre pressed the Terror so relentlessly that even the members of the Committees of Public Safety and General Security began to fear they would be the next victims. Robespierre lost his backing in the Convention, as more and more deputies came to favor moderation. The crucial day was the ninth of Thermidor, Year II (July 27, 1794), when shouts of "Down with the Tyrant!" drowned out Robespierre's attempts to address the deputies. The Convention ordered Robespierre's arrest, and on the next day the great fanatic went to the guillotine. Significantly, the sans-culottes of Paris made no move to rescue Robespierre, for the government had made a new attempt to enforce the "maximum" on wages only a few days before the ninth of Thermidor.

## The Thermidorean Reaction

The leaders of the Thermidorean Reaction, many of them former Jacobins, soon dismantled the machinery of the Terror. They disbanded the Revolutionary Tribunal, recalled the deputies on mission, and deprived the Committees of Public Safety and General Security of their independent authority. They closed the Paris Jacobin club and invited the surviving Girondin deputies to resume their old seats in the Convention. They took the first step toward the restoration of Catholicism by permitting priests to celebrate Mass, though under state supervision and without state financial support. The press and the theater recovered their freedom, and pleasure seekers again flocked to Paris, now liberated from the somberness of the Republic of Virtue. France was resuming a normal existence.

Normality, however, exacted a price. In southern and western France a counterrevolutionary "White Terror," equaling the great Terror in fury, claimed many lives, not only supporters of the Mountain but also purchasers of former church and noble lands. The men of Thermidor caused an acute inflation by canceling the economic legislation of the Terror. No longer checked even slightly by the "maximum," the prices of some foods rose to a hundred times the level of 1790, and the assignats sank so low in value that businessmen refused to accept them. Popular suffering was now more intense than it had ever been under the Terror. Desperate, half-starving Parisians staged several demonstrations against the Thermidoreans during 1795. Sometimes the rioters voiced their support of the discredited Mountain and its democratic Constitution of 1793, and sometimes they let themselves be used by royalist agents, but always they clamored for bread and lower prices.

The Thermidorean Reaction concluded with the passage of the Constitution of 1795, the last major act of the Convention. The men of Thermidor wanted both to retain the Republic and to assure the dominance of the propertied classes. The Constitution of 1795 therefore denied the

*The closing of the Hall of the Jacobins during the night of the 9th–10th Thermidor.*

vote to the poorest quarter of the nation and required that candidates for public office possess considerable property. It established two legislative councils, the Five Hundred and the Elders (who had to be at least forty years old and either married or widowed); both councils were to be elected piecemeal after the American practice of renewing one-third of the Senate every two years. Two-thirds of the initial members of the councils were to be drawn from the deputies of the Convention, who were therefore labeled "les perpetuels." The Council of Five Hundred nominated, and the Elders chose, five directors who headed the executive Directory, which was almost totally independent of the legislative councils.

The Constitution of 1795 marked the third great effort of the Revolution to provide France with an enduring government. It followed in part a classical example, for the two councils were patterned on the Areopagus and the Five Hundred of ancient Athens; it also followed the American precedent of 1787 and the French precedent of 1791. It embodied the separation of powers and deferred to the aristocracy of wealth, though not to that of birth. By abandoning the political democracy of the stillborn Constitution of 1793 and by reverting to the restricted suffrage of 1791, it demonstrated that the most radical phase of the Revolution had passed.

### The Directory

The new regime of the Directory, aided by good harvests which ended food shortages, made a vigorous attack on economic problems. It levied high protective tariffs, both as a measure of war against England and as a concession to French businessmen. Again responding to business pressure, it destroyed the plates used to print the assignats and in 1797 withdrew paper money from circulation. The return to hard money required stringent governmental economies. The Directory instituted these economies, made tax collection more efficient, and enjoyed considerable loot from France's victorious wars. It eased the crushing burden of the national debt by repudiating two-thirds of it and gave the veteran livre a new and lasting name, the franc.

The Directory suppressed with ease the amateurish "conspiracy of the equals" (1796–1797) sponsored by Gracchus Babeuf, who has come down in socialist legend as the first communist but who seems to have dreamt of a more equal society without realizing that rigorous organization would be needed to realize it. The Directory experienced much greater difficulty with the recurrent plots of royalists and Jacobins. Moreover, the directors and the legislative councils clashed repeatedly, each side seeking to turn the political balance in its own favor, and each, in consequence, violating the constitution. The councils sacked directors before their terms were finished; the directors refused to allow duly elected councillors to take their seats. Disgruntled politicians and apprehensive moderates, who feared that the Directory might be taken over by extremists, began to maneuver for the help of the army. The result of their maneuvering was the coup d'état of Brumaire in 1799 and the dictatorship of a general, Napoleon Bonaparte.

## IV Napoleon and France

Edmund Burke, the British political philosopher, foresaw very early the long process that culminated in Napoleon's dominance of France and Europe. In 1790, Burke warned the French —and his own countrymen—in his *Reflections on the Revolution in France:*

> Everything depends on the army in such a government as yours; for you have industriously destroyed all the opinions, . . . all the instincts which support government. Therefore the moment any difference arises between your National Assembly and any part of the nation, you must have recourse to force. Nothing else is left to you. . . .
>
> It is besides to be considered, whether an assembly like yours . . . is fit for promoting the discipline and obedience of an army. It is known, that armies have hitherto yielded a very precarious and uncertain obedience to any senate, or popular authority. . . . The officers must totally lose the characteristic disposition of military men, if they see with perfect submission and due admiration, the dominion of pleaders; especially when they find that they have a new court to pay to an endless succession of those pleaders. . . . In the weakness of one kind of authority, and in the fluctuation of all, the officers of an army will remain for some time mutinous and full of faction, until some popular general who understands the art of conciliating the soldiery, and who possesses the true spirit of command, shall draw the eyes of all men upon himself. Armies will obey him on his personal account. There is no other way of securing military obedience in this state of things. But the moment in which that event shall happen, the person who really commands the army is your master; the master . . . of your king, the master of your assembly, the master of your whole republic.*

In 1790, however, except for Burke, no one outside France paid much heed to the French army. It was widely believed that the very intensity of domestic problems made France incapable of a vigorous foreign policy. Catherine the Great predicted at late as 1792 that ten thousand soldiers would be sufficient to douse the "abominable bonfire" in France. Liberals everywhere hailed the peaceful promise of the Revolution. The capture of the Bastille delighted Charles James Fox, a leading English Whig: "How much the greatest event it is that ever happened in the world! and how much the best!"

*Everyman ed. (New York, 1910), pp. 215–217.

### The First Coalition, 1792-1795

The war that broke out in the spring of 1792 soon destroyed the illusions of French military weakness and French liberal purity. It deserves to be called the World War of 1792–1795, for almost all the European powers eventually participated, and the fighting ranged far beyond Europe. By the time the war was a year old, Austria and Prussia, the charter members of the first coalition against France, had been joined by Holland, Spain, and Great Britain. The British had both ideological and strategic interests at stake. They regarded the attack on the Tuileries, the September massacres, and the execution of Louis XVI as outrages against human decency and the institution of monarchy. And the French invasion of the Austrian Netherlands in the fall of 1792 raised the unpleasant prospect that this Belgian "cockpit of Europe" would fall under French control. The early campaigns of the war were indecisive. Late in 1792, the French followed up their success at Valmy by invading Belgium, only to lose ground again in 1793 after the defeat and desertion of Dumouriez. Then in 1794 the French definitely gained the advantage, and by 1795 French troops had occupied Belgium, Holland, and Germany west of the Rhine.

One reason for French success we have already seen—the Convention's energetic mobilization of national resources, which enabled France to have the unprecedented total of a million men under arms by the spring of 1794. Another reason, equally important yet easy to overlook, was the weakness of the first coalition. The partners in the coalition lacked a first-rate commander; nor did they achieve effective coordination of their efforts. The duke of Brunswick's failure to take Paris in 1792 resulted as much from his own deficient generalship as from the "miracle" of Valmy. Moreover, the partitions of Poland in 1793 and 1795 greatly assisted the French by distracting Prussia, Russia, and Austria. The pick of the Prussian army was diverted to occupation duty in newly annexed Polish provinces. By 1795 things had come to such a pass that the Prussians did not dare attack the French for fear of being assaulted from the rear by their nominal Austrian ally.

Prussia was the first member of the coalition to make peace. In the Treaty of Basel (1795) she ceded to France the scattered Prussian holdings west of the Rhine on the understanding that she might seek compensation elsewhere in Germany. Spain and Holland soon deserted the coalition also. In 1795, then, France at last secured her "natural frontiers." In addition to Belgium and the Rhineland she had also annexed Savoy and Nice, thereby extending her southeastern border to the crest of the Alps. These conquests, however, belied the ideals of the Revolution. In declaring war on Austria in 1792, France had sworn to uphold the promise of the Constitution of 1791: that she would never undertake a war of conquest. This was to be "not a war of nation against nation, but the righteous defense of a free people against the unjust aggression of a king." But the conquering armies of the First Republic brought closer the day when nation would fight nation—when the European nations would invoke "the righteous defense of a free people against the unjust aggression," not of a king, but of revolutionary France.

### Napoleon's Early Career

At the close of 1795, only Britain and Austria remained officially at war with France. To lead the attack against Hapsburg forces in northern Italy, the Directory picked a youthful general who was something of a philosophe and revolutionary as well as a ruthless, ambitious adventurer. He was born Napoleone Buonaparte on Corsica in 1769, soon after the French acquisition of that Mediterranean island from Genoa. He retained throughout his life the intense family loyalty characteristic of the rather primitive society of Corsica and bestowed on the members of the Bonaparte clan all the spoils of conquest, even thrones.

As a boy of nine Napoleon began to attend military school in France and, though he now spelled his name in the French style, was snubbed as a foreigner by some of his fellow cadets. He immersed himself in his studies and in reading (Rousseau was his favorite) and dreamed of the day when he might liberate his native island from French control. Later, however, his zeal for Corsican independence faded in consequence of the rupture between the Bonapartes and the hero of Corsican nationalism, Paoli, who was an ally of Britain. When the Revolution broke out, the young artillery officer helped to overthrow the Old Regime in Corsica and then went back to France to resume his military career. He defended the Convention, but more out of expediency than from conviction, and commanded the artillery in December 1793, when the forces of the Convention recaptured the Mediterranean port of Toulon, which had fallen to the British earlier in the year. After Thermidor he fell under a cloud as a suspected "terrorist" and came close to going with a French team of experts to advise the Ottoman Empire on modernizing its army. But he settled for a desk job in Paris and was available to rescue the Thermidorean Convention, in the last moments before the Directory took over (October 1795), by mowing down royalist rioters with the famous "whiff of grapeshot." Then he married Josephine de Beauharnais, a widow six years his senior and an intimate of the ruling clique of the Directory. The combination of Josephine's connections and Napoleon's own demonstrated talent gained him the Italian command in 1796.

In the Italian campaign, Major General Bonaparte, still in his twenties, cleared the Austrians out of their strongholds in the space of a year and made them sue for peace. He showed a remarkable ability to strike quickly and by surprise before his opponents could consolidate their defenses. He also showed a gift for propaganda and public relations, as this proclamation from the early phases of the campaign will illustrate:

> Soldiers! In two weeks you have won six victories; you have made 15,000 prisoners; you have killed or wounded more than 10,000 men.
>
> Deprived of everything, you have accomplished everything. You have won battles without cannon, negotiated rivers without bridges, made forced marches without shoes, encamped without brandy, and often without bread. Only the phalanxes of the Republic, only the soldiers of Liberty, would have been capable of suffering the things that you have suffered.
>
> You all burn to carry the glory of the French people; to humiliate the proud kings who dared to contemplate shackling us; to go back to your villages, to say proudly: 'I was of the conquering army of Italy!"
>
> Friends, I promise you that conquest; but there is a condition you must swear to fulfill: to respect the people whom you are delivering; to repress horrible pillaging.
>
> Peoples of Italy, the French army comes to break your chains; greet it with confidence; your property, religion and customs will be respected.*

It was characteristic of Napoleon to promise all things to all men. He encouraged the nationalism of underpaid and underfed French soldiers; yet he appealed also to the nationalism of the Italians, promising them liberation from Austria and guaranteeing the orderly conduct of the French army. He did not, of course, tell the Italians that they might be exchanging one master for another, nor did he publicize the money that he seized from Italian governments and the art treasures that he took from Italian galleries and shipped back to France.

In the Treaty of Campoformio (1797) terminating the Italian campaign, Austria acknowledged the loss of Belgium and recognized the two puppet states that Napoleon set up in northwestern Italy, the Ligurian Republic (Genoa) and the Cisalpine Republic (the former Austrian possession of Lombardy). In return, the Hapsburgs received the Italian territories of the Venetian Republic and a secret French assurance that Prussia, despite the specific promise made to her in 1795, would not be permitted to compensate for her losses in the Rhineland by taking lands elsewhere in Germany.

Only Britain remained at war with France. Napoleon decided to attack her indirectly through Egypt, then a semi-independent vassal of the Ottoman Empire. This would-be Alexander the Great, seeking new worlds to conquer, talked grandly of digging a canal at Suez, which would give French merchants the monopoly of a new short trade route to India and exact belated retribution from Britain for Clive's victory in the Seven Years' War. Since Napoleon shared the passion of the Enlightenment for science and antiquity, he invited about one hundred archaeologists and other experts to accompany his army and thereby helped to found the study known as Egyptology. Frenchmen discovered the Rosetta Stone, the first key to the translation of ancient Egyptian hieroglyphics, and later deciphered by Champollion. Napoleon's experts established in Egypt an outpost of French cultural imperialism that lasted until the twentieth century.

From the military standpoint, however, the campaign failed. Having eluded the British Med-

* Abridged from *Le Moniteur Universel,* May 17, 1796. Our translation.

iterranean fleet commanded by Nelson, Napoleon landed in Egypt in July 1798 and quickly routed the Mamluks, the ruling oligarchy. Then disaster struck. On August 1, 1798, Nelson discovered the French fleet moored at Abukir Bay along the Egyptian coast and destroyed it before its captains had time to weigh anchor. Nelson's victory deprived the French of both supplies and reinforcements. After a year of futile campaigning in the Near East, Napoleon suddenly left Egypt in August 1799 and returned to France.

### Brumaire

Napoleon found the situation in France ripe for a decisive political stroke. The Directory was shaken by a strong revival of Jacobinism. Several hundred deputies in the legislative councils belonged to the Society of the Friends of Liberty and Equality, essentially the old Jacobin club. Under their influence, the councils in 1799 decreed a forced loan from the rich and passed a Law of Hostages, designed to make the émigrés behave by threatening their relatives in France with reprisals if they engaged in activities hostile to the French Republic. Moderates feared that a new Reign of Terror would soon be unleashed.

Abroad, the Directory had established four new satellite republics with classical names—the Roman, the Parthenopean in Naples, the Batavian in Holland, and the Helvetian in Switzerland. But this new success of French imperialism upset the European balance and provoked the formation of the second coalition, headed by Britain, Austria, and Russia. The Hapsburgs resented the extension of French influence in their former Italian preserve, and Czar Paul I (1796–1801) feared that Napoleon would damage Russia's Mediterranean interests. The eccentric czar was head of the Knights of Malta, a Catholic order dating back to the Crusades, whom Napoleon had expelled from their headquarters on the island of Malta. In the campaign of 1799, Russian troops fought in Italy and Switzerland, and the Russian general Suvorov, who defeated the French repeatedly, became the hero of western Europe. By August 1799 the French had been expelled from Italy, and their puppet republics—Cisalpine, Roman, and Parthenopean—had been dismantled.

In these circumstances, Napoleon got a rousing reception on his return from Egypt. Soon he was engaged in a plot to overthrow the Directory, with the complicity of two of the five directors, Roger-Ducos and Siéyès, the old champion of the third estate. On November 9 and 10, 1799 (18 and 19 Brumaire by the revolutionary calendar), the plot was executed. The three directors not in the plot resigned, and the two legislative councils named Napoleon military commander of Paris. He was then to persuade the councils to entrust to the two remaining directors and himself the task of drafting a new constitution. Napoleon came close to failure. In the Elders he made a poor impression by mumbling almost incoherently about "volcanoes, tyrants, Jacobins, Cromwell." In the Council of Five Hundred, where there were many Jacobin deputies, he was greeted with cries of "Outlaw him," received a pummeling, scratched at his own face in anxiety till he drew blood, and then fainted. His brother Lucien, the presiding officer of the Five Hundred, saved the day until a detachment of troops loyal to Napoleon expelled the hostile deputies.

The coup d'état of Brumaire ended the Directory. The Bonapartist minority in the council vested full power in the victorious triumvirate of Roger-Ducos, Siéyès, and Napoleon, of whom only Napoleon really counted. It had all happened just as Edmund Burke had predicted:

> In the weakness of authority, . . . some popular general shall draw the eyes of all men upon himself. Armies will obey him on his personal account. . . . The person who really commands the army is your master.

### Napoleonic Government

The Constitution of the Year VIII, drawn up after Brumaire, was based on Siéyès' autocratic maxim "Confidence from below, authority from above." It erected a very strong executive, the Consulate, named, like other bodies set up by the constitution, after institutions of republican Rome. Although three consuls shared the executive, Napoleon as first consul left the other two only nominal power. Four separate bodies had a hand in legislation: (1) the Council of State proposed laws; (2) the Tribunate debated them but did not vote; (3) the Legislative Corps voted them but did not debate; (4) the Senate had the right to veto legislation. The members of all four bodies were either appointed by the first consul or elected indirectly by a process so complex that Bonaparte had ample opportunity to manipulate candidates. The core of this system was the Council of State, staffed by Bonaparte's hand-picked choices, which served both as a cabinet and as the highest administrative court. The three remaining bodies were intended merely to go through the motions of enacting whatever the first consul decreed. Even so, they were sometimes unruly, and the Tribunate so annoyed Napoleon that he finally abolished it in 1807.

Meantime, step by step, Napoleon increased his own authority. In 1802, he persuaded the legislators to drop the original ten-year limitation on his term of office and make him first consul for life, with the power to designate his successor and amend the constitution at will. France was now a monarchy in all but name. In 1804, he took the next logical move and prompted the Senate to declare that "the government of the republic is entrusted to an emperor." A magnificent coronation took place at Notre Dame in Paris on December 2. The pope consecrated the emperor, but, following Charlemagne's example, Napoleon placed the crown on his own head.

Each time Napoleon revised the Constitution in a nonrepublican direction he made the republican gesture of submitting the change to the electorate. Each time, the results of the plebiscite were overwhelmingly favorable: In 1799–1800, the vote was 3,011,107 for Napoleon and the Constitution of the Year VIII, and 1,562 against; in 1802, it was 3,568,885 for Napoleon and the life Consulate, and 8,374 against; in 1804, 3,572,329 for Napoleon and the Empire, and 2,579 against. Although the voters were exposed to considerable official pressure and the announced results were perhaps rigged a little, the majority of Frenchmen undoubtedly supported Napoleon. His military triumphs appealed to their growing nationalism, and his policy of stability at home insured them against further revolutionary crises and changes. Confidence did indeed seem to increase from below as authority increased from above.

If by any chance confidence failed to materialize below, Napoleon had the authority to deal with the recalcitrant. He wiped out the local self-government remaining from the early days of the Revolution. In place of locally elected officials, he substituted those appointed by himself—prefects in departments, subprefects in arrondissements, mayors in communes—and all were instructed to enforce compliance with the emperor's dictates. Napoleon brought the old French tradition of centralization to a new peak of intensity.

Men of every political background staffed the imperial administration. Napoleon cared little whether his subordinates were returned émigrés or ex-Jacobins, so long as they had ability. Besides, their varied antecedents reinforced the impression that narrow factionalism was dead and that the empire rested on a broad political base. Napoleon paid officials well and offered the additional bait of high titles. With the establishment of the empire he created dukes by the dozen and counts and barons by the hundred. He rewarded outstanding generals with the rank of marshal and other officers and civilian officials with the Legion of Honor. "Aristocracy always exists," Napoleon remarked. "Destroy it in the nobility, it removes itself to the rich and powerful houses of the middle class."* The imperial aristocracy gave the leaders of the middle class the social distinction that they felt to be rightfully theirs.

### Law and Justice

Napoleon revived some of the glamor of the Old Regime but not its glaring inequalities. His series of law codes, the celebrated Code Napoléon (1804–1810), declared all men equal before the law without regard to their rank and wealth. It extended to all the right to follow the occupation, and embrace the religion, of their choosing. It gave France the single coherent system of law which the philosophes had demanded and which the revolutionary governments had been too busy to formulate.

The Code Napoléon did not, however, embody the full judicial reform program of the Enlightenment; it incorporated from the old Roman law some practices that strengthened the absolutism of the empire. It favored the interests of the state over the rights of the individual, and it permitted some use of torture in trial procedure. Judges were no longer elected, as they had been

* Quoted in H. A. L. Fisher, *Napoleon* (New York, 1913), Appendix I.

under the Constitution of 1791, but appointed by the emperor; jurors were selected by his prefects. Though Napoleon confirmed the revolutionary legislation permitting divorce by mutual consent, the code canceled other revolutionary laws protecting wives, minors, and illegitimate children. The man of the family regained his old legal superiority. At times confirming the principles of 1789, and at times betraying them, Napoleonic law and justice offered a fair summary of the fate of the Revolution under the empire.

A similar ambiguity clouded Napoleon's attitude toward civil liberties. He practiced religious toleration of a sort and welcomed former political heretics into his administration. But his generosity stemmed always from expediency, never from any fundamental belief in liberty. If he failed to get his way by conciliation, he used force. In the western departments, where royalist uprisings had become chronic since the revolt in the Vendée, he massacred the rebels who declined his offer of amnesty in 1800. In 1804, he kidnapped the duke of Enghien from the neutral German state of Baden because the duke was believed to be the choice of monarchist conspirators for the throne of France. Though Napoleon immediately discovered the duke's innocence, he had him executed none the less.

Napoleon cared little for freedom of speech. In July, 1801, for example, he directed his librarian to read all the newspapers carefully and

> make an abstract of everything they contain likely to affect the public point of view, especially with regard to religion, philosophy, and political opinion. He will send me this abstract between 5 and 6 o'clock every day.
>
> Once every ten days he will send me an analysis of all the books or pamphlets which have appeared. . . .
>
> He will take pains to procure copies of all the plays which are produced, and to analyse them for me, with observations of the same character as those above mentioned. This analysis must be made, at latest, within 48 hours of the production of the plays.*

And so on—through "bills, posters, advertisements, institutes, literary meetings, sermons and fashionable trials"—no segment of public opinion escaped Napoleon's manipulation. He reduced by five-sixths the number of Paris newspapers and pestered theater managers with suggestions for improving the patriotic tone of plays. When he wanted to arouse French feelings, he simply started a press campaign, as in this instance from 1807:

> A great hue and cry is to be raised against the persecutions experienced by the Catholics of Ireland at the hands of the Anglican Church. . . . Bishops will be approached so that prayers will be offered entreating an end to the persecutions of the Anglican church against the Irish Catholics. But the administration must move very delicately and make use of the newspapers without their realizing what the government is driving at. . . . And the term "Anglican church" must always be used in place of "Protestants," for we have Protestants in France, but no Anglican church.*

## Religion

Political considerations colored all Napoleon's decisions on religion. "I do not see in religion the mystery of the incarnation," he said, "but the mystery of the social order. It attaches to heaven an idea of equality which prevents the rich man from being massacred by the poor."† Since French Catholics loathed the anticlericalism of the Revolution, Napoleon sought to appease them by working out a reconciliation with Rome.

The Concordat negotiated with Pope Pius VII (1800–1823) in 1801 accomplished the reconciliation. It canceled only the most obnoxious features of the Civil Constitution of the Clergy. The French state, while agreeing to pay clerical salaries, also agreed to suppress the popular election of bishops and priests. The bishops were to be nominated by the government and then consecrated by the pope; the priests were to be appointed by the bishops. At this point, Napoleon's concessions stopped. By declaring that Catholicism was the faith of the "great majority of Frenchmen," rather than the state religion, the Concordat implicitly admitted the toleration of Protestants and Jews. Also by implication the

* Quoted in J. M. Thompson, ed., *Napoleon's Letters* (London, 1954), pp. 93–94.

* *Lettres Inédites de Napoléon* (Paris, 1897), I, 93–94. Our translation.

† Quoted in H. A. L. Fisher, *Napoleon* (New York, 1913), Appendix I.

*Napoleon in 1798: an unfinished portrait by David.*

pope accepted such important measures of the Revolution as the abolition of the tithe and the confiscation of ecclesiastical lands.

Finally, the Concordat made the activities of the Church in France subject to the "police regulations" of the state. These regulations were spelled out in the Organic Articles, which Napoleon appended to the Concordat without consulting the pope. The French government was to supervise the publication of papal bulls, the establishment of seminaries, the nature of catechisms, and a host of other details. The Articles also reaffirmed the principle of the special autonomy enjoyed by the Gallican church within Catholicism. Despite all this, the anticlericals opposed the Concordat, and it took all Napoleon's pressure to obtain ratification of the Concordat by the legislative bodies of the Consulate.

The Concordat, then, made the Church a ward of the French state. Though it antagonized anticlericals, it did conciliate large numbers of Catholics, and it remained in force until 1905. The Concordat, however, did not bring complete peace between France and the Vatican, for Napoleon insisted that the pope should render to Caesar the things that were Caesar's. When Pius VII objected to Napoleon's making a French satellite of the Papal States, the new Caesar lectured him on the proper division of authority between the spiritual and temporal powers. Pius passed the last years of the Napoleonic regime as Bonaparte's prisoner, first in northern Italy and then in France.

### Education

The Revolution and Napoleon cost the Church its monopoly over education. The Constitution of 1791 had promised France a system of state schools. The Thermidorean Convention, while doing little to apply this principle to primary education, did set up institutions for advanced training, like the famous Ecole Polytechnique in Paris for engineers. In each department of France it also established a "central school" to provide secondary education of good quality at relatively low cost to students. Napoleon abolished these central schools in 1802 and replaced them with a smaller number of *lycées* open only to the relatively few pupils who could afford the high tuition or who received state scholarships. The change had a political motive, for Napoleon intended the lycées to groom capable and loyal administrators. The students wore uniforms and marched to military drums, and the curriculum, too, served the ends of patriotic indoctrination. To provide for the superintendence of all schools, lay and clerical, Napoleon founded in 1808 a body with the misleading name "University." He neglected primary schooling almost completely; yet building on the revolutionary base, he did advance the construction of secular schools. The educational competition of church and state, so often a bitter issue in nineteenth-century France, dated back to the Revolution and Napoleon.

### Economics

Political aims likewise governed the economic program of an emperor determined to promote national unity. The French peasants wanted to be left alone to enjoy the new freedom acquired in 1789; Napoleon did not disturb them, except to raise army recruits. The middle class wanted a balanced national budget and the end of revolutionary experiments with paper currency and a controlled economy. Napoleon continued the sound money of the Directory and, unlike the Directory, balanced the budget, thanks to the immense plunder that he gained in war. He greatly improved the efficiency and probity of tax collectors and established the semiofficial Bank of France (1800) to act as the government's financial agent. He strengthened the curbs placed on strikes and labor unions by the Le Chapelier Law of 1791 and obliged every workman to carry a written record listing his jobs and his general reputation. Though seaports suffered from the decline of overseas trade, rich war contracts and subsidies kept employment and profits generally high. As the war went on and on, however, Napoleon found it increasingly difficult to keep the peasantry and the bourgeoisie contented. Despite the levies on conquered countries, he had to draft more soldiers from the peasantry and increase the already unpopular taxes on salt, liquor, and tobacco.

In summary, the domestic policies of Napoleon I had something in common with the methods of all the celebrated one-man rulers. Like Caesar in Rome, Napoleon rendered lip service to the republic while subverting republican institutions; he used prefects to impose centralized authority as Louis XIV had used intendants; and, like modern dictators, he scorned free speech. Yet Napoleon was also a genuine enlightened despot. His law code and some of his educational reforms would have delighted the philosophes. He ended civil strife without sacrificing the redistribution of land and the equality before the law gained in 1789 and the years following. Abandoning some revolutionary policies, modifying others, and completing still others, Napoleon regimented the Revolution without wholly destroying it.

## V Napoleon and Europe

To many Frenchmen, Napoleon was the Man of Destiny, the most brilliant ruler in their country's long history. To most Europeans, on the other hand, Napoleon was the sinister Man on Horseback, the enemy of national independence, the foreigner who imposed French control and French reforms. As French conquests accumulated, and as nominally free countries became French puppets, Europe grew to hate the insatiable imperialism of Napoleon. Napoleonic France succeeded in building up a vast empire, but only at the cost of arousing the implacable enmity of the other European nations.

### The War, 1800-1807

Napoleon had barely launched the Consulate when he took to the field again. The second coalition, which had reached the peak of its success in August 1799, was now falling to pieces. Czar Paul of Russia alarmed Britain and Austria by his interest in Italy, and Britain offended him by retaining Malta, the headquarters of his beloved Knights. The czar launched against Britain a Baltic League of Armed Neutrality linking Prussia, Sweden, and Denmark with Russia. He even contemplated joining with France to drive the British out of India; this fantastic scheme collapsed when he was murdered in 1801 and succeeded by his son, Alexander I. The League in the Baltic disintegrated after Nelson violated Danish neutrality to bombard the Danish fleet in port at Copenhagen. Meanwhile, in the spring of 1800 Napoleon crossed the Alps with much fanfare, acting as though no one had ever made the passage before. He defeated the Austrians in Italy and negotiated the Treaty of Lunéville (1801), whereby Austria recognized the reconstituted French satellites in Italy and agreed that France should have a hand in redrawing the map of Germany.

After Lunéville, as after Campoformio four years before, Britain alone remained at war with France. British taxpayers, however, wanted relief from their heavy burden; British merchants longed to resume trading with continental markets partially closed to them since 1793. Though Britain had been unable to check Napoleon's expansion in Europe, she had very nearly won the colonial and naval war by 1801. She had captured former Dutch and Spanish colonies, and Nelson's fleet had expelled the French from Egypt and Malta. The British cabinet was confident that it held a strong bargaining position and could obtain favorable terms from Napoleon. But in the Peace of Amiens (1802) the British promised to surrender part of their colonial conquests and got nothing in return. The French failed either to reopen the Continent to British exports or to relinquish Belgium, which remained, in Napoleon's phrase, "a loaded pistol aimed at the heart of Britain."

The one-sided Peace of Amiens provided only a year's truce in the worldwide struggle of France and Britain. Napoleon aroused British exporters by a more stringent tariff law (1803) and jeopardized British interests in the Caribbean by a grandiose project for a colonial empire based on the island of Haiti and on the vast Louisiana territory ceded back to France in 1800 by Spain. In Haiti the Consulate enraged the blacks by attempting to restore slavery. A rebellion broke out, led by the able Toussaint l'Ouverture, whom the French defeated; but continued black resistance and an outbreak of yellow fever took a fearful toll of French troops and forced Napoleon to abandon the American project. In 1803, he sold to the United States for 80,000,000 francs (about $16,000,000) all of Louisiana, which later formed the whole or part of thirteen states.

When the Louisiana Purchase was completed, France and Britain were again at war. Napoleon interned many of the British tourists who had flocked to Paris since the Peace of Amiens, thus striking a new note of "total" war, contrasting with the eighteenth-century custom that permitted enemy citizens to circulate relatively freely even during hostilities. From 1803 through 1805, Napoleon actively prepared to invade England. He assembled more than a hundred thousand troops and a thousand landing barges on the French side of the Straits of Dover. In 1805, he sent Admiral Villeneuve and the French fleet to the West Indies to lure the British fleet away from Europe. Then Villeneuve was to return posthaste to convoy the French invasion force across the Channel while Nelson was still vainly combing the Caribbean. Villeneuve failed to give Nelson the slip; back in European waters, he put in at a friendly Spanish port instead of heading directly for the Channel as Napoleon had ordered. Nelson engaged the combined French and Spanish fleets off Cape Trafalgar at the southwest corner of Spain (October 1805). He lost his own life but not before he had destroyed half of his adversaries' ships without sacrificing a single one of his own. The hapless Villeneuve, long aware of French naval inferiority, committed suicide. The Battle of Trafalgar gave the British undisputed control of the seas and blasted French hopes of a cross-Channel invasion.

By the time of Trafalgar, Austria and Russia had joined with Britain in the third coalition. Austria, in particular, had been alarmed by Napoleon's efforts to promote a major revision of the political map of Germany. In 1803 the Reichsdeputationshauptschluss (a fine German word, "chief decree of the imperial deputation") abolished more than a hundred of the Germanies, chiefly city-states and small ecclesiastical principalities. The chief beneficiaries of this readjustment were the south German states of Bavaria, Württemberg, and Baden, which Napoleon clearly intended to form into a "third" Germany, dominated by France, as opposed to the "first" and "second" Germanies of Austria and Prussia, respectively.

Bonaparte routed the continental members of the third coalition in the most dazzling campaign of his career. At Ulm, on the upper Danube (October 1805), he captured 30,000 Austrians who had moved westward without waiting for their Russian allies. He met the main Russian force and the balance of the Austrian army near the Moravian village of Austerlitz. The ensuing battle (December 2, 1805) fittingly celebrated the first anniversary of Napoleon's coronation as emperor. Bringing up reinforcements secretly and with great speed, Napoleon completely surprised his opponents; their casualties were three times greater than his own. Within the month he forced the Hapsburg emperor, Francis II, to sign the humiliating Treaty of Pressburg, giving

*A supposed Napoleonic scheme for the invasion of England, by sea, air, and cross-Channel tunnel; the kites are Britain's anticipation of antiaircraft defense.*

the Austrian Tyrol to Bavaria and Venetia to the Napoleonic puppet kingdom of Italy.

A still harsher fate awaited the Prussians, brought back into the war for the first time since 1795 by Napoleon's repeated interventions in German affairs. The fact that the inept duke of Brunswick was still the Prussian commander, thirteen years after he had lost the battle of Valmy, indicated how much the army had deteriorated since the days of Frederick the Great. In October 1806 the French pulverized the main Prussian contingents in the twin battles of Jena and Auerstädt, and occupied Berlin. Napoleon postponed a final settlement with Prussia until he had beaten his only remaining continental opponent. Russia went down at Friedland (June 1807).

Napoleon's great string of victories against the third coalition resulted partly from the blunders of his enemies. The miscalculations of Austrian, Prussian, and Russian generals contributed to French successes at Austerlitz and at Jena. Furthermore, the French army was the most seasoned force in Europe. Its soldiers of every rank were well trained. New recruits were furnished by conscription, which raised an average of 85,000 men a year under Napoleon, and were quickly toughened by being assigned in small batches to veteran units—a process called the *amalgame* and developed during the Revolution to meet the emergencies of the war against the first coalition. French officers were promoted on the basis of ability rather than seniority or influence, and they were, on the whole, more concerned with maintaining the morale of their men than with imposing strict discipline. Bonaparte seldom risked an engagement unless his forces were the numerical equal of the enemy's; then he staked everything on a dramatic surprise, as at Austerlitz. Yet even this seemingly invincible French army had defects. The medical services were poor, so that a majority of deaths on campaigns were the result of disease or improperly treated wounds. Pay was low and irregular, and supplies were also irregular, since it was French policy to have men and horses live off the land as much as they could to save the expense and delays of bringing up elaborate supply trains. Though eventually serious in their impact, these shortcomings did not prevent Napoleon's ascendancy over Europe in 1807.

### The Tilsit Settlement

Napoleon reached the pinnacle of his career when he met Czar Alexander I on a raft anchored in the Niemen River at Tilsit, on the frontier between East Prussia and Russia. There, in July 1807, the two emperors drew up a treaty dividing Europe between them. Alexander acknowledged France's hegemony over central and western Europe and secured in return the recognition of eastern Europe as the Russian sphere. Napoleon pledged Russia a share in the spoils if the Ottoman Empire should be dismembered. He demanded no territory from the defeated czar, only a commitment to cease trade with Britain and to join the war against her. The Tilsit settlement, however, made Alexander bitterly unpopular at home, where Russian propaganda had been denouncing Napoleon as Antichrist.

While the two emperors negotiated on the raft, Frederick William III (1797–1840), the Prussian king, nervously paced the banks of the Niemen. He had good cause to be nervous, for Tilsit cost him almost half his territory. Prussia's Polish provinces formed a new puppet state, the Grand Duchy of Warsaw, which Napoleon assigned to a French ally, the king of Saxony. Prussian territory west of the Elbe River went to Napoleon to dispose of as he wished. Napoleon also stationed occupation troops in Prussia and fixed the maximum size of its army at 42,000 men.

### Empire and Satellites

Under this latter-day Caesar almost all Europe could be divided into three parts. First came the French Empire, including France proper and the territories annexed since 1789. Second were the satellites, ruled in many cases by relatives of Napoleon. And third came Austria, Prussia, and Russia, forced by defeat to become the allies of France. The only powers remaining outside the Napoleonic system were Britain, Turkey, and Sweden. In 1810, Bernadotte, one of Napoleon's marshals, was invited by the Swedes to become crown prince for their childless king, but he, too, guided Swedish policy against France.

The frontiers of the French Empire at their most extensive enclosed Belgium and Holland; the sections of Germany west of the Rhine and along the North Sea; the Italian lands of Piedmont, Genoa, Tuscany, and Rome; and finally, physically detached from the rest, the "Illyrian Provinces," stretching along the Dalmatian coast of the Adriatic, taken from Austria in 1809, and named after a unit of the old Roman Empire. The annexed territories were usually subdivided into departments and ruled by prefects, just like the departments of France proper.

The satellites flanked the French Empire. The Kingdom of Italy, an enlarged version of the Cisalpine Republic, included Lombardy, Venetia, and the central Italian lands not directly annexed by France. Napoleon was the king, and his stepson, Eugène de Beauharnais, was viceroy. In southern Italy, Napoleon deposed the Bourbon king of Naples in 1805 and gave the crown first to his brother Joseph and then to Joachim Murat, the husband of his sister Caroline. Joseph moved from Naples to Madrid in 1808 when Napoleon deposed the Spanish Bourbons, forcing the Spaniards to remain in the war against Britain.

In central Europe, Napoleon energetically pursued his project of a "third" Germany. He decreed a further reduction in the number of German states, and in 1806 aided the formal dissolution of that museum piece, the Holy Roman Empire. Francis II, the reigning Hapsburg, last of the Holy Roman emperors, now styled himself emperor of Austria. To replace the vanished empire, Napoleon created the Confederation of the Rhine, which included almost every German state except Austria and Prussia. At the heart of this confederation Napoleon carved out for his brother Jerome the Kingdom of Westphalia, which incorporated the Prussian holdings west of the Elbe seized at Tilsit. Two states completed the roster of French satellites—Switzerland and the Grand Duchy of Warsaw. Europe had not seen such an empire since the heyday of imperial Rome.

Napoleon longed to give dignity and permanence to his creations. It was not enough that his brothers and his in-laws should sit on thrones; he himself must found a dynasty, must have the heir so far denied him in fifteen years of childless marriage. He divorced Josephine, therefore, and in 1810 married Marie-Louise, the daughter of the Hapsburg Francis II. In due time, Marie-Louise bore a son, called "the king of Rome," but destined never to rule in Rome or anywhere else.

Throughout the new French acquisitions and the satellites Bonaparte and his relatives played the part of enlightened despots, curbing the power of the Church, abolishing serfdom, building roads, and introducing the metric system and the new French law codes. Everywhere, however, they exacted a heavy toll of tribute and subjection. In the Kingdom of Italy, for instance, Napoleon doubled the tax rate previously levied by the Austrians; half the revenues of the kingdom went to defray the expenses of the French army and the French government. Napoleon flooded his relatives with instructions on the government of their domains and brought them abruptly to heel whenever they showed signs of putting local interests above those of France. When Louis Bonaparte in Holland dared to disobey the imperial orders, his brother delivered a crushing rebuke:

> In ascending the throne of Holland, Your Majesty has forgotten that he is French and has stretched all the springs of his reason and tormented his conscience in order to persuade himself that he is Dutch. Dutchmen inclining toward France have been ignored and persecuted; those serving England have been promoted. . . . I have experienced the sorrow of seeing the name of France exposed to shame in a Holland ruled by a prince of my blood.*

* *Letters Inédites de Napoléon* (Paris, 1897), I, 382–383. Our translation.

Louis's boldness cost him his throne; his Dutch kingdom was annexed to France in 1810.

### The Continental System

Nowhere was Napoleon's imperialism more evident than in his Continental System. This attempt to regulate the economy of the whole Continent had a double aim: to build up the export trade of France and to cripple that of Britain. The collapse of Napoleon's cross-Channel invasion plans led him to expand the earlier tariff measures against Britain into a great campaign to bankrupt the nation of shopkeepers. The defeat of the third coalition gave him the opportunity to experiment with economic warfare on a continental scale and to carry mercantilism to extremes.

The Berlin Decree, issued by Napoleon in November 1806, forbade all trade with the British Isles and all commerce in British merchandise. It ordered the arrest of all Britons on the Continent and the confiscation of their property. Britain replied by requiring that neutral vessels wishing to trade with France put in first at a British port and pay duties. This regulation enabled Britain to share in the profits of neutral shipping to France. Napoleon retaliated with the Milan Decree (December 1807), ordering the seizure of all neutral ships that complied with the new British policy. The neutrals, in effect, were damned if they did and damned if they didn't.

Napoleon's vassals and allies had to support the Continental System or suffer the consequences. Of all the "un-French" activities countenanced by Louis Bonaparte in Holland, the worst, in Napoleon's view, was his toleration of Dutch smuggling of English contraband. The emperor likewise expected the satellites to feed French industrial prosperity. When Italians objected to the regulation of their silk exports, Napoleon lectured his viceroy, Eugène, on the facts of economic life:

> All the raw silk from the Kingdom of Italy goes to England. . . . It is therefore quite natural that I should wish to divert it from this route to the advantage of my French manufacturers: otherwise my silk factories, one of the chief supports of French commerce, would suffer sub-

stantial losses. . . . My principle is: France first. . . .

It is no use for Italy to make plans that leave French prosperity out of account; she must face the fact that the interests of the two countries hang together.*

The gigantic attempt to make "France first" failed almost totally. Only a few French industries benefited from the Continental System; the cessation of sugar imports from the West Indies, for example, promoted the cultivation of native sugar beets. But the decline of overseas trade depressed Bordeaux and other French Atlantic ports, and the increasing difficulty of obtaining raw materials like cotton caused widespread unemployment and produced a rash of bankruptcies. The new French markets on the Continent did not compensate for the loss of older markets overseas; the value of French exports declined by more than a third between 1805 and 1813.

The Continental System did not ruin Britain, although it did confront the British with a severe economic crisis. Markets abroad for British exports were uncertain; food imports were reduced; while prices rose sharply, wages lagged behind; and specie was in such short supply that not enough coins could be minted to keep pace with the demand. Both farm workers, already pinched by the enclosure movement, and factory workers suffered acutely. Yet Britain, fortified by her leadership in the economic revolutions and by the overwhelming superiority of her navy and merchant marine, rode out the storm. Every tract of land at all capable of growing food was brought under the plow. Factory owners improvised substitute payments for their workers when coins were unavailable. Exporters not only developed lucrative new markets in the Americas, the Ottoman Empire, and Asia but also smuggled goods to old customers on the Continent. Napoleon lacked the vast naval force to apprehend smugglers at sea, and he lacked the large staff of incorruptible customs inspectors to control contraband in the ports. Moreover, since the French army simply could not do without some items produced only in British factories, Napoleon violated his own decrees by authorizing secret purchases of British cloth and leather for uniforms.

* Quoted in J. M. Thompson, ed., *Napoleon's Letters*, pp. 241–242.

The Continental System antagonized both the neutral powers and Napoleon's allies. French seizure of American vessels in European ports under the terms of the Milan Decree put a dangerous strain on Franco-American relations. But British restrictions likewise bore heavily on the Americans. British impressment of American seamen on the pretext that they were deserters from the Royal Navy, together with the designs of American expansionists on Canada, produced the indecisive Anglo-American War of 1812–1814.

## The Peninsular War

In Europe, the political and military consequences of the Continental System formed a decisive and disastrous chapter in Napoleonic history. The chapter opened in 1807 when the emperor decided to impose the System on Britain's traditional ally, Portugal. The Portuguese expedition furnished Napoleon with an excuse for the military occupation of neighboring Spain. In 1808 he lured the Spanish royal family away from Madrid and made his brother Joseph king of Spain. But every measure taken by Napoleon—the removal of the ineffectual Bourbons, the installation of a foreign monarch, the attempted enforcement of the Continental System, and, not least, the suppression of the Inquisition and the curtailment of noble and clerical privileges—violated Spanish customs and offended Spanish nationalism. The irreconcilable Spaniards began fighting Napoleon when the population of Madrid rose in revolt on May 2, 1808.

While the rising in Madrid was soon repressed, the Peninsular War (named after the Iberian peninsula) rapidly grew from a minor irritation to a deadly cancer on the body of the Napoleonic Empire. The Spaniards employed ambushes and poisoned wells and used other guerrilla devices. The expedition that Britain sent to assist them upset all the rules about British inferiority in military, as opposed to naval, matters. It was ably commanded by Sir Arthur Wellesley (later the duke of Wellington) and generously supplied from home. Napoleon poured more than 300,000 troops into the Peninsular campaign, but his opponents gained the upper hand in 1812, when he detached part of his forces for the invasion of Russia. In 1813, King

*Goya's "Unhappy Mother."*

Joseph left Madrid forever, and Wellington, having liberated Spain, crossed into southern France.

## German Resistance

Napoleonic imperialism also aroused a nationalistic reaction among the traditionally disunited Germans. Intellectuals launched a campaign against the French language and French culture, which had long exerted a powerful influence. Johann Grimm and his brother Wilhelm contributed not only their very popular—and very German—*Fairy Tales* (1812) but also philological researches designed to prove the innate superiority of the German language. The philosopher Fichte delivered at Berlin the highly patriotic *Addresses to the German Nation* (1807–1808), claiming that German was the *Ursprache,* the fountainhead of language. And the Germans themselves, Fichte continued, were the *Urvolk,* the oldest and the most moral of nations.

All this did not constitute the dramatic mass political awakening sometimes pictured by enthusiastic German historians. The response came largely from the social and intellectual elite of Germany at first, but nationalistic awareness did begin to trickle down and make its impact felt when Austria reentered the war against France in 1809.

For the first time, the Hapsburg monarchy now attempted a total mobilization comparable to that decreed by the French Convention in 1793. While the new spirit enabled the Austrians to make a better showing, they were defeated by a narrow margin at Wagram (1809) and for the fourth time in a dozen years submitted to a peace dictated by Napoleon. The Treaty of Schönbrunn (1809) stripped them of the Illyrian Provinces and assigned their Polish territory of Galicia to the Grand Duchy of Warsaw. Francis II gave his daughter to Napoleon in marriage, and his defeated land became the unwilling ally of France. Leadership in the German revival passed to Prussia.

The shock of Jena and Tilsit jarred Prussia out of the lethargy that had overtaken her since the death of Frederick the Great in 1786. The new University of Berlin, founded in 1810 to compensate for the loss of Halle by the Tilsit settlement, attracted Fichte and other prophets of German nationalism. Able generals and statesmen, most of them non-Prussian, came to power. General Scharnhorst (who came from Hanover) headed a group of officers who abolished the inhuman discipline of the army and improved its efficiency. The ceiling of 42,000 soldiers imposed by Napoleon was evaded by the simple device of assigning recruits to the reserve after a fairly brief period of intensive training and then inducting another group of recruits. By 1813, Prussia had more than 150,000 trained men available for combat duty.

The social and administrative reorganization of the Prussian state was inspired by the energetic Stein—Baron vom und zum Stein, an enlightened aristocrat from the Rhineland. Stein conciliated the middle class by granting towns and cities some self-government. To improve the status of the peasantry, he sponsored the edict of October 1807, at long last abolishing serfdom in Prussia. The edict, however, did not break up the large Junker estates or provide land for the liberated serfs, many of whom now led a precarious existence as day laborers. Nor did it terminate the feudal rights of justice exercised by the Junker over his peasants. Stein and the others eliminated only the worst abuses of the Old Regime and left authority where it had traditionally rested—with the king, the army, and the Junkers. The Hohenzollern state was not so much reformed as restored to the traditions of absolutism and efficiency established by the Great Elector and Frederick the Great.

## The Russian Campaign

The event that enabled a developing German nationalism to turn its force against Napoleon was the French debacle in Russia. French actions after 1807 soon convinced Czar Alexander that Napoleon was not keeping the Tilsit bargain and was intruding on Russia's sphere in eastern Europe. When Alexander and Napoleon met again at the German town of Erfurt in 1808, they could reach no agreement, though they concealed their differences by a show of great intimacy. French acquisition of the Illyrian Provinces from Austria in 1809 raised the unpleasant prospect of French domination over the Balkans, and the simultaneous transfer of Galicia from Austria to the Grand Duchy of Warsaw suggested that this Napoleonic vassal might next seek to absorb the Polish territories of Russia. Meanwhile, Napoleon's insistent efforts to make Russia enforce the Continental System increasingly incensed Alexander. French annexations in northwest Germany completed the discomfiture of the czar, for they wiped out the state of Oldenburg, where his uncle was the reigning duke. All these factors caused the break between the czar and the emperor, and the famous invasion of Russia by the French in 1812.

For the invasion Napoleon assembled the Grande Armée of nearly 700,000 men, a majority of whom, however, were not Frenchmen but unwilling conscripts in the service of a foreign master. The supply system broke down almost immediately, and the Russian scorched-earth policy made it very hard for the soldiers to live off the land and impossible for horses to get fodder, so that many of them had to be destroyed. As the Grand Army marched eastward, one of Napoleon's aides reported:

> There were no inhabitants to be found, no prisoners to be taken, not a single straggler to be picked up. We were in the heart of inhabited Russia and yet we were like a vessel without a compass in the midst of a vast ocean, knowing nothing of what was happening around us.*

Napoleon marched all the way to Moscow without ever managing to strike a knockout blow. He remained in the burning city for five weeks (September-October 1812) in the vain hope of bringing Czar Alexander to terms. But Russian obduracy and the shortage of supplies forced him to begin a retreat that became a nightmare. Ill-fed and inadequately clothed and sheltered, the retreating soldiers suffered horribly from Russian attacks on stragglers and from the onslaughts of "General Winter." Less than a quarter of the Grand Army survived the retreat from Moscow;

* A. A. L. de Caulaincourt, *With Napoleon in Russia* (New York, 1935), p. 62.

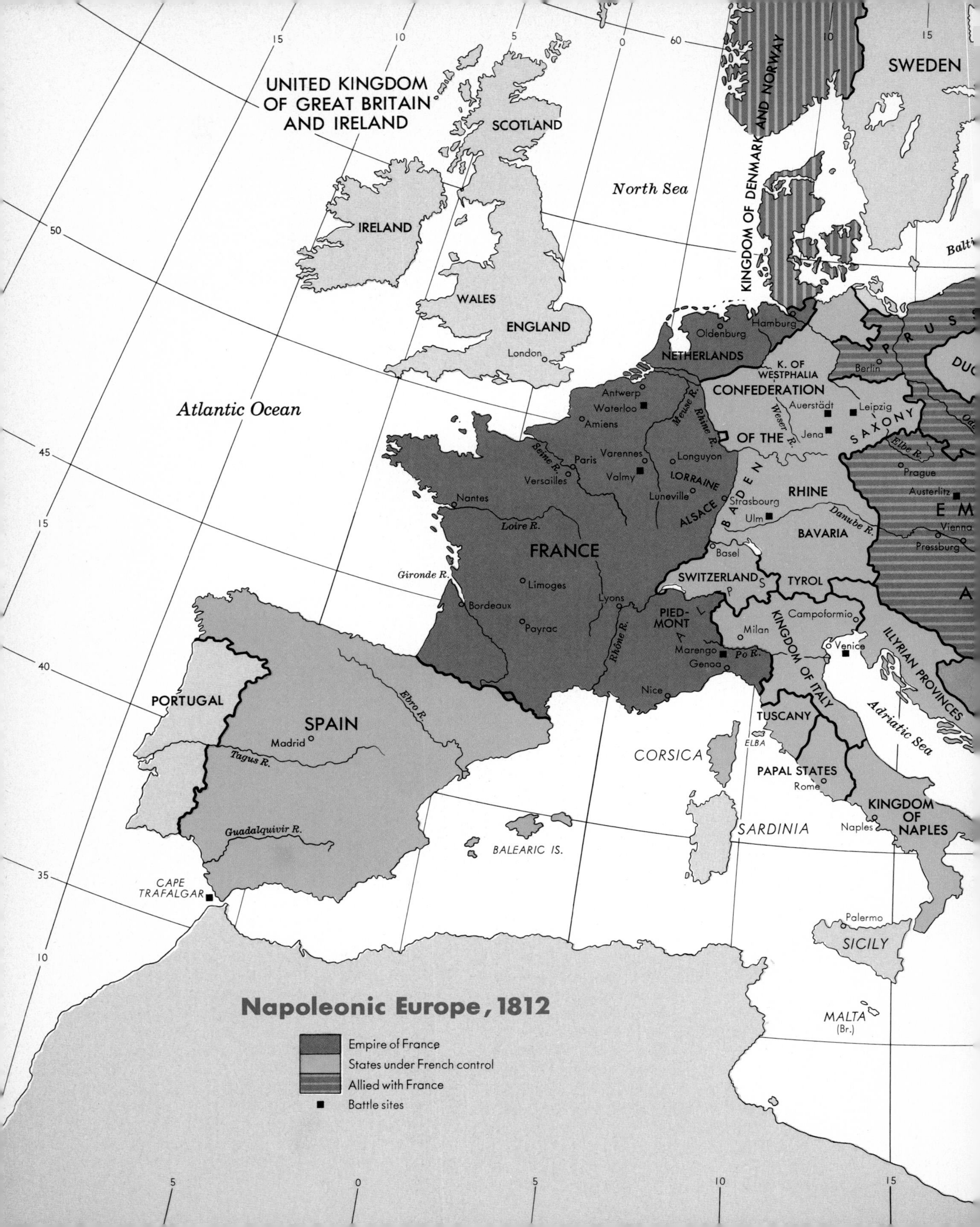

UNITED KINGDOM OF GREAT BRITAIN AND IRELAND
SCOTLAND
IRELAND
WALES
ENGLAND
London
North Sea
KINGDOM OF DENMARK AND NORWAY
SWEDEN
Atlantic Ocean
NETHERLANDS
Oldenburg
Hamburg
K. OF WESTPHALIA
CONFEDERATION OF THE RHINE
Berlin
Antwerp
Waterloo
Amiens
Auerstädt
Leipzig
Jena
SAXONY
Paris
Versailles
Varennes
Valmy
Longuyon
LORRAINE
Luneville
ALSACE
BADEN
Strasbourg
Ulm
Prague
Austerlitz
Vienna
Pressburg
BAVARIA
Nantes
Loire R.
Seine R.
Meuse R.
Rhine R.
Weser R.
Elbe R.
Danube R.
FRANCE
Basel
SWITZERLAND
TYROL
Gironde R.
Limoges
Bordeaux
Payrac
Lyons
Rhône R.
PIED-MONT
ALPS
Milan
Campoformio
Venice
Marengo
Po R.
Genoa
Nice
KINGDOM OF ITALY
ILLYRIAN PROVINCES
PORTUGAL
SPAIN
Madrid
Ebro R.
Tagus R.
Guadalquivir R.
TUSCANY
ELBA
CORSICA
PAPAL STATES
Rome
Adriatic Sea
SARDINIA
KINGDOM OF NAPLES
Naples
BALEARIC IS.
CAPE TRAFALGAR
Palermo
SICILY
MALTA (Br.)
Napoleonic Europe, 1812
Empire of France
States under French control
Allied with France
Battle sites

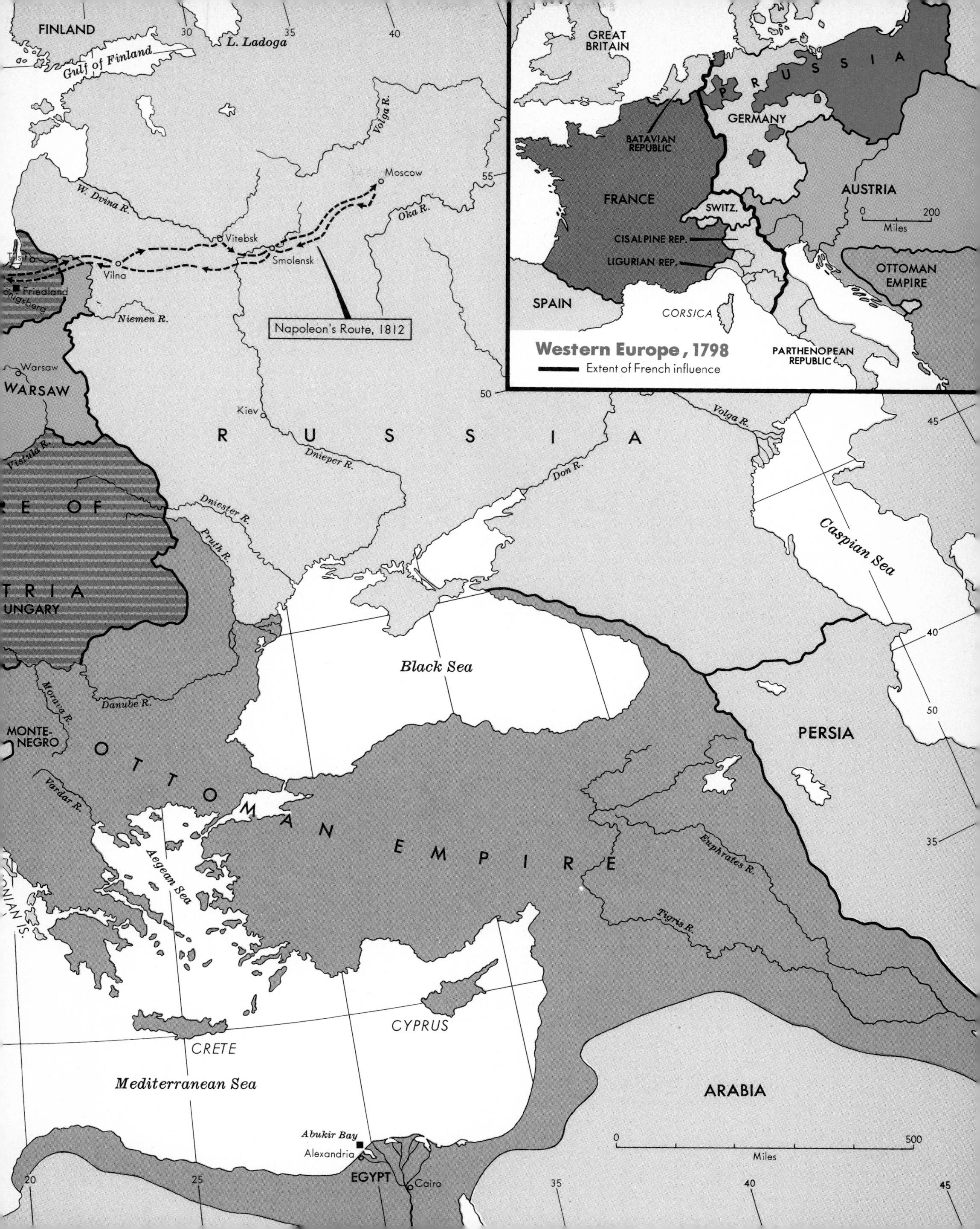

FINLAND
L. Ladoga
Gulf of Finland
Volga R.
Moscow
W. Dvina R.
Oka R.
Vitebsk
Smolensk
Tilsit
Vilna
Friedland
Königsberg
Niemen R.
Napoleon's Route, 1812
Warsaw
WARSAW
Kiev
R U S S I A
Dnieper R.
Vistula R.
Don R.
Volga R.
Dniester R.
Pruth R.
E OF
TRIA
UNGARY
Caspian Sea
Black Sea
Danube R.
Morava R.
MONTE-NEGRO
O T T O M A N E M P I R E
PERSIA
Vardar R.
Aegean Sea
Euphrates R.
Tigris R.
IONIAN IS.
CYPRUS
CRETE
Mediterranean Sea
ARABIA
Abukir Bay
Alexandria
EGYPT
Cairo
0
500
Miles
GREAT BRITAIN
PRUSSIA
BATAVIAN REPUBLIC
GERMANY
FRANCE
AUSTRIA
SWITZ.
CISALPINE REP.
LIGURIAN REP.
OTTOMAN EMPIRE
SPAIN
CORSICA
PARTHENOPEAN REPUBLIC
Western Europe, 1798
Extent of French influence
0
200
Miles

the rest had been taken prisoner or had died of wounds, starvation, disease, or the cold.

The Russian leaders had feared that Napoleon would liberate the serfs and turn them against their masters. But the peasants, despite the ill-treatment to which they had been subject for so long, formed guerrilla bands, harassed Napoleon's forces, and proved that their patriotic sentiments outweighed their class grievances. Kutuzov, the victorious Russian commander, now wanted to allow Russia's allies to prosecute the war. But Alexander insisted on pursuing the French, and sent Russian armies westward beyond the Russian frontiers on the track of Napoleon's forces.

### The Downfall

The British had been the first to resist Napoleon successfully, at Trafalgar and on the economic battlefields of the Continental System. Then had come Spanish resistance, then Russian. Now in 1813 almost every nation in Europe joined the final coalition against the French. Napoleon raised a new army, but he could not replace so readily the equipment squandered in Russia. In October 1813 he lost the "Battle of the Nations," fought at Leipzig in Germany, and by April 1814 the forces of the coalition occupied Paris. Faced also with mounting unrest at home, the emperor abdicated. After attempting suicide by poison, which turned out to have lost much of its strength since he had procured it for the Russian campaign, he went into exile as ruler of the minute island of Elba not far from the western coast of Italy.

The statesmen of the victorious coalition gathered in the Congress of Vienna to draw up the terms of peace. The Bourbons returned to France in the person of Louis XVIII, a younger brother of Louis XVI. Realizing that he could not revive the Old Regime intact, the new king issued the Charter of 1814 establishing a constitutional monarchy. The returned émigrés, however, showed no such good sense. They unleashed a new "White Terror" against the Revolution and all its works. Then, on March 1, 1815, Bonaparte pulled his last surprise: He landed on the Mediterranean coast of France.

For a hundred days, from March 20, 1815, when Napoleon reentered Paris, the French Empire was reborn. Once again the emperor rallied the French people, this time by promising a truly liberal regime, with a real parliament and genuine elections. He never had time, however, to show whether his promise was sincere, for on June 18, 1815, the British under Wellington and the Prussians under Blücher delivered the final blow at Waterloo, near Brussels. Again Napoleon went into exile, to the remote British island of St. Helena in the South Atlantic. There, in 1821, he died. Bonapartism, however, did not die in 1815 or 1821, any more than the Caesarism of ancient Rome had died on the Ides of March. A Napoleonic legend arose, fostered by the emperor himself on St. Helena. It glossed over the faults and failures of the emperor, depicting him as the paladin of liberalism and patriotism, and paved the way for the advent of another Napoleon in 1848.

## VI The Legacy of the Revolution

The Napoleonic legend, with its hero worship and belligerent nationalism, was one element in the legacy bequeathed by revolutionary and Napoleonic France. A second, and much more powerful element, was the great revolutionary motto—Liberté, Egalité, Fraternité. The motto lived on to inspire later generations of Jacobins in France and elsewhere, and to give this era its reputation of being, as R. R. Palmer claims, "The Age of the Democratic Revolution." Behind the motto was the fact that Frenchmen, though not yet enjoying the full democracy of the twentieth century, possessed a larger measure of liberty, equality, and fraternity in 1815 than they had ever known before 1789.

The Revolution founded a potent new tradition of liberty. True, Napoleon's censors and prefects gave new force to the old traditions of absolutism and centralization, but the middle class had won its freedom from obsolete restraints, and Protestants, Jews, and freethinkers had gained toleration both in France and in

French-dominated countries. While French institutions in 1815 did not measure up to the liberal ideals expressed in the Declaration of the Rights of Man, the ideals had been stated, and the effort to embody them in a new regime was to form the main theme of French domestic history in the nineteenth century.

The revolutionary and Napoleonic regimes established the principle of equal liability to taxation. They provided a greater degree of economic opportunity for the third estate by removing obstacles to the activity of businessmen, big and little, and by breaking up the large landholdings of the clergy and nobility. These lands passed mainly to the urban bourgeois and the well-to-do peasants; the only gesture toward equality of property was the Laws of Ventôse of 1794, and they were never implemented. Marxist historians have a case for arguing that the Revolution was an important step in the ascendancy of middle-class capitalism, both urban and rural. In this sense the work of the Revolution was not truly democratic, since the sans-culottes had apparently gained so little. Yet it must be remembered that the Code Napoléon did bury beyond all hope of exhumation the worst legal and social inequalities of the Old Regime. There was a good deal of truth in Napoleon's boast:

> Whether as First Consul or as Emperor, I have been the people's king; I have governed for the nation and in its interests, without allowing myself to be turned aside by the outcries or the private interests of certain people.*

The Revolution and Napoleon promoted fraternity in the legal sense by making all Frenchmen equal in the eyes of the law. They advanced fraternity in a broader sense by encouraging nationalism, the feeling of belonging to the great corporate body of Frenchmen who were superior to all other nations. French nationalism had existed long before 1789; Joan of Arc, Henry IV, and Louis XIV had all been nationalists in their diverse ways. But it remained for the Convention to formulate a fervent new nationalistic creed in its decree of August 23, 1793, providing for total mobilization. The Napoleonic Empire then demonstrated how easily nationalism on an unprecedented scale could lead to imperialism of unprecedented magnitude. A century ago, Alexis de Tocqueville, the great French student of democracy, wrote:

> The French Revolution was . . . a political revolution, which in its operation and its aspect resembled a religious one. It had every peculiar and characteristic feature of a religious movement; it not only spread to foreign countries, but it was carried thither by preaching and by propaganda.
>
> It roused passions such as the most violent political revolutions had never before excited. . . . This gave to it that aspect of a religious revolution which so terrified its contemporaries, or rather . . . it became a kind of new religion in itself—a religion, imperfect it is true, without a God, without a worship, without a future life, but which nevertheless, like Islam, poured forth its soldiers, its apostles, and its martyrs over the face of the earth.*

Its early adherents were fanatics—Robespierre and the Jacobins. Its later exponents—the men of Thermidor and Brumaire—modified the creed in the interests of practicality and moderation. Even in the hands of Napoleon, however, the Revolution remained a kind of religion, demanding political orthodoxy and punishing heretics, as King Louis Bonaparte of Holland, by political excommunication. And after 1815, as we shall see in the next chapter, the "new religion" of the Revolution continued to pour forth "its soldiers, its apostles, and its martyrs over the face of the earth."

* Quoted in Caulaincourt, *With Napoleon in Russia,* p. 364.

* A. de Tocqueville, *The Old Régime and the Revolution* (London, 1888), Part I, Ch. 3.

## Reading Suggestions on the French Revolution and Napoleon

GENERAL ACCOUNTS

G. Lefebvre, *The French Revolution,* 2 vols. (Columbia Univ. Press, 1962, 1964), and *Napoleon,* 2 vols. (Columbia Univ. Press, 1969). Full accounts, ranging beyond France itself, by an eminent French scholar.

C. Brinton, *A Decade of Revolution, 1789–1799* (*Torchbooks), and G. Bruun, *Europe and the French Imperium, 1799–1814* (*Torchbooks). Comprehensive volumes by American scholars, in the "Rise of Modern Europe" series; with full bibliographies.

R. R. Palmer, *The Age of the Democratic Revolution,* 2 vols. (*Princeton Univ. Press). Detailed exposition of the thesis that the French Revolution was part of a general democratic revolution in the West.

Jacques Godechot, *France and the Atlantic Revolution, 1770–1799* (Free Press, 1965). A ranking French scholar comes to conclusions similar to Palmer's.

P. Amann, ed., *The Eighteenth-Century Revolution: French or Western?* (*Heath). Selections both hostile and sympathetic to the Palmer-Godechot interpretation.

L. Gershoy, *The French Revolution and Napoleon* (Appleton, 1964). Lucid textbook account, stressing events in France.

THE REVOLUTION

A. de Tocqueville, *The Old Régime and the Revolution* (*Anchor). A celebrated essay of interpretation, stressing continuities between the old and new regimes.

F. A. Kafker and J. M. Laux, *The French Revolution: Conflicting Interpretations* (*Random House). A good sampling of recent scholarship.

J. Kaplow, *New Perspectives on the French Revolution* (*Wiley). Another sampler of recent scholarship, stressing historical sociology.

J. M. Thompson, *The French Revolution* (*Galaxy). Good solid account by a British scholar.

N. Hampson, *A Social History of the French Revolution* (*Univ. of Toronto Press). Well-balanced synthesis.

A. Mathiez, *The French Revolution* (*Universal). Narrative treatment to 1794, by an eloquent French scholar sympathetic to the Jacobins.

G. Lefebvre, *The Coming of the French Revolution* (*Vintage). Masterly short study of the causes of the revolution and of its course to October 1789.

G. Salvemini, *The French Revolution, 1788–1792* (*Norton). Colorful narrative by an Italian scholar of warm, liberal convictions.

G. Rudé, *The Crowd in the French Revolution* (*Oxford Univ. Press). Fascinating study of the great revolutionary "days" by a capable Marxian scholar.

A. Soboul, *The Parisian Sans-Culottes and the French Revolution, 1793–1794* (Clarendon, 1964). Translation of a portion of an important monograph, based on Paris police records; by another capable Marxian scholar.

C. Tilly, *The Vendée* (*Wiley). Revisionist study showing that much more was involved in the revolt than royalism and Catholicism.

A. Cobban, *The Social Interpretation of the French Revolution* (*Cambridge Univ. Press). A lively critique of attempts to view the revolution as a class struggle.

C. Brinton, *The Jacobins* (Macmillan, 1930), and M. J. Sydenham, *The Girondins* (Oxford Univ. Press, 1961). Careful studies greatly revising popular notions about the nature of revolutionary factions.

R. R. Palmer, *Twelve Who Ruled* (*Atheneum). Highly readable collective biography of the Committee of Public Safety.

J. M. Thompson, *Robespierre and the French Revolution* (*Collier); G. Bruun, *Saint-Just: Apostle of the Terror* (Houghton, 1932); L. Gottschalk, *Jean-Paul Marat* (*Phoenix). Enlightening biographies of major revolutionary figures.

NAPOLEON

P. Geyl, *Napoleon, For and Against* (*Yale Univ. Press). Full survey of judgments passed on Bonaparte by historians.

D. H. Pinkney, ed., *Napoleon: Historical Enigma* (*Heath). A briefer introduction to the contrasting interpretations of the man.

J. M. Thompson, *Napoleon Bonaparte: His Rise and Fall* (Oxford, 1952), and F. Markham, *Napoleon* (*Mentor). Readable biographies by careful scholars.

H. A. L. Fisher, *Napoleon* (*Oxford), and A. L. Guérard, *Napoleon I* (Knopf, 1956). Good shorter biographies.

R. B. Holtman, *The Napoleonic Revolution* (*Lippincott). Emphasizing institutional changes under Bonaparte.

D. G. Chandler, *The Campaigns of Napoleon* (Macmillan, 1966). Recent scholarly account.

O. Connelly, *Napoleon's Satellite Kingdoms* (Free Press, 1965). Informative studies of Spain, Holland, Westphalia, Italy, and Naples.

F. Markham, *Napoleon and the Awakening of Europe* (*Collier). Brief survey, arguing that European nationalisms were as yet underdeveloped.

SOURCES

J. H. Stewart, *A Documentary Survey of the French Revolution* (Macmillan, 1951). Excellent collection of constitutional texts and other official documents.

A. Young, *Travels in France* (*Anchor). Lively diary by an English farm expert who journeyed throughout France, 1787–1789.

E. Burke, *Reflections on the Revolution in France* (*several editions). The celebrated indictment of the destructive character of the Revolution.

J. M. Thompson, ed., *Napoleon's Letters* (Everyman). A fascinating collection, arranged chronologically.

J. C. Herold, ed., *The Mind of Napoleon* (*Columbia University). Another fascinating collection, arranged topically.

A. de Caulaincourt, *With Napoleon in Russia* (*Universal), and its sequel, *No Peace with Napoleon* (Morrow, 1936). Memoirs by one of Bonaparte's chief aides.

FICTION

A. France, *The Gods Are Athirst* (Roy, n.d.). Fine novel about a fanatical Jacobin.

C. Dickens, *A Tale of Two Cities* (*many editions). Deficient in accuracy, but unsurpassed in color.

P. Weiss, *The Persecution and Assassination of Jean-Paul Marat as Performed by the Inmates of the Asylum of Charenton under the Direction of the Marquis de Sade* (*several editions). The play depicting the intensity of the revolutionary experience.

Victor Hugo, *Ninety-Three* (Harper, 1874). The last novel by the famous French Romantic; long and overdrawn, but catches some of the drama going on at the Convention and in the countryside in the year when the Terror began.

L. Tolstoy, *War and Peace* (*several editions, often abridged). The epic novel about the Russian campaign.

# Illustrations

# Index